D0284513

DICTIONARY
OF
CONTEMPORARY SLANG

Tony Thorne

BLOOMSBURY

Ref
PE
3721
.T53x
1997

This edition published 1997

First published in 1990 by
Bloomsbury Publishing Plc
38 Soho Square
London W1V 5DF

Copyright © 1990, 1994, 1997 by Tony Thorne

A copy of the CIP entry for this book is available from the British Library

ISBN 07475 2856 X

All rights reserved: no part of this publication may be reproduced, stored in a
retrieval system, or transmitted in any form or by any means, electronic,
mechanical, photocopying or otherwise, without the prior written permission
of the publisher.

10 9 8 7 6 5 4 3 2 1

Designed by Ian Merrill

Typeset by Market House Books Ltd, Aylesbury
Printed in Great Britain by Clays Ltd, St Ives plc

INTRODUCTION

Slang…an attempt of common humanity to escape from
bald literalism, and express itself illimitably … the
wholesome fermentation or eructation of those processes
eternally active in language, by which froth and specks are
thrown up, mostly to pass away; though occasionally
to settle and permanently crystallise.

Walt Whitman, 1885

What is slang?

Most of us think that we recognise slang when we hear it or see it, but exactly how slang is defined and which terms should or should not be listed under that heading continue to be the subject of debate in the bar-room as much as in the university seminar. To arrive at a working definition of slang the first edition of this dictionary approached the phenomenon from two slightly different angles. Firstly, slang is a style category within the language which occupies an extreme position on the spectrum of formality. Slang is at the end of the line; it lies beyond mere informality or colloquialism, where language is considered too racy, raffish, novel or unsavoury for use in conversation with strangers … So slang enforces intimacy. It often performs an important social function which is to include into or exclude from the intimate circle, using forms of language through which speakers identify with or function within social sub-groups, ranging from surfers, schoolchildren and yuppies, to criminals, drinkers and fornicators. These remain the essential features of slang at the end of the 1990s, although its extreme informality may now seem less shocking than it used to, and its users now include ravers, rappers and net-heads along with the miscreants traditionally cited.

There are other characteristics which have been used to delimit slang, but these may often be the result of prejudice and misunderstanding and not percipience. Slang has been referred to again and again as 'illegitimate', 'low and disreputable' and condemned by serious writers as 'a sign and a cause of mental atrophy' (Oliver Wendell Holmes), 'the advertisement of mental poverty' (James C. Fernal). Its in-built unorthodoxy has led to the assumption that slang in all its incarnations (metaphors, euphemisms, taboo words, catchphrases, abbreviations and the rest) is somehow inherently substandard and unwholesome. But linguists and lexicographers cannot stigmatise words in the way that society may stigmatise the users of those words and, looked at objectively, slang is no more reprehensible than poetry, with which it has much in common in its creative playing with the conventions of language, its wit and inventiveness. In understanding this, and also that slang is a natural product of those 'processes eternally active in language', Walt Whitman was ahead of his time.

More recently some writers have claimed that the essence of slang is that it is language used in conscious opposition to authority, but slang does not have to be subversive, it may simply encode a shared experience, celebrate a common outlook which may be based as much on (relatively) innocent enjoyment (by, for instance, schoolchildren, drinkers, sports fans, Internet-users) as on illicit activities. Much slang, in fact, functions as an alternative vocabulary, replacing standard terms with more forceful, emotive or interesting versions just for the fun of it: **hooter** or **conk** for nose, **mutt** or **pooch** for dog, **ankle-biter** or **crumb-snatcher** for child are instances. Still hoping to find a defining characteristic other experts have seized on the rapid turnover of slang words and announced that this is the key element at work; that slang is concerned with faddishness and that its here-today-gone-to-morrow components are ungraspable and by implication inconsequential. Although novelty and innovation are important in slang, a close examination of the whole lexicon reveals that, as Whitman had noted, it is not necessarily transient at all. The word **punk**, for example, has survived in the linguistic underground since the seventeenth century and among the slang synonyms for money – **dosh**, **ackers**, **spondulicks**, **rhino**, **pelf** – which were popular in the City of London in the 1990s are many which are more than a hundred years old. A well-known word like **cool** in its slang sense is still in use (and has been adopted by other languages, too), although it first appeared around eighty years ago.

Curiously, despite the public's increasing fascination for slang, academic linguists in the UK have hitherto shunned it as a field of study. This may be due to a lingering conservatism, or to the fact that it is the standard varieties of English that have to be taught, but whatever the reasons the situation is very different elsewhere. In the US and Australia the study of slang is part of the curriculum in many institutions, in France, Spain, Holland, Scandinavia and Eastern Europe slang, and especially the slang of English, is the subject of more and more research projects and student theses; in all these places slang is discussed in symposia and in learned journals, while in Russia, China and Japan local editions of this dictionary can be found on school bookshelves and in university libraries.

Slang Lexicographers

The first glossaries or lexicons of European slang on record were lists of the verbal curiosities used by thieves and ne'er-do-wells which were compiled in Germany and France in the fifteenth century. A hundred years later the first English collections appeared under the titles *The Hye Waye to the Spytell House*, by Copland, *Fraternite of Vacabondes*, by Awdeley, and *Caveat for Common Cursetours*, by Harman. Although dramatists and pamphleteers of seventeenth-century England made spirited use of slang in their works, it was not until the very end of the 1600s that the next important compilation, the first real dictionary of slang, appeared. This was *A New Dictionary of the Terms ancient and modern of the Canting Crew* by 'B. E., Gent', a writer whose real identity is lost to us. In 1785, Captain Francis Grose published the first edition of his *Classical Dictionary of the Vulgar Tongue*, the most important contribution to slang lexicography until John Camden Hotten's *Dictionary of Modern Slang, Cant and Vulgar Words*, 1859, which was overtaken in its turn by Farmer and Henley's more sophisticated *Slang and its Analogues* in 1890. All these were published in Britain and it was the New Zealander Eric Partridge's single-handed masterwork *A Dictionary of Slang and Unconventional English*, also published in London, in 1937, that, despite its lack of citations and sometimes eccentric etymologies, became the yardstick of slang scholarship at least until the arrival of more rigorously organised compendiums from the USA in the 1950s. Since then several larger reference works have been published, usually confining themselves to one geographical area and based mainly on written sources, together with a number of smaller, often excellent specialist dictionaries dealing with categories such as naval slang, Glaswegian slang, rhyming slang, the argot of police and criminals and the jargon of finance and high technology.

The Bloomsbury Dictionary of Contemporary Slang

The *Bloomsbury Dictionary of Contemporary Slang* was first produced with the idea of combining the enthusiasms and instincts of a user of slang – someone who had been part of the subcultures and milieux where this language variety has flourished (and in later life still ventures into clubs, bars, music festivals, football matches and homeless shelters) – with the methods of the modern lexicographer and applied linguist. The first edition set out to record the 6,000 or so key terms and 15,000-odd definitions which formed the core of worldwide English language slang from 1950 to 1990: this new, updated edition extends the time-frame almost to the millennium and expands the number of entries by two thousand, losing a few obscure, doubtfully attested or just plain uninteresting terms in the process. The dictionary aims to pick up the elusive and picturesque figures of speech that really are in use out there in the community, and many terms which appear in the following pages have never been recorded before. In keeping with the modern principles of dictionary-making, the headwords which are listed here are defined as far as possible in natural, 'user-friendly' language. The modern dictionary ideally moves beyond mere definition and tries to show how a term functions in the language, who uses it and when and why, what special associations or overtones it may have, perhaps even how it is pronounced. Where possible a history of the word and an indication of its origin will be included and its usage illustrated by a quotation or example.

As with all similar dictionaries, this volume is based to some extent on consulting written sources such as newspapers, magazines, comic books, novels and works of non-fiction. Other secondary sources of slang are TV and radio programmes, films and song lyrics. Existing glossaries compiled by researchers, by journalists and by Internet enthusiasts were also checked, but treated, like fictional texts and broadcasts, with caution; investigators may be misled by their informants and, as society becomes more self-conscious in its treatment of new and unorthodox language, varieties of so-called slang appear that are only partly authentic, such as the gushing 'teen-talk' in UK magazines like *Just Seventeen, My Guy* or *Sugar* directed by twenty- and thirty-something journalists at their much younger readers, or the argot developed by writers for cult movies such as *Bill and Ted's Bogus Journey, Wayne's World* and *Clueless*. The embellishing or inventing of slang is nothing new; Damon Runyon, Raymond Chandler and P. G. Wodehouse all indulged in it, as did British TV comedy writers for *Porridge, Minder, Only Fools and Horses*, etc., over the last three decades. For this dictionary terms have been admitted if they can be verified from two or more sources, thereby, sadly, shutting out examples of idiolect (one person's private language) and nonce terms (one-off coinages).

Any description of slang that is based purely on secondary or written sources (and most still are) cannot hope to do justice to a language which is primarily transmitted orally. Slang terms may exist in spoken usage for many years, even for centuries, before being written down; some are never committed to paper, so there is an absolute need for work 'in the field' with primary sources; eavesdropping on and interviewing the users of slang themselves, and, where they are not able to report objectively on the words and phrases they are using, their neighbours, parents, colleagues, fellow-students and friends must be mobilised. This is the most exciting part of lexicography, if sometimes the most risky. The modern language researchers going undercover to listen in on conversations or setting up networks of informants at street-level can imagine themselves as successors to the pioneering anthropologists of the last century, rather than 'harmless drudges' (Dr Johnson's definition of the lexicographer) toiling alone in dusty libraries or staring at flickering screens.

Slang at the Millennium

The traditional breeding grounds of slang have always been secretive, often disenfranchised social groups and closed institutions with their rituals and codes. This has not changed, although the users in question have. Where once it was the armed forces, the public schools and Oxbridge that in Britain dominated socially and linguistically, now it is the media, the comprehensive playground and the new universities which exercise most influence on popular language: the office, the trading-floor and the computer-room have replaced the workshop, the factory and the street-market as nurturing environments for slang. The street gang and the prison, whence came nearly all the 'cant' that filled the early glossaries, still provide a great volume of slang, as do the subcultures of rave, techno and jungle music, crusties and new agers, skaters and snowboarders. Football metaphors and in-jokes have long since ousted the cricketing imagery of yesteryear.

Some special types of slang including **pig-latin** and **backslang** seem virtually to have disappeared in the last few years, while the rhyming slang which arose in the early Victorian age continues to flourish in Britain and Australia, replenished by succeeding generations, and the even older **parlyaree** lingers on in corners of London's theatre-land and gay community. The effect of the media and more recently of the Internet means that slang in English can no longer be seen as a set of discrete localised dialects, but as a continuum or a bundle of overlapping vocabularies stretching from North America and the Caribbean through Ireland and the UK on to South Africa, South and East Asia and Australasia. Each of these communities has its own peculiarities of speech, but instantaneous communications and the effect of English language movies, TV soaps and music means that there is a core of slang that is common to all of them and into which they can feed. The feeding-in still comes mainly from the US, and to a lesser extent Britain and Australia; slang from other areas and the slang of minorities in the larger communities has yet to make much impression on global English, with one significant exception. That is black slang which buzzes between Brooklyn, Trenchtown, Brixton and Soweto before, in many cases, crossing over to pervade the language of the underworld, teenagers, the music industry and showbusiness. Within one country previously obscure local slang can become nationally known, whether spread by the bush telegraph that has always linked schools and colleges or by the media: *Brookside*, *Coronation Street*, *Rab C. Nesbitt* and *Viz* magazine have all helped in disseminating British regionalisms. This mixing-up of national and local means that past assumptions about usage may no longer hold true: the earnest English traveller, having learned that **fag** and **bum** mean something else in North America, now finds that in fashionable US campus-speak they can mean cigarette and backside. In the meantime the American in Britain learns that cigarettes have become **tabs** or **biffs** and backside is now often rendered by the Jamaican **batty**.

Speakers of English everywhere seem to have become more liberal, admitting more and more slang into their unselfconscious everyday speech; **gobsmacked**, **O.T.T.**, **wimp** and **sorted** can now be heard among the respectable British middle-aged; terms such as **horny** and **bullshit** which were not so long ago considered vulgar in the extreme are now heard regularly on radio and television, while former taboo terms, notably the ubiquitous British **shag**, occur even in the conversation of young ladies. In Oakland, California, the liberalising process reached new extremes with the promotion of so-called **Ebonics**; black street speech given equal status with the language of the dominant white culture.

Youthspeak

The greatest number of new terms appearing in this edition of the dictionary are used by adolescents and children, the group in society most given to celebrating heightened sensations, new experiences and to renaming the features of their world, as well as mocking anyone less interesting or younger or older than themselves. But the rigid generation gap which used to operate in the family and school has to some extent disappeared. Children still distance themselves from their parents and other authority figures by their use of a secret code, but the boomers – the baby boom generation – grew up identifying themselves with subversion and liberalism and, now that they are parents in their turn, are unwilling either to disapprove of or to give up the use of slang, picking up their children's words (often much to the latters' embarrassment) and evolving their own family-based language (**helicopters**, **velcroids**, **howlers**, **chap-esse** are examples).

The main obsessions among slang users of all ages, as revealed by word counts, have not changed; intoxication by drink or drugs throws up (no pun intended) the largest number of synonyms; **lashed**, **langered**, **mullered** and **hooted** are recent additions to this part of the lexicon, these are followed by words related to sex and romance – **copping off**, **out trouting**, **on the sniff** and **jam**, **lam**, **slam** and the rest – and the many vogue terms of approval that go in and out of fashion among the young (in Britain **ace**, **brill**, **wicked** and **phat** have given way to **top**, **mint**, **fit** and **dope** which are themselves on the way out at the time of writing). The number of nicknames for money, **bollers**, **boyz**, **beer-tokens**, **squirt** and **spon** among them, has predictably increased since the materialist 1980s and adolescent concern with identity-building and status-confirming continues to produce a host of dismissive epithets for the unfortunate misfit, some of which, like **wendy**, **spod**, **licker**, are confined to the school environment while others, such as **trainspotter**, **anorak** and **geek**, have crossed over into generalised usage.

Other obsessions are more curious; is it the North American housewife's hygiene fetish which has given us more than a dozen words (**dust-bunny**, **dust-kitty**, **ghost-turd**, etc.) for the balls of fluff found on an unswept floor, where British English has only one (**beggars velvet**)? Why do speakers in post-industrial Britain and Australia still need a dozen or more terms for the flakes of dung that hang from the rear of sheep and other mammals, words like **dags**, **dangleberries**, **dingleberries**, **jub-nuts**, **winnets** and **wittens**? Teenagers have their fixations, finding wigs (**toop**, **syrup**, **Irish**, **rug**) and haemorrhoids (**farmers**, **Emma Freuds**, **nauticals**) particularly hilarious. A final curiosity is the appearance in teenage speech of fashionable vogue terms which are actually much older than their users realise: once again referring to money British youth has come up with **luka** ("filthy lucre" in a new guise), Americans with **duckets** (formerly "ducats").

Acknowledgements

Sincere thanks are due to the very large number of informants, correspondents and other enthusiasts who have contributed words, phrases, clarification, advice and criticism. The following deserve special mention (and apologies are proferred to anyone else whose name has disappeared from the files).

For black slang, thanks go in particular to Danielle Dodoo. For the slang of English schoolchildren, to Mathew Casey and to the pupils of Waldegrave School. For British student slang, the students of King's College, London, in particular Hattie Webster, Sarah-Jane Winter, Jake McClure, John Clarke, Karen Kelly, Helen Pettet, Matthew Gill, Rosalie Carew, Paula Little, Christopher Grantham, Charlotte Dawson and Sarah McGibbon. For South African terms, Mark Perl, Geoffrey Neilson and the *Cape Sunday Times*. For Canadian terms, Rosamund Oxlade and Christopher J. Moss. For Australianisms, Fiona Lloyd, Jennifer Hor, Chris and Liz Corbel. For slang from the USA, among many others, Dan Rowe, Connie Fletcher, Christopher Schwartz and the students of Richmond College and Syracuse University. Also Richard Littlejohn, Derek Jameson, Roland White, Simon Donald of *Viz*, Mick Kenning, John Davison, Alan Byrne, M. D. Evans, Barry Gayton, Leslie Dunkling, B. T. of Ilkley, James Parkin, Gerard McLoughlin, Simon Potter, W. J. McManus, Herbert Layton, Clive Exton, Vadim Kurapov, D. E. T. Read, Richard Cooper, Anne Darroch, Paul Heselton, Ron Fox, Mathilde le Bailly, Nicholas Jenkins, Michelle Woods, and also to all those who sent contributions to my "Last Word" column in the *Sunday Express*.

Introduction

I am especially grateful to the leading authority on US student slang and author of the seminal *Slang and Sociability*, Professor Connie C. Eble, of the University of North Carolina at Chapel Hill, for making available extracts from her ongoing tally of campus terms; to Ken George of the University of Buckingham; to Professor Félix Rodríguez González and Antonio Lillo Buades of the University of Alicante, and to Professors Janet Bately and Jane Roberts of King's College, London, for their encouragement of my own research.

Suggestions from Readers

The *Dictionary of Contemporary Slang* is an ongoing project; a survey which by virtue of its subject must be constantly updated to keep track of new coinages and changes in the status of existing terms. The idea of a reference work as something sternly authoritative and unreachably remote from its users is outmoded; thanks to electronic communications a dictionary can now interact with its readers. This is the first interactive slang dictionary and the compiler and the publishers would be very grateful for any contributions or suggestions from readers who can either mail material to Bloomsbury Publishing or communicate with the author via e-mail at *elc@kcl.ac.uk*. Information about new slang terms should ideally include, as well as the meaning, details of when and where the word or phrase was used and a direct quotation if possible, together with the name of the contributor, who will be acknowledged in the next edition.

TT, London, May 1997

HOW TO USE THIS BOOK

A typical entry in the dictionary will contain the components described below (with the typefaces explained in brackets):

The HEADWORDS are entered in alphabetical order (in primary bold face), together with any variant spellings or alternative forms. Next the PART OF SPEECH is given (in italics): these have been somewhat simplified so that an adjectival phrase appears as an adjective, noun phrase as a noun. Unless a word is used in all parts of the English-speaking world, it is given a REGIONAL LABEL (in italics). This indicates the country of origin, or the country in which the term is most prevalent. If a particular term has more than one quite separate meaning, these meanings are NUMBERED (in bold type). If one overall sense of a term is commonly subdivided into several slightly different meanings, these are indicated by LETTERS (in bold type: a, b, c, etc.). The headword, part of speech and regional label are followed by a DEFINITION (in roman typeface). This in turn is followed by more information about the use and origin of the term (in roman typeface). In the explanations foreign words are placed in italics and slang terms found elsewhere in the dictionary are shown in bold (these act as cross references throughout the dictionary). Many definitions are followed by an ILLUSTRATIVE PHRASE or sentence (in italics). If this example is an actual citation, its source follows in brackets.

a...

aardvark *n British* hard work, onerous tasks. A probably ephemeral pun heard among university students in the late 1980s.

↳*'They're giving us too much bloody aardvark, that's the problem.'*
(Recorded, undergraduate, London University, 1988).

aardvarking *n American* having sex. This term, popular among college students in the 1990s, often applies to sex in a public place, possibly evoking the animal's grubbing or rooting around in the earth or simply, as with **wombat**, heard in the same milieux, used for the sake of exoticism.

↳*'This semester her number-one hobby has been aardvarking every chance she gets.'*

'abdabs *n pl British See* **screaming (h)abdabs**.

abo *n Australian* an Aboriginal. A standard shortening used by whites which is now considered condescending or abusive: it is often part of offensive comparisons, as in *'to smell like an abo's armpit/abo's jockstrap'*.

Acapulco Gold *n* a strain of marihuana or **grass** from the foothills above Acapulco in west-central Mexico. The golden leaves, imported into the USA in large quantities from the late 1960s, are sought after for their supposed potency and quality.

AC/DC *adj* bisexual. From the label on electrical appliances indicating that they can be used with either alternating or direct current. The slang term originated in the USA and spread to Britain around 1960.

ace *n* 1 a best friend or good person. Used by males to other males, usually as a greeting or a term of endearment. In this sense the term probably spread from black American street-gangs in the 1950s to working-class whites in the USA, Australia and, to a lesser extent, Britain.

↳*'Hey, ace!'*

2 *Australian* the anus. By association with **arse** and the black mark on a playing card.

ace, ace out *vb* 1 to outmanoeuvre, outwit or defeat.

↳*'I had it all figured, but those guys aced me!'*
(*The A Team*, US TV series, 1985).

2 *American* to succeed, win or score very highly.

↳*'She aced out/aced the test.'*

ace, aces *adj* excellent, first class. Used extensively since the late 1950s in the USA, since the mid-1960s in Australia, and by the 1970s, especially by teenagers, in Britain. The origin of the term is obviously in the highest value playing card, the meaning now extended from 'best' to 'smartest', 'cleverest', etc.

↳*'An ace car/that film was really ace/she's aces!'*

ace boon coon *n American* (in the language of black males) one's best friend. An item of black street talk combining **ace** and **coon** with 'boon' to provide the suggestion of a cherished companion and the rhyme, which was included in so-called **Ebonics**, recognized as a legitimate language variety by school officials in Oakland, California, in late 1996. A similar usage is the phrase '*ace boom boom*'. During the 1960s and 1970s the variant form '*ace coon*' was heard, often ironically referring to a self-important black male or an individual who had achieved some success, e.g. in a work-group, department, etc.

↳*'You my ace boon coon!'*

ace in the hole *n* an advantage held in reserve until it is needed. From American stud-poker terminology, an ace (the most valuable card) dealt face down and not revealed.

aces *n pl See* **ace**.

acey-deucy *adj American* both good and bad, of uncertain quality. The term is at least pre-World War II, but still heard occasionally, especially from middle-aged or elderly speakers. It comes from a card game similar to backgammon in which aces are high and deuces (twos) are low.

acher *n See* **acre**.

acid *n* **1** LSD-25, the synthetic hallucinogenic drug. From the full name, Lysergic Acid Diethylamide. This has been the standard term by which users refer to the drug since its first popularity in California in 1965, in spite of the appearance of more picturesque but ephemeral alternatives. In the late 1980s, adherents of the **acid house** cult adopted the word as a slogan (usually a cry of *a-c-e-e-e-d!*) and to refer to LSD or **ecstasy**.
2 *British* sarcasm, snide comments, or cheeky exaggeration, especially in the expression '*come the old acid*', popular in working-class usage in the 1950s and 60s and still heard. In such phrases as '*his acid comments*' the adjectival meaning is similar, but cannot be described as slang.
✥'*Don't come the old acid with me!*'
3 *Australian* **put the acid on**, to demand money or information (from someone).

acid flash *n* a sudden recurrence of a much earlier experience of the drug LSD. Some users are disturbed months or years after taking the drug by sudden disorientation which lasts from seconds to hours and which may or may not be due to its effects.

acid head, acid freak *n* a user, especially a heavy or habitual user, of the drug LSD. The terms are not pejorative, and were used from the late 1960s to the mid-1970s by takers of LSD or other hallucinogens about themselves and each other.

acid house *n* a youth cult involving synthetic electronic dance-music (**house**) and the taking of euphoric hallucinogens such as **ecstasy** and LSD (**acid**). This fashion, celebrated in clubs and large impromptu parties, and with garish clothing and lighting effects, succeeded hip-hop, **rap** and other fads in 1988. '*A-c-e-e-e-d!*' (an elongated version of **acid**) was a rallying cry of celebrants, shouted and written on walls.
✥'*The redeeming features of last year's summer of Acid-House were that it generated energy and ideas for both the fashion and the music industry.*'
(*Independent*, 11 July 1989).

acid test *n* a party or informal ritual at which a group of people take food and/or drink laced with LSD. The expression and the practice were originated by Ken Kesey and the Merry Pranksters, a group of hedonistic travellers in the USA in the early 1960s who were successors to the **beats** and precursors of the **hippies**.
✥'*The Electric Kool-Aid Acid Test.*'
(Title of a book by Tom Wolfe, 1969).

acid trip *n* a period under the influence of the drug LSD, or **acid** (which produces an altered state of awareness and, sometimes, hallucinations). The experience lasts 4–6 hours at an average dose.

ackers *n British* money. The word, which has been in armed-forces and working-class use since the 1920s, has been revived, in common with synonyms such as **pelf**, rhino, etc., for jocular use in the 1980s by middle-class speakers. It comes from the Egyptian word *akka*: a coin worth one *piastre*.

acre, acher *n* **1** buttock(s). In this sense the word is common in Australia, normally in the singular.
2 testicle(s). Usually in the plural, this sense of the word is typically used by British schoolboys.
Both senses of both words stem from the simple play on the word 'ache' which has formed part of many different puns and dirty jokes, during the last forty years, involving sensitive parts of the (male) anatomy.
✥'*I told the estate agent I couldn't afford any land, so he kicked me in the balls and said, "There's a couple of achers for you".*'
(Schoolboy joke, London, 1965).

action man *n British* a devotee of military exercises or strenuous physical activities, or someone who makes a show of (relentless) energy. The term is applied derisively, originally by members of the armed forces to unpopular or excessively **gung-ho** colleagues, and now by extension to anyone who is showily or mindlessly **macho**. The satirical magazine *Private Eye* referred to Prince Andrew by this name in 1986 and 1987. The origin of this piece of sarcasm is the 'Action Man' doll – a poseable commando scale model in full kit sold to children in Britain since the 1960s.
✥'*Right little action man i'n' 'e? 'E simply wants to be prepared when the east wind blows 'ot.*'
(*Minder*, British TV series, 1988).

A.D. *n* drug addict. From the first two letters of 'addict', or a reversal of the initials of 'drug addict' to avoid confusion with 'District Attorney'. The term was quite popular among addicts themselves and the police in the USA. (In Britain **D.A.** was the 1960s vogue version.)

adam *n British* the drug MDA; methyl diamphetamine. Adam is an acronym from the initials, used by middle-class Londoners during the vogue for the drug since the mid-1980s. MDA is more commonly known to the press and non-users as **ecstasy**; to users it is also **E, X, xtc, Epsom salts**.

adam and eve *vb British* to believe. Well-established rhyming slang which is still heard among working-class Londoners and middle-class imitators, usually in the expression of astonishment '*Would you adam 'n' eve it?*'.

aerated *adj* angrily over-excited or agitated. Perhaps originated by educated speakers who were familiar with the technical senses of aerate (to supply the blood with oxygen or to make effervescent), but usually used nowadays by less sophisticated speakers who may mispronounce it as 'aeriated'.
↳'*Now, don't get all aerated.*'

african lager *n British* Guinness. A jocular London term of the 1970s, coined in the tradition of the earlier **african woodbine**. Lager has become the most popular beer served in southern English pubs; Guinness is of course black. The synonymous term 'Nigerian lager' has also been heard from the late 1980s.

african woodbine *n British* a cigarette containing cannabis, a **joint** or **reefer**. Woodbines are a well-known and long-established brand of cheap cigarette, particularly popular in the 1950s and 1960s.

afro *n* a hairstyle consisting of a mass of tight curls which was worn by Afro-Caribbeans and imitated (often by perming) by white **hippies**, particularly between 1967 and 1970.

-age *suffix American* a termination that became popular among older adolescents in the early 1990s in creating mock-serious nouns from existing slang and standard bases. **Buffage, grindage,** and **tuneage** are examples. The tendency was popularized by its use in such films as *Bill and Ted's Bogus Journey*, *Wayne's World* and *California Man*.

ag-fay *n American* a male homosexual. Usually used pejoratively and almost always by heterosexuals, this example of **pig Latin** is based on **fag**. Unlike the superficially similar **ofay**, this expression is predominantly used by white speakers.

ag, agg *n British* violence, aggression. A shortened form of **aggro**, heard in provincial adolescent slang from around 1990, and previously used by older prison inmates and members of the underworld. Like aggro, the word may be employed with the weaker sense of trouble or irritation.
↳'*If you go to the market precinct these days it's just ag.*'
↳'*His old lady's been giving him far too much ag over this.*'

aggers *n British* backside, buttocks. An item of provincial slang recorded in the *Observer* newspaper, 23 July 1994. Its derivation is uncertain.

aggie *n British* a marble (as used in children's games). An old term, usually for a striped marble, still heard in the 1950s. From agate, the banded stone from which marbles were originally made. *See* **alley**.

aggravation *n British* serious trouble, victimization or mutual harassment. A colloquial extension of the standard meaning of the word, used by police and the underworld. Aggravation is, like **bother** and **seeing-to**, a typical example of menacing understatement as practised in London working-class speech.

aggro *n British and Australian* **aggravation**. Originally the slang term was a euphemism for threatened or actual violence, offered typically by **skinheads**, although it is not clear whether they or their (typically **hippy**) victims first adopted the shortened form at the end of the 1960s. (Whichever is the case, the word is a derivation of aggravation in its colloquial sense as used by police and criminals since the 1950s.) Aggro, like **bother**, is a typical example of the use of menacing understatement in British working-class slang. The word was soon taken up by other users and in informal English has now reverted to something like its original unspecific meaning of annoyance or trouble. In Australian usage aggro can be used as an adjective as in '*I guess I was a bit aggro last night*'.

aggro *adj American* wonderful, excellent. This probably ephemeral term was recorded among teenagers in New York and California in late 1987. It is probably based on a misunderstanding or deliberate shifting in the meaning of the earlier British term.

A.H. *n American*
asshole (usually in the metaphorical rather than literal sense). A euphemistic abbreviation. *Compare* **a-hole**.

a-hole *n American* a euphemism for **asshole**, usually in the literal rather than metaphorical sense.

aim archie at the armitage *vb Australian* (of a male) to urinate. A later version of the widely known **point percy at the porcelain**, popularized in Barry Humphries' *Barry McKenzie* cartoon series. ('Armitage Ware' is a brand name of toilet bowls.)

aimed *adj American* identified, singled out, and/or victimized. A slang version of 'targeted' which probably originated in the argot of black street-gangs. It is now used in milder contexts by teenagers.

> ✎'*There's no way we'll get out of this; we've been aimed ...*'

airball *n American* a dim-witted, eccentric or unpleasant person. This mildly pejorative term of the 1980s is a combination of **airhead** and the more offensive **hairball**.

airbrained *adj American* silly, frivolous, empty-headed. Slightly less derogatory than the noun **airhead**, this term has not been imported into Britain to any significant extent, perhaps because of possible confusion with 'hare-brained' which is still in widespread use.

> ✎'*She's not just some airbrained bimbo, you know.*'

airhead *n* a fool; a silly, empty-headed person. An American teenager's term heard since the mid-1970s, used for instance by **Valley Girls**; it has been adopted by British teenagers in the 1980s.

> ✎'*The usual crowd of airheads, phonies, deadlegs, posers, bimbos, wallies, wannabees, hangers-on and gate-crashers...*'
> (Christena Appleyard, *Daily Mirror*, 11 May 1989).

air hose *n American* shoes, typically loafers (leather moccasins), worn without socks. A **preppie** term for a preppie sartorial convention, punning on the American sense of 'hose' meaning socks, stockings, etc. and the compressed air pipe at a filling station.

airs *n American* trainers. The word is a shortening of the trademark label *Air Jordans* which was generalized to denote any sports shoes and widely heard in 1991 and 1992. (The rare use of '*airing*' in black speech to mean walking or leaving is an unconnected earlier usage, probably based on 'open air').

a.k.a., aka *preposition, n* also known as, alias, in other words. Initials used by law enforcement agencies in the USA when giving suspect's aliases in official bulletins. The term was extended in America to a more general 'also' or 'alternatively' in writing and in speech (it is spoken as the three letters), and is sometimes used as a noun as in '*what's his a.k.a.?*'. In Britain a.k.a. was picked up by rock music journalists in the 1970s but has not entered the spoken jargon.

Alan Whickers, Alans *n pl British* knickers, panties. The terms are non-working-class rhyming slang, heard among young people, particularly students, in the 1970s and 1980s. The reference is to Alan Whicker, a well-known punctilious and dapper television interviewer.

> ✎'*There was this huge pair of Alan Whickers hanging on the line.*'

alec, aleck *n* a swindler's victim, dupe. This term from the early 20th century is still heard in the USA and Australia. It is not clear whether alec derives from 'smart alec' or vice versa. The word was used for instance in the film *House of Games* (1987, David Mamet), which dramatizes the world of small-time American gamblers.

aled, aled-up *adj British* drunk. A mild and acceptable term which although short and to-the-point can be used in polite company or family newspapers. The expressions probably originated in the north of England where ale has been and remains a common all-purpose word for beer.

> ✎'*He's aled again.*'

alf *n Australian* a common, foolish person. In the 1960s this term briefly vied with **ocker** as the generic term for un-couth manhood.

alkie *n* an alcoholic, especially one who lives rough or frequents the streets. The obvious term, which usually carries over-tones of contempt, has been widespread in the USA at least since the Depression; it was adopted after World War II in Aus-tralia and since the 1960s has been in limited use in Britain.

alley, allie *n British* a marble (as used in children's games). Like **aggie**, the word is approximately a hundred years old and refers to a pale or white marble. Although rarely heard today, these terms probably survive where the traditional game is still played. The most likely ori-gin of the term is a shortening of 'ala-baster', from which some Victorian mar-bles were made.

alley apple *n American* a lump of horse manure. A less common version of the expression **road apple**, which is now an international English term.

alley cat *n* a person who frequents the streets, particularly at night, a carouser, roisterer or promiscuous per-son. Those using this term, usually with disapproval, may have the cliché '*to have the morals of an alley cat*' in mind. Alley cat may be applied to either sex and, al-though heard in Britain and Australia since the 1960s, is originally pre-World War II American.

alleycat *vb* to prowl the streets, par-ticularly late at night.

✎ '*There's Arthur Smith alleycatting around, trying to pick up chicks.*' (Kit Hollerbach, *The 39,000 Steps*, Chan-nel 4 documentary on the Edinburgh Festival, July 1989).

alligator shoes/boots *n pl* old footwear with the toes gaping open. A jocular play on (expensive and luxurious) alligator-skin shoes.

all mouth and trousers *adj British* blustering and boastful, showing off without having the qualities to justify it. A commonly heard dismissive phrase, typically said by women about a loud or assertive man. There is a suggestion that this is a corruption of a more logical, but rarely heard expression, '*all mouth and no trousers*', meaning full of talk but de-ficient in the sexual area. A less racy ver-sion is '*all talk and no action*'. There is an

analogy with other colourful expressions, now mostly archaic, such as '*all my eye and Betty Martin*', meaning nonsense, and more abusive versions such as **all piss and wind**.

✎ '*Oh him! He's all mouth and trousers, that one.*'

all over the shop/show/lot/ ballpark *adj, adv* disorganized, in chaos or disarray. The first two versions are British, the last two American. This is a more colourful extension into slang of the colloquial phrase '*all over the place*', and the first version at least dates from the 19th century. ('Shop' is a working-class catch-all for any workplace.)

all piss and wind *adj* full of blus-ter and noise, but without real substance. This expression can have a similar mean-ing to **all mouth and trousers**, but can be applied for instance to a politician's speech or a theatrical performance, as well as to an individual. '*All piss and vine-gar*' is a rarer synonym.

all right, awright *interjection American* an exclamation of recognition, greeting, approval or admiration. The 'right' is emphasized, high-pitched and elongated when shouted. Used in this way the phrase was originally black Ameri-can; it was picked up by whites, espe-cially hippies, in the late 1960s.

alls-bay *n pl American* testicles. An item of **pig Latin** based on **balls**.

all that *n, adj American* (a person who is) exceptional, admirable. The phrase is almost invariably used dismis-sively or to express derision as in '*She thinks that she's all that*'. It occurs in black working-class speech and in black and white campus usage, and is probably a shortening of '(*not*) all that much' or '*all that great*'.

almonds, almond rocks *n pl British* socks. A London rhyming-slang term which is still in use. (Almond rock cakes were a popular working-class treat early in the 20th century.)

alms (-house) *adj British* rude, dis-respectful. This item of British street slang of the late 1990s is a variant form of **arms**. The reference is unclear, but the expression may have arisen in Caribbean usage.

alpha geek *n American* the most technically proficient and/or knowledgeable member of a group. The term, usually but not invariably applied to males in an office or work-group, is inspired by the categorizing of animal group-leaders as 'alpha males'. It was defined in *Wired* magazine in September 1995.

> ✎*'You gotta just identify the alpha geek and fire all your questions at him.'*
> (Recorded, financial trader, New York, 1996).

amagent *n South African* an alternative form of **ma-gent**.

amber fluid, amber nectar *n* beer, Australian lager. A facetious euphemism used by Australians in the 1970s which was popularized in Britain first by Barry Humphries' *Barry McKenzie* comic strip, then by TV advertisements featuring the actor Paul Hogan for Australian beer in the 1980s. The term was enthusiastically adopted by some middle-class British drinkers, themselves fond of mock-pompous coinages.

ambulance chaser *n* a lawyer, literally one who specializes in claiming on behalf of accident victims. The phrase is also applied, facetiously or critically, to any lawyer who is known for sharp practice or unethical methods. This term was originally American (dating from the beginning of the century) but is now employed in other English-speaking areas.

> ✎*'My daddy's a lawyer. Well, we often say he's an ambulance chaser.'*
> (Recorded, young woman, Chicago, 1983).

amp *n* 1 an ampoule (of a drug). An obvious shortening by drug users.

> ✎*'I scored a couple of amps of meth[edrine].'*

2 an amplifier. A common shortening used by musicians and hi-fi enthusiasts since the 1960s.

> ✎*'He rammed his guitar into the amp.'*

amped (up) *adj American* excited or agitated. This term from black street slang, which can also indicate excited anticipation, may derive from ampoule (of a narcotic) or from 'amphetamine(d)' but is equally likely to derive from the musicians' jargon 'amped-up', meaning with amplifiers fully rigged.

> ✎*'While they were keeping me waiting I was getting more and more amped up ...'*
> (Recorded, musician, New York City, 1995).

'ampsteads *n pl British* teeth. Cockney rhyming slang referring to the London beauty spot Hampstead Heath. The term (which is still heard) is invariably used with the dropped aspirate.

> ✎*'A lovely set of 'ampsteads/kicked in the 'ampsteads.'*

amscray *vb* scram, go away. One of the few examples of backslang or **pig Latin** which is actually used in speech, albeit rarely. The word is a pre-World War II Americanism which has been heard in Australia and in Britain since the 1950s.

> ✎*'We'd better amscray before he gets back.'*

amyl *n* amyl nitrite (sometimes called amyl nitrate), a very powerful stimulant drug inhaled from a broken phial, or **popper**. Amyl nitrite is prescribed for the treatment of angina pectoris; it has been taken for fun since the 1950s, and for its supposed sexually stimulating effects, especially by **gay** men, since the late 1970s.

anal *adj American* irritatingly pedantic, fastidious, conscientious, etc. This shortening of the popular psychological categorization 'anal retentive', was a vogue term among US college students in the 1990s.

> ✎*'Don't be so anal!'*
> ✎*'That was such an anal thing to do.'*

anchors *n pl British* brakes. Originally part of the jargon of pre-war professional drivers. The term was popular with some middle-class motorists throughout the 1950s and 1960s, usually in the phrase '*slam on the anchors*'; to brake suddenly. It now sounds rather dated.

the Andrew *n British* the navy. A dated term which is a shortening of 'Andrew Miller' (or 'Andrew Millar'). The eponymous Andrew is said to have been a press-ganger whose name was taken as a nickname for a warship and later for the whole service.

angel *n British* 1 in theatrical parlance, a financial backer of a production.

2 a nurse, in colloquial usage.

3 a dot on a radar screen. The term was commonly used in this context until the late 1950s.

angel, angela, angelina *n a*

passive male homosexual. These are slang terms used by homosexuals themselves and (usually pejoratively) by heterosexuals. The words may originate as terms of affection, as feminine nicknames, or possibly from earlier slang usage denoting a (female) prostitute.

angel dust *n* the drug **PCP**. A powdered (usually home-made) version of an animal tranquillizer which is smoked or sniffed through a tube and which produces in the user unpredictable and extreme physical and psychological effects. Users are capable of acts of violence, hallucinations and periods of imperviousness to pain and superhuman strength. PCP is easy to produce in home laboratories and became a severe social problem in US cities after 1975, principally among poorer teenagers. Fears of its spread to Britain and elsewhere were groundless. Its milieu is now largely given over to **crack**.

↳ *'For 15 years Washington has been struggling with abuse of PCP, also known as Angel Dust.'*
(*Independent*, 24 July 1989).

angel-drawers *n British* a term of endearment, used especially by middle-class speakers. The phrase is typical of the jocular compounds favoured, e.g. in St Valentine's Day dedications printed in newspaper small ads, but, unlike many of these, it is spoken.

anglo *n American* a person of (mainly) anglo-saxon ethnic origin. The term came into widespread use in the 1970s, especially among Hispanics. This was the first attempt by Americans from other ethnic backgrounds to categorize white anglo-saxons as a sub-group. (**WASP** was first coined by wasps themselves; **honky**, **pinkie**, etc. are terms of abuse.)

↳ *'They're mainly anglos out on Long Island these days.'*
(Recorded, suburban New Yorker, 1977).

animal house *n American* any dwelling, but especially a college fraternity house, whose occupants are excessively dirty and rowdy. This late 1950s campus term was revived by the film *National Lampoon's Animal House*, starring the late John Belushi in the role of a typical **animal** in 1978.

animal night/act *n Australian* a planned or self-conscious bout of bad behaviour or excess. The term is typically used (by and about males) with pride or admiration rather than distaste.

ankle *vb* to walk, stroll, saunter. A raffish expression heard in the USA and occasionally in Britain since the 1980s.

↳ *'Let's ankle down to the off-licence.'*

ankle *n American* an attractive female or females. This use of the word appears to predate its popularity among black youths and on campus in the late 1990s. The provenance is unclear and it may be a jocular reference to the archaic phrase *'a well-turned ankle'* as a Victorian notion of beauty.

↳ *'She's some cute ankle.'*

↳ *'Check out the ankle around here.'*

ankle-biter *n* a child, usually baby or a toddler. Commonly used with mock distaste by parents, sometimes with real distaste by others, ankle-biter was heard in all social classes in Britain and Australia in the late 1970s and 1980s. Synonyms are **leg-biter**, **rug rat** and **crumb-snatcher**.

annihilated *adj* helplessly drunk, drugged or exhausted. A middle-class teenager's colloquial expression, popular in the 1970s and 1980s.

anorak *n British* an unfashionable, studious or tedious person, usually a young male. A campus expression from the 1980s, based on the characteristic dress of these fellow-students. A sub-genre of jangling guitar pop music, supposedly beloved of such students, was dubbed 'anorak rock' in the music press in the mid-1980s.

↳ *'An anorak is one of those boring gits who sit at the front of every lecture with their Pringle jumpers asking the lecturer their clever questions.'*
(Graffito in the toilets at King's College, London University, July 1988).

ante up *vb* to pay one's contribution, put one's money in the common pot. This expression, not to be confused with *'up the ante'*, comes from the preliminary stage in a poker game when one or all of the players must put a stake in the pot. By extension ante up is sometimes used to mean settle accounts or (reluctantly) hand over something demanded.

↳ *'OK, you guys, it's time to ante up.'*

an't it? *question tag British* a variation of **innit?** which, like that term, originated in black British usage and was

adopted by adolescents and later by younger schoolchildren in the 1990s.
ॐ *'We're going to the park an't it?'*
ॐ *'An't it he's the one.'*

antsy *adj*

a nervous, jumpy, agitated.
ॐ *'She's been getting a little antsy lately – wants me to leave my wife.'*
(*The Secret of my Success*, US film, 1987).
b eager for sex.

Both senses of antsy are derived from the older, humorous colloquial expression '*to have ants in one's pants*' (meaning to be restless or agitated). Antsy is a fairly common and inoffensive term in the USA and Australia, but rare in Britain.

ape(shit) *adj, adv* out of control,

berserk, used especially in the expression **go ape**; the image is of a person reduced to a primal state, either by infatuation, excitement or, especially, anger. An American teenagers' term from the late 1950s now in general currency.
ॐ *'He's apeshit about her.'*
ॐ *'I go ape ev'ry time I see you smile.'*
('I Go Ape', written and recorded by Neil Sedaka, 1960).
ॐ *'After I'd left my last school, I pinched a wallet full of credit cards and went apeshit in about five different counties.'*
(*Sunday Times* magazine, Stephen Fry, August 1989).

ape-hangers *n pl* extra-high han-

dlebars for motorbikes or bicycles. The style was popularized by **bikers** in the USA in the 1950s, spreading to Britain where **rockers**, **greasers** and schoolchildren had adopted the style and the term by about 1959.

apple-polisher *n* a flatterer, some-

one who curries favour. The term comes from the image of the ingratiating pupil who polishes an apple carefully before presenting it to a teacher. The tradition of '*an apple for the teacher*' was really practised in the rural USA before World War II, but the term is common in all English-speaking areas. It is sometimes in the form of a verb as in '*she's been apple-polishing again*'; in Britain it is often shortened to **polisher**.
ॐ *'I had few qualifications for Hollywood; I was immoderately slothful, had no facility for salesmanship or apple-polishing, and possessed a very*

low boiling point.'
(S.J. Perelman, quoted in *Groucho, Harpo, Chico & sometimes Zeppo*, Joe Adamson, 1973).

apples *n pl* **1** breasts.

2 testicles.

Apples, like almost all other round fruits, have readily been used as euphemisms for these bodily parts. This type of metaphor may occur as a spontaneous coinage in any English-speaking community.

apples *adj Australian* fine, perfect,

OK. Often used in the expression '*she's apples*', meaning 'everything is all right'. This use of the word may originate in 'apples and rice' or 'apples and spice', obsolete British and Australian rhyming slang for 'nice'.

apples and pears *n pl British*

stairs. One of the best known examples of Cockney rhyming slang which, although authentic, is rarely heard these days.

apricots *n pl British* testicles.

ॐ *'Hot water has always made my apricots sag.'*
(Pensioner Ron Tuffer, quoted in the *Eastbourne Herald*, 7 May 1994).
ॐ *'So there 'e is, in this bird's bedroom, in up to 'is apricots, givin' it six-nowt ...'*
(*The Viz Big Fat Slags Book*, 1994).

April fools *n pl British* tools. Cock-

ney rhyming slang still heard occasionally in workshops, garages and factories.

April showers *n pl British* flowers.

An item of London working-class rhyming slang which survives in market traders' jargon.

arab *n* **1** a wild or shiftless person. In

Britain and Australia this is generally a derogatory term, although it can be used semi-affectionately, as by parents to unkempt children. This usage, no longer consciously racist, stems from the contempt felt by some members of the armed forces, stationed in colonies or protectorates, for 'street arabs', or from envious suspicion of the supposedly undisciplined lifestyle of the desert arabs.

2 a foreigner. A catch-all term generally used by uneducated speakers.

Archer *n British* £2,000. A probably

ephemeral invention by an anonymous wit in the tradition of a **monkey**, a pony, etc. It refers to the sum paid by the author and Tory politician Jeffrey Archer to Miss Monica Coughlan, a prostitute, to enable her to go abroad. Her return in 1987 resulted in Mr Archer bringing a libel case against the *News of the World*, which he won. (The synonym **Jeffrey** was also heard.)

✎ *'The usual two Archers in a plain envelope.'*
(*Weekending*, BBC Radio 4, 9 March 1990). *See also* **the Spanish archer**.

Aristotle, arry, arris *n* 1 a bottle. Rhyming slang, probably dating from the 19th century, but still occasionally heard in the London area and in Australia.

2 **'arris** (usually in the sense of 'courage, nerve').

arm *n* 1 *British* power, influence, coercion. A colloquial coinage on the lines of 'hold' or 'grip' or 'strong-arm'.

✎ *'This should give us some arm.'*

2 *See* **on the arm**.

3 *South African* a measurement of **dagga**. (Recorded as an item of Sowetan slang in the *Cape Sunday Times* on 29 January 1995).

armpit *n* a very unpleasant place. The word usually forms part of the expression *'the armpit of the universe'*; that is, the most unpleasant place in existence (a milder version of *'arsehole of the universe'*).

arms *adj British* offending codes of behaviour, breaking unwritten rules. This code term among teenage gangs was defined by one of its users as 'out of order'. The term was recorded in use among north London schoolboys in 1993 and 1994. It may in fact derive from the equally mysterious **alms(-house)**, which is heard in black British speech denoting rudeness or **dissing**.

✎ *'This is/he's arms.'*

'arris *n* 1 backside, buttocks. A cockney elaboration of **arse** sometimes adopted by middle-class speakers who want to avoid the offensive term.

✎ *'A kick in the 'arris.'*

2 courage, nerve (sense 3 of **arse**). A London working-class term.

✎ *'Loads of 'arris.'*

Both senses derive from a double rhyme; 'arris from **Aristotle**, meaning bottle, while 'bottle and glass' gives **arse**.

arse *n British* 1 backside, buttocks, anus. This word is not, strictly speaking, slang, but an ancient term ('aers' in Anglo-Saxon, descended from Germanic nouns related to an Indo-European ancestor meaning tail) which since the 17th century has been considered too vulgar for polite conversation. Australia follows the British spelling, while in the USA and Canada the word is spelled **ass**.

2 a foolish or contemptible person. A fairly mild term of exasperated contempt, popular in upper- and middle-class speech until the 1960s, now generally replaced by stronger or more colourful alternatives. *'Silly arse!'* was a favourite British rebuke.

3 **a** courage, nerve or cheek. This has been a popular working-class usage in London and Australian slang. In Britain it has, since the 1960s, largely been supplanted by more colourful terms such as **'arris** or **bottle**, which are derived from it, or by synonyms such as **balls**.

b *Australian* good luck. This usage, which is more commonly expressed by the adjective **arsy**, probably derives from the previous sense, with the implication that the good fortune came as a result of daring or impudence.

4 **the arse** *Australian* a synonym for 'the heave-ho', the **elbow** or 'the boot', usually in the expression **give someone the arse**.

5 *'My arse!'* 'Nonsense!', 'I don't believe it!', or 'It's not true!' An exclamation of angry or impatient disbelief, dating at least from the 18th century. It is probably a shortening of a longer phrase such as the following.

6 *'kiss my arse!'* an exclamation of defiance or contempt.

7 *'not to know one's arse from one's elbow/a hole in the ground'* to be incapable or incompetent, stupid.

8 *'the sun shines out of his/her arse'* he or she is wonderful, perfect or the favourite. The expressions are used contemptuously or enviously of a person who, in their own opinion or that of others, can do no wrong.

arse about *vb* to fool about, behave in an irresponsible or silly way. A favourite expression of many schoolmasters, especially in the 1950s and 1960s.

✎ *'Stop arsing about in there and get on with your work!'*

arse about face *adj, adv* back to front, the wrong way round or wrongly

ordered or organized.

arse bandit *n British* a male homosexual. The humorous but not affectionate term suggests an aggressive, predatory or desperate enemy. It is very much a term of jovial male abuse (there is no record of women saying it) in public schools, the army and the pub. Slightly less vulgar versions are **bum bandit** and **trouser bandit; chocolate bandit** is another synonym.

arsed *adj British*
See **can't be arsed**.

arse-end *n* the end, back or bottom of anything. A common vulgarism also used in the phrase '*the arse-end of nowhere*', a very remote and/or unpleasant place. '*Arse-end Charlie*' is a more robust version of the colloquial 'tail-end Charlie', as applied to a straggler.

arsehole *n British* **1** anus. **asshole** in American English.
2 '*the arsehole of the universe/earth/ world*' an extremely unpleasant place, especially one that is dirty, smelly and hot, but now by extension anywhere awful. The phrase was probably coined by troops stationed overseas, prompted by such captions as 'the pearl of the Orient' or 'the gateway to the Pacific'.
3 an extremely unpleasant person, especially one who combines offensiveness with stupidity. The term when used in Britain or Australia is stronger than the American equivalent **asshole**, and slightly different in emphasis. It shows real distaste and dislike rather than mild contempt.

arsehole *vb* **1** *British* to 'crawl', flatter or curry favour in a nauseating way. Typically used at work about a fellow employee, this is probably inspired by the now dated expressions **arsehole-crawler** or **arsehole-creep**.
✎'*There he goes, arseholing again. It makes me sick.*'
2 *Australian* to throw someone out, to get rid of (an unwanted lover). The word is often used plaintively or resentfully by jilted teenagers.
✎'*I can't understand it. Robyn arseholed me last night.*'

arseholed *adj British* **1** very drunk. A popular word among students, younger members of the armed forces and other heavy drinkers from the 1960s to the pre-sent. The image is of someone disgustingly or helplessly drunk, as in the expression '*pissed as an arsehole*'; but the term is neutral, not usually pejorative, and is used by all social classes.
✎'*Once a month he gets completely arseholed and then comes home and asks me to forgive him.*'
(Recorded, housewife, Devon, 1986).
2 *Australian*
a dismissed from one's job.
b ejected, especially from a bar.
c rejected by one's partner.

arseholes *exclamation British* nonsense. A term expressing brusque dismissal or defiance which now seems to be falling into disuse. The singer Ian Dury included it in a stream of abuse featured on a 1978 record.

arsehole to breakfast time *adj, adv British* **1** completely disorganized, 'at sixes and sevens'. A picturesque if fundamentally meaningless expression sometimes heard in Britain, especially in the north of England.
✎'*It's no good, it's all arsehole to breakfast time in that office at the moment.*'
2 thoroughly, constantly, or the full distance, as for instance in the expression '*he kicked him from arsehole to breakfast time*'. This may be an allusion to the complete digestive process (breakfast time referring to the mouth) but the origins of the phrase are obscure.

arse-licker *n* a flatterer or toady, someone who is nauseatingly sycophantic. This ancient image and phrase is paralleled in many European languages (*Arschlecken* in German, *lèche-cul* in French).

arse-man *n* **1** a man whose favourite part of a woman's anatomy is the buttocks as opposed to a **leg-man** or **tit-man**.
2 a skilled or habitual seducer. An old-fashioned phrase.
3 a male homosexual. This usage is now confined mainly to public-school or armed-services slang.

arse over tip/tit *adv* head over heels, upside down. The expression is typically cockney, but widespread in Britain and Australia. The American version is '*ass over tincups/teacups*'.
✎'*She tripped and fell arse over tit down the stairs.*'
(Recorded, plumber, London, 1987).

arse up *vb British* to make a mess of, mix up or spoil. A less common variation of **balls up** and the verb form of **cock-up**.

↳*'He managed to completely arse up the whole job.'*

arse-up *n British* a synonym for **cock-up** and **fuck-up**, which became popular from the mid-1990s, in common with most compounds based on **arse**.

↳*'It [a student union function] was quite well planned this year – unlike the last one, which was a complete arse-up.'*
(Recorded, London University student, October 1996).

arsy *adj Australian* lucky. Usually said grudgingly or enviously about someone who has managed to get away with something. (**Arse** in Australian slang may signify luck as well as brazenness.)

artichoke *n Australian* an elderly and/or unattractive (female) prostitute.

artillery *n* needles, hypodermic syringes and other paraphernalia used by heroin addicts. The image of an arsenal of deadly equipment is typical of addicts' own self-dramatizing slang (as in **shooting gallery**, **harpoon**, etc.).

↳*'Have you got the artillery ready, man?'*

artist, -artist *n, suffix* an expert in, or devotee of, a particular activity. The word can be added to many others, but the most popular are bull(shit)-artist, **burn-artist**, con-artist, **piss-artist**, **ripoff artist** and **sack artist**.

This pattern entered modern British slang via the armed forces in the 1950s and 1960s, and separately via American **hippy** terminology of the late 1960s and early 1970s. The ultimate geographical origin of the usage is obscure; it may have come into use spontaneously in several English-speaking areas, perhaps prompted by the Edwardian habit of pompously applying 'artist' or 'artiste' to performers in various fields of expertise.

arty-farty, artsy-fartsy *adj* pretentious, affected, more decorative than useful. A more vulgar parallel of the innocuous 'arty-crafty', which is Edwardian in origin and was usually applied to the pseudo-rustic, as in the Arts and Crafts design movement of the late 19th century.

arvo *n Australian* afternoon. An example of the Australian tendency to abbreviate even the most mundane everyday words. The tendency is shared by nursery slang in general and, in Britain, especially the slang of Liverpool. (Arvo is, however, uniquely Australian.)

↳*'There's no excuse for being in that state in the middle of the arvo!'*
(Recorded, Australian tourist, London, 1989).

asap, assap *adv* immediately, as soon as possible. The spoken form of the commonly-used initials a.s.a.p. (sometimes also used in speech, pronounced letter by letter).

ass *n American* **1** backside, buttocks, anus. The American spelling of the British **arse**.
2 sexual gratification. Usually used by men referring to women as anonymous sex objects.

↳*'I'm going to grab me some ass/good ass.'*

3 oneself, especially when thought of as an item to be manipulated.

↳*'You gonna get yo' ass killed!'*

4 *'Your ass is mine!'* You are in my power! A phrase used triumphantly, typically by representatives of authority to their victims.

5 *'Your ass is grass'* you are in very serious trouble. Usually said seriously as part of a threat, or ruefully by a victim.

↳*'Get it right or your ass is grass!'*

6 *'have one's ass in a sling, ass on the line'* to be in trouble, held responsible. *See also the entries following and* **badass, candyass, chew ass, kick ass**.

assap *adv See* **asap**.

asshole *n American* **1** anus. The American version of the British and Australian **arsehole**.
2 a very stupid person, someone who is pathetically or offensively foolish. This American word always implies contempt, but can also convey pity, unlike **arsehole**, which has overtones of real dislike. Since the 1960s, British and Australian speakers have adopted the American term in this sense, with its different spelling and pronunciation, for their own use. The word has become very widespread in the late 1970s and 1980s and has simultaneously become a vulgarism rather than a taboo term.

✎'*It didn't take very long to realize that he wasn't a threat, just a total asshole.*'
(Recorded, US executive, London, 1988).

3 a very unpleasant place.

✎'*On top of a bleak, snow-swept hillside in Hermon, Maine, which, if not the asshole of the universe, is at least within farting distance of it.*'
(Stephen King, *Sunday Times* magazine, 15 October 1989).

asshole buddy *n American* a very close friend or ally, a 'bosom pal', a term that is used in both jocular and unfriendly contexts. It was coined by, and usually about, heterosexual men.

ass-kicker *n American* an aggressive person, a disciplinarian; someone who **kicks ass**. An armed-forces term which has been adopted by students and school pupils, among others.

ass-kisser *n American* a sycophant, flatterer or toady. The expression is based on **kiss ass**.

ass-licker *n American* the American version of **arse-licker**.

ass-out *adj, adv American* a synonym of **balls-out** heard in the 1990s.

✎'*We've got to go ass-out to win this thing.*'

✎'*It was a whole ass-out crazy attempt to just finish the job on time.*'
(Recorded, art dealer, Chicago, May 1996).

ass over tincups/teacups *adv American* head over heels. A folksy American version of the British **arse over tip**.

ass-wipe *n American* **1** toilet paper. A working-class, blue-collar or armed-forces term.

2 a worthless, contemptible person. A term popular in the 1970s and 1980s.

at it *vb British* **1** having sex. A coy euphemism typically used by schoolchildren or the middle-aged.

2 committing a crime or crimes, or engaged in a confidence trick. A mild euphemism typically used by police or criminals themselves, from the common colloquialism 'at it again' referring to any repeated and troublesome activity.

attitude *n American* bad attitude, antisocial behaviour, sullen hostility. This use of the word without 'an' or 'the' probably derives from the black American prisoners' shortening of the white authority figures' phrases '*bad/negative/antisocial attitude*' or their accusation, '*You've got an attitude problem*'.

Audi! *exclamation American* goodbye. This announcement that one is leaving is probably a playful deformation of the phrase '*I'm out of here*', punning on the brand of German luxury car coveted by young males. It almost certainly originated in black street slang where the variant form '*Audi 5000!*' or simply **5000!** are also heard. By the mid-1990s, the term was also in use on campuses and among high-school students.

Aunt Nelly, Aunty Nelly *n* belly. A rhyming-slang term in use in Britain and Australia, particularly in the 1950s when belly was a taboo word in many households.

Aunty *See* **Auntie**.

Aussie *adj* (an) Australian.

autograph *n* a signature. Autograph is underworld argot, typically denoting a signature on a cheque or document, whether forged or genuine.

away-day *n British* a single dose of LSD or another hallucinogenic drug. A pun on the notion of a **trip** and the name of a cheap excursion ticket on British Rail.

away with the fairies/pixies *adj, adv* distracted, absent-minded, in a reverie. The first version of the phrase is common in Scottish usage, the second is more often heard in Australia. Both derive ultimately from the folk belief that forces from the fairy world can abduct, enchant or derange human victims.

awesome *adj* wonderful, excellent, very impressive. A popular teenage word, first used in the USA in the late 1970s and 1980s as part of the vocabulary of **Valley Girls**, **preppies** and hip-hop music enthusiasts, among others. This use of the adjective has been imported into Britain in the 1980s, especially by teenage skateboarders and **rap** music enthusiasts.

awol, A.W.O.L. *adj* missing, not present when needed. The expression has been extended, especially by British middle-class speakers, from its original meaning in army jargon of 'absent without leave' to inexplicably absent, either with the implication of fleeing to avoid responsibilities, or wandering uncontrolled or running amok.

✤ '*Ollie's gone awol again; he disappeared with a bottle and no one's seen him for days.*'
(Recorded, upper-class youth, London, 1985).

awright! *interjection* an alternative spelling of **all right**. With drawn-out pronunciation, this forms an exclamatory expression of appreciation, agreement or solidarity in American English.

aws *adj American* an abbreviated form of the fashionable slang sense of **awesome**, popular with college students, particularly females, during the 1990s.

axe *n* a guitar. The word in this sense was enthusiastically adopted by white rock musicians in the late 1960s. Black blues and jazz musicians had originally applied it to any instrument (such as a saxophone) that was held in both hands and 'wielded'. By the early 1970s the white use of the word, which had always had an element of self-consciousness, was mainly confined to rock music journalists or fans.

aya! *exclamation American* an excla-mation of amazement in vogue among teenagers in 1987 and 1988. The word may be a hearty cry or, more often, an affected shriek (possibly in imitation of Hispanic speech).

aye-aye, shepherd's pie/ Popeye! *exclamation British* these jokey expressions of agreement or compliance originated among primary and junior schoolchildren, but during the early 1990s were adopted as catch-phrases by adults, particularly those working in advertising, the media and finance in London. *Compare* **okey-dokey, artichokey**

Aztec two-step, the Aztec two-step *n* an attack of diarrhoea, particularly one suffered while travelling abroad. The image is of the agitation caused by impending diarrhoea, or more specifically the frantic and undignified clenched shuffle to the nearest toilet or bush. This parody of a dance title was coined by Americans who tend to suffer while on holiday in Mexico, and is a late 1970s alternative to **Montezuma's revenge** or the British **gyppy tummy** and **Delhi belly**.

B *n American* friend, peer. The abbreviation of buddy and/or bro(ther) is used as a greeting between males, particularly in black street usage. *Compare* **G**.

✍'*Hey B, how're they hangin'?*'

B.A. *n American* a troublesome, violent or anti-social person. An abbreviation of **badass**, or 'bad attitude'. The letters were used as the initials of the surly black hero 'B.A. Baracas' played by Mr T in the US television series *The A-Team* in the 1980s.

babe, babes, baby *n*

a sweetheart, lover. A usage imported from the USA into Britain via films, pop songs, etc. The word had begun to be used unself-consciously in Britain in the late 1970s, particularly in the form **babes** and mainly by working-class speakers. It is used by both sexes, but when used by men to women it can be considered patronizing or offensive.

b in the form 'babe', an attractive female. The word became a key term in male adolescent speech first in the USA and, later, elsewhere in the late 1980s. *See also* **robobabe**.

babe-magnet *n* an attractive or

supposedly irresistible male. A common characterization from the 1990s. **Fanny-magnet** is a more vulgar British variant.

(the) babes *n, adj* something excel-

lent, superlative. The usage, based on 'babes' as a term of endearment and by analogy with the colloquial expression 'the tops', has been recorded in Scotland and is sometimes heard elsewhere.

✍'*I tell you, it's the babes!*'
✍'*The do round Kirsty's last night was babes!*'

babia-majora *n American* an ex-

tremely attractive woman or women. A jocular item of ersatz slang invented for the cult US TV comedy sketches and movie *Wayne's World*, by alteration of the Latin designation of the outer female genitals *labia majora*.

baby blues *n pl* eyes. A humorous

adult phrase from the clichéd, twee or amorous description, 'baby-blue eyes'.

Babylon *n British*

a racist white society, Britain. The term originates in the biblical imagery of the **rastas**, but has spread, largely via the medium of reggae music, to other black youth and disaffected whites.

b the **Babylon** the police force, as tokens of oppression or white racist authority. A specific usage of the more general term for society, now widely heard among white youth.

baccy *n British* tobacco. This now

rather dated alteration of the standard term replaced the previous forms 'bacca' and 'bacco' early in the 20th century. (Cannabis was known jocularly in the 1960s and 70s as **wacky baccy**.)

bach/batch out *vb* to behave

and/or live like a bachelor. The term, which refers to living an 'unstructured' existence, was heard from the early 1990s.

✍'*He wasn't sure if he should go to Ireland or whether he should bach out at Pete's place.*'
(Recorded, American visitor to London, July 1994).

back *n American*

a buttocks, backside, especially if large or prominent. This term from black American usage became popularized via the **rap** lyrics to 'Baby Got Back' by Sir Mix-A-Lot (1991).

b a female or females seen as potential or real sexual partners. As in the case of **ass**, the preceding sense quickly became generalized in this way.

back-assed *adj American*

a backwards, reversed.
✍'*You got it all back-assed.*'
b perverse or clumsy.
✍'*A back-assed way of doing things.*'

backdoor *vb*

a to commit adultery (with).
✍'*In Australia, you'd never get away*

*with some of the things I've seen here
because you'd get a punch in the
mouth. We don't go in for backdooring
someone else's woman.'*
(Jamie Addicoat, fitness instructor, *Observer*, 30 April 1989).

b to act illicitly, covertly or deviously, to
deceive or betray.

backdoor man *n*

a a secret lover, especially a married
woman's lover. The term is originally
black American slang dating from at least
the 1950s.

✎*'I'm your backdoor man ... the men
don't know, but the little girls understand.'*
('Back Door Man', recorded by the
Doors, 1968).

b a man who sodomizes. This usage is
mainly applied to and by heterosexuals.
The Australian 'backdoor merchant'
means a homosexual.

backdoor work *n* a euphemism
for anal intercourse.

backfire *vb* to **fart**. A term which is
in use in Australia and has been heard occasionally in Britain, especially among
schoolchildren, since the 1950s.

back garden, back way, backdoor *n* the anus. Predictable
euphemisms which are invariably used
in a sexual context, usually by heterosexuals.

the back of Bourke *n Australian*
the 'back of beyond'. Bourke is a remote
town in Northern New South Wales.

backsiding *n British* chastising, denigrating, punishing. Heard in black British
usage, this term probably originated in
Caribbean patois.

✎*'She give him a real good backsiding.'*
(Recorded, black female student, London, January 1997).

backslang *n* backslang, in which a
word or alteration of a word is reversed
enjoyed some popularity in Britain,
chiefly among members of the underworld, the sub-proletariat and certain
trades such as meat portering. It is also
sometimes used by schoolchildren to disguise taboo conversations. Forms of backslang exist in other European languages,
notably in the Parisian *verlan* which is
still thriving. The only well-known 'mainstream' example of backslang is **yob** from

boy. *Compare* **pig Latin**.

back way *n See* **back garden**.

bacon *n American* a police officer or
the police. One of s several terms in underworld and student usage inspired by
the 1960s epithet **pig**. It can occur in the
form of '*(the) bacon*' for the police in general or '*a bacon*', denoting an individual
officer.

✎*'If you ask me he's bacon.'*
✎*'It's the bacon, let's book!'*

bad *adj* good. Originally from the terminology of the poorest black Americans,
either as simple irony or based on the assumption that what is bad in the eyes of
the white estaishment is good for them;
this usage spread via jazz musicians in
the 1950s to teenagers in the 1970s. It is
still primarily a black term, although occasionally used, rather self-consciously,
by white teenagers in the USA and, under
the influence of **rap** and hip-hop, in
Britain since the early 1980s. This use of
bad is normally distinguished from its opposite, literal meaning by a long drawn-out pronunciation. The superlative form
is 'baddest'.

✎*'In hip hop slang "That's bad" can
mean "that's good", depending on the
tone of voice.'*
(*Evening Standard*, 11 November 1987).

bad *n American* fault, mistake. A key
item of black street slang that was
adopted by white adolescents in the
1990s, usually in the form '*my bad!*', an
acknowledgement of guilt or blame.

badass *n, adj* (an) aggressive, antisocial or worthless (person). The word, first
popular among black Americans, is almost always now used with an element of
approval or admiration, albeit sometimes
grudging. The 'ass' component simply signifies 'individual'. In the 1970s the term
came into use among whites, but has not
spread to Britain or Australia.

✎*'Their badass biker style.'*
✎*'He's been a badass since he was a
kid.'*

bad-boy *n British* a youth, especially
a tough or admirable male. A 1990s synonym for **rude-boy** or **roughneck** first
used by black gang members before being
adopted by other teenagers and younger
schoolchildren. Like those terms, it is typical of the tendency by transgressive subcultures to adopt for the purposes of irony

and bravado the pejorative language of their critics (as in **bad**, **wicked**, etc.).

badmouth *vb* to insult, denigrate or disparage. An Americanism, probably originating in black speech, which has been imported into British usage since the 1970s.

bad news *n* a person who is unwelcome or disliked, a bore or troublemaker. A usage that was imported to Britain from the USA at the end of the 1960s.

bag *n* **1** an unattractive and/or unpleasant woman. This usage originated in the early 20th century with the idea of a shapeless, heavy or burdensome female, previously expressed as 'baggage'.
2 one's special interest or current preoccupation, sphere of activity. This usage came into vogue in Britain among the **beatniks** and later **hippies** in the 1960s. It was derived from black American jazz terminology, where it meant 'category' or 'style'. By the early 1980s the term had become distinctly dated.
✎ *'Papa's Got a Brand New Bag.'*
(Song title, James Brown, 1965).
3 *American* a package or some measured amount of marihuana or another drug. The custom of American street dealers of **grass** was, and is, to sell small amounts in paper envelopes or cellophane bags, typically **dime bags** or 'nickel bags'. *See also* **bagger**, **double bagger**.
4 *British* the sum of £1000 in the slang of city traders. Unlike **bar**, **pony**, and other similar terms, this seems to be a fairly recent coinage.
✎ *'It'll cost you at least a bag.'*

bag *vb* **1 a** to arrest or catch. This subsense of the word is encountered in police usage, from the terminology of hunters.
b to have or take. In this sense the word is used as a synonym for 'grab' or 'cop' in such instances as *'let's bag some beers'*. The usage also occurs in American adolescent argot which includes phrases such as **bag some z's/rays**.
2 a *American* to conceal or suppress.
b to give up or abandon.
✎ *'Maybe I should bag this tugboat business and go into politics.'*
(*Legwork*, US TV series, 1986).
c to dismiss, fire.
These usages, popular especially among teenagers, are all related by their suggestion of discarding someone or some-

thing with the trash. Similar meanings of bag were heard occasionally in Britain before 1950.
3 *Australian* to criticize. A **bagging** is a verbal attack or strong criticism.
4 *American* also **bag up**, to divide marihuana into small amounts and/or packages before selling it.
5 *See* **bag one's face**.

bagaza *n South African* a gun, especially a handgun.
(Recorded as an item of Sowetan slang in the *Cape Sunday Times* on 29 January 1995).

bagel-bender *n* a Jew. A derogatory nickname, used principally in the USA, based on the name of the baked bread rings that are a Jewish culinary delicacy. *Compare* **spaghetti-bender** and **taco-bender**.

bagger *n American* an ugly, repellent person. The term is a shortening of **double bagger** and, like that phrase, is in use among adolescent and pubescent speakers in the 1990s.

baggies *n* long, wide shorts as worn by surfers since the 1960s.
✎ *'We'll be wearin' our baggies,*
huarache sandals, too.'
('Surfin' USA', the Beach Boys, 1963).

bagging *n* **1** *British* a packed lunch, as carried by workers. A term heard especially in the north and midlands. **Snap** is an alternative.
2 *Australian* a criticism. *See* to **bag 3**.

baggy *n British* **1** (a devotee of) the **Madchester** music scene of the early 1990s. The so-called '*baggy scene*' probably took its name from the very loose clothing affected by devotees of **rave**, **acid house** and **indie** subcultures.
✎ *'For a while we were really into*
baggy.'
2 an unfashionable, unattractive individual. In this pejorative sense the word, recorded among students and young adults in the later 1990s to refer to a supposed frump or **drabbie**, is either an elaboration of the colloquial '(old) bag', influenced by the homely images of 'baggy cardigans/tweeds' or possibly by **bag lady**.

bag job *n* a theft or burglary. An underworld term heard in Britain but more widespread in the USA; not to be confused with a **paper bag job**.

bag lady *n* a female vagrant, specifically one who through obsession or necessity collects junk and carries it in bags. The term originated in the USA in the early 1970s; by the late 1980s it was occasionally also being used, there and elsewhere, to denote any excessively scruffy female.

bag man *n* **1** someone who collects, or looks after, money made illegally. An underworld and police term originating in the USA between the world wars and first applied to those sent by gangsters to collect extortion payments, illicit revenues or bribes.

↳ *'Before I got promoted I used to be a bag man for Kellom – just nickel and dime stuff.'*
(*The Big Easy*, US film, 1986).

2 a (male) tramp or vagrant, specifically one who collects and carries garbage in bags.

bag on (someone) *vb American* to insult or deride. A term from black street slang from the 1990s, it is probably adapted from earlier slang senses of **bag** as dismiss, abandon, etc. but is unlikely to be related to the similar Australian use of **bagging**.

bag one's face/head *vb American* to hide one's face or oneself. Invariably used as an imperative as in *'Go bag your face!'*. This expression is popular among **Valley Girls** and other middle-class teenagers. It implies that the person in question is too hideous to contemplate and should put a bag over their head. *See also* **bag someone's ass**.

bagpipe *vb* to engage in sexual stimulation using the armpit rather than the usual orifices. A term whose rarity presumably corresponds to that of the practice.

bags *n* **1** trousers. The word has had this meaning since the mid-19th century and survives, usually in a humorous context.

2 *American* breasts.

bag someone's ass *vb American* to leave, go away, 'get lost'. The expression literally means to thrust into a garbage bag and throw away.

↳ *'She had no intention of having lunch with him and that was that … Why couldn't she simply tell him to bag his ass?'*
(*The Switch*, Elmore Leonard, 1978).

bag some z's *vb American* an alternative version of **cop some z's**.

bagsy *exclamation* a schoolchildren's term that indicates the speaker's choice of seat, cake, bed, etc.

↳ *'Bagsy the one with the chocolate icing!'*

bag up *vb American* to divide marihuana into small amounts and/or packages (typically nickel or dime **bags**), before selling it.

bahookie *n British* the anus. The term, of unknown derivation, was used by the comic Scottish character Rab C. Nesbitt in the BBC 2 TV comedy of the same name in 1994.

baidie *adj British* bad-tempered, aggressive, provocative. An obscure term which is probably a dialect version of **batey**.

baigel *n South African* a spoilt young male. The term, which is derived from Yiddish (*bagels* are the baked bread rings often taken as emblematic of Jewish exiles' culture), has a female counterpart, which is **kugel**. Both refer to the notion of young Jewish people epitomizing chic urban circles in South Africa in the late 1990s.

bail *vb American* to leave (in a hurry). A teenagers' shortening of 'bail out'. The word has been fashionable among **Valley Girls** and others since the late 1970s.

bail/bale on someone *vb American* to oppress, burden or trouble. The bail or bale in question may derive from cotton picking as in the words from 'Ole Man River'; *tote that barge, lift that bale, get a little drunk and you lands in jail*, or may refer to bailing as in dumping water (on). The expression is typically used by teenagers and students.

bait *n* an attractive potential sexual partner. This term was used alone in the 1950s and 1960s or in compounds such as **bed-bait** and the surviving **jailbait**.

bake *n British* a hideaway or refuge. This example of the jargon of cat burglers was recorded in *FHM* magazine in April 1996, and defined there as 'a place to lay low while the constabulary run hither and thither in pursuit'. The precise origin of the term is uncertain, but it may come from the notion of the prison bake-house as a place where inmates can with-draw or hide illicit objects.

baked *adj American*
stoned. The term usually refers to the effects of marihuana and implies a milder intoxication than **fried**.

the baked bean *n British* the Queen. An authentic item of rhyming slang.

baksheesh, bakshee *n* a bribe, tip or payment. From the colonial era, the word is from Persian *bakshish*; something given.

bald *adj American* terrible. A vogue term among American teenagers in 1987 and 1988. The origins of this kind of appropriation from standard English are unrecorded, but often begin in gang code or street jargon.

bald-headed hermit *n American* the penis. A humorous euphemism now used typically by adolescent males, although the expression seems to have originated in educated British slang of the 19th century. (Also, perhaps coincidentally, in US slang of the turn of the century 'bald-headed' as well as its literal sense could mean both foolish and deceitful.)

Baldwin *n American* an attractive male. This vogue word among Californian high-school students was featured in the 1994 US film, *Clueless*, with its female counterpart **Betty** and its antonym **Barney**. The choice of the proper name may be arbitrary or may be inspired by the name of a celebrity (such as Alec Baldwin, star of romantic TV mini-series and Hollywood movies).

Bali belly *n Australian* diarrhoea. The Australian traveller's equivalent of **Delhi belly, Montezuma's revenge, gyppy tummy**, etc.

ball *vb American* 1 to have sex. An American term which, apart from a brief vogue in the **hippy** era, has rarely been used in Britain or Australia. Originally an item of black argot, it gained wider popularity in the early 1960s and, as its anatomical origin suggests, is generally a male usage.

⚘'*Presley fired me because I balled his old lady.*'
(The singer P. J. Proby, interviewed in 1965).

2 to behave in a boisterous, fun-loving and uninhibited way; to 'have a ball'. The term usually implies dancing, but also a degree of Bacchanalian, even orgiastic revelry far beyond that signified by the standard English (hunt or charity) ball.

⚘'*Good golly, Miss Molly, you sure like to ball!*'
(Little Richard, [ambiguous] song lyrics, 1958).

ball *n American* a stupid and/or obnoxious person. The slang for testicle has also been used as an insult by British junior-school pupils.

ball and chain *n* a spouse, usually one's wife. This jocular and obvious phrase has been heard in English-speaking areas throughout the 20th century.

ball-breaker, ball-buster *n*
a a very aggressive, dominant or demanding woman.
b an excessively hard taskmaster or martinet.
c an exhausting, demanding task.
All these terms were adopted in Britain and Australia in the 1970s from American usage. *Compare* **ball-tearer**.

ball-face *n American* a white person, particularly an unattractive male. A derogatory term from black street language based on the supposed similarity between the texture and colour of testicles and the colour of a typical Caucasian face.

ballistic *adj* furious, uncontrollable. This use of the term, often in the phrase '*go ballistic*', has become a common expression in the 1990s. It probably originated, unsurprisingly, in the slang of the armed forces, where it is still common.

⚘'*I totally choked; my father is going to go ballistic on me.*'
(*Clueless*, US film, 1995).

balloon *n British* a boastful or loud-mouthed individual, **blowhard, puff-bucket**. The term is heard particularly in the Scottish lowlands and the north of England.

⚘'*Aw, take no notice of the big balloon.*'

balls *n pl* 1 testicles. A predictable use of the word, balls was first used as a euphemism in Renaissance England, later becoming a standard, if coarse synonym.
2 rubbish, nonsense. This use of the word,

except perhaps as an exclamation, is surprisingly acceptable in middle-class speech (in such phrases as '*it's all balls*'), considering its derivation.

↳'*He was awarded a campaign medal, "but I didn't go to get mine. I wasn't interested; I thought it was all balls".*' (Falklands war veteran quoted in the *Observer* review of *The Fight for the Malvinas* by Martin Middlebrook, 9 April 1989).

3 courage, nerve. In this sense the word may now be applied to women in spite of the anatomical inconsistency.

4 *n* a mess. This is a modern mainly middle-class shortening of **balls-up**, usually in the phrase to '*make a balls of it/something*'.

5 *American* money, dollars. This usage was recorded in the later 1990s among adolescents. **Bollers** and **boyz** are British synonyms.

↳'*It's gonna cost you mucho balls.*' (Recorded, teenager, North London, June 1995).

balls-ache *n British* something or someone which is very tedious or trying.

balls-out *adj* full-scale, full-tilt. A vulgar version of all-out, this fairly uncommon intensifying expression is normally used by males.

balls up *vb* to make a mess of. In this mainly British expression, **balls** performs as a regular verb (**ballsing up** and **ballsed up** being conjugated forms). To **ball up** is an American alternative.

balls-up *n* a mess, mistake, disaster. This expression has been in use in Britain since the turn of the century.

ballsy *n* courageous, spirited. A vulgar alternative to **gutsy**. The word can be applied to either sex.

ball-tearer *n Australian* **1** a very demanding or exhausting task.

2 something spectacular or sensationally impressive. These are versions of the international English **ball-breaker**.

ball-tearing *adj Australian* **1** very demanding or exhausting.

2 spectacular, sensationally impressive.

Balt *n Australian* an immigrant (to Australia), a 'new Australian'. Not all so-called Balts were in fact from the Baltic states, which was the origin of the term,

commonly used in the early 1950s.

baltic *adj* cold, freezing. It is not clear where and when this usage originated, but it has been recorded among US college students and UK adults in the late 1990s.

↳'*It's bloody baltic in here!*'

bammy *n, adj British* (someone who is) crazy, eccentric. The term, originating as a dialect version of the colloquial 'barmy', is heard particularly in the Scottish lowlands and the north of England.

bam-stick *n British* a foolish or crazy person. The phrase is derived from **bammy** (the dialect version of 'barmy'), and is used particularly in the north of England and lowland Scotland. The 'stick' component may be a combining form denoting a person, or may refer to an actual stick used to pick up barm (the froth on fermenting yeast).

banana *n* **1** a foolish person. This childish term of mild abuse is now obsolescent in Britain, but predictably is still heard in post-colonial English in the Indian subcontinent, Malaysia, the Caribbean, etc. The 1950s **nana** was a shorter form.

2 penis. The mock nursery term **tummy banana** is more common.

3 *American* a light-skinned black woman. A term used by black men which is both appreciative and offensive.

4 an oriental person who affects white manners or collaborates with the white establishment. A term used by both white and oriental-language speakers, e.g. in Hong Kong and on US campuses.

bananas *adj* crazy or berserk. This now common colloquialism originated either in the notion of 'softness' (in the head) or from the archaic 'banana oil', 'soft soap', or 'balderdash'.

banana truck *n American* a crazy person. An expression which evokes a whole truck-full of bananas, hence an excess of 'softness' (in the head).

bandit *n British* **1** a homosexual. A dismissive or derisory term used by avowedly heterosexual males and deriving from longer expressions such as **trouser bandit, arse bandit, chocolate bandit**, etc.

2 -bandit. An ironic or jocular combining word, added to suggest a desperate or reprehensible character, or in police jargon, literally a criminal. In his *Field Manual for Police* (1977) David Powis cites '*milk bandit*' as an ironic term for penniless milk-bottle thieves; '*gas-meter bandit*' is self-explanatory.

band rat, band moll *n* a

groupie, girl who has sex with members of rock groups, especially one who follows or travels with them. Band rat is an American term from the mid-1960s, while band moll is Australian and from the early 1970s.

B and T *n British* 'bum and tit'. A

schoolboy abbreviation, popular especially in public schools in the early 1970s. The phrase usually refers to a glimpse of, or brief contact with, the mentioned parts, but can mean sexual experience in general.

♦'*He looks a bit tired; it's too much B and T.*'

bandy *adj British* bow(or 'bandy')-

legged as a result of sex. A working-class term used scornfully or jeeringly about a girl or woman by men. The term is not meant literally but the suggestion is that a girl has just had sex or has sex constantly. '*She's bandy!*' was shouted in the street by London **mods** and **skinheads** in the late 1960s.

bang *vb* 1 to have sex (with), **fuck**. The

association with striking (as in the origin of the word 'fuck' itself) is said to suggest the masculine role in sex, but in practice the unaffectionate term can also apply to women, especially in Australian usage where it is more common than in America. In Britain bang in this sense has only been widely understood since the late 1960s. It was introduced via the phrase **gang bang** and the following expression.

♦'*You're banging a major witness in a case you're trying?!*'
(*The Last Innocent Man*, US film, 1987).

2 *American* to be an active gang member. From the parlance of Los Angeles street gangs of the late 1980s, derived from the specific sense of **gangbanger**.

♦'*He's been banging for two years now.*'

bang *n* 1 a a sexual act. An unaffec-

tionate term used more often by men. In this sense the word does not seem to be older than the 20th century.

♦'*A quick bang.*'

b a person rated as a sexual partner.

♦'*A good bang.*'

2 *Australian* a brothel. The word is now rather archaic, but is still heard among older speakers.

3 a an exciting experience, a thrill. In this sense the word goes in and out of vogue, particularly among schoolchildren in many parts of the English-speaking world.

b a great success, very popular person or thing.

c an injection of illicit drugs, especially heroin, morphine or amphetamines, or the resulting jolt of pleasure. From the lexicon of drug users and addicts, originating in the 1940s or earlier and related to the more recent verb **bang up**.

bang *vb* to have sex (with).

banged-up *adj British* imprisoned,

shut away. From the second sense of the verb to **bang up**.

♦'*A banged-up man's no good to me. I want to enjoy life, not spend it in prison waiting-rooms.*'
(Recorded, drug-dealer's girlfriend, London, 1984).

banger *n* 1 a sausage. The word has

been common in this sense since the 1940s. It derives of course from the explosion of the skin during frying.

2 an old and/or decrepit vehicle.

banging *adj* exciting, powerful. Like

its contemporaries **kicking** and **slamming**, this term was in vogue from the early 1990s, especially among devotees of **rave** culture.

♦'*I tell you, it was banging.*'

banging *n American* a shooting. An

item of black street slang of the 1990s.

bangles *n pl*

a breasts.

b testicles. By association with the idea of adornment, as in **family jewels**, and with 'dangle'.

Both usages are most often heard among teenagers and schoolchildren all over the English-speaking world.

bang on *vb British* to nag, harangue

or talk incessantly and boringly. A popular term which has appeared in the 1980s in 'respectable' usage.

♦'*She's been banging on about her bloody job all evening.*'

bang/bash one's bishop *vb* to

masturbate. An old vulgarism once again

in vogue among middle- and upper-class males in Britain in the 1980s.

bang to rights *adj, adv British* red-handed, without hope of escape. This 19th-century expression (paralleled in American English by **dead to rights**) is usually heard in the form '*caught bang to rights*' or '*we've got him/her bang to rights*' (i.e. helpless, indefensible). Until the 1970s the term was part of the restricted codes of the police and underworld; since then the phrase has been given wider currency, particularly by the realist plays of G. F. Newman.

bang up *vb* 1 to inject oneself (with heroin or another hard drug). One of many drug-users' terms with overtones of bravado. Popular in Britain in the late 1960s and early 1970s.

2 *British* to imprison, shut away. A working-class, police and prisoners' term.

↘'*Being banged up's no joke, even in an open prison.*'
(Recorded, remand prisoner, 1986).

bang-up *adj American* excellent, exciting. The term occurs particularly in campus usage in the later 1990s, but was also recorded in British slang in the early 19th century where it was a shortening of a phrase such as '*bang up to the mark*'.

banjaxed *adj Irish* defeated, overcome or overwhelmed. A humorous term from the early 20th century, often used ruefully by husbands floored or humiliated in a domestic dispute. This Irish word, probably formed by association with 'banged', 'bashed', 'smashed', has been popularized in Britain by the Irish broadcaster, Terry Wogan, who used it as the title of a book in 1980. It can now be extended to mean stunned, flummoxed, amazed, drunk, etc.

banjo *vb British* to force entry, break in, especially by means of the battering device, to which the name has been given, based roughly on its shape. (Previously, shovels were known as banjos.) An item of police slang heard in the 1990s.

↘'*We're going to go round and banjo the house.*'
(Police officer, *Network First*, ITV documentary, February 1996).

banjo'd, banjoed *adj British*
a hopelessly drunk or under the influence of drugs. A jocular invention, perhaps influenced by **banjaxed** and some-

times heard among students and schoolchildren in the 1970s and the 1980s.

↘'*...stupid how they strut, smoking Woodbines till they're banjoed smirking at the Swedish smut*'
(*Psycle Sluts*, poem by John Cooper Clark, 1978).

b defeated, beaten. An armed-forces term of the late 1970s and 1980s. There may be a connection with **banjaxed** or with the archaic use of 'banjo' to mean a shovel or weapon.

bank *n American* money. A teenage vogue word of 1987 and 1988. The term was picked up by British **rap**, hip-hop and **acid house** enthusiasts and was still in use in the late 1990s.

↘'*Got any bank?*'

bank *adj American* inferior, unpleasant. A fashionable pejorative in black street slang of the 1990s, the term may be a blend of, or inspired by, terms such as **bunk**, **rank** but the noun 'bank' was used to mean 'toilet' in black slang of the 1940s and 50s, and yet another proposed derivation is from bankrupt.

BAP *n American* a 'black American princess'. A coinage based on the earlier JAP. Compare **buppie**.

baps *n pl British* female breasts. The expression, used typically by young males in the Midlands and north of England and Scotland, borrows the name of the small, round bread bun sold in various regions of the UK. **Muffins** is an equivalent North American usage.

bar *n British* one million pounds or one million dollars in the argot of London City traders. Used in this sense the word is probably a revival of the Romany *bar* or '*baur(o)*' which used to mean one sovereign or one pound and was still heard among street traders and prison inmates in the 1960s. See also **half a bar**.

bar! *exclamation British* an exclamation of dismissal or refusal, synonymous to its users with the colloquial 'no way'. The term was recorded in use among north London schoolboys in 1993 and 1994.

barb *n* a barbiturate. A shortening employed by drug abusers since the late 1950s.

↘'*We did a load of barbs and spent the rest of the day nailed to the floor.*'
(Recorded, student, Faversham, Kent,

1974).

barbie *n Australian* a barbecue. A common term since the late 1960s, now spreading via Australian TV soap operas to Britain where it has been adopted by **yuppies** in particular.

↳'*Australia was full of easy-going characters like Paul Hogan, who spent the day drinking Fosters and putting a shrimp on the barbie.*'
(Michael Parkinson, *Daily Mirror*, 17 April 1989).

Barbie (Doll) *n* a vacuous passive and/or conformist young woman. Barbie is the trademark name of the well-known plastic doll originating in the USA.

barf *vb American* to vomit. A popular student term dating from the 1950s. The word is imitative in origin and is sometimes used as an exclamation of disgust.

barf bag *n American*

a a disgusting or very unpleasant person. A teenagers' slightly less offensive version of **scumbag**.

b an airsickness bag. The term is rarely used in this sense, which derives from the verb **barf**: to vomit.

↳'*Word on the street is that you barf bags are giving the kids in the 7th grade a hard time.*'
(*Vice Versa*, US film, 1988).

barf city *n, adj American* (a) disgusting, revolting (place). The expression from **barf** (to vomit) is usually used as an exclamation of revulsion, typically by schoolchildren and teenagers.

barf (someone) out *vb American* to disgust, nauseate. A **Valley Girl** and teenagers' term, usually heard as an exclamation, as in '*It totally barfs me out!*'. It derives from **barf** meaning 'to vomit'.

bark *n British* cannabis. An item of prison slang based on the resemblance between the two substances, and recorded in the early 1990s.

bark *vb Australian* to vomit. By extension from the earlier use of bark as a humorous synonym for 'cough'.

barking *adj British* demented. A short form of '*barking mad*', evoking utter howling craziness, this expression is typically heard in upper- and middle-class speech, often preceded by 'absolutely'.

↳'*A friend in the Business was hugely amused when told of a forthcoming interview with Carla Lane. "She's quite barking, you know," he warned cheerfully …*'
(*Sunday Times* magazine, 4 March 1990).

barm pot *n British* a crazy, silly or eccentric person. A mild term of (often affectionate) abuse. Barm pot was on the way to becoming obsolete in the 1960s and 1970s but has enjoyed a revival in some circles in the 1980s. The phrase may either refer to a literal pot of barm (see **barmy**), or be an invention based on barmy, perhaps influenced by 'potty'.

barmy *adj* crazy. Barm is the froth of yeast formed on fermenting drinks such as beer (the word itself is related to the 'ferm' of ferment). The image of frothing lightheadedness and relation to intoxication gave rise to the term which is now a common colloquialism.

barnet *n British* hair, head of hair. A rhyming-slang term (from 'Barnet Fair'; both the event and the phrase in its full form were popular among Londoners in the second half of the 19th century) which is still widely used by working-class speakers and their imitators in and around London.

↳'*I'm stayin' in tonight and washin' me barnet.*'
(Recorded, social worker, Willesden, London, 1987).

barney *n British* an argument, fight or disturbance. Perhaps surprisingly the origin of this common term is obscure. It is assumed to derive from the male forename, but the connection between Barnaby and brawl or scuffle is unclear.

↳'*I like a bit of a barney from time to time – it helps to clear the air.*'

Barney *n American* an unattractive male. This pejorative term for a boy who is not categorized as a **Baldwin** was featured in the 1994 US film *Clueless*. The reason for the choice of proper name is uncertain, but may be inspired by the character Barney Rubble in the cartoon series and film *The Flintstones*, hence a primitive person.

baron *n British* a prisoner enjoying a degree of power and influence over his fellow-inmates. The source of the power is usually economic, with the baron controlling trade in cigarettes (a 'tobacco baron'), drugs or other prison currency.

barrel *n American* a gun. An item of street jargon from the 1990s employing the rhetorical device of synechdoche, or naming the whole from a constituent part.

꙳'*Teachers report that teenagers talk about "packing a barrel" or "chilling someone with a pipe".*' (*Sunday Times*, 31 August 1992).

barsy, barzy *adj British* mad, lunatic. A blend of barmy and crazy favoured by some middle-class speakers since the mid-1970s.

base *n*
crack. The term is a shortening of **freebase**, a system of smoking purified cocaine which pre-dated the use of the more refined and potent crack. The word base was in use among British users in 1989, together with many other nicknames.

base *vb American* to denigrate, criticize. A term from black street slang of the later 1990s used in the same way as **diss**.

base *adj American* unpleasant, disgusting, inferior. The standard term as in 'base behaviour' was appropriated, perhaps via black street slang, by high-school and college students in the 1980s. It is popular among female speakers.

꙳'*That new diner in the mall is, like, so base!*'

basehead *n American* a drug-user who **freebases** cocaine or smokes **crack**. The term dates from the early 1980s, the practice from the 1970s.

basements *n pl South African* shoes. The term is usually applied to trainers as worn by young males and was recorded in 1994.

bashed *adj American* drunk. One of a large number of synonyms evoking the idea of the drunkard as damaged or chastised.

bash the bishop *vb* (of a male) to masturbate. The phrase, recorded in the 19th century with its synonym 'flog the bishop', was probably the precursor of many similar jocular euphemisms such as **box the jesuit**, **spank the monkey**, etc. heard in the 20th century.

basher *n British* a shelter or shack made of cardboard, paper, plastic, etc. and lived in by a tramp or homeless person. The word is used by the 'gentlemen of the road' or **dossers** themselves.

꙳'*Their "bashers" (shacks) will be forcibly removed by police to make way for developers who want to "yuppify" the Charing Cross area.*' (*Observer*, 16 August 1987).

basing *n See* **freebasing**.

basket *n* **1** bastard. A euphemism used in Britain and Australia, particularly in the 1950s and 1960s, and especially by middle-class speakers.
2 *American* the male genitals. A male homosexual term, heard in the late 1970s and early 1980s.

basket case *n* a helpless invalid, a person who is mentally and/or physically incapacitated. Originally an Americanism, this expression (a variant of **cotcase**) has become widespread in recent years. It is now often used in journalists' jargon to refer to an irrevocably ruined enterprise.

bastard *n* the standard term for an illegitimate person has been used as a term of abuse, disapproval, pity, or even affection (particularly in British and Australian usage) since the early years of the 20th century.

꙳'*Targets: banks, shops, DHSS, cop-shops, Job Centres, rich bastards.*' (*Observer*, 3 April 1988).

bate *n British* a rage, fury, bad temper or state of agitation. An upper-class schoolboy word still preserved in the public-school vocabulary. The earlier spelling was usually bait, which gives a clue as to the origin of the word; it is thought to be a back-formation from baited (in the sense of teased, harassed or provoked), and not as is sometimes claimed from 'debate'.

batey *adj British* bad-tempered, irascible. A piece of dated but not yet archaic public-school slang deriving from the obsolescent use of **bate** to mean strife or argument.

bath bun *n British* **1** the sun. A less common alternative to **currant bun**.

꙳'*All this bleedin' rain. I've forgotten what the old bath bun looks like.*' (Recorded, street trader, London, 1988).
2 son.
Both uses are London working-class rhyming slang from the sweet fruit bun

originating in the city of Bath.

bath-dodger *n British* an un-washed or habitually dirty individual. **Soap-dodger** is a synonym.

bath(e)os *n pl South African* shoes. The term is usually applied to trainers, and probably derives from bath-house or bathing. Recorded as an item of Sowetan slang in the *Cape Sunday Times*, 29 January 1995.

batphone *n British*
a a walkie-talkie.
b a mobile telephone. The nickname, in-spired by the gadget featured in the *Batman* TV series of the 1960s, was first recorded among police officers in the early 1990s. **Squawker** is a synonym.

batso *adj British* crazy. The word, used typically by middle-class schoolchildren and adults, is an elaboration of the collo-quial 'bats' or 'batty', both based on the older expression 'to have bats in one's belfry'.
▷'*It seemed to me to be a completely batso idea.*'
(Recorded, London journalist, February 1995).

batter *n British See* **on the batter**.

battle-cruiser *n British* a **boozer**, the pub. This London rhyming-slang term originated, not surprisingly, in the 1940s, but is still heard, although **rub-a-dub** is probably more popular.

battler *n Australian* a resolute, ener-getic, or otherwise impressive person. The term (which used to denote a prosti-tute operating independently of a pimp) often applies to someone who is admired for triumphing over adversity. It also oc-curs in the form **bottler**.

batty *n Jamaican* backside, buttocks. The word, usually used in a sexual con-text, is an item of patois based on 'bottom' which has spread into white urban slang in the 1990s.

batty-boy *n British* a male homo-sexual. Nearly always used pejoratively, this is one of many terms from Jamaican patois using **batty**, a form of bottom, to denote sexuality.

batty-riders *n British* extremely short shorts or **hot-pants** worn by fe-males. The term was associated with the ragga or dance-hall reggae movement of the early to mid-1990s whose female ad-herents wore provocative clothes reflect-ing the salacious lyrics of the music.

batty-seed *n British* a male homo-sexual. This term from Jamaican patois (one of many based on **batty** meaning backside) was picked up like the more common **batty-boy** by London school-children in the 1990s. The origin of the 'seed' element is obscure.

bazillion *n American* a very large number or quantity. An alternative form of **zillion**, **squillion** and **gazillion**.
▷'*There are about a bazillion poems about trees.*'
(*Clarissa Explains It All*, US TV comedy, 1994).

bazooka'd *adj British* drunk. One of the many synonyms based on the no-tion of the drunkard as ruined, destroyed, etc.

bazumas, bazungas *n pl* female breasts. Supposedly humorous coinages (also rendered in other forms such as **gazungas**, **mazoomas**, etc.) which may have originated in an elaboration of 'bosom'.

bazza *n South African* friend, fellow gang member. Recorded as an item of Sowetan slang in the *Cape Sunday Times* 29 January 1995.

B-boy *n American* a participant in **hip-hop** street culture. This vogue term (the counterpart is **fly girl**) became wide-spread around 1982, but was first coined in the late 1970s. The initial probably stood for 'brother' as a term of address, or for 'break-dancer'.

beak *n* **1** nose. Beak has been used in this obvious sense since at least the be-ginning of the 19th century, although other terms, such as **hooter, bugle, conk** etc. are more popular.
2 a person in authority, especially a judge or schoolmaster. This old usage is now obsolete in American English but is re-tained in Britain in public-school slang and in the expression '*up before the beak*' (appearing before a magistrate or some-one else sitting in judgment). Attempts have been made to derive this meaning of beak from a Celtic term for judgment, but the more obvious derivation is from the intrusive beak (nose and/or mouth) of au-thority. The *Tatler* magazine reported in August 1989 that beak was still the stan-

dard Etonian slang for schoolmaster.

⮑ *'Finally the beak turn his beetling brow to them and his xpression [sic] become suddenly soft, his stern eye mild.'*
(Geoffrey Willans and Ronald Searle, *Back in the Jug Agane*, 1959).

beamer *n American* a BMW car. A **yuppie** nickname.

bean-bag *n British* a mild term of abuse among younger schoolchildren. Bean bags were used in throwing games and sports.

beaner, bean, bean-eater *n American* a Hispanic American, a Mexican or **Chicano**. A 1970s and 1980s term, highly offensive in the USA, which refers to poor Latin Americans' diet of *frijoles* or refried beans.

beans *n pl American* dollars. A humorous synonym possibly influenced by the colloquialism *'a hill of beans'* meaning something worth very little.

⮑ *'At least we're sitting on around a hundred beans from my brilliant idea.'*
(*Planes, Trains and Automobiles*, US film, 1987).

bear *n American* a police officer, especially in the vocabulary of CB radio. This usage derives from the US Forest Services' fire-warning posters showing 'Smokey the Bear' in the uniform of a ranger. It was adopted by CB enthusiasts in the mid-1970s.

beard *n* a male escort posing as a boyfriend, lover, husband, etc. The term (heard from the mid-1970s in showbiz and 'society' circles) may refer to a lesbian's 'official' partner, with whom she is seen in public.

beardie *n British* a bearded **beatnik**. A mildly derogatory term, often coupled with **weirdie** in the 1960s.

beast *n American* 1 a girl or woman. The term, typically used by male college and high-school students, may be either pejorative or appreciative.
2 the beast heroin. A drug users' ironic nickname.
3 a sex offender, in prison slang. A more recent synonym for **nonce**.

⮑ *'20 prison officers in riot uniform were observed banging their shields in unison and chanting "Beast, beast, beast!".'*

(*Observer*, 8 April 1990).

beast *vb British* to bully, oppress, humiliate. The word is part of the jargon of prisoners and prison officers.

beastie *n, adj American*
a (a) disgusting, coarse or disreputable (person).
b (something or someone) impressive, powerful or enormous. This expression, used typically by female teenagers, was a vogue term among blacks and whites in the USA in the 1980s and was adopted ironically in the name of the white **rap** group the Beastie Boys.

beasting *n British* a 'dressing-down', humiliation or instance of physical bullying. The noun, like the verb 'to beast', is formed from the use of **beast** in British prison slang to signify an authority figure.

beast(-man) *n British* a police officer or prison officer and, by extension, any figure of authority. The word was adopted by teenage schoolchildren in the 1990s.

beat *n* someone who is a member of the 'beat generation' or aspires to its values. The term, coined by the influential American writer Jack Kerouac and first published by John Clellon Holmes in his novel *Go*, is derived both from the notion of being beaten, downtrodden, or poor, and from the notion of beatitude, or holiness. The phrase 'the beat generation', coined in imitation of other literary groups such as the Lost Generation of the 1920s, originally applied to a relatively small group of writers, artists and bohemians in America immediately after World War II, whose activities and beliefs were minutely chronicled in autobiographical, mystical and experimental prose and poetry by Kerouac, Holmes, Gregory Corso, William Burroughs and Allen Ginsberg, among others.

The term **beatniks** (employing the Slavonic '-nik' suffix disparagingly) was applied to these and later followers by members of **straight** society, hostile to what they saw as the licentious, irreligious and communistic aspects of the beat lifestyle. In Britain the beats were a youth subculture of the early- to mid-1960s, which co-existed with **mods** and **rockers** and metamorphosed into **hippies**.

⮑ *'The most beautifully executed, the clearest and most important utterance yet made by the generation Kerouac*

*himself named years ago as "beat",
and whose principal avatar he is.'*
(Gilbert Millstein, *New York Times*, 5
September 1957).

beatnik *n* someone following a **beat**
lifestyle or modes of dress. The term was
coined by newspapermen to deride the
self-styled members of the beat generation but was later adopted by beatniks
themselves; the **-nik** suffix came from
Russian and was meant to identify the
beats with Godless Communism (as well
as being a derogatory word-ending in Yiddish terms such as **nudnik**). Aspects of
the beatnik lifestyle included scruffy dress
(often black), berets, modern jazz, coffee
bars, a slightly more liberal attitude to
sex than their contemporaries, at least a
pretence at interest in modern arts and
literature and a youth cult. Beatniks had
passed their peak by 1960, but many of
them (who incidentally referred to themselves simply as **beats**) were absorbed
into the **hippy** movement in the mid-
1960s.

✎ *'A petition signed by 2,321 residents
and holidaymakers at St Ives, Cornwall was handed to the Mayor, Ald.
Archie Knight during the weekend. It
calls for tighter vagrancy laws to rid
the town of beatniks.'*
(*Daily Telegraph*, 21 July 1969).

beat off, beat one's meat *vb*
(of a male), to masturbate. The first expression is primarily American, the second international.

beat one's boats *vb American* to
depart, run away. A jocular term heard in
the 1990s and based on **boats** as a slang
synonym for shoes or feet.

beaucoup *adj See* **bokoo**.

beaut *adj Australian* excellent, first-
rate. A well-known Australianism which,
although dated, is still in use.

beaver *n* **1 a** the female genitals. An
American term meaning the pubic hair
and vagina ('a beaver').

b an American term meaning a woman or
women seen exclusively as sex objects
('beaver').

✎ *'Let's get some beaver!'*
These terms became known, though
rarely used, outside the USA via pin-up
magazines in the late 1960s.

2 a beard, especially a full or luxuriant
one. A light-hearted 19th-century usage,

still heard among adults.

✎ *'He's sporting a handsome beaver.'*

Bedfordshire *n British* a bed or
bedtime. A nursery joke-form of the standard words, from the parents' catchphrase '*up the wooden hill to Bedfordshire*', meaning '(go) up the stairs to bed'.
This usage is in fact 200-year-old peasant
humour.

Beeb, the Beeb *See* **Auntie**.

beef *n* a complaint or grudge. This use
of the word has occurred in American
English since the early years of the 20th
century, originating in the speech of criminals, pugilists and marginals, etc. Since
the 1940s British speakers have also employed it. The relationship between this
sense of the word and its literal meaning
is not clear; the colloquial notion of
'brawn' may be involved.

✎ *'I just wanna tell you, I got no beef
about last night.'*
(*Miami Vice*, US TV series, 1987).

beef *vb* **1** to complain. In the 19th-cen-
tury language of street sellers, and later
in the theatre, beef was associated with
shouting, yelling and hence complaining.
By the early 20th century the word was in
use in the USA in the sense of a grudge or
complaint, but it is unclear whether the
usages are related.

2 *American* to **fart**. The usage may be inspired by the rhyme or pun on 'beef-
heart' (a meat product).

beef (someone) *vb* to have sex
with. A vulgarism in use all over the English-speaking world. Beef has had sexual
connotations, deriving from its use as a
synonym for flesh, for hundreds of years.
From the 1980s, as a verb **pork** is more
common.

beef bayonet *n* penis. A humorous
euphemism on the lines of **mutton dagger**, etc. The phrase was first popularized
in Britain by Barry Humphries' *Barry
McKenzie* comic strip, in the satirical
magazine *Private Eye* in the 1960s.

beef curtains *n pl* the female genitals. A late 1980s vogue term among
some male teenagers, particularly those
affecting 'street credibility'.

✎ *'Man, look at the beef curtains. Yeah,
the blonde one, know what I mean.'*
(Recorded, youth, Baker Street station,
London, 1985).

beersucker *n*
a the mouth.
b a heavy drinker.

beer-tokens *n pl British* one-pound coins or money in general, in the argot of students and other adolescents in the late 1980s. 'Beer-vouchers' is an alternative form.

bees 'n' honey *n British* money. A piece of London rhyming slang which, while never being a popular term, is still heard occasionally.

bee-stings *n pl* small female breasts. A jocular term employed by both sexes.

beetle *vb British* to hurry. A dated colloquialism revived by **Sloane Rangers** in the early 1980s. It is inspired of course by the scuttling of the insects.
✎'*I had to beetle along to Jonty's before lunch.*'

beetle-crushers *n pl British* heavy work boots. A humorous phrase often extended to refer to heavy or large shoes or footwear in general.

beevo(s) *n American* beer. A college students' term probably distantly related, via 'beverage', to the British **bevvy**. The fact that the Czech word for beer is *pivo* may be coincidental.

beggar *vb, n* a euphemism for **bugger** (except in the 'respectable' idioms '*beggar the imagination*' or '*beggar description*' when the meaning is to render impoverished or surpass).

beggar's velvet *n American* another term for **dust bunny**.

begonias *n pl American* the female breasts. The term is coined by analogy with other multi-syllable synonyms beginning with the letter 'b', such as **bazumas**, **bazungas**.

beige *adj American* dull, boring, insipid. A vogue term in the affected slang of west-coast adolescents heard since the 1980s. It may have originated as a **gay** disparagement of straight taste in decor, clothing, etc.

bell *vb, n British* (to make) a telephone call (to someone). A working-class usage which has become almost universal since the 1970s in the form '*give someone a bell*' or more racily, '*bell someone*'. It is also in Australian use.
✎'*I got a bell from old Milward yesterday.*'
(Recorded, businessman, London, 1988).

bell-end *n British* (tip of the) penis. A vulgarism popularized by the comic *Viz*. **Helmet** is a synonym.
✎'*He's scared to get his bell-end out!*'
(*Away The Lads*, BBC 2 TV documentary, February 1993).

bellyflop *n*
a a dive, landing stomach-first on water.
b an ignominious or total failure.

belter *n* something wonderful, excellent or exciting. An expression of enthusiasm heard predominantly in the north of England which can be applied equally to a girlfriend, a car, party, etc. This noun derives from the colloquial senses of the verb 'to belt' denoting thrashing, speeding, etc.
✎'*Just look at her. She's a right belter isn't she?*'

bender *n* **1** a bout of heavy drinking, a riotous spree. The term may have originated in North America in the mid-19th century when 'hell-bender' meant any event or spectacle which was outrageous, aggressive or exciting. An alternative derivation is from **bend the elbow**. In its narrower sense of unrestrained spree, the word was introduced in Britain at the end of the 19th century.
✎'*When his marriage collapsed, Dick went on a four-day bender.*'
(Recorded, business executive, London, 1986).
2 *British* a homosexual. A term of contempt, originally for a passive male homosexual who supposedly **bends over**. The term is now probably heard less frequently than in the late 1960s and early 1970s.
✎'*It's not every day that a man wakes up to find he's a screaming bender!*'
(*Blackadder II*, BBC TV comedy, 1988).
3 *British* a makeshift shelter. The word derives from the 'bender tents' used by gypsies or other travellers and made by stretching cloth or tarpaulin over bent-over saplings. It was brought into common currency by the women peace protesters camped outside the US base at Greenham Common in the mid-1980s.

bend over, bend down *vb*
a to submit to, or invite **buggery**. A eu-

phemism popular among all social classes in Britain in the 1960s and early 1970s.

✍ '*He'd bend over on Blackfriars Bridge for ten bob.*'
(Recorded, public schoolboy, London, 1970).

b (by extension) to yield or submit to abuse or attack. A term popular among businessmen in the 1980s. This may be a shortening of the phrase '*bend over backwards*' and is a brusquer version of '*take it lying down*'.

✍ '*I'm certainly not going to bend over for them.*'
(Recorded, company director responding to take-over attempt, London, 1988).

bend the elbow *vb* to drink alcohol. A hearty euphemism used by habitués of bars since the 19th century all over the English-speaking world.

bennie *n* a tablet of Benzedrine, trade mark for a variety of amphetamine used and abused from the 1940s to the 1960s.

Benny, Bennie *n British* a foolish, clumsy person, misfit. The name of a slow-witted male character (played by Paul Henry) in the long-running TV soap opera *Crossroads* was adopted as a nickname for unfortunate males and lasted into the late 1990s. The word became notorious when it was applied by British servicemen to inhabitants of the Falkland Islands in 1983. *See also* **still; throw a bennie**.

Benny Hill *n British* a till or cash box. An item of market-traders' rhyming slang based on the name of the late comedian and recorded in the mid-1990s. A synonym from the same environment is **Buffalo Bill**.

✍ '*Just hold on while I unlock the Benny Hill.*'

bent *adj* **1 a** criminal, crooked, dishonest. This usage has been widespread in Britain at least since the beginning of the 20th century. It is still used by the police to refer to anyone who is not **straight**, and by criminals and others to refer to corrupt police officers (often by the cliché phrase '*a bent copper*' – 'bent coppers' were damaged coins that could not be used in public lavatories in the 1950s and 1960s). A more colourful embroidery sometimes heard in Britain is '*bent as a butcher's hook*'.

✍ '*Remember, this happened in the 1960s when many detectives were bent.*'
(Former detective quoted in *Inside the Brotherhood*, Martin Short, 1989).

b stolen, forged.

✍ '*A bent motor.*'

2 sexually deviant, homosexual. A common term in Britain, mainly in working-class usage, since the 1940s. A London variant popular in the 1960s was '*as bent as a nine bob note*' (a non-existent, obviously forged denomination).

3 *American* drunk or under the influence of drugs. This usage is rather archaic, but the longer '*bent out of shape*' is still heard among college students and **preppies**.

4 *American* angry, furious. This seems to be an armed-forces term in origin. It is also more usual in the form '*bent out of shape*'.

be out! *exclamation British* an all-purpose cry of encouragement or enthusiasm in use among dancefloor-culture devotees in London in the mid-1990s.

beresk *adj* berserk, out of control. A humorous corruption perhaps inspired by a genuinely mistaken pronunciation, perhaps by the influence of 'bereft'. An alternative is **besrek**. Both forms have been heard, mainly among middle-class speakers in Britain and Australia – students and rugby players are typical users – since the early 1970s.

berk *n* a fool. This word, which has been widespread since the early 1960s, in Britain and Australia (where it was introduced via British TV comedies), is used as a form of mild derision by many speakers who would be shocked by its original meaning in rhyming slang. The origin is 'Berkeley hunt' or 'Berkshire hunt', meaning **cunt**, which in the late 19th and early 20th century was a Cockney synonym for fool.

✍ '*And how does he* [Paul Thompson] *see himself? Amiable berk? Complete nonentity? Heart-throb?*'
(*Evening Standard*, 2 September 1988).

bertie *n British* **1** a male homosexual. The connection between the name and the subject is unclear.

✍ '*He looks a bit of a bertie to me.*'

2 a fool, dupe. In this sense the word (probably based on the names Albert and **Herbert** as supposedly epitomizing foolish individuals) is typically used in London working-class speech.

✎ *'We're going to get a right pounding and they [the IRA]'ll make berties of us.'*
(Londoner calling a *LBC* radio phone-in programme, 25 October 1993).
3 *See* **do a bertie.**

berties *n pl British See* **take berties.**

besrek *n See* **beresk.**

best! *exclamation British* an ambivalent exclamation that may indicate approval or the sarcastic reverse; in these senses it has been defined by one of its users as *'that's good, ain't it? Not!'*. The term was recorded in use among north London schoolboys in 1993 and 1994.

betty *n* a girl, particularly a non-participant in sports such as skateboarding. A mildly derisory usage among some teenagers, possibly inspired by the character played by Michelle Dotrice in the TV comedy series *Some Mothers do 'ave 'em*. In the late 1980s betty became a vogue word in the US, often used to mean an attractive or popular girl. (In East Anglian dialect betty – perhaps coincidentally – is a prefix signifying 'female', as in *'betty-cat'*.

Betty Bracelets *n British* the police or a police officer. A jocular and ironic nickname bestowed by members of the **gay** community from the later 1950s. (Bracelets is archaic slang for manacles or handcuffs.)
✎ *'I was sitting there minding my own business when up comes Betty Bracelets looking all obstreporous ...'*
Recorded, male transvestite, London, 1992).

bevvied *adj British* drunk. From the increasingly popular use of the noun and verb shortenings of 'beverage'.

bevvy, bevvie *vb, n British* (to take) an alcoholic drink. A predominantly working-class abbreviation of 'beverage' in use since the 19th century, usually referring to beer. It seems to be gaining new popularity among students, etc. at the end of the 1980s.
✎ *'We had a few bevvies on the way here.'*
(Recorded, workman, York, 1986).
✎ *'They've been bevvying since lunchtime.'*

beyond the black stump *adj Australian See* **black stump.**

Bezz, Bezzie *n British* a cloddish, unsophisticated person. This term from the 1980s street slang of Manchester probably derives from an eponymous individual who bore this nickname, such as Mark Berry of the band the Happy Mondays. The music impresario Tony Wilson, when reminiscing, commented of the band New Order, *'They were all Bezzies.'*

B.F., b.f. *n British* 'bloody fool'. A pre-World War II, mainly middle-class euphemism, now sounding rather dated. The initials have sometimes been used with more vehemence, probably on the assumption that the 'f' in question stood for **fucker**.

B-52 *n American* a beehive hairstyle (as worn in the early 1960s and occasionally revived). The nickname borrowed the designation of a World War II bomber plane. A well-known avant-garde rock group from Macon, Georgia, adopted the expression as their name in the late 1970s.

B-girl *n American* **1** a prostitute or woman of dubious morals who frequents bars.
2 the female counterpart of a **B-boy. Fly-girl** is a more common synonym.

bi- *adj, n* bisexual.

bible *n See* **Tijuana bible.**

bible-basher an over-enthusiastic evangelist Christian. *See also* **jesus freak** and **god squad.**

bicycle *n See* **town bike.**

biddy *n* **1** a woman, especially an old or middle-aged one. The word was originally applied as a term of endearment. It is an affectionate form of Bridget.
2 wine. Usually a short form of **red biddy.**

bif, biff *n British* **1** a cigarette. A vogue term among adolescents in the later 1990s, the derivation of which is obscure.
✎ *'Chas's just caned my biffs.'*
2 an Internet user deemed to be embarrassing or unfortunate, in the patois of **cyberpunks** and **netheads**. This categorization is defined in *Surfing on the Internet*, by J. C. Hertz (1994), as 'the archetypal ultimate loser-cum-cyberpunk-wannabee stuck in the fantasy world of low-end equipment, limited software and all-caps mode'.

biff *vb British* to have sex. A rarer alternative form of **boff**, heard particularly among male adolescents in the early 1990s. The word can be used both transitively and intransitively.

biftad *n American* a male **preppie**. This comic but probably ephemeral coinage was recorded in use among American teenagers in 1987. It is a combination of two supposedly archetypal preppie nicknames as in the exchange:
'*Say, Biff...*'
'*Yes Tad?*'

biffie *n Canadian* a toilet. The origin of the word, heard in the 1960s and currently popular among male adolescents, is obscure. It might possibly be a corruption of the French *buffet* in the sense of bench or stool.

the big A *n Australian* Shortened form of the phrase '*the big arse*', meaning the 'heave-ho' or giving someone 'the elbow'. *See* **arse 4**.

the Big Apple *n American* the nickname for New York City. It seems to have originated among jazz musicians, perhaps from the notion of '*a bite of the apple*' meaning a chance of success.

big bamboo, the big bamboo *n* penis. In Caribbean English (and joky white imitations thereof from America to Australia) this euphemism has featured since the 1950s.

the big cack *n Australian* a wild celebration, enjoyable experience. **Cack** in this case is probably a short form of cackle with a nod to its other ruder sense. The term was popularized by Australian revellers in London in 1994. It denotes, according to the *Sunday Express*, 'the holy grail of funlovers, the ultimate party experience'.

big E *n* the **elbow**. *See also* **arse 4**.

big enchilada *n American* an important or self-important person, the boss. A humorous phrase from the 1970s. An enchilada is a Mexican filled pancake. The term is a later imitation of the pre-World War II colloquialisms, '*Big cheese/potato*'.

big girl's blouse *n British* a weak, ineffectual or pathetic male. A phrase usually heard in the north of England. It first came to prominence in the late 1960s.
↳'*Naff ballet roles – the big girl's blouse in* Les Sylphides.'
(*The Complete Naff Guide*, Bryson *et al.*, 1983).

big hair *n American* a spectacular teased or bouffant female hairstyle. This Americanism, dating from the 1950s, has begun to be used in other English-speaking areas in the 1990s, usually sarcastically.

the big house *n American* a prison, especially federal prison. This underworld euphemism was publicized by its use as the title of an Oscar-winning film of 1930 starring Wallace Beery.

big jobs *n British* excrement, defecation. A mainly middle-class nursery term, in use since the 1940s.

big man on campus *n American See* **B.M.O.C.**

big-note *vb Australian* to boast or to praise. The term probably referred originally to large denomination bank notes.
↳'*I big-noted myself.*'
(Mel Gibson, Australian actor, 1987).

big-noter *n Australian* a braggart, boastful person. From the verb form.

the big O *n* orgasm, particularly female orgasm. A journalese catchphrase probably originating in therapy and feminist circles in the USA in the early 1970s.

the big spit *n* an act of vomiting.

big (someone) up *vb British* to boost someone's confidence, praise. This fairly widespread slang phrase of the late 1990s probably originated in black British usage.
↳'*She were biggin' 'im up, goin' gwaarn, gwaarn! at 'im ...*'
(Recorded, black teenage girl, London, March 1997).

Big Swinging Dick *n* forceful, powerful individual. The term evokes a large virile male and is in use particularly among financial traders, first in Wall Street, and subsequently in the City of London. Impressive female colleagues were known in London as *Honorary Big Swinging Dicks*. The term was sometimes disguised as **B.S.D.**

bike *n See* **town bike**.

biked *adj British* deceived or de-frauded. This item of taxi-drivers' jargon often refers specifically to the driver's dilemma when the passenger disappears into a building without paying. It was recorded in the *Evening Standard*, 22 April 1996.

biker *n* a motorcycle rider, a member of a motorcycle gang. This American usage was unknown in Britain until the late 1960s when biker style and hard-ware began to be imitated.

bikie *n Australian* the Australian ver-sion of **biker**.

bilk *vb* to cheat someone, especially by withholding due payment. This word was in use in the late 17th century, also hav-ing the meaning of frustrate. (It may therefore be related to balk and baulk.)

bill, the Bill, the Old Bill *n British* the police. A working-class Lon-don term which slowly entered common currency during the 1970s, partly owing to television police dramas. The term's origins are obscure. It seems to have passed from **Bill** or **Old Bill**, a mock af-fectionate name for individual policemen, via **the Old Bill**, a personification of the police force as a whole, to **the Bill**. It can also be used in expressions such as *'(look out) (s)he's Bill!'* – he or she is a police of-ficer. Coincidentally or not, in 1917 the Metropolitan Police used Bruce Bairnsfa-ther's famous cartoon figure 'Old Bill' (he of *'If you know of a better 'ole, go to it'*) on a recruiting campaign. It may also be sig-nificant that when the Flying Squad was first motorized, all their licence plates had BYL registrations.

 ✎ *'A banner was draped from cell win-dows* [at Wandsworth prison where police had taken over from striking warders] *reading: support the screws – Old Bill out.'*
 (*Guardian*, 3 January 1989).

bill *vb American* to depart, leave. One of many fashionable synonyms in use in black street slang, later adopted by white adolescents in the late 1990s. It is prob-ably an alteration of the earlier **bail**. A va-riety of euphemisms (like its contempo-raries **bail**, **book**, **jam** and **jet**) for 'run away' are essential to the argot of gang members and their playground imitators.

 ✎ *'Someone's coming, we better bill!'*

Bill and Ben *n British* yen (Japan-ese currency). An item of rhyming slang

from the lexicon of London City traders in the 1990s. The names are those of the two 'Flowerpot Men', heroes of a 1950s children's TV puppet show.

billiards *n pl See* **pocket billiards**.

billies *n pl American* money, dollar bills. A popular term among **Valley Girls** and other teenagers since the early 1980s.

Billy (Bunter) *n British* an ordi-nary member of the public, customer. This item of rhyming slang from '*Billy Bunter*', meaning **punter** – borrowing the name of the fat schoolboy hero of chil-dren's stories – was widely used in service industries in the 1990s.

 ✎ *'Billies is our name for the clients ... no disrespect.'*
 (Club 18–30 representative, *Sunday Times Magazine*, 24 September 1995).

bim *n* a shortened form of **bimbo/bim-boy**.

 ✎ *'He wanted some bim to be skating down the slopes in a bikini.'*
 (*Blind Date*, TV dating show, March 1997).

bimbette *n* a silly, empty-headed young girl. A jocular diminutive of **bimbo**, popular in the mid-1980s, first in the USA and then, via magazine articles, in Britain, where it has been enthusiastically taken up and over-used in the tabloid press.

bimbetude *n* combined physical at-tractiveness and intellectual vacuity. This humorous combining of **bimbo** and 'pul-chritude' was briefly recorded in the early 1990s.

bimbo *n* **1** a silly, empty-headed or frivolous woman. This is the sense of the word in vogue since the late 1980s, im-ported to Britain and Australia from the USA. The origin is almost certainly a vari-ant of *bambino*, Italian for baby. In the early 1900s a bimbo, in American collo-quial use, was a man, especially a big, un-intelligent and aggressive man or a clumsy dupe. By the 1950s the word was used as a nickname for boys in England, perhaps inspired by a popular song of the time. By the 1920s bimbo was being ap-plied to women, especially by popular crime-fiction writers, and it is this use that has been revived in the 1980s with the return to fashion of glamorous but not over-cerebral celebrities. In the late

1980s the word was applied again occasionally to males, although with less brutish and more frivolous overtones than earlier.

✎ *'Darryl Hannah plays an interior designer and Gekko's part-time mistress who turns her attention to Bud Fox's apartment and bed. She's meant to be a rich man's bimbo.'*
(Oliver Stone, US film director, *Sunday Times* magazine, February 1988).

2 *British* bottom, backside. A nursery and schoolchildren's word of the 1950s, now rarely heard.

bimboid *adj* vacuous, having the attributes of a **bimbo**.

bimboy *n* a male **bimbo**. This humorous item of journalese is a synonym for the (possibly more common) **himbo**.

bin *n* a pocket, usually in trousers. This example of the jargon of cat burglars was recorded in *FHM* magazine in April 1996.

bin *vb British* to throw away, reject. A sharper or more imperious version of 'chuck it' or 'dump it' is *'bin it'*, heard since the late 1980s, especially in offices and in a broader business context.

the bin *n British* a mental hospital or asylum. A shortening of **loony bin**.

✎ *'If she goes on like this she's going to end up in the bin.'*
(Recorded, housewife, London, 1988).

bindle *n American* a package of illicit drugs in the form of a small bundle or packet. This item of early 1960s drug-users' slang derives from bindle; a bundle of bedding carried by a hobo, which in turn comes from the German *Bündel*; bundle (or from the German pronunciation of the standard English word).

bindlestiff *n American* a migrant hobo. (For the origin of bindle, see above.) This dated term is still heard.

bingo *n British* an arrest, a successful search. A customs officers' term employing the triumphal cry from the popular game of chance.

✎ *'We got a bingo finally after three weeks.'*

bins *n British* **1 a** glasses, spectacles. A Cockney shortening of binoculars, sometimes spelled **binns**. The term has been in use at least since the 1930s and is still heard.

b eyes. An extension of the previous usage.

2 a headphones. Part of the jargon of recording engineers and rock musicians in the late 1960s; the term was eagerly picked up by hi-fi enthusiasts and **musos** in the 1970s, although **cans** is more prevalent in this context.

b hi-fi or concert speakers. By extension from the above.

bint *n British* a girl, (young) woman. *Bint* is Arabic for daughter or girl; the word was adopted by soldiers serving in Egypt and became widespread in Britain from the 1920s to the 1960s. In English the word nearly always had, and has, deprecatory overtones.

✎ *'I've got to keep him and that Russian bint one step ahead of the police.'*
(*Room at the Bottom*, TV comedy, 1987).

bio-head *n American* an unstylish person, **nerd**. The expression was recorded in the late 1990s among college students and Internet users.

bird *n British* **1** a girl. A very common term in the late 1950s and 1960s, it is now somewhat dated and considered offensive or patronizing by most women. The word was first a 19th-century term of endearment, ultimately from Middle English, in which bird could be applied to young living things in general, not merely the feathered variety.

2 a prison sentence. From the rhyming slang 'birdlime'; time.

✎ *'He's doing bird in Wandsworth.'*

birdbath *n British* a silly person. A humorous variant form of the colloquial 'birdbrain' typically used since the 1970s by parents and children.

bird droppings *n British* an adolescent euphemism for **chickenshit** in the sense of something derisory or pitiful.

birding *n British* chasing or trying to 'pick up' women. A northern English working-class term of the 1960s and 1970s, from the more widespread use of **bird**.

birf *n British* a coy or jocular shortening of birthday, used typically by teenage-magazine journalists in the 1980s.

birl *n See* **burl**.

Birmingham screwdriver *n British See* **Brummagem screwdriver**.

biscuit *n American* **1** an attractive person. The term heard in the late 1990s, can be used by and of either sex. *Compare* **earth biscuit**.

↳*'Wow, a total biscuit!'*

2 the head.

↳*'The result was, Chrissie bumped her biscuit.'*

biscuits *n American* the buttocks.

↳*'Man, scope those biscuits.'*

bish-bash-bosh *adv, adj British* quickly, efficiently, in quick succession. A vogue catchphrase in use among fashionable young professionals in London in the mid-1980s.

↳*'It was bish-bash-bosh/a bish-bash-bosh job.'*

bishop *n See* **bang/bash one's bishop**.

bit *adj American* disappointed, resentful. A folksy version of 'bitter' or 'bitten' used by country people and poor blacks (in pre-war slang it usually meant 'cheated'); adopted as part of **preppie** language in the 1970s.

↳*'She sure was bit when she found out she hadn't been chosen.'*

bit *n* **1** activity, scene, subject. In **hip** talk and the argot of **beatniks**, as in *'the whole religion bit'* or *'he did his mysticism bit'*.

2 A **bit** is used as a euphemism for sexual activity, as in *'a bit on the side'*.

bitch *n*

a a pejorative term for a woman which although not strictly speaking slang is normally highly offensive. As a term of denigration bitch, like its alternatives 'sow', 'vixen' etc. has been widespread since the Middle English period. In black American speech 'bitch' can be used with proprietorial or condescending overtones rather than with personalized malice.

↳*'Ultimately, it [N-W-A's album]'s just another extension of the black underclass machismo which casts all women as "bitches".'*
(*Independent*, 8 September 1989).

b a spiteful or vindictive male homosexual.

c an infuriating or gruelling task.

d something impressive, admirable. This is another example of a negative term being employed in a contradictory sense (compare **bad**, **wicked**, etc.). It usually occurs in the appreciative phrase '**it's a**

bitch' in American speech.

bitchin' *adj American* excellent, first class. From the colloquial phrase *'it's a bitch!'*, expressing great enthusiasm.

biting *n* selling a graffiti artist's pen name to another young person. Usually seen in this form rather than the verb 'bite'. It is a specialization of the colloquial sense of bite meaning coercion.

bit of fluff/stuff *n British* a woman, seen as attractive but frivolous, or not to be taken seriously. A condescending male term from the early 1900s, still fairly widespread in the 1960s and not yet obsolete.

bit of rough *n British* a lover, of either sex, who exhibits or feigns primitive, aggressive or socially inferior characteristics. A phrase often used jocularly in the 1980s, originally a variation of the prostitutes' and homosexual term **rough trade**.

↳*'She's always preferred a bit of rough.'*

bitser, bitza *n* a mongrel (usually a dog). A witticism based on the idea that the animal's pedigree is composed of 'bits of this and bits of that'. The expression, which probably originated in Australia, can also be applied to anything put together from disparate components.

bivvy *vb British* to bivouac, make camp. A shortening used by scouts and the armed forces in the 1970s and 1980s.

bivvy *n British* **1 a** a bivouac, camping place.

b a tent, especially a small tent. Both terms are, predictably, part of the vocabulary of soldiers, scouts, campers and ramblers, etc.

2 an alternative form of **bevvy**.

biz, the biz *n*

a the **biz** show business. A term used by the self-consciously theatrical, originating as 'show biz' in the style of journalese popularized by *Variety* magazine.

b any sphere of activity, such as the music biz, the public relations biz, etc., by extension from the first sense. It is often used ironically to add a sheen of cheap glamour to difficult or thoroughly mundane jobs. In the company of cognoscenti, any such group may be referred to as **the biz**.

c a term of approbation, as in *'this is the*

biz' or *'he's the biz'*.

blab *vb* to inform (on someone), to tell tales or reveal information. The term often has the sense of a garrulous or inadvertent revelation of a secret or confidence. Like blabber, the word has meant '(to engage in) voluble or indiscreet talk' since the 16th century.

blabber *n Australian* a TV remote control. This item of domestic slang of the 1980s refers to the mute capability. No universal slang term for the remote control has yet emerged, though **zapper** is a recorded alternative.

black bag job *n American* a break-in or other covert operation carried out by a government agency. A piece of jargon from the time of the Watergate scandal.

black bombers *n pl British* capsules of Durophet (a form of amphetamine popular among drug abusers in the 1960s), named from their colour and their powerful effects.

blackie *n British* a cannabis **joint** containing an amount of cocaine.
↳*'So when I was offered a blackie ... I accepted and enjoyed it.'*
(*News of the World*, 21 October 1990).

blackjacks *n pl American See* **cosh** boy.

black maria *n* a prison van or police car or van. The nickname originated in the USA in the mid-19th century (Maria is probably an arbitrary borrowing of a female name as a familiarizing device).

black rat *n British* a traffic patrol officer. An item of police slang recorded by the *Evening Standard* magazine in February 1993. The black refers to the uniform and the rat to other officers' and motorists' dislike of the traffic police.

black stuff *n American*
a a drug user's euphemism for opium.
b *British* tarmacadam.

black stump *n Australian* the mythical starting point for the 'back of beyond'. *See also* **woop-woop**.

bladdered *adj British* drunk. An increasingly common term among middle-aged speakers as well as students, etc. since the early 1990s. It has been used in the TV soap opera *Brookside*.
↳*"What I like to do on a Monday night*

is go out and get bladdered," says Mick.'
(*Telegraph Magazine*, 15 June 1996).
↳*'... the conversation begins to steer bladderedly through a number of topics ...'*
(*Q* magazine, March 1997).

blade *n* a knife, particularly when used for protective or offensive purposes.

blag *n, vb British*
a (to carry out) a robbery. This is the sense of the term familiar to most people since its use in TV shows of the 1970s giving a realistic perspective on criminal milieus.
b to scrounge, cadge, deceive or bamboozle, or the booty from such an activity. The word blag has been in widespread use in both senses in underworld and police circles since the early 1950s. It is presumed that it derives from the French *blague*: a joke or blunder, but the details of this etymology are unclear. There have been suggestions that it is more simply an elaboration of to **bag**.

blah *n, adj* (something) dull, tedious, listless, inert. A pejorative term deriving from an exclamation of boredom or resignation. The word spread from the USA to Britain before World War II.

blair, blare *vb British* to criticize, denigrate, belittle. A word of obscure origin (it precedes the media attention paid to the Labour leader Tony Blair). It may have originated in black speech and may simply be an appropriation of the standard meaning of blare, i.e. to shout, trumpet. The term was recorded in use among North London schoolboys in 1993 and 1994.

blank (someone) *vb British* to snub, refuse to speak to someone or acknowledge them. A mainly working-class expression becoming increasingly popular in London since the later 1980s. The past participle form 'blanked' in particular is a vogue term among schoolchildren.
↳*'Donna went to see her and she totally blanked her.'*
(*EastEnders*, British TV drama series, March 1988).

blast *n* **1 a** a party or celebration.
b any enjoyable or exhilarating experience.
2 an inhalation of cannabis or another euphoric drug.

blat *n Australian* a short trip on a bicycle. The word, which was featured in the long-running soap opera *Neighbours* in 1996, has been adopted by British schoolchildren.

blatant *adj British*

a excessive, outrageous. A vogue term (invariably used to indicate approval) among adolescents in the mid-1990s.

↳ '*Crispin was being blatant again as usual when we went to TuTu's.*'
(Recorded, London University student, December 1996).

b Blatant! an exclamation of agreement.

blatherskite, blatherskate, bletherskite *n*

a a boastful or bombastic person, a 'windbag'.

b a villainous or disreputable person.

This picturesque word is the American and Australian version of the Scottish dialect word 'bletherskate'. Although it is a fairly innocuous term of mild abuse it derives from 'blether' meaning a bladder or to blather, and 'skate', a dialect variant of **shit**. The image evoked is of someone who is '*full of shit*'. During the War of Independence, Americans became familiar with the word from the Scottish song, 'Maggie Lauder'.

blatted *adj British* intoxicated by drugs or alcohol. A popular word among adolescents in the 1990s. Like many synonyms, the word evokes the notion of someone struck (down) or punished (which has been rendered by '*blat*' and '*blatter*' in dialect for centuries).

bleeder *n British* an individual, particularly an unfortunate or despicable person. This working-class term often conveys strong dislike or contempt. It dates from the 19th century, but has lost popularity since the 1960s.

bleeding *adj British* an intensifying term, currently out of fashion, but widespread in the 1960s when it was significantly stronger than **bloody**. This usage probably dates from the 19th century in working-class speech.

Blighty *n British* Britain. An anglicization of the Hindustani *bilayati*, meaning foreign. The word was originally used with some affection by the pre-World War I colonial army, but is now used only to suggest mock jingoism.

↳ '*I was blown through the door and put my hand to my head. It was covered in blood, but we had no thoughts of Blighty. We didn't want to go back, we'd only just come.*'
(World War I veteran David Watson, *Independent*, 12 November 1988).

blim *n British* a very small portion of a drug, usually hashish. A rare and obscure coinage, recorded among drug users and dealers in London in the late 1980s.

blimp *n* **1** *British* a pompous, old-fashioned, ineffectual person. The term was used to describe army officers of 'the old school' around 1939 and originated in Colonel Blimp, a character invented by the cartoonist David Low, probably inspired by blimp as the name of a small World War I barrage balloon. The word was commonly used in this sense in the 1950s.

↳ '*The Life and Death of Colonel Blimp.*'
(Title of a British film by Powell and Pressburger, 1941).

2 a fat person. A favourite American college-student term of derision, also heard among British schoolchildren and others in the 1980s. From the name of the World War I barrage balloon.

↳ '*When I was playing tennis I was just a fat blimp waddling round the court.*'
(Annabel Croft, *Today*, 7 February 1989).

blimp out *vb American* to become sated and/or collapse from overeating. An elaboration of **blimp** in the sense of fat person. In black street slang of the 1990s it is often shortened to 'blimp'.

blind *adj South African* unpleasant, painful. Recorded as an item of Sowetan slang in the *Cape Sunday Times*, 29 January 1995.

blinder *n British* an impressive or exciting action, thing or person. The word, which is often used for a sporting feat, commonly in the phrase to '*play a blinder*', implies something 'visually stunning'.

Blind Freddie *n Australian* the personification of a slow-witted, ignorant individual. The term is usually employed in phrases such as '*even Blind Freddie knows that*'.

blinding *adj British* excellent, outstanding, astonishing. This old term of approbation from the language of middle-aged Londoners was adopted as a vogue term by adolescents in the 1990s, sometimes in the form of an exclamation. (The colloquial **blinder**, meaning a dazzling feat, has been popular since the 1970s.)

✤*'It was a totally blinding bop.'*

✤*'Recently I bought a copy of the* Big Issue. *The man took the money and then, instead of the usual "Cheers!" or even "Thank you!", he said, "Blinding!"'*
(*Telegraph Magazine*, September 1996).

blissed-out
adj ecstatic, euphoric or in a trance, specifically as a result of religious experience. The term is from the jargon of transcendent 'fringe' or alternative religious cults of the late 1960s.

blitzed
adj very drunk or **stoned**. The usage ultimately derives from the German *Blitz* (lightning) *Krieg* (war).

✤*'Jesus, she was completely blitzed, absolutely out of her head.'*
(Recorded, photographer, London, 1989).

blob
n British 1 a corpse, road-accident victim. An unsympathetic term used by ambulance men, the police and tramps.

2 an ulcer, excrescence.

3 a bodily protuberance, a breast or a testicle.

4 a condom.

The second and third senses of the word are recent mock-childish coinages in use particularly among schoolchildren and students.

In archaic British slang, blob has been used in a variety of sexually related contexts, e.g. *'on blob'*, meaning sexually aroused, and *'blobbing'*, meaning suffering from a venereal infection. *See also* **on the blob**.

blobocracy
n British members of middle management or office workers, especially those considered unimaginative and undynamic. This dismissive epithet was heard in the office slang of the 1990s, typically used by senior executives of their subordinates.

✤*'If you want to get anything done, the simplest thing is just avoid the blobocracy and push it upstairs as fast and hard as you can.'*
(Recorded, advertising sales executive, London, 1995).

blob wagon
n British an ambulance. From the language of tramps and **dossers**.

✤*'Being rescued by the "blob wagon" for*

hospital treatment.'
(*Observer*, August 1987).

block
n British 1 head. Since the early 1950s this old term has only been used as part of phrases such as *'knock someone's block off'* or *'do one's block'*.

2 **the block** solitary confinement. A prisoners' term which is a shortening of 'punishment block'. **Down the block** denotes being (sent) into solitary confinement.

block (in)
vb British to have sex (with). A working-class male vulgarism heard from the late 19th century until the 1960s. It may now be obsolete.

blocked
adj British under the influence of drugs, especially **'pep pills'** or amphetamines. This word was popular in the early 1960s among **mods**, who used it to refer to the state of intoxication caused by 'pep pills' or amphetamines, such as **purple hearts**, **blues**, **black bombers**, etc. The origin is probably in the idea that one's **block**, or head, was completely taken over, and partly incapacitated by the drug. This is reinforced by the fact that a side-effect of amphetamines is to make the user tongue-tied, so that communication is literally blocked.

✤*'Does that mean you're blocked out of your mind on stage?'*

✤*'It means we're blocked out of our minds all the time.'*
(Pete Townshend of The Who, interviewed on the television programme *A Whole Scene Going*, 1966).

block it
vb British to take illicit drugs, become stupefied by drugs. A fairly rare usage heard among drug users in the 1960s. The phrase is related to the adjective **blocked**.

bloke
n a man. The most widespread slang term in Britain and Australia from the 1950s, when it superseded 'chap' and 'fellow', to the 1970s, when 'guy' began to rival it in popularity among younger speakers. The exact origin of the word is mysterious. It seems to have entered working-class slang from vagrants' jargon; either from Shelta, the Irish travellers' secret language, or from Romany. Romany has a word *loke* which is derived from the Hindustani for man; in Dutch *blok* means a fool. Whatever its ultimate origin, bloke entered British usage early in the 19th century and is still thriving in colloquial speech.

✤*'I went into the boozer the other day*

and there was this bloke I hadn't seen for 25 years.'
(William Donaldson, *Independent*, 26 August 1989).

blood *n American* a term of endearment or address used by black males to fellow males, it is a shortening of 'blood brother', or a version of 'young blood' as applied to tribal warriors.

blood-house *n Australian* a squalid, disreputable establishment, usually a bar, pub, café or hotel. The term probably arose in the 19th century. An East London theatre specializing in gory melodramas was nicknamed 'The Blood-hole' in the late 1800s.

bloody *adj British* an intensifying adjective which is now considered fairly mild, but which was held to be taboo in many circles until the later 1960s. The standard folk etymology is from the oath 'by our lady', but the word is more probably a simple extension of the literal meaning.

blooper *n American* a mistake, blunder. A coinage influenced by bloomer.
↳*'TV Censored Bloopers.'*
  (US TV programme featuring humorous out-takes from films and TV series, 1988).

blooter *n British* a failure, mess, instance of excessive behaviour, the origin of the word is unclear, but is presumably related to bloomer and **blooper**.

blootered *adj British* drunk. The term is heard particularly in the Scottish Lowlands and the north of England, and is perhaps influenced by the noun **blooter** or by **blotto**.

blot *n Australian* one of many Australian vulgarisms for the anus.

blotto *adj* drunk. The word appeared around 1905. It implies that the person in question had soaked up alcohol in the manner of blotting paper.

blow *vb American* **1** to leave, go. A shortening of 'blow away'.
↳*'I better blow town before the cops come looking for me.'*
2 to perform fellatio (upon someone). In this sense the term may derive from **blow job** or may be the source of that expression.
↳*'Who blew and were blown by those*

human seraphim, the sailors, caresses of Atlantic and Caribbean love.'
(*Howl*, poem by Allen Ginsberg, 1956).
3 a to smoke. In this sense the verb is typically used by devotees of cannabis.
↳*'Let's get together and blow a couple of numbers.'*
b to sniff, **snort**. A cocaine (and occasionally amphetamine) users' term for inhalation.
4 to be repellent; a rare synonym of to **suck**, heard among school and college students.
↳*'Man, that study program really blows.'*
5 to play a musical instrument (not necessarily a wind instrument) in **hip** talk.

blow *n* **1 a** cannabis for smoking (hashish or marihuana). A drug users' term.
b tobacco. A usage encountered especially in the speech of prison inmates.
Both instances are based on the use of the verb **blow** to mean to smoke.
2 cocaine. The use of blow to mean cocaine (from the slang use of the verb **blow** to mean both inhale and consume) spread from the USA to Britain in the later 1970s.

blow (someone) away *vb* to kill, especially by shooting. A widespread euphemism originally in American underworld and military usage.

the blower *n British* a telephone. A slang term which was common by the 1940s and is still heard. It may originate in 'blow' as an archaic term meaning 'to talk', or from the habit of blowing into an old telephone mouthpiece before speaking.
↳*'Get Nelson on the blower, will you.'*

blowfurt, blowfoot, blue foot *n British* a white person who affects black manners, clothing, etc. A highly pejorative term of uncertain derivation used by black teenagers in the early 1990s: it may originate in Caribbean patois. Mild disapproval is indicated by the more widespread **wigga**.

blowhard *n* a pompous and/or aggressive person, a blusterer. The term seems to have arisen in American speech but is now heard in all English-speaking regions. **Puff-bucket** is a near synonym.

blow-in *n Australian* a newcomer and/or interloper. The noun, usually referring to an unwelcome visitor, is based on the colloquial verb 'to blow in' meaning to arrive unexpectedly.

֍*'I've got enough to do without having to deal with bloody blow-ins.'*

blow job *n* an act of fellatio. This term, now widespread in English-speaking countries, spread from the USA in the 1960s. A puzzling misnomer to many, to **blow** in this context is probably a euphemism for ejaculate, a usage occasionally recorded in the 1950s. This may itself be influenced by the *there (s)he blows* of whaling cliché. An alternative and equally plausible derivation of blow job is from the black jazz musicians' **hip** talk expression **blow** meaning play (an instrument). This term probably caught on in Britain and Australia simply because there was no well-known alternative in existence.

blown away *adj* 1 killed. A cold-blooded euphemism on the same lines as **dusted**.

2 (pleasurably) surprised, 'transported', **gob-smacked**.

blown out *adj* 1 *American* tired, exhausted or hung over. A high-school and **preppie** term probably adapted from the following sense.

2 *American* intoxicated or euphoric after taking drugs, **high**. This use is still heard, but less commonly than during the **hippy** era.

3 *American* ruined, failed. Used typically of an event or an opportunity.

4 full of food, gorged. From the verb to **blow out**.

5 rejected, cast aside, expelled. From the verb to **blow out**.

֍*'Her past is littered with the corpses of blown out lovers.'*

blow off *vb* 1 *British* to fart. A children's term of the 1950s revived in the 1980s.

֍*'We were right in the middle of the restaurant and Kitty blew off in front of them all.'*
(Recorded, father, London, 1986).

2 *American* to reject, get rid of. A less common variant of **blow out**.

֍*'We had to blow off the trip after all.'*

3 *American* to absent oneself, avoid, waste time. The verb, popular in campus usage, can be employed transitively or intransitively.

֍*'We decided to blow off the class and hit the beach.'*

֍*'Don't go to the office today; blow off instead.'*

blow one's cookies/dough-nuts/groceries/lunch/grits *vb American* to vomit. Colourful euphemisms from the lexicon of high-school and college students.

blow one's mind *vb* to be transported beyond a normal state of mental equilibrium, experience sudden euphoria or disorientation. A key term from the lexicon of drug users of the 1960s, this phrase was rapidly generalized to cover less momentous instances of surprise, awe, admiration, etc. Now dated, the expression is still in many people's passive vocabulary, allowing it to be used, for example, in advertising copy as late as 1989.

֍*'Happiness is hard to find – we just want peace to blow our minds.'*
(Lyrics to *Revolution* by Tomorrow, 1967).

֍*'She blew my nose and then she blew my mind.'*
(*Honky Tonk Woman*, Rolling Stones, 1971).

֍*'The way she came on to me – it completely blew my mind.'*
(Recorded, student, London, 1976).

blow out *vb* 1 a to reject someone (especially a lover), or something. From the image of violently expelling something.

b to cancel, especially unexpectedly. In this sense the phrase applies typically to a pop group cancelling a tour or concert.

2 to over-eat as a matter of sensual indulgence. From the image of the stomach being blown out like a balloon.

blow-out *n* an occasion of over-indulgence, particularly excessive eating and drinking.

֍*'Have a blow-out at Les Trois Marches.'*
(*Mail on Sunday*, 'You' magazine, March 1988).

blowser *n British* a glue-sniffer. A rare vogue word from the early 1980s.

blowsing *n British* glue-sniffing. This obscure term was used in the 1980s by young solvent abusers themselves. 'Blowsed-up' means under the influence of glue. The word is an invention, perhaps influenced by 'blow'.

blow someone's mind *vb*

a to give someone a hallucinogenic drug.
b to astound, transport, bamboozle or overwhelm someone, or in some other way to radically and rapidly alter their mood or consciousness. An extension of the first sense. Both senses of the phrase were part of the **hippy** lexicon of the 1960s and are now dated. (The Beatles were castigated for their ambiguous use of '*I want to blow your mind*' in the lyrics of 'A day in the life' in 1967).

ᗏ'*We're not out to blow people's minds however. We're out to get through to them.*'
(Pete Townshend, *Oz* magazine, June 1969).

blow the gaff *vb* to give away information, reveal a secret, inform on someone. This picturesque phrase was derived from the archaic 'gaff' meaning a trickster's strategy or paraphernalia. Although it dates from the early 19th century, and often evokes the world of **spivs** or gangsters, the expression is still used. Confusingly, blow the gaff could conceivably also now mean 'leave (**blow**) the premises (**gaff**)'.

blub *vb British* to cry, weep. A middle-class children's and public-school term typically used derisively. It is a shortening of the colloquial 'blubber'.

ᗏ'*But the boiled egg made his gorge rise, and it was as much as he could do to stop himself blubbing over the toast and marmalade.*'
(*Scandal*, A. N. Wilson, 1983).

bludge *vb Australian* to cadge, scrounge, shirk or loaf. Originally the word meant to bully and was a shortening of bludgeon. It later meant to live off immoral earnings. The word, which has given rise to the more common **bludger**, has been introduced to Britain via Australian TV soap operas in the late 1980s.

bludger *n Australian* a cadger or scrounger, disreputable or despicable person. (A **dole-bludger** is the Australian equivalent of the British 'dole scrounger'.)

blue *n* 1 *Australian* a violent row or fight.

ᗏ'*They got into a blue – Kelly pushed Charlene into a gooseberry bush.*'
(*Neighbours*, Australian TV soap opera, 1987).

2 *British* an amphetamine tablet. A term from the 1960s when these tablets were light blue in colour and also known as **French blues** and **double-blues**. (Strictly speaking blues were tablets of drinamyl, a mixed amphetamine and barbiturate preparation, prescribed for slimmers.)
3 a police officer. A rare usage, but occasionally heard in all English-speaking countries; it is usually in the plural form.
4 *Australian* a red-headed man. A nickname mentioned in Rolf Harris's well-known song 'Tie me kangaroo down, sport!'.

blue balls *n* a condition of acute (male) sexual frustration, jocularly supposed to bring on a case of orchiditis, the testicles swelling to bursting point. This American expression of the 1950s, popular then among college students, has since spread to other English-speaking communities.

bluebottle *n British* a police officer. A term popular in the 1950s and still heard. It has been used in Britain since the 16th century, well before policemen wore uniforms, and indeed existed in any organized form, which suggests that the original reference was to an annoying pestilential presence.

ᗏ'*Before you could turn round the place filled up with bluebottles.*'
(Recorded, pub habitué, London, 1987).

blue foot *n British* a prostitute. An ephemeral word of uncertain origin.
(Recorded by Deputy Assistant Commissioner David Powis in his *Field Manual for Police*, 1977).

bluie, bluey *n* 1 *British* a five-pound note; from its colour.
2 *Australian* a red-headed man. A common facetious nickname also rendered as **blue**.

blunt *n* a marihuana cigarette, **joint**. This term, fashionable in the US and the UK since the early 1990s, originally referred to a cigar hollowed out and filled with a combination of cannabis and cocaine.

ᗏ'*We prefer to spark up a blunt and kick back.*'

B.M.O.C. *n American* 'big man on campus'; a **preppie** and student term for an influential fellow student.

B.M.W. *n American* a successful black male. The initials, punning on the brand

name of a favourite German car, stand for '*Black Man Working*'. An item of black street talk included in so-called **Ebonics**, recognized as a legitimate language variety by school officials in Oakland, California, in late 1996.

B.N.I.C. *n American* a successful or dominant black male. The initials stand for '*Boss Nigger In Charge*'. An item of black street talk that was included in so-called **Ebonics**, recognized as a legitimate language variety by school officials in Oakland, California, in late 1996. *Compare* **B.M.O.C.**

boak *vb British*

๛to vomit. The term, probably echoic in origin, is heard particularly in the Scottish Lowlands, the north of England, and Northern Ireland. It occurs in the work of the Scottish novelist James Kelman and the Northern Irish poet Tom Paulin.

๛'*It makes me want to boak.*'

๛'*We could hear him boaking in the next room.*'

boat *n American* a desirable, attractive individual. This item of adolescent slang is a clipping of the colloquial **dreamboat**.

boat (race) *n British* face. A piece of London rhyming slang which is still heard in both the shortened and full form. (The Oxford and Cambridge boat race provided an annual excursion for many East Enders.)

๛'*Nice legs, shame about the boat race.*' (Sexist catchphrase from the 1970s).

bob *n Canadian* a fat or well-built woman. The term, which can be used pejoratively or with mild affection (usually condescending), is an abbreviation of '*big 'ol bitch*'.

bob *vb American* to have sex (with). This fairly inoffensive term, heard among American adolescents, is also in use by younger speakers in Scotland and the north of England in the late 1990s. Like many similar terms (**boff**, **biff**, etc.) it probably derives from the use of the same word (in this case in British dialect) to denote jab or punch.

๛'*You hear lads saying they just want to bob her. Not me, mate.*' (*Guardian*, 15 July 1996).

bobbins *n British* rubbish, worthless items. This usage arose in the north of England referring originally to the waste bobbins in the wool mills and is still heard in the 1990s in its generalized sense.

bobby *n British* a policeman. A widely known nickname, usually applied to constables or uniformed officers. Rarely heard except in jest since the 1960s, the word derived from the Christian name of Sir Robert Peel, who founded the Metropolitan Police in 1828.

bobbydazzler *n British* something or someone impressive or dazzling. The word dates from the late 19th century.

bobby soxer *n American* a teenage girl. The phrase referred to the short white socks worn as part of a standard ensemble in the 1930s and 1940s. The term itself survived until the 1960s.

Bob Hope *n British* cannabis, **dope**. Rhyming slang from the name of the British-born American comedian. The term is usually said in full, as in '*We've run out of Bob Hope, let's call the man*'. The 'H' is often dropped, in self-conscious imitation of the appropriate accent (compare the self-conscious glottal stop in for example **bottle**). This is an example of rhyming slang used, and probably coined, by young middle-class soft-drug users in imitation of traditional working-class cockney rhyming slang.

bock *n British* bad luck. This obscure term, cited as an example of the jargon of cat burglars, was recorded in *FHM* magazine in April 1996.

bod *n* 1 body. The short form is usually heard in American speech as in '*check out his great bod*'. In British middle-class speech it refers to an individual as in '*odd-bod*'.

2 *British* a tedious, intrusive, pretentious or otherwise irritating person. A vogue term among the fashionable young in the later 1980s. The word may be a shortening of the synonymous '*wimp-bod*'.

๛'*We are going to create a club without bods ... No bods. Bods being the sort of chaps who've got onto the scene and just stuck like glue.*' (*Evening Standard*, 12 June 1989).

bodacious, boldacious *adj* fearsome, enormous, impressive, **feisty**. The word is now often used in black speech and by teenagers and has spread from American usage (where it originated) to the language of British teenagers. It appears to be a blend of bold and audacious, but Chapman's *New Dictionary of American Slang* derives it from 'body-atiously'; bodily.

bodge *n, vb British* (to do) a slapdash job, especially in constructing something. The term may be a back-formation from 'bodger', a rural craftsman who works out-of-doors in primitive conditions roughly shaping and turning chair-legs and spindles for example, or may be from the related standard verb, botch.

bodge-up *n British* 1 a makeshift repair, a ramshackle construction. The result of someone bodging a job.
2 a mess or disaster. A variant of **balls-up** or 'botch-up' influenced by meaning above.

bodgie *n Australian* a male member of a youth cult, similar to the British **teddy boys** of the 1950s. (The female counterpart was a **widgie**.) In the 1930s bodgie was apparently used in American **jive talk** to denote a male jitterbug (dance) fanatic; some authorities dispute this and derive bodgie from the British and Australian verb to **bodge**.

bodgy *adj British* inferior, malfunctioning or out of order. A late-1980s adolescent term based on **bodge-up**.
↳'*Hey mate, your machine's bodgy!*'
(Recorded, video arcade habitué, 1989).

body *n* a person, suspect, victim or 'arrestee'. A term used particularly by police in counting up arrests or numbers of detainees. **To have a body** means to have a suspect in custody for a particular outstanding offence.
↳'*The other frequently used term, "body", suggests detachment and indicates the appropriateness of behaviour that tends to deny or ... ignore the motivation and humanity that a detained person might reveal.*'
(*Inside the British Police Force*, Simon Holdaway, 1983).

B.O.F., b.o.f. *n British* a 'boring old fart'. An expression of derision institutionalized by rock-music journalists in the mid- and late 1970s, usually applied by devotees of **punk** music to musicians of the **hippy** era who were entering middle age.
↳'*Taking all my B.O.F. records and paperbacks down to [the] jumble sale....*'
(*Sincerely yours, Biff*, Chris Garratt and

Mick Kidd, 1986).

boff *vb* 1 to hit, to punch; a nursery variant of biff, occasionally used semi-facetiously by adults.
2 to have sex (with), **fuck**.
The term boff came to temporary prominence in Britain in 1974 when newspapers reported it as current among the upper-class set of which Lord Lucan (fugitive and alleged murderer) was a member. This gentle-sounding word, with its suggestions of 'puff', 'buff' and 'buffer', next appeared as a convenient euphemism employed in US TV series, such as *Soap*, of the late 1970s and 1980s, where verisimilitude would demand a brusquer alternative. It is unclear whether the word is American or British in origin or a simultaneous coinage. It may derive from its nursery sense of 'to hit'.
↳'*He's a logical choice.*'
'*So the fact he's boffing her has nothing to do with it?*'
(*Vice Versa*, US film, 1986).

boff *n* 1 *British* the backside, buttocks.
↳'*A kick up the boff.*'
(*Only Fools and Horses*, British TV comedy series, 1989).
2 a *American* a successful joke.
b *American* a hearty laugh.
Both senses of the word are part of the jargon of the entertainment industry and are probably imitative of an explosive chortle, or else like 'biff' denote a 'hit'.
3 *British* a **swot**. The word is probably a shortening of the colloquial 'boffin'.
↳'*Some took so much pride in never being seen with a book, they had virtual slaves carry their books to and from school ... the worst thing you could be was a "boff" or an "anorak".*'
(*Independent*, 17 November 1996).

boff *adj American* a variant of the vogue term **buff**.
↳'*You sure look boff to me.*'
(*California Man*, US film, 1992).

boffo *adj American* excellent, first-rate. A piece of jargon from the entertainment world (derived by most experts from 'box-office') which has entered popular journalese.

boffola *adj, n American* an uproarious joke or laugh. The word is a form of **boff** with the Spanish '-ola' suffix denoting large-scale or extra.

bog *n British* a mess, disaster. The word occurs in the phrase 'make a bog of (something)', popular in the 1980s.

bog(s) *n British* a toilet. A widespread vulgar term, probably coined by students or servicemen in the 19th century in the form of 'boghouse' to describe foul communal lavatories. The term is used in Australia, too.

꙰'"I ran into Shane", said Spider Stacey, "at a Ramones gig at the Roundhouse. He was standing on top of the bog, for some reason".'
(*Evening Standard*, 17 March 1988).

bog (up) *vb British*
a to make a mess of, spoil. Usually heard in the form '*bog it*' or '*bog it up*'. A term especially popular in public schools and the armed forces.
b to make the end of a cigarette or **joint** wet and mushy while smoking it.

bog-all *n British* a synonym for **fuck-all** or **bugger-all**, **naff-all**, etc.

bogart *vb* to monopolize or fail to pass on a **joint** or cigarette during communal smoking. This popular **hippy** term of the late 1960s was prompted by the actor Humphrey Bogart's habit in films of keeping a cigarette in his mouth for long periods. The verb originated in the USA and quickly spread to the other English-speaking areas.

꙰'*Don't Bogart that Joint.*'
(Song title, The Holy Modal Rounders, featured on the soundtrack to the film *Easy Rider*, 1969).

bog-brush *n British* a nickname or term of abuse applied by schoolchildren to a fellow pupil with cropped or spiky hair. ('Dunny-brush' is the Australian equivalent.)

bogey *n* **1** *British* a police officer. From the notion of the 'bogey man'.
2 an enemy aircraft or other enemy presence; a service term from the notion of the 'bogey man'.

꙰'*As they take evasive action, the "bogies", slang for the Libyan jets, continually come at them. "Bogies have jerked back at me again for the fifth time! They're on my nose now," one pilot says.*'
(*Evening Standard*, 6 January 1989).

3 *British* a piece of mucus from the nose.

bogging *adj British* stinking. The

term is heard particularly in the Scottish Lowlands and the north of England, and is probably based on **bog** in the sense of toilet.

boggo *adj, n British* standard, ordinary (merchandise). This variation of the colloquial 'bog-standard' has been recorded among adult speakers in the 1990s.

꙰'*It makes me laugh all this fuss in the papers about Porsches and Mercs being what we're after – we're coming for your boggo stuff.*'
(Car thief, quoted in the *AA Magazine*, 1995).

bog in *vb Australian* to begin (a meal), to eat with relish. A vulgar, alternative form of the colloquial 'tuck in'.

bog off *vb British* go away. Nearly always used as an aggressive exclamation or instruction. A vulgar term that existed in armed-service use before becoming a vogue successor to **naff off** around 1980. In spite of the brusque nature, the phrase is not taboo and is used by women.

꙰'*If he's going to treat her like that he can just bog off.*'
(Recorded, secretary, York, 1981).

bog-roll *n British*
a a toilet roll.
b paperwork or computer printout.

bog-trotter *n British* an Irish person. A pejorative term heard since the 17th century. The alternative form 'bog-hopper' is sometimes used in the United States.

bogue *adj American* **1** suffering from drug withdrawal. An obsolescent term of unknown origin from the jargon of narcotics addicts.
2 a worthless, counterfeit. From underworld usage.
b unpleasant, insincere. An adolescent term.
c inferior, ersatz. A vogue term among adolescents, it is a shortening, like the two preceeding senses, of **bogus**, itself a key item of fashionable youth slang.

bog-up *n British* a mess, a badly improvised job. A more vulgar form of botch-up and **bodge-up**.

bogus *adj American* unpleasant, unacceptable. The standard meaning of bogus (the word is said to have been the name of a counterfeiting machine) was adapted in adolescent usage to become an all-purpose vogue term of disapproval.

↳'*Bill and Ted's Bogus Journey*'
(title of US movie, 1991).

bog-wagon *n Australian* a private van, particularly one which has been customized and/or decorated inside. Like **shaggin' wagon**, it sometimes denotes a vehicle equipped for seduction.

bog-wog *n British* an Irish person. The racist term, a more recent variant of **bog-trotter**, is usually applied to Irish Catholics.

boho *adj* bohemian, often in the sense of scruffy and/or irresponsible. This Americanism was fashionable from the late 1980s among London journalists.

bohunk *n American* an East European immigrant. This old term deriving from Bohemian/Hungarian is offensive and occasionally still heard. It is synonymous with 'oaf'.

boiler *n British* a woman. A contemptuous, derogatory term, implying a lack of both attractiveness and intelligence, commonly used by young working-class males. The phrase 'dodgy boiler' suggests the extra possibility of sexually transmitted diseases. The word in this sense originated pre-World War II when it referred to an older woman with the dimensions and explosive attributes of the contraption. An alternative derivation is from boiler as used to denote a tough or scrawny chicken.

boink *vb American* to have sex with, **fuck**. A 1980s variation of **bonk**, sufficiently inoffensive to be used in TV series such as *Moonlighting*.

bokoo *adj American* very. This facetious adoption of the French '*beaucoup*' ('much' or 'many') probably originated in black **bebop** or white Cajun usage, but by the 1990s was fashionable among hip-hop aficionados and white adolescents. (Some authorities claim alternatively that it was adopted by US servicemen from the French-speaking Vietnamese. The same French word appeared in British slang after World War I in the form 'boko', now obsolete.)

↳'*The program was, like, bokoo boring.*'

bokoo *n American* a large quantity or a number of items. The noun form is probably less common than the adjectival.

↳'*She said how much did you want and I said, bokoo.*'

bold *adj British* flamboyant, daringly fashionable. A vogue word of the mid-1960s originating as a **camp** code word for a fashionable or overt **gay**. The word was adopted by **mods** as a term of approbation in 1965 and was used as the name of a chain of men's boutiques.

bollers *n British* money, the term is probably a humorous alteration of dollars, perhaps influenced by **boyz**. It may mean simply money or a large quantity of money as in '*He's got bollers*'. The term was recorded in use among north London schoolboys in 1993 and 1994.

bollixed, bollixed-up *adj* ruined, messed up. A derivation of **bollocks** which, in American English, is used as a less offensive version of 'ball(s)ed-up'.

bollock *n British* a ball (in the sense of dance). A **Sloane Ranger** witticism said quite unselfconsciously by girls as well as boys, Hunt bollocks and Charity bollocks being regular features in the annual social calendar.

bollock *vb British* to chastise, severely scold or dress down. The word has been used in this way since the early years of the 20th century.

bollocking *n British* a severe telling-off, chastisement or dressing-down.

↳'*If you are late for two days running on early turn you expect a bollocking from the skipper.*'
(*Inside the British Police*, Simon Holdaway, 1983).

↳'*He was all set for giving me a bollocking for parking where I shouldn't.*'
(*Guardian*, 12 December 1987).

bollock-naked *adj British* completely nude. A more vehement version is '*stark bollock-naked*'. In spite of its etymology, the expression may on occasion refer to women.

bollocks *n pl* 1 testicles. A version of this word has existed since Anglo-Saxon times; in Old English it was bealluc, a diminutive or familiar elaboration of bula: ball. For much of its existence the word, usually spelled 'ballocks', was standard (if coarse) English.

2 *British* rubbish, nonsense. Often used as an exclamation or in expressing derision

or dismissal such as '*a load of (old) bollocks*', this sense of the term has existed since the early 20th century.

↳'*Never Mind the Bollocks, Here's the Sex Pistols.*' (Title of LP, 1977).

↳'*That's a lot of bollocks. There aren't any styles, there's just good music and bad music, and that's ALL.*'
(*Evening Standard*, 17 March 1988).

3 the bollocks *British* something superlative. The usage, fashionable in the late 1990s is a shortening of the phrase (It's) **the dog's bollocks**. *See also* **bollock**.

bollocky *adj*

bollock-naked; a variant form from Australia.

bolt *vb American* to leave, go away. A **Valley Girl** and teenager's expression usually denoting a leisurely departure.

bolted-up *adj British* a synonym for **fitted up** or **framed**, in criminal jargon of the late 1980s.

↳'*I've got about 30 previous – about half of those, I was bolted up.*'
(Recorded, bag snatcher, London, 1988).

the bomb *n Australian*

See **have the bomb**.

bomb *vb* to put one's **tag** (personal signature) on a building. From the jargon of graffiti 'artists'.

↳'*Welcome to a freshly-bombed station.*'
(Graffito, East Putney underground station, London, 1988).

bombed *adj* drunk or **stoned** on illicit drugs. '*Bombed out of one's mind/skull*' is a common elaboration.

↳'*Harvey decided his only real option was to get bombed out of his skull; some things never went out of style, thank God ...*'
(*The Serial*, Cyra McFadden, 1976).

bomber *n* **1 a** a pill or capsule of an illicit drug, especially amphetamines (see **black bomber**).

b a **joint**, especially a large or powerful one.

2 a graffiti artist. From the verb to **bomb**.

3 *South African* a train. Recorded as an item of Sowetan slang in the *Cape Sunday Times*, 29 January 1995.

bona *adj, exclamation British* excellent, fine, the real thing. An all-purpose term of approbation increasingly heard among working-class Londoners in the 1980s, probably derived from bona fide or from the Spanish and Italian words for good (*buena* and *buona*). In the 1960s bona was part of the **camp** lexicon (popularized in Kenneth Horne's radio comedy shows), originating in theatrical performers' and prostitutes' argot of the 19th century, in which it often meant 'beautiful'.

↳'*A bona geezer.*'

bonce *n British* head. Bonce was a mid-19th-century dialect and schoolboy term for a big marble. The word was soon adapted to mean head, and in that sense remained popular in young people's usage until the 1960s. It now sounds old-fashioned or affectedly upper class, but may be due for revival, in common with other obsolescent but 'jolly' words.

bone *vb* to have sex (with). This usage, originating in American speech and common from the mid-1980s, may be a backformation from **boner**.

↳'*You were boning her, weren't you?*'
(*Night Moves*, US movie, 1992).

↳'*I hate them.*'
'*Yeah but would you bone them?*'
(*Buffy the Vampire Slayer*, US film 1992).

bonehead *n British*

a a complete fool.

b a **skinhead** of unusually low intelligence and/or extremely right-wing views. The expression is used by skinheads themselves to characterize their more brutal fellows, who may also differentiate themselves by having almost completely shaven heads.

boner *n* **1** a clumsy error, serious mistake. The origin of the term is not clear; it may be inspired by 'bone-headed' or by a 'bone-jarring' blow.

2 an erection. 'Bone', 'hambone' and 'jigging bone' are all archaic slang terms for the penis.

bones *n pl* dice.

boneyard *n* a cemetery.

bong, bhong *n* a water-pipe for smoking cannabis, strictly one with a carburation hole so that the smoker can add air at will to the smoke. The typical bong is smaller than a hubble-bubble but larger than a pipe. A part of late 1960s drug paraphernalia. In the late 1980s the

word referred also to a **crack** pipe.

bong, bong on *vb*

a *Australian* to smoke cannabis in a water pipe (a **bong**).
b *American* to smoke **crack**.

bonged *adj*

stoned after smoking cannabis or **crack**.

bongo'd *adj British* thoroughly intoxicated by an illicit drug or, less commonly, alcohol. A variant form of synonymous terms such as **bombed**, **banjo'd**.

bonk *vb British* to have sex (with). A vogue word of the late 1980s; first heard in the late 1970s and quickly picked up by the media as a useful, vigorous, but printable euphemism for **fuck**. (The word was first broadcast in a British TV comedy series; at a later date, the tennis champion Boris Becker was dubbed 'Bonking Boris' by the gutter press.) It is a childish synonym for hit: the sexual sense may derive from the sound of energetic bouncing. Alternatively an extended correspondence in *Private Eye* magazine suggested that this had long been a schoolboy term meaning masturbate or ejaculate. It may also be significant that the immediately precedent vogue word for copulate among teenagers was **knob**, which in **backslang** would give bonk.

♥ '*They do call it bonking after all, which as everyone knows, is THE word used by promiscuous people who DON'T REALLY LIKE SEX.*'
(Julie Burchill, *Elle* magazine, December 1987).

bonkers *adj* crazy. A common colloquialism in Britain since the mid-1960s (it seems to have existed in restricted use since the 1920s), bonkers has more recently been adopted by American teenagers. The inspiration behind it is uncertain but may refer to a bang ('bonk') on the head.

bonnet *n British* an all-purpose nonsense term, heard in late 1990s London speech.

bonzer *adj Australian* excellent, great. A word sometimes adopted for humorous use by British speakers. It may derive from bonanza or from latinate words for 'good'.

boo *n American* marihuana. A former blackslang word, adopted by **hippies** in the late 1970s. It is possibly a pre-World

War II adoption of *jabooby*, an African term for fear, or else from the adjectival sense.

boob, boo-boo *vb* to blunder, commit a gaffe or error. The verb, based on the earlier nouns **booby** and **boob** in the sense of fool, has been in use since before World War II, the reduplicated form boo-boo since the 1960s.

boob *n British* jail. An item of prison slang from the 1990s, probably a shortened version of **booby hatch** in the sense of an institution in which one becomes crazy.

boobs *n pl* breasts. The only slang word for breasts which is currently acceptable in 'polite circles'. (It is also used in the singular form, 'boob'.) It is a less brusque variant of the more vulgar **bubs** or **bubbies** which probably derive from the noises made by suckling babies. Boobs has been a fashionable term since the mid-1960s; bubbie since the 17th century.

♥ '*Gimme the good old days – when a pair of boobs was a couple of dumb guys.*'
(*Smokey and the Bandit III*, US film, 1983).

booby hatch *n* a psychiatric hospital. A jocular term, originally from North America. The association with **boob** and **booby** is obvious; hutch or hatch is an archaic term for many different enclosures and containers.

boo-coo(s) *n, adj* variant forms of **bokoo**.

boof, boof-head *n Australian* a stupid person. The terms are heard throughout the English-speaking world, but probably originated in Australian usage before World War II.

booger *n American* a piece of mucus from the nose, the American version of **bogey**.

book *vb American* to depart, leave. A fashionable term of the 1990s in black street usage and also heard among white adolescents. A variety of euphemisms (like its contemporaries **bail**, **bill**, **jam** and **jet**) for 'run away' are essential to the argot of gang members and their playground imitators. The origin of this usage is not certain; it may derive from an earlier phrase 'book it', meaning that someone has to return home quickly in order

to record a transaction.

boom *n* **1** *American* a stereo cassette player, particularly one fitted in a car. A teenagers' term recorded in California in 1987.

2 a party. A teenagers' term in use in Britain and the USA since the early 1980s.

boomer *n Australian* **1** a particularly large kangaroo. Boom is an archaic term meaning to rush or move forcefully.

2 something excellent, admirable, exciting.

3 *American* a member of the so-called baby-boom generation born between 1945 and 1960. The term came into prominence in the 1990s as the adult lifestyle of this age-group came under renewed scrutiny.

boom-ting *n British* something excellent or impressive. An item of black British slang adopted by adolescents during the 1990s, combining the colloquial senses of boom and the Afro-Caribbean pronunciation of 'thing'.

boondocks, the boondocks *n American* an out-of-the-way place, a rural community, the back of beyond, **the sticks**. In Tagalog, a language spoken in the Philippines, *bundok* means mountain (area). The word was picked up by US service personnel in World War II.

✎'*He comes from somewhere out in the boondocks.*'

boong *n Australian* a coloured person. An offensive racist epithet based on an Aboriginal word, but used as a catchall term regardless of nationality. *Compare* **choong**.

the boonies, booneys *n pl* shorter forms of **boondocks**.

boost *vb* **1** *American* to steal. Originally from black slang, perhaps influenced by **lift**, **hoist** and **heist**, the term is now in general use among young people. It usually refers to petty theft, often shoplifting.

✎'*Some gals go in for boosting, or paper-pushing or lifting leathers. Others work the chloral hydrate.*'
(*Wild Town*, Jim Thompson, 1957).

2 *South African* to assist or help. Recorded as an item of Sowetan slang in the *Cape Sunday Times*, 29 January 1995.

boot *vb American* to vomit. This **preppie** expression is echoic or a blend of **barf** and 'hoot'.

booted *adj American* expelled, 'booted out' (of school or college). A **preppie** term of the 1970s.

booze *vb, n* (to drink) alcohol. '*On the booze*' may mean habituated to alcohol or on a drinking binge. The word originated in Middle English as bousen, from Middle Dutch and Flemish *busen*; a word based on the root *bus-*; swelling.

booze-up *n* a drinking bout or drinks party.

bop *vb* **1 a** to dance.
✎'*Bop till you drop.*'
(Record title, Ry Cooder, 1974).

b to move in a fast but relaxed way. This usage became popular in Britain in the late 1960s and is still heard.
✎'*Why don't we bop down to the supermarket and grab some beers.*'

2 to hit or punch.
✎'*Say that again and I'll bop you a good one.*'

bop *n* **1** a fast **cool** style of modern jazz introduced in the 1940s; also known as **bebop**. Bop was accompanied by rapid nonsense lyrics and dancing.

2 a dance. A word from America of the 1950s, revived in the 1970s and still popular in Britain, among teenagers and students in particular.
✎'*Are you going to the art school bop?*'

bopper *n* **1** *American* a **cool** musician, dancer or devotee of **bop**.

2 a **teenybopper**. This shortened form of the word was especially popular in Britain in the 1970s to describe a vivacious, party-loving (usually small or childlike) young girl, a **raver**.

boracic, brassic(k) *adj British* penniless, broke. The word is a shortening of the rhyming slang 'boracic lint': 'skint'. A genuine example of London working-class argot, this term was adopted into raffish speech in general in the early 1970s. (Boracic is an older name for boric acid used as a weak antiseptic impregnating bandages, etc.)

born-again *combining form British* an intensifying phrase used to prefix another pejorative term, the usage (which may have arisen in armed services' speech) is based on the notion of a '*born-again Christian*' being a particularly extreme or intense example of the variety. *See also* **ocean-going**.

✎'*In my humble opinion he behaved like a born-again bastard.*'
(Recorded, executive, Guildford, England, 1995).

boss *adj* excellent, first-rate, superlative. Currently a fashionable word among teenagers all over the English-speaking community, boss originated in American black street-jargon of the early 1960s. It was picked up by other speakers, but it remained an Americanism. (The music industry attempted to promote the 'Boss town sound' in order to establish Boston as the US equivalent of Liverpool in 1964; Duane Eddy had a 1960s hit with *Boss Guitar*.) In the 1970s and 1980s the usage spread through the language of disco, **funk** and **rap** to the young of Britain and Australia.

bot *vb, n Australian*
a (to behave as) an irritant or cadger. A shortening of bot-fly (a native parasite) or botulism.
b *British* shortened form of bottom, **arse**.

bother *n Britain* trouble, violence, aggression. A typical example of menacing understatement as it occurs in London working-class speech (**spanking**, **seeing-to**, **have a word with (someone)** are other examples). The use of bother by police and thugs as a euphemism for violence reached public notice in the late 1960s when it became a **skinhead** rallying cry, usually rendered as **bovver**.

bottle *n British* courage, bravery, 'nerve', especially in the phrases to 'have a lot of bottle', to **lose one's bottle**, 'his/her bottle's gone'. It derives from 'bottle and glass', rhyming slang for **arse**. Most users of **bottle** are ignorant of its derivation (compare the earlier **berk**). The word is long-established in the repertoire of south and east London rhyming slang, but surfaced in widespread usage only in the mid-1970s (probably via television renderings of police or criminal speech) to enjoy a vogue culminating in the adoption of the slogan 'Milk has gotta lotta bottle' for a nationwide advertising campaign in 1985. The word is pronounced with a medial glottal stop by cockneys and their imitators.

✎'*If you've got an old PC trained twenty years ago and he's got no bottle, then you have to have somebody chase and get it [a stolen car].*'
(*Inside the British Police*, Simon Holdaway, 1983).

bottle *vb British* **1** to hit with a bottle. A widespread brawler's tactic which seems to have become less widespread since the 1960s.
2 to collect money on behalf of a **busker** or other street entertainer.

bottle it *vb British* a later synonym for the more widespread expression **bottle out**, recorded among London football hooligans in the late 1980s.
✎'*Just don't bottle it at the last minute, OK?*'

bottle out *vb British* to lose one's nerve. From **bottle** in the sense of courage.

bottler *n Australian* a powerful, forceful or impressive person. It is probably an alteration of **battler**.
✎'*You're an absolute bottler, you are – the most powerful woman I've ever ...!*'
(*Let The Blood Run Free*, Australian TV comedy, 1993).

bottom burp *n British* a **fart**. An example of 'schoolboy humour' not confined solely to schoolchildren.

bottom-feeder *n* an individual engaged in 'doubtful', or sordid or disreputable activities. The image evoked is of a scavenging fish (swimming in murky waters) and the phrase is used in the slang of the workplace, sometimes as a synonym for **bottom-fisher**.

bottom-fisher *n* a trader in cheap and/or disreputable shares or commodities in the jargon of financial traders of the 1990s.
✎'*The bottom-fisher pulled an archer from his bag.*'
(*London Evening Standard*, 9 December 1994).

boulder-holder *n* a brassiere. A supposedly humorous phrase used invariably by males since the 1960s.

the bounce *n*
a the sack (from one's job) or a rejection (by a sweetheart). A later version of 'the boot'.
b one's fate, an inevitable result. Usually in expressions of resignation, such as '*that's the bounce*'.

bounced (out) *adj* fired from one's job, ejected, expelled or rejected. The image is one of forcible and speedy ejection resulting in one bouncing off one's backside on the floor or pavement.

bouncer *n* a dud cheque, in debt collectors', underworld and police jargon all over the English-speaking world.

bounce-up *n British* a fight, brawl. A short-lived synonym for 'punch-up' in the slang of **teddy boys** and toughs of the 1960s.

✎ *'A bounce-up in the Old Bailey – whatever next? You must control yourselves.'*
(*Hancock's Half Hour*, British TV comedy, 1959).

bouncy-bouncy *n* sex. A coy or joking euphemism invented by adults in imitation of children's language. It is usually in the expression *'play bouncy-bouncy'*.

bounty bar *n British* a black person who apes white manners or collaborates with white society, an **Uncle Tom**. The bounty bar, derived from the trademark name of a type of confectionery, like the synonym **coconut**, implies that such people are dark (like the chocolate) outside and white inside. The term is typically used by black or Asian teenagers.

Bourneville boulevard *n* the anus. The vulgarism (Bourneville is a trademark for Cadbury's chocolate) is heard in such phrases as *'cruising the Bournville boulevard'* referring to 'active' and 'predatory' male homosexual behaviour, and was reported by the former *Sun* journalist and *LBC* radio presenter, Richard Littlejohn. **Marmite motorway** is a contemporary British synonym and **Hershey highway** is the American equivalent.

bovver *n British* trouble, **aggro**. A spelling, in imitation of a London accent, of **bother** in its menacing euphemistic sense of physical violence or extreme aggravation. *'You want bovver?'* was the standard challenge issued by **skinheads**.

bovver-boots *n pl* heavy boots as worn as part of the **skinhead** uniform in the late 1960s. Skinheads first wore army surplus boots, later adopting 'Doc Martens' (DMs).

bovver-boy *n*

a a youth, particularly a **skinhead**, who enjoys fighting and conflict and is always attempting to provoke trouble. A coinage based on the noun **bovver**, from the late 1960s.

b someone who is brought in to do a difficult job, a trouble-shooter. By humorous analogy with the above.

bow-and-arrow *n British* a sparrow. An authentic item of London rhyming slang which seems to have survived into the 1990s.

bowser *n British* an ugly or unattractive woman. A male term of contempt coined on the basis of **dog** and the later **bow-wow**.

bow-wow *n*

a an unattractive woman.

b anything inferior, unappealing or worthless. Both senses of the nursery word are more recent synonyms for **dog** in its (originally American) slang sense. In city slang 'bow-wow stocks' are poorly performing shares.

bow-wows *n pl American* **dogs** in the sense of feet.

box *n* **1 a** the anus. An old term popularized by male homosexuals in the 1970s.

b the male genitals. A term occasionally used by British schoolboys (influenced by 'cricket box', a protective shield for the genitals), and by male homosexuals.

c the vagina. An uncommon, but persistent, usage since the 1950s in all parts of the English-speaking world. The origin may be an unaffectionate reference to a 'container' or may derive from 'box of tricks'.

2 a a coffin.

b a safe. Used by criminals, among others, throughout the 20th century.

3 the box television. No longer really slang, but a common colloquialism, especially in Britain.

4 a guitar. This usage was adopted by British rock musicians in the late 1960s from America, where it was originally used by black jazz and rock musicians in the 1950s.

5 *American* a portable cassette/radio player. A version of the longer **ghetto/beat/rasta box**, heard in the later 1970s.

boxed-up *adj British* **1** comfortable,

content. This vogue term of the early 1990s probably derives from the notion of a homeless person comfortably accommodated in a squat or a **basher**, etc., but was generalized to refer to any state of contentment. **Made-up** is a near synonym from northern English speech.

↳ *'A new girlfriend and a flat and a car; I'm well boxed up.'*

2 *American* intoxicated by drugs or alcohol. This usage may be related to the earlier '*boxed out*', meaning uninhibited, wild (by contrast with the colloquial 'boxed-in').

boxhead *n Australian* a stupid person. The term was one of many insults employed by the Australian Prime Minister, Paul Keating, in outbursts in Parliament during the 1990s.

box the jesuit *vb American* (of a male) to masturbate. The phrase was coined by analogy with the earlier **bash the bishop**, and was adopted as the name of a 1990s rock band.

boy *n* heroin. Although this coded use of the standard word became common in the 1990s, it originated in US street slang of the 1920s. Its ultimate derivation is obscure, but may possibly evoke the image of a boy as an ever-present servant or term of address for a slave.

↳ *'He was trying to score some boy.'*

boyf *n*

a a boyfriend.

b a boy. The abbreviation may have occurred in teenage usage, but in the UK was notable as an example of journalese attempting to replicate adolescent speech. The more generalized later sense mirrors this.

boy racer *n British* an irresponsible young car owner. A term of contempt applied to youths who characteristically decorate or customize cars and drive dangerously.

boystown *n* the male homosexual **scene**, the **gay** milieu or part of town. A code term from the 1970s gay lexicon derived from the cult 1938 film *Boys' Town*, dealing sentimentally with juvenile delinquents.

boyz *n British* £1. The term always appears in the seemingly plural form, so that one boyz = £1, ten boyz = £10. It was recorded in use among north London

schoolboys in 1993 and 1994. **Bollers** and **luka** are contemporary synonyms.

bozo *n* a buffoon, a clumsy or foolish person. A mild term of contempt which can sometimes sound almost affectionate. It has been widely applied to the former US president Ronald Reagan. Originally from the USA and Canada, and dating from at least the 1920s, the word is now in limited use in Britain and Australia. Before the 1960s it meant man or simple fellow; since then it has been adopted as a name for circus clowns for example. Attempts have been made to derive the word from Spanish origins such as *vosotros* (the familiar plural form of 'you') or a Mexican slang term for facial hair. In Italian, **bozo** means lump or bump.

↳ *'Capable of putting up with every bozo and meathead who comes his way.'* (Jonathan Keates reviewing Malcolm Bradbury's *Unsent Letters*, *Observer*, 5 June 1988).

bozo-filter *n* an alternative name for a **killfile**, in the 1990s patois of **cyberpunks** and **net-heads**.

brace *vb American* to accost, **shake down**. A rather old-fashioned underworld term.

brackers *adj British* broke, penniless. A word heard in the 1980s which is an invention based on **boracic** or a deformation of 'broke'.

Brahms (and Liszt) *adj British* drunk. Rhyming slang for **pissed**. A fairly popular Cockney term since the 1930s, which was given wider currency by its use in television comedies of the early 1970s.

brainbox *n British* an exceptionally intelligent person. A term typically used derisively or enviously by children of, or to, fellow pupils.

brainless, braindead *adj British* drunk. The term is heard particularly in the Scottish Lowlands and the north of England.

brains department *n British* the CID. A usually derisive term applied by members of the **button mob**. An item of police slang recorded by the *Evening Standard* magazine, February 1993.

brandy *n British* backside, buttocks. Used in this sense the term was heard among the London **gay** community since the 1960s and may have originated from the rhyming slang, '*brandy and rum*: **bum**.'

brasco *n Australian* a toilet.

brass *n British* **1** money. Brass has been an obvious metaphor or euphemism as long as the metal has been used in coins. The word is currently more widespread in northern England.
2 a prostitute. Originally 'brass nail', this working-class usage is rhyming slang on **tail**, in the sexual sense.
3 a shorter form of **brass neck**.

brass *adj British* broke, penniless. Pronounced to rhyme with 'gass', never southern English 'class', this is a short form of **boracic** or **brassick** heard among teenagers in 1990.

brass eye *n British* the anus. This obscure vulgarism, used by schoolboys, was adopted as the name of a controversial satirical TV comedy in 1997.

brassick *adj British* broke, penniless. An alternative spelling of **boracic**.

brass-monkeys *adj British* extremely cold. A shortening of '*brass-monkey time*' or '*brass-monkey weather*', this phrase refers to the widely known vulgar saying '*cold enough to freeze the balls off a brass monkey!*'. A rather far-fetched explanation of the catchphrase is that a 'brass monkey' was a rack of cannonballs on board a warship.

brass neck *n British* an intensive form of **neck** in the sense of 'cheek' or 'nerve'.

bread *n* money. In the 1960s this usage supplanted the earlier **dough** in **hip** parlance; by the late 1970s the word was dated and in the 1980s has largely been replaced by a variety of colourful alternatives (in Britain, **dosh**, **rhino**, etc.).
↳'*This year two chicks and I got enough bread together and flew to Eilat (Israel) to see what was happening out there.*'
(Reader's letter in *Oz* magazine, February 1970).

breadbasket *n* the abdomen. A pugilists' euphemism, first recorded in 1753.

breadhead *n* someone who is motivated by money, a mercenary person. A term of disapproval from the **hippy** era, applied to those professing loyalty to the counterculture who openly or covertly sold out to commercialism or profit.
↳'*Bob Geldof, then an impoverished photographer's assistant, sold him photos of Jagger and Pete Townshend which are still reproduced. Goldsmith, always an unrepentant "breadhead", parted with ten quid.*'
(*Sunday Times* magazine, June 1989).

breakfast *n See* **dingo's breakfast**, **dog's breakfast**, **Mexican breakfast**.

break it down *vb British* to enjoy oneself, act boisterously. A vogue term among teenagers and devotees of dancefloor and **acid house** culture from the end of the 1980s. The term, perhaps American in origin, was also recorded in use among north London schoolboys in 1993 and 1994, sometimes as an exclamation.

break north *vb American* to depart, leave. A vogue term in black street slang of the 1990s, the origin of the term is obscure but may evoke the escape of a slave from the southern states. A variety of euphemisms (like its contemporaries **bail**, **book**, **jam** and **jet**) for 'run away' are essential to the argot of gang members and their playground imitators.

breed *vb American* to make (a woman) pregnant. An item of black speech probably originating in the Caribbean. It occurs in the cult novel *Yardie* (1993) by Victor Headley.

breeder *n* a heterosexual. A pejorative term in use among **gay** speakers, quoted by the San Francisco writer Armistead Maupin.

breezy *adj American* excellent. The term was fashionable among adolescents in the early 1990s, often used as an all-purpose exclamation of approval.

brew *n* **1** beer, or a beer. A word used by northern British drinkers (usually without the indefinite article) and by American college students (usually in the form 'a brew').
2 *British* tea. A term popular in institutions, especially in the 1950s.

brewer's, brewer's droop *n phrase* impotence, usually temporary, caused by drinking alcohol. The term is common in Britain, where it is now sometimes shortened to **brewer's**, and in Australia. (Brewers featured in many comic or ribald expressions from the 16th to the 19th centuries.)

brewski *n American* a beer. An elaboration of **brew** popular with students.

Brian *n British* a boring, vacuous person. Supposedly a typical name for an earnest and tedious working-class or lower-middle-class male. The term has been given humorous currency in the late 1970s and the 1980s by joking references to TV sports commentator Brian Johnson and a well-known sketch in the TV series *Monty Python's Flying Circus* concerning footballers. However, it was already heard among schoolboys in London in the late 1960s.

↳'*Educating Brian.*'
(Title of an article on 'academic' footballers, *You* magazine, March 1988).

brick it *vb British* to be extremely nervous, overcome with fear. A recent usage derived from the vulgarism **shitting bricks**.

↳'*Although I was bricking it, when the light came on on top of the camera, it was like this fifth gear…*'
(*Evening Standard*, 2 September 1988).

brief *n British* 1 a lawyer. Derived from the briefs, or documents containing a resume of each case, with which the lawyer is prepared or 'briefed'. A working-class term used since before World War II by both police and criminals.

↳'*One eight-year-old white boy brought in after being caught red-handed mugging in the area, astonished officers by refusing to say anything until he had seen "his brief".*'
(*Observer*, 22 May 1988).

2 a passport. A word from the lexicon of drug smugglers, among others.

↳'*They picked him up with a suitcase full of cash and three false briefs.*'
(Recorded, convicted cocaine smuggler, London, 1987).

brights *n American* intelligence, awareness. The term is a near synonym for **smarts** and is often used in the admonition '*turn up your brights!*'

brill *adj British* wonderful, exciting. A teenagers' shortening of brilliant, used as an all-purpose term of approval since the late 1970s.

↳'*They are a wicked group and steam up the charts with brill singles in the US.*'
(Heavily ironic reader's letter, *NME*, 8 July 1989).

↳'*I am having a completely utterly brill time…*'
(Postcard from a 9-year-old, London, 1989).

brillo-pads *adj British* excellent. An elaborated form of **brill**, used by London schoolchildren from the late 1980s borrowing the trademark name of kitchen scouring pads.

bring down *vb* to depress or disappoint. A black American and **beatnik** term, like the other phrasal verbs come down and **put down**, adopted in Britain in the early 1960s by jazz enthusiasts among others. The phrase became one of the standard items in the **hippy** vocabulary. The past form brought down was also used in Britain to mean suddenly depressed, especially after an initial drug **high**.

↳'*Don't Bring Me Down.*'
(Title of song by the Pretty Things, 1964).

bringdown *n*
a a disappointment, a depressing experience. A black American and **beatnik** term popular among **hippies** in Britain. The word implies high expectations unfulfilled, or depression following elation.

↳'*What a Bringdown.*'
(Title of song recorded by Cream, 1969).

b a depressing or morose person.

↳'*Don't invite John – he's a real bringdown since Sally dumped him.*'

bristols *n pl British* breasts. A common vulgarism, from the rhyming slang 'Bristol City': **titty**. (Bristol City is the name of the city's chief football team.)

bro' *n American* a term of address used typically by black Americans to each other. It is a shortening of brother.

broad *n American* a woman. A disparaging term in that it is exclusively used by men and implies a lack of respect for the woman in question. The origin of the word is not documented but is probably from 'broad-**ass**' or something similar, denoting an accommodating woman. (Immorality is not an integral part of the meaning in modern usage.)

↳'*We've got Dustin Hoffman fighting Meryl Streep for a four-year-old in "Kramer vs Kramer"…Thirty years ago, the Duke would have slapped the*

broad around and shipped the kid off to military school.'
(*Real Men Don't Eat Quiche*, Bruce Feirstein, 1982).

brok *adj British* broken, damaged, in disarray. This alteration of broke(n) probably originated in black dialect. It was a vogue term among teenage gangs (**bruck[ers]** is an alternative form). The term was recorded in use among north London schoolboys in 1993 and 1994.

Bronx cheer *n American* a **farting** noise made with the lips and tongue, a **raspberry**. The Bronx is a mainly working-class borough of New York City.

broom-broom *n British* a car. A nursery word sometimes used facetiously by adults.
⮑*'He's got himself a new broom-broom.'*

broomhead *n* a dunce, stupid person. A homely term of (usually mild) abuse, used typically by parents and children.
⮑*'You broomhead! Why didn't you tell me?'*
(*Degrassi Junior High*, Canadian TV series, 1987).

brothel creepers *n pl British* shoes with thick crepe soles, fashionable among **teddy boys** and others in the 1950s ('brothel stompers' is an American version). Brothel creepers has sometimes also denoted suede shoes or 'desert boots'.
⮑*'Red tiger-stripe brothel-creepers are all the rage.'*
(*Tatler*, March 1987).

brother *n British* a lesbian. Although a fairly predictable coinage, it may in fact be an ironic male response to the feminist use of 'sister' to indicate solidarity.
⮑*'They're all brothers in the canteen.'*
(Recorded, London student, September 1995).

brown *n American* the anus. In this sense the word is probably an abbreviation of **brown-eye**.
⮑*'In/up the brown.'*

brown *vb American* to sodomize, perform anal intercourse.
⮑*'The idea of browning really geeks me out!'*

brown bread *adj British* dead. A rhyming-slang expression which probably

originated in the 1960s and which is still in working-class use in London.

brown envelope *n British* a full confession. The term, used by criminals and police in the 1990s, derives from the phrase '*to give (someone) a/the brown envelope*' and typically describes the action of a 'supergrass', who confesses in return for a light sentence. The envelope in question probably evokes a mysterious package (e.g., containing a note or payment).

brown eye *n* the anus. An Australianism also heard in Britain, not to be confused with **big brown eyes**.

brown hatter *n* a male homosexual. A derogatory term from the 1950s, still occasionally heard. The term refers both to the idea of contact between the head of the penis and excrement and to the archaic upper-class notion that the wearing of brown hats on certain formal occasions marked out a man as socially unacceptable.

brownie *n British* a Scotch, drink of whiskey. A word used by middle-class and usually middle-aged drinkers.

brownie-hound *n* a male homosexual. One of several 1980s epithets combining humour and hostility and evoking an image of a predatory sodomite ('chasing' or 'stealing' excreta). **Turd burglar** and **chocolate bandit** are synonyms.

brownie points *n pl* credit for good deeds, an imaginary award for virtuous actions. An American colloquialism which has caught on in Britain since the late 1970s.

brown-nose *vb, n* to flatter, behave sycophantically (towards). A vulgarism common in all English-speaking countries at least since World War II. 'Brown-noser' is an alternative version of the noun form. From the image of kissing another person's backside. (*Private Eye*, the satirical magazine, has instituted a regular column in which the 'order of the Brown Nose' is awarded for nauseating sycophancy.)
⮑*'Brown-nosing the boss.'*
⮑*'Now he is on his knees, brown-nosing with the rest of them.'*
(*Private Eye*, 1 April 1988).

brown trousers *n, adj British* (a) very frightening (situation). A light-hearted reference to the terrified person losing control of their bowel movements. Now mainly middle class in usage, the term probably dates from World War II, but has not previously been recorded in writing.

ॐ*'Getting up in front of all those people was brown trousers.'*

ॐ*'A brown trouser job.'*

bruck *adj British* broken, destroyed. A dialect form of 'broken' in the speech of the southern United States and of the Caribbean, this term passed from black British usage into general adolescent usage in the 1990s. *'Bruckers'* is an elaborated form of the same word.

Brummie, Brummy *n, adj British*

a (someone) from Birmingham. From the city's nickname **Brummagem**.
b the speech of Birmingham.

brush *n British*

a pubic hair.
b sexual activity or potential sex partners. The word is almost invariably used by men of women.

Brussel Sprouts, Brussels *n pl British* (boy) scouts. An item of authentic London rhyming slang recorded in the late 1980s.

brutal *adj* excellent. A typical appropriation of a negative (compare **bad**, **wicked, chronic**) as a faddish adolescent form of all-purpose approval. Brutal has been recorded at different times in the UK, USA and Australia.

B.S.D. *n*
See **Big Swinging Dick**.

bubba *n American* a young man, especially an uncomplicated extrovert. The jocular term, evoking beer- and sport-loving, possibly well-to-do **redneck** youths, was applied in the mid-1990s to US President Bill Clinton and there was a brief attempt to promote the idea of a new social category under the same name (a magazine called *Bubba* was published) along the lines of the **laddish** tendency in the UK. The word originated as a 'baby-talk' pronunciation of 'brother' used as a nickname or term of endearment applied to young adult males in the southern states of the USA.

bubble *n British* a Greek. Rhyming slang, from 'bubble and squeak', an inexpensive dish of fried leftover mashed potatoes and greens. The term probably dates from the 19th century, but is still in use in London. In spite of its friendly sound, bubble is not a jocular term and can be used abusively.

ॐ*'They also call him* [George Michael] *the bubble with the stubble.'*
(*News of the World*, 29 May 1988).

bubble *vb British* to weep. The term is now heard particularly in the Scottish Lowlands and the north of England. It occurred in public school slang as long ago as the 1920s.

ॐ*'For God's sake, stop your bubbling, you big softie!'*

bubble-head *n* a version of **airhead**.

bubbly *n* Champagne, or any other sparkling wine.
ॐ*'A bottle of bubbly.'*

bubkes *n See* **bupkes**.

buck *n* **1** *American* a dollar. A buckhorn knife handle was used apparently as a counter in 19th-century card games and buckskins were earlier traded and used as a unit of exchange in North America.
2 a young male gang member. A term adopted by British black youth and football hooligans from the streetgangs of the USA, who themselves appropriated a word applied to young Red Indian braves.

bucket *n* **1** a pejorative or humorous term for a car or boat.
2 *British* mouth. In this sense the word is typically heard in working-class speech in such phrases as *'shut your bucket!'* or *'stick this in your bucket!'*, recorded in the mid-1990s.
3 *American* an unfortunate person. An item of possibly ersatz slang from the lexicon of the cult 1992 film, *Wayne's World*. **Pail** is a synonym.

bucket *vb* **1a** to move quickly. Usually but not always in the phrase **bucketing along**. This usage dates from the 19th century.
b to pour (with rain). Usually heard in the expression *'it's bucketing down'*.
2 *Australian* to criticize or denigrate. This use of the word probably arose from the image of tipping a bucket, e.g., of excrement over a victim, although the noun

'bucketing' was recorded in England in 1914 in the sense of a harsh or oppressive task.

bucket shop *n* an establishment selling cheap and/or low quality items in large quantities. The phrase has become a standard British colloquialism for a cut-price travel agency. The expression originated in the USA in the 1880s when it was referred to share-selling operations, by analogy with cheap saloons.

Buckley's hope/chance *n Australian* no chance at all or very little chance. The eponymous Buckley was an escaped convict who surrendered to the authorities after 32 years on the run, dying one year later in 1956.

buckshee *adj* free, without charge. Like baksheesh, meaning a bribe or tip, this word derives from Persian *bakshish*; something given, a gift, and dates from the colonial era.

buck-wild *adj American* uncontrolled, uncontrollable, running amok. The term uses the intensifying combining form 'buck-' which probably originated in the speech of the southern US.

bud *n American* cannabis, marihuana. The use of the word is probably inspired by the appearance of the flowering heads and round seeds of marihuana plants.

buddha sticks *n pl* another name for **Thai sticks**.

buddy *n*
a *American* a male friend, from 'butty', a British dialect or gypsy diminutive of brother. 'Butty', or 'but', is heard in parts of Wales to mean a close friend (of either sex).
b a volunteer companion to an AIDS patient.

buff *n* 1 an enthusiast, expert or aficionado. An American term which, in forms such as film-buff, opera-buff, etc., has become established in other English-speaking countries. The word is said (by American lexicographer, Robert L. Chapman among others) to be inspired by the buff-coloured raincoats worn by 19th-century New York firemen, later applied to watchers of fires, hence devotees of any activity.
✤ *'Having your life dragged through the popular press for scrutiny by a nation of voyeurs and trivia-buffs....'*

(*London Australasian Weekly*, 4 September 1989).
2 the buff the nude. From the colour of (white) skin.

buff *adj American* excellent, attractive. A vogue term of appreciation or approval in use among adolescents in the early 1990s and associated with **slacker** and **grunge** subcultures as well as the language of college students. **Boff** is a variant form.
✤ *'She's buff!'*
(*Sneakers*, US film, 1993).

buffage *n American* an attractive person or persons. A vogue term of 1993 using the -**age** suffix as in **grindage**, **tune-age** with the vogue term **buff**, especially in the appreciative description or exclamation *'major buffage!'* popular particularly among females.

Buffalo Bill *n British* a till or cash box. An item of market traders' rhyming slang recorded in the mid-1990s. A synonym from the same environment is **Benny Hill**.
✤ *'Just hand it over and I'll bung it in the old Buffalo Bill.'*

buffaloed *adj American*
a bullied, cowed, overwhelmed or bamboozled.
b knocked flat or knocked out. Both senses of the word evoke the crushing force of a stampede.

bug *n*
a an insect.
b a covert listening device.
c a virus or infection.
d a fault or flaw in a machine or system.
e an enthusiast, devotee. A racier synonym of **buff**.
The word bug originates in Middle English 'bugge' meaning hobgoblin or scarecrow.

bug *vb American* to irritate or annoy. The image is of a crawling, buzzing or biting insect. The use of this term spread to Britain in the **beatnik** era but has never fully established itself.
✤ *'Stephenson said Mark Allen had "kept bugging them to burn down his neighbour's flat".'*
(*Independent*, 1 November 1989).

bugged *adj* 1 angry, irritated. From the verb to **bug**.

2 suffering from abscesses. A prisoners' and drug addicts' term.

bugger *n* **1** a sodomite. The Bogomil ('lovers of God') heretics sent emissaries from their base in Bulgaria in the eleventh and twelfth centuries to contact heretics in Western Europe. These travellers were known as *Bulgarus* (late Latin), and *bougre* (Middle French), a name which was imported into Middle English along with a loathing of the heretics and their practices. One offence which heretics of all persuasions were accused of was unnatural vice, hence the transformation of Bulgarians into buggers. The word is now a very mild pejorative often meaning little more than 'fellow'.

↳*'So, if trying to persuade the local authority to stop discriminating and accept its responsibilities in a multiracial society makes us "buggers" or "pompous prats", as Mr Flounders contemptuously calls us, then we are proud to be so.'*
(Reader's letter, *Independent*, 26 August 1989).

2 an awkward or difficult task or person.
↳*'This is a bugger to get open.'*

bugger *vb* **1** to sodomize.
2 to ruin, wreck, incapacitate, thwart. This figurative application of the term is several hundred years old.

bugger-all *n British* nothing, none. A synonym of **sod-all** and **fuck-all**. It occasionally denotes almost or virtually nothing.

buggeration *n British* ruin, confusion. The word is often used as an exclamation of impatience by middle-class and upper-class speakers.

buggered *adj* incapacitated, ruined, useless. This usage is encountered in British and Australian speech.

buggerize *vb Australian* to damage, mishandle, etc. The term is also used in the phrase *'to buggerize around'*, meaning to waste time.

bugging *adj American* irritated, agitated, discomfited. This vogue term, fashionable among adolescents at the end of the 1990s, may have originated in prison or underworld usage, itself derived from the verb **to bug** or the adjective **bugs** in the sense of crazy.

↳*'Those guys were all looking at me like I was a freak and I didn't belong there and I was like totally bugging ...'*
(Recorded, female student, California, 1995).

bugger off *vb* to leave, go away. A common verb and expletive in British and Australian speech.

a bugger's muddle *n British* an absolute mess. A phrase which was in armed-service and middle-class use in the 1950s and although sounding dated, survives.

buggery *n* **1** anal intercourse. The word is still, in Britain, the official designation of the act in legal terminology.
2 *British* oblivion, destruction, ruin. The word usually appears in phrases such as *'all to buggery'*.

buggins' turn *n British* an automatic privilege that comes in turn to members of a group, regardless of merit, seniority, etc. A piece of bureaucrats' slang. Buggins is an imaginary name, perhaps inspired by **muggins**. The term probably dates from the 1940s and is still heard in local government and civil-service circles.

↳*'The committee's leader is still selected on the principle of Buggins' turn.'*
(Recorded, member of Brent Council, London, 1987).

bug house, bug hutch *n American* a mental hospital.

bugle *n* nose. An old London working-class usage, paralleled in Canada, Australia and elsewhere.

↳*'If you go on doing all that cocaine, you'll perforate your bugle!'*
(Recorded, artist, Vauxhall, London, 1976).

bugle-duster *n* a handkerchief.

bug out *vb American* to leave hurriedly. The **bug** component in this adolescent expression is essentially meaningless.

bugs bunny *n British* money. A rhyming-slang term heard in raffish and underworld use since the 1960s.

buick *vb, n* (to) vomit. An imitative term employing the name of an American make of automobile and recalling such words as **puke** and **hoick**.

builds *n British* the components needed to construct a **joint**. The term may apply to cigarette papers alone or to the tobacco, cardboard, etc.

↳*'I've got the puffy, I just need the builds.'*
(Recorded, university student, London 1995).

built *adj* 1 physically well-developed; statuesque or strong. An American term of the 1970s, now heard in Australia and Britain. It is used to express appreciation of sexual attractiveness by men of women and vice versa.

↳*'Man, is she built.'*
2 built like a brick shithouse heavily, strongly or solidly built. The term is used usually of people; when referring to men it is generally appreciative, when used of women it is more disparaging. This is a very popular expression in Australia, but used throughout the English-speaking world. In polite company 'outhouse' can be substituted for 'shithouse'.

bull *n* 1 a uniformed policeman. A 200-year-old term still heard in North America and Australia, but never in Britain.

↳*'But Butch, you can't stay here. This is the first place the bulls will look for you.'*
(*Going Bye Bye*, film starring Laurel and Hardy, 1934).
2 a shorter and more acceptable version of **bullshit**. In armed-service usage it particularly refers to excessive regimentation of unnecessary formalities; in civilian speech it often denotes empty talk.
3 *American* a sexually active or aggressive male. A rarely heard 1970s and 1980s alternative to **stud**. *See also* **shoot the breeze/bull**.

bull and cow *n British* a noisy argument, a fight or brawl. Still thriving London rhyming slang for row.

↳*'There was a right bull and cow in the pub last night.'*

bull artist *n* a more polite form of 'bullshit-artist'.

bulldyke *n* a masculine, dominant or aggressive lesbian. An offensive term which was commonly heard until the late 1960s (by which time **gay** women's styles had largely moved away from imitation of male roles). Bulldyke was almost invariably used by men and was invariably pe-

jorative; it was sometimes extended to apply to any lesbian. *See also* **dyke**.

bull session *n* a period of earnest or bombastic but shallow conversation. The expression usually refers to energetic group discussions between friends (usually males), talking **bull**.

bullsh *n* an abbreviated, euphemistic version of **bullshit**, which seems to have originated in Australian usage.

bullshit *n* nonsense, or falsehood, especially when blatant or offensive; empty, insincere or bombastic speech or behaviour; tedious attention to detail. The term has become particularly widespread since the late 1960s before which it was more often heard in American speech than British (where it was, however, a well-known part of armed-service language).

↳*'I'm not allowed to talk about it ...*
[Roald] *Dahl grumbled from his Buckinghamshire home. It has something to do with security or some such bullshit.'*
(*Evening Standard*, 8 September 1989).

bullshit *vb* to try to impress, persuade, bamboozle or deceive with empty, boastful or portentous talk. Whereas the noun form is sometimes shortened to the less offensive **bull**, the verb form, especially in American speech, is shortened to **shit(ting)**, (as in *'come on, you're shittin' me'*).

↳*'Don't try to bullshit me, I know the score....'*

bullshitter *n* a bombastic, verbose or insincere person; a habitual source of **bullshit**.

↳*'"Mi-Lords! Laydees! and Gentlemen!!!" A VOICE FROM THE DARK SHOUTS, "Go home you Welsh bullshitter!"'*
(Spike Milligan, *Adolf Hitler, My Part in his Downfall*, 1971).

bum *n* 1 *British* bottom, backside, buttocks. From the Middle English period to the end of the 18th century it was possible to use this word in English without offending respectable persons. By the 19th century it was considered rude, perhaps unsurprisingly in that its suggested origin was in 'bom' or 'boom', an imitation of the sound of flatulence.
2 a tramp, down-and-out, wastrel. This sense of the word is probably unrelated to the previous one. It is a 19th-century

shortening of bummer, meaning an idler or loafer from the German *Bummler*, layabout (derived from *bummeln*, to dangle, hang about). *See* on the bum.

↳'*It kind of upsets me that they talk about him as if he's a hopeless bum.*' (Recorded, Canadian teenage girl, London, April 1996).

3 a sodomy or the opportunity thereof. A vulgarism used mainly by heterosexuals, referring to homosexual activity.

b sex. A heterosexual synonym for **tail**.

bum *adj*

a worthless, inferior, bad.

↳'*A bum cheque/trip.*'

b incapacitated, out of order.

↳'*A bum ankle.*'

These usages are inspired by the American noun sense of tramp, idler.

bum *vb* to cadge or scrounge. From the noun form **bum** meaning down-and-out or beggar. This use of the word is predominantly British.

↳'*Can I bum a cigarette from you, man.*'

Bum and tit *See* B and T.

bumboy *n British* **1** a homosexual or a youth (not necessarily homosexual) who consents to buggery. A term of contempt, originating several hundred years ago and widespread since the 1950s, especially among schoolchildren.

2 a sycophant, an **arse-licker**. The term is rather archaic, having been supplanted by stronger alternatives.

bum chum *n* a male homosexual partner. A schoolchildren's term, usually used jokingly to jeer at close friends.

↳'*Those two are supposed to be definite bum chums.*' (Recorded, female care-worker, London 1993).

bumf, bumpf, bumph *n British* information on paper; forms, instructions, brochures, etc., especially those considered unnecessary, annoying or in excessive quantity. This term is now an acceptable middle-class colloquialism although its origin is more vulgar. It derives from 'bum fodder', a pre-World War II public-school and armed-forces term for toilet paper. This was applied scornfully in wartime to excessive bureaucratic paperwork. In Australia the usage is sometimes extended to mean unnecessary or verbose speech. The phrase 'bum fodder' in full is now obsolete, but was used from the 17th century to refer to waste paper.

↳'*A glimpse of the unpestered life you lead at Cap Ferrat, deluged with fan mail, besieged by the press, inundated with bumpf of one sort or another.*' (Ian Fleming in a letter to Somerset Maugham, quoted in John Pearson's biography, 1966).

bumfluff *n British* light facial hair on a pubescent boy. Usually a term of mild derision, especially referring to a youth's first attempts to grow a moustache or beard.

bummed out *adj American* disappointed, dejected, having suffered a **bummer**.

bummer *n* a bad experience, a disappointment. An American expression (said to have originated in the jargon of the racetrack where it meant a loss which reduced one to the status of a **bum**) which spread to Britain and Australia in the **hippy** era of the late 1960s. It is still heard, although in the late 1980s it was dated. The meaning of the term was reinforced by the expression a **bum trip**, an unpleasant experience with LSD.

↳'*So okay, it looks like a bummer. But maybe...maybe you can still get something out of it.*' (Elmore Leonard, *The Switch*, 1978).

bump *vb* **1a** to remove someone surreptitiously from a waiting list, in order to substitute a more favoured client. A piece of jargon from the world of air travel which entered the public consciousness in the late 1980s due to the prevalence of the practice.

↳'*We were bumped at the last moment.*'

↳'*They offered to bump someone to get us on.*'

b *British* cheat, swindle. This sense of the word, popular among London schoolchildren in the mid 1990s, may derive from the earlier jargon sense.

↳'*Yeah! He's trying to bump you.*'

↳'*We got bumped.*'

2 *American* kill. An item of street slang, abbreviating the now dated colloquialism 'bump off'.

3 a shortening of **bump 'n grind** used by adolescents and **rappers** in the mid-1990s.

bumper *n Australian* a cigarette end.

bumpers *n pl* **1** breasts.
2 tennis shoes or baseball boots, especially those (in the style of the 1960s) with extra-thick rubber round the toe-caps resembling the bumpers of American automobiles.

bumph *n* an alternative spelling of **bumf**.

bump 'n grind *vb, n* (to make) pelvic motions in simulation of sexual thrusting, usually as part of dancing or of 'heavy petting'. The term is North American in origin.

bump off *vb* to kill. A 'tough-talking' euphemism now largely replaced by more sinister locutions such as **blow away**, **waste**, etc.

bump one's gums *vb American* to talk, speak or converse. An item of black street talk which was included in so-called **Ebonics**, recognized as a legitimate language variety by school officials in Oakland, California, in late 1996. A variant of the earlier **flap/snap one's gums**.

bumps *n pl* breasts. A mock-childish term.

bump start *vb, n British* (to assist in) a sudden rousing to action, whether physical or metaphorical. The expression, employing the image of push-starting a reluctant car, is a fashionable colloquialism in the 1980s, often in a business or sexual context. **Kickstart** is a more popular alternative in American speech.
✤'*The poor old boy needed a bump start!*'
✤'*We had to bump start the bloody project by ourselves.*'

bump tummies *vb* to have sex. A humorous euphemism invented by adults in imitation of nursery language. Usually said by middle-class speakers.

the bum's rush *n* an unceremonious ejection. This is North American saloon terminology of the early 20th century, referring to barmen or doormen grabbing undesirable customers (such as **bums**) by the collar and the seat of the pants and bodily hustling them out into the street. The phrase is almost always used in the expressions '*give someone the bum's rush*' or '*get the bum's rush*'.
✤'*Personally I think Ange should have given Den the bum's rush.*'
(*Biff* cartoon, 1986).

bum tags *n pl British* another term for **dingleberries**.

bumwad *n* toilet paper. A vulgarism heard in Britain and Australia.

bunce *n British* money or profit. A word dating from the 19th century and almost obsolete by the 1960s, except among street traders and the London underworld. In the late 1980s the word was revived by middle-class users such as alternative comedians in search of colourful synonyms in a climate of financial excesses. Bunce may originally have been a corruption of 'bonus'.

buncey, buncy *adj British* profitable, lucrative. The adjectival use postdates the noun.

bunch of fives *n British* a fist. A 19th-century pun on a hand of cards (or, later, a handful of banknotes), typically used in describing threatening or violent behaviour.

bunch-punch *n American* a **gangbang** or **train**.

bunco *n American* a swindle, fraud. A version of bunk or bunkum which has not been exported.

bundle *n* **1** a large quantity of money or of something else desirable, such as narcotics.
✤'*I lost a bundle.*'
2 *British* a fight, brawl or rough-and-tumble. Used especially by schoolchildren from the 1950s onward, typically as a cry or chant to attract onlookers to a playground or street fight, it is the British equivalent of the American **rumble**. Bundle is also used as a verb.
3 the male genitals, normally as seen through tight clothing. A term used by homosexuals and heterosexuals since the mid-1960s.
4 *American* an attractive woman. A condescending term which is probably a shortening of 'bundle of joy'. *See also* **drop a bundle**.

bung *n British* a bribe. A term used by police and criminals, almost always to refer to a bribe being given to a policeman. This normally implies something more substantial than a **drink**. The earlier verb form **to bung**, meaning to pay a bribe or protection money is now rare but not obsolete.

❖'He wants a bung of a monkey to square it.'

bung (someone) *vb British* to bribe, pay protection money. An item of underworld and police jargon.

❖'We're going to have to bung him if we want to stay out of trouble.'

Bungalow Bill *n phrase British* a name applied by wits to a male who is either considered to be rather unintelligent (i.e. there is 'nothing upstairs') or genitally well-endowed (i.e. 'everything is downstairs'), or both. The nickname was applied by the UK press in 1987 to the actress Joan Collins' companion, the property developer, Bill Wiggins.

bunghole *n* the anus. A vulgarism found in the works of the celebrator of low life, Charles Bukowski, among others.

bunghole *vb* to sodomize, **bugger**.

bung it on *vb Australian* to behave in a presumptuous or pretentious manner. The term denotes 'putting on airs' from which phrase it may derive.

bung on a blue *vb Australian* to lose one's temper, indulge in a display of irritation.

bungy, bungie, bunjie *n British* a rubber eraser. A schoolchildren's term since at least World War II, it was in use among office workers as early as the 1930s. The sound of the word is intended to convey the shape and consistency (influenced by words such as bung and spongey). The 'g' is usually soft.

❖'If i thro a bit of bungy at peason he will bide his time and thro an ink bomb back [sic].'
(*Back in the Jug Agane*, Geoffrey Willans and Ronald Searle, 1959).

bun in the oven *n British* 'to have a bun in the oven' has meant to be pregnant in working-class British usage since the 19th century. The comparison of the stomach or abdomen with an oven is older still.

bunjie *n British* an alternative form of **bungy** (rubber eraser).

bunk *adj American* unfashionable, **uncool**. A teenage vogue word from 1987 which is a deliberate shifting of the standard sense of bunk and bunkum (as signifying nonsense). *See also* **bank**.

❖'That's bunk, man.'
❖'A real bunk thing to do.'

bunk *vb American* to cheat. A verb formed from the colloquial nouns bunk and bunkum and the slang **bunco**.

bunk in *vb British* to gatecrash, enter illicitly or surreptitiously. Bunk occurs in many contexts as a version of bung, meaning throw forcibly; here the image evolved is of being lifted or hoisted through a window, for example.

❖'I told him I'd never been to drama school, so he said: "RADA [the Royal Academy of Dramatic Arts] *is just down the road. Let's go and bunk in".'
(Philip Roth, *Observer*, section 5, 9 April 1989).

bunk off *vb British* to play truant or absent oneself. A term now heard mainly among schoolchildren, bunk off is a variant of '*do a bunk*' which has been a common expression since the 19th century. There is no connection with bunk bed, but rather with the sense of bunk (like 'bung') as to hoist or toss.

bunk (someone) up *vb British* to lift someone or otherwise help them to climb over an obstruction, such as a wall. A schoolchildren's word of the 1950s, still occasionally heard, it was less common than the form to give someone a bunk-up. This is another example of bunk in the sense of hoist or throw *See* **bunk in**, **bunk off**, **bunk-up**.

bunk-up *n British* 1 an act of sexual intercourse, especially when furtive and/or brusque. A term influenced more by the notion of being **up someone** than the erotic possibilities of bunk beds.

❖'A bunk-up behind the bike sheds.'
2 a lift, help in climbing something.

❖'Give me a bunk-up over this wall and I'll scrump us some apples.'
Both uses were common schoolchildren's currency in the 1950s and 1960s. The sense of bunk is hoist or throw; it is a variant form of bung.

bunny *n British* 1 incessant talking, chatter. This is a later version of **rabbit** (a shortening of the rhyming slang 'rabbit and pork'; talk). As rabbit entered non-cockney colloquial speech, so working-class Londoners adopted this more raffish alternative. It is sometimes used in verb form.

2 a *Australian* a dupe or victim. Partridge

dates this usage to the 1920s, although the word was briefly used in a similar sense by British **teddy boys** in the 1950s and by the US novelist Sinclair Lewis.

b a girl or young woman. A patronizing male term with similar implications to the previous sense.

buns *n pl* **1** *American* buttocks. A popular term since the early 1970s which is not particularly vulgar and which is not in popular usage outside North America. The origin may be an obsolete northern British dialect term for 'tail', a variation on **bum**, or simply refer to the parallels in form and texture with edible buns.

2 *Australian* sanitary towels or tampons. A shortening of 'jam buns' used almost exclusively by men. ('To have the buns on' is to be menstruating.)

bupkes, bupkiss *n American*

a an insignificant amount or trivial matter.

b nothing or none. The word is a borrowing from Yiddish, which adopted it from the Russian for 'beans', a term widely used colloquially (in expressions such as 'not worth a hill/row of beans', **bean-counter**, etc.) to suggest items of little value.

buppie *n* a member of the black middle class, a black **yuppie**. An American categorization of the late 1980s also heard in Britain and still in use a decade later.

↳*'Establishing a black middle class won't help anybody except a few buppies – all yuppies, black and white, are scum.'*
(Reader's letter, *NME*, 8 July 1989).

the burbs *pl American* suburbs. A vogue word of the later 1980s.

burg *n American* a town, place. From the Germanic component added to many American place-names.

↳*'Let's split this burg for good.'*

burl *n Australian* a try. Usually in the phrase **give it a burl**; to make an attempt at, to try (a task or activity). Probably a blend of the colloquial expressions '*have a bash*' and '*give it a whirl*'. Give it a burl is one of many Australian expressions given currency in Britain by the cartoon strip *The Adventures of Barry McKenzie*, written by Barry Humphries, which ran in the satirical magazine *Private Eye* between 1965 and 1974. Some of the more colourful of these expressions were in fact coined, or embellished, by Humphries himself, but this phrase was well-established in Australia by the early 1960s.

burly *n, adj American* (something) difficult, hard to achieve, problematical. A teenage vogue term from 1987, in use among the successors of **Valley Girls** and **preppies**, among others. It may originate in black street-slang where standard terms are often appropriated for use as gang code words or from surfers' slang.

burn *n* **1 a** tobacco.

↳*'Got any burn.'*

b a cigarette.

c a smoke.

↳*'A quick burn.'*

The first sense is in use in prisons in the UK; the others are also heard in other English-speaking areas.

2 *American* a **hit** of crack.

↳*'I just need a burn.'*

burn (someone) *vb* **1** to cheat financially. An Americanism that was part of the **hippy** vocabulary (typically referring to selling phoney drugs) and hence spread to the UK. It is now archaic in Britain. **2** *American* to kill. A 'tough guy' euphemism.

burner *n* a firearm. An item of American teen gang language probably postdating the verb form to burn, reported in *The Sunday Times*, 8 March 1992.

burn off *vb British* to overtake, outstrip and thus humiliate another driver. A term from the language of **ton-up boys** and **boy racers**.

burnt *n British* glass. The term is a shortened form of the London rhyming slang '*burnt grass*', meaning glass, or '*burnt cinder*', 'winder' or window (both derivations have been suggested by its users) and is used in the jargon of criminals and glaziers, decorators, etc. to refer to glass panels in windows and doors. The word was cited as an example of the jargon of cat burglars recorded in *FHM* magazine in April 1996.

burnt *adj American* terrible, hopeless. A teenage vogue term of the late 1980s which is an extension of the earlier slang senses of cheated or 'burnt out'.

bush *adj* provincial or primitive. A term that can mean rural, or second-rate, or both. Much used in Australia in expressions such as 'bush scrubber' and 'bush lawyer' and, to a lesser extent, in the USA where it is often in the form 'bush league', small-town or small-time.

bush *n* 1 area of pubic hair. The term is used more often by men of a woman's pubic hair than vice-versa.

✎ *'Naff things the French do on a beach: ...display enormous pubic bushes.'*
(*Complete Naff Guide*, 1983).

2 marihuana, **grass**. A common term among smokers in the Caribbean and Britain. Bush refers especially to cannabis leaves and seeds sold unsorted and uncleaned.

✎ *'Prisoners cut off the cannabis leaves and dry them before smoking the drug in a form known as "bush".'*
(*Observer*, 12 June 1988).

bush-boogie *n American* a derogatory term for a black person. Boogie alone has had this meaning since the 1950s at least; the addition of **bush** adds the idea of provincialism.

bushed *adj* exhausted. A 20th-century version of the 19th-century senses of disorientated, lost in the wilderness.

bushie *n Australian* a provincial, rural or barbaric person; yokel.

✎ *'He thought the stereotype of the sporty, outdoorsy Australian began with the romantic 19th century image created by artists like Banjo Paterson, who had tried to convince us that we were "bushies".'*
(*Southern Cross* magazine, July 1987).

bush-league *adj American* provincial, amateurish, unsophisticated, inferior. The term derives from the categorization of minor-league baseball teams, and is sometimes shortened to **bush**.

✎ *'I can't handle the shit anymore.'*
'You're bush-league, that's why.'
(*Pay Dirt*, US movie, 1992).

business *n* 1 *British* the business. The very best, the acme of excellence.

✎ *'You should try some of this gear – it's the business.'*

2 *British* the business a thrashing, a thorough dressing down or beating up.

✎ *'We gave him the business. He won't try that again.'*

3 a hypodermic syringe. A drug user's euphemism.

4 defecation. To 'do one's business' was a nursery expression epitomizing Victorian notions of duty and hygiene.

busk it *vb British* to improvise. From the standard English **busker**, a wandering street musician. **Busk it** at first was a musician's, later a theatrical performer's term, referring to improvisation (*'I don't know it, but if you hum a few bars I'll busk it'*) but is now widely used in other forms of endeavour, such as business. The word 'busk' seems to have originated in an 18th-century borrowing from a Latin language: the Spanish *buscat*: to search; the archaic French *busquer*: to cruise; etc.

✎ *'If they don't accept our agenda we'll just have to busk it.'*

bust *n* 1 an arrest, especially for possession of illicit drugs. An item of **hippy** jargon which originated in the early 1960s and which by the late 1980s had become a common enough colloquialism to be used in the written and broadcast media. In American streetgang and underworld usage the word already had the sense of '*catch in the act*' by the late 1950s.

✎ *'The busts started to happen. People started to go to prison. People started to die. But by then you were too far in.'*
(Female ex-drug addict, *Independent*, 17 July 1989).

2 *American* a spectacular achievement or successful coup. A teenage term of approbation of the late 1980s, coming from the jargon of basketball, where it means a good shot.

3 a wild party or celebration.

4 **a** *Australian* a break-in, burglary.

b a break-out, escape from prison.

bust *vb* 1 to arrest, particularly for possession of drugs. In the USA the word was being used in this sense by the 1950s.

✎ *'And then I went and got busted, my old mother was disgusted. I'm never ever going to be trusted, by anybody anymore.'*
(Lyrics to 'Busted' by the Bonzo Dog Band, 1970).

✎ *'What I say [is] if guys get busted in North Africa and end up in their shitty prisons they got to be dumb in the first place.'*
(Letter to *Oz* magazine, June 1969).

2 *American* to demote. The word is used in this sense in armed-forces jargon as in '*busted down to sergeant*'.

bust on (someone) *vb American*

to punish, attack, kill. An item of youth slang of the late 1980s. Christian Brando, son of the actor, Marlon Brando, was reported by his sister Cheyenne to have said he was going to bust on her boyfriend, Dag Drollet, whom he was later convicted of shooting and killing.

bust one's buns *vb American* to

exhaust oneself by working, to make great efforts. **Buns** in this expression means buttocks, and the phrase is roughly equivalent to the British 'work one's arse off'.

butch *adj*

a tough, strong and assertive. The term is now often used humorously or to express mild derision; it probably comes from 'Butch' as a male nickname first heard at the end of the 19th century in the USA, which in turn probably derives from butcher.

b assertively masculine in behaviour and/or appearance. The term, typically applied disapprovingly or derisively, is used about heterosexual women, lesbians and **gay men**. During the 1950s the word had a narrower sense of a 'masculine' (active) rather than a 'feminine' (passive) partner in a homosexual relationship, or of a lesbian who behaved and dressed like a man; in this sense butch was also used as a noun.

butcher's *n British* a look. Nearly al-

ways in the phrases '*have a butcher's*' or '*take a butcher's (at this)*'. From the rhyming slang 'butcher's hook', which is at least eighty years old, and is still heard in the unabbreviated form.

butch up *vb* to become more as-

sertive, tougher or more masculine. This relatively recent expression (heard since the early 1980s in Britain) is often used as an exhortation, normally to a man who is behaving in a weak or cowardly way. (The antonym is **wimp out**.)

butt *n* backside, buttocks. In the United

States, butt is the most common colloquial term for this part of the body. Although slightly vulgar and generally the monopoly of male speakers, butt unlike **ass** is permissible in 'polite society' or broadcasts. It is rarely heard in Britain or Australia. Butt is historically related to

'buttocks' and in British, Australian and American English is still used to denote the thick end of something, as in the butt of a cue or a rifle, or simply the end, as in cigarette butt.

butterball, butterbutt *n Amer-*

ican a fat person, a **lard-ass**.

butters *adj British* ugly. A term from

black Caribbean usage that was adopted by adolescents in the mid-1990s. It is probably related to 'buttocks'.

✎ '*It's not surprising she got upset; they were called out at her, "Hey, butters!"*'
(Recorded, London schoolgirl, 1994).

butters, but-a-boy *n British* a

newly qualified taxi driver. This item of taxi drivers' jargon may derive from the catchphrase 'a driver now – but for how long?'. The term was recorded in the *Evening Standard*, 22 April 1996.

buttfuck, butt-fuck *n American*

a a male homosexual. A heterosexual term of abuse.

b a despicable or contemptible person.
Both senses of the term play on the idea of someone who will submit to anal intercourse.

buttfuck, butt-fuck *vb Ameri-*

can to sodomize, **bugger**. An expression typically used by heterosexual males who are repelled or fascinated by the practice.

✎ '*"Go butt-fuck yourself, Fruitfly." Milo smiled tightly.*
"If I were you, I'd worry about my own anal sphincter, Ernie".'
(Jonathan Kellerman, *Over the Edge*, 1987).

buttie, butty *n British* a sandwich.

From Liverpool working-class slang (a shortening of 'buttered bread'). The term was spread throughout Britain in the 1960s, largely through the influence of the 'Mersey boom'.

✎ '*A chip buttie/A jam buttie.*' See also
buddy.

buttinsky, buttinski *n Ameri-*

can someone who interferes, someone who butts in. A humorous imitation of a Yiddish or a Slavic surname. The jocular -**ski** suffix is popular among high-school and college students, for instance.

✎ '*This is probably not any of my business, in fact I'm sure that it's not my business, and you're probably going to*

get very mad at me for being a buttin-ski, but I really couldn't live with myself if I didn't say something.'
(*Moonlighting*, US TV series, 1989).

button *n* **1 a** clitoris. An obvious reference which has been recorded in English since 1879. It gave rise to the now archaic buttonhole for the vagina.
b chin. Most often heard in the phrase '*right on the button*', used of a punch that finds its target.
2 a section of the peyote cactus resembling a button, ingested for its hallucinogenic effect.

button it *vb* to shut up, keep quiet, **zip one's lip**. A shortening of **button one's lip** which is heard as a peremptory imperative.

button mob *n British* members of the uniformed branch of the police in the derisive term of the plainclothes CID.

button one's lip *vb* to shut up, keep quiet.

butt out *vb American* to stop interfering, keep out, leave. Usually in the form of an instruction to remove oneself, butt out is a fairly mild if brusque expression. The **butt** component is interesting in that it is probably inspired by 'butt in' in which case it derives from butt meaning strike or push with the head. (It is commonly assumed to derive from **butt**, backside.)

buttplug *n American* a term of abuse among schoolchildren. A slightly milder version of **buttfuck**.
✎'*Sit on this, buttplug!'*
(*My Science Project*, US film, 1985).

butt-ugly *adj American* a stronger version of the colloquial 'plug-ugly'.

butt-wad *n* a foolish and/or contemptible person. The insult, originating in the US, employs the widespread combining form -**wad**.

buy a woof ticket *vb American* to pretend to make a threat. An item of black street talk that was included in so-called **Ebonics**, recognized as a legitimate language variety by school officials in Oakland, California, in late 1996. The verb 'woof', now somewhat dated, has

been used in black slang to mean aggress or threaten.

buy it *vb* to die or meet disaster. A euphemism often ascribed to airforce pilots in war comics and films. It may derive from the expression to buy or pay dearly (i.e. with one's life) or may be a shortening of the American **buy the farm**.
✎'*I'm sorry, Madge, but Archie's bought it.'*

buy the farm *vb American* to die. An expression which is said to have originated with barnstorming or fighter pilots. The farm in question is either a 'worm farm' (i.e. a grave) or an ironic reference to a symbol of retirement (if a pilot survived he would often literally buy a farm).

buzz *n* **1** a rumour. A usage now so widespread as to be a colloquialism rather than slang.
2 a pleasurable sensation, stimulation. In the jargon of drug users, especially the **beats** and later the **hippies**, the word referred to a surge of lightheadedness, a **rush** or **high**. It sometimes also refers to the use of alcohol.

buzz *vb* **1** *British* to become intoxicated from sniffing solvents. The term is heard particularly in the Scottish Lowlands and the north of England. (**Huff** is an American synonym.)
2 to experience a sense of exhilaration, **rush** or **high**.

buzz-crusher *n American* a killjoy or 'wet blanket'. A teenage vogue term of 1988.

buzzed, buzzing *adj* excited, exhilarated, stimulated.

buzz-kill(er) *n American* a variant form of **buzz-crusher**.

B.V.D.s *n American* men's underwear. From a trademark name.
✎'*I was standing there in my B.V.D.s.'*

by the cringe *exclamation British* a more moderate or joking euphemism for 'by Christ'. It appeared in the north of England in the 1960s and was popularized by, among others, the TV comedy series *The Likely Lads* and the soap opera *Coronation Street*.

C...

C *n* cocaine. A rare usage, cocaine having a wealth of more colourful nicknames, from **snow** to **Peruvian marching powder**.

cabbage *n British* **1** money; a lighthearted 1950s expression rarely heard today. The term was used for instance by 'Flash Harry' (played by George Cole) in the film *The Pure Hell of St Trinians*, in 1960. **Lettuce** was a more popular alternative, with the same derivation from the 'green and leafy' nature of banknotes.
2 a brain-damaged or inert, incapable person.

cable *n American* a golden chain worn as decoration especially by males. The use of the word and the practice arose in the **hip hop** black street subculture of the early 1980s in which heavy gold chains (also known as **ropes**) and (often improvised) medallions were an essential part of the paraphernalia.

ca-ca *n British* excrement, **shit**. A word generally used by parents and children in the home. For the derivation see **cack**.

cack *n, vb*
shit, defecate. A word which in Britain is fairly rare (it is heard more often in the north of England than in London and the south-east), but remains common in Australia. Cack is a variation of **ca-ca**: both are usually 'nursery words' and come from a common and very ancient Indo-European base. There are equivalents in Latin (*cacare*) and many modern European languages – *caca* in French, *kaka* in German, *kakani* in Czech. 'Cakken' was the middle English verb.
↳ *'He cacks on your "originals", you pee-pee on his boots.'*
(*Psycle Sluts*, John Cooper Clarke, 1979).

cack-handed *adj British* clumsy, inept. The term originally meant left-handed, probably deriving from the idea of handling **cack** (excrement). Although the connection seems obvious, this expression is probably too old to be influenced by reports of the Muslim practice of eating with the right hand, wiping away excrement with the left. This pejorative adjective seems to be country dialect in origin; it is now fairly widespread and not particularly offensive.
↳ *'A cack-handed attempt at patching up the dispute.'*

cad *n British* An unprincipled, contemptible fellow. A word applied in the 19th century by privileged school pupils and students to their 'common' counterparts. It came to mean an often plausible but dishonourable male. Unknown to most of its users, the word is a short form of 'caddie', a Scottish and northern English dialect word meaning junior or unskilled helper, itself from the French *cadet*. It remains an emblematic term of the period from the 1920s to the 1950s, suggesting to many the blazered and cravat-wearing character personified by the comic actor Cardew ('the Cad') Robinson.

Caddy *n American* a Cadillac car.

caff *n British* a café, particularly a cheap, unpretentious one. An important word in the vocabulary of **teddy boys**, **ton-up kids**, etc., the word was later given the racier alternative pronunciation **kayf**.

caj *adj See* **cas**.

cake *n American* money. The term has occurred particularly in adolescent and campus usage since the 1980s, but was first recorded in adult black street slang of the 1960s.

cake-boy *n American* a **gay** male. An item of black street slang adopted by high school and college students in the 1990s, probably from the earlier term 'cake (-eater)' meaning a 'ladies' man' or fop.

cakehole *n British* mouth. A slang term which was extremely widespread (and considered by many to be vulgar) in the 1950s and 1960s. It survives in the argot of schoolchildren.

call *vb Australian* to vomit. A shortening of **call for Hughie/Charlie/Ruth**, etc.
↳ *'I've got to call.'*
↳ *'He's called all over the stairs.'*

call for Hughie/Charlie/ Ruth, etc. *vb* to vomit. These are variations of **cry Hughie**, etc.

call-girl *n* a prostitute who makes assignations by telephone. The term became popular after streetwalking was outlawed in Britain.

camel toes *n American* the female genitals as visible through tight clothing. The phrase, which appeared in the late 1990s, is the counterpart of the male **basket** or **packet**.

camp *adj* homosexual, effeminate or affectedly theatrical in manner, gesture, speech, etc. A word which emerged from theatrical slang into general use in the 1960s. The sense of the term has moved from the specific ((male) homosexual) to the general (affected, exaggerated, parodic).

The word was adopted by the theatrical world some time after World War I from London slang, but the ultimate derivation of the adjective is obscure. It may come from the French *camper*, meaning to portray or pose, or from the dialect term 'kemp', meaning uncouth. In the late 1970s the gay phrase '*as camp as a row of tents*', referring to a person who is outrageously or blatantly camp, crossed over into general usage. The word camp was adopted in Australia and the USA before World War II.

↳'*To be camp is to be mannered, affected, theatrical. To be camp is to be effeminate.*'
(*About Town*, magazine, June 1962).

camp, camp about, camp it up *vb* to behave in a **camp** way, using exaggerated, 'effeminate' gestures, speech mannerisms, etc. The phrase '*camp it up*' is particularly used to indicate a scene-stealing or outrageous piece of theatrics (literal or figurative) without necessarily any sexual overtones.

camping *adj British* exciting, stimulating, dynamic. The term, heard in the late 1990s, is a facetious pun on the (vogue) term 'intense' (from 'in tents').

↳'*Wow, that movie last night was mega camping.*'
(Recorded, London student, March 1996).

can, the can *n* **1 the can** a toilet. Now a less-than-respectable term, but originally an accurate description of the buckets, tin containers, etc. used in outdoor lavatories, for example. The word was more common in the USA than Britain (except in armed-forces usage) until the 1970s.

2 the can a jail, prison. In this sense dating from the late 19th century, the word is more common in Australia and America than it is in Britain.

3 *American* backside; buttocks. An inoffensive euphemism.

↳'*She fell on her can.*'

can *vb American* **1** to dismiss from a job, fire. The term probably derives from the American sense of **can** meaning buttocks, **ass**, and the notions of kicking one's **ass** out, or thrown out on one's **ass**.

↳'*I got some more news, I got canned last week.*'
(Recorded, female executive, Chicago, 1983).

2 to stop, suppress or conceal something. This sense is normally expressed in the phrase '*can it!*'.

canary *n* an informer. An underworld term originating in the USA, based on the notion of **singing** (like a bird).

↳'*Mob canary slain in Rolls – Had testified in bootleg gas probes.*'
(*New York Daily News*, 3 May 1989).

cancer stick *n* a cigarette. A middle-class irony, used by smokers and non-smokers alike since the late 1960s.

candy *n American*
a an illegal drug, particularly cocaine, heroin. This use of the word originated before World War I as a specialization of the figurative use of candy as anything enjoyable. (The word was used in black street slang with sexual connotations.)
b a dose of liquid LSD on a sugar cube. This vogue term was heard in Britain about 1967 when LSD was still taken in this form. *See also* **nose candy**.

candyass *n American* a weak or effete person, usually male.

candyman *n American* a **pusher** or **dealer** of illicit drugs, especially heroin or cocaine. Originating in black street usage, in which candy could also signify sexual gratification, this expression became part of the addicts' lexicon in the USA by the 1950s. (The original 'candyman' was an innocent peddler of sweets in the early 1900s.) The word features in numerous blues and folk songs.

cane *vb British* **1** to beat up, assault. A working-class brawler's and prisoners' term. It is probably a back formation from the more widespread colloquialism a 'caning', meaning a trouncing or defeat.

2 to devour or consume. A vogue term from the language of adolescents in the later 1990s, it is an extension of the colloquial sense of cane as meaning to punish or subject to heavy use. Among students it typically applies to excessive or spectacular use of cocaine, cigarettes, etc.

↪'*Rachel was telling Phil off for caning the blow.*'

3 to cadge, borrow. A vogue term among British adolescents in the later 1990s, this is an extension of the preceding sense of the word.

↪'*Can I cane some chuddie off you?*'

caned *adj British* intoxicated by drugs or drink. A popular term among adolescents during the 1990s, like many synonyms evoking the notion of punishment.

canned *adj* drunk. The word seems to have originated in the USA, but had spread to other English-speaking countries before the 1950s.

cannibal *n American* a person who performs fellatio or cunnilingus.

cannon *n See* **loose cannon**.

canny *adj British* sharp-witted, 'street smart', attractive. This term from standard English is applied, particularly in Newcastle and the north of England, as a general term of approval, especially in the phrase '*a canny lad/lass*'. Canny is an irregular adjectival form of the verb 'can', thus meaning able, probably influenced by the dialect 'ken', to know (how).

cans *n pl American* female breasts. Although the names of receptacles are often appropriated as euphemisms for breasts, this usage may in fact be an alteration of **cones**.

cantaloupes *n pl American* breasts. (The cantaloupe is a type of melon.)

can't be arsed *phrase British* a vogue term since 1993 used, e.g., by the Scottish stand-up comedian Bruce Morton. The word **arse** and compounds including it became extremely popular, especially with middle-class adolescents in the mid-1990s, possibly prompted by their use by the comedian John Sparkes in the Scottish TV comedy *Absolutely*.

This, the most widespread of such usages, is a vulgar variant of 'can't be bothered' and as such was emblematic of the idler and **slacker** subcultures.

Canuck *n* a Canadian. The only widespread slang term for Canadians, whether French or English-speaking, it is rarely used by the British. The word has usually been used in a derogatory sense. (The -uck ending is probably an imitation of an Amerindian form, as in Chinook, the name of a North American Indian tribal group and jargon.)

canvas *n See* **on canvas**.

cap *n* a capsule of an illicit drug. The word appeared in the 1960s and was sometimes applied to a dose of LSD even when this did not come, strictly speaking, in capsule form.

↪'*She scored a few caps of acid.*'

cap *vb American* **1** to insult, humiliate, **put (someone) down**. A teenage vogue term of the late 1980s. It presumably originates in the idea of capping someone's best stories or achievements, i.e. going one better.

2 to kill. An item of underworld and street gang parlance. **Tag** and **clip** are contemporary synonyms.

capeesh?, capeeshee?, coppish? *question form American* do you understand? The words are anglicizations of the Italian *capisci*?

↪'*You dig? capeesh? understand? dig? Didn't they teach you that in Kiev?*' (*Red Heat*, US film, 1988).

capella *n British* a hat. Part of the **parlyaree** lexicon, used, e.g., by London **gays** in the 1960s, it is from the Italian *cappello*.

↪'*She's swishing about in her bona capella.*'

Captain Cook *n British* a look. An old piece of rhyming slang which shows signs of a revival in the late 1980s, as middle-class speakers fashionably imitate working-class usage. It is typically used in expressions such as '*take/have a Captain Cook (at this)*'.

cardie *n British* a cardigan.

cark, cark it *vb Australian* to die. The origin of the word is obscure; it may be a deformation of **croak** or of **cack**. Like other items of current Australian slang, the word has been introduced to Britain via TV soap operas.

↳ *'They break down in the middle of nowhere and before you know it they've carked it.'*
(Recorded, Australian visitor, London, 1988).

carked *adj* 1 (of a situation) ruined or destroyed.

2 (of a person) exhausted, **pooped**.
This word may simply be an invention, or may be derived from **croak**, **cocked (up)**, or, more plausibly, **cack** (excrement, **shit**, by analogy with **poop**). It is heard in Britain and Australia, but not in the USA.

carn *n British* cash, money. A distorted pronunciation of coin, probably taken from, or in imitation of, black speech. The word was heard in teenage circles from at least 1990.

↳ *'You got nuff* [enough] *carn, guy?'*

carpet *n British* 1 a period of three months' imprisonment. This term, dating from the early years of the 20th century, is based on the supposition that it would take three months for an inmate to weave a carpet.
2 the sum of three pounds. In use among gamblers, market traders, etc. This sense of the word may be inspired by the preceding one.

carpet-muncher someone who performs cunnilingus. The term is usually used by males referring to **gay** women. **Rug-muncher** is a synonym.

carpet rat *n* a less common version of **rug rat**.

carpy *n British* incarceration. This item of prisoners' jargon refers to the period of the day in which prisoners are locked in their cells. It has been derived from the Latin injunction *carpe diem* ('seize the day') but may alternatively be a form of **carpet**.

↳ *'I just need a scratcher for a burn, before carpy.'*
(*Evening Standard*, September 1995).

carrot-top *n* a red-haired person. The expression is used all over the English-speaking world; in Britain the earlier carrot-nob, like **copper-nob**, is now almost obsolete.

carrying *adj* 1 in possession of illicit drugs or firearms. An international Eng-lish usage.

2 *British* solvent, 'flush', having plenty of cash on one's person. A London working-class term.

car surfing *n* riding on the roof of a moving car. A dangerous teenage fad of the late 1980s, influenced by the US film *Teenwolf*. *See also* **train surfing**.

carsy, carzie *n British* alternative spellings of **khazi**.

carve *vb British* to attack with a knife, to slash or cut (someone). From the vernacular of thugs, street gangs and professional criminals.

↳ *'They threatened to carve him.'*
↳ *'She got carved.'*

carve-up *n British* 1 a swindle or conspiracy that ruins one's chances. A rueful London working-class term probably inspired by a greedy carving up of a chicken or joint of meat and the use of **carve** to mean slash (a person) with a knife. The word was especially popular in the 1950s.

↳ *'Wot A Carve-Up!'*
(Title of British comedy film, 1962).

2 a sharing-out of loot or booty. A term used by criminals and police, especially in London.

carvie-diesel *n British* tea. The term is heard among inmates referring to the tea brewed in a prison canteen. It was recorded in the 'London Lingo' section of the *Evening Standard* in 1995. Diesel is a mocking reference to the consistency of the brew, 'carvie' is archaic slang for a fellow-inmate (itself from the earlier 'carving-**china**': 'friend who shares').

cas, caj, caz *adj* 1 *American* relaxed, nonchalant.

2 *American* good, acceptable.
Both senses of the word, which is a shortening of casual and pronounced 'cazz' or, more frequently, 'cazh' or 'caj', are teenage terms of approbation from the late 1980s.

3 *British*
a a shortening of 'casual' in the sense of a relationship which is not yet serious. The term is part of the teenage dating lexicon of the later 1990s.

↳ *'Is this a cas thing you've got?'*
↳ *'Are you two just caj?'*

b a shortening of 'casual' in the sense of

informal as applied to clothing or appearance. The word is usually used mockingly between adolescents.

✎ *'A caj jacket/outfit.'*
✎ *'She's trying to look très cazh tonight.'*

case *n See* **get on someone's case.**

case *vb* to reconnoitre (premises) in preparation for subsequent robbery. The well-known phrase *'case the joint'* has existed in underworld slang since before World War II. It originated in American usage, first being used with a generalized meaning of to assess.

cassava *n American*
a the female genitals. A euphemism used by men and heard in the 1980s. It may come from the Caribbean, where the cassava root is eaten as a staple.
b a woman, especially an available one. By extension from the more specific first meaning.

casual *n British* a member of a working-class sub-group of the early 1980s who were to some extent successors to **skinheads** and **suedeheads**. The characteristic of a casual was that he or she wore fairly expensive designer sports clothes in imitation of Italian or US **preppie** looks. The musical accompaniment to this style was generally home-produced soul or disco music. Casuals were a more materialistic and conformist manifestation from the skinhead and **mod** milieux. Optional elements of the lifestyle included football hooliganism and shoplifting for clothes or profit. Casuals were personified by the 1988 comic character Eddie Loadsamoney, created by Harry Enfield.

casual *adj South African* excellent. The standard adjective has been borrowed for use as a fashionable all-purpose term of approbation among younger speakers in the 1990s.

cat *n* **1** a person. In the parlance of **beatniks**, **hipsters**, etc. Deriving from black musicians' argot, cat was an approving form for a fellow (almost always male – females were **chicks**). The word is still in use, unself-consciously among American blacks and jazz aficionados, and self-consciously in **hip** circles in Britain and Australia.

✎ *'All the cats and chicks/gonna get their kicks/at the hop.'*
(Lyric to *At the Hop*, recorded by Danny and the Juniors, 1959).

2 a spiteful woman. This sense is now so widespread as to be a colloquialism, rather than true slang. It is probably derived from 'catty' rather than vice versa, although cat meant prostitute until the end of the 19th century.
3 *American* the female genitals. A rarer alternative to **pussy**.
4 *Australian* a passive male homosexual. This sense of the word probably, although not certainly, originated as an abbreviation of catamite.

the catbird seat *n American* a very advantageous or privileged position. The catbird is a black and grey songbird which characteristically sings from a high perch.

catch a cold *vb* to suffer a financial loss or setback. This expression from business jargon, implies a temporary rather than terminal affliction.

catch some z's *vb American* a version of **cop (some) z's.**

cathouse *n* a brothel. A widely known expression, although it is mainly used in the USA; cathouse is based upon cat in its now archaic sense of prostitute (current in British English from the 16th to the early 20th century).

cavalier *n British* (a male with) an uncircumcized penis. This term is from the argot of schoolchildren. *Compare* **roundhead**.

caveman mode *adj* obsolete, outdated. A dismissive term from the jargon of computer users in the mid-1990s.

cementhead *n American* a stupid person. A coinage on the lines of **rubble-head**, **rock-head**, etc. (The notion of 'rocks in one's head' in place of brains is a well-known American concept.)

century *n* one hundred pounds or one hundred dollars, the word has been common in the argot of criminals, among others, for the last hundred years.

✎ *'I put a century on it and it lost.'*

cereb *n American* a **swot**, in the language of the more sophisticated **preppies**. The word is from cerebral and may be pronounced 'see-reb' or 'sarebbe'.

cessy *adj British* foul, repugnant, disgusting. A fairly rare, and usually middle-class usage, derived from cesspool or cesspit.

↳'*Honestly, the whole thing was cessy!*'

chad *n* rubbish, debris, worthless information. The term derives from computing jargon in which it denotes the waste paper discarded from a printer.

chai *n British* a girl, female. An item of **parlyaree** first recorded in the 19th century and still used by older members of the **gay** community in London in the 1980s. An alternative spelling is **chy**. The term derives from Romany.

chai-klom, chy-clom *n British* a female wig or hairstyle. An item of **parlyaree** recorded since the 1960s. The second part of the compound is of uncertain origin. The first is the **parlyaree** (originally Romany) term for girl.

the chair *n American* the electric chair, used for the execution of criminals in many parts of the world.

Chalfonts *n pl British* haemorrhoids. Rhyming slang for piles, from the small town of Chalfont St Giles in Buckinghamshire. **Farmers** and nauticals are synonyms.

↳'*Stan was around yesterday, complaining about his Chalfonts.*' (Recorded, pensioner, Bristol, 1989).

chalked *adj American* murdered, killed. This item of 1990s street slang derives from the marking out of a corpse by a chalked outline.

challenged *adj American* a shortening of 'mentally challenged'.

chandies *n South African* a difficult situation, trouble. Recorded as an item of Sowetan slang in the *Cape Sunday Times*, 29 January 1995.

channel surfing *n* changing TV channels randomly or in search of a programme to watch. An Americanism describing the activities of **couch potatoes** that became a widespread colloquialism in all English-speaking areas in the later 1990s.

chap *vb American* to irritate or provoke. A term heard in adolescent usage since the 1980s, deriving from the sense of the standard term signifying 'to chafe'.

↳'*Quit chappin' me!*'

chap-esse *n British* a woman. The word became popular in ironic and facetious middle-class speech and in the slang of the armed services in the early 1990s.

↳'*Now here's something special for all you chaps and chap-esses out there ...*'

char, cha *n British* tea. The words for tea in almost all eastern languages from slavonic through Indian to Chinese, are variants of 'ch'a' or 'chai'.

↳'*A nice cup of char.*'

chara' *n British* a motor coach. From the word charabanc (French *char à bancs*, carriage with benches), widespread from at least the 1920s into the 1950s as a rather pretentious alternative to coach, and used by tour operators and their customers. The word in full was pronounced 'sharrabong' or 'sharrabang', and the shortening likewise. Elderly speakers still occasionally use the term.

charfing *n South African* joking. Recorded as an item of Sowetan slang in the *Cape Sunday Times*, 29 January 1995.

charge *n British* hashish or marihuana. The word was popular in the 1950s and 1960s, especially among **beatniks**, students, etc., who generally did not use hard drugs. This term, no longer heard, refers (rather inappropriately perhaps in the case of cannabis) to the 'charge', or sudden electrifying sensation felt by the drug user, possibly reinforced by **charas**. In American usage it was originally applied to the effect of a heroin injection.

↳'*Got any charge, man?*'

charity-bang/girl/moll *n* a woman who gives sexual favours gratis (especially when she might be expected to demand payment, or when the favour is inspired by pity). The 'moll' version was heard in Australia in the 1950s and early 1960s.

Charles *n British* cocaine. *See* **charlie**.

charlie *n* 1 *British* a foolish person. This innocuous word, often encountered in the expression '*a right/proper charlie*', is in fact derived from the more vulgar cockney rhyming slang Charlie Hunt: **cunt**. In pre-World War II cockney usage **cunt** merely meant fool, rather than the modern sense of a thoroughly unpleasant person.

2 cocaine. A euphemism from the international alphabet designation for the letter 'C', or simply a nickname. (The full

form of the proper name, Charles, is occasionally used, usually facetiously, in Britain in this sense of the word.)

✎ '*She came steaming into the room when I had a massive great pile of charlie drying out on the floor.*'
(*News of the World*, 29 October 1989).

3 *American* the Viet Cong personified. During the Vietnam war the military alphabet designation 'Victor Charlie' was shortened thus.

4 *South African* a friend. Recorded as an item of Sowetan slang in the *Cape Sunday Times*, 29 January 1995.

charlie *adj British* cheap and nasty, flashy or in bad taste. A public-school and **Sloane Ranger** term of disapproval, heard in the early 1980s.

✎ '*He's really awfully charlie.*'
✎ '*The flat's a bit charlie, if you ask me.*'

charlies *n pl* breasts. A word used (almost exclusively by men) since the 19th century. There have been many attempts to explain this term by deriving it from rhyming slang (Charlie Wheeler: **sheila**), from Romany or from the habits of Charles II. It is more probably simply a personification which implies affectionate familiarity.

Charlie's dead! *exclamation British* your slip/petticoat/underwear is showing. A schoolchildren's cry since the 1950s. Inspired by the notion of flags at half mast (in mourning for a deceased husband).

charver, charva *vb, n British* (to have) sexual intercourse. A word that is almost unknown in the 1980s, but which was used in criminal, theatrical and other circles in the 1950s and early 1960s. It is Romany in origin (*charvo* meaning to interfere with), and refers to the 'taking' of a woman by a man, so by extension it has been used to signify a woman as a sex object.

chase the dragon *vb*

a to take heroin by smoking it. The specific meaning of this expression (the arrival of which coincided with an influx of cheap heroin into the UK in the late 1970s) is to inhale fumes from a piece of the vaporizing drug through a tube, often literally chasing the smoke across the sheet of foil on which the drug is 'cooked'.

✎ '*Carmella never injected heroin, her serious involvement came with "chasing the dragon", inhaling a burning*

trail from a piece of tin foil.'
(*Independent*, 17 July 1989).

b to flirt with death by using heroin. This more generalized meaning of the sinisterly colourful phrase was adopted by middle- and upper-class drug users when heroin spread to these circles in the early 1980s.

chateau'd *adj British* drunk. A colourful upper-class and **yuppie** expression of the late 1980s playing on 'shattered' and implying that it is an expensive claret (Bordeaux) or other château-bottled wine which has caused the inebriety.

cheaters *n pl American* sunglasses or glasses. A word now popular with schoolchildren but which probably originated with cardsharps who supposedly used 'magic spectacles', or with fraudsters who wore dark glasses as disguise.

check *interjection American* yes. A jargon expression of affirmation (based on the mark of verification on a checklist, for instance) carried over into popular speech.

✎ '*Hey you, stay cool!*'
'*Check!*'
(*Panic on the 5.22*, US film, 1974).

check out *vb* to die. The notion of leaving a hotel or motel carried over into an eternal context. An old euphemism in American English which is now international.

cheese *n Australian* one's partner or one's wife. *See* **cheese and kisses**.

cheese, the cheese *n* **1** an important person. In the form a cheese or the cheese this is a short term of the colloquial 'big cheese'.

2 something or someone unpleasant or unsavoury, particularly distasteful bodily secretions. From the smell and texture of ripe cheese.

3 *exclamation British* another spelling and/or pronunciation of **chiz**!

4 a Dutch person. A humorous or derogatory term heard in one form or another ('*cheese-head*' or '*John Cheese*' are alternatives) since the 19th century.

cheese and kisses *n Australian* one's wife. This rhyming slang for 'the missus' is probably the origin of the synonymous **cheese** and **old cheese** referring to a mother.

cheeseball *n* an unsavoury or contemptible person. An all-purpose term of abuse borrowing the name of the cocktail biscuit and the notion of **cheesy**.

cheese it *vb American* to beware, hide or to run away. This old phrase, normally used in the form of an exclamation such as '*cheese it – the cops!*' has become a comic cliché in the USA. It may once have been used by members of the underworld (in Britain) or it may be a pre-1900 invention by writers or journalists. In any case it is actually heard in use today, usually somewhat facetiously by adults, and straightforwardly by children.

cheesy *adj* unpleasant, unsavoury, squalid, disreputable, underhand. The original notion of smelly cheese has encompassed a number of nuances of distaste. The word became extremely fashionable in 1990s' youth slang.

�ᗉ'*A cheesy place.*'

↣'*a cheesy thing to do.*'

↣'*It was a degrading, lying, cheating piece of cheesiness.*'
(John Lydon [characterizing Alec Cox's film *Sid and Nancy*], BBC television, 1989).

cherries *n pl American* flashing lights on a police car. '*Hit the cherries!*' is the command to turn them on.

cherry *n* 1 a maidenhead, virginity. The word is usually part of the phrase '*to lose one's cherry*', said normally of girls but occasionally of boys. The expression is old (dating at least from the late 19th century) but has not been superseded. It derives from the supposed similarity of the fruit to the hymen.

b a young girl, virgin. This is an extension of the preceding sense, although modern users of the word may derive it simply from the notion of sweet or delicious.

c *South African* an attractive young female. Recorded as an item of Sowetan slang in the *Cape Sunday Times* on 29 January 1995.

2 *British* the tip of a lit cigarette. *See also* **cherry 'og**.

cherry *adj* new, fresh and attractive. A term used by teenagers and young adults since the 1970s in the USA and subsequently elsewhere. It evokes both the shininess of the fruit and the figurative sense of virginity.

chevy *n American* a Chevrolet car.

chew (someone) out, chew (someone's) ass *vb American* to chastise, tell off, give someone a severe 'dressing-down'. A colloquial expression heard typically in educational institutions and the armed services.

chi-ack, chi-ike, chiake *vb* to tease or taunt. A rather dated term derived from 'to cheek'. It has been more common in Australia where the noun form, meaning impudence or insolence, is also heard.

chiba *n* cannabis, marihuana. A fashionable term heard among **hip hop** and **rap** aficionados since the early 1990s. It was first recorded in the 1970s and may derive from Hispanic slang.

Chicano *n* a Mexican American. *Méjicano* or *Méxicano* in Spanish has been anglicized to this word which by the 1980s has few pejorative overtones. It has to a large extent been superseded by **Latino** or 'Hispanic'.

chi-chi *adj* excessively cute, pretentious or twee. The word is a direct borrowing from French.

chick *n*

a a girl, girlfriend. The word has been used as a term of affection for hundreds of years, but was readopted by British slang from America in the **teddy boy** era. It was used unself-consciously by **hippies** until the mid-1970s, since when it has been disapproved of by the majority of women. The term is now dated.

↣'*This year two chicks and I got enough bread together and flew to Eilat (Israel) to see what was happening out there.*'
(Reader's letter, *Oz* magazine, February 1970).

b also **chickie, chicken** *American* a passive homosexual partner or sodomized victim of a **rooster**. An American prison term of the 1970s and 1980s.

chicken *n* 1 a coward. In this sense the word has been in use for several centuries, although the children's taunt or exclamation was an Americanism of the early 1950s.

2 a a young male who is, or is likely to be, preyed on by an older homosexual (**chickenhawk**), in **gay**, police and prison usage.

b an under-age girl as a sex object or partner, in the jargon of pornography. ('Chicken' was a common term of endearment especially to a younger or vulnerable lover in the 19th and early 20th century.)

3 a game in which young people dare one another to attempt something dangerous (e.g. to stand in the path of an oncoming train or car); the chicken, or first to withdraw, is the loser. When motor vehicle races are involved **chicken run** is the usual phrase.

chicken *adj* afraid, cowardly.

chickenhawk *n*

a a male homosexual who 'preys on' younger men. This American term from the **gay** lexicon was given wider currency by press articles in the late 1980s, when Scott Thurston, the entertainer Liberace's lover, referred to him as a chickenhawk in revelations after his death.

b a heterosexual seducer or exploiter of under-age girls.

✎ '*Lolita at twelve, thirteen, fourteen, fifteen – and chickenhawk Charlie* [Chaplin] *never far away, mistily watching the bud unfold.*'
(Kenneth Anger, *Hollywood Babylon*, 1975).

chicken neck, chicken's neck *n British* a cheque. An unusual piece of rhyming slang recorded in the late 1980s. An alternative is **Gregory (Peck)**.

✎ '*He suggested that £25,000 would be enough for him to spill the whole story … He then dropped his price to £5,000 and added "I'll take a chicken's neck".*'
(*Daily Mirror*, 31 March 1989).

chicken run *n American* a teenage game in which drivers aim their cars at each other to see which one will swerve first; **chicken** here is in the colloquial sense of coward(ly).

chickenshit *n* anything worthless, petty or contemptible. In American usage the word originally had the specific meaning of oppressive minor regulations and other effects of bureaucracy, particularly in the armed forces in World War II. The noun sense is now rarer than the adjectival use of the word, except when describing paltry amounts of money.

chickenshit *adj*

a cowardly, afraid. An Americanism which was adopted in Britain, mainly by schoolchildren and teenagers, in the late 1980s.

b petty, contemptible. This sense derives from the American and Canadian armed forces expression to describe small-minded regulations, orders, etc.

chickie, chicky *n American*

a a young girl.

b a young partner or victim of a dominant male homosexual, particularly in prison. Both senses of the word are (often sinister) adaptations of an original term of endearment.

chief, chief-bod *n* a foolish or obnoxious individual, misfit. A vogue term from the language of adolescent gangs, also recorded in the late 1980s among aficionados of dance culture. The term was in use among north London schoolboys in 1993 and 1994, sometimes shortened to **chief**. ('*Chief*' occurs in North American usage, the '*bod*' form is exclusively British.)

chill *vb* **1** to kill. A 'tough-guy' euphemism originating in US street slang.

✎ '*Teachers report that teenagers talk about "packing a barrel" or "chilling someone with a pipe".*'
(*Sunday Times*, 31 August 1992).

2 to relax, become calm. This shortening of the earlier **chill out** (itself adopted from American usage) became popular among British adolescents during the 1990s.

chill *adj British* relaxed, relaxing, unstressed. Derived from the verb form, this adolescent vogue term was in use during the 1990s.

✎ '*Feeling chill.*'
✎ '*A chill party.*'

chilled *adj* excellent, admirable. A teenage vogue word of the later 1980s. The term is a synonym for **cool**, influenced by the verb form to **chill out** (relax, unwind). British fans of **rap**, **acid house** music and skateboarding introduced the word to schoolchildren's slang.

the chilled article *n Australian* a cold beer. A mock-pompous euphemism used by drinkers.

chillin' *vb American* relaxing. A teenagers' shortening of **chill(ing) out** recorded in the late 1980s.

chill(ing) out *vb American* to relax, take it easy. A popular phrase in the 1980s, first among teenagers but later

among adults, too, it comes from black street talk and is a later variation of **cool out**.

chillum *n* a type of container (usually ceramic but sometimes made of wood or stone) which is packed with marihuana or hashish (often mixed with tobacco) for smoking. This item from the lexicon of **hippies** and other cannabis users is not a pipe, but a hollow cone held cupped in both hands, with a 'chillum stone' lodged in it to prevent the contents being sucked into the lungs of an enthusiastic user. Chillum is not, strictly speaking, a slang word, but Hindi in origin. It is, however, the only name for the object in question.

chilly *adj British* excellent, fashionable, a British teenagers' term of all-purpose approval based upon **chill (out)** and **chilling**, recorded in 1991.

chimney-wok *n British* a satellite dish affixed to the exterior of a house. The jokey nickname was heard from the early 1990s, sometimes abbreviated to **wok**.

chin *vb British* to hit someone (by implication on the face or head, although not necessarily on the chin). An old working-class term still heard in or around bar brawls, playground fights, etc.
↳'*He called me a poof, so I chinned the bastard.*'
(Recorded, pub habitué, London, 1988).

china *n British* a friend, 'mate'. Rhyming slang from 'china plate'. An example of London rhyming slang which has survived from the 19th century and is still in working-class use today, albeit often ironically or self-consciously. It is usually part of the phrase '*me old china*'.

Chinese *adj See* **get chinese**.

chink *n* **1** a Chinese person. The word (possibly inspired by Chinese words for their own country and people, actually pronounced 'Joong-') has been used in American and Australian speech since the turn of the century; in Britain it is slightly more recent.
2 money, change. From the sound of coins.

chinkie, chinky *n British*
a a Chinese restaurant or take-away food service.
b a Chinese meal.
↳'*I don't feel like cooking. Let's grab a*

chinky on the way home.'
c a Chinese person. A more patronizing or dismissive version of **chink**.

chinless wonder *n British* an effete or gormless youth, particularly a vacuous upper-class male. The pejorative expression is applied to those literally weak-chinned, but more often to young men, usually in a privileged position, who are irresolute, offensively presumptuous or absurd. **Deb's delight**, **pedigree chum**, and **wimp** have similar overtones.

chintzy *adj American* inferior, tasteless, unfashionable. The term, which may have arisen independently from the colloquial (and milder) British usage, was heard among university students in the early 1990s, sometimes generalized as an all-purpose pejorative covering notions such as stinginess and pettiness. Whereas in Britain chintz is emblematic of (lower-)middle-class conformity in decor, in the US it suggests cheap, garish clothing. The word itself, denoting patterned cotton cloth, comes from the Hindi *chhini*, itself from Sanskrit *citra* meaning spotted and/or bright.

chip *vb British* to leave, run away. Like its synonym **duss**, a vogue term among teenage gang members in the 1990s.
↳'*Let's chip, it's the beast.*'
(Recorded London schoolboy, 1994).
↳'*There are more of them [flying ants], we'd better chip.*'
(Recorded black youth, Holland Park, London, 1994).

chippie, chippy *n* **1** *British* a fish and chip shop. A nickname which appeared to spread from Liverpool in the early 1960s.
2 *British* a carpenter.
3 *American and Australian* a prostitute or promiscuous woman. The etymology of this sense of the word is unclear.

chipping *n American*
a the occasional use of illicit drugs (as opposed to regular use by addicts).
b secret and sporadic use of illicit drugs while under surveillance, for instance in prison or while undergoing a drug rehabilitation programme.

chippy *adj* aggressive and hypersensitive, irritatingly resentful. The word is based on either the 19th-century '*chip in*', to interfere; or the later notion of having '*a chip on one's shoulder*'.

&'*He's chippy. I find that small people are often chippy.*'
(Recorded, Sloane Ranger, London, 1984).

&'*Mr Kinnock appears to be sinking under a barrage of criticism to the effect that he is an ill-educated Welsh windbag carried high by chippy class hatred.*'
(*Evening Standard*, 25 July 1988).

chips *n pl British* money. Rather than referring to the tokens used for gambling, this is probably derived from the earlier and synonymous use of **potatoes**. Like that term it occurred several times in the telephone conversations between Sarah Ferguson, Duchess of York, and her psychic advisor, Madame Vasso, published in Vasso's memoirs and in the UK press in 1996.

chirps *adj British* engaged in 'chatting up', **on the pull**. A fashionable term among adolescents in the 1990s. Its derivation is uncertain.

chiv *n, vb* (to) knife (someone). A word originating in Romany (gypsy) speech, used particularly in criminal argot of the 1950s. The word, also written and pronounced **shiv**, often referred to a homemade knife or razor blade used for instance by prisoners or street gangs.

chiz *n, exclamation British* a blend of cheat and 'swizz'. A schoolchildren's word of the 1950s kept alive by its liberal use in the *Molesworth* series of books by Geoffrey Willans and Ronald Searle.

&'*"Let me take you by the handy pandy" and she do chiz chiz chiz chiz while all St Custards cheer.*'
(*Back in the Jug Agane*, Geoffrey Willans and Ronald Searle, 1959).

choad, chode *n Canadian*

a penis.

b a stupid and/or obnoxious person. The origin of this term is unclear, but (particularly in the second, figurative sense) it has become popular among college students and Internet users in the late 1990s, also in combinations such as '*dick-chode*', '*chode-lick/wad*'.

choad, chode *adj Canadian* unpleasant, worthless, inferior. The adjectival form derives from the noun. It was defined on the Internet by *Play Time* in March 1997 as 'so bad it's good'.

chocaholic *n* a person with an inordinate fondness for chocolate in all its forms. A jocular term punning on alcoholic. Colloquial and slang terms relating to food and indulgence (**foodie**, **couch potato**, etc.) were a feature of the 1980s.

chocolate bandit *n British* a male homosexual. Like **brownie hound**, **turd burglar**, etc., this unaffectionately jocular term portrays the sodomist as a covert thief of excrement.

chocolate cha cha *n American* anal intercourse. One of many vulgarisms in use among heterosexuals and based on the faecal aspects of (not necessarily homosexual) sodomy.

&'*If you ask me, they've been doing the chocolate cha-cha.*'

chocolate city *n American* a town or city district run by black officials. An item of black street talk which was included in so-called **Ebonics**, recognized as a legitimate language variety by school officials in Oakland, California, in late 1996.

chocolate-dipper *n* a male homosexual. One of many supposedly humorous but pejorative phrases, invariably used by heterosexual males and based on the faecal aspects of sodomy. (**Brownie-hound**, **chutney-ferret** are others.)

chocolate drop *n* a black or coloured person. A usually unaffectionate term used mainly by schoolchildren.

chocolate frog *n Australian* 1 a foreigner, immigrant, not necessarily non-white. A piece of purely Australian rhyming slang for **wog**.
2 an informer, **stool pigeon**. In this sense the word is probably rhyming slang for dog, as in '*dirty dog*', '*low dog*', etc.

chode *n, adj Canadian See* **choad**.

choirboy *n American*

a an innocent, naïve or young male.

b a new recruit to the police force, a **rookie**.

c someone feigning innocence or naïvety. In this ironic sense the word was used by the ex-police officer Joseph Wambaugh as the title of his 1973 novel, *The Choirboys* (filmed in 1977).

choke a darkie *vb Australian* to defecate. A vulgarism heard since the

1960s. *See also* **strangle a darkie**.

choked, choked-off *adj British*
overcome with indignation, fury, rancour
or another strong emotion. Choked is a
very widespread working-class usage,
especially in London speech. Choked-off
is a less common, and more recent variant.
↳'*I tell you I was choked, really bloody
choked when she told me they'd given
the contract to someone else.*'

choke (someone) off *vb British*
to discourage, repudiate or reject someone. This term is used in a fairly specific
sense in the context of prisons where it
usually means to frustrate someone who
is attempting an official complaint or application.

choke the/one's chicken *vb*
(of a man) to masturbate. A teenagers'
and students' variant of **jerkin' the
gherkin, flogging the lizard**, etc.

choky, chokey *n British* prison or
a cell. A word which is still in use in the
late 1980s, although it now sounds rather
dated. The term comes from the Hindi
chauki, meaning a shed or police compound, and was imported from India in
the mid-19th century by members of the
armed forces.

choking *adj British* desperate (for relief, typically in the form of alcohol or
sex). The widespread term, popular e.g.
among university students in the late
1990s, is a shortening of the colloquial
phrase 'choking for (the specified item)'.
The phrase '*choking for it*' invariably
refers to sex. **Gagging** is a contemporary
synonym.

chomp *vb* to eat or bite. An imitative
term.

chompers *n pl* teeth. A jocular term
inspired by the verb to **chomp** and the
earlier **choppers**.

chones *n pl American* testicles. A corruption of the Spanish **cojones**.

choo-choo *n* a train. Like **chuffer**
or **chuff-chuff** this is a nursery phrase
often used facetiously by adults.

chook *n Australian* a chicken. This is
an alternative pronunciation of an old dialect term, imitating the clucking of hens,
which gives **chuck** in British English.
↳'*I hope your chooks turn to emus and*

kick down your dunnee.'
(Rural Australian curse).

choom *n Australian* an English person. Now usually pejorative, the term
seems to have appeared during World
War I and was probably an imitation of
the northern English pronunciation of
'chum'.

choong, chung *n Australian* a Chinese person. A derogatory racist term,
which may be an imitation of oriental
speech or a deformation of **chink** or **jungle (bunny)**.

chop *n* a cut-down, customized motorcycle. A shortening of **chopper 2a**.
↳'*Sarah belongs to the distinctly laid
back, Harley-Davidson inclined
"lifestyle" bikers. Soon she will be appearing on a customised 550 cut-down
"chop".*'
(*Independent*, 6 April 1988).

chopped hog *n* a customized motorcycle. The term originally referred
specifically to the Harley Davidsons with
lengthened front forks ridden by Hell's
Angels.

chopper *n* **1** a helicopter. This was
probably originally a children's version
of the longer word, reinforced by the
sound and scything action of the rotor
blades. It was adopted by adults in World
War II.
2 a a customized motorbike, usually having high **apehanger** handlebars and
lengthened front forks, as ridden by Hell's
Angels. It is derived from **chopped hog** or
chopped (meaning cut down, altered).
Nowadays it is often shortened to **chop**.
b a young person's tricycle or bicycle designed and manufactured to look like a
customized motorbike, that is with a large
back wheel and long front forks. From
the 1970s when such bikes became popular.
3 *British* penis. A working-class vulgarism
dating from at least the 1940s and still
heard.
4 *American* a machine gun. Although this
use of the word is familiar to many people through films and crime fiction, it has
been obsolete in spontaneous speech
since before World War II.

choppers *n pl* teeth. A lighthearted
term used all over the English-speaking
world, often referring to false teeth.
↳'*A new set of choppers.*'

chops *n* mouth or jaws. The word has been heard since the 18th century before which it was usually in the form 'chaps', referring to the jaws of animals.

⮑ *'The punishing dancebeat of late-'80s London smacks you hard in the chops.'*
(*Time Out*, 26 July 1989).

chop shop *n American* a customizing workshop for cars or motorbikes. To **chop** is in this case to cut down or alter.

chopsy *adj British* garrulous, inclined to talk out of turn, argumentative, **mouthy**. From the use of **chops** to designate mouth or jaws.

⮑ *'Spurs have turned into a really chopsy team since Venables took over.'*
(Recorded, Welsh football supporter, London, 1989).

chow *n* **1** food. The word is about a century old and derives either from far eastern pidgin English 'chowchow', meaning a mixture, or from *jiao(ze)* (pronounced 'jowzer'), Mandarin Chinese for a dumpling.
2 a Chinese person. The term is usually used derogatively.

chow down *vb American* to eat, sit down to a meal, 'tuck in'. From **chow** meaning food.

⮑ *'While we're here let's chow down, hey?'*
(*Real Men*, US film, 1987).

Christmas! *exclamation* an inoffensive euphemism for Christ, mainly used by British and Australian speakers.

Christmas-crackered *adj British* exhausted, worn out. Rhyming slang for **knackered**; a less common version than **cream-crackered**.

chrome-dome *n* a bald person. A humorous derogatory term referring to the polished sheen of a hairless head. In their book *The Boy looks at Johnny* Julie Burchill and Tony Parsons consistently referred to the balding musician Brian Eno as a chrome-dome.

⮑ *'Who's the chrome-dome?'*
'I never saw him before.'
(*Cheers*, US TV series, 1987).

chronic *adj American* excellent, powerful. One of many appropriations of negative terms as vogue terms of approbation in adolescent speech, such as **bad**, **wicked**, **brutal**. Chronic appeared in the late 1990s.

⮑ *'Wow, this sure is some chronic blow.'*

chubbette *n* a 'well-built' or shapely young woman. A vogue term of the early 1980s among some American and British speakers.

chubby *n American* an erection. An item of teenage slang often heard in the phrase *'crack or pop a chubby'*. It may derive from the earlier synonym **crack a fat**.

⮑ *'Hi boys, don't pop a chubby on our account.'*
(*Meet the Applegates*, US film, 1991).

chubby-chaser *n* someone who is sexually interested in or attracted to large or obese people. '*Chubby checker*' has also been recorded in London speech for a male who enjoys looking at 'well-built' women. The phrase was an Americanism of the early 1960s and was adopted as the nick-name of the American soul singer who popularized the 'twist'.

chuck *n* a term of endearment literally meaning chicken, in northern English speech. It was originally a rural dialect term imitating the sound of clucking, (**chook** in modern Australian).

chuck *vb* **1** to vomit. A moderately respectable euphemism probably abbreviated from the more common **chuck up**.
2 to throw out; specifically in police and underworld jargon to reject (an appeal) or dismiss (a case) or acquit (a defendant).
3 *British* stop, desist. In this sense the word has been used particularly in working-class slang of the north of England.

⮑ *'Chuck hassling me, will ya!'*
(*Your Cheating Heart*, British TV drama, 1990)

4 to eat excessively, in this case the verb is synonymous with 'chuck out', or **pig out**.
5 fuck. The variant form is used euphemistically as an exclamation or intensifier.

⮑ *'They say it is, is it chuck!'*
(Gary Crowley, *The Beat*, British TV music programme, 25 October 1993).

chuck a cheesy *vb Australian* to grin. The colloquial cliché 'a cheesy grin' has given rise to this more recent expression, in use since the mid-1980s among adolescents.

chuck a mental *vb* to become enlarged, agitated, disoriented. The term was featured in the Australian soap opera *Neighbours* in 1991, and is also in use among British and Scottish schoolchildren.

chuckle-dust *n American* any illicit drug in powder form. The phrase seems to originate from the early 1990s when it was used to refer to **angel dust** or cocaine and was subsequently also recorded among north London schoolboys in 1993 and 1994.

chucklehead *n American* a foolish, silly or eccentric person.

chuck out *vb* to eat to excess. This less common synonym for **pig out** has been recorded in Australian and American usage.

chuck up *vb* to vomit. **Upchuck** is a later variant form.

chuck you Farley! *exclamation American* a variation of *'fuck you Charlie!'* used by high-school and college students, **Valley Girls** and others as a cry of contempt or defiance.

ᗷ *'Howdy Mr Flakey Foont, gimme some skin baby.'*
'Chuck you Farley!'
(Cartoon by Robert Crumb in *Head Comix*, 1968).

chuddie *n* chewing gum. In the form *'chuttie'* the term was first recorded in American speech as long ago as the 1920s; it was very probably originally a nursery form of the verb to chew. In the late 1990s it has become a vogue term among UK adolescents.

chuff *n British* **1** anus, backside. A word which has been heard since the 1940s, and which is innocuous enough to use where other synonyms are taboo. The etymology of the word is obscure, but it may be from dialect meaning plump (which is related to **chuffed**; pleased).

ᗷ *'As tight as a badger's chuff.'*
(*Room at the Bottom*, British TV series, 1988).

2 a **fart**. A schoolchildren's and students' vulgarism recently popularized by *Viz* magazine. *See also* **chuffing**.

chuff-chuff *n British* a synonym of **chuffer**.

chuffed *adj British* delighted, pleased.

The word's meaning stretches from flattered to excited. It probably originates in northern English dialect (meaning puffed-up and proud) and is still most frequently heard in the north and midlands. Embellished forms are *'dead chuffed'*, *'chuffed pink'* and *'chuffed to arseholes'*. The TV soap opera, *Coronation Street*, which is set in the north of England, has *'chuffed to little mint-balls'*.

chuffer *n British* a train. A quasi-nursery word used facetiously by adults.

ᗷ *'I'm catching the chuffer down to Bath.'*
(Recorded, journalist, 1987).

chuffing *adj British* a polite or disguised form of **fucking** as an intensifying adjective. It is heard most often in the north of England.

chuff-nuts *n pl British* another term for **dingleberries**.

chug *vb British* to drink (alcohol). A coinage, derived from the drinkers' toast or chant 'chug-a-lug', fashionable among young people in London in the late 1980s.

ᗷ *'Sloane Rebs all support Chelsea F.C., and can be seen every other Saturday lunchtime "chugging brew" and getting hammered at any number of pubs in the Fulham Road, before charging down to Stamford Bridge for a "frightfully good game of footy".'*
(*I-D* magazine, November 1987).

chummy *n British* a term of address used typically by police officers to or about suspects. This condescending word is representative of the menacing use of terms of endearment, understatement, etc. favoured by London police and underworld.

ᗷ *'I think chummy here has got something he wants to tell us.'*

chump *n British See* **off one's chump**.

chump *vb American*
a to cheat or dupe.

ᗷ *'The guy was chumpin' me.'*

b to steal, appropriate. In both senses the term was popular in black street slang of the 1990s. It is formed from the colloquial noun sense denoting a 'sucker'.

ᗷ *'First they chumped my car, then they came back for the fuckin' furniture!'*

chunder *vb Australian* to vomit. This term, in use among Australian **surfies**

and others in the 1960s, was imported into Britain later in the decade by the strip cartoon *The Adventures of Barry McKenzie*. The writer, Barry Humphries, derives it from the warning cry *'Watch under!'*, perhaps used by sailors. An alternative derivation is from 'Chunder Loo' as rhyming slang for spew, from the name of a character used in advertisements for boot polish fifty years earlier. Already established in Britain, especially among young sportsmen and drinkers, there are signs that this and other Australianisms are making headway in the USA following the success of the Australian comedy film *Crocodile Dundee* in 1987.

chunk *vb American* to vomit. The term, used by adolescents, is probably a shortening of the widespread phrase **blow chunks**.

↳*'Cissie chunked all over the couch.'*

chunky *adj British* an all-purpose term of approbation briefly in vogue among London **mods** in 1966 and 1967.

chunter, chunner *vb British* to nag or complain, especially incessantly and in an undertone. Chunter is a common form throughout Britain, while chunner is a northern and midland variant. The word is imitative of the sound.

↳*'What are you chuntering on about?'*

church key *n* a bottle opener. A (mainly middle-aged) drinkers' witticism.

chutney-ferret *n British* a male homosexual. One of a set of synonymous phrases (**fudge-nudger**, **turd-burglar**, etc.) based on the faecal aspects of sodomy.

chutney-locker *n British* the anus. A euphemism appearing in London speech around 1990.

chutzpah *n* daring effrontery, impressive cheek. The word, pronounced 'hootspar', is via Yiddish from the Hebrew *huspah* (brazenness, audacity); it has been in use among non-Jewish Americans since at least the mid-1960s, but only appeared in the mid-1970s in Britain.

↳*'I have valued my fleeting acquaintance with Larry Adler over the years because it has always given me an easy way of explaining the meaning of the Jewish word* chutzpah *to those who have not met this valuable term. As far as I can define it briefly, it's an*

elegant opportunism, so fast as to deceive the eye, and so successful as to be totally disarming. Or what cockneys call bloody cheek.'
(Miles Kington, *Independent*, 27 January 1989).

chy *n British* a variant form of **chai**.

cider-punk *n British* a **crustie**. The phrase was used (unlike crustie itself) by members of the early 1990s subculture which included militant beggars, homeless vagrants and their weekend emulators. Cider was a preferred (cheap) stimulant and **punk** the music of choice.

cig, ciggie *n* a cigarette.

cirp, curp *n British* alternative possible spellings of **kirp**.

clackers *n pl Scottish*
balls (in both the literal and figurative slang senses). The word, recorded in the early 1990s, was the name of a fashionable children's toy of the 1970s consisting of two plastic balls on a string wound round the fingers and knocked together. **Conkers** is a synonym of similar provenance.

clack *n, vb British* (to) chatter, talk incessantly. A mainly working-class word, popular in the north of England. **Clack on** is an alternative verb form.

clag *n British* bad weather. A rural dialect term for clay or mud, **clag** was first adopted in airforce slang to refer to thick cloud or fog. More recently, TV weather forecasters have employed the term lightheartedly.

clam *n American* 1 a dollar. Invariably used in the plural, this is a racier alternative to **buck**, etc.

2 *see* **spear the bearded clam**.

clambrain *n American* a foolish or stupid person. The image evoked is of someone with the brain power of a mollusc.

clam up *vb* to keep quiet, refuse to speak. Originally an Americanism (clams are a popular oyster-like seafood), the term is now widespread.

clang *vb British* to commit a gaffe, make a mistake. A back formation from the colloquial phrase '(drop) a clanger', which shares the meaning of the shortened form.

clap, the clap *n* venereal disease, gonorrhoea. The only widespread slang term for the condition, this word was derived from French (*clapoir*, meaning a swelling, or *clapier*, brothel) in the late 16th century. It became a taboo and therefore slang term only in the 19th century. The specific reference to gonorrhoea had widened to include other venereal diseases by the 1950s.

✧*'For while he nibbles at her Am'rous*
Trap
She gets the Mony but he gets the
Clap.'
(*Poor Pensive Punck*, poem by John Dryden, 1691).

✧*'Ain't got the clap have you?'*
'God no! It's just a sense of cosmic boredom.'
(Robert Crumb, cartoon in *Head Comix*, 1968).

clapped, clapped out *adj* worn out, exhausted. The second of these essentially British terms has been adopted in the USA since the 1950s. They are normally applied to machines, particularly cars, although they derive originally from the idea of a person debilitated by the **clap**, or venereal disease. As the origin is forgotten, the terms are now colloquial rather than vulgar.

clapped, clapped up *adj* infected with venereal disease, suffering from gonorrhoea. These rather old-fashioned forms have largely been replaced by *'got the clap'*.

claret *n British* blood. Originally an upper-class theatrical and boxing euphemism, this word is now heard mainly in London police and underworld circles.

✧*'If you prick me do I not spill claret?'*
(The character 'Arthur Daley' in *Minder*, British TV series, 1983).

clart, clarts *n British* trouble, a mess. This dialect term from the north of England and Scotland – probably a variety of 'clot' or 'clod' (of mud, slime, excrement) – is heard occasionally in other parts of Britain, usually in expressions such as *'too much faff and clart'* or *'(dropped) in the clarts'*. 'Clarty', the dialect adjective meaning dirty, sticky and messy, is also still heard.

clat *n British* a dirty and/or obnoxious person. The term, which is related to the dialect **clart**, is heard particularly in the Scottish Lowlands and the north of England.

✧*'The little clat gets right up my nose.'*
(Recorded, middle-aged woman, York, 1995).

clat-tale *n British* a tell-tale. A northern English children's variant of the standard terms *'tattle-tale'* or *'tell-tale'*.

clattering *n British* a kicking. The term is from the jargon of football fans and refers not to kicks in the course of play, but a personal attack by one or more players during a match and by extension also by brawlers, hooligans, etc., off the field.

clemmed *adj British* starving, hungry. An old word which is a survival of northern dialect (from Middle English 'clemmen', to pinch). It is still heard occasionally among older speakers (and, incidentally, in the TV soap opera *Coronation Street*).

clever *adj British* acceptable, satisfying. The standard term has for many years been used in colloquial, especially working-class speech, as a generalized synonym for good, pleasant, etc., usually, however, used in a negative context.

✧*'The night life's not that clever.'*
(*Away the Lads*, BBC 2 TV documentary, February 1993).

✧*'The weather wasn't too clever that weekend.'*

clever-clogs *n British* a know-all, **smartarse** or over-achiever. A now common colloquialism probably originating in the north or Midlands where clogs were until recently part of working-class folklore. *See also* **pop one's clogs**.

✧*'The exhibition has all the hallmarks of a rushed and ill-considered job, knocked together by a clever-clogs rather than an art historian.'*
(*Evening Standard*, 17 March 1988).

click *n American* a clique, small group of friends or confederates. A favourite word with high-school and college students.

clink *n* **1 a** jail, prison. The most common (in Britain) and least racy synonym; it was the name of a prison on Clink Street in Southwark, London, from at least 1509 until the 18th century. The term may also be inspired by the sounds of metal keys, doors and manacles.

✧*'You'll end up in clink.'*

b *British* detention, in schoolchildren's jargon.

✎*'I'm in Saturday morning clink again.'*

2 *British* money. Like **chink** it is imitative of the sound of cash.

✎*'I'm a bit short of clink.'*

clinker *n American* a failure. A word used particularly with reference to a film or play. In this sense it has been adopted by some British writers; in the USA it may occasionally denote other types of failure or incompetence. The slang use is based on the word's standard meaning of coal residue or cinder.

✎*'Most of Hollywood, and especially John's brother Jim, refused to have anything to do with this clinker, adapted from the book by crusading Bob "I've been played by Robert Redford" Woodward.'*
(*Tatler*, October 1989).

clinkers *n pl British* another term for **dingleberries**.

clip *vb* **1** to take (someone's) money dishonestly by sharp practice, deceit or fraud. The word is a euphemism from the jargon of tricksters, with the image of 'trimming' someone of their 'excess' wealth.

2 *British* to hit someone a glancing blow with an open hand, to smack.

✎*'I clipped him round the ear.'*

3 *American* to kill, execute. An item of black street slang from the early 1990s. One of many short 'tough-guy' euphemisms such as **tag**, **cap**, **off**, etc.

clip artist *n American* a fraudster, cardsharp or confidence trickster. A dated term derived from the verb to **clip 1**.

clip joint *n* originally a club or bar which employs hostesses who encourage clients to buy them (inevitably hugely overpriced) drinks in the expectation, rarely fulfilled, that their generosity will be reciprocated with sexual favours. The phrase may now be applied to any overpriced low-quality establishment. **Clip**, like 'trim', is an old euphemism for 'relieve someone of their money'.

clippie *n British* a bus conductress or conductor. The word obviously derives from the clipping of tickets; it originated in Britain and Australia around the outbreak of World War II and is still heard wherever these professions survive.

clipping *n British* a particular kind of cheating in which a prostitute takes a client's money but does not provide sex. A specific sense of the more general slang meaning of **clip**.

clobber *n British* clothes, accessories or equipment. The word is now so widespread as to be colloquial rather than slang. It dates from the 19th century but its origin is obscure; it may be an invention, a dialect form of 'clothes', or from the Yiddish *klbr*.

clobbered-up *adj British*

a dressed, dressed-up.

b burdened, encumbered.

clock *vb British* **1** to notice or see, to look at. A working-class usage widespread, especially in south-east England, since World War II. The middle-class fashion in the late 1980s for imitating working-class speech has brought the word into some prominence and greater respectability. It probably derives from the obsolete use of **clock** to mean a person's face.

✎*'Villains call it clocking in Leeds, eyeballing in Manchester and screwing in London's East End ... It came as a shock: juries can be intimidated by a stare.'*
(*Sunday Times*, 5 June 1988).

2 to hit. A usage that was and is popular in Australia and which has been adopted in Britain (where it may have originated) and the USA. This term, used almost exclusively by men, probably also derives from the archaic **clock** meaning face; hence the verb, meaning to punch (in the face).

✎*'He finally lost his temper and clocked him one.'*

3 to tamper with the mileometer of a car in order to show a low mileage. A piece of dealers' jargon which has passed into common currency due to the wide extent of the practice.

clocking *n American* selling **crack**. A street-slang term of the late 1980s.

✎*'Some of them wear tiny gold charms that look like miniature watch faces – a dealer's trademark, which is probably where the term clocking came from.'*
(*Sunday Times*, 10 September 1989).

clock it *vb* to defeat one's opponent, win a contest. The term derives from the jargon employed in the Nintendo Game Boy computer games.

clodhopper *n*

a a clumsy or boorish person. The term originally (two hundred-odd years ago) referred to a ploughman or rustic (treading clods of earth in the fields).

b *British* a policeman. Rhyming slang from **copper**, rather than a simple pejorative.

clog *vb British* to kick.

clog, cloggy *n British* a Dutch person. This humorous or derogatory word may date from the 1940s when clogs were still widely worn. **Cheese** is a synonym.

clogger *n British* someone who kicks people. The term is usually used dismissively of soccer players whose game is based more on violence than competence.

↳ *'That team are nothing but a bunch of cloggers.'*

cloggy *n See* **clog**.

clogs *n pl See* **pop one's clogs**.

clone *n*

a a **gay** man of stereotyped appearance. In the gay male community of the 1970s a 'uniform' of working clothes, leather caps, moustaches, etc. developed. Indistinguishable conformists to this standard code were referred to by others and themselves as clones. In this sense the word is not necessarily pejorative.

b any fashion-follower or imitator who is indistinguishable from others, or blindly conformist to a dress code. A derogatory term since the late 1970s, often added to a prefix to form such epithets as '*Madonna-clone*', '*Michael Jackson-clone*', etc.

clone-zone *n* the male homosexual milieu or **gay** area of a town where **clones** congregate. A term from the late 1970s.

closet case/queen *n* a homosexual who conceals his or her homosexuality; the second version of the phrase refers only to men. Originally part of underground **gay** terminology, this phrase became well known in the early 1970s when many previously secretive homosexuals decided to **come out**. The term was first widely used in the USA although its precise time and place of origin is obscure. The connection between closet and

secrecy is obvious; compare the phrase with the well-known '*skeleton in the cupboard*'.

Club Fed *n American* prison, especially a Federal, rather than state institution. A 1980s pun on Club Med(iterranée), which continues the time-honoured metaphor of a prison sentence as a vacation.

clucky *adj Australian* broody, pregnant. From the image of a mother hen clucking over her clutch of eggs, the word has now extended to mean pregnant, wanting to be pregnant, or merely eagerly anticipating something.

clue-ie *adj Australian* bright, alert, well-informed. The term is derived from the colloquial 'clued up' and has been used in Australian TV programmes such as *Police Rescue*, also broadcast in the UK.

↳ *'When it comes down to it, she's not too clue-ie, is she?'*

clueless *adj American* unfashionable, unpopular, unattractive. The standard colloquialism was adopted as a vogue term among Californian high-school students in the early 1990s, often in order to categorize a person excluded from the in-group. The word provided the title of the 1994 US movie which featured the pampered successors to the earlier **vals**.

clumping *n British* a beating or maiming. The term, used typically by criminals to indicate physical punishment or a revenge attack, was recorded in the ITV documentary, *The Cook Report*, 6 June 1995.

clunk *n American* **1** a stupid, dull-witted person.

2 an old, dilapidated car or truck.

clutch *n British* a cheek-to-cheek or arm-in-arm dance. A 'society' word used by **Sloane Rangers** among others, which is a specialized use of the colloquial meaning of 'embrace'.

clutched *adj American* tense, agitated. The term refers to the physical symptoms of anxiety in the form of tension in the abdomen and chest.

↳ *'There's no need to get so clutched, it's only a math test.'*

Clyde *n See* **Clydesdale**.

Clydesdale *n American* an attractive male. A humorous term of the late 1980s based on the supposed suggestion of heroic **WASP** maledom inherent in the Christian names Clyde and Dale. The word, which probably originated on the streets ('Clyde' was used by **hipsters** in the 1950s to categorize an archetypal **square**), was used by **Valley Girls** and **preppies** among others in the early 1980s. (The literal meaning of Clydesdale is a form of large, handsome, pedigree horse; strong, hardworking and enormously expensive.)

c-note *n* a hundred dollars or a hundred pounds (not necessarily always in the form of a hundred-denomination bill). From the Latin numeral C: one hundred, this amount is also known as a **century**.

coasting *adj American* under the influence of illicit drugs, moving around in a drug-induced daze or stupor. By extension, being in a euphoric state after listening to jazz, rock music, etc.

coating *n British* abuse, insults. This use of the word has been recorded in the 1990s among middle-aged speakers and either refers to the grabbing by the lapels or is based on the notion of 'pasting', and the slang sense of **paint**. The archaic verb 'coat' was also recorded in Britain and Australia in the sense of to reprimand.

cob *vb, n American* (to give someone) a pinch or poke in the buttocks. In this sense the word, originally a dialect term for a lump or a protrusion, can be dated back to the English slang of the later 18th century. *See also* **get/have a cob on**.

cobber *n Australian* friend, mate. An unsophisticated term of address among men, which is now virtually obsolete. There are two possible derivations proposed for this well-known Australianism: the archaic English dialect verb 'cob', to take a liking to (someone) or the Yiddish word *chaber* (from Hebrew, meaning comrade).

cobblers *n British* nonsense, rubbish, **balls**. A popular example of rhyming slang (from 'cobbler's awls') which is often used in ignorance of its vulgar derivation. Formerly used literally by cockneys to mean testicles, the word is old, but was given widespread currency in the 1960s by such TV comedies as *Steptoe and Son*.

↳ '*He is dismissive about awards: "A load of cobblers".*'
(*Observer, Section 5*, 9 April 1989).

cock *n British* **1** a term of address (for men). It probably derives from 'cock-sparrow', or from the image of a brave-fighting cock. Typically, the word is used in an affectionate, bantering way in expressions such as the dated Cockney '*wotcher cock!*', or '*(my) old cock*'. Cock has been used in this general sense for at least three hundred years.

2 nonsense, rubbish. This sense of the word has been in use since the 1940s and may be a shortening of poppycock (from the Dutch *pappekak* – 'soft shit' or absolute rubbish), or 'cock and bull', or a euphemistic variant of **cack**.

3 penis. In this sense the word is used all over the English-speaking world. In Britain the usage dates from the 17th century. Its origin is in the image of the male member either as a strutting fighter or as resembling a chicken's neck or water-valve. (In the USA the word rooster is usually prudishly substituted when referring to the male bird.)

cock diesel *n American* a powerful, attractive male. The term, usually employed appreciatively but sometimes ironically, is heard in black street slang and on white campuses in the 1990s. The 'diesel' element (as in **diesel-dyke**) suggests the unrefined power of a diesel-engined vehicle.

cocker *n* an affectionate term of address to a male usually in the form '*my old cocker*'. This London working-class expression dates from the 19th century and possibly referred to a fellow devotee of cockfighting.

cocksmoker *n Canadian* someone who performs fellatio. A more recent form of **cocksucker**, heard among adolescents and used as a more acceptable vulgarism on the Internet.

cocksucker *n* a despicable, contemptible person. This expression is almost always used in this sense rather than its literal meaning of someone who performs fellatio; it is generally an Americanism, applied to males as a term of abuse. The implication is of a person who is willing to stoop (metaphorically) to disgusting, debasing acts.

cock-tease, cock-teaser *n* a slightly more polite version of **prick-tease(r)**.

cock (something) up *vb British* to make a mess of, to mismanage disastrously. As in the noun **cock-up** the precise origin of the expression is uncertain. It is common in Britain and Australia, but not in the USA.

cock-up *n British* a mistake, blunder or shambles. Many different sources have been posited for this expression; cock may refer to some obscure piece of professional jargon (it occurs in the vocabularies of printers, hunters, brewers and others), or to the penis; it may be an alteration of **cack**. Alternatively cock may simply have been chosen as a more acceptable complement in a phrase synonymous with **balls-up** and **fuck-up**.
↳'*Mercifully these cock-ups don't happen too often.*'
(Jeremy Paxman, Breakfast TV, November 1988).

coco *n British* a black or coloured person. A pejorative or patronizing term used especially by middle- and upper-class speakers since the 1960s.
↳'*And there were two cocos changing a wheel in the outside lane.*'
(Recorded, public schoolboy, London, 1971).

coco, cocoa *vb British* almost always used in the phrase '*I should coco(a)!*', expressing disbelief or indignation. This is London rhyming slang for 'say so' (as in '*I should say so!*').

cocoa-shunter *n British* a male homosexual. One of many vulgarisms (**fudge-nudger**, etc.) playing on the notion of sodomy and faeces, this expression was used in the TV comedy spoof *Brass Eye* in March 1997.

coconut *n* **1** *British* a non-white person who collaborates with the white establishment, an **Uncle Tom**. This expression, used by young Asians and blacks in the 1980s, refers to the idea that such people are, like the coconut, black on the outside but white on the inside. **Bounty bar** is an alternative.
2 one's head. An obvious but probably obsolescent usage.
3 *American* a dollar.

cocooning *n American* staying at home with one's partner and children (as opposed to going out or socializing in the evening). A **yuppie** term from the late 1980s.

↳'*The latest trendy American word for spending an evening at home in front of the TV with your partner is "cocooning". The Yanks say it's a natural new-age protective reaction to the stresses of late 20th century life.*'
(*Daily Mirror*, 16 February 1989).

cods *n pl British* testicles. The singular form cod is an archaic word for the scrotum; it is an anglo-saxon word meaning bag (seen in the obsolete terms peasecod and codpiece). Since the era of Middle English the plural has had this meaning in British and later Australian usage, although not in the USA.
↳'*He got kicked in the cods for his efforts.*'

codswallop, cods *n British* nonsense, worthless rubbish. A dismissive term, typically applied to something purporting to be true. There is more than one theory as to the origin of the word; the most fanciful is that it referred to the wallop (gassy drink) produced by Mr. Codd (inventor of a patent ginger-beer bottle). Alternatively it may refer to testicles (**cods**) as in **balls**.
↳'*Equal opportunities? That's a load of old codswallop!*'
(Recorded, office worker, London 1986).

coffee-bar cowboys *n pl British* young men who frequent coffee bars and cafés. The equivalent of America's **drugstore cowboys** and Australia's **milkbar cowboys**, this term was used derisively or disapprovingly of the young (**corner-boys**, **teddy boys**, **ton-up kids**, **rockers**, etc.) who congregated in such places throughout the 1950s and 1960s.

coffin-dodger *n British* an elderly person. A sometimes humorous pejorative.
↳'*My four sons and their friends, all in their mid-twenties, refer to the likes of me, a mere 60 year old, as "nearly-deads" and "coffin-dodgers".*'
(Readers' letter to the *Independent*, 4 September 1992).

coffin nail *n* a cigarette. The jocular term pre-dates the public concern over the effects of smoking on health in the last three decades.

cog *n British*
a a gear, in the jargon of motorcyclists and other drivers.
↳'*Drop down a cog and rev up.*'

b power, acceleration.

✎ *'Give it some cog.'*

cog *vb British* to move, go, act energetically. The word also occurs in the verbs **give it some cog** and **get cogging**. The term, used in this way particularly in working-class speech, is derived from sense **b** of the noun form.

cojones *n pl*

a courage, 'guts'. A word (pronounced 'co-honays') introduced to many English speakers by Ernest Hemingway, it is the Spanish slang word for **balls** in both literal and metaphorical senses.

b testicles. The word sometimes has its literal sense in American English, especially when spoken by Hispanics.

✎ *'She kicked him in the cojones.'*

coke *n* cocaine.

✎ *'If somebody come and sell coke on our street we kill 'em or beat 'em up bad.'*
(13-year-old US dealer, *Independent*, 24 July 1989).

cokehead, cokie *n American* a (habitual) user of cocaine. *See* **head**.

cold *adj* untraceable. The opposite of **hot** in its criminal sense, often applied to weapons or cars.

✎ *'It's OK, these guns are cold.'*

cold turkey *n* a sudden withdrawal from hard drugs, typically heroin, with attendant hot and cold flushes, goosepimples, discomfort, etc. The expression is originally American, from the 1940s or earlier, and in the late 1980s was increasingly used, often ironically, to describe a sudden withdrawal from any habitual activity. The phrase refers either to 'goose flesh' or to the general pallor and consistency of cold turkey meat.

✎ *'To go cold turkey/go through cold turkey.'*

✎ *'They gave him cold turkey treatment.'*

✎ *'When you've got cold turkey you think: "If I just had a little bit, I would be perfectly all right".'*
(Ex-drug addict, *Independent*, 17 July 1989).

collar *n, vb* (to) arrest (someone). The noun form is a later coinage from the verb, meaning to catch, and the idiomatic expression *'to feel someone's collar'*, meaning to arrest them. Collar is another police jargon term which has passed into general use.

✎ *'Forget it Friday, this is our collar.'*
(*Dragnet*, US film, 1987).

come *vb* to experience an orgasm. A Victorian euphemism for a physiological fact that has no other name (apart from the also-euphemistic 'climax') in standard English; this use of the word in fact dates back at least as far as Shakespeare and occurs subsequently in the (now archaic) form *'come off'*.

come, cum *n* semen. A later derivation from the verb to **come**.

come across *vb* to consent to sex, especially after initial reluctance. A phrase widespread in the English-speaking world since the 1960s, originating from the more general sense of come across, meaning to accede, give, agree.

come a gutser *vb Australian*

a to have an accident.

b to commit a blunder, fail, the phrase functions similarly to the colloquial 'come a cropper', the 'gutser' originally denoting a heavy fall onto one's stomach.

comedown *n* a period of physical and mental depression and exhaustion following a bout of elation from drugs, specifically the after-effects of amphetamine use.

✎ *'That stuff's terrible – the comedown lasts longer than the high.'*

come it *vb British* to behave in a presumptuous, provocative or aggressive way, to show off. A working-class phrase popular with **skinheads**, who used it to mean 'invite aggression'.

✎ *'Don't come it with me you cheeky little bleeder or I'll give you a clip round the ear.'*
(Recorded, park keeper, London, 1958).

come on *vb* to start to menstruate. A euphemism used by women and men.

come out *vb* to reveal oneself as a homosexual, declare one's homosexuality. The expression is a shortening of *'come out of the closet'*, dating from the period in the early 1970s when liberalization encouraged more openness among **gay** men and women in their relations with each other and the **straight** world. The term has sometimes been extended in the later 1970s and the 1980s to mean 'to declare one's real position' in non-sexual contexts.

come the raw prawn *vb Australian* to try to take advantage of, or deceive someone. This colourful expression probably originated in the 1940s and is still heard. The precise connection between the uncooked crustacean and deceitfulness is not clear, but the suggestion is of cadging by feigning innocence or naïvety.

completely cute *adj American* suitably attractive, handsome and/or sexy. An expression used by upper- and middle-class young women to indicate approval of a potential male partner. A code term in the **preppie** lexicon.

compo *n Australian* (unemployment) compensation. A typical Australian shortening. (*Compare* **arvo**, **convo**, etc.)

con *vb, n* (to perpetrate) a swindle or fraud, obtain money by false pretences. This venerable colloquialism (regarded as slang in the 1950s) is simply a shortening of 'confidence-trick'.

⬧ '*A crazy au pair girl planned to con super-star Eric Clapton out of a fortune by claiming another couple's baby was THEIR love child.*' (*News of the World*, 1988).

con *n American* a convict or ex-convict, felon or prisoner.

conch *n American* a **swot**. A **preppie** shortening of conscientious.

conchie *n* an alternative spelling of **conshie**.

condo *n American* a condominium (an apartment complex which is jointly owned by its tenants).

cone-head *n American*
a an intellectual or **swot**.
b a stupid, socially inept person. The term is a more recent version of **pointy-head**. Its latter sense, as used in adolescent speech, was adopted as the title of a comedy film starring Dan Ayckroyd in 1993.

cones *n pl* breasts.

conk *n* 1 a a nose. The generally-quoted origin for this comical word is the conch shell (often collected as a curio since the 17th century), or a learned play on the Latin *concha*, meaning shell in general, or trumpet.

⬧ '*This face, embossed as it is with a vast fleshy conk.*'

(*Observer* magazine, 15 May 1988).
b head. A less common use of the word.
2 *American* a 'process' hairstyle (one where the hair is straightened by the application of chemicals and/or heat) as worn by **hip** young blacks from the 1930s until the 1960s when it was superseded by the racially affirmative **afro** styles.

conkers *n pl Scottish*
balls (in both the literal and figurative slang senses). Like its contemporary synonym **clackers**, the expression borrows the name of a children's game.

connection, connexion *n* a drug supplier, a **dealer** or **pusher**. Originally from the language of American drug users of the late 1950s and 1960s, the term has become part of the international jargon of illicit drug users. It particularly refers to a source of heroin. (Connection was used ambiguously as the title and in the lyrics of a 1967 song by the Rolling Stones.)

conniption *n* a fit of irritation, agitation. The geographical origin and derivation of the word is obscure (it is fairly common in Australian and North American speech) but it is most often heard among middle-aged speakers.
⬧ '*To have/get into a conniption.*'

coochie *n American*
a the female sex organs.
b a female or females as sex objects. This item of black slang is probably a shortening of **hoo(t)chie-coochie**, which has denoted sexual activity since the 19th century.

cookie-pusher *n American* an unmanly man, an effete or sycophantic male. The image is of someone who spends his time (the word never seems to be used of women) passing cookies at tea parties, either because he enjoys such 'effeminate' activities, or in order to curry favour or further his career.
⬧ '*Some little State Department cookie-pusher trying to persuade them all to play ball.*'

cooking *adj American* going well, moving fast, succeeding. Originally from pre-World War II street language, this usage spread, especially via jazz musicians, to young whites. It is still often used to refer to musicians performing well and generating excitement. A stronger form is '*cooking with gas*'.

cool *adj*

a unflappable, imperturbable.

b excellent, admirable, acceptable. One of the key items in the vocabulary of jazz musicians, **hipsters**, beatniks and **hippies**, cool, with its original suggestion of calm disinterested serenity, is a word which has not dated. It is as much in vogue with teenagers in the late 1980s as it was among the 1930s jazz musicians who probably coined it (to denote gentler, progressive jazz, as opposed to 'hot' jazz).

cool *n* sang froid, imperturbability. A back-formation from the adjective.

cool it, cool out *vb* to relax, unwind, defuse a situation. A **hipsters'** term which has become a common colloquialism.

coon *n* a black person. Originally (and still) a term of racist abuse common in the Southern states of the USA, from raccoon (a black-faced rural pest). The word has been adopted in Britain and Australia to refer to a person of any supposedly inferior race. In Britain it is a widespread racist epithet in use by the police and other working-class whites; **egg and spoon** is the rhyming-slang version.

↳'*There were a couple of coons shouting at each other and it's difficult in these circumstances, I suppose.*'
(Police officer, quoted in *Inside the British Police* by Simon Holdaway, 1983).

cootie *n American* a head or body louse. The word was originally armed-forces slang, from the Polynesian *kuty*, meaning 'parasite'.

↳'*Here you are.*'
'*No, not if it has cooties on it.*'
'*I don't have cooties!*'
(*Roseanne*, US TV comedy series, 1989).

cooze *n American*

a a woman. A fairly vulgar term, used almost exclusively by men, and having overtones of 'sex object', 'victim' or 'slut'.

b the female sex organs. The origin of the word is obscure.

cop *n* a police officer. A shortening of **copper**. In Britain until the 1960s cop was felt to be an Americanism and only in the late 1980s did it find its way into print, albeit in the gutter press.

↳'*Don't cry/Gotta go bye bye/SUD-*

DENLY: DIE DIE/COP KILL A CREEP! pow pow pow.'
('Concentration Moon' written by Frank Zappa, recorded by the Mothers of Invention, 1967).

cop *vb* to buy illicit drugs, to **score**. A specialization of the general use of cop to mean obtain.

↳'*You wanna take a walk,*
You wanna go cop,
You wanna go get
Some chinese rock?'
('Chinese Rock' by Dee Dee Ramone and Richard Hell, recorded by the Heartbreakers, 1977).

copacetic, kopasetic *adj American* excellent, satisfactory, hunky dory. Used usually of a situation or state of affairs, copacetic is as likely to be said by a college professor as a New York **cop**. The college professor might think he is using a newish slang term; the cop may suspect that a word ending in -ic derives from Greek or Latin. Both would be wrong. This bizarre word has rarely been written down, but was recorded as early as 1919. Attempts have been made to derive it from Latin, Yiddish or even Amerindian roots, but its true origin is unknown. It has not crossed the Atlantic in its comparatively long history.

↳'*What's your sign love?*'
'*Stop*'
'*Well that's copacetic.*'
(*Beach Party*, US film, 1981).

↳'*You stick with me and everything will be copacetic.*'
(*The Secret of My Success*, US film, 1987).

cop a feel *vb American* to grope (someone) sexually; succeed in heavy petting. A (mainly male) teenagers' term from the 1950s, when this might be the goal, rather than a way-stage in the process of seduction.

↳'*I didn't even get to cop a feel.*'
↳'*Then when they start gettin' passionate, start coppin a few feels.*'
(High-school student, *IT* magazine, June 1972).

cop a plea *vb American* to plead guilty to a lesser offence than the one which is charged to speed up the judicial process (for the prosecutors) and avoid a heavier sentence (for the defendant). A strategy which forms the basis of plea bargaining, a peculiarity of the US legal system.

⇪*'The guy copped a goddam plea and only went down for three.'*

cop off *vb British* to find a sexual partner, to **pull** someone. A term from the north of England that had become widespread elsewhere by the 1990s.

⇪*'Down on the disco floor/They make their profits/From the things they sell/To help you cop off.'*
(Lyric of 'At Home He Is a Tourist', written and recorded by The Gang of Four, 1979).

⇪*'Cop off … that beautiful moment when you finally get some snog action …'*
(*Just Seventeen* magazine, August 1996).

cop-out *vb, n* (to be guilty of) an evasion, avoidance of responsibility. This expression (almost always heard in the noun form) was American slang until the late 1970s at which time it suddenly gained widespread currency, even among 'respectable' speakers in Britain. The phrase arose in the 1960s meaning specifically to 'duck out' of one's obligations to one's peers.

copper *n* a police officer. The word originated in Britain in the 1840s, from 'to cop' as a humorous or racier alternative to 'to catch'.

copper-nob *n* a red-headed person. An affectionate nickname, now dated but still common in the early 1960s.

coppish *question form American* an alternative spelling of **capeesh**.

copshop *n British* a police station. Currently mainly a children's expression.

cop (some) zees *vb American* to sleep. The phrase, which also occurs in the form **stack some zees**, uses the repeated letter 'z' as a cartoon representation of snoring.

corgis *n pl British* (a) 'couple of really ghastly individuals'. Another in the series of jokey acronyms (on the lines of **yuppie**, **dinkie**, etc.) coined by professionals and the media to epitomize special subgroups of the population in the late 1980s.

cork up *vb British* to keep quiet. A phrase briefly in vogue among adolescents in the mid-1960s, usually in the form of a brusque imperative.

corn *n* money. A variant form of the Caribbean form **carn** which was said to be the favourite word of the black British boxer Frank Bruno in 1992.

corn-dog *n American* a **swot**. One of many synonyms used in the USA (**throat**, **grind**) and UK (**wendy**, **spod**) principally by male school students to ostracize misfits. The reference is to a bland-tasting variety of hot-dog.

corner-boy *n British* an idle or shiftless youth, a layabout. From their habit of hanging around on street corners. This adult and journalese term of disapproval from the 1950s was applied to supposed hooligans and **teddy boys**. As long ago as the 1880s *'corner-cove'* and *'corner man'* were in use with a similar meaning.

cornflake *n American* an eccentric, crazy or silly person. An elaboration of the widespread term **flake** (which has the same meaning). The pun is on the name of the breakfast cereal; 'corn' is otherwise meaningless.

corn-hole *n American*
a the anus.
b a pinch or poke in the anal region. In this sense the phrase has been recorded since the early years of the 20th century.

Cornish pasties *n pl British* a style of man's shoe considered deeply unfashionable or indicative of a certain social subgroup in the 1970s and 1980s (specified by Judy Rumbold, fashion editor of the *Guardian*, as 'maths teachers countrywide'). The pastie was so-called because of the supposed resemblance of the moulded-soled, heavily stitched shoe to the meat and vegetable savoury.

corpse *vb British* (in acting) 1 to be rendered unable to speak or act by the onset of uncontrollable hysterical laughter, in rehearsal or before an audience. The word has been used in the theatre since the 19th century.
2 to cause another actor to break down with laughter or giggling during rehearsal or performance.
These meanings are also true of performers in operas and musicals.

cory, corey *n British* penis. A vulgarism used particularly by marginals and the poorer elements of the working class. The word, which is from the Romany word for thorn, *kori*, was more widely used in the 1950s and 1960s than today.

cosh boy *n British* a young male thug. A journalese phrase from the early 1950s when criminals frequently carried coshes (US: blackjacks) with which to attack people. The phrase was used as an alarmist codeword for a **mugger**. Ian Fleming (in a letter to Somerset Maugham in 1953) referred jokingly to his first James Bond novel as a 'Cosh-boy's Own Paper'.

costume *n See* in costume.

cosy *n British* an act of sex. A **Sloane Ranger** euphemism, used by girls and perhaps revealing of sexual attitudes in this milieu.

cot-case *n* an invalid or someone who has been mentally and/or physically incapacitated. A usually heartless and often derogatory expression, used in Britain and Australia typically by health-care personnel or relatives. The similar term 'stretcher-case' has become an acceptable colloquialism, whereas **basket case** remains slang.

cottage *n British* a public lavatory, in the language of the homosexuals who made contact there. The word and the practice were more common in the 1950s and 1960s before the liberalization of anti-homosexual laws, but are still in evidence. The term is also used in Australia.

cottaging *n British* visiting, or hanging around in, public lavatories to make sexual contacts. A male homosexual's term from the 1950s, still in use in the late 1980s.

couch potato *n American* a lazy, greedy person. This expression from the late 1980s describes a person whose only activity is to lie in front of a television and eat and drink. (Couch is an American synonym for sofa.)

> '"Couch-potato," according to Lindsey Bareham "is American for a television addict": the potato, once again, is defamed as a symbol of dull lethargy.'
> (Patrick Skene Catling, *Daily Telegraph*, Christmas Book Review, 1989).

cough *vb British* to confess to a crime, to reluctantly give up information. A police and underworld term influenced by the notion of coughing up something stuck in the throat.

> 'Look, many times I have known prisoners who have coughed to seven or eight jobs when they have been given a quick thump.'

(Police officer quoted in *Inside the British Police* by Simon Holdaway, 1983).

cow *n British* **1 a** an unpleasant or obnoxious woman.
b a placid, drab or humiliated woman. The word is often used with real malice, or alternatively can be said with fellow feeling by a sympathetic woman, especially in the phrase '*poor cow*'. Cow is not a universal term of abuse (in French for instance it can be a term of affection). It is said that the synonym **moo** was used in the 1960s because cow was still considered beyond the pale for family TV.

> 'When she went bust the Revenue let her keep her bed because it was a tool of her trade. She was a rude old cow but I liked her and we'll all be dead soon.'
> (William Donaldson, *Independent*, 26 August 1989).

2 an unpleasant or extremely irritating task, experience or sensation, etc. In this sense the word is often used in the phrase '*a cow of a job*', etc. *Compare* **mare**.

cowboy *n*
a a reckless or irresponsible person, especially someone young, inexperienced and/or wild. The term is typically used by older workers referring to younger ones, or by police about a delinquent loner. The term originated in the 1950s, drawing comparisons with western film heroes or with pre-war gangsters' use of 'cowboy job' or the verb 'to **cowboy**' to refer to a particularly messy or violent crime.
b *British* a bad workman. The meaning of **cowboy a** has been extended and popularized in colloquial language to mean anyone who does a shoddy job in order to make a quick profit.

> 'Cowboy plumber/plasterer.'

cowboy *vb British* to behave or perform recklessly. The word is now used in two main senses; to drive dangerously or to perform a professional task in a slapdash and/or hazardous way.

cowboy job/operation *n* **1** an unauthorized scheme, as in, for instance, the field of espionage.
2 *British* a badly finished or skimped example of workmanship. *See* **cowboy**.

cowboy outfit *n British* a firm or organization which specializes in shoddy workmanship or dubious business practices. The punch-line of a familiar joke among disgruntled businessmen is that a doting millionaire when asked by his infant son for a cowboy outfit, buys him the company in question.

cow college *n American* a college in an obscure town or remote place.

cow-horns *n pl British* high curved handlebars on a motorcycle or bicycle. A synonym for **ape-hangers**.

coyote *n American* a person who preys on those illegally immigrating to the USA from Mexico. The word (literally, prairie wolf) is used in Spanish to describe unscrupulous agents, mainly Mexican, who offer to help **wet backs** cross the border, but rob, defraud, denounce or even kill them instead. A term from the late 1970s and 1980s.

cozzer *n* a police officer. An item of London working-class slang. The word might have originated in the archaic market porters' term '*cozza(r)*' from the Hebrew *chazar* meaning pork or pig. London's first black policeman, Norwell Roberts, was known as '*Nozzer the cozzer*'.

⬥'*I didn't want to see the shit-eating grins on the cozzers' faces.*'
(Jimmy Robinson, released prisoner, speaking on the BBC TV programme *Panorama*, 24 February 1997).

crabs *n pl* pubic lice, a case of *pediculosis pubis*. The louse is popularly known as the crab louse from its resemblance when viewed under magnification.

⬥'*A dose/case of crabs.*'

crack *n* 1 a purified, addictive form of cocaine. Pellets of crack are smoked; they fizz and crackle, which is probably the origin of the name, reinforced by the precedent of **smack**. The drug became popular in the USA in 1985, but was first described in *The Gourmet Cookbook, a complete guide to Cocaine*, published in California in 1972.

⬥'*Crack – cocaine mixed with baking soda and cooked in microwave ovens – has been described as the "fast food of drugs".*'
(*Independent*, 24 July 1989).

2 the vagina. An obvious vulgarism, occasionally heard in all English-speaking areas.

3 *Irish* and *British* a good time, from the adjective cracking and the Irish notion (sense **4**).

⬥'*It's a right crack.*'
(Snooker hall manager, ITV telethon, May 1988).

4 the crack *Irish* and *British* what's going on, the latest news, or the current ambience. This word is used all over Ireland and in the late 1980s spread to Britain. The all-purpose term, usually in phrases such as '*what's the crack?*' or '*that's the crack!*', seems to combine two very old popular unorthodox senses of the word: talk, gossip or boast, as in **crack on**; and first-rate, excellent – **crack** as an adjective.

⬥'*This is the only place to live. I tried Australia but I came back because I missed the crack.*'
(Belfast resident, *The Crack: a Belfast Year*, Sally Belfrage, 1987).

⬥'*Big Alex is a minder and a fixer. In his words, he knows all the crack.*'
(*Guardian*, 12 December 1987).

crack *adj British* top-notch, first-rate. A shortening of the colloquial 'cracking'.
⬥'*A crack outfit/a crack team.*'

crack a brown *vb Australian* to fart. A fairly rare post-World War II male vulgarism.

crack a chubby *vb See* **chubby**.

crack a fat *vb Australian* to have an erection. A vulgarism known in Britain through Barry Humphries' *Adventures of Barry McKenzie*. There are a number of mostly obsolete expressions in Australian English using the word 'crack' meaning achieve or produce.

crack a stiffie *vb British* to have an erection. An expression used in **Sloane Ranger** and **yuppie** circles, among others.

cracker *n American* 1 a white person. In black street argot the term, from the colour of savoury biscuits, is almost invariably pejorative and often refers to an unsophisticated or bigoted white.

2 a computer programmer who breaches systems for fun or profit, in the patois of **cyberpunks** and **netheads**. Compare **hacker**.

crackerbox *n American*
a a psychiatric hospital.
b a crazy person. The terms are a pun on the colloquial adjectival sense of 'crackers'.

⬥'*I'm stuck in some private crackerbox.*'
(*Man Trouble*, US film, 1993).

crack house *n* a place where the drug **crack** is prepared, sold or consumed.

↪'*In the depressed inner-city areas of Los Angeles or New York, crack is frequently consumed in "crack houses" or "rock houses" – derelict buildings, often occupied by squatters, where addicts can buy and consume the drug.*'
(*Sunday Times*, 10 September 1989).

crack it *vb British* to succeed in a seduction. Used by and about men, this is a specific use of the general colloquial sense of to succeed, especially to suddenly succeed after long effort, as in 'cracking' a safe or a code.

crackle *n British* money, banknotes. A word used by street traders, bookies, **spivs**, etc., particularly in the 1950s and 1960s. An alternative to **crinkle**, similarly inspired by the sound of crisp new notes.

crackling *n British* an attractive female, or women in general seen as sex objects. This male expression was particularly popular in the 1950s and early 1960s, usually in the phrase '*a bit of crackling*'. It derives from the idea of pork crackling being a 'tasty morsel', perhaps reinforced by the vulgar sense of **crack** (*see* **crack**, sense 2).

crack on *vb British* 1 to talk incessantly, browbeat or boast. The phrase, which is now generally used by middle-class speakers, is a successor to a colloquial use of **crack** to mean gossip, brag or tell tales which is at least 300 years old and survives in Scottish and American speech.

↪'*He was cracking on about his job and his responsibilities.*'
(Recorded, city financier, London, 1987).

2 a to establish contact with a potential romantic partner, seduce.

↪'*You can't crack on to that many people here.*'
(*Away The Lads*, BBC 2 TV documentary, February 1993).

b 'crack on someone' flirt with, have and/or express an infatuation with. An item of slang in use in girls' public schools in the early 1990s.

crack wise *vb* to make witty or cheeky remarks. A back-formation from the noun and verb 'wisecrack'.

crank *n* 1 penis. A rare usage, mainly heard in the USA among sailors, **truckers**, **hard-hats** and others in the 1960s.

2 **speed** (methedrine or amphetamine), heroin. A drug users' term from the late 1960s which could also be used to refer to any drug which '*cranks up*' or re-stimulates a person's system.

3 *American* an irritable, bad-tempered person. The slang noun is derived from the colloquial adjective cranky (itself from the Scottish dialect word for bent or distorted).

cranking, cranked *adj* exciting, stimulating, powerful. The words come from the image of cranking up an engine and, by extension, the colloquial 'cranking up the volume'.

crank up *vb* to inject (a dangerous drug). A **junkies'** term from the early 1970s derived from the image of inserting a handle into an engine to jerk it back into life.

↪'*They're going to crank up/to crank up some smack.*'

crap *n* 1 a excrement, **shit**.
b dirt, rubbish.
c worthless nonsense, **bullshit**.

In modern usage crap is generally seen as a more moderate synonym for **shit**; in fact the word comes from Middle English 'crappe', which meant scrapings, scale, residue or chaff; this in turn came from words existing in Old French, German and Dutch, distantly related to 'crop' and 'crabbed'. (The fact that the flush toilet was invented by a Thomas Crapper appears to be pure coincidence.)

2 oppressive, petty or unpleasant behaviour; by extension from **crap 1 a** and **b**. This idea is usually expressed in such phrases as '*he doesn't take any crap from anyone*' or '*she's not going to put up with this crap any more*'.

crap *vb* to defecate, **shit**. The verb form, which began to be used in the late 18th century, is derived from the earlier noun **crap**, which originally meant rubbish, rather than excrement.

crapola *n American* misleading or worthless information, pretentious, contemptible behaviour. An embellishment of **crap**. (The suffix **-ola**, as in **payola**, etc., is an imitation Spanish/Italian word-ending which adds the sense of big, bad, flagrant, etc.)

crap on *vb British* a near synonym for the verb to **bang on**, with the added suggestion that the content of the monologue or harangue in question is worthless or frivolous.

✎ *'The only moments of light relief we get are when you come in and we crap on about anything we like.'*
(Recorded, London University student, July 1988).

crapper, the crapper *n* toilet. This vulgarism appears to derive from **crap** and not from the name of Thomas Crapper, a Victorian manufacturer of lavatories who is claimed to be the inventor of the flush toilet.

crappy, crappo *adj* worthless, contemptible, of very low quality. From **crap**. Crappo is a more recent variant.

crash *vb* 1 also **crash out** to go to sleep, lie down and lose consciousness. This word was very popular in the **hippy** era, perhaps because the suggestion of sudden collapse coincided with drug-induced sleep or simply curling up on a floor, exhausted. Crash sounds rather dated in the late 1990s; it originated in armed-services slang in World War II, probably among airmen, and was adopted by bohemian travellers and **beatniks** during the 1950s.
2 to gatecrash. A word made especially popular by the teenage custom (from the 1960s onward) of arriving uninvited at parties.
3 *British* to cadge or borrow. In use among working-class speakers and members of the armed services in the 1950s, this term became popular among adolescents in the 1990s. The term is heard particularly in the Scottish Lowlands and the north of England.

✎ *'Can you crash me a tenner?'*

✎ *'I just wanted to crash a couple of biffs.'*

crash and burn *vb* to fail spectacularly. A military metaphor which became an item of journalese in the early 1990s.

crasher *n British* a (crashing) bore. An upper-, and more recently middle-class term. It has existed in limited circulation since the 1950s, has been fashionable among **Sloane Rangers**, **yuppies**, etc.

crash-hot *adj Australian* excellent, first-rate. This fairly popular expression is probably a euphemism for **shit-hot**.

crashpad a place to sleep (temporarily). This term, combining **crash**, meaning to sleep, and **pad**, meaning home or shelter, was popularized by the **hippies**; it usually referred to a communal building where sleeping space was available to travellers.

crater-face *n* a person suffering from facial acne or spots. **Pizza-face** is a synonym, similarly used by or of adolescents.

cream *n South African* an attractive, young female. Recorded as an item of Sowetan slang in the *Cape Sunday Times*, 29 January 1995.

cream, cream one's jeans *vb* to have an orgasm, or to become sexually excited (while dressed). The vulgarism can be used of either sex (and now, by extension, can even sometimes mean to become over-excited or over-enthusiastic without the sexual connotation). Cream has been a euphemism for semen or sexual lubricant for at least a century. **Cream one's jeans** dates from the late 1960s.

cream-crackered *adj British* **knackered**; exhausted, worn out. A humorous rhyming-slang version of the more common word. It was probably coined in the 1970s, inspired by the savoury dry biscuits called 'cream crackers'.

crease *n British* the anus, buttocks, female genital area. The vulgarism, in use especially in the northwest of England, is often heard in phrases such as '*a kick up the crease*'.

creature-features *n* a mild term of abuse among schoolchildren. It may originate in 'creature-feature', a show-business jargon term for a horror film of the 1950s.

creatures, the creatures *n pl British* prison warders. A prisoners' term conveying more bitterness than the more usual **screws**.

cred *adj, n British* (having) 'street credibility'. A 1980s adolescent vogue term inspired by the earlier cliché.

creeping Jesus *n* an unpleasantly insincere, untrustworthy or complaining person, a creep, sneak or **whinger**. This strange expression of distaste is mainly heard among middle-class speakers in Britain and Australia; it dates according to the *Oxford English Dictionary* at least to 1818.

creep (someone) out *vb* to disgust, disquiet. Formed from the colloquial 'creepy', the phrase is popular among younger teenagers.

↳*'I don't care: he creeps me out, plus he smells gross ...'*
(*The X-Files*, US TV series, 1996).

creepshow *adj* frightening, grotesque, or merely unpleasant. An American teenagers' word, from the title of a horror film released in 1982. The adjective is an elaboration of '*creepy*' and the earlier '*creepsville*', and has been heard among British teenagers from the late 1980s.

↳*'A creepshow party.'*
↳*'Her creepshow boyfriend.'*

cremated *adj British* ruined, destroyed, defeated, trounced. A coinage of the 1980s combining the notions of 'killed' and **burned**. The term was briefly in vogue among **yuppies**.

↳*'If the market moves in a big way we'll get cremated.'*
(*Serious Money*, Caryl Churchill, 1987).

crew *n*

a *British* a gang. A word used since the 1960s by street gangs, especially **skinheads** and football hooligans, to refer to themselves. It was a synonym for band (of ruffians) 300 years earlier.

b *American* a group of young people. Unlike the British sense which implies violence, this 1980s usage usually refers to **hip-hop** artists, break dancers or **scratch** musicians.

crew *vb American* to belong to a gang or social group. An item of black street slang of the 1990s, the verb is formed from the earlier noun usage.

crib *n American* home. A common term in black street slang sometimes adopted, usually facetiously, by white adolescents.

crim *n* a criminal. A term heard increasingly from the late 1980s; it is probably originally an Australian usage.

crim, crimble, crimbo *n British* Christmas. These are adults' nurs-ery words (probably originally from Liverpool) which were popularized, particularly by radio disc jockeys, in the 1970s.

↳*'Stevie's determined to have a well wacky Crimble do – even by his standards.'*
(*Just Seventeen*, magazine, December 1987).

cringe (someone) *vb British* to embarrass, discomfit or excruciate. A mainly middle-class usage of the late 1980s.

↳*'Would it cringe you too much if I used my* [cell-]*phone here?'*
(Recorded, yuppie to companion in opera-house bar, London, June 1988).

cringe-making *adj British* sickening, embarrassing. The use of '-making' as a suffix in this way is typical of British middle- and upper-class usage in phrases such as this and sick-making.

↳*'I couldn't bear to watch; it was just too cringe-making.'*

crinkle *n British* banknotes, money. This term was used by bookies, **spivs**, and the like in the 1950s and is now probably obsolete. **Crackle** was a synonym.

↳*'I need some crinkle in a hurry.'*

crinkly *n British* **1** an elderly person or adult. A young person's dismissive (or sometimes grudgingly affectionate) term. It forms part of the group of post-1970 vogue terms which includes **dusty**, **crumbly** and **wrinklie**.

2 a banknote, especially a £1 banknote. The term was used by **Sloane Rangers** in the late 1970s.

crispy *adj American* **1a** suffering from a hangover. A teenage and adolescent vogue word of 1988. Its provenance is uncertain; it may evoke the notion of 'brittle' or 'fragile'.

b unpleasant, inferior. The generalized term in use among American adolescents in the 1990s seems to postdate the more specific sense above.

2 *American* smart, neat.

croak *vb* **1** to die. An unsentimental term derived presumably from the choking death rattle, or rasping dying words. The usage dates from the 19th century.

↳*'He croaked before he could tell us anything useful.'*

2 to kill. An American gangster and prison term.

↳ *'The guy threatened to croak his business partner.'*

croaker *n British* a doctor who prescribes for addicts. A drug addicts' and prisoners' term in use since the 1960s, although the notion of the death-dealing doctor thus expressed goes back to the 19th century.

croc(k) *n British* a stupid and/or irritating person. The word occurred in the speech of London schoolchildren in the early 1990s. Its exact etymology is uncertain, although in early-19th-century dialect the word denoted a worthless or worn-out animal and it was later used in public school slang to refer to a weak or unsporting fellow pupil.

crock, crock of shit *n American* nonsense, something worthless and unpleasant. *'It's a crock!'* is an expression (inoffensive enough to be used on TV) employed in the 1970s and 1980s to dismiss, deride or reject something such as false information. In North America the word crock for container is not archaic as it is in Britain and Australia.

crocked *adj* 1 *American* drunk. A word used for example by college students in the 1980s. It probably comes from the old use of crocks as containers for pickling or preserving in alcohol or, particularly in Canada, as containers for whiskey. Alternatively, the derivation may be the same as that of the following sense.
2 *American* angry. This use of the word is connected with an archaic or dialect use of 'crock' and 'crook' to mean an old, infirm, cantankerous and complaining person.
3 *British* broken or injured; used particularly of sportsmen incapacitated through injury. From the standard English sense of crock as potsherd or from a dialect term for a decrepit animal.

cron(z) *n American* a gun. The term, which usually refers to a handgun, originated in black street argot in the 1990s. Its derivation is obscure.

crook *adj Australian* unwell, unhealthy, wrong, dubious. A common term in Australia, crook is either an alteration of archaic slang 'cronk' (from German and Yiddish *krank*) meaning ill, or of crooked, meaning bent out of shape. By 1988 the word could be used in a British newspaper or magazine, due to the influence of Australian soap operas (it has not as yet penetrated British speech).

crow *n British* a new army recruit. The word originally referred specifically to a troublesome recruit in either army or navy and was probably inspired by the synonymous 'rook' or 'rookie' (which itself was a deformation of the word recruit, or perhaps derived from 'rook', to cheat).

crucial *adj British* a Jamaican code word from the radical self-dramatizing slang of **rude boys** and reggae devotees, crucial became a vogue term of appreciation in London around 1979, first among black youth and later white imitators. Lenny Henry, the black comedian, brought the word to a wider audience by including it in the scripts of his television series, in the mouth of the character 'Delbert Wilkins'.

crud *n*
a anything filthy, disgusting or worthless, including excrement, any encrusted or coagulated substance and (in American English) the effects of skin infection. Crud is from Middle English 'crudde', a dialect word related to the standard English curd.
b a worthless, despicable person (usually male). A word used widely in the 1960s, in place of taboo synonyms such as **turd**.

cruddy *adj* unpleasant, inferior, worthless. A word in vogue in the mid-1960s. It is now heard mainly among schoolchildren.

cruel *vb Australian* to spoil, frustrate, defeat. This use of the word often occurs in the phrase *'to cruel it'* meaning to ruin or jeopardize an enterprise.

cruise *vb*
a (used intransitively) to move around in search of a sexual partner. The word was first used by prostitutes seeking clients, then in the 1960s by **gays** and subsequently in the 1970s by heterosexuals, especially those frequenting singles bars.
b (used transitively) to actively try to attract a particular potential sexual partner. The overtones of cruising a person are a discreet display of oneself with some unmistakable hints or **come-ons**.

crumb (it) *vb American* to ruin, mess up. From crumble in its standard sense, reinforced by the notion of acting like a **crumb**, and by **crummy**.

♭'*You crumbed the play.*'
(*House of Games*, US film, David Mamet, 1987).

crumble *n British* a generic term for old or senile people. Used in the 1980s in the expression '*a bit of crumble*' for instance, or by nursing staff to refer contemptuously to their elderly patients.

crumbly, crumblie *n British*
a an old person. In spite of the suggestion of crumbling or falling apart, the term is only mildly contemptuous and may even be used affectionately. Coincidentally, the 1960s French slang term for old or 'past it' was *croulant*, meaning crumbling.
♭'*Senior citizens, inevitably, watch 37 hours a week. "Audiences are getting crumbly," says Street-Porter in media-speak.*'
(*Independent*, 23 March 1988).
b a parent or adult. Used by children and teenagers since the mid-1970s. A fairly inoffensive middle- and upper-class word favoured by **Sloane Rangers** among others. *See also* **wrinklie, crinkly, dusty**.

crumb-snatcher *n American* a baby or small child. Like **ankle-biter, rug-rat**, etc., the phrase can be used affectionately and/or ruefully.

crummy, crumby *adj* dilapidated, dirty, worthless. By the mid-19th century this word was in use in Britain as a literal and figurative synonym for lousy, apparently due to the resemblance of body lice to crumbs. The word (usually spelled with double 'm'), has remained in widespread use in Britain and the USA.

crumpet *n British* a woman, or women viewed collectively as sex objects. **Crumpet** or '*a bit of crumpet*' date from the last decade of the 19th century and conform to a much older pattern of likening women to cakes (**tart**), delicacies (**crackling**), etc. The terms 'crumpet' or 'a bit of crumpet' are now likely to offend most women although both are still widespread, mainly in working-class usage. Women are now beginning to use the terms to refer to males.
♭'*I don't think we should condemn a doctor simply because he made a wrong diagnosis of what is, or is not, crumpet.*'
(*Carry on Again, Doctor*, British comedy film, 1969).

crumpet man *n British* a woman-

izer, seducer. A working-class expression of the 1960s.

crunchie *n American* a lesbian, particularly a lesbian with austere habits and 'utopian' views. 'Crunchies' were one faction of lesbians at Yale University in the late 1980s, the other being so-called **lipsticks**.

crusher *n British* a boring, tedious person, a ('crushing') bore. An alternative to **crasher**, typically used by middle- and upper-class speakers in the 1980s.

crust *n British* (one's) head. This London working-class usage is almost always heard in the forms **off one's crust** or '*do one's crust*'.

crustie *n British* a homeless person and/or beggar, especially a member of a militant subculture of importunate vagrants of the early 1990s centred on the English West Country who practised deliberate self-degradation and embraced personal filthiness (hence the name, from the encrustations on bodies and clothing). Other names for members of the same subculture were **fraggles, hedgers, scrotes, smellies, soap-dodgers** and **cider-punks**.
♭'*The Crusties of Bath are, with their counterparts at the other end of the social spectrum, the smooth lawyers and medics, considerably more redolent of the city Jane Austen knew than anything else the tourist is likely to see.*'
(Reader's letter to the *Independent*, November 1991).

crut *n* dirt, distasteful material or unpleasantness in general. A version of **crud** (normally felt to be less offensive than that word).

crutching, crotching (it) *vb British* smuggling illicit substances (tobacco, drugs, etc.) in bodily crevices. An item of prison slang recorded in the 1990s.

cry Ruth/Hughie/Ralph *vb* to vomit. All these humorous equivalents attempt to imitate the sound of hearty or sudden retching. They have been popular, particularly with students, all over the English-speaking world since the 1960s.

crystal *n* amphetamine or cocaine. An item of drug users' jargon.

cube *n* an extremely **square** person. A

derogatory **hipsters'** and **beatnik** term last heard in the early 1960s.

cubehead *n American* a user of LSD (lysergic acid diethylamide), the hallucinogenic drug. A term used in the mid-1960s, when LSD was frequently taken orally on sugar cubes.

cuff *vb* to add an additional item to a bill, list of expenses, etc. The word seems to have arisen in pre-World War II underworld usage in the USA with the meanings of swindle and cadge. It may have been inspired by the image of keeping a tally written on a shirt cuff or on a card concealed beneath it.

cull *n American* an unfashionable, unpopular person. The term, in use particularly on campuses since the 1980s, is of uncertain origin, although 'cull' or 'cully' were used as early as the 17th century to denote a dupe or a 'blockhead' (deriving ultimately from the French for testicles or from the related Italian *coglione*, a fool).

cum *n See* **come**.

cunt *n* **1 a** the vagina. This taboo word has ancient origins; related words (French *con*, Spanish *coño*, etc.) exist in other European languages and it seems that in the unwritten prehistoric Indo-European parent languages 'cu' or 'koo' was a word base expressing 'feminine', 'fecund' and associated notions.
b a woman, or women in general. An extension of the above which is probably most commonly heard in the USA.
2 a very unpleasant person. As well as being the most 'obscene' of the common set of sexually-related taboo words, cunt is also used to indicate extreme distaste or dislike. This usage, which is more noticeable in British and Australian English than American, is presumably inspired by deep-seated fear and loathing of women's sexuality, although in practice the word is usually applied to men.
From Anglo-Saxon times until the 14th century the word was in standard use, but was then replaced by euphemisms in all but rural dialect speech. Most dictionaries refused to acknowledge the word until the 1960s and it is probably the only word that is still banned from British newspapers and television.

cupcake *n American* **1** a cute or attractive woman. A deliberately humorous or (consciously or unconsciously) patronizing male term of endearment. Cup-

cakes are small, usually iced, buns.
2 an eccentric person.

curling *n British* drinking alcohol, especially beer. The expression is a synonym for **bend(ing) the elbow**, heard in the Midlands and north of England.

currant bun *n British* **1 a** the sun.
b son.
Both rhyming-slang uses have been in evidence in London working-class use since at least the 1940s.
2 a nun. A rare item of rhyming slang heard occasionally from at least the 1950s.

curry queen *n* a gay male who is attracted to South Asian partners. Compare **rice-queen**.

curse, the curse *n* menstruation, a monthly period. This is the standard term used by schoolgirls and women; its probable origin is in Genesis, in which Eve is 'cursed' by God who promises to *'multiply thy sorrow and thy conception: in sorrow thou shalt bring forth children'*. The 'curse of Eve' thus became a euphemism for the most troublesome aspect of femininity.
↳ *'I've got the curse, I'm afraid.'*

cushdy, cushti, kushti *adj British* fine, wonderful. An all-purpose term of approbation or agreement. This working-class term (recently brought to a wider audience by the television comedy *Only Fools and Horses*) is related to cushy, the colloquial term for easy or comfortable. Both words derive ultimately from an archaic Persian word *khosh*, meaning pleasant, either via Hindustani, *khush*, or Romany, *kushto*, or both.

cuss (someone) off *vb* to criticize, denigrate. The phrase is in black usage in Britain and the US and may have originated in Caribbean speech.

cut *vb* to dilute or adulterate (illicit drugs), usually with the intention of increasing weight and hence profit.
↳ *'The coke was cut with lactose.'*

cut *adj* circumcized.
↳ *'Everyone knows what cut and uncut means.'*
(Male prostitute, Channel 4 documentary, *Hookers, Hustlers, Pimps and their Johns*, October 1994).

cut (someone) a little slack

vb American to relax regulations, to make allowances for or give room to move. The image is of tailoring something for relatively unrestricted ease of movement.

꙳*'Come on, cut me a little slack, will you?'*

cut a rug *vb* to dance.

A lighthearted expression which was fashionable in the jitterbug era and in the post-war language of rock and **jive**. It still survives in jocular use.

cute *adj See* completely cute.

cut it *vb* to succeed, manage.

A shortened form of *'cut the mustard'* or *'cut some ice'*.

꙳*'Her experience among women rappers trying to cut it in the macho world of Hip Hop, led Charlotte to look again at the girl groups from the Seventies she'd always loved.'*
(*Ms London Magazine*, 4 September 1989).

cyberpunk *n* an enthusiast for information technology, **net-head**.

The term arose in the 1980s to describe young fans of the science-fiction writer William Gibson, who combined a fascination for computing and youth culture with a supposedly **punk** attitude. In the later 1990s the word usually referred to a nonconformist user of the Internet.

꙳*'Just launched, Cyberseed describes itself as Britain's first Cyberpunk event, which will, it is hoped, one Friday every month, present a vision where man, music and machine contrive to be one.'*
(*Sunday Times*, 12 December 1993).

d...

D n **1 dope,** illicit drugs. The predictable abbreviation was typically used by British cannabis smokers in the early and mid-1970s.

↳ *'Hey, man, got any d?'*

2 *Australian* detective. This abbreviation dates from the 19th century and is now almost archaic. It has metamorphosed into **demon.**

D.A. *n British* **1** a hairstyle in which the hair is scraped back and greased into a curl on the nape of the neck. It is an abbreviation of **duck's arse.** The style was popular among **teddy boys** in the 1950s and, to a lesser extent, with the **rockers** of the early 1960s.

2 drug addict. An abbreviation used, generally facetiously, by drug users themselves in the mid- and late 1960s.

dabs *n pl British* fingerprints. The term has been used by police, criminals and crime writers since the 1930s at least. It derives from the fingerprinting process in which the suspect presses his or her fingers on an ink pad.

↳ *'We managed to lift some dabs from the wine glasses.'*

daddio, daddy-o *n* (old) man. A variant of Dad and Daddy, used as a term of address. It originated in the **jive talk** of black jazz musicians in the 1940s, and was adopted by the **beatniks** of the 1950s. The word implied a degree of respect or affection, usually for someone older or in authority. In later use, by British **teddy boys** and **beatniks** for example, it was often a teasing or mocking form of address.

daddy *n British* **1** a dominant inmate among prisoners.

2 an older and/or dominant male homosexual, in a relationship, group or institution.

dag *n Australian* **1** (a piece of dried) sheep dung. This sense of the word dates from the 16th century, but has become archaic in Britain. It usually refers to the dried flakes adhering to tail wool.

2 a stupid or unpleasant person, by extension from the first sense. In the late 1980s dag has become a fairly mild all-purpose insult or description, freely used for instance in television soap operas such as *Neighbours.*

dagga *n South African* cannabis, marihuana. This is the most common term for these drugs in South Africa, and derives from local African languages. It is occasionally heard elsewhere among drug users.

daggy *adj Australian* stupid, unpleasant. From **dag.** A brusque but fairly mild expression of distaste (deemed suitable for inclusion in the script of TV soap operas, for instance).

dago *n*

a a person of Hispanic origin (Spanish or Latin American). This derogatory meaning is probably the original sense of the word in that it derives from the Hispanic proper name Diego (James). The word usually has this sense when used by British speakers.

b an Italian. This has become the most common American sense of the word. Dago is sometimes used as an indiscriminate insult to persons, usually male, of Mediterranean origin.

dainties *n pl* (women's) panties, knickers. A jokily coy euphemism heard in both America and Australia in the mid-1970s.

dairybelle *n South African* an attractive woman, especially one with large breasts. The term is an adoption of the brand name of milk and cheese products.

daisy *n* a male homosexual or an effeminate man. The word in this sense is not common but occurs occasionally in British, American and Australian usage.

daisy chain *n* a group of people taking part in 'serial' sexual activity; cunnilingus, fellatio, penetration etc. in series.

daisy roots, daisies *n pl British* boots. A well-known, but now rarely heard, piece of cockney rhyming slang which dates from the late 19th century. The meaning of the term was sometimes extended to shoes.

daks *n pl* trousers. From the trademark name of a brand of casual trousers sold since the 1930s in Britain and Australia. The word's popularity was boosted by its use in the *Barry McKenzie* cartoon series in *Private Eye* magazine, usually in the phrase '*drop one's daks*'.

damage *n* expense, cost, charge. This sense of the word is at least two hundred years old and today hardly qualifies as slang.
↳'*What's the damage?*'

dame *n* a woman. An Americanism usually identified with the criminal, musical, etc. milieus of the 1920s, '30s and '40s. The usage obviously derives from the original British 13th-century title of Dame (itself from Latin *domina*, via Old French), which quickly became a synonym for woman in dialect and rural speech. Like **doll**, **broad** and to some extent **chick**, the term now sounds dated.

damp *adj* **1** *British* a middle-class synonym for **wet** in the sense of ineffectual, feeble.
↳'*I always found Jenny's husband a bit damp.*'
2 sexually aroused (of a woman).
↳'*On the Jonathan Ross show one night I saw a female comic asked how she viewed the prospect of the next guest, a renowned male hunk. "I'm damp," she replied, and went on to repeat the assertion a few times. "Damp. Yes, I'm really damp." There was no joke as such, no turn or twist or wit, just a blank description.*'
(Sebastian Faulks, *Independent* magazine, 28 October 1989).

d and d *adj* drunk and disorderly. The phrase in full is police or judicial jargon; the abbreviation is a euphemism used by police in the USA and in Britain facetiously by drinkers.
↳'*Terry was completely d and d again last night.*'

dang *n American* **1** penis. A rare variant of **dong**.
2 a euphemism for damn.

dangleberries *n pl* a variation of **dingleberries**.

dangler *n* **1** a penis. A nursery euphemism also used facetiously among adults.
2 *Australian* a **flasher**, a male sexual exhibitionist.
3 *British* a trailer, when attached to a truck or tractor.
4 *American* a trapeze artist.

danglers *n pl* testicles. An old and predictable euphemism heard, for example, in British public schools and the armed forces.

dap *adj American* elegant, smart, fashionable. The term, heard in black and campus speech, is a shortening of dapper.

dap-dap *n, adj American* (an individual considered) attractive, well-dressed, fashionable. An elaboration of **dap** favoured by younger teenagers in California and featured in the 1996 US film, *Clueless*.

dappy *n, adj British* (a person who is) silly, clumsy, eccentric. This blend of dippy and daffy was in use among schoolchildren and teenage speakers in the early 1990s.

daps *n pl British* tennis shoes, plimsolls. The word may echo the sound of light footfalls or derive from an archaic dialect verb meaning to dart or pad. Daps was a particularly popular term among teenagers and schoolchildren in Wales and the southwest in the 1960s.

darb *vb British* to have sex. In this sense the word was recorded among London schoolgirls in 1993. Its origins are unknown and it seems not to be related to the identical American noun.

darb *adj American* an excellent or admirable person or thing. The word seems to have originated in the 1920s and is said to derive from Ruby Darby, the name of a popular showgirl.

dare *adj British* good. A vogue term in use among teenage gang members. The term, sometimes in the form of an exclamation of approval, was recorded in use among north London schoolboys in 1993 and 1994.

dark *adj British* behaving harshly, unfairly or unpleasantly (to another person). Used in this way the term is part of the slang code heard among London teenagers in the 1990s. It probably originated in the black Caribbean community, although the same word was employed to mean stupid or obtuse in 17th-century English slang.

⋈ *'I didn't like it that he was actin' dark.'*
(Recorded, North London schoolboy, 1993).

dash *n* money, a bribe or tip. The term is from West Africa, where it derives from *dashee*, a local African dialect term. It may be the origin of the more common **dosh**.

date *n* 1 *Australian* also **date-locker** the anus. Presumably by association with the colour of the fruit, or just possibly from the archaic British rhyming slang 'date and plum' meaning **bum**.
2 *British* a stupid, silly or weak person. This rare usage (probably by association with the texture of an over-ripe date) is now nearly obsolete, but was heard until the 1960s, especially in the phrases 'you soft date' and 'you soppy date'. Such phrases now survive only in nursery language.
3 a prostitute's assignation with a client. An item of police slang recorded by the London *Evening Standard* magazine, February 1993.

date roll *n Australian* a toilet roll. Derived from **date 1**.

David *n British* semen. This 1996 term from the language of adolescents puns on the surname of the sports hero and Arsenal and England goalkeeper, David Seaman.

David (Gower) *n British* a shower. An instance of educated rhyming slang which borrows the name of the cricketer, heard among university students in the 1990s.

Davy Crockett *n British* pocket. A piece of rhyming slang inspired by the cult film about the American pioneer for which there was a craze in 1956. **Sky rocket** and **Lucy Locket** are synonyms.

daylighting *n* working (usually illicitly) at a second job during daylight hours. An obvious derivation from the colloquial 'moonlighting'.

deadass *n, adj American* very boring, feeble or very stupid (person).
⋈ *'He's a real deadass.'*
⋈ *'What a deadass town.'*

dead bang *adv, adj American* caught in flagrante, or red-handed. An American police version of **dead to rights**, or the British **bang to rights**.
⋈ *'I got you dead bang for breaking into Eddie's apartment.'*
(*The Rockford Files*, US TV crime series, 1979).

deadbeat *n*
a a poor or homeless person.
b a penniless scrounger, freeloader.
c a worthless or stupid person.
All these senses derive from a 19th-century Americanism in which 'dead' means 'completely', and 'beat' is not 'exhausted' but 'loafer' or **hobo**.

dead-crack *adj British* penniless, broke.

deadhead *n* 1 a very stupid, lifeless or boring person. An obvious derivation of its component parts, this phrase is reinforced by its 19th-century American meaning of non-paying passengers or non-participants (from dead head of cattle).
2 *Australian* an idle person, good-for-nothing.
3 a fan or devotee of the San Francisco rock group The Grateful Dead, which was popular in the late 1960s and early 1970s, and enjoyed a revival in the 1980s. Supposedly archetypically **hippy** in their attitudes, The Grateful Dead, known to their fans simply as The Dead, inspired unusual levels of commitment in their followers.

deadhead *vb American* to run or drive (a vehicle) empty or without passengers. This meaning, a relic of 19th-century cattle drives, is now rarely heard. (*See also* **deadhead 1**.)

deadleg *n, vb British* 1 a feeble, lazy or disappointing person. This word has been used from the 1950s and may derive from an earlier armed-forces term **deadlegs**, meaning a cripple or someone who refuses to rise from bed.
⋈ *'The usual crowd of airheads, phonies, deadlegs, posers, bimbos, wallies, wannabees, hangers-on and gate-crashers.'*
(Christena Appleyard, *Daily Mirror*, 11 May 1989).
2 a numb feeling in the leg following a kneeing in the thigh by an attacker or, when used as a verb, the action of knee-

ing someone in this way. A popular school playground tactic.

dead meat *n* a person who is dead, about to die or inevitably doomed. Dead meat is an old and heartless euphemism for a corpse. Now the phrase usually forms part of a threat.

↳*'Do that, baby, and you're dead meat!'*

deadneck *n American* a variant of **deadhead**, **deadbeat**, etc.

deadshit *n Australian* a contemptible or very unpleasant person. The word is also sometimes used as an adjective as in, *'That was a deadshit party'*.

dead soldier *n* an empty bottle (of alcohol). The phrase was first used by members of the British armed forces about 200 years ago, likening the aftermath of a drinking bout to a battlefield littered with corpses. In American usage the term is sometimes extended to leftovers other than bottles.

↳*'I'll clear up the dead soldiers while you fumigate the place.'*

dead to rights *adv, adj American* an American version of the British **bang to rights**. Dead to rights is probably the original form of the phrase, dating from the 19th century and now rarely, if ever, heard in Britain.

('Dead' is used in its common colloquial meaning of 'completely'.)

deal *n British* a portion or amount of a drug, especially hashish. Before decimalization in 1971, very small amounts of cannabis were bought or referred to as a **five-bob deal** or **ten-bob deal**.

deal *vb* to sell (drugs). The verb is used intransitively, *'does he still deal?'*, and transitively, *'she deals dope at the weekend'*.

dealer *n* a supplier of illicit drugs. The term, imported into other English-speaking areas from the United States in the early 1960s, is a neutral one, implying someone who sells on demand without coercion. It replaced the earlier, pejorative word **pusher** among users themselves.

dealing *adj British* involved in a relationship, 'seeing someone'. A term from the older adolescent's lexicon of dating, heard in the later 1990s.

deb *n* **1** a debutante; that is, a young girl being introduced into the social season. Although principally identified with an upper-class London milieu, the adoption of *débutante*, French for 'beginner', may have occurred in the USA in the first decade of the 20th century.

2 *American* a female member of a street gang. A term used in the 1960s, usually in the plural, probably originating in debutante, perhaps reinforced by the prevalence of the Christian name Deborah or Debbie. Deb resurfaced in the gang argot of Los Angeles in the 1980s.

de-bag *vb British* to remove (someone's) trousers. The phrase originated among 19th-century university students but quickly spread to schoolboys for whom the ritual humiliation of fellow pupils by de-bagging was a popular diversion up to the late 1960s at least. **Bags** was a 19th-century slang term for trousers which survived until fairly recently.

debs' delight *n British* an upper-class young man, especially one who might be considered an eligible partner or escort by parents (of debutantes), in spite of low intelligence. The phrase was used pejoratively and/or enviously and was popular in the 1960s. A more recent version is **pedigree chum**.

deck *vb* to knock (someone) to the ground. A variant of to floor.

deck *n* **1** a portion or package of illicit drugs, especially heroin. The term, from American addicts' jargon of the 1960s, spread to Britain and Australia where the meaning was sometimes amended to refer to an injection, or the amount (of heroin) necessary for an injection.

2 a skateboard or surfboard, in the jargon of aficionados.

deck up *vb* to prepare for injection, or to inject a drug, usually heroin. A phrase from the jargon of drug users and prisoners in the UK. The verb derives from the noun **deck**, meaning a quantity of a narcotic.

decorators *n pl British See* **have the decorators in**.

de-dyke *vb* to remove or conceal evidence of lesbianism. In British lesbian households of the 1980s, de-dyking generally preceded a visit by heterosexual parents.

deep sea diver *n* a £5 note, 'fiver'. A piece of London rhyming slang heard occasionally since about the mid-1970s.

deep six *vb American* to bury, dispose of. The verb form, which has been common in American speech since the 1950s, derives from the earlier noun form **the deep six**, an underworld euphemism for the grave. The ultimate origin is nautical; burials at sea have to be made in water that is more than six fathoms deep.
↳ *'I've got to exchange all this* [money]*!'*
↳ *'You can deep-six it, sir.'*
    (*M.A.S.H.*, US TV series, 1977).

def *adj* excellent, wonderful, the real thing. A late 1980s vogue term of approbation deriving from the language of **hip hop**. The word is a shortening of definitive or definite. The use of the word as the title of a BBC2 'youth slot' programme (*DEF II*) in 1988 may mark its apogee.
↳ *'This month's music selections are frightfully def, totally treach and all those other hip hop clichés.'*
    (*I-D* magazine, November 1987).

de facto *n Australian* a live-in lover, one's unmarried partner. This phrase is one Australian solution (since the 1970s) to the problem of finding an acceptable term to describe what the British judicial system calls a 'common-law spouse'.
↳ *'My de facto's out buying groceries.'*
    (Recorded, young woman, Melbourne, 1978).

de-frosted *adj American* heated, agitated. An adolescents' term, inspired by the opposite notion of **cool** or **chilled out**.
↳ *'Come on, don't get all de-frosted.'*

dekko *n British* a look, glance. A word that probably originated in the jargon of tramps, taken from the Romany word for look, *dik*, in the late 19th century. British soldiers overseas also encountered the Hindustani version *dekko*. The word is now less popular than in the 1950s but is still heard in the phrases **take** or **have a dekko (at)**. The word is not unknown but is rare in American slang, where it has been recorded as **'decko'**. *See also* **dick**.

Delhi belly *n* diarrhoea. Since the era of British colonialism this has been the South Asian equivalent of **gippy tummy**, **Montezuma's Revenge**, etc.

dementoid, demental *n, adj American* (a) crazy, demented (person). A high-school term of the 1980s that expresses contempt, grudging admiration or both. The word is also used adjectivally as in *'that was a totally dementoid movie'*.

demo *n* 1 a political demonstration.
2 a demonstration tape or record made by musicians in the hope of gaining work.
3 a demolition job or a demolition worker.

demon *n Australian* a detective. This probably originated in the simple abbreviation D, which then passed via 'd-man' to demon. The word is fairly rare; when it does occur it is often in the plural form.

dennis *n British* hashish or marihuana. The term is a shortened version of the rhyming slang '*Dennis Law*', meaning **draw**. The name of the footballer was evoked by adolescents at the end of the 1980s.

derk, durk *n British* a stupid person. Used by younger teenagers, the words are formed from or influenced by **dork, nerd, durr-brain**.

dero, derro *n Australian* a homeless person or tramp, a derelict. The term has been in use for about twenty years. It is also heard as a (fairly mild) insult among children and adolescents.

derro *n British* 1 an unfortunate, inferior or unpleasant person. A derivation from 'derelict', used either of vagrants or of someone pitied or disliked.
↳ *'And touching someone when you're dancing, Caris intimates, is the act of a derro, a flo-to-tin' yup, a deadbeat, a homebug and a commuter.'*
    (*Observer*, Section 5, 7 May 1989).
2 a **derry** (derelict building).

derry, deri *n British* a derelict building or similar location, used as a temporary shelter by tramps, etc.
↳ *'It's not a derry, guy, there are people living there.'*
    (Recorded, vagrant, Waterloo, London, 1988).

Desmond *n British* a lower second university degree, a 2/2 (two-two). This is a student's witticism playing on the name of the black South African community leader Bishop Desmond Tutu. The word was in vogue in 1986 and gave rise to a number of other joky euphemisms, such as **Douglas, Pattie, Taiwan, Richard**.
↳ *'We all expected Penny to get a James*

but she ended up with a Desmond.'
(*Evening Standard*, June 1988).

des. res. *n British* a 'desirable residence'. The spoken form of the abbreviation used in estate agents' advertisements (pronounced 'dezz-rezz') is usually used enviously, of a genuinely attractive home, or ironically of a squalid one.

destroyed *adj* completely intoxicated by alcohol or illicit drugs. A widespread colloquialism which has been particularly popular among middle-class speakers since the late 1960s. The word continues the tendency evidenced by usages such as **smashed**, **bombed**, **wrecked**, etc.

detox *n, vb* (to undertake) a course of withdrawal from 'hard' drugs or alcohol, detoxification, detoxify. A term from health workers' jargon which is now standard among drug users and patients.

deuce *n*

a two dollars or two pounds.

↳'*Just let me have a deuce till tomorrow.'*

b a two-year prison sentence.

↳'*He pulled a deuce in Club Fed.'*

devo *adj American* apparently 'robotic' or de-personalized. The name of the avant-garde late-1970s band (who presented themselves as near-automatons and semi-retards due to 'devolution') is now used to describe a 'somnambulistic', expressionless person or behaviour. **Stepford** is used in a similar context.

↳'*I don't know what her problem is but she is so devo.'*

↳'*Acting devo.'*

dex, dexie, dexo *n* a pill or capsule of Dexedrine, an amphetamine (**pep pill**) frequently prescribed and abused in the 1950s and 1960s. Yellow pills of Dexedrine (a trademark) were popular among English **mods** of the mid-1960s. Dexy's Midnight Runners, a phrase adopted as the name of a late 1970s white soul group, was an elaborate nickname for the drug.

Dezzy *n British* an alternative form of Desmond.

dialog(ue) *vb* to engage in conversation, particularly with intent to trick, seduce, etc.

diamond *adj British* first-rate, superb, admirable. A London working-class and underworld term, often heard in the appreciative phrase 'a diamond geezer'.

dib *n* a contribution, portion, amount of money. This word was in use in Britain in the late 19th century, but is now heard mainly in the USA, typically in children's street or playground games. The plural form was common in England until the late 1950s and survives especially in the expression 'to have dibs on something', to reserve or have first rights to.

dib *vb, n British* a partly-smoked cigarette saved for relighting later, or the act of extinguishing it. This term, which may originate in a dialect verb meaning to pinch or to stub, is used for instance by workmen, labourers and the armed forces.

dick *n* **1** penis. This use of the word has been widespread in the English-speaking world since the end of the 19th century. It is probably in origin an affectionate personification in the same way as **willie**, etc. This sense of the word is sometimes extended to mean sex in general, as in '*Suzy loves dick*'.

↳'*Not all women in pop are or ever have been, brainless bimbos lured into lurex by cynical rock business shitheads with one eye on their cheque books and the other on their dicks.'*
(*Ms London* magazine, 4 September 1989).

2 a fool (invariably male). Dick has this secondary sense in common with most slang terms for the male member, such as **prick**, **tool**, etc.

3 nothing at all. A vulgar emphatic more commonly heard in America, and in vogue since the mid-1970s. Its sense is roughly equivalent to the British **bugger-all**.

↳'*What do those gimps do all day?'*

↳'*They do dick.'*

4 a detective. Almost invariably in the phrase **private dick**. This Americanism, popularized in crime fiction, originated in underworld jargon as a corruption of the word detective itself. *See also* **dickless Tracy**.

dick *vb* **1** to have sex (with), penetrate. A predictable but rare term, generated from the noun sense of **dick**.

2 *British* to look at. A variation of the Romany *dik*, to look, from which **dekko** may be derived. This rare term is occasionally heard among tramps, street traders, etc. *See also* **dekko**.

3 to mess up, mess around (with). A variant of **dick around** or **dick up**.

↳*'She completely dicked the project.'*

dick around *vb* to mess around (with), behave in a disorganized or aimless way. The expression employs **dick** (penis) in the same way as **cock**, **prat** around, etc.

dickbrained *adj* stupid, extremely foolish. A term popular among young people in the 1980s. The adjective is American in origin and the sense of **dick** deriving from 'penis' may be reinforced by the German sense of 'thick'.

dickhead *n* a fool, idiot. An old, folksy Americanism which became a vogue term among British youth from around 1980. It may be applied to males or females. Abusive compound words ending in '-head' have proliferated since the end of the 1970s.

↳*'The outcome of being a dickhead is that I don't possess any Aretha Franklin singles and make do with compilations.'*
(John Peel quoted in *New Musical Express*, 7 February 1987).

dickless Tracy *n Australian* a policewoman. A humorous coinage playing on **dick** (penis) and Dick Tracy, the American comic-strip detective hero created by Chester Gould.

dick up *vb* to make a mess of. A variant of **cock up** occasionally heard in Britain and Australia.

dick-wad, dick-weed *n* a despicable, obnoxious or contemptible person. Teenage insults using the combining form **-wad** and its euphemistic version **-weed**.

dicky *adj British* shaky, insecure, faulty. A colloquialism whose origin is obscure but which dates back at least 150 years. Its original meaning of 'ill' survives in the modern phrase 'a dicky heart'.

↳*'Oh, my dicky ticker!'*
(Catchphrase from *'Allo 'Allo!*, British TV comedy series of the 1980s).

dicky bird *n British* a word. A piece of London rhyming slang which has become a widespread colloquialism, especially in the phrase 'not a dicky bird'. Unlike most modern examples of rhyming

slang, it is invariably used in full, presumably to avoid confusion with 'dickie' and **dick**.

dicky dirt *n British* a shirt. A piece of cockney rhyming slang which was obsolescent by the early 1970s but was resuscitated and given wider currency in London by the opening of a chain of cut-price clothing stores under the same name.

did *n British* a form of **didicoi**.

diddle *vb* **1** *British* to cheat. A common colloquialism recorded since the early 1800s. In Old English 'dydrian' meant to deceive or delude; Jeremy Diddler was a fictional swindler (in the 1803 farce *Raising the Wind* by James Kenney).

↳*'Comedian Ken Dodd insisted on cash for shows to diddle the taxman, his former agent told a jury yesterday.'*
(*Daily Mirror*, 5 July 1989).

2 a to have sex with. This sense probably derives from a nursery sense of diddle meaning fiddle with or agitate (*see* **diddle 2b**).

b to sexually stimulate (a woman) with the fingers. (In Middle English 'dideren' meant to quiver.)

diddlo, didlo *adj British* crazy, silly or unhinged, 'daft'. An inoffensive Londoners' word popularized by the ITV series *Minder* from the late 1970s.

↳*'Right bunch of diddlos, this lot!'*
(*Minder*, British TV series, 1986).

diddly(squat) *n American* nothing at all, or something very insignificant, petty or small. Diddly is a nursery term akin to tiddly. The word has been used by adults, alone or in conjunction with other nursery terms (**squat**, **shit**, 'whoop', 'doo', etc.) to express dismissive contempt. A variant form is **doody** or **doodly (squat)**.

diddly-dum *adj British* perfect, fine. A term used typically by students in the 1970s and 1980s, usually in phrases such as *'everything's (just) diddly-dum'*. The phrase resembles other mock-nursery inventions such as **dinky-di** and **fair dinkum**.

diddy *n British* **1** a fool. A lighthearted term of abuse, heard particularly in Scotland and the north of England.

↳*'You're a genius! How much did he promise?'*
'Nothing.'

'You're a diddy!'
(*City Lights*, British TV series, 1989).

2 a **didicoi**.

diddy *adj British* small, cute and appealing. A variant of **diddly**, popularized by the Liverpool comedian, Ken Dodd.

didicoi, diddicoy, diddyguy, did *n British* a gypsy or a half-gypsy. The word derives from the Romany *didakeis*, meaning the offspring of a marriage between a full-blooded gypsy and an outsider. The word, which can be spelt in many ways, is often used in country districts to denote any type of gypsy or traveller.

✥*'There was this didicoi used to go down our snooker club – couldn't sign his own name but he always had a roll of money on him.'*
(Recorded, carpet fitter, London, 1989).

diesel (dyke) *n* a lesbian who behaves aggressively and/or who is of rough masculine appearance or heavy build. The word, which is pejorative and generally used by men, carries overtones of engineers, engines, trucks and other **butch** associations and perhaps also refers to the overalls, dungarees, etc. worn by some lesbians. The term originated in the USA but was heard in Britain in the 1980s as a pejorative term and also as a simple descriptive phrase used by lesbians themselves.

dig *vb* to understand, appreciate or enjoy. A word from the slang of American swing and jazz musicians which was adopted by the beat generation and thence by teenagers all over the English-speaking world. It is now almost always used ironically or facetiously (except in the question form, *'you dig?'*). The ultimate origin is perhaps a metaphorical or religious sense of dig (into), meaning to apply oneself to (a task).

✥*'The Seventies were not a decade in which a young artist could kid himself his creative idealism could best be fulfilled grovelling in a muddy field digging Hendrix through a bad acid haze.'*
(*Platinum Logic*, Tony Parsons, 1981).

digger *n Australian* an Australian. The word was used by gold prospectors in the latter half of the 19th century to address or describe one another. It was adopted by British, Canadian and American servicemen in the First World War.

Aussie has largely replaced digger since the 1960s.

digs *n British* excitement, thrills. A more recent synonym for **kicks**, used by adolescents during the later 1990s.

dike *n* a variant spelling of **dyke**.

dilbert *n British* a foolish person. A teenage term of mild abuse from the late 1980s, it is probably a blend of **dill** and the (supposedly comical) Christian names Gilbert or Herbert.

✥*'No I'm not – and definitely not with a dilbert like you.'*
(Recorded, schoolgirl, London, 1989).

dildo *n* **1** an artificial penis. The word is approximately 200 years old and probably originates in *diletto*, Italian for (a) delight or darling. Alternatively the term may simply be an invention.

2 a fool, an offensively stupid person. This sense of the word, popular among teenagers since the mid-1970s, may be an embellishment of **dill** as much as a derivative of **dildo 1**.

✥*'Oh, come on, he's such a dildo!'*
(Recorded, schoolboy, London, 1988).

dill *n* fool, idiot, silly person. A word which has been recorded in Australia and the USA since at least the early 1950s, and in Britain since the mid-1970s when it was popular among schoolchildren. The word may be a shortening of dill pickle (gherkins may also be the source of **wally**, used to describe a fool), or of **dilly**.

dillberries, dilberries *n pl* a variant of **dingleberries**.

dilly *n* **1** something remarkable, impressive or outstanding. Typically used in an admiring phrase such as 'that's a dilly!' The word may be an invention, a corruption of 'delight(ful)' or a survival of a lost dialect word.

2 a fool. Possibly influenced by dull/silly, this term is most commonly heard in Australia.

dimbo, dimmo *n* an unintelligent or dull-witted person. These embellishments of dim (also influenced by dumb, **dumbo** and **bimbo**) have been favourite words with British schoolchildren since the late 1970s.

✥*'You little dimbo, you've got no idea have you?'*
(*On Approval*, British TV play, February 1989).

✎'*He* [Bruce Springsteen] *is just dead popular with a lot of dimmos because of the unchallenging nature of what he does.*'
(Alexei Sayle, *Great Bus Journeys of the World*, 1988).

dim bulb *n American* a dimwit or dullard. The phrase evokes a low-wattage light bulb.

dime (someone) *vb American* to inform on someone, betray to the police. A back-formation from **dime dropper**, used especially by prison inmates.

dime dropper *n American* an informer. An underworld phrase derived from the dime (ten cents) dropped into a payphone when calling the police.

dimp *n, vb British* a cigarette end which can be retrieved, typically from the street, and relit. The word, now part of the language of tramps, is also heard as a verb meaning to extinguish (for later smoking). The term seems to be an invention, possibly influenced by crimp and damp.

dimstick *n British* a stupid person. The word, used by younger teenagers in the 1990s, is a blend of **dimbo** and **dip-** or **bam-stick**.

din-dins *n* dinner or another meal, food. A nursery word which like many others ('choo-choo', **gee-gee**, **wee-wee**, etc.) is used facetiously by teenagers and adults. The conversion of dinner into din-din is by a familiar process known as reduplication.

ding *n Australian* an Italian person or person of Italian descent. The word, of obscure origin and usually pejorative, was also used in the 1940s and 50s to refer to Greeks.

ding *vb* 1 to hit.
2 to single out for a reprimand, rejection or for an onerous duty. This use of the word occurs in institutional life in both Britain and America, but its origin is obscure.
✎'*They dinged me.*'
✎'*He was dinged.*'

dingaling, ding-a-ling *n* 1 an eccentric, crazy or foolish person. A word which originated in the USA and was enthusiastically adopted by schoolchildren in Britain in the late 1960s.

2 penis. This obscure nursery word was popularized by Chuck Berry's hit song of 1972, 'My Ding-a-Ling'.

dingbat *n* 1 an eccentric, crazy or foolish person. Originally this was an Australian word, probably derived from 'dingbats' as an adjective (an embellishment of the colloquial 'bats'). The word is now popular in Britain and the USA.
✎'*In fact, editing and voice-over combine to ensure that the man never looks a real dingbat.*'
(*Independent*, 23 December 1988).
2 *Australian* a Chinese person.
3 a any unnamed or unnameable thing. This mainly American sense is influenced by the Dutch and German *Ding*: thing.
b a typographical symbol, printers' device. A specialized use of the previous sense.

dingdong *n* 1 a a noisy to-and-fro shouting match or fight; from the image of bells clashing or being struck.
b a rowdy party. This sense is probably British in origin; ding-dong has been working-class London rhyming slang since the turn of the century for 'sing-song' and hence musical gathering and party.
✎'*Let's have a Ding-Dong.*'
(Title of rock and roll record by American group Freddie Bell and the Bell-Boys, 1958).
2 a fool or eccentric person. A variant of **dingaling**.
3 penis. A nursery word also used facetiously by adults.

dingleberry *n* 1 a piece of dung or excrement clinging to hair or wool around the anus. This originally rural notion (applied to sheep and by extension to humans) has curiously given rise to a very large number of colourful terms throughout the English-speaking world. Others are **dangleberries**, **dillberries**, **clinkers**, **winnets** and **wittens**, **bum tags**, **chuffnuts**, etc.
2 a crazy or eccentric person, a fool. Most commonly heard among American high-school and college students; it is inspired by the previous sense (although users may be unaware of the fact).

dingo *n British* a stupid person. This schoolchildren's word of the 1990s is an alteration of **dimbo**.

dingo's breakfast *n Australian* a

piss and a look around. A humorous coinage on the lines of **Mexican breakfast** or 'pelican's breakfast'.

dingus *n* a thing, an obscure or un-named object. Originally a South African and American version of 'thingy' or 'thingummy', it derives from the Dutch *ding*, meaning thing.

dingy *adj American* eccentric, crazy, foolish. The term, rhyming with 'ring', is probably a back-formation from **ding-a-ling**.

dink *n* 1 a silly person, fool or eccentric. The word has been used especially by children and young people in both Britain and America, although possibly coined separately in each.
2 **a** South-East Asian person. The racist term, probably an arbitrary alteration of **chink**, has been applied in Australia to people of Chinese origin and in the US to Japanese and Vietnamese.
3 *American also* **dinky** one of a childless **yuppie** couple; an acronym for 'double (or dual) income, no kids', coined in New York in 1986. Dink is an example of the American use of acronyms to describe social sub-groups. This tendency, which produced **WASP**, **JAP** and later **yuppies** in the 1970s, became a vogue among New Yorkers in the mid-1980s. In spite of enthusiastic use by some journalists and imitation by their London counterparts, this term, like **droppie**, **guppy**, etc. has achieved only limited currency.
↳*'Take Dink, for instance, which I always thought meant idiot. The other day I heard a girl refer to a yuppie couple as "dinks".'*
(*Evening Standard*, 22 January 1987).
4 *American* **a** a penis. A fairly rare teenage term.
b nothing at all. In this sense the equivalent of **dick**.

dinkum *adj Australian See* **fair dinkum**.

dinky *n* 1 *British* a car, particularly a large, impressive car. Said self-deprecatingly or admiringly by nouveau-riche working-class speakers and **Sloane Rangers**. Dinky Toys were a brand of miniature model cars popular among children in the 1950s and early 1960s.
2 a **dink** (*see* **dink 3**).
↳*'I have had my year of being a dinky (double income, no kids) and I lost all my friends of any worth to it.'*

(Richard Jobson, *The Sunday Times*, 9 July 1989).

dinky-di *n*
a *Australian* the real thing (pronounced 'dinkee-die'). Perhaps an embellishment of **fair dinkum**.
b *British* fine, perfect (pronounced 'dinkee-dee'; the spelling is arbitrary). A pseudo-nursery term like **diddly-dum**, probably invented by students.
↳*'Don't worry, everything's dinky-di.'*

dip *n* 1 a fool. This word, first heard in the 1970s, is either a back-formation from **dippy** or a short form of **dipstick** or **dipshit**.
↳*'All those people out there, they're just complete dips.'*
(Recorded, American teenager, London, 1988).
2 *also* **dipster** a pickpocket. A Victorian term, still in police and underworld use.
3 *British* an act of sex. The vulgarism usually refers to male sexual activity and was used for example by the stand-up comedian Frank Skinner in stage monologues in 1992. It is derived from the phrase **dip one's wick**.

dip (out) *vb American* to depart, leave. A vogue term from black street slang of the 1990s. The variant form '*do the dip*' has also been recorded. A variety of euphemisms (like its contemporaries **bail**, **book**, **jam** and **jet**) for 'run away' are essential to the argot of gang members and their playground imitators.

dip one's/the wick *vb* (of a man) to have sex. A vulgar euphemism which is about a century old. Wick is either a shortening of the rhyming slang **Hampton Wick**: **prick**, or a straightforward metaphor from candle-wick. Originally British, the term is now used, albeit less commonly, in the USA and Australia.

dip out *vb Australian* to fail.

dipping *n* picking pockets. The term has been in use since the middle of the 19th century.

dippy *adj* eccentric, silly, or slightly deranged; daft. A British term now in use throughout the English-speaking world. It seems to be an invented word rather than a derivation.

dipshit *n* a fool. This vulgarism is sometimes said to be a euphemism for male homosexual or male member (compare **dung-puncher**, etc.) but may simply be an elaboration of **dip**.

dipso *n* an alcoholic or drunkard. A shortening of the term dipsomaniac (from the Greek *dipsa*, thirst).

dipstick *n* a fool. The word is probably a euphemism for **dipshit**, but with less unpleasant overtones. It has been popularized by television series and films in both Britain and the USA since the early 1980s and is a favourite with teenagers.

dipsy *n, adj American* 1 (an) alcoholic or drunk. In this sense the word is based on dipsomaniac (*see also* **dipso**) and/or 'tipsy'.

2 (a) foolish person.

dirtbag, dirtball *n American* a despicable person. These terms of abuse, being strong but not obscene, are frequently heard in films and TV programmes, such as the police series *Hill Street Blues*.

✧*'All right dirtbags, I've had enough.'*
(Psychopath in *Beer*, US film, 1985).

dirty *adj* 1 **a** possessing or containing illicit drugs, a jargon term used by police, customs officers and drug users.

✧*'His suitcase came through dirty.'*

b *British* unsafe, illicit, **hot**. This general sense is employed typically by criminals and the police.

2 *Australian* annoyed, resentful. In this sense the word is often used in the phrase 'to be dirty on (someone)'.

dirty old man *n See* D.O.M.

disco-biscuits *n British* tablets of ecstasy. The nickname was in use from 1990, and provided the title for an anthology of drug-related writing published in London in 1997.

discombobulated *adj* confused, discomfited or distracted. An invented pseudo-latinate verb, normally heard in the adjective form. It dates from the 19th century when such portmanteau words were popular.

✧*'I've been feeling discombobulated since we got back.'*

discuss Uganda *vb British* to have sex. A euphemism coined in the 1970s by the British satirical magazine *Private Eye*. It has become one of the magazine's long-

running jokes and is said to stem from a party at which a female journalist was alleged to have explained an upstairs sexual encounter by saying *'We were discussing Uganda'*. (Idi Amin's régime was in the news at the time.) The term Ugandan Affairs is also derived from this source.

disgusto *n, adj* (a) repellent (thing or person). A favourite term of **JAPs** and **Valley Girls** among others, this Americanism has been adopted, or separately coined, by British and Australian schoolchildren.

✧*'Oh look at all the disgustos* [baby crabs]*! We don't have them by Lake Michigan.'*
(Recorded, American Jewish girl, Brittany, 1982).

dish *n* 1 **a** a very attractive woman. This appreciative term (though offensive to most modern women) is one of many that liken a woman to a tasty snack or meal. Unlike **tart** or **crumpet**, for example, dish was introduced, or perhaps reintroduced (the metaphor was not unknown in earlier times) into Britain from the USA in the 1930s.

b a very attractive man. Since the mid-1960s the word has also been used of men by women and this usage may now be more common than the original.

✧*'And those photographs of Mustapha – he was so unattractive, and because you'd had him they said "what a dish".'*
(Kenneth Halliwell, quoted in Joe Orton's diary, 2 May 1967).

2 *American* gossip. From the phrase **dish the dirt**.

✧*'Oh my, this is prime dish. I can't wait to tell the girls.'*
(*Cheers*, US TV comedy series, 1989).

dish *vb* to defeat, destroy or ruin. The original sense of this British term of the 18th century was to swindle, deceive or make a fool of. The image behind the expression was probably that of 'serving up' something (or someone) that has been well and truly 'processed', exploited, etc.

dish the dirt *vb American* to spread scandalous or malicious gossip. 'Dish' here is, of course, dish up in the sense of serve to an eager audience.

dishy *adj* very attractive, handsome or beautiful. The adjective form of **dish** is currently more often used by women than men and is so common in Britain as to be a colloquialism rather than true slang.

diss *vb* to scorn, snub, belittle. This vogue word of the late 1980s entered adolescent speech via the hip-hop and **rap** sub-cultures originating in the USA. A typical 'clipping', like **def**, **treach**, etc., it is based on the verbs dismiss, disapprove or disrespect [sic] (perhaps influenced by **dish**).

ditsy, ditzy *adj* silly, eccentric, twee, or frivolous. An invented term, popular especially in the USA, since the mid-1970s. The word which is obviously influenced by dizzy is generally applied to females.

ditz *n* a silly, eccentric and/or frivolous person, someone who is **ditzy**. An Americanism picked up by some British speakers in the mid-1980s.

div *n British* a person who is odd, stupid, weak or deviant in some way. This shortening of **divvy** has become popular among young people of all classes in the 1980s. Before that it was part of the lexicon of criminals, tramps, street-traders and workmen.

✎'*Him, he's a bit of a div, isn't he?*'
(Recorded, student, London University, 1986).

dive *n See* **take a dive**.

divebombing *n British* **1** attacking something with spray paints in order to cover it with graffiti. From the late 1970s the term has been used by young graffiti artists, or vandals.
2 picking up cigarette ends from the street (to relight and smoke). A term used by vagrants in the 1980s.

diving *n American* **1** picking pockets. An underworld term which is the equivalent of the British **dipping**.
2 *See* **pearl-diver**.

divot *n American* a toupée, or hairpiece. The standard word denoting a clod of earth and grass dug out by a golfing stroke has become part of the adolescent lexicon of mockery (like its UK counterparts **syrup**, **irish**, etc.). Divot itself is an old Scottish word of unknown origin.

divvy *adj British* odd, stupid, deviant, weak or pathetic. This term, of uncertain origin, has existed in the vocabulary of society's 'marginals' since at least the late

1950s (it is unlikely to derive from deviant, but may be related to daft or daffy, or even by a tortuous etymology from 'divine' in the sense of possessed). It has recently been revived as a vogue term by schoolchildren, although the short noun form **div** is more common. (Divvy itself has occasionally been recorded as a noun.)

✎'*Who's your friend with the glasses? 'E looks a bit divvy.*'
(Recorded, street-gang member, London, 1967).

diz *n American* a foolish, eccentric or disoriented individual. The term in usage among US teenagers in the 1990s is probably a variant form of **ditz** or may be based upon 'dizzy'.

d.k. *vb American* to snub someone or renege on something, to feign ignorance of someone or something. The letters (pronounced 'dee-kay') are an acronym of **don't know**.

✎'*He d.k.'d me.*'
(*Wall Street*, US film, 1988).

d.m.'s *n pl British* 'Doc Marten's' footwear. An abbreviation of the trademark name of the boots worn by skinheads in preference to **bovver boots** in the 1970s and by **punks** and other youth groups. From the late 1980s, D.M.s were worn by young women as part of conventional dress and had lost much of their youth-group connotations. The term is used to refer to a style of footwear rather than solely to the authentic trademarked item.

do *vb* **1** to have sex with. More a shorthand vulgarism than an evasive euphemism, the term was widely used in the USA from the late 1960s and in the 1990s is popular among adolescents in Britain.

✎'*Debbie does Dallas*'
(Title of 1970s US porno film).

✎'*Is she really doing that dreamboat in the sixth form?*'
(*Just Seventeen* magazine, August 1996).

2 to kill. A term used by criminals and street gang members and their fictional counterparts.

✎'*He didn't say a goddam word, he just went and did her.*'

do *n American* a hairstyle. This shortened form of hairdo originated in black slang.

do, doo *n* excrement. A nursery word used all over the English-speaking world, although in Britain the plural form **dos** is probably more common. The word in this sense is probably pre-World War II and derives from the Victorian notion of doing or performing one's bodily functions (dutifully).

do (drugs) *vb* to take drugs. The term can apply to single instances or to habitual use. Originally an Americanism, it was adopted by British speakers in the **hippy** era.

↳'*Well the one* [trip] *that stopped me from doing acid forever was when I dropped seven tabs.*'
(Zodiac Mindwarp, *I-D* magazine, November 1987).

D.O.A. *adj* unconscious, inert. A facetious use of the American police and hospital jargon 'dead on arrival' to mean 'dead to the world', particularly after taking drugs or alcohol.

do a Bertie *vb British* to turn Queen's Evidence, to inform on one's accomplices. A fairly rare piece of criminal jargon of uncertain origin. It is possibly from the Edwardian era, when turning King's Evidence would have been joining 'Bertie's' side, and seems to have existed before the days of Bertie Smalls, a 1970s criminal supergrass (high-level informer).

do-able *adj American* sexually attractive. This term, used to categorize a potential partner, was popular among female Californian high-school students in the 1990s and was featured in the 1994 US film *Clueless*.

↳'*There's no getting round the style question. If you want to be "do-able" … you cannot afford to dress "random".*'
(*Sunday Times Style Magazine*, 22 October 1995).

do a duck *vb British* to escape, conceal oneself. A term that may originate from the colloquialism 'ducking and diving' or simply 'ducking out of sight', was used by London criminals, including Johnny Bradbury, a member of the Richardson gang of 1960s notoriety.

do a job on (someone) *vb* to deceive, thoroughly overwhelm, devastate. Originally an Americanism, this unspecific phrase is now in fairly widespread use in Britain and Australia.

do a number on (someone) *vb* to cheat, frustrate, defeat, demoralize. Like the previous phrase, this expression, the precise meaning of which depends on its context, originated in the USA and is now used elsewhere.

↳'*A talk that made it clear that Ari intended "to do a number on Bolker, he wanted to hurt the fellow, not do him in, but certainly to harm him in some way".*'
(Nigel Dempster, writing in *The Sunday Times*, 24 September 1989).

do a runner *vb British* to escape, run away or disappear. A phrase from semi-criminal and subsequent working-class usage which has become a generally popular term since the early 1980s. It originally referred specifically to the practice of leaving a restaurant, bar, etc. without paying.

↳'*I decided to "do a runner", i.e. to leg it out of the restaurant without paying the bill.*'
(*Great Bus Journeys of the World*, Alexei Sayle, 1988).

do a train (on someone) *vb British* to have serial sexual intercourse (with one partner). A 1980s alternative to **gang bang** with the implication that the sexual partner is consenting.

dob, dob in, dob on *vb Australian* to inform (on someone), tell tales. A schoolchildren's term since the late 1970s which was previously, and still is, part of underworld terminology. Dob was a British dialect word meaning something between drop and lob (it survives in the noun form in colloquial expressions such as 'a dob of butter'). Dob in has been introduced to British audiences by Australian soap operas of the 1980s.

↳'*I tell you what you do, dob her in to the governor.*'
(*Prisoner, Cell Block H*, Australian TV series, 1982).

dock asthma *n British* gasps of (usually feigned) surprise and disbelief by prisoners in the dock. A part of police and prison jargon since at least the 1950s.

docker *n British* a partly smoked cigarette, put out for later relighting. This word, which is more common in the north of England than elsewhere, originates in dock: to cut short, or the related archaic use of dock, meaning the solid part of an animal tail.

Doctor Feelgood *n American* a doctor or other person who freely prescribes pleasurable drugs. The name has been used in several blues and soul songs since World War II, but probably predates them as a black underworld term, where it had a more generalized meaning of someone who could provide euphoria or comfort. It was later applied as a nickname, for example to Dr Max Jacobson, physician to President Kennedy, famous for his disbursement of amphetamines to New York high society.

doctors and nurses *n* sexual activity or sex play. To **play (at) doctors and nurses** is a humorous euphemism, sometimes used by adults, deriving from the children's game which often involves sexual experimentation.

dodgy *adj British*
a doubtful, suspect. A common term in British English and nowadays hardly slang. It arose in the later 19th century and derives from the sense of dodge as an artful or risky ruse. In the 1960s 'dodgy!' was the counterpart of 'swinging!' in the catchphrases of TV compere Norman Vaughan.
b stolen, illegal. A narrower sense of **dodgy a**, common since the 1960s in such euphemisms as **dodgy gear/merchandise**.

dodgy job, dodgy one *n British*
a criminal case or arrest which is difficult to substantiate, in police jargon. An expression employing the colloquialism **dodgy** in its sense of both uncertain and illicit.

↳'*A dodgy job is a case in which the circumstantial evidence is slight or the arrest has been provoked by the behaviour of the suspect …rather than by evidence of some other substantive offence.*'
(*Inside the British Police*, Simon Holdaway, 1985).

doer *n American* a perpetrator of a crime, suspected criminal. The term, a synonym of **perp**, is probably a shortening of wrongdoer in police jargon.

dog *n* **1 a** an ugly, unpleasant or unattractive woman or girl. This sense of the word was in common use in the USA from the 1950s. It was adopted by British speakers in the mid-1970s.

b *American* something unpleasant or worthless. Expressions in which dog expresses distaste or contempt are almost all American in origin, presumably reflecting the cliché that the British are a nation of dog lovers. Nevertheless there are occasional instances of this sense in British English.

↳'*This car's a dog!*'

c a company or share that performs badly on the stock exchange, a worthless piece of stock (these are also known as **bow-wow** stocks).

2 *British* a wig, toupee. The word usually implies a ragged, ill-fitting or generally unconvincing hairpiece. It has been in use among teenagers at least since the early 1970s.

3 a rogue, (likeable) reprobate. A 19th-century usage, now a colloquialism usually surviving in the form **(you) old dog!**

4 a **dog-end**.

5 *See* **dogs**.

dog *vb American* to abandon, reject, get rid of. The word in this sense has been used by teenagers and college students since the late 1980s.

↳'*Dog the dorm rules now!*'
(*A Different World*, American TV series, 1987).

dog (and bone) *n British* telephone. An example of rhyming slang which is still used today. It is usually used of the appliance rather than the action.

↳'*Get on the dog to him and find out when he's coming.*'

dog (it) *vb British* to play truant. The term is heard particularly in the Scottish Lowlands and the north of England.

dog-and-boned *adj British*
stoned. A cannabis smoker's term from the 1960s and early 1970s, now heard in the form **doggo**.

dog (someone) around *vb American*
a to pester. An expression inspired by the same images as to 'dog someone's heels'.
b to behave badly, cruelly, irresponsibly or unfaithfully, especially to one's partner. This Americanism seems to have its origin in black street talk of the late 1950s, perhaps inspired by the notion of an errant or 'dirty dog'.

dog-ass *adj American* worthless, inferior, bad. A vulgarism in use for in-

stance among military personnel and college students since the 1950s.

dog-botherer *n British* a humorous and meaningless term of abuse, inspired by **god-botherer**, but without connotations of religious zeal, bestiality or indeed specific wrong-doing.

dog-box *n British* a mess, confused situation. An item of middle-class family slang heard in the 1990s.

dog-end *n British* a cigarette end. The word usually describes a stubbed-out butt, rather than a partly-smoked cigarette put aside for later relighting (see **dimp** and **docker**). It has been in use since at least World War II.

dog-esse *n American* an obnoxious and/or unattractive woman. A supposedly humorous synonym for **bitch**.

dogface *n American* a common soldier, infantry private in the US army. A term from World War II. It is presumably derived from a hangdog or cowed expression.

(all) dogged-up *adj* dressed smartly or extravagantly. The term is probably inspired by 'decked out' or 'dolled up', or by the expression **dog's dinner**.

↳*'I don't want to have to get all dogged-up just to go out to dinner.'*

dogger *n British* a truant. The term is heard particularly in the Scottish Lowlands and the north of England, and derives from the earlier verb to **dog (it)**.

doggett *vb British* to scrounge. An arcane piece of London rhyming slang. Thomas Doggett, an actor, on the occasion of George I's accession in 1715, endowed a prize for an annual race for Thames watermen between London Bridge and Chelsea. The prize for the race, which is still rowed, is a coat and badge, hence 'Doggett's Coat and Badge': cadge. The word is also used as a noun to mean a scrounger.

↳*'He's meeting me at the Hong Kong. He's only trying to doggett a Chinese* [meal].'
(Recorded, pensioner, Bristol, 1989).

doggie-do/dos *n*

a dog excrement.

b something worthless and/or repellent. Both meanings are used, generally face-

tiously, among adults, though the term originated as a nursery word.

doggie-fashion, doggy-fashion *adv* (sexual intercourse) involving penetration from the rear.

↳*'They like to do it doggy-fashion.'*

doggo *adj* **1** *American* worthless, inferior, bad. A variation of **dog-ass**.

2 *British* intoxicated by marihuana. This unusual term derives from a now obsolete piece of rhyming slang **dog-and-boned**: **stoned**, perhaps reinforced by the immobility and furtiveness implied in the colloquial phrase to 'lie doggo'.

dog it *vb American* to perform badly, fail to do one's best. A campus and high-school expression from the 1970s.

↳*'If you dog it again this time, you're off the team.'*

dog out *vb American* to get (**all**) **dogged up**.

dogs *n pl* **1 a** feet. Of obscure origin, this usage has persisted in British and American usage at least since World War II. It usually implies tired, sore feet.

↳*'Ooh, that feels better – my dogs are barking today!'*
(*Planes, Trains and Automobiles*, US film, 1987).

b slippers, shoes or boots.

c *American* trainers. An item of black street talk that was included in so-called **Ebonics**, recognized as a legitimate language variety by school officials in Oakland, California, in late 1996.

2 the dogs *British* greyhounds or greyhound racing.

the dog's bollocks *n British* a superlative thing, situation, etc. This widespread vulgarism was given wider currency from its use in *Viz* magazine from the early 1990s, and its first broadcast use in the TV comedy series, *Hale and Pace*, in 1997.

dog's breakfast *n* a mess, confused mixture. From the image of a mishmash of unappetizing scraps. The expression (compare the roughly contemporaneous **dog's dinner**) is commonly applied to a misconceived or botched plan or display. The phrase dates from the 1930s.

↳*'My god, he made a real dog's breakfast of that presentation.'*
(Recorded, publisher, London, 1986).

dog's breath, dogsbreath *n*

a repellent, contemptible or unpleasant person. A term of abuse popular in the 1980s, probably because it is colourful without being obscene; another factor in its spread is its usage in TV shows, particularly by the cult character Mick Belker in the US TV police series *Hill Street Blues*. It originated in American teen usage in the late 1970s (*see* **dog**). This term is sometimes heard as **dogbreath**.

dog's dinner *n*

a an extravagant display, especially a vulgar, misguided or unsuccessful attempt at smartness. The expression, which dates from the late 1920s, usually forms part of a phrase such as 'all done up like a dog's dinner'.

b a mess. In this negative sense **dog's breakfast** is currently more fashionable.

do-hickey *n American*

a an unspecified thing, thingummy.

b a spot, pimple or skin blemish. **Hickey** alone is a common teenage term for spot or lovebite; the prefix is an embellishment.

c penis. A children's term that is probably a specific application of **do-hickey a**.

doink *vb* 1 to hit.

2 to have sex. The term is a variant form of **bonk** and **boink**.

do it *vb* to have sex. An evasive or coy euphemism used by children, those too embarrassed to be more explicit, or, often, facetiously by adults.

do-it fluid *n American* alcoholic

liquor. An item of black street talk which was included in so-called **Ebonics**, recognized as a legitimate language variety by school officials in Oakland, California, in late 1996.

dole-bludger *n Australian* a person

who claims unemployment pay which they are not entitled to, a 'dole scrounger' (*see* **bludger**). This common term is sometimes extended to encompass any idle or shiftless person.

> '*Newspapers are always whingeing about the dole bludgers.*'
> (*Girls Night Out*, Kathy Lette, 1989).

doley, dolie *n Australian* someone

who is on the dole (drawing unemployment pay).

doll *n* woman. A fairly dated Ameri-

canism adopted into British working-class usage in the 1950s and again in the 1970s, since when it may also be used by women of men. The word has condescending or proprietorial overtones when used by teenagers.

dollar *n British* five shillings (in pre-

1971 non-decimal British currency). This usage derives from the fact that the former five-shilling coin resembled a silver dollar and that at various times in the 20th century the rate of exchange of the US dollar stood at five shillings (25 pence after decimalization).

doll city *n American*

a a beautiful person (of either sex but implying idealized cuteness, femininity or passivity).

> '*Wow check the new boy out – doll city!*'

b a pleasant situation or attractive idea. The expression is often an exclamation of approval.

> '*Paris in the fall – doll city!*'

Both instances of the phrase typically occur in adolescent speech.

dollface *n American* an attractive or

cute person. A term of affection used especially by women to men.

dolls *n pl American* pills of ampheta-

mine or barbiturate drugs. A term adopted by middle-class users of (often prescribed) drugs. The word was popularized (and probably invented) by the author Jacqueline Susann in her sensationalist novel *The Valley of the Dolls* in 1965. The inspiration for the term is presumably the fact that the pills and capsules are colourful and comforting.

dolly *adj British* excellent, attractive,

cute. A vogue word of the mid-1960s, enshrined in the title of Adam Diment's fashionable novel *The Dolly Dolly Spy*. The word passed from **camp** theatrical and homosexual use to general currency for a year or so. It survives in middle-class speech, as an ironic or scathing synonym for twee.

dolly bird *n British* an attractive girl.

This expression, which would now appear hopelessly dated and offensive to many women, briefly epitomized the ideal gamine of the mid- to late 1960s. The word was used only fleetingly by the fashionable young themselves before becoming a journalistic cliché.

dolly-mixtures *n pl British* pictures. Often used by criminals and police to describe mugshots, crime-scene photographs, etc., the rhyming slang refers to sweets popular among children since the 1950s. As an example of the jargon of cat burglars the phrase was cited in *FHM* magazine in April 1996.

D.O.M. *n* a 'dirty old man'. A middle-class and **Sloane Ranger** version of the colloquial expression. D.O.M. is applied, usually by females, to anyone male and lecherous regardless of age.

do me something! *exclamation British* a phrase used by teenage gangs as a provocation or invitation to fight. A synonym is **what to go**? Both phrases are often followed by **then?!**. The term was recorded in use among north London schoolboys in 1993 and 1994.

don *adj* excellent, fashionable, admirable. A vogue term of approbation, which originated in American usage in the early 1990s and by 1995 had been adopted for fashionable speech by British and Australian adolescents. It may derive from **the Don** in the sense of a powerful or exceptional individual.

don, the Don *n British*
a a pre-eminent, successful or admirable person.
b an excellent thing, the best.
Both senses of the word derive from the use of the word to refer to a criminal boss, originally from the title of a Spanish gentleman.

don *vb British* to steal, defraud. In this sense the term was used by London schoolchildren in the early 1990s. Its derivation is uncertain. One user defined it as 'a rip-off' and claimed it as a deformation of **con**.

donah *n* a girl. A 19th-century usage derived via tramps, showmen, market traders and petty criminals from Italian and Spanish (*donna*, *doña*, meaning lady). The word had virtually died out in British English by the 1950s, but was still in use among street-gang members in the USA, and more generally in Australia.

Donald Duck, Donald *n* a **fuck**. A piece of rhyming slang, based on the cartoon character, that is heard in Australian and British English.

dong, donger *n* 1 penis. This word is common in current Australian English but is also heard in Britain and North America. Its origin is unclear but it resembles synonyms such as **whang**, **schlong**, etc. Unlike most similar terms its use has not been extended to mean a fool. This hearty, brusque word is usually used by males.
2 a blow, strike, from the verb form.

donging *n British* living outside society in makeshift shelters, teepees, trees, etc. The term is a back-formation from the 'Dongas Tribe' of environmental protesters who came to prominence in the summer of 1994.

donk *n Australian* 1 a car engine. This is probably a shortening of donkey, which the late Eric Partridge recorded as being in use in British navy jargon for a ship's engine. The term 'donkey engine' is often used for small, portable or auxiliary engines such as an outboard motor or miniature shunting locomotive.
2 a foolish person.

donnybrook *n* a brawl, free-for-all. Donnybrook Fair held near Dublin was often the scene of uproarious behaviour.

doob *n* 1 *British* an amphetamine pill. The singular form of the more common **doobs**.
2 penis. This rare usage is either an invention or a shortening of **doobry**.

doobie, dooby *n* 1 *American* a marihuana cigarette, a **joint**.
2 *British* a stupid or foolish person. The term is heard particularly in the Scottish Lowlands and the north of England.

doobry *n British* 1 an unspecified thing, thingummy, or a person whose name is forgotten or unknown. This invented word has existed at least since the 1950s.
2 an amphetamine tablet, or other pill. This is probably a narrowing of the preceding sense and was popular among the **mods** of the 1960s, although the plural **doobs** was the more common alternative. Doobry in this drug-related sense has also been derived from **double-blues**, a particular type of **pep pill**.

doobs *n pl British* tablets or capsules of amphetamine (later known generically as **speed**). This was the 1960s mods' own favourite term for the pills known to the popular press as **purple hearts** or **pep pills**.

doodad *n* an unspecified thing, thingummy. The word is American, dating from before World War II. **Doodads** are bits and pieces, odds and ends.

doodah *n* an unspecified thing, gadget, thingummy. The British and Australian form of the American **doodad**.

doodle *n* 1 penis. A nursery word.
2 nonsense, rubbish or excrement.

doodly squat *n American*
a excrement.
b nonsense, nothing at all. The expression is a common variant form of **diddly (squat)**.
↳ '*Shoot – I wouldn't tell you doodly squat after the way you've behaved.*'
(*Night Game*, US film, 1988).

doody, doo-doo, do-do *n American* excrement. A nursery word used facetiously by adults, this is one of many similar words, perhaps inspired by the older usage, **do** or **dos**.

doody-wacker *n Australian* a gadget or unnamed object. The phrase is an arbitrary coinage on the lines of **doodad**, **do-hickey**, etc.

doofer, doofa *n* 1 an unspecified thing, thingummy.
↳ '*Hand me that doofer.*'
2 a partly-smoked cigarette; a pun on '(it will) do for later'. A war-time term that remained in use in the 1960s and may still survive.

doofus *n* an alternative spelling of **dufus**.

doofy *adj American* foolish, clumsy. The term is probably derived from the earlier term **doofus**.
↳ '*He looked pretty doofy to me.*'
(New York paparazzo talking of actor Michael J. Fox in *True Stories*, Channel 4 TV, April 1993).

dook *n* a hand, fist. A variation of the better-known **duke(s)**. In rustic and working-class Australian speech this form survives from archaic British usage. *See* **dukes, duke it, duke on it**.

doolally *adj British* deranged, crazy. A very popular term derived from the location of a colonial army sanatorium and

rest camp at Deolali, Bombay, where soldiers exhibiting signs of fatigue, heat exhaustion, etc. were sent. An early form which is still heard occasionally was **do(o)lally-tap**, the *tap* meaning fever in Hindi.

dooley, doolie *n British* a stupid or contemptible person. This term of abuse, probably originating in Scottish usage, was featured in the ITV drama *Your Cheating Heart*, written by Johnny Byrne in 1990. The term is now heard particularly in the Scottish Lowlands and the north of England.

do one *vb British* to run away. A recent usage posted on the Internet by *Bodge World* in February 1997.

do one's fruit *vb British* to become enraged, lose control. A variant of the colloquial version 'do one's nut', punning on the fruit-and-nut chocolate bar, this item of middle-class, middle-aged jocularity was recorded in the early 1990s.
↳ '*When they finally said the train was cancelled, I just did my fruit ...*'
(Recorded, male commuter, London 1991).

do one's nut/block/crust/ pieces/taters *vb* to lose control, to become furious. Originally working-class alternatives for to 'lose one's head' or to 'blow one's top', all in use in Britain and Australia; the more colourful second, third, fourth and fifth variants are currently in vogue among young people.
↳ '*Funny you should say that, because these days I find I do my nut very easily.*'
(*Alfie*, British film, 1966).
↳ '*They were freaking about those lost trannies* [transparencies]; *David was doing his crust.*'
(Recorded, art director, London, 1989).
↳ '*Men are always saying they can count the number of times they've cried on the fingers of one hand. Well, I reckon women can count the number of times they've really done their blocks.*'
(*Girls Night Out*, Kathy Lette, 1989).

doover *n* an alternative form of the first sense of **doofer**.

dooze *n American* 1 something which is very easy to accomplish, an attractive proposition.
2 an alternative form of **doozer**.

dooze *vb American* to bamboozle, flatter.

doozer, doozie, doozy *n* something or someone very impressive, remarkable or exceptional; a 'humdinger'. This is probably an invented word (though some authorities derive it from a spectacular pre-World War II car, the Duesenburg). The term is certainly American in origin.

dope *n* 1 an illicit drug, narcotics. The word was first applied to stupefying drugs such as opium and heroin at the turn of the century, and remained limited to this context until the 1960s. In the late 1960s **hippy** drug users began to apply the then almost archaic form ironically to their preferred soft drug, cannabis (marihuana and hashish), and this remains the most common use today.

✎ *'He said: "You know how you leave dope lying around? Well, she ate some and she went berserk. She hasn't liked it much since".'*
(*News of the World*, 29 October 1989).

2 information, news. In this sense the word has been used at least since World War I, especially in America. The word is derived from the idea of something dense or viscous, embodied in the Dutch word *doop*, meaning dip (in the sense of a sauce in which other food may be dipped).

3 a foolish or stupid person.

dope *adj* excellent, fashionable, admirable. A vogue term of approbation, which originated in American usage in the early 1990s and by 1995 had been adopted for fashionable speech by British and Australian adolescents.

✎ *'He's dope – I'd go out with him.'*
(*California Man*, US film, 1992).

✎ *'Bangin' sounds and dope d.j.s.'*
(Disco poster at King's College, London University, September 1995).

dope out *vb* to work out, discover information. A phrase derived from **dope 2**, it is more common in American English where it originated before World War II.

doped-up *adj* under the influence of a (stupefying or tranquillizing) drug.

doper *n* a user of illicit drugs. The word, from **dope**, has been in vogue since the early 1970s. It is used about, rather than by drug users, and is applied indiscriminately to users of hard and soft drugs.

✎ *'He's a doper from way back.'*

dopper *n British* 1 penis.

2 a fool or contemptible person. The earlier sense seems to have fallen into disuse but, like many synonyms (**prick, plonker**, etc.), has been adopted to denote a stupid person. The word dopper itself occurred in Norfolk dialect meaning a thick blanket or sweater, but this is unlikely to be the origin of the derogatory usage which is probably related to the archaic 'dobber', male member.

do-re-mi *n American* money. A pun on **dough**.

Doris *n British* a frumpy or unattractive older woman in the slang of City traders in the 1990s. Such women, especially if thought to be unglamorous or too serious, are typically dismissed by males as *'a bit of a Doris'*. **Nora** is a synonym.

dork *n* 1 penis. A term popularized first among American adults then among teenagers in the 1970s, it is probably inspired by **dick** and, perhaps, **pork**.

2 a fool, offensive buffoon. This is a predictable second (and now more widespread) sense of the word, on the same pattern as **dick, prick**, etc. It is not used affectionately (as **plonker** for instance is), but is only mildly offensive. Since the late 1970s this term has been in vogue in Britain and Australia as well as in its country of origin.

✎ *'I love your husband, but he's a real dork.'*
'Yes, but he's my dork.'
(*Someone to Watch Over Me*, US film, 1987).

dorky *adj* dull, offensively gauche, silly. From **dork 2**.

dos *n pl* a version of **do** (in the sense of excrement).
(It is pronounced 'dooze'.)

dose *n* a venereal infection. Until the 1960s the word most often referred to a bout of gonorrhoea.

✎ *'Don't Give A Dose to the One You Love Most.'*
(Song written and recorded by Shel Silverstein, 1972).

dosed (up) *adj* 1 infected with a venereal disease.

2 drugged illicitly (as in the case of a greyhound or racehorse, for example) or un-

wittingly (in the case of a human). The expression is in this sense a synonym for **spiked**, and in the 1970s often referred to LSD.

dosh *n British* money. This is a working-class term from the early 1950s which was falling out of use in the 1960s, but which, like many similar words (**bunce, loot, lolly,** etc.), was revived in the money-conscious late 1980s. It is a favourite with alternative comedians and 'professional cockneys'. The original would seem logically to be the old African colonial term **dash**, denoting a tip or bribe, but other authorities claim that it is influenced by **doss**, in the sense of the price of a bed (for the night).

doss *vb*

a to sleep.

♧'*I need a place to doss for a couple of nights.*'

b to move from place to place, sleeping in borrowed or low-class accommodation.

♧'*Old Shawie's been dossing for the last three weeks.*'
(Recorded, student, London, 1988).

A 19th-century term which may derive from the Latin *dorsum*, for back. The verb, as opposed to noun forms of the word, are mainly encountered in British English.

doss *n* 1 a a place to sleep, especially a temporary, free and/or makeshift bed. This word from 19th-century tramps' jargon was probably originally a corruption of *dorsum*, Latin for 'back'. Tramps are unlikely to have coined the term; it may have come from the jargon surrounding pugilism (meaning 'flat on one's back') which was a sport subscribed to by aristocrats and students, among others.

b a period of sleep, nap.

2 a very easy task, pushover. In this sense the word, although based on the notion of lying down, may be influenced by 'toss', as in easily tossing off a piece of work.

♧'*You mustn't see this purely as a doss.*'

doss around *vb British* to do nothing in particular, lead an aimless existence. From **doss 2**.

dossbag *n British* 1 a sleeping bag.
2 a scruffy, lazy or slovenly person.

doss down *vb British* to lie down to sleep (usually on the floor), bed down.

♧'*Just doss down anywhere you like.*'

dosser *n British*

a a homeless person, vagrant, or down-and-out who sleeps wherever space is available.

♧'*Leftovers of our present society, the dossers and meths-heads, the socially inadequates, the power-seekers and the bread-lovers.*'
(*International Times* (*IT*), April 1968).

♧'*We are not tramps, winos or even dossers, we are gentlemen of the road – and we refuse to be moved.*'
(Homeless man, *Observer*, 16 August 1987).

b a slovenly, irresponsible person. A favourite term of affectionate abuse between young (usually male) people in the 1980s. (From the noun **doss** or the verb **doss around**.)

doss house *n* a dormitory for vagrants or a cheap, shabby hotel.

♧'*I felt like pissing off and spending the night in some Arab dosshouse.*'
(Joe Orton's diary, 14 May 1967).

♧'*I don't know how you manage to live in this doss house you call a flat.*'

dot *vb* to hit. Usually used in the phrase to **dot (someone) one**, meaning to land a heavy and precise (on the 'dot') blow, or to black someone's eye.

do the wild thing *vb American*

a to run amok.

b to have sex. An item of black slang which may have given rise to the widely reported **wilding**.

do time *vb* to serve a prison sentence.

double-bagger *n American* a hideous or repellent person. A phrase from the vocabulary of **Valley Girls** and other American teenagers from the mid-1970s, probably originating in earlier surfers' slang. The image evoked is of a person who must wear a bag over their head – and provide one for the onlooker too, or alternatively wear *two* bags. The expression in this humorous usage was first borrowed from the language of baseball, where it describes a hit which allows the hitter to advance two bases, or 'bags'.

double result *n British* in the jargon of football hooligans, this denotes a victory against both an opposing team's supporters and the police.

douchebag *n American* a contemptible or very unpleasant person. The expression is usually a strong term of abuse, indicating real distaste, although like comparable words it is sometimes used lightheartedly, typically by high-school and college students. Rubber bags were a part of douching paraphernalia when that form of contraception was widespread, especially among prostitutes. The word is applied to males and females.

✎ '*OK, we're going in there and anyone who doesn't act elegant is a douchebag.*'
(*Satisfaction*, US film, 1988).

dough *n* money. This was the most popular American slang term for money from the 19th century until the mid-1960s when it was supplanted by **bread**.

doughboy *n* 1 *American* an army private. The word was most popular at the time of World War I but is still occasionally used. The original doughboy was a sort of suet dumpling served in the armies and navies of the 19th century in Britain and the USA.

2 *British* a blow, heavy punch. In working-class and cockney jargon this rare sense of the word is occasionally recorded. Its derivation may be from the (heavy) dumpling referred to above.

✎ '*He landed him a real doughboy round the chops.*'

dough-brain *n American* a slow-witted person. The term derives from the old notion of 'soft in the head'.

Douglas *n British* a 3rd (third-class) university honours degree. A student witticism of the late 1980s playing on the name, Douglas Hurd, of a long-serving member of Mrs Thatcher's Conservative cabinet (a **Richard** is a synonym). *Compare* **Desmond**, **Pattie**, **Taiwan**.

do up *vb* 1 to inject or inhale (a drug). An embellishment of **do** in the sense of take (drugs) common among illicit drug users since the early 1970s.

2 *see* **done up**.

done up *adj British* an alternative form of **fitted up** or **stitched up**.

dout, dowt *n British* a cigarette end or stub. A word like **dub**, used by vagrants and working-class speakers. The *Oxford English Dictionary* first recorded the word in use in Glasgow in 1975. It may be a dialectal form of 'dowse(d)' or a contraction of 'stubbed-out'.

down *adj American* authentic, trustworthy, sound. The usage may derive from the appreciative sense of **down-and-dirty** or the phrase **down with** (someone).

✎ '*You're a down girl.*'
(*Clueless*, US film, 1995).

down-and-dirty *adj American*
a deceitful, corrupt, savage. An exclamation used in poker (when cards are dealt or slapped on the table) extended to describe base or brutal behaviour.

b basic, primitive, authentic, 'rough and ready'. In this sense the phrase is usually appreciative rather than pejorative; in rock-music jargon it denotes healthily authentic or **funky**.

downer *n* 1 a tranquillizing or sedative drug (especially a barbiturate) in the language of illicit-drug users (as opposed to **uppers** or stimulant drugs).

✎ '*She's on downers.*'

2 a depressing or boring experience. From the slang of American **hipsters** of the 1950s, widespread in the English-speaking world since the 1960s, but now sounding rather dated in British English; although the phrase **on a downer** (going through a depressed or unlucky phase) is currently widespread.

downhome *adj American* rustic, ethnic or (agreeably) simple and neighbourly. The word was first used by urbanized northern blacks to refer to their southern roots.

downstairs *adj, adv* (in) the genital area or the buttocks. A coy euphemism which was probably inspired by the earlier **upstairs**, relating to the brain or head.

down the block *adj, adv British* in solitary confinement, being punished. A prisoners' term.

down the road *adj, adv British* dismissed, rejected. An item of working-class slang.

✎ '*I want him down the road as soon as possible.*'
(Recorded, labouring gang leader, London, 1992).

down the tubes/flush/chute
adv ruined, abandoned, beyond hope. These are racier versions of 'down the drain', 'down the pan' or 'down the toilet', heard in the USA since the late 1970s and

in Britain since the early 1980s.

↳*'Bright enough to realise he is going down the tubes, he is still drawn to a prodigal self-destruction.'*
(*The Sunday Times*, 26 July 1987).

down with *adj* close to, supportive of. An item of black street argot popular among **rappers** and hip-hop aficionados.
↳*'My crew, they're all down with me.'*

dozy *adj British* slow-witted, foolish. The word is now a colloquialism; in the 1950s it was part of 'vulgar' speech. Originally it meant sleepy or lazy and was (and still is) a favourite term of abuse employed by sergeant majors and officers in the armed forces, teachers and other authority figures.

drabbie *n British* a 'frump', 'bluestocking' or puritanical person, usually female. A middle-class term of mild derision or disapproval, based on drab and applied, often by journalists, in the 1980s to literary, academic or other professional women who deliberately eschew a glamorous appearance.

drack *n Australian* rubbish. An Australian variant form of the more common **dreck**.

drack *adj Australian* scruffy, shabby, dowdy. The adjective is formed from the earlier noun, itself a variant of **dreck**.

drag *n* 1 women's clothing, as worn by men, especially homosexuals, transvestites, female impersonators. Originally theatrical slang of the early 20th century in Britain, signifying a long dress (dragging along the ground), the phrase **in drag** crossed into popular terminology in the early 1960s. In the case of women wearing masculine clothing **man-drag** or **male drag** is usually specified.
↳*'Marlene in man-drag.'*
(Caption to photograph of Marlene Dietrich in Kenneth Anger's *Hollywood Babylon*, 1975).
2 a thing, event or person considered to be boring or depressing. An Americanism, probably originating in the late 19th century, and remaining in marginal use until the 1960s, it was adopted into teenage currency in Britain and Australia in the late 1950s and was widespread by the mid-1960s.
↳*'What a drag it is getting old.'*
(*Mother's Little Helper*, Rolling Stones, 1965).

3 *British* **a** an inhalation of cigarette smoke, a puff.
↳*'Give me a drag on that.'*
b a marihuana cigarette, a **joint**. A prisoners' term.
4 a street, especially a long or important street, usually in the form **main drag**. This Americanism gave rise to **drag racing** to describe unofficial races from a standing start over a short, straight stretch of public road. Drag racing is now also an organized sport run over custom-built private **dragstrips**.

drag ass *vb American* 1 a variant of **haul ass**.
2 to move unwillingly, lazily or slowly.

drag-ass *adj American* boring, tedious, onerous. The word is applied to people as well as to tasks.

dragged-up *adj*
a dressed in **drag**.
b dressed, clothed (especially in flamboyant or unusually expensive clothing). By extension from the first sense to the heterosexual world (although the term does not seem to be applied to women). Dragged-up is a racier version of 'dolled-up'.
↳*'Here he comes, all dragged-up in his best things.'*

draggin' wagon *n American* 1 a tow-truck.
2 a car or van used to impress, seduce or transport members of the opposite sex. A high-school and college-boy term of the late 1970s, inspired by the preceding sense.

draggy *adj* tedious, slow or depressing, from the second sense of **drag**. The word is now rather dated. In the 1960s and 1970s it was more popular in Britain than in the USA.
↳*'It was a totally draggy scene.'*

dragon *n British* a formidable (and therefore unattractive and/or unavailable) female. The earlier colloquialism was adopted as a code term by male financial traders in the City of London and was recorded (with other categorizations such as **oof**, **mum**, etc.) by psychologist Belinda Brookes in the *Independent on Sunday*, 9 July 1995.

drag queen *n* a male homosexual who wears women's clothing. The phrase now has overtones of flamboyant, exhibitionist 'femininity' rather than mere cross-dressing.

⮩*'Kenneth Williams then gave a long portrait of a dismal drag queen writing a witty letter requesting employment.'*
(Joe Orton's Diary, 13 April 1967).

⮩*'The most important week in my life and I'm going to be spending it with a drag queen?!'*
(*He's My Girl*, US film, 1987).

drainpipes, drainpipe jeans, drainies, drains *n pl*
British very tight trousers fashionable in the 1950s among **teddy boys** and, later, **rockers**. Although the terms have been fashionable subsequently (during the glitter craze and **punk** era, for instance), they are now more rare.

drain the lizard/dragon/snake *vb*
to urinate. Colourful euphemisms popular with (invariably male) college students, hearty drinkers, etc. These expressions entered the slang lexicon of teenagers and college students in the late 1960s and early 1970s, although they are probably older, adult coinages on the pattern of **siphon the python**. It is not clear where in the English-speaking world the pattern originated, but it is thought by many to be typically Australian.

⮩*'He can't come to the phone right now, he's in the can draining his lizard.'*
(*Friday 13th Part VI*, US film, 1986).

draipsing *n*
British extorting money or items of value from a weaker person. The synonym of **taxing** was employed in the 1970s among comprehensive-school pupils in London and referred to using a threat rather than actual violence to bully younger pupils into giving up items of value. Its derivation is uncertain.

drama queen *n*
a self-dramatizing or hysterical person. The expression was originally (in the 1960s) applied by male homosexuals to their fellows. In the 1970s the phrase was adopted by heterosexuals and applied to women and, sometimes, to **straight** as well as **gay** men.

drape(s) *n*
a clothes, a suit or outfit. The word was in use in the USA (where 'drapes' are curtains) in the 1950s among black musicians, **hipsters** and **beatniks**. It was then adopted by **spivs** and prisoners in

Britain, where it is still heard.

b British a drape jacket, the top half of a **zoot suit** and part of the uniform of the **teddy boy** in the 1950s. (The drape has wide shoulders, and is almost as long as a frock-coat, but loose and unwaisted.)

draw *n British*
a tobacco. In this sense the word, derived from the action of inhaling, dates from the 1950s. It occurs in prison jargon in particular.

b cannabis (hashish or marihuana). Since the mid-1970s this word has been in vogue for smokable cannabis.

⮩*'By the time he returned home hours late, Robert was intoxicated with cider and high on 'draw' (cannabis cigarette).'*
(*Sunday Times*, 28 January 1996).

draw *n*
British a 'two-one' honours degree in the late 1980s parlance of university students. (The joke is that a draw means 'two won'.) Alternative names for the same award are **made-in** or **Taiwan**. *See also* **Desmond, Douglas, Pattie, Richard**.

dread *n*
Jamaican a Rastafarian, someone who wears **dreadlocks**.

dread *adj*
Jamaican an all-purpose word implying authentic, impressive, etc., in connection with the black reggae and **ganja** culture and Rastafarian religion of Jamaica. The word first conveyed the power and awe felt and inspired by the (**dreadlock**-wearing) devotees of Rastafarianism.

⮩*'He's dread/It's real dread.'*

dreadlocks *n pl*
hair in long, tight ringlets that are never cut, as worn by devotees of Rastafarianism (**Rasta**), the Jamaican religion. The style has been adopted by some non-religious black and white exponents of 1980s youth culture. The word is now usually shortened to **locks**.

dreamboat *n*
a very attractive person of the opposite sex. The word, redolent of Hollywood in the 1940s, is still used, especially in the USA and usually, but not always, facetiously as a description or term of endearment.

dreck *n*
rubbish, a worthless thing, **shit**. From the Yiddish *drek* and German *Dreck*, which have the same meaning.

⮩*'Here's some news to gladden the*

hearts of all devotees of dreck – the world première of Prisoner Cell Block "H".'
(*Time Out* magazine, July 1989).

dreg *n British* a despicable or worthless person. A middle-class term of abuse or disapproval which has been rare since the late 1960s. It is a modern back-formation from the standard plural dregs, which itself derives from an Old Norse term for oil or wine residues.

dreich *adj Scottish* dreary. A dialect term which is occasionally heard as a colourful new colloquialism in self-conscious use amongst middle-class inhabitants of England in the late 1990s.
♦*'The weather is rather, as they say, dreich.'*

drift *vb* leave, go away, escape. The word is sometimes in the imperative form, meaning 'get lost'; otherwise it is a cool or 'tough-guy' synonym for to go.

drill *vb* 1 *British* to sleep. A middle-class and public-school term deriving from the phrase 'blanket drill', a facetious army expression for sleeping.
2 to shoot (usually to kill). A now dated Americanism adopted by crime and Western movies and fiction.
3 to have sex with. A rare usage on the same pattern as **screw**.

drink *n British* a small bribe, tip or other financial inducement. Originally, in London working-class usage, it meant literally the price of an (alcoholic) drink. Now it usually refers to a more substantial sum and is sometimes extended to a share in an attractive venture, or a 'piece of the action'. As an item of British police and underworld slang, it was given wider currency by TV series such as *Minder*.
♦*'Brian will need a drink, too.'*

drinkable *adj British* attractive and/or available. The term was popular among City traders, **Sloanes** and **yuppies** from the later 1980s and could be applied equally to a potential sex partner, usually by males, or to an investment opportunity.

drinking vouchers *n pl British* coins or banknotes. An alternative version of **beer vouchers/tokens**.
♦*'Our Rebels are more likely to be huddled inside an SW William Hill putting plenty of "drinking vouchers" (cash*

money) on Chelsea thrashing Man United. They can often be spied at pubs like the White Hart.'
(*I-D* magazine, November 1987).

drip *n* an insipid, unassertive or boring person. This common colloquialism is probably British in origin, but is also used, especially by school and college students, in the USA and Australia. It is one of many terms (**wet**, **damp**, **dripping**) equating weakness with water.

the drip *n British* hire purchase, paying by instalments. The phrase is usually part of the longer expression **on the drip**.

dripping *adj British* weak, irresolute, pathetic. An upper- and middle-class term of mild contempt from the late 1970s. It is inspired by the popular colloquialism **wet**.
♦*'Her husband's absolutely dripping.'*

drive the porcelain bus/ great white bus/big bus *vb American* to vomit. A popular expression among college and high-school students. The image is of a helpless drunk or hangover victim kneeling before the toilet pedestal, clutching the rim of the bowl in both hands like an oversize steering wheel, as the room spins. (**Kiss the porcelain god** is an alternative form.)

droid *n American* a stupid, slow or completely unimaginative person, in the language of teenagers and students. It is a shortening of 'android', of which both the full and abbreviated forms have been used extensively in science-fiction books and films since the mid-1970s.
♦*'Man, he's a total droid.'* (*Zombie High*, US film, 1987).

drone *n* a dull, lifeless and/or parasitic person. This word is an unusual example of a term which existed as an educated colloquialism, but may have been reinvented as slang by speakers who were unaware of it. In the 1920s and 1930s it was applied to idle, upper-class, young men about town – **debs' delights** – as in the novels of P. G. Wodehouse. The image was of the male bee who never works but serves only to continue the line. The modern reinvention, heard among adolescents in the 1980s in the USA and Britain, may be inspired by the standard senses of 'monotonous hum' or 'unmanned flying target'.

drongo *n* a foolish, unfortunate or unpleasant person. An Australian word which was adopted by British speakers in the early 1970s, probably introduced to it by an influx of young Australian travellers. It is a term of scathing contempt which may have been inspired by a spectacularly unsuccessful racehorse of the same name in the 1920s, although drongo is also the name of an Australian bird. The word seemed to be declining in popularity in the late 1980s.

droob *n Australian* a dullard. This word is probably a blend of **drip** and **boob(y)**.

drooly *adj* very attractive, appealing or appetizing. A less usual synonym of **dishy** or **yummy**, often used by adolescent females.

drop *vb* 1 to take (an illicit drug) orally. The word was most often encountered in the phrase **drop acid**; to take LSD by mouth. Originally an American term, 'drop' replaced the neutral 'take' in Britain around 1966.

↳'*Well, the one that stopped me from doing acid forever was when I dropped seven tabs. I completely lost my mind and went to Muppetland – the whole trip lasted for about six months.*'
(Zodiac Mindwarp, *I-D* magazine, November 1987).

2 to knock (a person) down.
↳'*He threatened to drop him.*'

3 to give birth to. A shortening of **drop a pup**.
↳'*Has she dropped it yet?*'
↳'*She's going to drop in August.*'

drop *n British* news, requisite information. The word usually occurs in the question '*What's the drop?*', recorded among UK adolescents in the early 1990s.

drop a bollock *vb British* to commit a blunder; a vulgar alternative to the colloquial 'drop a brick' or 'drop a clanger'.

drop a bundle *vb* to lose a large amount of money (by gambling or speculative investment, for instance). *See also* **drop one's bundle**.

drop a pup *vb Australian* to give birth. A vulgar and/or humorous euphemism used mainly by men.

dropdead *adj* stunning, extreme,

sensational. A vogue word since the mid- to late 1980s among those concerned with fashion. The usage is American in origin.
↳'*A dropdead blonde.*'
↳'*dropdead gorgeous.*'

drop-kick *n Australian* a 'low', worthless or miserable person. This relatively mild epithet, used in television soap operas of the 1980s for example, is probably a descendant of the vulgar rhyming slang (based on soccer), 'dropkick and punt': **cunt**.
↳'*This makes me seem like a real drop-kick or something.*'

drop off the twig *vb* to die. A lighthearted expression in vogue in Britain in the late 1980s. Bird imagery features in several colourful, predominantly working-class phrases in British colloquial use, such as 'sick as a parrot', or **rattle someone's cage**.

drop one out *vb British* to exclude someone (such as a suspect) from one's list, surveillance or enquiry. A piece of police jargon presumably based on the notion of people being in or out of the **frame**.

drop one's bundle *vb Australian* to panic. The bundle in question may originate in a **hobo's** pack, or may be a reference to fright's tendency to empty the bowels.

drop one's daks *vb Australian* to take off one's trousers. An Australianism (Daks is a trademark for a brand of casual slacks especially popular in the early 1960s in Britain and Australia). A catch-phrase from *The Adventures of Barry McKenzie*, the cartoon strip published in *Private Eye* magazine in the late 1960s was '*drop your daks and say the magic word*'.

drop out *vb* to withdraw from conventional society, opt out. The motto of the **hippy** movement, coined by Dr Timothy Leary in 1967, was '**turn on, tune in, and drop out**' (take drugs and/or become enlightened; make contact with like-minded people or the life force; and leave society behind). The phrase survives in the specific sense of abandon one's education.
↳'*Since I dropped out in September last year I have come to the conclusion that the city drop-out scene is a pa-*

thetic one.'
(Letter to *Oz* magazine, June 1968).

drop-out *n* someone who has opted out of society. In this sense the word, and the concept, date from the late 1960s when **hippies** renounced capitalism, the education system, etc. to form an 'alternative society'. The term was quickly picked up by the press and others who disapproved and became a pejorative description. In the USA in the 1950s and early 1960s drop-out was used to refer specifically to those who had left full-time education before graduating from high school.

dropped on *adj* punished, reprimanded. The expression in full is **dropped on from a great height**; the 'dropping' in question may refer to the weight of authority, or may be a euphemism for **shitting**. Predominantly a middle-class term, it is generally used in the context of a hierarchy.

drop trou *vb American* to take down one's trousers, usually as part of an undergraduate ritual or **hazing**, as an expression of high spirits sometimes, but not necessarily, involving **mooning**; or in preparation for sex. A **preppie** term.

druggy, druggie *n* a user of illicit drugs. The term has been used by disapproving commentators, such as concerned parents, teachers, etc. since the mid-1960s, when **beatniks** were the culprits.

drum *n* 1 *British* a house, home or building. The word, which is used especially in police and underworld circles, may come from the Romany word *drom*, meaning highway, but is possibly a backformation from **drummer**, someone who knocks (drums) on people's doors, either to buy or sell goods or to find somewhere unoccupied to rob. In the past the word has also meant prison cell and brothel, especially in Canada and Australia respectively.

↪ *'Go and turn over his drum while we keep him locked up here.'*
(Recorded, Detective Sergeant, Canterbury, 1971).

2 *Australian* a tip, piece of information or news, probably from the notion of 'jungle drums'.

↪ *'I got a drum that she was in town.'*

drummer *n*

a a door-to-door salesperson, peddler or buyer of junk.

b a housebreaker or burglar.

This now obsolescent term derives either from knocking (drumming) on doors or from **drum** as a vagrants' and criminals' synonym for house.

drumming *n British*

a selling door-to-door.

b housebreaking or burglary.

Both senses of the word derive from **drum** as a slang term for house or home, or from drum in the sense of knock.

drumsticks *n pl South African* legs. The word is used typically by young males commenting mockingly on young females. It was first recorded in this sense in English slang of the 18th century and later in black American argot of the 1940s.

dry *n British* rubbish, **shit**. The origin of this vogue term among adolescent gangs is uncertain. The term was recorded in use among north London schoolboys in 1993 and 1994.

dry-hump, dry-fuck, dry root *n, vb* a sexual activity (often performed standing up) in which the partners simulate intercourse while they (or at least their genitals) are fully clothed. The term usually describes the behaviour of consenting heterosexuals rather than 'perversions' such as frottage (where the activity is performed on an unwilling victim, as for instance in a crowded lift or train), tribadism (between lesbian partners) or frication (between male homosexual partners). Dry root is an expression peculiar to Australian speakers.

↪ *'You can't dry hump good in the car. Unless you're a midget.'*
(High-school student, *IT* magazine, June 1972).

the D.T.s. *n* delirium tremens; trembling as a result of alcohol abuse.

dub *n* 1 a kind of heavy reggae-music in which instrumental tracks already recorded are electronically altered and overlaid ('dubbed' one on another) with vocals and sound effects to create a new piece of music. The form was popular in Jamaica and Britain in the late 1970s and early 1980s.

2 *American* a cigarette.

3 a fool, incompetent. An almost archaic word which survives among older speakers in the USA and Australia.

dub *adj American* fashionable, aware. In this sense, the word was a vogue term of the lexicon of the grunge movement originating in Seattle in 1993 and functioned as a synonym of **hip** and **dope**, etc.

dubbed (up) *adj British* locked up, incarcerated. A 1950s underworld usage probably deriving from an archaic use of dub to mean key or lock. **Tucked up** is a more recent alternative.

dubber *n American* a cigarette. The word's etymology is unclear.

dubbo *n Australian* a fool. An embellishment of the archaic **dub** meaning an awkward or incompetent person, especially a rustic simpleton.

ducats *n American See* **duckets**.

duchess *n British* a woman, usually one's wife. The image is of a dignified, respectable female who is no longer young. This cockney usage is still in evidence although roughly a century old. The word is either a straightforward simile or a shortening of a rhyming-slang phrase, 'Duchess of Fife': wife.

duck, duck egg *n* a score of nil or zero in sport, especially cricket. The term is at least a century old and derives from the resemblance between the written or printed 0 and the egg.

duckburg *n American* a rural, provincial town. A mildly contemptuous term.

duckets *n American* money, dollars. An appropriation of the archaic ducats (Venetian gold coins used all over Renaissance Europe) heard in black street argot and campus slang, and high-school slang in the 1990s.

↳'*He earns minor duckets in a thankless job.*'
(*Clueless*, US film, 1995).

ducks, ducs, duc-duc *n American* variant forms of **duckets**.

duck's arse *n British See* **D.A.**

duck's breakfast *n* a drink of water. A humorous expression on the pattern of **Mexican breakfast**, 'pelican's breakfast', etc. The geographical origin of the phrase is obscure.

duck shoot *n American* an exceptionally easy task. From the image of shooting sitting ducks.

duck-squeezer *n American* an enthusiast for environmental issues. A pejorative categorization heard particularly on campuses, the term is part of a set including **eagle-freak**, **tree-hugger**, **earth biscuit**, **granola** etc.

ducky *adj* cute, delightful. A word which today is almost invariably used ironically or facetiously. It derives from duck as a term of endearment.

dude *n* a man. The 19th-century American sense of dude as 'fop', overdressed city dweller, etc. (familiar from Westerns and 'dude ranches') gave rise to a 20th-century black usage meaning first pimp or 'fancy man', then simply (male) person. The term came into vogue in the 1970s and spread to Britain, where in 1973 it was briefly adopted by the **gay** and teenage milieux (appearing for instance in the title of the David Bowie song 'All the Young Dudes'). In the late 1980s the word has again surfaced in teenage parlance, inspired by its continuing presence in black American street speech. Dude was originally a German rustic term for a fool.

↳'*There were more commercials ... but no more crime ... nothing about two dudes in Halloween masks breaking into a Bloomfield Village home.*'
(*The Switch*, Elmore Leonard, 1978).

duds *n pl* clothes. A word (the plural is usually used) which is approximately three hundred years old, deriving from the Middle English 'dudde', meaning a coarse cloth cloak. The plural of the word later came to mean rags or clothes and now sometimes has the extended sense of an outfit and/or set of accessories.

duff *n* 1 backside, buttocks. Duff is a 19th-century word for boiled dumpling or pudding (surviving in the British 'plum duff'), from which this usage was probably derived.

↳'*Come on you turkeys, get off your duffs and give me some info.*'
(*Buck Rogers in the 25th Century*, US film, 1979).
2 *see* **up the duff**.

duff *adj* useless, inferior. The word derives from a piece of 18th-century thieves' jargon meaning worthless or counterfeit, related to **duffer** which originally denoted a seller of supposedly stolen goods.

duff *vb Australian* to steal. A verb formed from the generalized negative sense of **duff**. The usage is now fairly rare.

duffies *n pl Australian* underpants, usually male.

duff up/over *n British* to beat up. Mild-sounding terms for what may be anything from a children's scuffle to a murderous attack. The modern sense, in vogue since the 1950s, seems to derive from an earlier sense meaning to ruin which is related to the adjective **duff**.

↳*'Michael threatened to duff him up if he ever did anything like that again.'*
(Recorded, teenage girl, London, 1986).

duffy *n See* **duppy**.

dufus *n American*

a an eccentric person.

b a foolish or gauche person.

c a gadget, intriguing object, thingummy. All three senses are typically used on college campuses. The origin of the term is obscure. It is probably an invented word with a mock Latin suffix, although there is a possible connection with *doofart*, a Scandinavian word for fool.

duke it, duke it up/out *vb* to fight, brawl or box. Later formulations from the noun **dukes**; fists.

duke on it *vb* to shake hands. A slang version of 'shake on it', from **dukes**, fists.

dukes *n pl American* fists. This has been part of the jargon of streetfighters and pugilists since the turn of the century. It originates either in the rhyming slang Duke of York: fork, i.e. hand or finger; or from a Romany word meaning palm or hand. The word is most commonly heard in the challenge **put up your dukes** or the phrase **duke it out** (to engage in a fist-fight).

dumbass *n, adj American* (a) stupid (person). A relatively modern extension of dumb (*see* **dumbo**).

dumb cluck *n* a stupid or gormless person. In origin a rustic Americanism, probably inspired by the supposed stupidity of chickens (*see* **dumbo**).

dumbell *n American* a stupid person (See **dumbo**).

dumb-head *n* a stupid person. An elaboration of the American sense of dumb which is a direct translation of the German *Dummkopf*: fool.

dumbo *n, adj* (a) stupid (person). The American use of dumb for stupid, reinforced by the German *dumm*, is as old as the British sense of mute. Since the 1960s the American sense has been adopted in colloquial British English. This variant word may have been reinforced by the Walt Disney film *Dumbo* (which was itself inspired by 'Jumbo', the name of an elephant at London zoo).

dumdum, dum-dum *n* a stupid person. An embellishment (by the linguistic process known as 'reduplication', which is common in nursery words) of dumb (*see* **dumbo**).

dummy *n American* a fool, simpleton or dupe. From dumb in the American sense (*see* **dumbo**).

↳*'The dummy got too chummy in a Bing Crosby number.'*
(*Salome Maloney*, John Cooper Clarke, 1978).

dummy up *vb* to keep silent; refuse to speak. A more robust alternative to **clam up**, used for instance by underworld characters in fact and fiction.

dump *n* **1** a dirty, messy or dilapidated place. The word in this sense is now so common as to be a colloquialism rather than slang (which it would have been considered to be, say, in the 1950s).

2 an act of defecation, usually in a phrase such as 'take' or 'have a dump'.

↳*'What are you doing back there, taking a dump?'*
(*Friday 13th Part VI*, US film, 1986).

dumper *n American* a violent, male devotee of aggressive sexual practices. The term is used by police and pornographers to describe males indulging in rough sexual treatment of women.

dump on (someone) *vb* to criticize or chastise, heap blame or responsibility on, denigrate. This expression is now often used as an innocuous colloquialism, although it derives from the decidedly vulgar sense of **dump 2** above.

↳*'Stop dumping on me, dad.'*
(*Vice Versa*, US film, 1988).

dung-puncher *n* a male homosexual. A highly pejorative term paralleling

fudgepacker, brownie-hound and **turd burglar** in the reference to the faecal aspects of sodomy.

dunkie *n British* a girl. The word is probably an abbreviation of 'dunkin' donut', a trademark name of an American chain of doughnut and coffee shops, although there may be a connection with the sexual sense of **dunking**. The overtones of the expression, used by teenagers in the 1970s, were not respectful.

dunking *n British* sex. A euphemism which was in middle-class and 'society' use in the early and mid-1970s. It now seems to have fallen out of use but might be revived (on the pattern of similarly predictable terms which are periodically rediscovered). The origin is of course in the practice of dunking biscuits (Britain) or doughnuts (America) in tea or coffee.

dunky *n British* a condom. The term is a back-formation from **dunk** as a sexual euphemism.

dunnee, dunny *n Australian* a toilet, especially an 'outhouse' or outside lavatory. The word was reintroduced to some British speakers via the Australianisms in the cartoon strip *The Adventures of Barry McKenzie* in *Private Eye* magazine in the late 1960s. In fact this term has existed for approximately 200 years in British English as 'dunnakin' (spelt in various ways, including 'dunnigan' in Ireland) and had become obsolete. The ultimate origin of these words is obscure but seems to be related to archaic dialect words for excrement such as 'danna', or its colour (dun).

Durban poison *n* the nickname of a particularly highly-prized strain of marihuana from the Republic of South Africa.

Durex *n British* a condom. The trademark name of the popular brand is often used generically. **Trojan** is the US equivalent.

durk *n British See* **derk**.

durr-brain *n British* a foolish, slow-witted person. This popular term of abuse among schoolchildren probably imitates the hesitation noise supposedly made, e.g., before the responding of a simpleton or dullard, but might possibly be a version of the American **dough-brain**.

duss, dust *vb* to depart, leave. In this sense the word dust was recorded among black Americans as long ago as the 1930s, the expression deriving from the image of a cloud of dust being thrown up. As duss, the term was fashionable among gang members and schoolchildren in the UK in the mid-1990s.
  ▷*'It's the beast-man, let's duss!'*

dust *n*
angel dust, PCP. Among young people the shortened form was considered 'cooler' than the full phrase in the late 1980s.
  ▷*'Johnny does dust.'*
  (Graffito, Hammersmith, London, 1987).

dust *vb American* to kill. A 'tough-guy' euphemism implying the casual elimination of nuisances, typically in a gangland or military context. The origin is probably in a now-obsolete use of dust, meaning to hit, which survives in the expression 'dust-up'.

dustbin lids *n pl British* children, kids. A piece of fairly modern rhyming slang which has spread beyond its working-class London context. The singular form exists, but is rare. **Saucepan lids** is an alternative form.

dust bunny *n American* a ball of fluff lurking in undusted parts of a household. (Also known as **dust kitty** and many other terms.)
  ▷*'She won't make the bed, she won't sweep up the dust bunnies or nothin'.'*
  (*The Rockford Files*, US TV series, 1980).

dust kitty *n American*
a a ball of household fluff, found for instance under a bed or in other undusted parts of a home. This domestic phenomenon has given rise to a number of colourful expressions in American English (**dust bunny, beggar's velvet**, 'house moss' and **ghost turds** are others), but none in British English.
b the navel. So-called due to its being a repository for fluff, etc.

dusty, dustie *n British* **1** an old person. A term of mild contempt or even affection to their elders among **Sloane Rangers** and other young people of the late 1970s, becoming more widespread since. A less common alternative to **wrinkly**. In *The Official Sloane Ranger Handbook* (1982) Ann Barr and Peter York attempt to define the ages of adults as follows: **wrinkly** (40 to 50 years old); **crumbly** (50 to 70 years old); and **dusty**

(70 and above).

2 a dustman. Not as common an abbreviation as **postie** for postman, for instance.

dutch *n British* 1 wife. This hundred-year-old piece of Cockney usage is still heard (invariably in the form **my old dutch**) although now often used facetiously or self-consciously. It may be a shortening of **duchess** (originally 'duchess of Fife', rhyming slang for wife), or she may be so-called after 'an old Dutch clock' (a homely piece of furniture with a broad open dial). There is no recorded proof for these etymologies and it is possible that this sense in fact has the same origin as the following, reflecting the use of 'mate' to mean wife.

2 friend, mate. A second Cockney sense of the word comes from the rhyme 'Dutch plate'.

Dutch, dutch fuck *vb American* to have sex by putting the penis between the female breasts. Dutch here is used as in other expressions like 'Dutch auction', 'go dutch', etc., to mean unorthodox. In adolescent British armed service slang dutch fuck referred to lighting one cigarette from another. **Tittyfuck** is a synonym.

dweeb *n* a foolish, gormless or unpopular person. An American campus and high-school word of the late 1980s, adopted by British youth in 1988.

꙳*'I didn't even tell her my name – I am a dweeb!'*

(*18 Again!*, US film, 1988).

dwem *n* a 'dead white European male'. A key term in the 'politically correct' lexicon of the mid 1990s; a dismissive categorization of members of the supposed literary canon, such as Shakespeare.

dyke, dike *n* a lesbian. The only common slang term to describe a female homosexual; it was first used derogatorily by heterosexuals, but it is now used by **gay** women themselves, though often wryly. When said by a heterosexual the word usually still carries overtones of the 'aggressive masculine' stereotype of a lesbian. No one has satisfactorily explained the term's ultimate origin; it might be from an old pejorative euphemism for a woman's genitals. Another, rather far-fetched theory is that it is inspired by the story of the little Dutch boy with his finger in the dyke. Whatever its origin the word seems to have been imported into British English from America between the world wars.

dykie, dyky *n*
a like a **dyke**, lesbian.
b (of a woman) 'masculine' in behaviour and/or appearance.

dynosupreme *adj American* excellent, perfect, outstanding. Often an exclamation, this is a teenage vogue elaboration of supreme using a mock-prefix based on dynamo or dynamic, or a contraction of dynamite.

E *n* **1** (a dose of) the drug **ecstasy**. An abbreviation in vogue in the UK since the late 1980s.

2 *See* **the big E.**

▷ *'She's on E.'*

eagle freak *n American* an enthusiast for environmental issues. A pejorative categorization heard particularly on campuses, the term is part of a set including **duck-squeezer, tree hugger, earth biscuit, granola**, etc.

earache *n British* incessant chatter, complaining or nagging. The expression usually occurs in working-class speech.

▷ *'Will you stop giving me all this earache about being late and let me eat my tea in peace.'*

ear-basher/-banger/-bender *n* someone who talks incessantly, a person who harangues, nags or bores. Ear-basher is heard in Britain and Australia; ear-banger and ear-bender are predominantly American.

earlies *n British* underpants, knickers. A fairly obscure but surviving instance of 19th-century London rhyming slang. The rhyme is 'early doors': drawers. 'Early doors' is from theatrical jargon.

earner *n British* a scheme or situation which brings financial advantage, especially when unexpected or illicit. Originally from the language of police and thieves, the term, especially in the vogue phrase *'a nice little earner'*, has entered general circulation in the profit-oriented society of the late 1980s.

▷ *'The job's hard work, long hours and pretty boring – but at £70 a week it's a nice little earner if you're 15 and living at home.'*

(Teenage truant, *Observer*, February 1988).

earnings *n British* the proceeds of crime or dishonesty. An item from the language of adolescent gangs. The term was recorded in use among north London schoolboys in 1993 and 1994.

ear'ole *n British* a dull, gormless or exasperating person. A word used typically by working-class schoolchildren in the 1970s to refer to tedious fellow pupils or adults. The eighth edition of Eric Partridge's *Dictionary of Slang and Unconventional English* quotes a 1976 article in *New Society* which derives ear'ole from those (pupils) who listen and obey, as opposed to those who act or refuse to conform. This is likely to be a folk etymology (and probably spurious) as the word was in use as long ago as the 1950s as a nonspecific term of abuse.

ear'ole *vb British* **1** to 'buttonhole' (someone); in other words, to detain (someone) in conversation.

2 to scrounge; from **on the earhole**, which earlier in the century meant to try to swindle.

3 to nag, shout at, talk incessantly.

4 to listen to, eavesdrop.

All these senses of the word are in mainly working-class use and are most commonly heard in London.

earth biscuit *n American* an enthusiast for environmental issues. A pejorative categorization heard particularly on campuses, the term is part of a set including **duck-squeezer, tree hugger, eagle freak, granola**, etc.

earwig *vb British* **1** to eavesdrop, or listen out for news, danger, etc. A working-class word used by the underworld and, more innocuously, by or about neighbourhood gossips, etc.

▷ *'You cunning git! You was earwiggin' my conversation.'*
(*Only Fools and Horses*, British TV comedy series, 1989).

2 to understand, realize. A less common sense of the word in this rhyming-slang expression (from '**twig**').

ear-wigging *n British* a synonym for **ear-bashing**, punning on the earwig insect and the 19th-century colloquial use of 'wig' to mean scold.

▷ *'That didn't stop [David] Puttnam giving [Christopher] Patten a severe ear-*

wigging from the green pulpit last week.'
(*The Sunday Times*, 26 November 1989).

easy! *exclamation* 1 *British* a generalized cry of derision, triumph, joy, etc. The word is usually lengthened to 'eezee!' It originated on football terraces in the 1960s, and is often heard in repetitive crowd chants at sporting events.
2 an all-purpose greeting or farewell, which probably originated in gang usage whence it was adopted by adolescents in the 1990s. *Compare* **easy-seen!**

easy meat *n*
a a person who is easy to seduce or take advantage of.
b something easy to achieve or acquire. The phrase has been in currency since the 1920s.

easy-peasy *adj British* very easy indeed, posing no problem. A popular phrase with younger schoolchildren since the early 1980s, although common in Scotland and northern England for decades.

easy-seen! *exclamation British* an elaboration of **seen**, used as an all-purpose exclamation of greeting, thanks, approbation, etc. The term was recorded in use among north London schoolboys in 1993 and 1994.

eat, eat out, eat someone out *vb* to perform cunnilingus. These Americanisms of the 1960s are heard in Australia and to a lesser extent in Britain.

eat dirt *vb See* **eat shit**.

eat it! *vb, exclamation American* a euphemism for **eat shit!**

eat my shorts! *exclamation American* an exclamation of defiance or contempt, popular among male high-school and college students in the 1980s. The shorts in question are of course (unsavoury) male underwear.

eat shit/dirt *vb*
a to submit to humiliation, to abase oneself. Until recently the phrase had more currency in the USA and Australia than in Britain.
b **eat shit!** An American exclamation of defiance or contempt.

Ebonics *n American* a variety of English, mainly consisting of street slang, and in use among young blacks in the late 1990s. The word is constructed from 'ebony' and 'phonics'. The school board in Oakland, California, was the first to recognize Ebonics, also known as **black-speak** or **jive-talk**, as a legitimate language variety.

ecaf *n British* face. An item of **back-slang** which became part of the **parlyaree** in use among London gays since the 1950s.
↳*'Slap some rouge and mascara on your old ecaf ...'*

eckies, exes *n pl British* expenses. Shortenings of the standard word used by businesspeople. Nuances of rank may be ascribed to the terms; the first is most usually heard among sales personnel, the second among executives.

eco-freak, eco-nut *n* a person concerned with ecology and the environment. These dismissive or patronizing terms, used by critics or mockers, surfaced in the 1970s.

ecstasy *n* the drug MDMA (3,4 methylene dioxy methamphetamine). A preparation which was synthesized and patented in 1914 and rediscovered for recreational use in 1975 in the USA. The drug, related to **speed**, remained a minority taste until the early 1980s; it was used by Californian therapists among others and was legal until 1985. Since that time MDMA, which causes elation, wakefulness and comfortable sensations but is now known to be dangerous even in small doses, has been the favourite drug of aficionados of night clubs and discos, especially those subscribing to the British **acid house** cult. It is also known as **E**, **Epsom salts**, **X** and **adam**.
↳*'Every generation finds the drug it needs ... the cold, selfish children of 1985 think ecstasy will make them loved and loving.'*
(P. J. O'Rourke, *Republican Party Reptile*, 1987).

edge city *n* a sensation or situation in which one experiences tension, dread or anticipation. A dramatizing of 'edgy' heard among drug users and progressive music fans.

edged *adj American* nervous, anxious, irritated. This adaptation of the colloquial 'edgy' and the slang **edge city** was heard in black speech and campus slang from the early 1990s.

Edwardian *n British* a **teddy boy**. A variant form of the name used seriously on occasions by journalists and facetiously by teddy boys themselves.

eek, eke *n British*

a face. A word heard in London theatrical and **camp** slang from the late 1950s. The etymology is obscure. One suggestion, unfortunately rather far-fetched, is that it is from the scream of fright occasioned by glimpsing the said visage leering through the limelight.

b face-paint, make-up. Also a theatrical term, presumably derived from the first sense. **Slap** is a more common alternative.

eff *vb* a euphemism for **fuck** heard in America and Australia but more popular in Britain. It is most often encountered in the phrase '*eff off*' and '*effing and blinding*' (cursing, using bad language).

⏃'*Mr ... put his arms around my waist and tried to kiss my neck. I told him to eff off.*'
(Victim of sexual harassment, *Daily Mirror*, 31 March 1989).

effect *n See* in effect.

egg *n See* lay an egg.

egg and spoon *n British* a black person. Rhyming slang for **coon**; this picturesque working-class phrase, its origin in children's egg and spoon races, usually implies contempt and dislike.

eggbeater *n* an old or primitive motor or motorized vehicle. A helicopter, car, outboard motor, etc.

eggplant *n American* an Afro-Caribbean person. The analogy is with the shiny, dark skin-colour of the vegetable.

ego-trip *n* an exhibition of self-aggrandizement, self-indulgence or other selfishness. The term dates from the late 1960s and derives from the notion that under the influence of LSD (on a **trip**) enlightened persons will lose their ego, while the unenlightened may experience a concentration of selfish impulses. Trip later took on the generalized idea of be-

haviour or idée fixe, and ego, simply egomaniacal or egotistic.

Egyptian PT *n British* sleeping. A joking and contemptuous expression dating from before World War II. It derives from the feats of legendary laziness imputed to Arabs in general by the British forces overseas. The phrase survives, mainly in public-school and army slang.

elbow *vb British* to dismiss (someone), to dispose of or reject (something). A more modern version of '*give it/them the elbow*'. It is often in the passive form '*get elbowed*'.

⏃'*OK, elbow the buskers, we haven't got time.*'
(TV studio crew, *One Day in the Life of Television*, 1 November 1989).

elbow bender *n British* an habitual imbiber of alcoholic liquor; a drunk. From the phrase to **bend the elbow** (in lifting a drink to the lips).

⏃'*Sam Brown admits she became a big-time boozer when she was a schoolgirl and is still a solid elbow-bender.*'
(Photo caption, *People*, 23 April 1989).

electric soup *n* alcoholic drink, a strong alcoholic punch. The phrase is predominantly heard in middle-class circles. It belongs to a set of synonymous phrases including **lunatic soup** and **giggle water**.

elephants, elephant's trunk *adj British* drunk. A piece of 100-year-old London rhyming slang which is still heard, although usually used facetiously.

⏃'*I seen him down our local again – completely elephants.*'

el ----o *noun form American* a Spanish pattern applied jocularly to English words mainly by American speakers. The meaning is 'the supreme ----', 'the quintessential ----' or just 'the ----'. It appears in 'el creepo', 'el sleazo', 'el cheapo', etc. This tendency (in imitation of Hispanic 'low life' speech) has been in evidence since the early 1970s. *See also* the entries which follow.

el primo *n American* the very best, top quality. From Spanish in which it means the first (quality). The expression is used by **anglos**, blacks, etc. in imitation of Hispanic speech.

el ropo *n American* a cigar or **joint**, especially a large and noxious one, from the idea of low-grade tobacco resembling **rope**.

embalmed *adj* drunk. A now fairly rare, predominantly middle-class euphemism, it is an old usage, probably coined in the 19th century and inspired by balm (as a euphemism for comforting liquor), balmy (see **barmy**) and the early 20th-century Americanism 'embalming fluid', meaning whisky.

embrocation *n British* alcoholic drink. A humorous borrowing of the word for rub-on liniment, said mainly by the middle aged.

↘ *'I think a spot of embrocation might be in order.'*

Emma Freuds *n pl British* haemorrhoids. An item of rhyming slang popularized by the comic *Viz* in its feature 'Nobby's Piles'. The name is that of a female TV presenter.

emmet *n British* a tourist, an unwelcome stranger. A dialect word (meaning ant) used in Cornwall since the 1950s to refer disparagingly to swarms of holidaymakers. **Grockle** is another regional term with a similar meaning.

enchilada *n American See* **big enchilada**.

ends *n American* money. The term, probably originating in black street argot in the 1950s, was later adopted by college students. It may have begun as '*N's*' referring to (bank)-notes, or possibly derived from the cliché 'to make ends meet'.

endsville *n, adj American* the ultimate; the best or the worst. From the language of **hipsters** and **beatniks** in the late 1950s, already sounding dated by the 1960s.

Epsom salts *n British* the drug **ecstasy**. A vogue term on the **acid house** scene in 1989. The expression is borrowed from the name of the old-fashioned purgative medicine (hydrated magnesium sulphate).

ept *adj British* skilled, competent. A jocular back-formation from inept, heard in middle-class speech in the 1990s. *Compare* **ert**.

↘ *'I've got to say she's not very ept, is she?'*
(Recorded, office manager, London, 1996).

equipment *n*
a the male sex organs. An unromantic euphemism used by males and females alike.
b a woman's breasts. A rarer vulgarism, usually indicating unromantic appraisal.

'erb *n See* **herb**.

'erbert *n British* a foolish person, a cheeky, unwashed child. For many years, in London working-class slang, Herbert or 'Erbert was used to refer to any otherwise unnamed man or boy. Gradually, probably by being used in phrases such as *'silly 'erbert'*, it came to have the more pejorative sense. There probably never was an eponymous Herbert; it was merely a common working-class name from the Edwardian era.

erdie *British* a tedious, orthodox, **straight** individual. The origin of the term is mysterious: Eric Partridge's dictionary derives it somewhat unconvincingly from the German *Erde*, 'earth', as in earthbound.

↘ *'Most managers were erdies; agents ditto.'*
(Rolling Stones' manager Andrew Oldham in 1965, quoted in Christopher Sandford's *Mick Jagger: Primitive Cool*, 1993).

eric *n British* **1** an erection. A schoolboy term.
2 a foolish, gauche or unpopular male. This sense of the word also occurs in school argot and may be a corruption of **erk** or **oik**.

erk *n British* a vulgar, inferior or tedious person. A piece of armed service and public-school slang which some authorities derive from aircraft. It may in origin be a version of **oik**.

erp, earp *vb American* to vomit. The word is echoic and has been recorded among teenagers of both sexes.

↘ *'Someone's erped in the parking lot.'*

-ers *n word-ending British* a termination added to all or part of a standard word. In public-school, armed forces or middle-class speech it confers familiarity or affection. The core-word is sometimes preceded by **harry-**, as in **harry-starkers** for stark naked. This speech-pattern, found risible by many since the 1960s, arose at Oxford and in public schools in the late 19th century. *See also* **preggas, honkers, starkers**, etc.

ert *adj British* alert, lively, aware. A humorous back-formation from the standard term inert, heard in middle-class adult speech in the 1990s. *Compare* **ept**.

↳*'You've got to try to be a bit more ert!'*

Eurotrash *n* the European 'jet-set' and their hangers-on. A version of 'international **white trash**', heard in 'society' and journalistic circles.

↳*I enjoyed it, famous bits of Eurotrash enjoy it, but Miss Mouse might not feel altogether comfortable.'*
(Rupert Christiansen, *Harpers and Queen*, November 1989).

eve *n British* the drug MDEA, a stimulant related to **ecstasy** which is known as **adam** (from MDMA).

evil *adj American* impressive, admirable. This use of the word originated in the jargon of black musicians; a rarer variant of **bad** or **wicked**. It is now used by teenagers of all ethnic origins, in Britain and Australia as well as the USA.

ex *n See* X.

exercise the ferret *vb Australian* to have sex. An unromantic male expression equating the penis with the aggressive, hyperactive animal and its well-known proclivity for wriggling into crevices and tunnels.

exes *n pl British* expenses. A variant form of **eckies**.

extract the Michael *vb British* to **take the mickey**; to mock. A humorously pedantic version of the well-known colloquialism.

extract the urine *vb British* to **take the piss**; to mock. A mock-pedantic version of the common, more vulgar expression.

eyeball *vb* to look at, stare at or inspect. The expression probably originated in the USA in black usage in the late 1940s. By the 1970s it was heard in Britain and Australia, especially among teenagers and the police. In the form 'eyeballing' the term can have the specific meanings of staring threateningly or provocatively.

↳*'The male models in leopard-skin-print Gaultier jackets getting eyeballed by Sharons with Bucks Fizz haircuts and pound signs in their eyes at the Limelight.'*
(*Observer*, Section 5, 7 May 1989).

↳*'Villains call it clocking in Leeds, eyeballing in Manchester and screwing in London's East End … It came as a shock: juries can be intimidated by a stare.'*
(*The Sunday Times*, 5 June 1988).

eyeball *n British*

a a surveillance operation, in the jargon of the CID and the Flying Squad in particular.

↳*'We've been on eyeball for a week now.'*

b 'visual contact', a sighting. Another police term, employed for example during a stakeout or surveillance.

↳*'Do you have an eyeball on suspect one?'*
(Detective Sergeant, *Flying Squad*, British TV documentary series, February 1989).

eyetie *n, adj* (an) Italian. A rather unimaginative and dated soubriquet, but fairly inoffensive, as opposed to **macaroni** or **wop**. The term arose at about the time of World War I. In working-class pronunciation (in both Britain and the USA) the first syllable of Italian continues to be pronounced 'eye' (hence the Morris 'Ital', named by car workers after a poll).

f ...

F.A./Fanny Adams, sweet F.A./Fanny Adams *n British*

a nothing at all. Fanny Adams is a widespread euphemism for **fuck-all**.

b a pitifully small amount. In 19th-century naval slang, Fanny Adams was tinned or cooked meat, a sardonic reference to a girl of the same name who was murdered and dismembered in 1867. The name was later matched with the initials of **fuck-all** and used euphemistically in its place.

ᗺ*'He says Eve behaved like a complete bitch over the kids' custody ... and he'll get sweet F.A. out of the sale of the house.'*
(Party gossip in cartoon by Posy Simmonds, *Guardian*, 1979).

fab *adj* brilliant, wonderful. This abbreviation of fabulous was adopted as an all-purpose term of approbation by teenagers in the 1960s from **camp** adult parlance and a local usage in Liverpool. The word was revived in the late 1980s, at first ironically, but increasingly in its original sense.

fabe, fabe-o *adj British* variant forms of **fab**, occurring in London **parlyaree** in the 1960s and recorded in the TV documentary *Out* in July 1992.

face *n British* 1 an outstanding person, someone who is more sophisticated, better dressed, etc. than the rest. A vogue word among **mods** in 1963 and 1964, probably originating from the idea of a well-known or recognizable face in the crowd, or possibly from a 'face card', an expression occasionally heard in the USA, indicating an extraordinary, important or famous person. (The word also occurs in underworld and prison jargon, denoting a prominent personage.) The quintessential mod groups of the time were The Who (whose first and unsuccessful single was 'He's the face'), and The Small Faces.

2 a synonym for 'cheek' or **front** sense **1**. This use of the word was popular in raffish speech of the late 1980s.

ᗺ*'"A really good beggar makes maybe £50," Brian says. "I haven't got the face to do it".'*
(Homeless youth, *Independent*, 22 December 1989).

3 *See* **give someone face**.

4 *See* **jump in someone's face**.

faceache *n*

a an ugly person. A term of mild derision or abuse, now mainly confined to children's badinage.

b an indicated but unnamed person, **whatsisname**.

ᗺ*'Old faceache's back again.'*

face-case *n American* a teenage synonym for **faceache**, heard in the late 1980s.

faced *adj American* 1 drunk. A **preppie** term which is a milder shortening of **shitfaced**.

ᗺ*'Get a six-pack of tall-boys, get faced and hit on the girls.'*
(*3rd Rock From the Sun*, US TV Comedy 1996).

2 humiliated, snubbed. This teenage term of the late 1950s describes the result of having been **put down**: it derives from 'losing face'.

face man *n American* a male, especially an attractive male, considered to have a bland, insipid personality.

fade *vb* 1 *American* to leave (a place), go away. A piece of **hipster** and **beatnik** language from the 1950s which has been revived by teenagers in the 1980s.

ᗺ*'Come on guys, let's fade.'*

2 *American* to meet or cover a bet. From the language of the dice game craps.

ᗺ*'Ten bucks says he doesn't make it. Who'll fade me?'*

3 to kill, eliminate. A term from the argot of street gangs and other criminals.

ᗺ*'I feel like I can't be faded ... just the hardest nigger around!'*
(*Gang War*, Channel 4 TV documentary, August 1995).

fadge *n* the vagina. A vulgarism in use among adolescents in the 1990s and listed in *Viz* comic in 1994. **Vadge** is an alternative reading.

faff, faff about *vb British* to behave in a confused, disorganized or inde-cisive way. The expression usually indi-cates exasperation at another's incompe-tence.

↬ *'Stop faffing about and play the bloody thing forwards!'*
(Recorded, football spectator, North Lon-don, 1988).

fag *n* 1 *British* a cigarette. In Middle English 'fagge' meant, as a verb, to droop or, as a noun, a flap or remnant. These notions gave rise to 'fag-end' and subse-quently, in the 19th century, to fag as a stubbed-out or limp, low-quality ciga-rette. In the 20th century the word was generalized to refer to any cigarette.

↬ *"Come on darling give us a fag," says a brass to an elderly tom. "Have pity on a destitute prostitute!"'*
(*Sunday Times* colour supplement fea-ture on the East End of London, 2 June 1968).

2 *American* a male homosexual. This is generally taken to be a shortened ver-sion of **faggot**, but may pre-date it. (There is no discernible connection with the British public-school term meaning a ju-nior boy performing servant duties.)

↬ *'I'm led into a room where a short fag doctor and a big bull-dyke nurse are waiting for me.'*
(Bill Levy's journal in *Oz* magazine, Feb-ruary 1970).

faggot *n* 1 *British* an unattractive or disreputable woman. This now outdated term, some three hundred years old, is still heard in the phrase 'old faggot', but has otherwise largely disappeared due to the influence of the following American sense of the word.

2 *American* a homosexual man. It is not certain whether this term is an embell-ished version of **fag**, derives from the old British sense of the word (above), or is a native American invention. The second alternative appears the most likely.

↬ *'You know I'm a faggot? Well, congrat-ulations.'*
(*Kiss of the Spider Woman*, film by Hec-tor Babenco, 1985).

faggy *adj American*
camp, effeminate. The adjective is formed from the earlier noun.

↬ *'Just a faggy little leather boy with a smaller piece of stick.'*
('Memo from Turner', song recorded by Mick Jagger, 1969).

fag-hag *n* a woman who prefers the company of homosexual men. The ex-pression became popular in the late 1960s with increased awareness of the gay community among **straights**. The phrase quickly spread from the US to Britain and Australia. Although originally and usually used pejoratively, it can now be used neutrally, or by a woman of her-self.

↬ *'She [Edith Olivier] became the supreme fag-hag of the 1920s and 1930s, the older woman who acts as mother-confessor and salonnière to a group of young homosexual men.'*
(Bevis Hillier writing in *The Sunday Times*, 26 November 1989).

fag stag *n American* a heterosexual male who enjoys the company of **gay** males. The coinage is by analogy with the earlier **fag-hag**.

fag tag *n American* the outside loop at the back (at the top of the pleat) of a stan-dard American button-down Oxford shirt. The phrase is based on the jocular as-sumption that the 'tag' is there as an aid to homosexual assault. This college-stu-dent term, quoted in the *Official Preppy Handbook* by Lisa Bernbach (1980) has the alternative designations **fruit loop** and **ripcord**.

fains, fainites, faynits *excla-mation British* a cry demanding a truce or exemption from something (such as being caught or penalized in a playground game). The various forms of the word are a survival of the archaic 'fains' or 'fains I' which means forbid and is related to the standard English fend.

↬ *'The air echoed with cries of pax, unpax, fains, roter, shutup.'*
(Geoffrey Willans and Ronald Searle, *Back in the Jug Agane*, 1959).

fair dinkum *adj Australian* just, honest, equable, worthy of approval. This well-known Australianism originated in a Victorian British dialect version of 'fair play' or 'fair share'. (The exact origin of the 'dinkum' component is not clear.)

fair go/goes *phrase Australian* an interjection demanding fair or reason-able behaviour.

↬ *'Come on, fair goes, give us a break.'*

fair suck of the pineap-ple/sauce stick *phrase Australian* elaborations of the colloquial 'fair crack of the whip'.

fairy *n* a male homosexual. The word in this sense probably originated in the American West around the turn of the century. It was commonly heard in Britain by the 1920s.

fairy money *n British* vouchers or coupons. The derisive phrase appeared in the mid-1990s, often referring to the redeemable but almost worthless tokens given out with petrol sales in garages.

fall guy *n American* a dupe, victim or scapegoat. A pre-war Americanism deriving from the phrase 'to take a fall' (to be caught, arrested or imprisoned).

ϟ*'Two fall guys were to be arrested and charged in their place.'*
(Former detective *Inside the Brotherhood*, Martin Short, 1989).

falling-down juice *n British* alcohol. A popular term among students particularly in the west Midlands in the late 1990s.

falsies *n pl British* a padded brassiere or other padding worn to make a woman's breasts appear larger.

family jewels *n pl* the male genitals, more specifically the testicles. A jocular expression which may be Victorian in origin. Now sometimes shortened to **jewels**.

fan *n* 1 an aircraft propeller.
2 *American* backside. A shortening of **fanny** sense 2.
ϟ*'She fell on her fan.'*

fancy Dan *n British* a spectacular performer, especially one who shows off their skill. The phrase is typically used by football fans to express grudging admiration or sarcasm.

fang-farrier *n Australian* dentist. A humorous coinage: a farrier is a blacksmith.

fanny *n* 1 *British* the female genitals. This old and relatively inoffensive euphemism is possibly derived from the well-known erotic novel *The Memoirs of Fanny Hill*, by John Cleland, published in 1749, or is perhaps simply an affectionate personification of the sex organs, using the short form of Frances. The word is used by women as well as men.

2 *American* backside, buttocks. The American sense of the word probably derives from the earlier British sense. Fanny is sometimes confusingly used with this meaning by middle-class speakers in Britain, too.

fanny about *vb British* to **faff about**, dither. The **fanny** element may be present merely for its sound, or proximity to fuss or **faff**, or as a suggestion of femininity, rather than as a direct reference to buttocks or genitals.

Fanny Adams *n British See* **F.A./Fanny Adams**.

fanny-fit *n British* a bout of consternation or agitation. This term, based on fussing as described in the phrase **fanny about**, became popular in all age groups in the 1990s. **Hissy-fit** is a similar usage from the same period.

fanny-magnet *n British* an attractive young male. This racier version of the widespread phrase **babe-magnet** was posted on the Internet by Bodge World in 1997.

fanny merchant *n British* someone who behaves in an indecisive, weak or supposedly effeminate way.

ϟ*'Stop pratting about, Hoddle and get stuck in. You're nothing but a fanny merchant.'*
(Recorded, football supporter, North London, 1985).

fanny rat *n British* a womanizer or seducer. A term used with either contempt or admiration by other men.

ϟ*'A policeman accused of drowning his wife in a holiday villa's Jacuzzi bath was branded "King Fanny Rat" by his colleagues because of his womanizing.'*
(*Daily Mirror*, 15 April 1989).

fantabuloso *adj British* exceptionally good and/or spectacular, an item of **parlyaree** recorded in the TV documentary *Out* in July 1992.

farley, farly *n American* a man or boy, a **gay** male, a ridiculous or unattractive person. A **Valley Girl** term used in the early 1970s.

ϟ*'I can't get behind London. There are all these crazy farleys everywhere.'*
(Recorded, Californian teenage girl, 1970). *See also* **chuck you farley!**

Farmer Giles *See* **farmers**.

farmers *n pl British* haemorrhoids. Rhyming slang from Farmer Giles: piles. The eponymous farmer is a common personification of bucolic heartiness. The longer version, Farmer Giles, was heard, particularly among schoolchildren, until at least the late 1970s.

♭*'Send your farmers packing with "Preparation Ouch".'*
(*There's a Lot of it About*, British TV comedy series starring Spike Milligan, 1989).

far-out, farout *adj*
a extreme, eccentric, unconventional.
b wonderful, remarkable. By extension from the first sense, usually as an exclamation in the approval of anything extraordinary.
Both senses of the phrase, originally an Americanism, were beloved by **hippies** from the late 1960s, but far-out was sounding dated by about 1974 and if used in current conversation, would probably invite ridicule.

♭*'Marlene's entire range of expression was pretty much limited to "far out", "super" and "gross".'*
(*The Serial*, Cyra McFadden, 1976).

fart *n* 1 an expulsion of intestinal gas from the anus. Not really a slang term, but often included as such because of its vulgar overtones. (For the etymology see the verb form.)
2 a term of abuse, sometimes dismissive, now sometimes almost affectionate, heard especially in the expressions 'old fart' and 'boring old fart' (**b.o.f.**). Fart in this sense suggests someone inconsequential, ineffectual or otherwise worthy of mild contempt.

fart *vb* to 'break wind', expel intestinal gas through the anus. The word is a descendant of an old Germanic verb *ferzan* which in turn comes from an Indo-European root *perd-* or *pard-* (giving modern French *péter* among others). In English fart has never been genuine slang, but is sometimes considered to be so because it is taboo in polite company. This was not the case until the 18th century. As with other 'four-letter words' there is no neat equivalent term in polite standard English.

fart around/about *vb* to mess around, waste one's time or play the fool.

♭*'Come on you guys, stop farting around and get down to business.'*

fart-arse, fartarse about/ around *vb British* to waste time, behave ineffectually or indecisively. A common, mildly vulgar term in British and Australian English. It is an elaboration of **fart around**.

♭*'I wish they'd stop fart-arsing around and make their minds up.'*

fartleberries *n pl* another word for **dingleberries**.

fast-ass, fast-arse *n, adj British* (a person who is) clever, socially adept. A term of approbation from the slang of London schoolchildren in the 1990s, often pronounced (like the similar smart-arse/ass) in the American way.

♭*'Sarah just thinks she's such a fast-ass, but she isn't.'*

fat *adj* excellent, fashionable, **hip**. A vogue term of approval in youth subcultures of the 1980s. **Fattier** and **fattiest** are other terms. The word is sometimes spelled **phat**.

fat city *n American* 1 a state of contentment and/or material repletion, a very satisfactory situation.

♭*'Wait till you see the set-up there – he's in fat city.'*
2 obesity or an obese person. A high-school and college term of the 1970s and 1980s.

♭*'Get a load of fat city, here!'*

fat farm *n* a health farm or slimming centre.

fatso *n* a fat person. This unfriendly term from the USA largely superseded the more typically British 'fatty' in the 1960s.

fave, fave rave *n* a favourite thing or person. The expression was first used in the 1960s. Nowadays it is almost always used humorously or ironically, typically surviving in the journalese of teenage magazines.

faynits *exclamation British* an alternative spelling of **fainites**.

fax (someone) *vb British* to **fuck**. A euphemism heard in upper-class, media, and show-business circles.

♭*'But darling I'm quite sure she's faxing him.'*

-features *suffix* '-face'. In British and Australian English it is often added to other, usually offensive, words as an insult or mock insult as in **bum-features**, **creature-features**, cunt-features, etc.

feature with (someone) *vb*

Australian to have sex with, succeed in seducing. A favourite expression of Barry McKenzie. Popularized by the cartoon strip in *Private Eye* magazine in the 1960s, it was briefly current as a result among students and others. It is probably inspired by the journalese 'featuring' as in 'starring', or as in being the main protagonist of a scandal.

✎ *'If I don't feature with this tart tonight the Pope's a flamin' Jew.'*
(*Barry McKenzie*).

feck! *exclamation British* a euphemistic deformation of **fuck**. Used in the cult TV comedy *Father Ted* (and posted on the Internet by Bodge World) in 1996 and 1997.

Fed *n See* Club Fed.

the Feds *n pl American* law enforcers, FBI agents. The word, used especially by lawbreakers in the USA, was briefly and inappropriately picked up in Britain as a euphemism for police in the early 1970s.

feeb *n American* a feeble-minded person, **twerp**. A teenager's term. This is one of a series of expressions for social misfits or peergroup outcasts coined by American school and college pupils. Earlier words such as **wimp** and **nerd** have entered world English, others like **dweeb**, which immediately predated feeb, have not as yet.

feek *adj Irish* attractive, 'enchanting'. The word may be a variant form of fake used to mean magic(al).

feel *n* a sexual contact, a **grope** or caress. In American teen jargon the word is often heard in the phrase **cop a feel**.

feel froggy *vb American* to want to fight. An item of black street talk which was included in so-called **Ebonics**, recognized as a legitimate language variety by school officials in Oakland, California, in late 1996. It comes from the catchphrase used as a challenge to fight: *'If you feel froggy, leap!'*

feel one's oats *vb* to behave in a restive, spirited, assertive or aggressive manner. This phrase is viewed as slang by some speakers and as a colloquialism by others. It is sometimes felt to be less than respectable by analogy with the vulgar **get one's oats**, but in fact merely draws upon the image of a horse which has just been fed. According to the slang collector, Eric Partridge, the expression originated in the USA in the mid-19th century.

feel someone's collar *vb* to arrest or take into custody. An item of police jargon, now more often expressed by the noun **collar**.

feisty *adj* spirited, tough and assertive, quarrelsome. The word looks like Yiddish, but is in fact from a southern American English dialect word for a small, fierce dog (a 'feist' or 'fice'), the name of which is distantly derived from 'fist', a variant of **fart**. The adjective was exclusively American until the 1970s when, mainly through the journalistic language of film criticism, etc. it became known in Britain and Australia.

✎ *'It was this feisty creature* [Pamella Bordes] *who ended a relationship with Andrew Neil by redecorating the walls of his Kensington flat with obscene graffiti.'*
(*Private Eye*, February 1989).

felching *n*

a the insertion of a live animal into the anus as a form of sexual stimulation. The practice was reported from California in 1993 and the word briefly became a vogue source of humour among UK adolescents.

b the term may also be applied to other practices involving digital or anal contact with the anus.

felony shoes *n pl American* trainers, sports shoes. An item of black street slang reflecting the fact that trainers were standard footwear among gangs in the 1990s.

femme, fem *n, adj*

a a lesbian accustomed to playing a passive, female role in relationships; the opposite role to **butch**.

b an effeminate or passive male homosexual. Both terms are from the French for woman or wife (*femme*), and have been in fairly widespread use since the turn of the century. Femme (or fem) was a slang term meaning woman in the 17th, 18th and early 19th centuries.

fence *vb, n* (to act as) a receiver of or dealer in stolen goods. The word was generally considered slang until the 1960s; there being no equivalent shorter than the definition above. Fence is now a universally understood term. It as at least 350 years old, apparently originating as a shortening of 'defence', although the precise relationship to that word is unclear.

fender-bender *n American*

a someone who poses as a road-accident victim or stages an accident in order to claim compensation. A law enforcers' and lawbreakers' term.

b a minor traffic accident or 'shunt' in which a car or its wing or bumper is slightly dented.

ferret *n See* exercise the ferret.

fess up *vb American* to confess, own up.

⮑ *'We want the truth!' 'What time is it?' 'Time for you to fess up!'*
(*Out of the Dark*, US film, 1988).

fidget *n British* a secret, 'wrinkle', edge or angle. A mainly working-class term used, among others, by fraudsters and petty criminals.

⮑ *'He's got a few fidgets worked out.'*

fifi *n American* sex, sexual gratification. A humorous euphemism heard among middle-aged speakers often in the phrase *'getting some fifi'*. It was featured in the US movie *Extreme Prejudice*, 1987.

fifth wheel *n* a superfluous or intrusive extra person, an unnecessary thing. The phrase is American in origin.

fillet, fillet of cod *n British* a sod. A disguised rhyming-slang form of the term of abuse. The word (and phrase) is referred to by the comedian Ronnie Barker in his *Fletcher's Book of Rhyming Slang* 1979), but is not recorded elsewhere.

filleted *adj British* a late 1980s version of gutted. A fashionable way of conveying intense (or exaggerated) disappointment, bitterness, etc.

⮑ *'When she said she was going and taking the kids, I tell you, I was filleted.'*

fill someone in *vb British* to beat someone up. A phrase dating from before World War II.

F.I.L.T.H. *n British* an acronym for *'failed in London; try Hong Kong'*. A pejorative categorization applied by and to yuppies from the early 1980s and still in use just prior to the handover of Hong Kong to the Chinese authorities in 1997.

filth, the filth *n British* the police, especially those in plain clothes. A thoroughly derogatory term coined in the 1950s and enthusiastically adopted by radicals, student demonstrators and criminals alike in the 1960s.

⮑ *'I didn't realize he* [an ex-boyfriend] *was filth.'*
(Recorded, nurse, London, 1985).

⮑ *'They don't call us the filth for nothing.'*
(Comedian Julian Clary, in police uniform, on *Friday Night Live*, April 1988).

filthy *adj British* extremely wealthy. A shortening of 'filthy rich'.

⮑ *'I tell you, she's absolutely filthy.'*

fin *n American* a five-dollar bill. From the Yiddish *finif*, five. *See also* finski.

finagling *n* devious machination, manoeuvre or manipulation. The word, which is sometimes used as a regular verb ('to finagle'), is well-established in the USA. It is said to derive from the archaic British dialect word fainaigue (meaning to cheat).

financial *adj Australian* well-off, in funds, solvent.

⮑ *'He's fairly financial just at the moment.'*

finesse (someone) *vb American* to outmanoeuvre someone, cleverly manipulate or cheat. From the technique in contract bridge. Originally a cardsharps' term, now in general use.

finger *vb* to inform on someone. From the action of pointing out a culprit.

⮑ *'They fingered him for the Jamaica Avenue job.'*

finger, finger fuck *vb* to sexually stimulate (vaginally or anally) with the finger(s).

fink *n American* an informer or any untrustworthy, reprehensible person. In the late 19th century the word was used for spies, informers, policemen and strikebreakers. It is the German word for finch and was presumably imported by German or Yiddish-speaking immigrants, although the exact meaning is obscure. (It appears not to be related to 'singing like a canary'.) Less plausibly, the name of the Pinkerton detective agency has also been suggested as a source. *See also* **ratfink**.

finski *n American* a **fin** (five-dollar bill). An embellished form of the word used typically by high-school or college students. The '-ski' ending (in imitation of Slavic languages or Yiddish) is thought to add raciness to short everyday words.

✤*'See what a finski can do for a man's attitude?'*
(*Ferris Bueller's Day Off*, US film, 1986).

fired-up *adj*
a angry, furious.
b sexually aroused.
c stimulated by illicit drugs.
d enthused, aroused, excited.

All these senses of the word are American slang in origin, based on the firing-up or revving of an engine. The term is now a common colloquialism.

fireman's hose *n British* nose. A piece of authentic rhyming slang, still heard occasionally in London.

✤*'He had to stick his fireman's hose into it, didn't he.'*
(Recorded, hairdresser, Richmond, 1988).

firkin' *adj*
fucking. This word is generally thought of and used as a joky euphemism, inspired by the similarity of the taboo word with the archaic name for a cask of ale. In fact 'firk' existed as a verb in its own right in early modern English. It meant to strike, and also to copulate, and may even have been in origin a distortion of 'fuck'. The word is typically used as an intensifier, as in *'firkin' cold'*.

firm, the firm *n*
a *British* a criminal gang or organization. Also used by and of teams of football hooligans, such as the Inter-City Firm, a much-publicized gang of older West Ham supporters.
b an insider's, or would-be insider's euphemism for an official but clandestine organization, such as a secret-service department or undercover police group.

first base *n American* kissing, necking. The first stage in the process of seduction, as described by teenagers and students (usually from the male point of view). The image is taken from baseball, where to get to first base is the first step towards scoring a run; stretching the analogy, a **home run** or **homer** is full sexual intercourse.

fish *n* a woman. The term is typically used pejoratively by **gay** males, referring to the supposedly characteristic smell of the female genitalia.

fishing expedition *n* an attempt to gather information while purporting to be doing something else. An expression used in general conversation and, recently, specifically in business jargon where, for example, a company will advertise for personnel in order to interrogate interviewees about rivals' plans.

fishing fleet *n British* a group of females arriving *en masse* in search of partners or husbands. The expression is applied today mainly to visitors to the outpost of upper-class society in Hong Kong; it formerly referred to the same social phenomenon occurring in India, etc. in the colonial era.

fit *adj British* excellent, fashionable. A vogue term among adolescents in the early 1990s. Synonyms are **mint** and **top**.

fit *n* **1** a set of clothes
✤*'I say rid [get rid of] the fit right now!'*
2 *British* also **the fit** the materials needed to prepare and inject heroin; the ligature, burner and hypodermic. An item of prisoners' and addicts' slang.
In both senses the word is a shortening of 'outfit'.

fit up *vb British* to **frame**; to manufacture evidence to procure a (false) conviction for a criminal offence. A piece of police and underworld jargon, which by 1989 had become widely known through its use by journalists, scriptwriters, etc.
✤*'I know a CID sergeant who had fitted a bloke up with an indecent exposure. They just stopped him as he walked around a corner and gave it to him.'*
(Police officer, *Inside the British Police*, Simon Holdaway, 1983).
✤*'Would I be fitted up for betraying him?'*
(Former detective, quoted in *Inside the Brotherhood*, Martin Short, 1989).

fit-up, fit *n* a **frame-up**, a situation in which an innocent person is accused or incriminated on the basis of false evidence, perjury, etc. The noun derives from the verb form.

↳'*It was an obvious bloody fit-up, but they let it go through anyway.*'
(Recorded, pub customer, London, 1987).

five by five *n American* a short, fat person.

five-finger discount *n American* something stolen, especially a shoplifter's booty. This is the thieves' own term, popular, especially in New York, in the 1970s and 1980s.

Five-0 *n American* the police force or an individual police officer. The usage originated in the TV series *Hawaii Five-0*, broadcast in the early 1970s.

five thousand!, 5000! *exclamation American* goodbye. A variant form of **Audi!**

fix *n* an injection of a narcotic. Originally an Americanism, by the 1960s it was in use throughout the English-speaking world. The word is now also used metaphorically or ironically to describe any habitual action, such as taking a fix of nicotine, or any pleasure which the speaker would not willingly forgo, as in a weekly fix of a television programme.

flack *n See* **flak**.

flag *vb American* to fail. In high school and college usage, the term refers to an F grade attached to an assignment.
↳'*I knew they'd flag me.*'
↳'*Erin got flagged again.*'

flagged *adj American* nabbed, reprimanded, identified and/or warned. It is the custom in American-football matches for the umpires to throw a flag (a sort of yellow duster) when they spot an infringement, to mark the spot where it took place. This is known as there being 'a flag on the play'. Flagged sometimes has the very specific senses of having been refused further drinks in a bar or arrested.

flak *n* criticism, antagonism, aggression, trouble. The terms *Flugabwehrkanone* and *Fliegerabwehrkanone*, given to German World War II anti-aircraft guns, provided this acronym which was adopted as an English colloquialism. It is now sometimes spelled flack.

↳'*We've had to take a lot of flak over this.*'
↳'*They've been getting a lot of flak from head office recently.*'

flake *n* 1 *American* an eccentric or crazy person. A later formation from **flaky**. The origin is obscure.
↳'*Marx stands out as refreshingly creative and literate among a batch of flakes.*'
(Robert Conquest, *Independent*, 27 January 1989).
2 *Australian* shark meat.
↳'*Flake and chips.*'
3 *American* cocaine. High-quality Peruvian cocaine, for example, is often sold in the form of small flakes.
4 *Australian* an unscrupulous, untrustworthy person.
5 *Scottish* an unreliable or dangerous individual. *See also* **flaking**.

flaked, flaked out *adj* exhausted, collapsed.

flake out *vb* 1 *American* to leave (a place). An American teenagers' idiom in use since the late 1970s.
2 *American* to act eccentrically. From **flake** and **flaky**.
3 to collapse from weariness, fall asleep. In this sense the word is now a common colloquialism. Its derivation is uncertain.
↳'*After twelve hours in that damn factory all I want to do is come home and flake out on the sofa in front of the TV.*'

flaking *n American* doctoring, manufacturing or planting evidence to secure an arrest and/or conviction. Police jargon of uncertain derivation.

flaky, flakey *adj American* eccentric, crazy, unstable and irresponsible. This Americanism was given wider currency when President Ronald Reagan referred to Colonel Gaddafi as 'flaky' in January 1986; the word had to be translated in the press for British and Australian readers. The original connotations of the word are obscure. It seems to have existed in the above senses since the late 1960s, possibly originating in the argot of baseball players and sports journalists. Suggested derivations are from **flake** as a word for cocaine, or from flaking or crumbling stucco, stone, timber, etc. This second derivation, with overtones of disintegration and splitting or dividing, is more plausible.

flaky, flakey *n British See* **throw a flaky.**

flame *vb* to attack verbally and/or humiliate by sending an Internet or e-mail message. An item of **net-head** slang dating from the later 1980s.

↳ *'She got flamed.'*

flamer *n* **1** *American* **a** a flagrant or obvious solecism or blunder.

b a person who commits a gaffe or error. Both these sub-senses of the word are campus terms, used especially in **preppie** jargon.

2 a flagrant male homosexual, in American and Australian slang of the 1970s and 1980s. Since the beginning of the 19th century the word had been employed in British English to refer to something conspicuous.

flaming *n* **1** *American* (of gay males) behaving in a provocatively or flamboyant homosexual manner.

2a using computer links and networks to carry on obscene or sexually titillating conversations. A term of the late 1980s. This noun form preceded the later use of flame as a verb.

2b posting verbal attacks upon an Internet user, in the 1990s patois of **cyberpunks** and **net-heads.**

flaming *adj* an intensifying adjective; an alternative to **bloody** or a euphemism for **fucking.** The word is mainly heard in Britain, where it is rather dated, and in Australia, where it is fairly common. Especially in the north of England it forms part of several colourful but inoffensive oaths such as 'flaming heck', 'flaming 'eck' and 'flaming Nora'. In American usage flaming usually has the specific suggestion of 'flagrant' in a homosexual context.

flannel *vb, n* (to subject someone to) talk intended to flatter, deceive, bamboozle, cajole, etc. This term is now a well-known colloquialism for waffle or nonsense. It was originally (in the 19th century) a scathing term for the pretentious ornamentation on commercial letterheads, etc.

↳ *'He gave me a load of old flannel.'*

flapdoodle *n* fuss, agitation, con-

sternation. An invented nonsense word dating from the 19th century.

flap one's gums *vb American* to talk, speak or converse. An item of black street talk that was included in so-called **Ebonics,** recognized as a legitimate language variety by school officials in Oakland, California, in late 1996. **Flap one's lips** is a less common variant, **snap** and **bump one's gums** are synonyms.

flaps *n pl* **1** ears, especially large or protruding ears.

2 the female labia.

flash *n* **1** a glimpse of, or deliberate exposure of, the genitals, breasts, underwear, etc.

2 a the sensation felt immediately after the injection of a narcotic; the sudden, initial effect of a drug.

b also **acid flash.** A sudden recurrence of a previous experience of the drug LSD (lysergic acid diethylamide).

3 *British* a street trader's display of goods.

flash *adj* ostentatious, showing off. Since the 1960s, especially in Britain and Australia, this form has tended to replace the earlier 'flashy'.

↳ *'Why do you bring horses if not to sell? It's flash.'*
(Recorded, gypsy boy, Appleby horse fair, 1988).

flasher *n* a sexual exhibitionist, a man who deliberately exposes his genitals in public. The word was slang or police jargon until the 1960s when the prevalence of the activity and a lessening of verbal prudishness brought it into common currency.

Flash Harry *n British* a show-off, a flamboyant or boastful person. The identity of the eponymous Harry is unknown.

flash on (something) *vb* to be inspired by something, have a sudden bond with something, have a revealing intuition about something. A characteristically vague **hippy** term of the 1960s which is now rarely heard except in the context of the 'psychobabble' of alternative therapists, etc. It derives from the specific drug-related meaning of the noun **flash.**

flash the ash *vb British* to offer a cigarette. Usually the expression is in the form of a request or demand.

flat *adj British* penniless. A shortened form of the colloquial 'flat broke', heard in raffish speech of the late 1980s.

flatlining *adj* drunk. The term is medical jargon for the state of a patient whose vital signs have disappeared, leaving only a flat trace on monitoring screens; it was popularized by the 1990 US movie *Flatliners*. It usually denotes a state of drunken speechlessness or near-unconsciousness and is in use among American and Australian adolescents.

flave *adj American* fashionable, stylish, cool. A vogue term among rappers and hip-hop aficionados in the early 1990s, the word is an abbreviated form of the earlier word 'flavor', denoting personal style.

flavour of the month *n* the current favourite or fashionable person or thing. An expression which usually expresses a scathing or critical attitude to fads or ephemeral popularity. (It derives from the use of the phrase in advertising ice cream in the USA in the 1950s and 1960s.)

↳'*Looks like she's flavour of the month in the office at the moment.*'

↳'*Ecology, well it's flavour of the month.*'

fleabag *n*
a a cheap, dirty hotel.
b a scruffy, dirty person or animal.
c an old sleeping bag or bed.

fleapit *n* a cheap, dirty cinema. Originally the term usually referred to the front-stalls section and the 'pit' in front of the screen. Before World War II, in the case of rural cinemas especially, the term was often a literal description.

flex *n British* energy, enthusiasm. A term from the jargon of dancefloor and **acid house** aficionados in the 1990s.

↳'*Give it flex!*'

flick *n* a film. This word was first common slang, then trade jargon in the film business and now, via such American magazines as *Variety*, is emerging again as a general term for a movie. (For the derivation *see* **flicks**.) *See* **skinflick**.

flicking *adj British* an intensifying adjective, a euphemism for **fucking**. It is used for example by schoolgirls and adult women.

↳'*I can lay any amount of hands on them – no flicking danger.*'
(*An Evening with Victoria Wood*, British TV programme, 1988).

flicks, the flicks *n pl* the cinema, films. An early slang term in all English-speaking countries, derived from 'flicker' or from the homemade moving pictures made by flicking cards. This form of the word is now obsolete in the USA and has rarely been heard in Britain or Australia since the early 1960s. The singular form **flick** is still current.

↳'*We're going down the flicks tomorrow night.*'

flid *n British* a stupid person. The word was reported as being in use among schoolchildren by the sociolinguist Peter Trudgill in his 1990 work *Bad Language*, but seems to have arisen in the 1970s. It may be an arbitrary coinage or an obscure dialect term, or alternatively a conflation of 'flip one's lid' or, some suggest, of 'thalidomide (victim)'.

flim-flam *vb, n* (to attempt) trickery or deceit, specifically a confidence trick involving a tall story. The word, which is in use in Britain, but more widespread in the USA, probably comes, via Scottish dialect, from an old Scandinavian word *flim* meaning mockery. The added second syllable is an example of a common linguistic change in comical words (such as knick-knack, etc.) known as 'reduplication'.

↳'*I can smell flim-flam, right down to the paperclips you make me buy.*'
(*Columbo*, US TV series, 1976).

fling *vb, n British* **1** (to give someone) a bribe, illicit payment. A piece of criminal and police jargon which is a more recent coinage inspired by **bung**.

↳'*We'll have to fling him to square it.*'

↳'*I'd need a fling in that case.*'

2 an affair, usually extramarital.

flip, flip out *vb* to lose control, either through delight, anger, etc., under the influence of an illicit drug, or during the course of a nervous breakdown. Both words spread from American English to world English in the 1960s and derive from the earlier **flip one's wig** or **flip one's lid**, in use in the late 1940s and 1950s among **hipsters**, jazz enthusiasts and **beatniks**. To flip out was used to describe temporary insanity caused by LSD in the early days of the **hippy** era. The term is now old-fashioned (although surviving in French, particularly in the form *flippé*).

✎ '*He was worried about his mother, though. The old lady was flipping out.*'
(*Requiem for a Dream*, Hubert Selby Jr., 1979).

flipping *adj British* a euphemism for **fucking** used as a mild intensifier, especially in such phrases as **flipping hell** or **flipping heck**.

✎ '"*Stop standing there dreaming, lass", shouts Dad, "and get the top orf this flipping bottle of 'arp."*'
(*Town* magazine, May 1964).

floating *adj* euphoric, especially from the effects of illicit drugs. A now dated term common in the late 1950s and early 1960s.

flob *vb British* to spit. An echoic term heard among schoolchildren since the 1950s.

flog *vb* to sell. A common colloquialism in Britain which would still be considered slang by some speakers. The word originally referred to selling off military stores illicitly and is said to derive from a 19th-century army expression to 'flog the clock', meaning to put the clock forward to shorten the working day, later extended to other devious behaviour.

flog the lizard/log/dong/ meat/mutton/the bishop *vb* to masturbate. Colourful expressions used of, and usually by, men. The verb to flog was employed in the formation of a large number of slang terms in the 18th and 19th centuries.

floozy, floosie *n* a disreputable immoral, 'loose-living' or frivolous female. A late-19th-century word which is still in use (now usually said lightheartedly). The word originated in the USA, but by the end of World War II was in widespread use elsewhere. It is probably a deformation of 'flossy', an archaic word for a prostitute (itself deriving from flossy, meaning 'showy', or from the female nickname).

flop *n* 1 a place to sleep, a temporary bed or shelter. Especially in the USA the term is, and has been, used by vagrants since the early 20th century.

2 excreta. Probably originating in the USA, where **dogflop** is heard, this euphemism is paralleled by the British plop(s).

flop *vb* 1 (in this sense also **flop out**) to collapse exhausted, go to bed.

2 to consent to sex. In this sense the word has been used, albeit rarely, in the USA at least since Raymond Chandler's private eye Philip Marlowe said of a woman that she would 'flop at the drop of a hat'.

flophouse *n* a cheap hotel or dormitory for vagrants. Originally an Americanism, the word is now part of international English.

floss *n American* abbreviated female underwear, G-string, or thong. The colloquial shortening of 'dental floss' was used by females from the late 1980s to refer to ultra-brief backless panties.

flub *vb* to fail, blunder. The word, of uncertain origin, has been recorded among computer specialists and **rave** devotees in the 1990s.

fluff *n See* **bit of fluff**.

fluff *vb British* a euphemism for **fuck**, used in the form **fluffing** as an intensifying adjective or in the expression **fluff off!** (an exclamation delivered at journalists by Prince Philip in October 1987).

fluffing *adj British* a mild euphemism for **flaming** or **fucking**, when used as intensifiers.

fly *adj American* streetwise, fashionable. A vogue term in black street slang of the mid-1980s.

✎ '*You fly, you cool: too much macho man fu' one woman.*'
(*LA Takedown*, US film, 1989).

fly a kite *vb* to issue a worthless cheque. Originally an underworld term from the jargon of fraudsters, the expression is now a common colloquialism with the meaning of presenting any dubious scheme or idea for approval. It retains its original meaning in criminal and police parlance.

fly-girl *n American* the female counterpart of a **B-boy**.

fod *n British* forehead. A schoolchildren's conflation.

fodder *n British* food. A lighthearted or hearty usage, heard typically among middle- and upper-class speakers.

folderol *n* fuss, complications, 'argy-bargy'. 'Fol-de-rol' and 'falderal' are nonsense words used in popular songs in former times.

folding stuff, the folding stuff *n* money, bank notes. A common lighthearted euphemism.

↳ '*The Cali cartel has a gentler reputation, first offering large amounts of the folding stuff and abhoring murder unless it is absolutely necessary.*' (*Independent*, 12 September 1989).

fomp *vb American* to engage in sexual horseplay, heavy petting. The word is popular among college students in the later 1990s but its derivation is unclear.

fool around *vb American* to commit a sexual indiscretion, typically adultery. A common euphemistic use of the expression, heard particularly among middle-class and middle-aged speakers since the 1960s. The term in this specific sense has not caught on outside the USA.

footsie *n See* **play footsie**.

footy *n* football. An abbreviated form popular in Australasia and in Britain where it is now more common than the older **footer** (which persists in public-school usage).

↳ '*Ockers on the way out …these days more go to theatre than footy.*' (Caption to photo in *Southern Cross* magazine, July 1989).

foozling *adj*
a clumsy, bungled.
b trivial, footling. From the verb foozle meaning to play or move clumsily or bungle; itself from German *fuseln*, to work carelessly.

form *n British* a criminal record. A police and underworld term derived from the language of the racetrack where it refers to a record or reputation based on past performance.

↳ '*Has he got any form?*'

fornicating *adj British* a jocular euphemism for **fucking** (as an intensifying adjective).

↳ '*I'm fed up hearing about his fornicating job!*'

foul *adj American* immoral, unacceptable. The standard term was appropriated by black street slang as a general indication of disapproval.

four-by-two, forby *n British* a

Jew. London rhyming slang in current usage. A descriptive, rather than an intrinsically offensive term. A four by two is a standard size of timber plank ($4'' \times 2''$), used for rafters, etc. (In the US it is known as a two-by-four.)

four-on-the-floor *adj, adv* flat out, extremely, excessively. This term, used typically by the young in the 1980s, comes from the hot rodders' term for a 'stick shift' or four-speed gear system.

↳ '*When I realized I wanted it, I tell you, I went at it four-on-the-floor.*'

↳ '*She's a four-on-the-floor great girl!*'

fox *n* a person who is sexually attractive. The word was used in black American slang of the 1940s by men of women (who were also known as 'minks'). Fox was adopted by white speakers in the 1960s and can now also be said of men by women.

↳ '*She's a fox and she knows it too.*' (Lyrics to 'Deborah', written by Dave Edmunds and Nick Lowe, 1978).

foxy *adj* attractive in a 'feral', sexually exciting way. Usually but not invariably used of women by men. The word was originally a black Americanism derived from the noun form **fox**; it is now widely known and used.

↳ '*Young foxy looking chick; Mr Walker say* [sic] *she lays by the swimming pool without her top on.*' (*The Switch*, Elmore Leonard, 1978).

↳ '*Lookit all these foxy chicks! Everywhere I turn.*' (Robert Crumb, cartoon in *Head Comix*, 1970).

fragged *adj American* ruined, or badly damaged. The term derives from the Vietnam-era practice of 'fragging' or killing one's own officers, itself based on 'fragmentation grenade'.

↳ '*The fraternity house was totally fragged.*'

fraggle *n British* a new-age traveller or **crustie**. The term, from the lexicon of the homeless, neo-**hippies**, etc., denotes an unkempt and/or seemingly deranged youth. It is inspired by the TV puppet series *Fraggle Rock*.

frail *n American* a female. A now obsolete masculine term from the pre-war era of crime fiction (Raymond Chandler used the expression). The expression was condescending, but not at the time offensive. It is occasionally resurrected for humorous use particularly in parody or pastiche.

frame *vb* to falsely accuse someone, or contrive to have someone convicted of a crime they did not commit. The image is of a picture or portrait being fitted within a frame. It should probably not be confused with **in the frame**. The earlier version of the expression was to frame (someone) up which survives in the noun form **frame-up**; both date from the early 20th century and were exported from the USA before World War II.

♥'*He convinced me that they had both been framed so the two villains who had committed the crime could get off.*'
(Former detective quoted in *Inside the Brotherhood*, Martin Short, 1989).

framed *adj* falsely accused, incriminated or convicted of a crime. The term was first used in the USA in the early years of the 20th century.

frame-up, frame *n* a situation in which someone is **framed**. Originally an Americanism from the early years of the century.

francis, frances *n American* the buttocks. The derivation of this term, heard in the armed forces and on college campuses, is obscure but it may be a euphemism for **fanny**.

franger *n Australian* a condom.

frat *vb, n* 1 *British* a schoolchildren's alteration of **fart**.
2 (to indulge in) fraternization.

freak *vb* to lose control of oneself, become hysterical. A shortening of **freak out**, this term came, in **hippy** usage of the late 1960s and early 1970s, to have a negative connotation of alarm or over-reaction.

♥'*I told her I was leaving home and she completely freaked.*'

freak *n* 1 a **hippy**, a long-haired (if male), non-conformist member of the 'alternative society' of the late 1960s and early 1970s. Freak was originally a term of abuse directed by **straights** at homosexuals and later at those guilty of outlandish behaviour and/or bizarre appearance. The term was quickly adopted by the objects of abuse and used as a badge of pride in themselves. (Hippies al-

most never referred to themselves as hippies after 1966; freak remained the acceptable epithet until the movement faded in the early to mid-1970s.) The word has now reverted to its original derogatory sense and is applied for instance to sexual deviants.

♥'*I feel like lettin' my freak flag* [i.e. long hair] *fly.*'
(Song lyric, Crosby, Stills, Nash and Young, 1970).

2 (as a suffix -**freak**) an enthusiast, devotee. From the mid-1970s the word was used in this sense, as in health-freak, **eco-freak**, etc. It was originally a **hippy** usage, as in **acid freak**. The term now sounds dated and has partially been replaced by the less radical **buff**.

3 *American* a sexually active or promiscuous person. This item of black street slang may be used pejoratively or appreciatively.

freaking *adj* an intensifying adjective, a euphemism for **fucking**.

♥'*You're a narc, you're a freaking narc!*'
(*Magnum*, US TV series, 1981).

freak out *vb* to lose one's self-control, to behave in an outrageous, frantic way. The phrase first described the alarming effect of hallucinogenic drugs such as LSD on some users, but was soon extended to any wild behaviour (whether viewed positively or negatively) such as ecstatic dancing. The expression originated in the USA among the first **hippies** and quickly spread to other English-speaking areas; it was sounding dated by the mid-1970s.

freak-out, freakout *n* a bout or scene of wild abandon, self-expression or loss of control. Originally, in **hippy** terminology, it was the result of ingesting hallucinogenic drugs, but later came to refer to any simulation of their effects.

♥'*These guys that come up and say: "Wouldn't it be a mind-blower if we got 6,000 million kids in red uniforms and had a big freak-out in the middle of Ealing Common".*'
(Pete Townshend interviewed in *Oz* magazine, June 1969).

freak someone out *vb* to alarm, traumatize or 'transport' someone. A transitive form of **freak out**.

freaky *adj* 1a unorthodox, non-conformist, pertaining to **freaks**.

♥'*Their awful freaky dancing.*'

b amazing, outstanding, **far-out**. A term of approval used by **freaks**.

↳'*This freaky chick.*'

2 *American* upset, unsettled. A 1990s synonym for **freaked** or **freaking out**, used by neo-**Valley girls**, e.g., '*When I saw him I was, like, freaky*'.

freaky-deaky *adj* a later elaboration of **freaky** in both senses. This form of the word was generally used pejoratively, condescendingly or sarcastically.

freckle *n Australian* the anus. One of many Australian vulgarities (**ace**, **date**, etc.) to denote this anatomical feature.

freebasing *n* taking cocaine by mixing the crystals with various volatile solvents including ether to form a **base** which is then smoked in a pipe. This activity is also known as 'basing'.

↳'*…the technique known as freebasing, a method of separating the base cocaine from the hydrochloride salt … the result is pure crystals of cocaine…*'

(*Guardian*, 5 September 1989).

french *vb* **1** to perform oral sex. A jargon term from the world of prostitution and pornography. The word may refer to cunnilingus or fellatio and derives from the British notion that all forms of 'deviant' sexual behaviour are widespread among, if not invented by, the French. This may originate in the widespread accusation or supposition of the spreading of venereal disease by foreign neighbours.
2 to engage in **French kissing**, in the language of teenagers. In this sense the word is most commonly heard in the USA. *See also* **Frenching unit**.

frenchie, frenchy *n* a condom. From the now obsolescent 'French letter', one of many examples of ascribing anything with sexual connotations to the French. (In French the equivalent is *capote anglaise*; English bonnet or overcoat.)

Frenching unit *n American* the mouth or tongue. A humorous euphemism, popular among college students for instance, and derived from the verb, to **french**, in the sense of tongue kissing or oral sex.

French kiss *n* an openmouthed kiss with tongue contact. A phrase which appeared in British and American speech shortly after World War I, before which there was, perhaps significantly, no equivalent term. Later alternatives were **soul kiss** and **tongue sushi**.

French safe *n Canadian* a condom. The phrase has been heard since the 1970s.

fresh *adj American* excellent. A vogue term among teenagers in 1987 and 1988. Teenage argot is in constant need of new terms of approbation but this fairly obvious example (derived probably from its over-use in advertising hyperbole rather than its standard American colloquial sense of cheeky) was still heard in the late 1990s.

↳'*Hey, check the fresh car!*'

friar tuck *n British* an act of sexual intercourse. A rhyming-slang form of **fuck**.

fridge *n British* a male. An item of rhyming slang ('*fridge freezer*', meaning **geezer**), heard since the 1970s.

fried *adj* suffering from the effects of drug intoxication. The term probably derives from the notion of 'frying one's brains', and denotes a state of dangerous disorientation, physical collapse, etc. **Baked** and **toasted** are used in the US in similar senses.

frig *vb* **1** to masturbate (oneself or another person). The ultimate origin of the word is the Latin *fricare*, to rub (from which friction is derived), via the Middle English friggen.

↳'*Friggin' in the rigging 'cause there's fuck-all else to do.*'
(Chorus from the rugby-song 'The Good Ship Venus').

2 to have sex (with). Since the 19th century the word has been used as a slightly less offensive alternative to **fuck**, although this was not its original sense.
The verb is nowadays rarely used in either sense except in the noun or adjectival form **frigging**.

frigging *adj* an intensifier used with adjectives and nouns for emphasis in the same way as **bloody** or **fucking**. It is considered substantially more offensive than the former and slightly less offensive than the latter.

↳'*I was talking to my Canadian niece this very weekend; she (a devout Mormon, 22-ish, not given to profanity) used the word frigging and said, "I'm*

sorry. I keep forgetting it's a bad word over here" or words to that effect.'
(Recorded, editor, London, 1989).

the frighteners *n pl See* **put the frighteners on (someone)**.

frill *n American* a girl or woman. A condescending male term which may be related to **frail** rather than to a more obvious origin.

frog, froggie *n, adj* **1** (a) French (person). The only slang term for this particular nationality dates from the end of the 18th century when the French were known as 'frog-eaters'.
2 *Australian* a condom (*see also* **frenchie**).

frog (and toad) *n British* road. A piece of London rhyming slang which is occasionally still heard.
⇘ *'I'm off down the frog for a pint of pig's.'*
(Recorded, financial journalist, York, 1980).

froggy *adj American* aggressive, willing to fight. This item of black street talk was probably derived from the phrase **feel froggy** rather than vice-versa.

frogspawn *n British* semolina or tapioca pudding. A schoolchildren's word for one of the most hated items in the school lunch-menu of the 1950s and 1960s.

front, the front *n British* courage, cheek, effrontery, **chutzpah**. This use of the word, as opposed to the colloquial senses of bearing or façade, occurs in phrases such as 'loads of front' or 'he's got a front as big as Harrods' (a reference to the large, impressive frontage of the London store). *See* **front out**.

front (someone) *vb Australian* to confront. This abbreviated form from the speech of adolescents was featured in Australian soap operas from 1990.
⇘ *'Why don't you just front her about it.'*
(*Neighbours*, Australian TV soap opera, December 1991).

front bottom, front bum *n* the female genitals. A term used by young children of both sexes and, often jocularly, by some adults in Britain and Australia.

front out/off/it *vb*

a to face up to someone or something, either with courage or bluff.
⇘ *'She decided to front him out.'*
b also **front off, front it**. To behave aggressively or over-assertively. An activity of young working-class males, often containing an implicit invitation to violence.
The phrase in both its senses was popular in the 1980s in Britain, and became a vogue term in US black slang of the 1990s.
⇘ *'He was fronting out down our boozer, so me and a couple of mates gave him a good kicking.'*
(Recorded, youth, London, 1988).

front-wheel skid, front-wheeler, fronter *n British* a Jew. A racist London rhyming-slang term of the 1970s and 1980s. The rhyme is on **yid**.

frost *vb*
a to snub or ignore.
b to anger or irritate.
Both senses have been in use (based on social coolness, 'chilling' or 'freezing') since the 19th century. The word is currently fashionable in teenage use in the USA.

frost *n* **1** a failure, woeful example of inadequacy. This fairly rare usage of the word occurs in educated speech, particularly in reference to a disappointing performance (in the theatre for example; it may originate in a literary or Shakespearean 'killing frost').
2 a snub or silent rebuff. This sense of the word derives from the verb form, currently in vogue among adolescents, particularly in the USA.

frost-top *n American* an elderly person. This item of adult and family slang often refers to a relative. A synonym is **moss-back**.

fruit *n American* **1** a male homosexual. From the idea of exotic, 'ripe', etc. A common term of abuse in the USA since early in the 20th century.
2 an eccentric person. A shortening of **fruitcake**.

fruitcake *n* **1** an eccentric or crazy person. This is a term from the late 1960s, originating in the 1950s catchphrase, 'as nutty as a fruitcake'.
2 *American* a male homosexual. An elaboration of **fruit**.

fruit-fly *n American*

a a male homosexual. An elaboration of **fruit** and synonym of **fruitcake**.

b a woman who frequents or escorts male homosexuals, **fag-hag**.

fruit loop *n American* another college term for **fag tag**. A play on *Fruit Loops*, the name of an American brand of breakfast cereal.

fruity *adj* **1** *British* sexually suggestive or provocative. In the former sense the word has become a common colloquialism as in fruity jokes/stories, etc. In the latter sense it remains a more restricted slang term in use especially among British cockneys and their imitators.

2 *American* strange or eccentric. The word is often used adverbially as in **acting fruity**. It presumably derives from the noun **fruitcake**.

fry *vb American*

a to execute someone by electrocution in the electric chair.

b to punish or chastise someone. A college students' and armed-forces recruits' term, used in such expressions as 'he got fried' or 'they fried her ass'.

fubar *n* a spectacular instance of incompetence, hopeless mess. The term originated as an acronym standing for '*fucked up*' or '*fouled up beyond all recognition*'. It probably originated in armed-forces usage like the similar **snafu** and is now heard particularly in US campus and office speech.

fuck *vb* **1** to have sex with. The most commonly used 'four-letter' word, used intransitively ('*let's fuck*') and transitively ('*he fucked her/him*'); now also of women ('*she fucked him/her*'). Surprisingly, the age and origins of this word are obscure. It may not be Anglo-Saxon as is often supposed (it was not recorded in writing until the 16th century) and does not occur in Chaucer and Shakespeare, but may have been borrowed from Norse (*fukkar* in Norwegian, *fockar* in Swedish). Wherever and whenever the word entered English, it is certain that it is related to a pattern of words in Indo-European languages which give, among many others, *pungere* (Latin; to prick), *ficken* (German; to fuck or strike), *foutre* (French; to fuck). The common semantic feature of these words is that they contain the meaning strike, push or prick.

Fuck has always been a taboo word in all English-speaking countries and is still omitted from broadcasts and generally asterisked if written in the press. In the late 20th century the verb often has the more specialized sense of 'habitually copulate' or 'be sexually willing' as in '*does she fuck?*'.

2 to make a mess of, destroy. A 1980s' shortening of **fuck up** with slightly more emphatic or drastic connotations.

↳'*They fucked the experiment totally.*'

3 to damn or disregard.

↳'*Fuck art, let's dance!*'
(T-shirt slogan of the 1970s).

fuck *n*

a an act of sexual intercourse. The noun post-dates the verb by at least three hundred years.

b a person when evaluated as a sexual partner.

↳'*A good fuck/an easy fuck.*'

c a person, especially when viewed as a fool, victim, villain, etc.

↳'*The poor dumb fuck didn't have a chance.*'

fuck (someone) over *vb* to humiliate, discomfit, distress, or destroy someone or something.

↳'*Once the income tax guys get their hands on you they can really fuck you over.*'
(Recorded, self-employed male, London, 1988).

fuck-a-duck *exclamation* a virtually meaningless expression of surprise or disbelief.

fuck-all *n British* nothing or almost nothing. An emphatic vulgarism.

↳'*He walked away with two hundred thousand and I got fuck-all.*'
(Recorded, businessman, London, 1987).

fuck around/about *vb* to play the fool, behave irresponsibly or irresolutely.

↳'*OK let's stop fucking around and get down to work.*'

fucked *adj*

a (of things) ruined, destroyed, rendered useless.

↳'*This typewriter is completely fucked.*'

b (of people) completely exhausted, beaten or at a loss.

↳'*I'm feeling fucked.*'

fucked-up *adj*

a (of things or situations) in a mess, destroyed, spoilt or ruined. Originally the expression meant seduced and abandoned.

b (of people) psychologically disturbed, traumatized.

↪'*Sadowitz will soon revert to being the fucked-up nonentity he must have been before people like you started dressing him up in the Emperor's New Clothes.*'
(Letter to *Time Out*, December 1987).

c (of people) temporarily deranged by drugs or drink (not necessarily a negative term).

↪'*I got really fucked-up on that dope.*'

fucker *n* a person. the word does not invariably imply dislike or contempt, although it may.

↪'*The poor fucker never stood a chance.*' *See* **motherfucker**.

fuckhead *n* a stupid or unpleasant person. A term of abuse popular in the 1980s and usually applied to males.

fucking *adj* an intensifier used with other adjectives for emphasis. Like **bloody** it is also one of the very few examples of an 'infix' (a word component inserted before the stressed syllable in the middle of a polysyllabic word) in English.

↪'*Jesus, it's fucking cold in here.*'
↪'*Abso-fucking-lutely.*'

fuck-me shoes *n pl* provocative female footwear. This obscure term received extensive publicity at the end of 1995 when the former feminist writer Germaine Greer accused the *Guardian* columnist Suzanne Moore of betraying feminist principles by wearing 'fuck-me shoes' among other items. The phrase probably originated in American usage but may be a confusion with 'fuck-you shoes' implying a disregard for convention or propriety or 'fuck-off shoes' where fuck-off means both outsize and aggressive. Very briefly in the 1980s heavy boots as worn by rightwing **skinheads** were known as 'fuck-off boots'.

fucknuckle *n* a term of abuse, used of males. The second component is included merely for the purpose of reduplication of sound and signifies nothing.

fuck off *vb* to leave, go away. A vulgarism that is used in regular verb forms and as an interjection.

↪'*Why don't you just fuck off!*'

fuckoff *n American* a useless, hopeless or idle person.

fuck-off money *n* funds with which to escape, retire, etc.

fuckpig *n* a very unpleasant, worthless or contemptible person. This is the British version of the American **pigfucker**. It has been part of the London working-class slang repertoire since the 19th century.

fuck truck *n* another term for **passion wagon**.

fuck up, fuck (someone) up

vb **1** to make a mess of things, commit a serious error or blunder. *See* **snafu**.

↪'*Don't tell me, you've fucked up yet again.*'

2 fuck someone up to create an emotional disturbance (in someone), traumatize.

↪'*They fuck you up, your mum and dad.*'
(Philip Larkin, *This be the Verse*).

fuck-up *n*

a a disaster, blunder, error or failure.

b a bungler or blunderer.

c someone who is emotionally or psychologically disturbed.

fuckwit *n* an idiot, a halfwit. An Australianism which has caught on in British use since the late 1970s. It usually expresses exasperated contempt.

↪'*The guy's a complete fuckwit.*'
↪'*You've all been coining it for years. All you fuckwits in the City.*'
(Caryl Churchill, *Serious Money*, 1987).

fuckwitted *adj Australian* hopelessly stupid, dim-witted.

fudge-nudger *n British* a male homosexual. The term was one of many synonyms based on the notion of excrement (others include **turd-burglar**, **chutney-ferret**, and **jobbie-jabber**), denoting 'active' or 'predatory' homosexuality heard in the 1990s.

fudgepacker *n British* a homosexual. A derisive late 1980s term employing fudge as an image for excrement and equating homosexuality with buggery, on

the same pattern as **brownie-hound**, **chocolate bandit**, etc.

fudge-tunnel *n British* the anus. The vulgar euphemism was adopted as the name of a British **grunge** band in the early 1990s.

fuggin' *adj* a euphemism for **fucking**.

fugly *adj American* ugly, repellent. Although the word, which is popular in campus speech, is blended from '*fucking ugly*', it is generally milder than its components imply.

↳ '*God, that's some fugly dog she's got.*'

full (as a boot/bull/bull's bum) *adj Australian* drunk. Full or 'full as a tick' were euphemisms for drunk in Britain in the 19th century, but are now obsolete. Earlier Australianisms on the same pattern were '*full as an egg*' and '*full as a goat*'.

full as a state school *adj Australian* drunk. A more recent variation of expressions based on the notion of full (of drink), heard during the late 1980s, but perhaps older.

the full monty *n British* all that is desired and/or required. The previously obscure phrase suddenly became extremely popular in 1990 and 1991 and many derivations were proposed, ranging from a nickname given to inhabitants of the Potteries region of England to a comment on the quality of the wartime briefings given by the British General Montgomery in North Africa. In fact, the most likely explanation of the phrase is that it is a piece of gamblers' jargon meaning the entire kitty or necessary 'pot' to be bet, from the Spanish *monte* (mountain). In the US 'monte' was adopted as the name of a risky card game, while in Australian horseracing circles 'monty' used to mean an accurate tip or certain bet.

↳ '*We had starters, main course, wine, you name it – the full monty…*'.
(Recorded, financial consultant, London, May 1993).

full-on *adj, adv British* exiting, powerful, with maximum effort. A vogue term among students particularly in the Midlands during the later 1990s. The expression is used in the same way as the colloquial 'all-out'.

funbag *n*

a a woman, particularly an attractive woman or a potential sexual partner.

b *American* a prostitute, in 1980s police jargon.

funbags *n pl Australian* breasts. A vulgar term from the 1960s inspired by children's 'lucky dip' sweet packets on the same lines as **mystery bags**.

fun-bundle *n* a condescending term for a female.

fundage *n* money. One of many formations using **-age** for mock pomposity. This example was not confined to North America and has been recorded among British students in the 1990s.

fundamental *adj American* excellent. A fashionable usage often in the form of an exclamation among adolescents from the early 1990s.

fungus face, fungus features *n*

a a bearded man.

b a very unhealthy-looking or ugly person.

Both senses are popular with schoolchildren.

funk *n* 1 a heavily rhythmic, 'earthy' music, particularly soul or disco music. A term applied to varieties of urban black music since the 1950s.

b authentic feeling, earthiness, a quality of unsophisticated, raw vitality. The noun form is a back-formation from the adjective **funky**.

2 *British* cowardice, fearfulness, a fit of panic. A word which is quite unrelated to the musical sense. Funk here comes from the Flemish *fonck*, worry or agitation. (A blue funk is a state of extreme fear.) It has been in use since the 18th century.

funky *adj* 1 a earthy, raw in the style of **funk** music (characteristically having heavy rhythm and bass and simple repeated melodies). This term, applied to urban soul-music which contained elements of African, jazz, blues and rock music, has been heard since the 1950s. It is sometimes elaborated to funky-butt.

b vital, raw, energetic in an unsophisticated way. A term of approval applied to people, objects, ideas, etc. by extension from the musical sense.

2 smelly, fetid. This is the original sense of the word, dating from the early-17th-century British noun funk, meaning a

stink or 'fug' of tobacco smoke. This in turn probably derives from the Latin verb *fumigare* (to smoke or fumigate), via French. Senses **1a** and **b** originate in this meaning.

funny farm *n* a psychiatric hospital or home for mental patients.

♭'*They're coming to take me away, ha ha, to the funny farm, where life is beautiful all the time.*'
('They're coming to take me away, ha-haaa!', song by Napoleon XIV, 1966).

funny money *n*

a counterfeit money.

b worthless denominations.

c foreign currency.

d excess or unearned wealth. The words in this sense express disbelief or resigned acceptance in the face of 'unthinkably' large amounts of money.

furburger, fur-doughnut, furry hoop, fur pie *n* the vagina. Expressions which have been part of the male repertoire of vulgarisms since the 1960s. In the USA, furburger and fur pie are sometimes used to refer to a female or females in general.

furiously *adj American* extremely. A hyperbolic vogue term in use among the **Vals** of the 1990s and featured in the 1994 US film *Clueless*.

furphy *n Australian* a lie, malicious rumour, tall story. The term is said to originate in Irish usage, but has also been derived from a person of the same name, the contractor who supplied garbage disposal wagons for the army camps in Australia during the First World War. An alternative eponymous source is the writer Joseph Furphy.

fusion *n British* state of unhappiness, irritation or agitation. This term became popular among teenagers in the 1990s who had probably picked it up from an older generation among whom this shortening of the word confusion had become almost obsolete. The usage was recorded among north London schoolboys in 1993 and 1994.

♭'*She's in a fusion again.*'

futz *n American* **1** the vagina.

2 a disreputable and/or unpleasant male. These noun forms are related to the verb form.

futz *vb American* to mess or fool around. The word is a deformation of a Yiddish verb *arumfartzen*, meaning literally and metaphorically to **fart around**.

(the) fuzz *n* the police. A 1960s' buzzword nowadays only likely to be used by a hopelessly out-of-date adult attempting to communicate ingratiatingly with young people (who will either not understand at all, or regard the dated term with contempt). The meaning was originally contemptuous, but through widespread use in the late 1960s became a relatively mild epithet. It derives either from the likening of a worthless person to mould, fluff or dust, or it is a black reference to white men's 'wispy' head and body hair.

♭'*You're more likely to be damaged permanently in a tangle with the American fuzz though, if you see what I mean.*'
(Terry Reid, interviewed in *Oz* magazine, February 1969).

fuzz-butt *n American* a novice. The term is used especially to refer to inexperienced members of the armed forces and it refers to the notion of an adolescent with downy hair on the buttocks.

the f-word *n British* a coy reference to the taboo word **fuck**.

♭'*He was very coarse, always scratching himself and saying the f-word.*'
(Recorded, middle-aged female bus-passenger, London, 1989).

G *American* friend, peer. This all-purpose greeting used among black speakers (usually but not necessarily male) is probably an abbreviation of **guy** although **gangsta** has been suggested as an alternative.

G *n* **1** a gram (of some illicit substance). The abbreviation is typically used in referring to cocaine, which is sold in grams.

2 a thousand, a **grand**.

↳ '*It cost me two g's.*'

3 *American* friend, peer. The abbreviation (probably of 'guy') is used as a greeting between males, particularly in black street usage.

4 *American* an FBI agent. A 1990s abbreviation of **G-man** heard among criminals and street-gang members.

gadgie, gadgy *n, adj British* (an) old, infirm or senile (person). A schoolchildren's word mainly heard in the north of England. The source is in dialect of the 19th century or earlier but the precise original meaning is lost.

gaff *n British* a home or house. In 19th-century slang a gaff was a fair, fairground or any place of cheap entertainment. These notions were expanded in the argot of actors, tramps, market stallholders, criminals etc. and the word came to be used to describe any place or location, hence the current meaning which was racy underworld jargon from the 1920s to the 1950s when **spivs**, **teddy boys** etc. gave it wider currency. (It is still mainly used by working-class speakers.)

↳ '*If I was you I'd go round his gaff and pour brake fluid all over his paintwork – see how that goes down.*'
(*The Firm*, British TV play, February 1989).

↳ '*Nice gaff you've got here.*' See also **blow the gaff**.

gaffer *n*

a a boss. A rustic term of address or descriptive word for an old man or master current in Britain since the 16th century, gaffer is a contraction of grandfather. It is still widely used, particularly by working-class speakers.

↳ '*If I were you I'd go and fetch the gaffer; he's the only one who knows what's going on.*'

b an old man. This is probably the most common sense of the word in the USA, where it is also used to refer to a father (but rarely specifically a grandfather), and to a foreman as in the first sense.

c *British* a police officer. The term was recorded among London criminals in 1993.

gaffle *vb American* to confound, defeat, cheat. A term heard in black street slang in the 1990s, perhaps derived from the use of 'gaff' in black slang to mean a swindler or crooked betting scheme.

gag *vb* to vomit. A teenager's specialized use of the colloquial term for choking or retching. Its use is not entirely restricted to the speech of teenagers.

gaga *adj* senile, crazy, besotted. The word has come into world English from French, via upper-class or educated British English of the 1920s. In French it was probably originally a nursery word, influenced by *grand-père* (grandfather) and *gâteaux* (feeble-minded, infirm).

↳ '*She's gone completely gaga over this appalling creep.*'
(Recorded, wine bar habituée, London, 1986).

gage, gauge *n* marihuana or hashish. Gauge was a now obsolete slang term for an alcoholic drink and later also for a pipe or a pipeful of tobacco, coming presumably from the idea of a measure (of something intoxicating). The survival of these senses in American and Jamaican English led to the use of the same word for cannabis. In Britain gage was also heard among **beatniks**, prisoners, etc. in the 1960s when it was sometimes assumed to derive from 'greengage', an allusion to the colour of **grass**. The term is now dated.

↳ '*You want to blow that gage this way? We'd love it.*'
(Chrissie Hynde of the Pretenders rock group, shouting from the stage at Glastonbury music festival, 25 June 1994).

gagging *adj British* desperate (for relief, typically in the form of sex or alcohol). Like its synonym **choking**, gagging (literally, retching) became a popular vulgarism in all social circles during the 1990s. The phrase 'gagging for it' refers specifically and invariably to sex.

gag me with a spoon! *exclamation American* a favourite **Valley Girl** expression of exaggerated or thrilled disgust or astonishment.

↳'*Wow, gag me with a spoon! How gross can you get.*'

galah *n Australian* a fool, a silly, empty-headed person. The galah is a species of Australian cockatoo which characteristically congregates with others and 'chatters'. A rural catchphrase in currency before World War II, was '*as mad as a (gum)tree full of galahs*'. The word is pronounced with the stress on the second syllable.

↳'*Let's forget the whole thing, I feel like a right galah.*'
(*The Flying Doctors*, Australian TV series, 1987).

gallus *adj Scottish* cheeky, assertive, feisty. A Scottish dialect term applied particularly to women, it was used particularly to refer to TV presenter Muriel Gray in 1995. It is said to derive from the observation that someone was 'fit for the gallows'.

gam *vb British* to perform oral sex. A shortening of *gamahucher*, a 19th-century French term for this practice which was adopted into the specialist jargon of prostitutes, pornographers and their customers. The word is now a rather old-fashioned working-class and schoolchildren's vulgarism.

game *adj British* working as a prostitute, available for sex. The word in this sense is a back-formation from the earlier 'on the game'. It is used by **punters** and those involved professionally in prostitution.

↳'*She's game.*'

gams *n pl* legs, especially a woman's legs when considered shapely. A jocular word which now sounds old-fashioned, unsurprisingly in that it originates in the medieval heraldic term for leg, gamb, which in turn comes from Old Northern French dialect *gambe* (modern French is *jambe*, Italian is *gamba*). Gams is sometimes thought to come from gammon, a word which features in several cockney slang expressions; it does not, but it is distantly related etymologically. It is still heard occasionally throughout the English-speaking world.

↳'*Oo Nudge, check out those gams.*'
(*Beach House*, US film, 1981).

gander *n* a look. The word, which is usually part of phrases such as '*take/have a gander at this*', comes from the bird's characteristic craning of the neck.

ganef, gonef, gonof *n American* a thief, petty criminal. A word from the Hebrew *gannath*; thief, via Yiddish. In the 19th century variant forms of this word were heard in Britain and South Africa, but are now archaic.

↳'*I'm curious, what do you remember about the man who robbed you ... I want to know what the ganef looked like.*'
(*Hill Street Blues*, US TV series, 1986).

gang bang *vb, n* (to take part in) sex involving several males sequentially with one woman; group sex. The word received publicity in the 1960s, largely as a result of articles describing the rituals of Hells Angels and others.

gang bang *vb American* to take part in the activities of a street gang. A term from the 1980s which is a play on the well-known sexual term, and bang in the sense of gunshot. The word has been brought to public attention by TV documentaries describing the activities of such gangs in the era of **crack**. (The phrase is now sometimes shortened to **bang**.)

gangbanger *n American* a loyal and committed member of a street gang. This 1980s term is used by and about the members of street gangs in Los Angeles. The bang in question is a gunshot; shooting a victim is often part of the initiation process.

gangbusters *n, adj American* (something) superlative, excellent, impressive. A schoolchildren's word which is a shortening of the jocular adult phrase '*like gangbusters*', meaning very strongly, energetically or dynamically. The terms originate in the violently heroic actions of the anti-mob law enforcers (nicknamed gang-busters) of yellow journalism and crime fiction.

↳'*Hey you know, that set they played was gangbusters!*'

gangie *n Australian* a **gang bang** or group-grope.

ganja *n* marihuana. This is one of the many names for cannabis which has been heard in various milieus over the last fifty years or so. At present the term is popular in the Caribbean and among blacks and young white smokers in Britain. It comes originally from the Sanskrit *gañja*, via Hindi.

gannet *n British* a person who eats greedily, someone who bolts their food. Gannet is a 1970s and 1980s term derived, possibly via comics' adaptation of navy argot, from the voracious habits of the fish-gorging seabird.

✎*'If you've got any sense you'll keep the best stuff away from those gannets.'*
(Recorded, teacher, York, 1981).

gangsta *n, adj American* (a person) belonging to black street gang culture. The term, which denoted an admirable gang member, became generalized as an all-purpose categorization in street gang, hip hop and **rap** culture.

garbo *n Australian* a garbage man, dustman. The word's first use seems to have coincided with the height of the fame of the Swedish movie actress, Greta Garbo.

garbonzas *n pl American* breasts. One of many invented terms used lightheartedly by males (**gazungas** is another version). This may conceivably be influenced by the Spanish *garbanzos*; chickpeas.

✎*'After totting up the score-sheet of exposed breasts ["garbonzas"], mutilations, rolling heads, gross-outs, auto-collisions, he awards a number of stars and puts his seal of approval on a film.'*
(*Observer*, 9 April 1989).

gargle *n Irish and British* (an) alcoholic drink. A joke on the lines of **lotion** and **tincture** which is at least 100 years old and is still commonly heard in Dublin, for instance.

✎*'Fancy a gargle, John?'*
(Posy Simmonds cartoon, *Guardian*, 1981).

✎*'I'll have some gargle, if you don't mind, sir.'*
(Recorded, Irish pub habitué, London, 1987).

garms *n pl* clothes. The clipped form of 'garments' was an important part of the hip hop and **rap** subculture's lexicon from the 1980s, later crossing the Atlantic and eventually heard among UK adolescents. Older synonyms were **rags**, **threads** and **vines**.

✎*'Grab your flash garms!'*
(*Touch Magazine*, September 1993).

garn, g'arn *exclamation British* an old-fashioned Cockney term not widely heard since the late 1950s, garn is a form of 'go on!' or 'get on!', and was used as a shout of dismissal, defiance or irritation.

Gary Glitter *n British* the anus. The vulgarism uses the name of the enduring 1970s rock star as rhyming slang for **shitter**. (Previously the name of the cowboy star of the 1950s, Tex Ritter, had been employed.)

✎*'What male priests can do – give choirboys one up the Gary Glitter.'*
(Comedienne Jo Brand, Christmas 1994).

gas *n* 1 something which is exhilarating, stimulating or highly enjoyable. In the phrase *'it's a gas'* and *'what a gas!'*, this word became one of the clichés of the **hippy** vocabulary. It probably originated in American black street slang of the late 1950s, inspired by the exhilarating effects of nitrous oxide (laughing gas), although the same word, with the same meaning and origin, already existed in Irish speech.

✎*'But it's all right now, in fact it's a gas … I'm jumping Jack Flash, it's a gas, gas, gas.'*
('Jumping Jack Flash', Rolling Stones, 1968).

2 an idle conversation, period of empty chatter.

gas guzzler *n* an uneconomical car. A term originally applied to American non-compact cars of the 1970s.

gash *adj British* 1 spare, available. This now almost obsolete use of the word was common in the armed services in the 1950s and probably has the same origins as the following senses.

2 attractive, impressive. The origin of this sub-sense of gash is obscure but may be inspired by the attractiveness of 'spare' or available women. It was heard among working-class Londoners until the late 1960s.

3 useless, worn out, broken. In this sense

gash is still heard especially in London, among workmen, technicians, musicians, etc.

↳ *'There's nothing in there but a pile of gash tapes.'*
(Recorded, video technician, London, 1988).

The various meanings of the term probably all derive from a 19th-century adoption of the French word *gâcher* (to waste or spoil) or *gâchis* (mess) for rubbish on board ship. The meaning was ironically extended to cover extra portions, then anything spare. The original French is preserved in the third sense above.

gash *n*

a a woman or girl. A male term of sexual origin but not necessarily used with sexual connotations. The term existed in the argot of the streets in the 1950s both in the USA and in working-class Britain, (where it usually occurred in the phrase '*a bit of gash*'). It was revived in the 1980s by aficionados of **rap** music and hip hop as a fashionable synonym for girlfriend. The origin of the word lies in **b**, which is unknown to many users.

b a woman's genitals, or women as sex objects. The fearful or dismissive male image of a woman's external sex organs as a wound is an ancient one. Gash in this sense was a widespread vulgar euphemism in the 19th century.

gasper *n* 1 a cigarette. An ironic witticism from the days before the anti-smoking lobby, when shortness of breath was still a possible subject for levity. (It is probably unconnected with the more recent British cliché 'gasping for a fag'.) The word was at its most popular in the 1950s in the language of **spivs**, **cads**, etc., but is not yet obsolete.

2 *British* a devotee of self-asphyxiation as a sexual stimulus. The term, from the lexicon of prostitution, received publicity at the time of the death in 1994 of the Tory MP Stephen Milligan while indulging in this practice (known in slang as **scarfing**).

gassed *adj* drunk. A popular word among middle-class, middle-aged drinkers in the USA in the mid-1960s, gassed was also a synonym for tipsy in Britain after World War I (probably from laughing- rather than mustard-gas).

gasser *n* 1 something which is highly amusing or impressive. This sense of the word is inspired by the properties of laughing-gas and is used to denote a good joke, for example. This is an Americanism which is also heard in Britain and may have been coined there independently. It was first used before World War II, and is now heard particularly among teenagers.

2 *American* a depressing experience, person or situation. The word is rare in this sense, in which the image evoked is presumably of a poisonous, asphyxiating or anaesthetic gas.

gat *n* a pistol, revolver. A piece of obsolete underworld slang from the early 1900s derived from Gatling gun (an early revolving-barrel machine-gun). The word is occasionally resurrected by writers invoking the atmosphere of the gangster era, and was the trademark name of a cheap British air pistol of the 1950s.

gata *n* *South African* a police officer. Recorded as an item of Sowetan slang in the *Cape Sunday Times*, 29 January 1995.

gate fever *n* *British* terror at the prospect of release from prison. An item from inmates' jargon describing a familiar condition.

gauch out *vb* *British* *See* **gouch out**.

gay *adj* homosexual. In late medieval English 'gay' often had the sense of showy or affected as well as happy and light-hearted. In British slang of the 18th and 19th century it was a euphemism for sexually available or living an immoral life, and was invariably applied to women, usually prostitutes. In the early 20th century it was adopted as a code word by the British and American homosexual community, an innocent-sounding term which they could use of themselves and each other. The word had the secondary purpose of reinforcing homosexuals' positive perception of their sexual identity as opposed to the derisive or disapproving terminology of the heterosexual world. 'Gay' was widely used in the theatrical milieu by the mid-1960s and, when homosexuals began to assert themselves openly in the later 1960s, it supplanted all alternatives to become the standard non-discriminatory designation.

gaylord *n* *British* an effete or homosexual male. A schoolchildren's term of the late 1980s. The word, which is an embellishment of **gay**, may derive from Jamaican argot.

gazillion *n* *American* a very large

number or quantity. An alternative form for **zillion, squillion** and **bazillion**.

gazing *n British* relaxing. A fashionable term among adolescents in the later 1990s, the word may be related to 'shoe-gazing', a phrase earlier used to describe the posturing of **indie** musicians who would slouch almost motionless while performing staring down at the stage.

gazump *vb British* to cheat (in a house purchase) by raising the price at the last moment, after agreement has been reached but before contracts have been formalized. An old expression from the language of swindlers, revived to denote a practice which became widespread during and after the dramatic rise in property prices in 1972. The word formerly existed in several forms (gazumph, gazoomph, gazumf, etc.) and is from Yiddish.

gazunda, gazunder, gazunta, gozunder *n* a chamber pot. A perennial humorous euphemism heard in Britain and Australia, based on the fact that the un-nameable article in question 'goes under' the bed. By extension these words are sometimes used to refer to other un-named gadgets, containers, implements or contraptions.

gazungas *n pl* female breasts. A male term.

gear *adj British* excellent, absolutely right, first rate. An ephemeral vogue word that spread with the popularity of the Beatles and the 'Mersey sound' from Liverpool in 1963 to be picked up by the media (a fact which incidentally marked its demise as a fashionable term). It is related to 'the gear' meaning the 'real thing' or top quality merchandise.

gear *n* 1 clothes, accessories. Now a widely-used colloquialism, gear was slang, in the sense of being a vogue word in restricted usage, in the early 1960s, when its use paralleled the new interest in fashion among **mods**.
2 illicit drug(s). Since the early 1960s gear has been used by drug abusers, prisoners, etc. to denote, in particular, cannabis or heroin. In this sense the word is a typical part of the drug user's quasi-military or workman-like vocabulary (**works, equipment** and **artillery** are other examples).
▷'*Got any gear, man?*'
3 a top quality merchandise, the 'real thing'.

b stolen goods. A specific usage of the standard colloquial sense of the word.
▷'*Stash the gear in the garage.*'

gee *n American* a version of **G**.

gee-gee *n British* a horse. A nursery term adopted by adults to refer ruefully or facetiously to race-horses. In British films of the 1950s the word was characteristic of **spivs** and **cads**.
▷'*I lost thirty quid on the gee-gees.*'

geek *n American* a freak, insane or disgusting person. This old word originated with fairground or **carny** folk to describe someone willing to abase themselves or perform disgusting acts, such as biting the heads off live chickens, or a grotesque person exhibited for money. The word is now firmly established in teenage and schoolchildren's slang, helped by the preponderance of geeks in the horror films of the late 1970s and 1980s. It may be derived from German, Dutch or Yiddish words for 'to peep', or from Dutch and English dialect words for a fool.
▷'*I'm gonna marry the geek tycoon.*'
(*Cheers*, US TV series, 1988).

geek, geek out *vb American*
a to behave eccentrically, like a **geek**.
b to search desperately for drug remnants, particularly **crack**. This sense is a specialization of the first, used by drug users in 1989 to describe the actions of a crack addict *in extremis*.
▷'*You just want more and more. That's when you go geeking – looking for specks on the floor, just to get some more.*'
(Drug user, *Guardian*, 5 September 1989).

geek rock *n American* another name for **crack**. **Rock** is a generic term for narcotics in (lumpy) powder or granule form, **geek** is a crazy person.

geet *n British* a contemptible and/or tedious person.
▷'*Those geets at the ACF [Army Cadet Force] deserved what happened. If they want to join the army, why don't they go and do it.*'
(Delinquent youth quoted in the *Telegraph Magazine*, 15th June 1996).

geeze bag *n American* an old **fart**,

old **geezer**. A term of mild abuse or derision, mainly in adolescent use.

geezer *n* a man. A common word in Britain, where slang users often assume that it derives from a bathroom geyser (water heater), by analogy with **boiler**. In fact it probably originates in 'guiser' or 'gizer', a word for a masquerader or mummer who wears a (dis)guise. In the 19th century geezer could be applied to women. The word is also used in the USA, where it is regarded as rather colourful.

geezing *n American* injecting heroin, **shooting up**. An item of addicts' and underworld slang, also used by the police, which appeared in the 1960s.

gelt *n* money. The word is taken directly from Yiddish or German and has been used in all English-speaking areas since at least the 17th century, at first probably in allusion to Jewish money-lenders.

gendarmes *n pl British* the police. A middle-class appropriation of the French word in an attempt at raciness.
↳ '*Had a spot of bother with the gendarmes as I was driving down.*'

Generation X *n American* a journalese coinage describing the supposedly listless, apathetic post-**yuppie** generation of young people who were entering adulthood in the early 1990s. The phrase was borrowed, in 1992, by the Canadian author Douglas Copeland from earlier use as the title of a 1960s sociological analysis of youth rebellion and in the 1970s as the name of a would-be **punk** band.

gentleman of the road *n British* a tramp, vagrant. A euphemism first applied to highwaymen and later by tramps to themselves.

geordie *n British* a native or inhabitant of Newcastle or Tyneside in the north-east of England. The word is a Scottish dialect version of George and probably first arose as a nickname for one of the Hanoverian kings, used by and later applied to soldiers billeted upon Newcastle. The name refers also to the distinctive speech patterns of the area.

george *adj American* excellent, first-rate, fine. A word from teenage slang of the late 1950s which is periodically revived by modern schoolchildren and college students. It probably derives from

gorgeous or is an expansion of the letter g (for good).

george *vb American* to have sex, the term is used particularly by adolescents and refers to heterosexual activity by either sex.

George Melly *n British* belly, paunch. This item of rhyming slang employs the name of the corpulent old-Etonian jazz singer and writer.

George Raft *n British* a draught (of air). A fairly widespread piece of jocular rhyming slang inspired by the American actor of the same name (famous for his tough-guy and underworld roles on and off screen).
↳ '*Blimey, there's a bit of a George Raft in here, ain't there?*'

the gerbil *n British* the teachers' nickname for the Thatcher government's Education Reform bill which became law in 1988. Commentators who remarked on the benign choice of the name of a children's pet misunderstood the teachers' reading of the acronym; rodent-like and insatiable were more probably the qualities evoked.

germ *n British* an irritating, unpleasant or contemptible person. A schoolchildren's term of criticism or abuse, typically applied to fellow pupils or younger children.

gerry, geri *n British* an old person. A short form of geriatric, typically said without affection by teenagers or schoolchildren.

gertcha! *exclamation British* a cockney cry, roughly equivalent to 'get away!', 'give over!', or 'get out of it!' and expressing disbelief or gentle mockery. The dated expression was revived for use in the musical accompaniment (by Chas and Dave) to a television advertisement for Courage Best Bitter screened in 1983.
↳ '*"Gercher", wheezes Dad convulsively over the debris of the saloon bar.*'
(*Town* magazine, May 1964).

get *n British* a bastard, literally or figuratively; an unpleasant or stupid person. This word is more widespread in the Midlands and north of England, generally in working-class usage. In the south of England **git** is more common. Get was originally a derivation of 'beget' and meant a (begotten) child.

get a click *vb British* to succeed in picking up a partner. The term is heard particularly in the Scottish lowlands and the north of England.

�德'*I hear Jillie managed to get a click last night.*'

get/have a cob on *vb British* to become angry, display irritation. The term has been used in the Channel 4 TV soap opera *Brookside*. Eric Partridge dated the phrase to the 1930s: the 'cob' in question is probably originally a dialect term for a lump or a protrusion, and can be dated back to English slang of the later 18th century.

get a job *vb, exclamation American* (to) fulfil oneself. A joke variation on admonitions such as **get a life**, **get real**, which enjoyed a vogue in the 1990s.

get a life *vb, exclamation* (to) fulfil oneself. An admonition, originally American, that became a vogue term from the early 1990s. **Get a job** is a jocular alternative.

get a rift/rush/hustle on *vb British* to hurry up, make haste. These are more colourful working-class London variants of the colloquial '*get a move on*'.

get a twitch on *vb British* to become agitated and/or furious. An item of London working-class slang heard among, e.g., football supporters in the 1990s.

get behind *vb* approve of, support, empathize with. A phrasal verb (originating in the USA) of the sort popular with the 'alternative lifestyle' proponents of the early 1970s. Compare **get off**, **get down**, etc.

ᛞ'*I can't really get behind the idea of God as some bearded dude sitting on a cloud.*'

get boots *vb American* to have sex. A vogue term in black street slang in the 1990s. **Knock boots** is an alternative and probably original version of the phrase.

get Chinese *vb American* to get very stoned, become euphoric and/or semiconscious by smoking marihuana. This **preppie** expression is based on the premise that their stupefaction will rival that of Chinese opium addicts or that their

glazed serenity will result in an oriental demeanour.

get cogging *vb British See* **cog**.

get down *vb American* to let oneself go, begin something in earnest. This phrase was originally a piece of black slang, inspired by 'get down to business' (probably first used as a euphemism for beginning sexual activity, then transferred to musical activity). The expression is still heard in a musical context, referring for instance to musicians improvising successfully or to disco dancers 'letting go' (it is often used as a shouted exclamation, sometimes expanded into such forms as '*get down and get dirty*' or '*get down and get with it!*'). Around 1970 get down was adopted as a catchphrase by the white counter-culture, often with a generalized sense of 'start to communicate' or share experience.

get (someone) in *vb* to engage in lesbian sex.

ᛞ'*They're all getting each other in, didn't you know that?*'
(Recorded, London student, September 1995).

get in (someone's) eye/face *vb American* to aggress, behave intrusively and annoyingly (towards).

get into bed (with) *vb* to merge or agree to liaise closely with. A piece of jargon from the business world which has become widely known since the late 1970s.

get it on *vb*

a to succeed in having sex, to achieve (mutual) sexual gratification. An American euphemism, dating from the 1960s.

ᛞ'*I'm gonna ask you something right up front. Are you getting it on with that dude with the dog parlor or not?*'
(*The Serial*, Cyra McFadden, 1976).

b to succeed in something pleasurable or desirable. A generalization of the first sense which was used, sometimes as an exhortation, in the **hippy** era. Both senses became known, and to some extent used, in Britain after 1970, but had largely fallen out of use by the end of the decade.

get it together *vb* to organize oneself, one's life and/or environment. A vogue term and cliché from around 1969.

The 'it' refers to one's 'act', one's life, one's head, or to things in general.

get it up *vb* to achieve an erection. A common vulgarism.

get laid *vb* to have sex. A derivation from **lay**, which spread from the USA to Britain around 1968.

↳ *'Young guys in their twenties, of course they're going to try and get laid, and even if they don't succeed it's hardly big news.'*
(Lenny Henry, *Time Out* magazine, 26 July 1989).

get next to (someone) *vb* to strike up a relationship with someone. The phrase has been used by frequenters of discos since the late 1980s.

get off (on) *vb*

a to achieve satisfaction, exhilaration or inspiration (from). This American expression of the early 1970s is an extension of an earlier purely sexual sense of the phrase in which get off means to achieve orgasm. This concept was modified by the drug users' image of leaving terra firma, of flying or floating in a state of euphoria. Since the late 1970s the term has been heard (in Britain and Australia) generalized to include finding pleasure from more innocuous sources, such as music.

↳ *'Did you manage to get off on those mushrooms?'*
↳ *'I really get off on that guitar solo.'*
↳ *'Would you please define "got off on it"?'*
↳ *'He got a sexual thrill from beating the girls.'*
(*The Last Innocent Man*, US film, 1987).

b to **get someone off** retains the sexual sense of bringing someone to a climax: this use of the phrase is fairly rare.

get off one's case *vb British* to become intoxicated by drugs, to **get high**. An item of prison slang.

get one's act/head/shit together *vb* to organize oneself, arrange one's affairs, start to perform efficiently or effectively. A euphemism from the era of alternative therapy which likens one's behaviour to a performance (it may in fact have originated in theatrical or musical circles); unlike many such phrases it is still in widespread use.

get one's arse in(to) gear *vb*

to prepare oneself, get organized and get going. A phrase which appeared in Britain and America (with **ass**) seemingly simultaneously around 1974. It is usually employed as an exhortation to someone who is disorganized or wasting time.

get one's end away *vb British* to have sex, succeed in seduction. A masculine vulgarism in widespread use since the 1960s, this is a variation on '*get one's end in*', a euphemism dating from the early years of the 20th century.

get one's head together *vb* to collect one's thoughts, achieve a state of equanimity. A cliché of the 'alternative society' of the early 1970s (members of rock groups, suffering from the excesses of social and professional life, typically spoke of going to the countryside to get their heads together). This phrase is still heard, albeit more rarely, usually in the sense of pull oneself together or **get one's act together**.

↳ *'You know you really should try and get your head together if you intend to carry on in this business.'*

get one's jollies *vb* to derive enjoyment, obtain sensual satisfaction. The gratification referred to in this phrase is often less innocuous than the light-hearted nature of the words might imply.

↳ *'It's not my idea of a good time, but if that's how you get your jollies, I won't stand in your way.'*

get one's knickers in a twist *vb British* to become agitated, flustered or over-excited. This picturesque vulgarism originated in the late 1950s with a purely sexual sense. Now widely used, it is generally heard in the negative form, exhorting someone to calm down.

get one's knob polished *vb American* to receive fellatio.

get one's leg over/across *vb British* (of a male) to have sex, to succeed in seduction.

↳ *'You [Colin Moynihan, minister for sport] can be honest with us. Did you get your leg over or not?'*
(*Private Eye* magazine, April 1989).

get one's oats *vb British* to achieve sexual satisfaction. The phrase originates in the idea of 'sowing one's wild oats', especially in the sense of sexual adventuring outside marriage. Since the 1960s the phrase has been applied to both men and women, and to sex in general rather than adultery in particular. It is heard in all social classes in Britain and Australia.

✤'*If he plays his cards right, he should end up getting his oats tonight.*'
(Recorded, teenage drinker, London, 1986).

get one's rocks off *vb* to obtain

sexual satisfaction, achieve orgasm, ejaculate. An American vulgarism which became part of the **hippy** linguistic repertoire; some British users of the expression are unaware that **rocks** is a direct euphemism for testicles. (In American usage **nuts** or other terms could be substituted for rocks.) In the later 1970s the phrase was extended to mean to indulge oneself or enjoy oneself generally rather than in a specifically sexual sense. It now sounds dated.

✤'*But I only get my rocks off while I'm dreaming.*'
(Lyric from 'Rocks Off', The Rolling Stones, 1972).

get on one's wick/tits *vb*

British to irritate, annoy or vex. The 'wick' in question, unknown to many speakers, is a now rather archaic shortening of **hampton wick**, rhyming slang for **prick** (which is nowadays more usually shortened to **hampton**). In spite of the implied gender difference, both versions of the expression are used indiscriminately by both men and women.

✤'*It really gets on my tits when someone calls me a career woman.*'
(Recorded, female journalist, London, 1986).

get on someone's case *vb*

American to harass, badger or interfere. A phrase used with indignation or resentment, typically by an 'underdog' to or of an authority figure. The notion on which the expression is based is that of a judge or law-enforcer examining one's case. '*Get off my case*' is a widespread negative form.

get over *vb American* to become a

success in white society. An item of black street slang.

get real *vb, exclamation* to face up to

reality, to behave rationally. A vogue term originating in the United States and widespread elsewhere since the 1980s. Near synonyms are **get a life** and **get a job**.

get someone up *vb British*

a to bribe or pay off, 'square someone'.

b to entrap, **frame** or manoeuvre someone into a disadvantageous position.

Both senses of the rather vague euphemism have been in use in police and criminal parlance since the 1960s.

get tapped up *vb British* to suc-

ceed in meeting/seducing a partner. The phrase is used in working-class speech, particularly in the northeast of England.

✤'*Couldn't even get tapped up last night.*'
(*Away The Lads*, BBC 2 TV documentary, February 1993).

get the ass *vb American* to become

angry, irritated or furious. An item of black street talk included in so-called **Ebonics**, recognized as a legitimate language variety by school officials in Oakland, California, in late 1996.

get the horn *vb* to achieve an erec-

tion. A vulgarism employing the horn as a penis metaphor, heard more commonly in the adjective **horny**. Get the horn is now mainly heard in uneducated adult speech and the language of schoolchildren. To be 'on the (h)orn' is an alternative form.

get the hump *vb British* to become

bad-tempered, morose or offended. This common expression is at least 100 years old. The origin of this sense of hump is not clear, although it may refer straightforwardly to a hunchback's deformity, to a back bent with care, a head dropped in gloom, or a traveller's burden. In modern cockney usage the phrase is often abbreviated to the adjective **humpty**.

get the needle, get the dead needle *vb British* to become irritated,

bitter or vindictive. This expression is one of a number referring to needle in the sense of provoke or annoy. This particular form of words has survived as a working-class Londoners' phrase since the late 19th century.

get the salmon on prawn *vb*

British to have an erection. A piece of rhyming slang based on the phrase **on the horn**. The phrase was chosen as the title of an exhibition of paintings by the young artist Sarah Lucas in London in 1995.

get up one's nose *vb British* to ir-

ritate, annoy. A colourful vulgarism used by both sexes since its popularization in TV comedies of the late 1960s, notably *Steptoe and Son* and *Till Death us do Part.*

♦ *'It really gets up my nose the way he harps on about his work.'*

get wood *vb British*

to have an erection. A phrase popularized in the 1990s by *Viz* comic.

ghost *vb American* to depart, leave.

This item of black street slang, adopted also by white adolescents in the 1990s, is probably related to the phrase **git ghost**.

ghost turds *n pl American* another

expression for **dust bunnies**.

G.I.B. *adj American* sexually accom-

plished and/or sexually active. The euphemistic abbreviation of *'good in bed'* is spoken as its constituent letters, not as an acronym.

gibbing *n British* gate-crashing. This

term was in use among bouncers and security men during the 1990s. Its origin is obscure.

gig *n*

a a musical engagement or performance. One of many terms, originating among pre-World War II jazz musicians in the USA, which were adopted by the rock-music milieu in the 1960s. The exact origin of the word is obscure, but may be related to 'jig' in the sense of a dance.

♦ *'These lads are professional musicians and gigs are their bread and butter.'*
(*News of the World*, 29 May 1988).

b an appointment, session, stint or activity. Particularly in the 1970s the musicians' term was extended to refer to any one-off engagement or event (thus sometimes performing as a synonym of **trip** or **scene**).

♦ *'I've got the feeling this party isn't really my gig.'*

gig *vb* to perform at a **gig** or (more

often) a series of gigs. An item of musician's jargon.

♦ *'These guys* [The Grateful Dead] *will be gigging beyond the grave.'*
(*Independent*, 26 February 1988).

gigantic *adj British* excellent. A

vogue term among British adolescents in the 1990s as an adjective or exclamation.

giggle-stick *n* a **joint**, cannabis cig-

arette. A jocular expression, typically used by middle-class students or otherwise respectable adults since the early 1970s. It is not part of the lexicon of hardened drug users.

giggle water *n* alcoholic drink, par-

ticularly champagne or exotic spirits. An ingenue's jocular expression for the potential cause of unaccustomed hilarity.

gilbert *n British See* **green gilbert**.

gimme five! *exclamation* an invita-

tion to slap palms as a ritualized greeting or sign of solidarity.

gimmer, gim *n British* a foolish,

clumsy or unfortunate person. The words originated as Scottish and northern English dialect terms to a helpless young ewe or old sheep. They are still used primarily as contemptuous descriptions of females.

gimp *n*

a a crippled or lame person, especially an old one. The term is thought to derive from a blend of grandfather and limp. The adjective 'gimpy' is applied, often derisively, to anything or anyone clumsy or crippled.

b an awkward, ineffectual or clumsy person. By extension from the first sense above. The word is popular among schoolchildren.

ginchy *adj* excellent, skilful, smart,

elegant. A word of unknown etymology which entered the teenage lexicon in the early 1960s, first in Australia and Britain and shortly thereafter, in the USA. Ginchy is said to have originated in surfing slang, denoting for instance, an expertly executed manoeuvre. The noun form **ginch** also exists, but has been less common; both words are now rare.

ginger *n, adj British* a homosexual.

Rhyming slang from 'ginger beer': **queer**. A piece of pre-World War II London working-class argot which is very much alive in spite of the decline in ginger-beer drinking.

gink *n* 1 an awkward, ugly, foolish,

clumsy person. The word is at least 100 years old in Britain and America, but its origin is obscure; it may be an invention, or derive from either Scottish dialect or Turkish or Arabic via Romany. Before the

1950s the word also meant simply a person, without the pejorative overtones.

↳ *'Who's the shortsighted gink in the corner?'*

2 *n British* a bad smell, stink. The word, which is probably Lowlands Scots in origin, also occurs in the form of the verb *'to gink'*.

gippo *n See* **gyppo**.

gippy tummy *n See* **gyppy tummy**.

girl-cott *vb* to boycott. A feminist alternative, coined in the 1980s and used both facetiously and seriously.

girlfriend *n American* a female companion, member of one's circle or gang. This use of the word arose among black adolescents in the late 1970s and by the 1990s had become a common term of address among younger females across the US. The word is sometimes abbreviated to 'girlf'.

girlie *n British* a weak or effeminate person, sissy. A schoolboy expression of derision adopted facetiously by some adult males.

girl's blouse *n British See* **big girl's blouse**.

gism *n* an alternative spelling of **jissom**.

gismo, gizmo *n* a gadget, unnamed object. An American armed-forces term adopted in Britain since the 1960s.

git *n British* an unpleasant or worthless person. Many saloon-bar lexicologists have claimed that this word is an Arabic term of abuse, meaning 'pregnant camel', which was imported by servicemen who had been stationed in Egypt. The Arabic word does exist, but was probably noticed by British soldiers because the word git, a southern pronunciation of **get** (bastard or fool), was already part of their stock of vulgarisms.

↳ *'A frightfully clever chap called Stephen Fry, sending up all those smug gits who present kids' TV. (Hmmm ... comes across as a bit of a smug git himself.)'*
(*News of the World*, 15 May 1988).

git ghost *vb American* to behave discreetly, 'keep a low profile'. An item of black street talk that was included in so-called **Ebonics**, recognized as a legitimate language variety by school officials in Oakland, California, in late 1996.

git-go *n American* the outset, beginning. The term is usually heard in the phrase *'from the git-go'*.

git wid it *vb American* to become alert, streetwise, adapt to the current situation. An imitation of the earlier colloquial phase 'get with it' spoken with an Afro-Caribbean accent. An item of black street talk that was included in so-called **Ebonics**, recognized as a legitimate language variety by school officials in Oakland, California, in late 1996.

give (someone) a portion *vb British* to have sex. The vulgarism describes the sex act from the male point of view and has been popularized in the broadcast media, e.g., by the TV comedy series *Hale and Pace* in 1996.

give (someone) face *vb American* to affront, provoke, deride. An item of black street slang heard in the 1990s.

↳ *'Are you giving me face?'*
'What the hell does that mean?'
(*Made in America*, US film, 1993).

give head *vb American* (to be willing) to perform fellatio. A male term from the 1950s and 1960s, used typically by college students or servicemen during the **hippy** period of sexual experimentation. The phrase, and indeed the practice, seemed to assume a real and symbolic importance in male sexuality in the USA far greater than in Britain and Australia. The term has occasionally been applied to cunnilingus. (In the 1980s the words **skull** or 'some skull' have occasionally been substituted for head.)

↳ *'But she never lost her head, even when she was giving head.'*
('Walk on the Wild Side', written and recorded by Lou Reed, 1972).

give it a burl *vb See* **burl**.

give it large *vb British* an alternative form of **large** it.

give it one, give her one *vb British* to have sex (with a woman). A male vulgarism which has been commonly heard from the 1980s, both in boastful or assertive male conversation and in parodies thereof. A common elaboration is *'Give her one for the boys'*.

give it some cog *vb British* to accelerate, increase power and speed. A motorcyclist's term since the 1980s. **Cog** is jargon for gear.

give it some wellie *vb See* **wellie**.

give it toes *vb British* to run away, escape. Recorded from the mid-1980s and heard particularly in the Merseyside area, this is a synonym for the London criminal slang **have it away on one's toes**.

give it up! *exclamation*

a a demand by a mugger to give up one's money, possessions, etc.

b an exclamation of joy or solidarity. In the second sense the phrase became a fashionable cry uttered by aficionados of dancefloor culture in the mid-1990s.

give (someone) the arse *Australian* to get rid of, jilt or dismiss someone; a variation of **give someone the boot/elbow/heave-ho**.

give (someone/something) the wellie *vb British*

a to dismiss (someone) from work

b to reject (a partner).

c to discard (an object).

In all senses the expression is a variant form of the colloquial 'give someone the boot'. Compare **give it some wellie**.

give (someone) togg outs *vb British* to attack, beat up. An item of teenage playground slang of the 1990s, recorded among schoolboys in north London. The origin of the phrase is obscure: (tog(g)s might logically mean 'blows/ punches' but the word has not been recorded in that sense previously); it may have arisen in black British street slang.

given, givon *n British* an unpleasant, despicable or stupid person. A term of abuse heard in the 1950s and 1960s, mainly in working-class and schoolchildren's usage. The word is of obscure origin (one suggestion is that it is a corruption or misunderstanding of 'gibbon') and does not appear to have been recorded elsewhere.

glar, glah *n British* paint. A term used by house painters and artists in London, which has not apparently been previously recorded in writing. The origin is obscure, although some connection with glare, gloss or glue seems possible.

> ✎'*Go on, slop on some more of the old glar.*'
> (Recorded, mural artist, Vauxhall, London, 1974).

Glasgow kiss *n British* a head-butt. The term, sometimes also expressed as **Glasgow handshake** dates from the 1960s. **Gorbals kiss** is a synonym.

glass *n* diamonds or other gems, in underworld argot.

glasshouse *n British* an army prison. The military detention centre at Aldershot barracks had a glass roof in the early years of the 20th century and was notorious for the severity of its regime. Known as the 'Glass House' to inmates, it gave its name to other similar establishments.

glitch *n* a snag, unforeseen fault or malfunction. This piece of aerospace technicians' jargon from the late 1960s has entered the common vocabulary in the era of high technology, referring particularly to computer problems. It is either a blend of **gremlin** and hitch, or from a Yiddish version of German *glitschen*, meaning to slip.

glitz *n* glamour, (pseudo)sophisticated showiness. The word is a blend of glamour, ritzy and glitter and is probably a back-formation from **glitzy**. The term is usually used with a degree of implied criticism; it evokes superficiality and 'brittleness'. The word seems to have been an invention of journalists and writers in about 1984. In 1985 it was used as the title of a crime thriller by the American author Elmore Leonard.

> ✎'*Here* [Liberia] *there is little glitz to the evangelical churches.*'
> (*Sunday Correspondent*, 17 September 1989).

glitzy *adj* glamorous, showy. A vogue word from 1985 to 1987, used particularly by journalists evoking materialistic but superficial glamour. It is generally more negative than positive in its connotations (*see* **glitz**).

glop *vb British* to drink alcohol, particularly to swill beer. A student term of the 1980s.

> ✎'*Glop, don't stop.*'
> (Slogan in urinal, University of Essex, 1987).

glory-hole *n American* a hole in a partition between two toilet cubicles, enabling voyeurism or communication by (usually male) **gays**.

glug *vb, n* (to take) a drink or drinks of alcohol. A word which imitates the gurgle of pouring or swallowing.

G-man *n American* an FBI agent. The underworld and journalese term is either a contraction of 'government man' or a reference to G-division of the Dublin police force in which some New York City policemen had served. The phrase is now obsolete except when abbreviated for **G**.

gnarly *adj American* 1 excellent. 2 awful, inadequate. Both senses of the word have been beloved by **Valley Girls** and their teenage imitators in the USA since the mid-1970s. The word is thought to have originated in surfing jargon in the 1960s, referring to the texture of waves. By 1989 *Tatler* magazine reported the word as being in use among schoolboys at Eton. It is sometimes spelled **narly**.

go *vb* to be sexually active and/or enthusiastic. The word is used in this sense, particularly in Britain, of women by men; its vulgarity was highlighted in the 'Nudge nudge, wink, wink' sketch by Eric Idle in the British TV series, *Monty Python's Flying Circus* (1970), in which he badgers a fellow drinker with importunate questions such as:

↳ *'Your wife ... does she go? I bet she does.' See also* **goer**.

go ape *vb See* **ape**.

go at it *vb British* to have sex. A vulgar euphemism popular with adolescents in the mid-1990s. The colloquial phrase denotes any vigorous performance, but its meaning has become specified in slang usage.

↳ *'They can't wait to go at it, both of them!'*
(Recorded, London University student, October 1996).

gob *n British* mouth. The word was originally Irish and Scottish Gaelic for beak or mouth, becoming a British dialect term in about the 16th century. It is still more widespread (and considered less vulgar) in Ireland, in Liverpool, where the influence of Irish speech is strong, and in the north of England where the influence of post-Gaelic dialect lingers. In southern England it is mainly a schoolchildren's word.

gob *vb* to spit. The ritualistic spitting at groups performing on stage indulged in by **punks** from 1976 on was known as '*gobbing*'.

gobble, gobble off *vb, n* (to perform) oral sex, particularly fellatio. A vulgarism which is most widespread in Britain.

gobby *adj British* excessively loquatious, boastful. Based on **gob**, the term is a slang version of the colloquial 'gabby'.

go belly-up *vb*
a to die.
↳ *'Just another fat junkie who went belly-up.'*
(*Tatler*, October 1989).

b to fail or collapse. Said typically of a business or other venture.

These senses are based on the image of a dying fish or a supine dead animal.

↳ *'He lost all his equity when the firm went belly-up in the recession of '81.'*
(*Wall Street*, US film, 1987).

c to give in, yield, submit. This refers to the animal behaviour whereby the soft underparts are exposed to an adversary as a sign of submission.

gob-grabbing *n British* passing illicit objects or substances covertly from mouth to mouth. An item of prisoner's slang.

↳ *'If you went to hug a fellow-prisoner, wouldn't he suspect you of attempting a 'gob-grabbing'...?'*
(Will Self writing in the *Evening Standard* magazine, September 1993).

gob job *n British* an act of oral sex, usually referring to fellatio. A vulgarism from the late 1960s.

go Borneo *vb American*
a to get drunk.

b to behave outrageously, go too far.

Both senses are **preppie** terms indicating a regression to a supposed primitive jungle mentality, influenced by the numerous 'Wild men of Borneo' featured in travelling freak shows and the wrestling ring over the years. (The original tales of wild men living in the unexplored jungles of

Borneo probably arose from the first reports of the orang-utan.)

gobshite *n British* a contemptible person. A Liverpudlian and northern term of abuse which, since the 1960s, has spread to other areas of Britain including London. It usually indicates great distaste or contempt (**gob** is mouth and **shite** excrement; both are regional vulgarisms).

gobslutch *n British* a slovenly, messy person; someone with dirty personal habits, especially eating habits. A term from the north of England, heard in the long-running TV soap opera *Coronation Street*. (**Gob** is mouth, 'slutch' a variant form of slush.)

gobsmacked, gob-struck *adj British* astonished, struck dumb, left open-mouthed in amazement. From **gob**. These are originally Liverpudlian terms and are now widespread, used even by **Sloane Rangers** and **yuppies**, thanks initially to usage on TV comedies set in Liverpool. The expressions enjoyed a vogue in popular speech and journalistic use in 1988 and 1989. The phrases originally referred to a victim gaping after literally being punched in the mouth.

 ✎'*He had expected to pay one tenth of the price and was said to be "gobsmacked" at the final cost.*'
(*Independent*, 21 September 1989).

gobsmacking *adj British* astonishing. A more recent derivation of **gobsmacked**.

 ✎'*... but when Casaubon observes, "Life isn't simple, the way it is in detective stories," the gobsmacking banality can only be the author's.*'
(Hugo Barnacle reviewing Umberto Eco, *Independent*, 14 October 1989).

go bush *vb Australian* to go native, become countrified. *See also* **bush, bushie.**

god-botherer *n British* an excessively pious person or a clergyman. A mainly middle-class expression applied particularly to institutional holy men such as prison and army chaplains, or to members of evangelical movements. The phrase has inspired the more frivolous non-specific insult, **dog-botherer**.

god forbids *n pl* children, kids. The rhyming-slang phrase is synonymous with **saucepan lids** and **dustbin lids**, and was still in use in the late 1990s.

 ✎'*Try not to wake up the god forbids.*'

go down *vb American* to take place, happen. A phrase from black street slang which became widespread in the later 1960s.

go down (on) *vb* to perform oral sex. The term is used by and applied to both sexes; until the late 1960s it was a predominantly American expression. Elaborations used by high-school and college students included '*go down like water/like a submarine*' (usually indicating shock at a person's readiness to indulge in this behaviour).

the God squad *n British* the forces of organized religion, especially in evangelical form. The phrase has been applied scornfully to the Salvation Army, doorstep zealots and university Christian Unions alike, from the late 1950s to the present.

goer *n* a sexually active and enthusiastic person; in the past, almost always said of women by men. The word can express admiration and approval or astonishment, rarely moral disdain.

gofer *n* a minion or assistant who runs errands or delivers messages, etc. The word, originally an Americanism from the film industry (where it is now a job title), is a pun on 'go for (something)' and gopher, the North American burrowing rodent.

gogglebox *n* a television set. This term has been in use since the late 1950s. At first used pejoratively by those disapproving of TV, then ironically by viewing enthusiasts, the word is now semantically neutral.

goggles *n* spectacles, or someone wearing them. A schoolchildren's word.

goggy *n British* a misfit, pupil rejected by schoolfellows. This invented term was reported by the *Tatler* of September 1989 to be in current use at Eton College. (Synonyms are **gunk, spod, Wendy** and **zoid**.)

going for gold *vb British* expending maximum energy, displaying maximum effort. This 1990s usage borrows the cliché phrase from the language of sports and competitions.

 ✎'*Everyone's up by the speakers, going for gold.*'

(New Age tribal dancer, *Exodus: The Diary*, Channel 4 TV documentary, 12 November 1995).

going in *n British* 'chatting up' a stranger of the opposite sex. The term is part of the language of dating in use among adolescents in the later 1990s and was included in *Just Seventeen* magazine's 'lingo of lurve' guide to teenage jargon in August 1996.

going through *n British* engaging in an argument or dispute, usually with a romantic partner or close friend. The term is part of the language of adolescents in use in the later 1990s and was included in *Just Seventeen* magazine's 'lingo of lurve' guide in August 1996.

goit *n British* a foolish and/or grotesque person. The term, presumably based on 'goitre', was used in and possibly coined for the cult BBC TV comedy series, *Red Dwarf*.

goldbrick *vb American* **1** to shirk, idle or loaf. In this sense the word is often used in an armed service context.

2 to swindle. The reference is to painted 'gold' bricks sold by fraudsters.

gold-card *vb* to assert oneself, behave ostentatiously or resolve a situation by the use of wealth. This probably ephemeral **yuppie** term of 1989 is inspired by the use of 'gold' versions of credit and charge cards such as American Express.
⇘'*Old Milward just gold-carded him.*'

golden *adj American* exceptional, superlative. The standard adjective used figuratively (as in a 'golden opportunity') was adopted as a vogue term by Californian high-school students in the 1990s particularly to categorize a valued or admired friend. The term was featured in the 1994 US film *Clueless*.

golden showers *n* urine or urination. A jokey euphemism derived from the jargon of prostitution, in which urination is part of the sexual repertoire. An alternative term is **water sports**.

gome, gomer *n American* a tediously studious fellow pupil or student, a swot. A **preppie** and teenage term based on the name (Gomer Pyle) of a fictional comic television character who personifies cloddishness. Perhaps coincidentally,

gomeril or gomerel are archaic British dialect words for a simpleton.

gomey *n Irish* a stupid person. The word is related to the Scottish **gommie** and the American **gomer**, all deriving from older dialect words for a simpleton which in turn come from the Old English *guma*, meaning man, which is a cognate of the Latin *humanus* and the word from which (bride)groom derives.

gommie *n British* a foolish, stupid or gormless person. The term is heard particularly in the Scottish Lowlands and the north of England. It is related to the Irish **gomey** and the American **gomer**.

gone *adj*
a in a euphoric state; ecstatic from the effects of drugs or music. The term is from the slang of jazz musicians of the 1950s, adopted by **beatniks** and **hipsters**. It now seems comically dated.
⇘'*I tried talking him out of it, but he was totally gone on booze and reefer.*'
b inspiring ecstasy or euphoria; said especially of music and usually preceded by 'real'.
⇘'*Some real gone jazz.*'
⇘'*A real gone chick.*'

gonef *n American* an alternative spelling of **ganef**.

gong *n* **1** *British* a medal. The use of the word derives predictably from its resemblance to the metal gong which was ceremoniously sounded in colonial days, itself named from an echoic Malayan word.
⇘'*Tony Hart, Tory leader of Kent County Council, may not be in line for the usual gong dished out to holders of his office.*'
(*Private Eye*, April 1989).
2 *South African* a Chinese person. Recorded as an item of Sowetan slang in the *Cape Sunday Times*, 29 January 1995.

gongol *n British* an idiot, an unfortunate simpleton or buffoon. The word is a blend of **goon** and mongol and was briefly a vogue term among London schoolchildren from 1979.

gonk *n British* a dull-witted, buffoonish or grotesque person. Gonk was services slang in the 1950s for sleep (probably from 'conk out') but the word was used as a trademark name for troll-like dolls in the late 1960s. It is from this source that the word as a term of abuse or contempt arose, just as **muppet** did in the late 1970s. Gonk was applied by schoolchildren to unfortunate fellow-pupils and by hospital staff and police to the mentally retarded.

gonof *n American* an alternative spelling of **ganef**.

gonzagas *n pl American* female breasts. Gonzaga is a Spanish proper name, but is used in this sense by analogy with earlier humorous synonyms **garbonzas** and **gazungas**.

gonzo *adj* unrestrained, hedonistic, extremist as a style, particularly a journalistic style popularized by Hunter S. Thompson in his articles for *Rolling Stone* magazine in the early 1970s. Gonzo is said to be an earlier **hipster** term made up of **gone** and the '-o' ending (with a median s or z to aid pronunciation), but is more likely to be a straightforward borrowing of the Italian *gonzo*, meaning foolish.

✤ *'He was responsible for pioneering the style of modern journalism known as "Gonzo": the freewheeling and often self-indulgent method which has been copied by countless writers.'*
(*I-D* magazine, November 1987).

goobatron *n* a foolish person, **nerd**. An adolescent elaboration of **goober**, heard in the late 1980s.

goober *n American*
a a spot or pimple.
b a foolish person, especially one small in stature.
c a gob of spit. All senses of the word are derived from a Southern American term for a peanut which is an Americanization of the Kongo word *nguba*.

good afternoons *n pl South African* prominent buttocks. The term is used appreciatively and jocularly, invariably by males, of a female's posterior. It was recorded as an item of Sowetan slang in the *Cape Sunday Times*, 29 January 1995.

G.O.O.D. job *n* a job taken simply to 'get out of debt'. The implication is of a menial job abandoned when the debts are paid. The term was heard among **cyberpunks**, **net-heads** and **yuppies** in the early 1990s in the US and UK.

the good oil *n Australian* the truth,

an utterly accurate and/or admirable statement.

the goods *n* 1 the real thing, first rate merchandise.
2 incriminating information, evidence.

goody-goody, goody-two-shoes *n* an offensively virtuous or diligent person. The second phrase is more often heard in the USA; it derives from the heroine of a children's story, and implies a dislikeable prissiness.

✤ *'Superman's naïve, a goody-two-shoes. Batman busts heads.'*
(Joe Lihach of Village Comics, *Observer*, July 1989).

gooey *n American* girlfriend. A fashionable but probably ephemeral term among teenagers in late 1987 and 1988. It is probably influenced by 'gooey-eyes' (romantic looks).

✤ *'How's your gooey?'*

gooey nectar *n American* an attractive girl, a particularly good-looking girlfriend. A teenagers' vogue word from late 1987 combining **gooey** (girlfriend) with 'nectar' (pretty girl).

goof *n* a gormless, awkward or foolish person. Originally a rural British dialect word, goof became widely used between the two world wars all over the English-speaking world, particularly in the USA.

goof *vb American* 1 to blunder, make a mistake, fail. The verb post-dates the noun form of the word.
2 to stare or look vacuous. A teenage term from **goofy**.
3 to indulge in wordplay, improvise poetry. A word and an activity popular with the more literary **beats** in the 1950s.

goofball *n American* 1 a slow-witted and/or clumsy person. A mildly derogatory term derived from **goof** and **goofy**.
2 an illicit drug, typically a tranquilizer or barbiturate which renders the user slow or inert.

goof off *vb American* to avoid responsibility, refuse to take things seriously. An Americanism since the 1940s, the word was briefly adopted by British **beatniks** in the early 1960s but did not establish itself.

go off on (someone) *vb American* to criticize, denigrate, **diss**. An item of black slang of the 1990s, also adopted by younger white speakers.

goof up *vb American* to make a mistake, blunder. (An elaboration of **goof**.)

goo-gobs *n American* a large quantity of money, used in the phrase '*to make goo-gobs*'. An item of black street slang that was reported by US linguists to be obsolete by the end of the 1960s, but which has been revived in 1990s usage.

googy-egg, googie, goog *n Australian* an egg. A piece of 'baby talk' transferred from the nursery to facetious adult usage.

gook *n* 1 *American* a North Vietnamese or any oriental. A derogatory term widely used by American soldiers in the Vietnam war, but originating much earlier, probably in the Filipino uprising of 1899, in which US troops referred to Filipinos as 'gugus' from a native word meaning tutelary spirit. Coincidentally, *kuk* is a Korean word-ending meaning person, and gook was also heard in the Korean conflict.

✎ '...*dinks, gooks, slopes – all sorts of slang to dehumanize them.*'
(Veteran of My Lai massacre, Channel 4 TV, 22 June 1988).

2 an alternative spelling of **guck**.

goolies, ghoulies *n pl British* testicles. In northern Indian languages *gooli* means pellet or pill. The word was picked up by British colonial troops at the turn of the century as a euphemism for testicle. This sense was reinforced by a more circuitous route; the gypsies' language, Romany, also adopted the Indian word *gooli*, from which the English and Australian schoolchildren's word 'gully', a marble, derived. **Marbles** itself was a common euphemism for testicles.

✎ '*The temperature further increased each time we dipped a deep fried fish ball into the special Oh' Boy sauce. "It's enough to take your goolies off," gasped my sister-in-law.*'
(Craig Brown, *The Sunday Times* magazine, 8 October 1989).

goomba, gumba *n American* a friend or associate. The word has been widely used mainly by males in many social contexts. It is often assumed to have an Afro-Caribbean origin, but one authority, Robert L. Chapman, derives it

from a dialect pronunciation of the Italian *compare* ('comrade' or 'relation').

goon *n*
a a foolish, clumsy or clownish person. This sense of the word was popularized in Britain by the zany radio series *The Goon Show* in the 1950s, and was earlier used in the *Popeye* cartoons for 'Alice the Goon', a huge dull-witted character. This in turn was probably influenced by a pre-existing word in British dialect meaning vacuous or simple (and distantly related to 'yawn').
b a thug. The word was already being used in this sense in the USA in the late 1930s, typically of hired strike-breakers. It was later applied particularly to strong-arm men of low intelligence used by gangsters to intimidate or punish.
✎ '*Tell Simpson to get his goons to lay off – then we'll talk.*'
(*Rockford Files*, US TV series, 1978).

goony *n American* a foolish person. A variant form of **goon**, mainly heard among children and teenagers.

gooper *n American* a gob of spit. This is probably a variant form of **goober**.

goopy *adj* foolish, clumsy or unfortunate. An uncommon adjective influenced by **goop** and **goofy**.
✎ '*To keep goopy stills from love scenes out of circulation, his contracts stipulate that the studio can't release his photograph without his approval.*'
(*Elle* magazine, May 1989).

gooseberry *n British See* **play gooseberry**.

goosegog *n British* a gooseberry, in the literal sense. A nursery term also used by adults and teenagers.

go over the side *vb British* to leave one's post for illicit purposes, e.g., sex. The term is sometimes abbreviated to OTS, which explains its provenance; it is a pun on the official designation 'out taking statements'. An item of police slang recorded by the London *Evening Standard* magazine, February 1993.

go pear-shaped *vb British See* **pear-shaped**.

Gorbals kiss *n British* a headbutt. The phrase, a synonym of **Glasgow kiss**, refers to the formerly notoriously violent working-class district in that city.

gorilla-finger *n Australian* a **joint**, especially a large one. The phrase was recorded in the early 1990s.

↪ *'When we've packed up, we'll roll up the first gorilla-finger of the evening.'*
(Recorded, Australian sound engineer, London, September 1993).

gorked out, gawked out *adj American* incapable, intoxicated, disoriented. The word was featured in the 1990 US film, *Donor*.

goss *n British* gossip (in the sense of rumour, scandal and chatter, not of a person). A vogue term which appeared in 1988 and established itself in the language of teenagers and writers in teenage magazines. Although the shortened form resembles the abbreviated journalese of *Variety* magazine in the USA, it appears to be a native British coinage.

↪ *'A triff new weekly mag with all the goss on your fave TV stars.'*
(BBC TV advertisement for *Fast Forward* magazine, 1989).

goth *n British* a young person characterized by a devotion to a 'doom-laden' or bombastic style of 1980s post-**punk** rock music and the wearing of black clothing and quasi-medieval insignia, jewellery, etc.

go the full distance *vb* to be arrested, tried, convicted and sent to prison. A euphemism heard among the criminal fraternity and the police in the 1970s and 1980s. The metaphor is taken from boxing jargon.

go through the slips *vb British* to renege on (a deal), an item of underworld slang from the 1990s. The term refers either to a cricket ball passing near the wicket or to an escape near the 'slips' (wings) of a theatre.

go tits-up *vb American*
a to die
b to be ruined, bankrupted, defeated, etc. In both senses the expression is a vulgar version of the more common **go belly-up**.

go troppo *vb Australian See* **troppo**.

gouch out *vb British*
a to botch a drug **fix**, fail to hit a vein. A term used by drug addicts in the mid-1960s.
b to become semi-conscious, **nod out**. The difference between these two meanings seems to be based on a misunderstanding, but since the origin of the term is obscure (a rather far-fetched notion is that the supposedly somnolent South American gaucho is the inspiration, although gauchos in fact are anything but somnolent) it is not clear which is the 'true' meaning.

gouge *vb American* to intimidate, damage, do down. A business term of the 1980s.

gouged *adj British* intoxicated by drugs, the term especially denotes **stoned** on **Ecstasy**.

gouger *n Irish* a **yob**, lout or thug. The word is Dublin slang since the 1980s.

gourd *n American* head. The word is almost always heard in the phrase '*out of one's gourd*'.

governor *n British See* **guvnor**.

go walkabout *vb* to daydream, lose concentration. The term derives from the Australian aborigine practice of leaving the community to go into the bush on a mystical quest (when they are said to 'go walkabout'). It was applied by journalists to the tendency of the tennis player, Evonne Goolagong, to allow her concentration to slip during matches and now is applied to any sort of aberrant mental behaviour.

gozunder *n See* **gazunda**.

graft *n* 1 a work, particularly hard, unrelenting or persistent work.
b a job, one's occupation.
2 *American* dishonesty, bribery, or peddling influence in public or political life.
Both the British and American senses of the word ultimately derive from a British dialect word descended from the Anglo-Saxon verb *grafan*, related to grave, and meaning to dig.

graft *vb British*
a to work, in particular to work hard and constantly.
b to engage in clever, devious or dishonest money-making schemes, especially

those involving selling in street markets, fairs, etc.

c to pursue criminal activities.

All the senses of graft originate in a dialect word meaning to dig, from the Anglo-Saxon verb *grafan*.

grafter *n British*

a a worker, especially a humble, hard-working or long-suffering worker.

b a person who makes a living from clever, devious or dishonest schemes. This word is applied in particular to street traders.

c a criminal, particularly an habitual petty criminal. These senses all derive from the verb to **graft**.

grand *n* a thousand pounds or a thousand dollars.

The word originated in the jargon of American sportsmen, gamblers and, later, criminals. It was adopted in the same milieux in Britain by 1950.

↳ *'Zackerman rings and – this'll make you smile – he goes, he goes, I'll give you a hundred grand plus the car and that, and fifty in your hand.'*
(*Serious Money*, play by Caryl Churchill, 1987).

grand *adj South African* appreciate.

In this sense the word was recorded as an item of Sowetan slang in the *Cape Sunday Times*, 29 January 1995.

↳ *'Well, I don't grand your joke.'*

grandstand *vb American* to put on a bravura display, show off to an audience.

The expression comes from the world of sport and was originally an Americanism. It is often used as an adjective as in 'a grandstand play'.

granola *n American* a keen environmentalist or a person dressing like one.

This campus categorization (often pejorative) appropriates the name of a health-food cereal. It is a synonym for **earth biscuit**, **duck-squeezer**, etc.

grass *n* 1 herbal cannabis, marihuana.

British smokers traditionally preferred hashish, but began to import more marihuana in the mid-1960s. Grass was the predominant American term and had largely supplanted **bush**, **pot**, **herb**, etc. in British speech by 1970.

↳ *'Well, the first thing they wanted was some grass.'*
(Rockstar's minder, *Guardian*, 12 December 1987).

2 *British* an informer. Originally the expression was 'grasshopper' as rhyming slang for copper; the meaning was then transferred to the '*copper's nark*' or informer and by the 1940s grass had become established in the underworld lexicon. By the 1970s the word was also widespread among schoolchildren and others. 'Supergrass' was a journalese elaboration denoting a highly significant informer.

grass (someone up) *vb British* to inform (on someone), betray (someone) to the police or authorities.

The usage was originally to '*grass on someone*' or to '*grass to the authorities*'. In the 1980s the London underworld expression to **grass someone up** is widely used, not least among schoolchildren, who had adopted it from TV police dramas and documentaries. For the etymology see the noun, **grass**, sense **2**.

graze *vb* to eat while standing up and/or occupied in some other activity.

A piece of **yuppie** jargon from the late 1980s.

grease *n American* money.

An underworld term of the early 20th century, adopted by **beatniks** among others and, more recently, by teenagers. From the notion of greasing the wheels of commerce, or money as a social lubricant.

↳ *'If we had some grease we could hit town this weekend.'*

grease *vb American* to kill.

The word appears to have had the specific meaning of shoot (probably inspired by 'grease-gun') until the 1970s when it acquired its additional and more general sense.

↳ *'One move and we grease your friend.'*

greaseball *n American*

a a person of Hispanic or Mediterranean origin or appearance. An offensive term which has been in use since before World War II.

b a person, such as a cook or mechanic, who works in literally greasy conditions.

greaser *n* 1 *British* a **rocker**, motorcycle enthusiast, scruffy unfashionable person.

A scathing term adopted by **mods** and students to refer to **rockers** in 1964. The word has gradually fallen out of use since that time.

2 *American* an Hispanic or person of Mediterranean origin. The term refers to

a supposedly greasy complexion; it implies great contempt and causes offence.

🗩 *'Crazy greasers – they've always got bees in their panty hose about something.'*
(P. J. O'Rourke writing on Panama in *Holidays in Hell*, 1988).

3 a petty criminal, juvenile delinquent, etc., specifically one who wears hair oil, a leather jacket, etc.

4 a toady, sycophant or hypocrite, from the notion of greasiness equated with unctuous, devious behaviour.

greasy spoon *n* a transport cafe, diner or other cheap restaurant. A mildly derogatory but generally affectionate term for the kind of eating place where most if not all of the hot dishes are fried in animal fat. The expression seems to have originated in Canada or the USA in the 1930s.

🗩 *'There's nothing for breakfast except toast. Let's go down the greasy spoon – I fancy a good grease-up.'*
(Recorded, teacher, London, 1987).

grebo, greebo *n British* a scruffy young rock-music enthusiast, typically long-haired, unkempt and leather-jacketed. The word was coined in 1985 in the Midlands to describe a youth sub-group of gauche but earnest heavy-rock devotees. Grebo does not so much denote a separate cult (its proponents displayed characteristics of **rockers**, **hippies**, **goths** and **punks**) but a new term for a pre-existing phenomenon (as in the case of **anorak**).

🗩 *'Brummie "grebo" boors Pop Will Eat Itself sound frightful on paper and even worse (in the best possible sense, you understand) in the flesh.'*
(*Independent*, 11 May 1989).

🗩 *'Greboes drink stout and snakebite, smoke Players No.6 (packets of ten), wear y-fronts and dirty torn jeans, drive big bikes, and go out with girls who don't shave their armpits.'*
(*I-D* magazine, November 1987).

greek *vb, n American* (to engage in) anal sex. The term from the euphemism 'greek love' is invariably used for homosexual behaviour between males.

green, green stuff *n* money. Banknotes of all denominations are green in the USA (see also **long green**). In Britain, pound notes were green until replaced by coins in the 1980s.

greenback *n American* a banknote.

US paper money is predominantly green in colour.

greenback *vb American* to subsidize, underwrite, finance. A recent derivation of the well-established noun form, greenback is employed as a novel synonym for bankroll.

green gilbert *n British* a thick piece of mucus from the nose. A schoolchildren's term which has been in use since the 1950s and is now considered respectable enough to be said on television. The choice of Gilbert is due to the supposed inherent comicality of the name and to its echoes of gobbet, glutinous, etc.

greenie *n* **1** *British* a one-pound note. From the predominant colour.

2 *American* a (Heineken) beer. A **preppie** term, often extended to refer to other brands, from the colour of the bottle and label of the popular import.

green welly, green-welly brigade *adj, n British* (in the style of or characteristic of) upper-middle-class young people who indulge in country pursuits such as riding and hunting and who typically wear Barbour jackets and green wellington boots. The term **green-welly brigade** is used pejoratively to refer to wealthy townspeople who visit the country at weekends (usually staying in second homes), and comments of their habit of 'dressing-down' in a pseudo-country style. The urban equivalent is **Sloane Ranger**, although that term was out of favour by about 1988. The phrase 'green welly' was sufficiently well known to be used as a caption in a press advertisement for 'environment-friendly' Saab cars in 1989.

gregory *n British* a cheque. A piece of rhyming slang from the late 1980s, playing on the name of the film star Gregory Peck. The same rhyme has also been recorded with the alternative meaning of 'neck', but this, given the rarity of conversations concerning that part of the body, seems unlikely to supplant the financial sense.

🗩 *'I'm just popping out to sausage [and mash: cash] a gregory.'*
(Recorded, property speculator, Bath, 1988).

greldge, grelge *n American* an unpleasant substance, dirt. An item of middle-class slang used by adults as well as adolescents. It was recorded from the early 1990s and appears to be formed from such terms as grease, filth and grunge.

grem, gremmie *n Australian*

a a novice or incompetent surfer.

b a novice or incompetent skateboarder. A teenage term imported into Britain in the late 1970s. The variant forms are probably based on **gremlin**.

gremlin *n* an unexplained flaw, malfunction or error. A word used particularly by British soldiers in World War I, and American airmen, in World War II, evoking a malicious spirit. (The word is a form of the Irish *gruaimin* meaning a bad-tempered little fellow.)

grey, the grey *n British* **1 a** a conventional, conformist person. A vogue term in British counterculture circles from about 1966 to 1968. The word had the same dismissive or pitying overtones as **straight** which had supplanted it by the end of the 1960s.

b the grey denoted the collective mass of conformism, dullards and authority figures, as opposed to the (literally as well as metaphorically) colourful **hippies**.

2 *American* the 'white' man. A derisive term used by blacks.

greybar *n* a period of inactivity. An item of **net-head** jargon referring to sitting before a grey screen waiting for a display.

greybeard *n* an 'old-timer'. The word probably originates (as 'graybeard') in the USA where it is a jargon term for a long-serving senior officer in various fields, such as civil aviation, from the literary term for an old man. *See* **longbeard**.

grid *n British* mouth. The term, which is heard in northern speech, is almost invariably heard in the phrase '*shut your grid!*'.

G-ride *n American* a stolen car. An item of black street talk that was included in so-called **Ebonics**, recognized as a legitimate language variety by school officials in Oakland, California, in late 1996.

griefy *adj British* depressing, troublesome. A fairly rare middle-class teenage and student term from the early 1970s.

ᮗ'*I mean we've all tried to fly from up-stairs windows ... we know those griefy scenes, man!*'

('American ethno-botanist' in cartoon by Posy Simmonds, *Guardian*, 1980).

grievous *adj British* annoying. The standard term was adopted as a vogue term of disapproval by adolescents in the later 1990s.

grifter *n American* an untrustworthy, suspect or dishonest person, typically a gambler or minor fraudster. Grifter is a word from the early 20th century which is a blend of graft and drifter. It was used by Raymond Chandler in his detective fiction and was still occasionally heard in the late 1980s.

grill *vb* to interrogate. Police and armed-forces slang of the 1950s which has become a widely-used colloquialism.

grim *adj British* extremely unpleasant, disgusting. The standard term was adopted as a vogue term of disapproval by adolescents in the later 1990s.

grind *vb* to have sex. An unromantic description, widespread in the 1960s, via an earlier phrase 'bump and grind', describing sex or a suggestive dance, especially the motions of a striptease or burlesque artist. Grind in the noun form has been used in a sexual sense for approximately 400 years.

grind *n* **1** an act of sexual intercourse. A widespread vulgarism since the 1960s, the word has been used with a sexual connotation since the 16th century.

2 *American* a **swot**, a tediously diligent student, in high-school and college terminology.

3 the quotidian reality, oppressive routine, as in the 'daily grind'.

grindage *n American* food. One of many items of adolescent slang using the -age suffix, fashionable in the 1990s.

grizzer *n South African* mother, matriarch or elderly lady. Recorded as an item of Sowetan slang in the *Cape Sunday Times* on 29 January 1995.

gro, groe *n American* a black person. The racist epithet is a clipped form of 'negro'. In the UK **groid** has been used in the same way.

grobber *n British* an obnoxious, repulsive individual. The term was first recorded in the 1960s and may be related to the verb 'to grub'.

groceries *n pl See* **blow one's cookies/groceries**.

grockle *n British* an unwelcome outsider, tourist or visitor. A Devon dialect term applied contemptuously to summer visitors by local residents since the 1960s. The word has been adopted by the many non-native **hippies** and travellers living in the West Country to refer to anyone who is not approved of. (The term has also been heard in other parts of Britain.) Grockle is claimed to derive from the name of the famous clown Grock. In Cornwall the equivalent is **emmet**.

♦'*That unmistakable grockle smell – stale fat and farts.*'
(Recorded, resident of Torquay, 1976).

♦'*We never go in that pub – full of grockles.*'
(Recorded, resident of Parracombe, North Devon, 1986).

grody *adj American* an American version of **grotty**, used typically by **Valley Girls**. A word dating from the mid-1970s which now seems established in the teen lexicon. It is often intensified in the phrase 'grody to the max'.

grog 1 *vb, n* (to indulge in) alcoholic drink. The noun form, from the rum and hot water served in the British navy since the 18th century, can now refer to any strong drink, or even beer. It is generally heard among middle-aged speakers. The verb 'to grog' or 'grog up' (in Australian English to 'grog on') is rarer and restricted mainly to a younger age group. It implies heavy and constant imbibing. 'Old Grog' (from the grogram, or silk and wool cloak he wore) was the nickname of Admiral Vernon who aroused his sailors by ordering the dilution of their rum ration in 1740.

♦'*Not realizing one's dependence on the grog is where the wheels touch the road, eh?*'
('Edmund Heep' in a cartoon by Posy Simmonds, *Guardian*, 1979).

2 *vb British* to spit. The term is heard particularly in the Scottish lowlands and the north of England.

groid *n* a black person. This racist term of abuse, a shortening of the adjective negroid, was particularly prevalent in police usage in London in the late 1980s. It also exists in American speech.

♦'*Travelling around – being an International Knee-grow (or a "groid" as the Met would have it) – thanks chaps!*'
(Lenny Henry, *Time Out* magazine, 26 July 1989).

grommet *n British* 1 an imaginary fixture, component or part, an unspecified or unnameable object. A grommet is actually an eyelet or metal ring, originating in a nautical context and deriving from the archaic French *gourmette* or *groumette*, meaning bridle ring.

2 **a** a woman or women regarded as sex objects.

b sexual activity.

These now obsolescent uses of the word were in use in the 1950s among male speakers. They arise from the nautical term for ring or eyelet, used as a euphemism for the female genitals.

groove *n* an enjoyable experience or situation. An Americanism derived from the verb to **groove** (on) and the adjective **groovy**. The word was **hip** jargon of jazz musicians since the 1930s, later becoming part of the **hippy** lexicon and as such was also heard outside the USA until the mid-1970s. It now sounds very dated. *See* **in the groove**.

groove *vb* to experience a sensation of well-being, fellow-feeling, to feel in tune with one's surroundings. This well-known and characteristic **hippy** term originates in the slang of jazz musicians and others for whom being in the groove meant being at one with the melody, with one's fellow players, etc. (like a needle in the groove of a record). The word subsequently became a pivotal one for hippies, for whom it expressed a notion of enjoyable one-ness with one's environment that hitherto lacked a name. The expression was hackneyed by the time James Taylor was ridiculed by British rock journalists for his declaration at a mid-1970s concert at the Royal Albert Hall that he '*grooved to the vibes*'. To 'groove on something' was another typical form.

♦'*Groovin' down a crowded avenue/ doin' anythin/ we like to do.*'
('Groovin', recorded by the Young Rascals, 1967).

groover *n* 1 a fashionable, dynamic **hip** person. A 1960s formation from **groovy** and the verb to **groove**.

2 a tedious person, **swot**. A probably

ephemeral usage of the late 1980s, based on the newly pejorative teenage sense of **groovy**.

⮑ '*Charmless college swats are no longer known as "nerds" but are on the receiving end of a whole variety of new insults including "dweeb", "geek", "goober", "wonk", "corn-dog", "goob-a-tron" and "groover".*'
(*Independent* magazine, 24 December 1988).

groovy *adj* 1 satisfactory, satisfying, fine. A term of approval, sometimes in the form of a mild exclamation from the **hippy** era. The adjective is derived from the verb to **groove**; originally an American term, it was adopted by British rock musicians, **beatniks**, and, later, **hippies** from about 1965. It now sounds risibly dated, unless used ironically.

⮑ '*You see we have a lot of other groovy things going for us, and not just concerning music.*'
(Mick Jagger, *Record Mirror*, 26 August 1967).

2 *American* tedious, dull. A vogue word of 1988 among adolescents. It is probably inspired by ironic use of the dated term of approbation.

⮑ '*Another 1960s catchword, "groovy", has mysteriously turned into its opposite, now signifying stodgy or old-fashioned.*'
(*Independent* magazine, 24 December 1988).

gross *adj* disgusting, distasteful. An Americanism of the mid-1960s, particularly popular among teenage girls. It is a fashionable usage of the standard term (from Latin *grossus*, thick, via French and Middle English) in its sense of excessive, vulgar or obscene.

⮑ '*Like Joan's, Marlene's entire range of expression was pretty much limited to "far out", "super" and "gross".*'
(*The Serial*, Cyra McFadden, 1976).

gross-out *n American* a disgusting act or situation. A favourite term of teenagers since the mid-1960s, usually said with excited or exaggerated distaste.

⮑ '*After totting up the score-sheet of exposed breasts ("garbonzas"), mutilations, rolling heads, gross-outs, auto-collisions, he awards a number of stars and puts his seal of approval on a film.*'
(*Observer*, 9 April 1989).

gross (someone) out *vb American* to disgust or repel. The expression is normally used by a speaker to refer to their own distaste. It is a teenagers' term, popular since the late 1960s.

⮑ '*Would you move your socks. Like out into the patio or something? I mean they're really grossing me out.*'
(*The Serial*, Cyra McFadden, 1976).

Grosvenor Squares *vb British* rhyming slang for flares, i.e. bell-bottom trousers. This phrase was an ephemeral youth term of the late 1970s used contemptuously of the (by then) unfashionable style and the remnants of the **hippy** movement who still favoured it. London's Grosvenor Square, the site of the US embassy, was the scene of peace demonstrations by students and hippies during the Vietnam war. A later, more lasting alternative piece of rhyming slang for the same item was '**Lionel Blairs**', followed by **Tony Blairs**.

⮑ '*Belinda has discovered an important pair of "jeans" dating from the late 1960s. These are most certainly rare items, known by collectors as "Grosvenor Squares".*'
(Caption to cartoon by Posy Simmonds, *Guardian*, 1981).

grot *n British*
a dirt, squalor, unpleasantness. Although this word was a back-formation from the adjective 'grotty', it no longer reflects that word's origin in 'grotesque'.

⮑ '*I can't go on living among all this grot.*'

b a dirty, slovenly or disreputable person.

⮑ '*He really is an awful grot.*'

grotty *adj British* unpleasant, revolting or distasteful. The word became extremely popular in the early 1960s and quickly passed into the middle-class lexicon where it is still found. Grotty, a typically Liverpudlian shortening of grotesque, became popular among young people, via the influence of the 'Mersey boom' in the early 1960s. It was adopted by some Americans in imitation of British usage, although an American form, **grody**, arose in the 1970s.

grounded *adj American* confined to one's home, deprived of one's car keys. A popular parental means of chastising American teenagers. The image is of course that of a plane and/or pilot prevented from flying.

↳'*I can't go out tonight, I'm grounded too, you know.*'
(*The Stepford Children*, US TV film, 1987).

group-grope *n* a group 'heavy-petting' session. A teenagers' term from the early 1960s. The phrase was later applied to full scale **gang bangs** or orgies, and scathingly to group therapy sessions.

groupie *n* a girl who associates with or follows a musical group or star. The term originally assumed and still implies the sexual availability of the girl. The word and the phenomenon were publicized in the late 1960s, particularly in the semi-autobiographical book *Groupie* by the British writer Jenny Fabian in 1968 and the US film *Groupie Girl*, 1969. Groupie was a condescending or pejorative expression used by the musicians themselves, and by jealous or disapproving fans in the mid-1960s in Britain whence it spread. Nowadays the word is usually used in the general sense of devotee, admirer.

grouse *n, adj Australian* (something) excellent, superlative. This use of the word probably derives from the notion of the bird as a delicacy; also used figuratively to denote an attractive woman since the pre-war period.

grub *n* **1** food. The word has existed with this meaning since at least the 17th century, inspired by the action of grubbing around.

↳'*At the weigh-in, Reynolds, in the red corner, weighed eight stone, two pounds.*'

↳'*Give the poor sod some grub!*'
(Spike Milligan, *Adolf Hitler, My Part in his Downfall*, 1971).

2 a *Australian* a dirty, slovenly person. This sense of the word was in British use until the early 20th century, but is now obsolete there.

b *British* a younger child, especially a grubby or defiant one. From the terminology of prep and public schools.
Both these senses of grub derive from the lowly insect larva.

gruey, gruie *adj British* 'gruesome', distasteful, unpleasant. A middle-class

teenagers' and students' term from the early 1970s.

grunge *n American* **1a** anything dirty, distasteful, squalid or sordid. This adolescent coinage is now heard in Britain.

↳'*For Martin Amis is the Wodehouse of grunge...*'
(David Sexton, *Sunday Correspondent*, 17 September 1989).

b a boring or irritating person or task.

2 a genre of rock music and subsequently a youth subculture and fashion movement, originating in Seattle in 1992. The earlier senses of the word were applied to the heavy, fuzzy sound of the musical style and to the deliberately scruffy image cultivated by its adherents.

↳'*Sure, even before Kurt Cobain took his own life last year, whispers of grunge's death had been patently acknowledged.*'
(*Guardian*, 25 March 1995).

grunt *n American* **1 a** (dog) soldier, an army private. A derogatory term sometimes used ironically by the soldiers themselves, deriving from the supposedly low intelligence and predilection for grumbling of the humble enlisted man or conscript.

↳'*The grunts were conscious that they were involved in a drug-and-rock 'n' roll extension. Most of the combatants, black and white, came from the working class.*'
(Michael Herr, *Observer*, 15 January 1989).

2 power. The term is used particularly by car enthusiasts to refer to engine power.

↳'*The engine size has gone up from 3.4 to 3.6 so there's plenty of grunt.*'
(*Top Gear*, BBC 2 TV motoring series, 13 February 1997).

gruntled *adj* satisfied, gratified. A jocular back-formation from the standard disgruntled (in which 'gruntle' in fact means grumble and is related to grunt). This rare word is typically used by educated speakers, saloon-bar philosophers and amateur or professional comedians.

↳'*I was feeling extremely gruntled following my success.*'

grunt-work *n American* menial or demeaning job(s).

↳'*You know, I used to do the grunt-work around here. Now I own the place.*'
(*Double Cross*, US film, 1994).

G-thing, -thang *n American* **1** a subject or activity characteristic of a gangsta.
↳*'Nothin' but a G-thang.'*
(Title of a rap recording by Dr Dre, 1992).
2 a subject or activity characteristic of males, from the phrase *'it's a guy's thing'*.
↳*'You wouldn't understand: it's a G-thing.'*

gub *vb British*
a to hit (someone), especially in the mouth or face.
↳*'The geezer kept at him and finally Mickey gubbed him.'*
b to defeat.
↳*'Our team got well and truly gubbed.'*
Both senses of the verb derive from a dialect form of **gob** meaning mouth. The terms are heard particularly in the Scottish Lowlands and the north of England.

gubbing *n British* a beating. The term, from the verb to **gub**, is almost always used literally, but can also be used figuratively to mean a verbal attack.

gucci *adj* flashy, materialistic. The name of the Italian design company, usually employed with (mildly) critical intent, was adopted for use in street and later campus slang in the USA in the 1980s. Gucci shoes and handbags were part of the accessories favoured by devotees of the hip hop and **rap** subcultures. In the slang of the British Office Training Corps the phrase *'gucci kit'* is used to mock those who bring expensive luggage and accessories in training camps.

guck *n* a sticky substance, muck. A mainly American nursery word blending 'goo' and 'muck'. Also spelled **gook**.

guff *vb, n British* (to) **fart**. An old childish vulgarism which has been revived in the late 1980s as part of a vogue for pseudo-nursery slang among students and others.
↳*'The force of the gigantic guff you used has wrecked the entire drainage system.'*
(*Johnny Fartpants*, Viz Comic, April/May 1988).

guffie *n British* a **fart**. A variation of guff.

guinea *n American* an Italian. An offensive term, the origin of which is ob- scure, but which might derive from a proper name such as Gianni or Giovanni, or else by a tortuous process from the name of the African country (whence slaves were exported).

gumballs *n pl American* the flashing lights on the roof of a police car, from their supposed resemblance to multi-coloured chewing gum or boiled sweets.
↳*'He'd be on him before he hit Woodward, nail him with the gumballs flashing blue and siren turned up to high yelp.'*
(*The Switch*, Elmore Leonard, 1978).

gumbo *n See* **hippy gumbo**.

gumby *n* an aggressively gormless, clumsy and/or dull person. From the name of a character personifying these qualities in the TV comedy series *Monty Python's Flying Circus* in the 1970s (in turn partially inspired by Peter Cook's earlier invention 'E. L. Wisty'). The personification and name were taken up by British and American teenagers in particular.

gump *n American* **1** a foolish, clumsy person, simpleton. This widespread term pre-dated the 1994 movie *Forrest Gump*. It originated in English Yorkshire dialect in which it denoted a 'dolt' and was probably related to the colloquial 'gumption'.
2 a male prostitute, particularly a transvestite male prostitute, from the slang of Chicago police, recorded in the non-fiction work *Pure Cop*, 1991.

gumshoe *n, vb* a detective, private eye or plainclothes police officer. The term was first used in the USA early in the 20th century and referred to the silent rubber-soled shoes that detectives supposedly wore as opposed to uniformed police officers' heavy boots. Gumshoe (now a word largely confined to humorous or literary use) has also been employed as a verb meaning to plod the beat or follow a trail of clues.

gunge *n British* a sticky substance, muck. A slang term of the 1960s which has become a middle-class colloquialism.

gung-ho *adj* excessively eager, enthusiastic and/or assertive, especially in the context of patriotism, jingoism and military aggression. This phrase was thought to be a Chinese rallying cry. (The words 'gung ho' were part of the Chinese title of an Industrial Cooperative and were assumed wrongly to mean 'work together'.) It was adopted by the Marine Corps and later for general American military use in World War II. It became known outside the USA to a limited extent during the Korean war and more particularly during the Vietnam war, now being so well known as to constitute a colloquialism rather than slang term.

gunk *n* **1** muck, goo, sticky stuff. An American version of the British **gunge**, now heard in Britain, too. By extension it can also mean debris or rubbish.

2 *British* a school misfit. A schoolboy term reported to be in current use in Eton College by *Tatler* magazine in September 1989.

gunning sticks *n American* smoking cigarettes. A term used often with real or ironic bravado, particularly by younger adolescents in the 1990s.

gunsel *n American*

a a callow youth.

b a gunman.

The latter meaning is now more widely encountered, but the former, with overtones of punkishness, comes from the Yiddish slang for young man (*gantsel* or *ganzl*; gosling), and was the sense in which it was used in crime novels and *films noirs* in the 1930s. The second meaning is based on a misreading of the first.

gunship *n British* an unmarked police car, in the jargon of the late 1980s. Although partially ironic, the choice of term illustrates the shift in self-perception since the days of the **bobby** on his 'manor'.

※ *'They call their specially souped-up cars gunships and when the order comes to go in the command is: "Attack! Attack! Attack!".'*
(*Evening Standard*, 25 January 1992)

guns of Navarone *n pl South African* female breasts. The jocular expression from the 1990s borrows the title of a 1961 film featuring giant cliff-top cannons.

guppy *n* an environmental **yuppie**. An ephemeral journalese coinage blending green and yuppie, inspired by the popular tropical fish.

gurgle *n British* (an) alcoholic drink. A fairly predictable euphemism, used typically by pub habitués and other hearty drinkers. It is probably influenced by **gargle**.

※ *'Fancy popping down to the Swan for a bit of a gurgle?'*
(Recorded, middle-aged drinker, Pangbourne, 1986).

gurgler *n Australian* a toilet. The term is sometimes used figuratively in the phrase '*down the gurgler*', meaning ruined, lost or failed.

gurk *vb, n*

a *British* (to) belch, burp.

b *Australian* (to) fart.

Imitative words used, mainly by children, since the 1950s.

gurning *adj British* intoxicated by drugs or drink. The term was popular among adolescents and students in the later 1990s and refers particularly to someone feeling the ill-effects of drugs. It is inspired by the verb to gurn (from Middle English *girn*, a form of 'grin'), which means to pull grotesque faces.

gussied-up *adj* smartly dressed, neatly turned out. The term is common in American speech and is heard elsewhere. It may have originated in Australian usage and is possibly based on the names Augustus, Gus or Gussie as supposedly denoting an effeminate or fussy male.

※ *'Well, you're all gussied-up.'*
(*Curaçao*, US film, 1993).

gut-rot *n* cheap, low-quality alcoholic drink. This phrase is probably more widespread in Britain and Australia than the alternative **rot-gut**. Unlike rot-gut, it is occasionally also used to refer to food.

gutsache *n* a miserable, complaining person, **misery-guts**. The expression is particularly popular in Australia, but is also heard in Britain. The image evoked is of someone perpetually suffering from dyspepsia or provoking indigestion in others.

gutser, gutzer *n Australian* See **come a gutser.**

gutted *adj British*

a devastated, deeply disappointed, saddened or shocked. A vogue word among working-class and lower-middle-class speakers since the late 1980s, perhaps encouraged by the over-use of the word by sportsmen and sports commentators.

The concept has also been expressed subsequently by the alternatives **kippered** and **filleted**.

✎ *'24 hours before work on the commercial was due to start the answer came from Central. It was no. After all those years – just no. I was gutted.'*
(Paul "Benny" Henry, *News of the World*, 8 January 1989).

b used as an exclamation. By the end of 1990 the term had become a schoolchildren's catchphrase, used as a shout of victory or defiance, meaning 'I have humiliated you' or 'You have been shamed'. The form *'gutted out'* is also heard.

gutters *n British* an unattractive female. A synonym for **butters** and **dog**, in the jargon of clubland recorded in the early 1990s.

✎ *'An out and out gutters.'*
(*Touch Magazine*, September 1993).

gutty, gutsy *adj British* bold, brave or 'bolshie'. A late 1980s coinage, popular in unsophisticated speech, which is a back-formation from the well-established colloquial sense of guts as courage.

guv *n British* a respectful term of address to a male, in working-class usage. Said invariably by as well as to men, guv is a shortening of the almost equally widespread **guvnor**, meaning boss.

guvnor, governor *n British* a boss, chief or leader. A descriptive term or term of address used by, to and about males in working-class speech. This widespread colloquial form of governor arose in the early 19th century and shows no sign of dying out. Governor, then spelled correctly, was recorded as a slang term for one's employer as early as 1802; Charles Dickens later referred to it as a slang synonym for 'old man' or 'boss' when referring to one's father. In the 1980s it acquired a further nuance in the form *'the guvnor'* as an acknowledged expert or leading exponent (for instance among rock musicians and fans).

✎ *'I'll be alright 'cos I believe in the life hereafter. I mean, Jesus was the governor wasn't he?'*
(East Ender, *The Sunday Times*, 2 June 1968).

gweeb, gweebo *n American* a stupid, dull person. A late 1980s variation on **dweeb**, coined by teenagers. It is probably unrelated to the British **grebo**.

gwot *n American* a contemptible person. This high-school term of great distaste, heard since the late 1980s, is an invention, obviously influenced by other evocations of unpleasantness such as grotesque, **weed**, **twat**, etc.

✎ *'Oh god, not him, he's such a gwot.'*
(*Some Kind of Wonderful*, US film, 1987).

gyppo *n* **1** a gypsy.
2 an Egyptian. A neutral rather than pejorative term in origin, gyppo was, and is, sometimes extended in uneducated speech to encompass other Arabs or Muslims.

gyppy tummy *n British* an attack of diarrhoea. A phrase from the colonial era. The equivalent of **Delhi belly**, **Montezuma's revenge**, etc.

h...

H *n* heroin. This was the most popular term among British drug users in the 1950s and 1960s before being supplanted by **smack, scag**, etc.

↳ *'He's been on H for years.'*

habit *n* an addiction, a 'drug habit'. A drug user and law enforcer's term, sometimes extended to refer to more innocuous addictions.

↳ *'A $100 a day habit.'*

hack *n* 1 a journalist, professional writer. The word, inspired by the image of a worn-out workhorse, has traditionally denoted a disreputable, unprincipled, mercenary reporter or writer. Since the late 1960s, if not earlier, journalists have appropriated it to refer to themselves proudly rather than self-deprecatingly. Hack is still used in publishing as a simple descriptive term for a journeyman writer prepared to tackle any subject, as distinct from a specialist.
2 *British* an excessively ambitious student. In the slang of Oxford and Cambridge universities this is the undergraduate equivalent of the many schoolchildrens' synonyms for **swot**.
3 a cough, particularly a dry, rasping cough. The word imitates the sound in question.

hacked-off *adj* annoyed, irritated, resentful. From the late 1980s, this phrase has enjoyed something of a vogue as a replacement for the better-known 'brassed-off', 'cheesed-off' and as a euphemism for **pissed-off**. It has been recorded in both the USA and Britain since the early 1950s, sometimes shortened to **hacked** alone.

hacker *n* 1 someone who **hacks into** a computer system. The hacking in question is the evocation of a person chopping their way through dense undergrowth to their destination. Hacker in this sense appeared as part of data-processing jargon in the early 1980s. Spectacular instances of the penetration of computerized systems brought the word to public awareness.
2 a taxi driver. A 'hackney cab' (the archaic version of taxi cab) takes its name from 'hackney' meaning a horse used for transportation. The short version of the phrase survives in this sense.
3 a clumsy worker. Here hack evokes chopping clumsily, rather than handling or cutting finely.

hackette *n British* a female journalist. A jocular term coined by journalists (on the basis of **hack**) and popularized in the 1980s by *Private Eye* magazine (who referred to society gossip columnist Lady Olga Maitland as '*the fragrant hackette*') among others.

hack into *vb See* **hacker**.

hack it *vb* to succeed, to manage (in spite of adversity). A slang usage which remained relatively obscure until the early 1980s since when it has become a common colloquialism. The original sense of hack is uncertain here; it may mean to drive, to strive or to chop (one's way through). The phrase is a near-synonym for 'cut it' (which, however, probably derives from 'cut the mustard').

↳ *'The poor guy's finished, he just can't hack it anymore.'*

ha-ha *n British* marihuana or hashish (cannabis), or another 'euphoric' drug. A light-hearted reference by middle-class soft-drug users to the hilarity induced by smoking, ingesting or sniffing the chosen substance.

hairball *n American* an unpleasant and/or despicable person, by analogy with something vomited by a cat. The phrase owes its usage from the 1980s partly to the fact that, while offensive, it is not obscene and can therefore be used in television dramas and by children in the presence of adults.

hairy *adj* dangerous, frightening. The word was used in the early 20th century in Britain by university students to mean difficult, and later in the armed forces to mean dangerous. It is not clear whether the image inspiring the term is that of a hairy animal or monster, or of one's own hair standing on end.

↳*'That was a pretty hairy drive down to Donovan's place.'*

hairy, hairie *n British* a bearded, long-haired person and by extension a **beatnik**, 'bohemian' or intellectual. A disparaging term typically used by middle-class speakers in the mid-1960s.

↳*'Honestly, she spends her time with all these weirdos and hairies.'*

hairy, herry, herrie *n Scottish* a female. The term is almost invariably pejorative and often refers to an unattractive or troublesome young woman. It is said to derive from the fact that the poorer female inhabitants of Glasgow in the 1930s and 40s could not afford hats (then *de rigueur* for respectable women), thereby exposing their hair to onlookers.

↳*'Mick was off wi' a wee herrie, so I'm told.'*

hairy-arsed *adj British* wild, primitive, uncouth or rugged. A term in armed-forces and middle-class use which is often, but by no means always, appreciative in tone.

↳*'The place was full of hairy-arsed builders.'*

↳*'I am not some hairy-arsed Viking from the North bent on a bit of rape and pillage.'*
(John Ashworth, Director of the LSE, quoted in *The Independent*, 5 January 1995).

half a bar *n British* before decimalization in 1971 half a bar was ten shillings; since then it has meant fifty pence. The phrase is London working class or cockney. 'Bar' is an archaic term, still occasionally heard in London, coming from a Romany word (*bar* or *baur(o)*) meaning a sovereign and, later, one pound.

half-arsed, half-assed *adj* ill-considered, incomplete, ineffectual. An expression which appeared in British and American usage around the turn of the century. The term may originate in the notion of something which has less than a whole solid base or, according to a more fanciful theory, derive from a jocular deformation of 'haphazard'. In modern British speech it is sometimes used as a more vulgar version of half-hearted (its more probable inspiration).

↳*'A half-arsed attempt to take over the department.'*

hamburger *n British* the vagina. A vulgarism in use among adolescents in the 1990s and listed in *Viz* comic in 1994. **Furburger** is a (probably earlier) synonym.

hammer *n See* **put the hammer on.**

hammered *adj British* drunk. A briefly fashionable word among young people in 1986 and 1987.

↳*'Sloane Rebs all support Chelsea FC, and can be seen every other Saturday lunchtime "chugging brew" and getting hammered at any number of pubs in the Fulham Road, before charging down to Stamford Bridge for a "frightfully good game of footy".'*
(*I-D* magazine, November 1987).

Hampsteads *n pl British* a short form of the cockney rhyming slang 'Hampstead Heath': teeth.

hampton, Hampton Wick *n British* penis. Hampton Wick is a southwestern suburb of London, providing a rhyme for **prick**. In modern usage the short form of the phrase is usually preferred. Since the mid-1970s the term has been considered well-established and inoffensive enough to be used in television comedies.

↳*'Then there were these telephone calls from ... groupies. Somehow they'd learned a hell of a lot of cockney slang. They'd phone up and say "Hi Jeff [Beck], how's your 'Ampton Wick?" Ridiculous!'*
(Jimmy Page, *Oz* magazine, April 1969).

handbag *n British* a male escort, a 'walker'. Handbag refers to a 'decorative appendage' to a fashionable lady, often a homosexual male. The term was popular in high society and journalistic circles in the mid-1980s.

handbag *vb British* to frustrate, obstruct or attack. A jocular version of **sandbag** seen in the 1980s, often in journalistic references to Margaret Thatcher. The term evokes shrewish intransigence.

handbag situation, handbags at ten paces *n British* a scene of provocation, a confrontation, and/or feigned violence. These sarcastic phrases are typically used by football supporters to describe a scene in which players make a show of menacing or jostling each other. The reference is to a supposed brawl between middle-aged women.

↳ '*A handbag situation – when players square up and scuffle (supermarket style) but the ball is too far away for them to kick each other ...*'
(*Evening Standard*, 26 May 1994).

hand-job *n* an act of manual sexual stimulation, usually masturbation of a male by a female. A common vulgarism in use since the mid-1960s.

handle *n* a name, nickname, alias or title. The first sense of the word was that of title (an appendage to one's name) in the early 19th century.

handsome *adj British* excellent, impressive. An all-purpose term of approval used by cockneys and other Londoners, sometimes standing alone as an exclamation. The 'h' is usually dropped.

handy *adj British* **1** a catch-all London working-class term, invariably pronounced without the 'h' and signifying adept, devious, virile, brutal, etc., usually in a context of immorality or illegality.
2 a term from teenage sexual slang, invariably applied to boys and defined by *Just Seventeen* magazine in August 1996 as 'a bit too tactile under a girl's T-shirt for her liking'.

hang *vb American* **1** to consort with, frequent. This black street usage is a shortening of the colloquialism 'hang out' and was adopted by white adolescents in the 1990s.

↳ '*He's been hangin' with the homeboys.*'
↳ '*Those betties hang down at the mall.*'
2 to relax. This usage is probably a shortening of the phrase **hang loose**. Originating in black street slang, it was adopted by white adolescents in the 1990s.

↳ '*I'm inclined to tell them all to go to hell and just hang for a while.*'

hang a louie *vb American* to take a left turn. A teenage expression from the early 1970s.

hang a ralph *vb American* to take a right turn. A teenage expression from the early 1970s.

hang a yooie/u-ie *vb British* to make a U-turn when driving a car. A mock-racy expression from the 1980s.

hang five *vb* to ride a surfboard (at near-optimum speed or full stretch) with the toes of one foot hooked over the front. From the jargon of American surfers since the early 1960s. *See also* **hang ten**.

hang loose *vb American* to stay relaxed, keep **cool, chill out**. A vogue term from the late 1950s and early 1960s when it characterized the nonchalant state of detachment aspired to by **beatniks,** jazz musicians, etc. The phrase (still heard occasionally) is often an exhortation to a friend on parting. It probably originates in the use of **loose** to describe a free, unstructured style or mood (although some have interpreted it as referring to the male genitals in an unencumbered position).

hang one on *vb* an alternative form of **tie one on**.

hang one on someone *vb* to hit, punch. An expression, used particularly by brawlers, which may also be expressed with the verbs 'land', 'stick' or 'put'.

hang out *vb See* **let it all hang out**.

hang ten *vb American* to ride a surfboard (at near-optimum speed or full stretch) with the toes of both feet hooked over the front. From the jargon of American surfers since the early 1960s. The phrase is sometimes used figuratively to mean something like '*go full-tilt on a risky course*'.

hang-up *n* a neurosis, obsession. From the image of being hung on a hook. This **beatnik** term was seized upon by the **hippies** to describe the concerns of the **straight** world. Unlike many contemporary terms, hang-up has not dated significantly and is still in use today.

↳ '*He's got a hang-up about young chicks in uniform.*'

hank *adj British* extremely hungry. Recorded in London in 1994, the word is a shortening of the rhyming slang phrase '*Hank B. Marvin*', meaning starvin(g), borrowing the name of the lead guitarist of the Shadows pop group.

↳ '*Can you hurry up, we're all bloody hank in here.*'
(Recorded, builder, southeast London, July 1994).

hankie-head *n* an Arab. The term, which probably postdates the more widespread synonyms **rag-head** and **towel-**

head, was popularized by the comic writer P. J. O-Rourke in the 1980s.

ha'porth *n British* an inconsequential person. A person of no account or importance was likened to a halfpenny's worth. Usually in the phrase '*silly ha'-porth*' (with the 'h' often dropped) this mild expression of contempt or derision was common until the early 1960s.

happening *adj American* exciting, stimulating and/or up-to-date. A fashionable term from the vocabulary of teenagers since the mid-1970s. It is influenced by the earlier black catchphrase greeting 'what's happening?' and the **hippy** cliché, '*it's all happening*'.
 ✎'*A really happening band.*'

happy dust *n* a narcotic in powder form. The term has been applied to cocaine, **PCP** and amphetamines among others.

happy stick *n* a **joint** (cannabis cigarette). A rare euphemism.

hard-arse, hardass *n* a tough, unyielding and/or severe person, martinet. This noun form post-dates the adjectival form hard-arsed.

hardass *n American See* **hard-arse.**

hardball *n See* **play hardball.**

hardbody *n American* a young Californian male, especially one interested in physical culture and body-building. A vogue term of the late 1970s and 1980s heard among those frequenting the beach and boardwalk.

hardcore *adj* **1** thoroughly criminal, deviant or sexually debauched, this is a specific sense of the colloquial meaning of hardcore (committed or uncompromising, as applied for example to political beliefs or pornography). In the 1970s in the USA the word took on a narrower connotation in the jargon of the street and underworld, coming to mean irredeemably criminal. It was often used in this sense to indicate admiration or awe.
 ✎'*That guy's real hardcore.*'
 ✎'*The hardcore life.*'
2 *adj* excessive, outrageous, relentless. This vogue term in adolescent speech in the later 1990s is often used to indicate appreciation or admiration. It is based on the earlier uses of the word to characterize pornography and rock music,

and, according to its users (one of whom defined the usage as referring to 'somebody who stays up all night, is violent, or drinks everyone under the table or takes loads of drugs'), its antonym is **lightweight**.
 ✎'*A hardcore guy/scene.*'
 ✎'*Acting/playing hardcore.*'

hardcore *n* a style of fast, loud, aggressive music, a development of **punk**. The term originated in America in the early 1980s, perhaps influenced by the adjectival use of **hardcore** to mean (uncompromisingly) rebellious, anarchic or criminal, spreading to Britain around 1985. The genre has since spawned subcults such as '*deathcore*' and '*speedcore*'.

hard-off *n American* an unstimulating, disappointing person, experience or sensation. The term, coined by analogy with **hard-on**, is used by members of both sexes.

hard-on *n*

a an erection. To '*have a hard-on*' has been the most common way of expressing male sexual tumescence since the early 20th century. It derives from a slightly earlier adjectival form (to be 'hard-on') which follows a pattern of Victorian euphemism which includes '*fetch off*' (to have sex or orgasm), etc.
 ✎'*Don't go home with your hard-on/It will only drive you insane.*'
 (Lyrics from 'Don't go home with your hard-on', Leonard Cohen and Phil Spector, 1977).
b a sudden strong desire or affection. This specialized sense is a piece of **macho** business jargon from the late 1970s. It suggests an aggressive and uncompromising wish to acquire or cement relations with a business partner, for example.
 ✎'*I think Ingrams is nursing a hard-on for United Mills.*'

the hard word *n*
a a rejection or condemnation.
 ✎'*It was the one thing that would bring Christina [Onassis] and her father together again. It was only a matter of time before Christina gave me the hard word.*'
 (Joseph Bolker quoted in *Heiress*, by Nigel Dempster, 1989).
b a difficult request or ultimatum, particularly a demand for money or sex. The phrase is normally part of longer expres-

sions such as '*put the hard word on*' or '*give someone the hard word*'. The origin of the expression is obscure, but it is most prevalent in Australian use.

haricot (bean) *n Australian* a male homosexual. Rhyming slang on **queen**.

Harold (Lloyd) *vb British* to slip a lock using a strip of celluloid or plastic. A now archaic term for this practice, employed by housebreakers, etc. Since the 1960s **loid** has been the version preferred by police and criminals. (Harold Lloyd was a star comedian of the American silent cinema between the World Wars.)

harolds *npl Australian* trousers or underpants. The etymology of this jocular usage is unclear: it is thought to originate in rhyming slang based on a real or imaginary proper name such as 'Harold Tagg(s)' or 'Wragg(s)': **bags**.

harp, harpoon *n* a harmonica. Long known as a 'mouth harp' among black American blues musicians, the harmonica became known worldwide as a harp during the rhythm and blues boom of the early 1960s. Harpoon is a later and fairly rare elaboration.

⃗'*Seriously he* [Stevie Wonder]'*s a knockout harp player, but this singing-only effort is a swinger.*'
(*Rave* magazine, March 1966).

harpic *adj British* crazy, deranged. A pun which was popular for instance among schoolchildren in the 1960s. The person so described was '*clean round the bend*', from the slogan of the Harpic toilet cleaning preparation which claimed in a TV advertisement to '*clean round the hidden bend*'. The word was used on *Whacko!*, a parody of public-school life starring the late Jimmy Edwards.

harpoon *n* 1 a hypodermic syringe. Another example of the self-dramatizing language of drug abusers. *Compare* **artillery**, **shooting gallery**, etc.
2 a version of **harp** in the sense of harmonica.

Harris Tweed *n British* speed. This fairly rare example of drug users' rhyming slang, appropriating the name of the high-quality Scottish clothing fabric, was first recorded in the 1980s.

harry *n British* heroin. An addicts' term from the 1960s, personifying the drug in the same way as **charlie** for cocaine.

harry- *prefix British* a prefix used in public-school, university and armed-services slang, almost always by males, to add jocular familiarity to a standard term. It is often used in conjunction with the -er(s) word ending. The -er(s) form is probably earlier; 'harry-' seems to have originated in armed-forces speech pre-World War II.

⃗'*Fiona's harry-preggers again.*'

harry-starkers *adj British* naked. An upper-class or armed-services jocularity.

harsh *adj* 1 *American* unpleasant, inferior. An all-purpose negative, briefly a vogue term among Californian adolescents in the mid-1990s.
2 good, impressive. In this reversed or ironic sense, recorded among British mods of the 1960s and US high-school and college students of the 1990s, the word is one of a large set of near-synonyms including **savage**, **brutal**, **tough**, etc., which have been adopted into adolescent codes.

hash *n* hashish (cannabis resin). Hashish from North Africa, the Middle East and the Himalayas is the most widely-used form of cannabis in Britain, especially among white smokers, while **grass** (herbal cannabis) is more common in the USA. This shortened form of the word was probably the most widespread term in use among British cannabis smokers in the early 1960s. It was then largely supplanted by more colourful terms such as **charge, shit, dope**, etc.

⃗'*Hash smoking is now a widespread social habit, almost in the same class as whiskey and soda.*'
(Letter to *Oz* magazine, June 1969).

hassle *vb, n* (to subject someone to) bother, harassment, intrusive complications. This term had existed in American English since the 19th century; in the 1960s it formed part of the **hip** and counterculture jargon which became established throughout the anglophone community. In origin it is either a blend of harass or haggle and tussle or wrestle, or an Anglicization of the synonymous French verb *harceler*, or (more convincingly), a version of **hustle**. In Britain hassle replaced hustle as a vogue term among **beatniks** and **mods** in about 1967.

hat *n American* a condom. **Jim(my)-hat** is an alternative form.

hatch *vb British* to drink, drain (one's glass). A matter-of-fact beer-drinkers' term, derived from the exclamation 'down the hatch!'.
> ⮑ *'I think we'd better hatch these [beers] and get going.'*
> (Recorded, wedding guest, Bristol, 1988).

hatchback *n South African* a female with prominent buttocks. An appreciative term used by young males in the 1990s and inspired by the designation of cars.

hatstand *adj British* crazy, eccentric, deranged. The nonsense term was invented by the comic *Viz* for the character Roger Irrelevant and was adopted into student slang in the late 1990s.
> ⮑ *'He's completely hatstand and always has been.'*

hatter *n Australian* a crazy person. It is said that the usage grew up in Australia, particularly with reference to isolated workers who became eccentric or deranged. The expression is based on the colloquial phrase 'mad as a hatter' (which itself comes from the common supposition that English hat-makers of the late 18th and early 19th centuries were subject to mercury poisoning leading to brain damage).

haul ass *vb* to get moving, go into action. An Americanism, usually in the form of a command or exhortation, which is heard in British and Australian speech of the 1980s.

haul off *vb American* to get ready to strike someone or to launch an attack. The term may be used literally (of leaning back before aiming a blow) or figuratively.

have a lend (of someone) *vb Australian* to deceive, bamboozle, lie about. The phrase is related to older locutions such as 'get a lend of/have a loan of' which refer to a dishonest individual taking advantage of another by borrowing from them.
> ⮑ *'You better be sure he's having a lend of you.'*
> (Recorded, Melbourne bus driver to adolescent passenger, 1995).

have a scene (with someone) *vb* to have a sexual relationship, have an affair. This phrase, now sounding rather dated but as yet lacking a more fashionable alternative, was the standard term throughout the late 1960s and early 1970s for an unmarried relationship. The expression, particularly popular with middle-class British **hippies**, avoided the juvenile, frivolous or banal implications of 'going out with' and the middle-aged overtones of the word 'affair'.

have a word with (someone) *vb British* to beat up. A euphemism used by brawlers, street gang members and police officers, particularly in the late 1960s.

have it away, have it off *vb* to have sex. These phrases, which have been commonly used in Britain and Australia since the 1940s, seem to derive from an earlier sense of the same terms meaning to succeed in stealing or succeed in accomplishing (something illicit). There is also significant similarity with 19th-century sexual euphemisms such as 'fetch off'. Both expressions are used by all social classes.
> ⮑ *'He later told me he'd had it off with a photographer the previous night and so wasn't much concerned with having it away himself.'*
> (Joe Orton's Diary, 14 May 1967).

have it (away) on one's toes *vb British* to escape, run away. A phrase from the repertoire of criminals, prisoners and the police since the early 1950s. It is still current among these and working-class Londoners in the late 1980s.

have the bomb *vb Australian* to be exhausted. The phrase may be related to the use of **bombed**, meaning incapacitated by drink or drugs.

have the decorators in, have the painters in *vb* to menstruate. A women's euphemism; both phrases are heard in Britain and Australia, the second version in the USA.

have the hots (for someone) *vb* to nurse a sexual desire for someone, to lust after. The phrase is a variation of now obsolescent phrases ('to be hot for', to 'have the hot ass', etc.) in which hot equates with sexually excited. First heard in the United States in the 1960s, the term quickly spread to other English-speaking countries.

have (someone) over *vb British* **a** to trick, dupe, deceive. A working-class euphemism related to the colloquialism 'get one over on (someone)'.

✥*'Similar themes run through stories about social workers who are reckoned to be easily "had over" by "villains" and even by juvenile offenders.'*
(*Inside the British Police*, Simon Holdaway, 1983).

✥*'I was a young geezer and I was trying to have the police over.'*
(Vincent Hickey, released prisoner speaking on *Panorama*, 24 February 1997).

b to seduce. A specialized sense of the preceding usage, invariably referring to a male 'taking advantage of' a female.

Hawaii *n British* a £50 note or sum of fifty pounds. A raffish expression inspired by *Hawaii-Five O*, the title of an American TV crime series of the 1970s.

✥*'I got him to do it, but it cost me a Hawaii.'*

hawk one's fork, hawk the fork *vb Australian* to sell one's body, engage in prostitution. A colourful vulgarism playing on the medieval sense of fork as the join of the legs. In archaic British slang 'hawk one's mutton' and 'hawk one's meat' were terms with the same meaning.

hazing *n American* teasing or humiliation, especially as part of a student initiation rite. An American version of the British 'ragging', but often with less lighthearted overtones. The word originated in naval use where it meant to oppress or harass. It probably has no etymological connection with other senses of haze, deriving instead from the archaic French *haser*, to irritate.

head *n* 1 an aficionado of the drug-using counterculture drug-user. A word used by **hippies** to refer to themselves. The term originally simply meant a person or individual in the slang of black jazz musicians and, later, white **hipsters**. It became a suffix used to denote different categories of drug users ('pot-head', acid head, etc.) and subsequently was generalized again. It now sounds dated and has fallen out of use save among the remnants of the 'alternative society'.

✥*'Those were the days of heads and freaks. And if getting high was where it was at, then Vietnam was the ultimate trip.'*
(Michael Herr, *Observer*, 15 January 1989).

2 a toilet. This is the singular form of **the**

heads, the earlier designation for shipboard latrines.

3 oral sex, particularly fellatio. The word in this sense is usually encountered in the phrase **give head.**

headbanger *n*

a a devotee of heavy-metal rock music who expresses excitement by frenzied shaking and even literal banging of the head in time to the music. The practice and term originated in the early 1970s.

b a person who behaves in a relentlessly frenzied or dangerous way. This usage, deriving from the first sense of the term, usually expresses a certain shocked admiration. It has been current among British schoolchildren and students since the late 1970s, and is rapidly becoming 'respectable' by its use in the press and elsewhere by adults, typically with reference to political extremists.

✥*'I'd like to meet her father; he sounds like a right headbanger.'*
(Contestant on *Blind Date*, TV show, September 1989).

c a madman, psychotic, **headcase.**

✥*'Another bloody headbanger, that's all. Probably didn't get enough sugar on his cornflakes, so he takes it out on innocent folk.'*
(Victim of random shooting, *Daily Mirror*, 2 May 1989).

headbanging *adj*

a shaking or banging one's head in response to rock music.

b behaving in a wild, unrestrained, relentless or excessive manner. The second generalized sense is an extension of the first and was coined to describe the behaviour of (mainly male) rock-music fans in the early 1970s.

headcase *n* an unhinged or deranged person. The word, originally an Americanism of the early 1970s, is typically used by teenagers to indicate awe or dismissive contempt; it rarely refers to the genuinely insane.

head honcho *n* the top person in a hierarchy, the most important boss. *See* **honcho.**

✥*'I can't be bothered dealing with assistants. Who's the head honcho around here?'*

headlamps, headlights *n pl* breasts. These are jocular male terms from the earlier 20th century, when large, raised car headlamps were the norm. The first version is British, the second American and Australian. **Bumpers** and **hooters** are other slang terms for breasts using automotive analogies.

heads, the heads *n pl* a toilet, latrine. This plural form is now rather dated, except in armed services' usage. It originated in naval terminology where it referred to the for'ard location of the privies on a ship. (The) Head is more common.

headset *n* attitude, way of thinking. This version of the colloquial 'mindset', punning on headset as, e.g., a virtual reality helmet, is heard in British campus slang. It may have originated in the jargon of psychotherapy.

↳ *'If you want to understand them, you've got to try to relate to a completely different headset.'*
(Recorded, postgraduate student, Warwick University, November 1995).

headshrinker, headshrink *n* a psychiatrist, psychoanalyst. A jocular term of the 1950s originating in the United States and reflecting the mild contempt, tinged with fear, felt towards the practitioners of these professions. Since the late 1960s both terms have normally been shortened to **shrink**.

head trip *n*
a an instance or period of self-obsessed behaviour. An expression from the **hippy** lexicon, originally supposedly describing a specific category of LSD-influenced behaviour, which was later extended to describe any thoughtless egoism.

b an instance or period of delusion, incoherence, self-absorption or contemplation, especially one provoked by drugs such as LSD. In this sense the phrase is not necessarily pejorative, and was used in the **hippy** era to describe 'self-exploration'.

heat, the heat *n American* the police. A black street form of the early 1960s (using the image of heat as pressure, oppression, something stifling) which was adopted by **hippies**. *'The heat's on the street!'* was a warning among black communities and white activists alike.

↳ *'Her man got took away by the heat/we're lost and incomplete.'*
('Endgame', song by Doll by Doll, 1979).

heater *n American* a handgun. A pre-World War II term which was appropriated by writers of crime fiction.

heatseeker *n American* a dynamic person. The usage derives from the phrase 'heat-seeking missile' as used in news reports, etc., from the 1970s, and is heard in the 1990s in a professional context and among students.

heave *vb* to retch or vomit. A literal, rather than metaphorical usage.

heave-ho, the old heave-ho, heave-o *n* a rejection or dismissal. A worldwide English expression, typically referring to being jilted by a lover, or being fired from one's job. It originates in the shouts of exhortation made by men engaging in physical exertion. It was a sailors' call in the 17th century.

↳ *'It was evens ... four men had broken her heart and she had given another four the old heave-ho.'*
(*A Touch of Spice*, British TV comedy, 1989).

heaves, the heaves *n* an attack of retching or vomiting. A literal description of these spasms, although the expression is, by its context, considered slang.

heaving *n British* stinking. The term, in use in working-class speech in the north of England and Scotland, possibly evokes the notion of something so rotten as to be infested with maggots and literally pulsating, or else evokes the heaving (i.e., retching) of the person sensing the odour. Slightly less overwhelming experiences are evoked by **bowfing**, **minging** and **howling**.

↳ *'I couldn't stay in the flat more than five minutes – it was fuckin' heavin' in there ...'*

heavy *n* a thug, **minder**, someone employed for their intimidating physical presence rather than their intellectual qualities. Originally an Americanism, the term has spread to world English via crime fiction and films. In current British colloquial speech it is sometimes used in the phrase *'come the heavy'*, meaning to act in a threatening manner.

heavy *vb* to intimidate, threaten or pressurize (someone). The verb forms (expressed as *'to heavy someone, to heavy someone into (doing) something'* or to

'*come the heavy*') post-date the adjective and noun forms.

heavy *adj* **1** violent, oppressive, intimidating, powerful.
2 a (of a situation) emotionally charged.
b (of a person) difficult to cope with, having a powerful personality. These senses of the word, which were slang terms of the 1960s, have become common colloquialisms.

hebe, heeb, heebie *n* a Jew. Based on the word Hebrew, these words originated in the USA. They have been heard in Britain and Australia since the early 1970s, sometimes jocularly lengthened to **heebie-jeebies**. Hebe is less offensive than **yid**, **kike**, etc., but discriminatory nonetheless.

hedger *n British* a rural vagrant. The term, from the lexicon of the homeless, travellers, etc., denotes a **crustie** who prefers to live rough in the countryside. It was first recorded in the early 1990s, although phrases containing 'hedge'– like 'ditch' the scene of sordid or dishonest behaviour – were common from the 16th century.

heel *n American* someone who behaves in an unworthy or base way. This use of the word appeared at the turn of the century.

heesh *n American* an altered pronunciation and spelling of **hash** (hashish). The term was used on the street in the 1960s and 1970s, since when it has been adopted by schoolchildren and **preppies** in imitation of more louche speakers.

heifer *n*
a a young woman. A usage which is mainly restricted to the slang of the USA and Australia. In Britain the word was common in the 19th century, but has been archaic since before World War I.
b an unattractive, clumsy or unsophisticated young woman.
✥'*I feel like such a heifer.*'

height *adj American* excellent, first-rate. A term of approbation from the hip-hop youth culture of the 1980s, coined by black teenagers (as a shortening of 'height of fashion'), in the USA and spread with the music and dance trend to Britain. The word is ephemeral and perhaps unlikely to have outlasted the 1980s.
✥'*Don't reach for a tape measure the*

next time someone refers to your bullet-proof safari jacket as "height". They just mean it's cool.'
(Charles Maclean on New York terminology, *Evening Standard*, 22 January 1987).

heimie *n* an alternative spelling of **hymie**.

heinie *n American* backside, buttocks. A coy diminutive of hind(quarters) or behind, although spelled as if it were Yiddish. The term is innocuous enough to be used by mothers and children.
✥'*He hit me daddy – and then he kicked me in the heinie.*'
(*Date with an Angel*, US film, 1987).

heist *vb, n* (to commit) a robbery or hold-up. The word, redolent of American gangsterdom, dates from the first two decades of the 20th century. It is probably a variant form of **hoist**, like 'lift' a 200-year-old euphemism for steal, influenced by German and Yiddish speakers who would know the verb as *heisst*. Heist in its current usage usually suggests a carefully staged major robbery or criminal operation.

helicopter *n American* a temporary visitor. In middle-class adult slang of the 1990s the word may be applied to a neighbour who drops in just to eat and then disappears or, as in the phrase '*helicopter-parent*', by school staff referring to parents who stay only long enough for a brief consultation or complaint.

the helicopters *n British* a bout of dizziness, the **whirling pits**.

hella *prefix American* very. A variant form of 'helluva' and 'hellish', influenced by the fashionable prefix **mega**. The most popular use of the device is in the combination '*hellacool*', heard among American teenagers in 1987 and 1988.

hellacious *adj American*
a appalling, awful, horrifying. A hyperbolic term mainly used and presumably coined by educated speakers, this is an invented elaboration of 'hellish'.
✥'*Hellacious wet scene.*'
'*Multiple wounds?*'
'*Uh-huh.*'
'*Same as the other Slasher murders?*'
(*Over the Edge*, Jonathon Kellerman, 1987).
b impressive, excellent. The term, like **bad, wicked**, etc. has since the early

1980s been used by the young to indicate approval.

↳*'Hey, they're a hellacious band.'*

henry *n British* heroin. A personification used by addicts in the 1970s, perhaps influenced by the use of the name 'Henry the Horse' in the song 'For the Benefit of Mr. Kite' on the Beatles' 1967 LP, *Sgt. Pepper's Lonely Hearts' Club Band. See also* **Harry.**

hep *adj* aware, in touch with the latest (cultural) trends. An Americanism from the jargon of jazz musicians in the early part of the 20th century, hep was adopted by the white intellectuals of the **beat** generation in the mid-1950s and slightly later by teenagers. The word metamorphosed into **hip** (although the two terms coexisted in the early 1960s), which itself prompted the coinage of **hippy**. The precise dates and derivation of hep are somewhat obscure, although it almost certainly originates in a shout of exhortation or encouragement; either the noise used by riders, ploughmen, etc. to horses, or (perhaps more likely, given the importance of marching bands in the early history of jazz), that used by parade leaders, drill sergeants, etc. to keep time. To 'get hep' or 'be hep' then signifies to be working in harmony or in step.

hepcat *n* an aficionado of **jive**, jazz and other aspects of progressive popular culture of the 1940s and 1950s. Originally a black term combining **hep** (fashionably aware) and **cat** (man), it was adopted by white bohemians, intellectuals and proto-**beatniks** and used until replaced by such terms as **hipster** in the 1960s. British jazz fans also picked up the expression and used it self-consciously or humorously until the mid-1960s.

herb *n* 1 marihuana, herbal cannabis. This is probably the most common name for the drug in Caribbean use (usually pronounced **'erb**). The word has been given especial prominence since the early 1970s by reference to it (in popular songs and elsewhere) by Jamaican Rastafarians, for whom it is sacramental. White British cannabis smokers adopted the term as an alternative to the more commonplace **grass**, **bush**, etc. in the mid-1970s.

2 *British* a street urchin. A rare shortening of **Herbert**, typically pronounced 'erb.

3 *American* a dupe. This term, heard in

the 1990s in street argot, is probably taken from the proper name supposedly denoting a quintessential 'sucker'. **(H)erbert** is the British equivalent.

herbal, herbals *n* marihuana. The term is a predictable borrowing of one component of the official designation 'herbal cannabis' for the leaves and flowers of the plant sold and consumed loose, as opposed to compacted into hashish. It has partly supplanted the form **(h)erb** in the later 1990s.

↳*'If you guys are into herbal I think we can oblige with a spliff or two.'*

↳*'Didn't any of them enjoy a lug on the herbals?'*
(*Q* magazine, March 1997).

Herbert *n British See* **'erbert.**

her indoors *n British* one's wife, female partner or boss. A London working-class circumlocution which was popularized by its use in the TV series *Minder* (broadcast between 1979 and 1988). The expression has established itself as a facetious or ironic reference to an unseen (and by implication oppressive) female presence.

↳*'All right I'll stop off for a quick drink, but for God's sake don't tell her indoors.'*
(Recorded, teacher, London, 1988).

Hershey highway *n American* the anus. The expression, usually heard in connection with homosexual behaviour, uses the brand name of chocolate bars, like its British equivalent, **Bourneville boulevard.**

het *n, adj British* (a) heterosexual.

↳*'They wouldn't understand, they're all hets.'*

↳*'It's a strictly het affair.'*

hey diddle diddle *n* an act of urination, a **piddle**. A piece of rhyming slang in use in London and Australia. (**Jimmy Riddle** is a more common alternative.) The words are from the first line of a well-known nursery rhyme.

hickey *n American*
a a love bite.

↳*'I like your date, Sam. Be careful she doesn't lose a baby tooth when she's giving you a hickey.'*
(*Cheers*, US TV comedy series, 1986).

b a spot or other skin blemish.

Hicksville *n American* a backward provincial place. A racier version of 'hick town', based on 'hick' meaning rustic or unsophisticated. (Hick was originally a diminutive of Richard, influenced by 'hickory'.)

H.I.D. *n British* an abbreviated form of **her indoors** used by City financial traders during the 1990s.

hide the sausage/salami/ weenie *n phrase* to have sexual intercourse. Usually preceded by 'play', these phrases are adult imitations of baby talk, used facetiously since the late 1960s. The first version is British and Australian, the second and third American.

high *adj* intoxicated by alcohol or drugs, euphoric. The expression '*high as a kite*' preceded the shorter usage which became widespread in the late 1960s.

&'*I feel like getting high.*'
&'*High on life.*'

high five (someone) *vb American* to slap raised palms and fingers together as a ritual greeting. The custom and the expression appeared in the black community in the 1970s and was subsequently adopted by sportspeople and adolescents in general.

high-hat *vb American* to behave condescendingly or 'high-handedly' (towards someone). A fairly rare but long-established expression. The silent-film star Clara Bow claimed that more sedate members of the Hollywood community high-hatted her.

high muckamuck *n American* See **muckamuck**.

hike *vb, n* (to make) a departure or journey.
&'*Take a hike.*'
&'*It's time to hike.*'

hill-billy *adj British* chilly. An item of rhyming slang that probably originated in Glasgow rather than London.
&'*It's a bit hill-billy in here.*'

himbo *n* a male **bimbo**. An item of journalese that was adopted into general speech in the 1990s. **Bimboy** is a synonym.

hinky, hincky *adj American* 1 inspiring doubt, or suspicion; of uncertain loyalty, origin, etc. This term of unknown derivation is roughly equivalent to the British **dodgy**.
2 cute and/or neat.

hip *adj*
a in touch with current trends, up-to-date, culturally aware. This word coexisted with, and then supplanted **hep** in the 1960s in the argot of musicians, **beatniks** and other bohemians. It implied identification with an ideal of **cool** behaviour characterized by a nonchalant, enlightened detachment and a rejection of 'bourgeois' values. The word is still used in this sense, but is no longer a vogue term; it is rather a descriptive or ironic designation used typically by journalists and social commentators.

&'*Now, the truly hip stay at home with the baby and open a bottle of wine with a couple of friends; if they do go out, they dress down in T-shirts, jeans and sneakers.*'
(*The Sunday Times*, 9 July 1989).

b aware, 'in the know'. Hip, now divested of its counter-culture overtones, is used in popular speech to denote an unspoken understanding of a certain state of affairs.

&'*There's no need to give me all this bullshit, man. I'm hip to what's going down.*'

hippy, hippie *n* a proponent and member of the 'alternative society' or counterculture movement which opposed orthodox bourgeois values during the late 1960s. The hippy movement was a much wider-based successor to the **hipster** and **beatnik** tendency, reaching public notice in California in 1966. By the summer of 1967 (known as the 'Summer of Love') manifestations of hippiedom had spread to Britain. True hippies never referred to themselves as such (but rather as **freaks** or **heads**); the term was originally a slightly condescending nickname (based on **hip** or **hipster**) bestowed by older musicians and other bohemians. By 1975 the main impetus of the movement had ebbed, although, in the 1980s, recognizable hippies still existed, albeit as aficionados of a self-conscious style.

&'*In punk's style degradation, there is still no worse insult than "hippie".*'
(*Observer*, 24 May 1987).

hipster *n* a culturally aware person, a **cool** bohemian. Predecessors to the **hippies** of the late 1960s, hipsters were the aficionados of jazz, oriental philosophy, modernist art-forms, etc., who themselves succeeded the **hepcats** of the 1940s and 1950s. Hipster and **beatnik** are in a historical perspective almost identical, although the word hipster, unlike beatnik, was used by those in question to describe themselves. For the etymology of the word, see **hep**.

hissie-fit *n* a bout of hysterical anger, agitation, despair, etc. The term is used particularly by women and gay males and is obviously derived from the standard term hysterical. **Fanny-fit** is a similar phrase recorded in British speech of the 1990s.

✥'*Julian's having a hissie-fit.*'
(*Concierge*, US film, 1993).

hit *n* **1 a** a puff on a cigarette or pipe containing marihuana or another illicit drug.

✥'*Give me a hit on that joint.*'

✥'*It opens my head, opens my membranes. If you get a good hit, maybe you go comatose for ten minutes.*'
(Crack user, *Guardian*, 5 September 1989).

b a single dose of a drug, particularly LSD.

✥'*Laura just sold me three hits of acid for six quid.*'

✥'*At work it got more and more difficult. To start with she would have a hit in the morning, another in the evening, and then at night.*'
(*Independent*, 4 April 1988).

Both uses date from the late 1960s and are still current.

2 a killing, assassination. An underworld euphemism from the USA, since the early 1970s used or understood all over the English-speaking world. The term invariably refers to a professional murder.

hit *vb* **1** to assassinate or murder. The verb probably post-dates the noun form.

2 *American* to serve a drink to. Usually in a form such as '*hit me again with one of those*'.

3 to solicit money from, borrow from. A more robust version of the colloquial 'touch'. A racier and more recent American version is '*hit someone up*' *(for)*.

✥'*He hit me for $20.*'

hit it *vb* to have sex. In this sense, the term was used among aficionados of London dancefloor culture in the 1990s. It is

probably based on the notion of 'scoring a hit', or of 'hitting it off'.

✥'*When they all got together afterwards, I'm sure Max thought he was going to hit it with Lisa.*'
(Recorded, club habitué, London, April 1996).

hit-man *n* a professional killer, paid assassin, this euphemistic term from the jargon of the American underworld and law enforcers had spread to other English-speaking areas by about 1972.

hit on *vb American*
a to 'chat up', attempt to seduce, accost sexually or romantically.

b to aggress, bully or criticize.

c to importune or beg for money. All senses of the term became popular in the 1980s, especially among teenagers. The unorthodox verb form probably originates from an immigrants' error, or a deliberate elaboration by black speakers.

hit the bricks *vb American* a more fashionable version of the colloquial '*hit the road*' and later '*hit the street*' (to get going or appear in public). Originally the phrase specifically referred to released prisoners.

hit the hay/sack *vb* to go to bed, lie down to sleep. Both expressions have been widespread in English since the turn of the century and probably originated in tramps' jargon.

hit the toe *vb Australian* to depart, leave. Although the coinage seems transparent, Partridge records it as rhyming slang for 'go' and attributes it to the **surfie** subculture.

hit up *vb* **1** to inject oneself with an illicit drug, particularly heroin. An American addicts' expression of the 1960s, since adopted elsewhere. It may be used intransitively as in '*she's hitting up*', or transitively as in '*hit up some smack*'.

2 hit someone up *American* a racier version of **hit** in the sense of borrow (money) from.

hobo *n American* a tramp or vagrant. The word is now a common colloquialism and no longer considered to be slang by most speakers. Authorities disagree on the origin of the term; it may be from a greeting ('*Ho! Boy*' or '*Ho Bro'!*') or refer to 'hoe-boys' (agricultural migrant workers).

ho *n*

a a female prostitute, promiscuous and/or immoral woman.

b a female. The southern US and Afro-Caribbean pronunciation of **whore** became one of the best-known items of hip hop and **rappers'** slang, moving, like many pejorative terms in transgressive subcultures, to take on first ironic then straightforwardly neutral or appreciative connotations before crossing over into the generalized slang of adolescents in all English-speaking areas.

hobby-bobby *n British* a special
constable. The regular police officers' derisive name for part-time volunteer 'specials'.

hobson-jobson *n British* the linguistic process whereby foreign words or phrases are anglicized for use by English speakers. The practice was particularly noticeable during the colonial era and World War I. Hobson-Jobson is itself a rendering of the Moslem religious cry '*Ya Hasan, Ya Hosain!*' (praising or lamenting Hassan and Hussein, grandsons of Mohammed). **Plonk** (an alteration of the French *vin blanc*) and hocus-pocus (from the Latin *hoc est corpus*) are examples of this type of pun or folk etymology.

hock *vb* to pawn. The word comes from
the Dutch *hok*, the literal meaning of which is 'hook'. In 19th-century Dutch slang, *hok* meant both debt and the clutches of creditors or the law, whence the English term.

hockey, hockie, hockey *n*

a an act of (hawking and spitting).

b a gob of spit.

c a piece of any disgusting substance, such as excrement. The term is imitative either of clearing the throat and spitting or of a choking reaction to a disgusting sight.

d *American* nonsense, rubbish. A generalization of the previous senses.

hockshop *n* a pawnshop, pawnbrokers. An expression (from **hock**) used all over the English-speaking world.

hog *n* **1** a motorcycle. A word popular
with American Hell's Angels of the late 1950s and 1960s, and their British and Australian imitators. The word originally referred specifically and affectionately to Harley Davidsons, the Hell's Angels' preferred machines. (Hog is the standard American term for pig.) *See* **chopped hog**.

2 an angry or unpleasant woman. An Americanism which, unlike the similar **pig** or **dog**, has not been adopted in other English-speaking areas.

3 PCP, angel dust. This disorienting narcotic, phencyclidine, is an animal tranquillizer used on pigs, among other species.

hogans *n pl American* female breasts.
The word is probably an ignorant or facetious alteration of **ogens**.

↳'*Look at them hogans!*'
(*Herman's Head*, US TV comedy, 1993).

hog-tied *adj American* incapacitated,
rendered helpless. Hogs (the standard American word for pigs) were hobbled by having all four legs bound.

hog-whimpering *adj British*

a abject, bestial, helpless.

b abjectly or bestially drunk. A colourful term popular among **Sloane Rangers** in Britain since the mid-1970s. The word is probably an original public-school or army coinage, but may echo the many now obsolete slang terms containing the word 'hog' that invoke wallowing, snorting and other excessive behaviour; expressions such as 'hog-rubber' (peasant), 'hog-trough' (ship), 'hog-fat' (slovenly person), etc.

↳'*Old Ollie was absolutely hog-whimpering last night.*'

hog-wild *adj, adv* uncontrolled, unrestrained in behaviour. A folksy Americanism from the turn of the century which is normally heard in the form of '*go hog-wild*' or '*run hog-wild*'. (Hog is the standard term for pig in the USA.) The term was immortalized as the title of a Laurel and Hardy short film in 1930.

ho-hum *n, adj* (something) dull, tedious, of mediocre quality or little interest. When used by Americans this expression usually denotes boredom, by British speakers it may rather suggest uncertainty. In American English the adjective occasionally doubles as a noun, or more rarely a verb (meaning to be bored by or to declare boring).

↳'*As far as the presentation went, well it was kind of ho-hum.*'

↳'*A big ho-hum.*'

↳'*They ho-hummed the lecture course.*'

hoick *vb British* to spit, or to clear the throat and spit. The word is a more echoic version of the standard English 'hawk'.

↳'*He hoicked over the fence into the garden.*'

hoist *vb* 1 to steal, particularly by shoplifting or picking a pocket. The term is around 200 years old in underworld jargon, and was still heard in the late 1980s.

↳'*He managed to hoist a couple of watches.*'

2 *American* to raise and down a drink, usually beer. A masculine term with overtones of heroic or hearty drinking sessions. (The word may occasionally refer to eating, as in '*hoist some oysters*'.)

↳'*What say we go hoist a few?*'

hoist, hoister *n*

a a thief, specifically a shoplifter or pickpocket, or a thieves' accomplice.

b a robbery or an act of shoplifting or pickpocketing. The racier **heist** is a variant form of this 100-year-old expression.

hoisty *adj British* stolen, illicit, **bent** or **hot**. The term may have originated in TV scripts (based on the authentic slang senses of hoist and by analogy with **hooky**), rather than in underworld usage. It was featured in the Simpson and Galton comedy *Over the Rainbow*, 1993.

hoity-toity *adj* affectedly arrogant, condescendingly superior. A 19th-century term which derives from the earlier '*highty-tighty*' (meaning 'high and mighty') and is influenced by haughty.

hokey *adj American* phoney, counterfeit, of dubious quality, third-rate. A back-formation from **hokum**.

holding *adj American* In possession of illicit drugs. A legalistic, officialese term, also adopted by drug-abusers.

↳'*When they found him he was holding but they had to let him go on a technicality.*'

hold it down *vb British* to act in a commendably restrained manner, 'stay cool'. The phrase occurs in the language of teenage gangs and was recorded in use among north London schoolboys in 1993 and 1994.

hole *n* 1 **a** an anus or vagina. The word is barely a euphemism but a simple description of an orifice, in common use since at least Chaucer's *Canterbury Tales* (begun sometime in the later 1380s).

↳'*Dark was the night as pitch or as coal and at the window out she* [Alison] *put her hole.*'
('The Miller's Tale', *Canterbury Tales*, Geoffrey Chaucer).

↳'*Does anyone need another politician/ caught with his pants down/ money sticking in his hole.*'
(Lou Reed, 'Strawman', from the LP *New York*, 1989).

b mouth. In this sense the word is often used by schoolchildren, especially in the phrase '*shut your hole!*'.

2 **a** an unpleasant place. This term is now so common as to be a colloquialism rather than slang, as it probably would have been considered until the early 1960s. **Rat-hole** is a more vivid modern embellishment.

b a one-person cell, a place of solitary confinement.

3 an abbreviation of **asshole** (in the figurative sense of foolish/obnoxious individual). This term, originating in North American usage, was adopted by British adolescents in the later 1990s.

home, homes *n* shortenings of **homeboy**.

homeboy *n American* a street-gang member ready and old enough to defend his area or **turf**. The word, now part of the code of Los Angeles street gangs, was originally an innocuous American term for a good neighbour or good citizen.

↳'*And some homeboys looking for trouble down here from the Bronx.*'
(Lou Reed, 'Halloween Parade', from the album *New York*, 1989).

homegirl *n American* the female equivalent of the more common **homeboy**, recorded in black American speech as long ago as the 1930s. By the 1990s the term was often abbreviated to **homey**.

home run, homer *n American* an instance of sexual satisfaction or conquest; full sexual intercourse. This adolescents' expression, inspired by baseball and typically used by males, denotes the successful culmination of a heavy petting session or attempted seduction. Partial success is referred to as reaching **first base**.

↳'*Danny managed to score a home run.*'

↳'*He made a homer.*'

homey, homie *n* a shortening of **homeboy** or **homegirl**, which became popular in the 1990s and was also adopted by white adolescents to refer to their peers, first in North America and subsequently to a limited extent in the UK. When it first appeared approximately fifty years earlier the word was used by black American migrants as an affectionate term of address for anyone originating from the same hometown or city.

࿏'*I'm square with my homeys ...*'
(17-year-old black female suspected of the murder of another girl, quoted in the *Evening Standard*, 2 March 1997).

homeys, homies *n pl* 1 'homeloving young professionals'. This ephemeral coinage on the lines of acronyms such as **yuppie, dinky**, etc. describes the state following yuppie cohabitation in which partners become settled, homeloving and houseproud. It dates from 1988.

࿏'*Advertisers flood the show because it targets their pet plug: the "homie" generation. ('Homies' have much more disposable income than the yuppie generation).*'

2 homeboys.

homintern *n British* a social network of gay males. This humorous variation of Comintern (the international network of communist nations during the Cold War) was recorded among sophisticates in the 1990s.

homo *n* a male homosexual. This was probably the most common term in colloquial use among heterosexuals until the popular adoption of the non-discriminatory **gay** and its many pejorative alternatives in the late 1960s.

honcho *n* a boss, important person. This word from American English of the late 1950s is not, as is often supposed, Chicano in origin, but from the Japanese *hancho* meaning squad-leader; the term was adopted by Americans during the Korean War. It is now used typically in a business context, often in the phrase **head honcho**.

࿏'*He* [Reagan] *was surrounded in his own White House by the portly honchos of the Democratic Party. The message was unwitting but clear: these are the people who count in Washington today.*'
(*Observer*, 22 November 1987).

honeypot *n* the vagina. A euphemism

which was first recorded in the 17th century and is still employed today, particularly in the USA.

honk *vb* 1 to vomit. The term is echoic and has existed in British slang since the 1950s.

2 to stink. Related to the Liverpudlian **ronk**, this sense of the word is widespread in Australia and not unknown in Britain.

3 to drink (to excess). A middle-class and high-society term of the 1950s in Britain, now rarely heard. *See* **honkers** and **honking**.

honk *n* 1 **a** a stink, bad smell. A variation of **ronk**, perhaps influenced by **hum** and stink. A usage popular in Australia and to a lesser extent in Britain.

b an evil-smelling person or animal.

2 an act of vomiting, from the verb to **honk**.

3 a wild, noisy, drunken party. A British term of the 1950s, probably from **honk** meaning to drink and **honked**, drunk.

honked *adj British* drunk. The 'honk' in question may echo the hooting and vomiting of drunkards, or else the gulping or quaffing. **Honking** and **honkers** are synonyms.

honkers *adj British* drunk. A middle-class term perhaps originating in armed-service slang, where it has been heard since the 1950s. The **-ers** ending is typical of public-school and army expressions.

honkies *n American* backside or buttocks. An Americanism of the 1970s, derived from the colloquial verb to 'hunker down' (i.e. to squat), which in turn is related to the word haunches (in mock-rustic English 'hunkers').

honking *adj British* drunk. A middle-class usage, heard less often nowadays than in the 1960s, which may have originated in armed services slang. The 'honk' denotes either drinking in gulps, the braying made by drunken revellers or, more probably, vomiting.

honky, honkey, honkie *n American* a white person. A pejorative black term which became widely known in the early 1970s. The word's origin is unclear; it is said to be a deformation of 'hunk', meaning an immigrant (ultimately from 'Hungarian'), but may equally well be inspired by the honking of pigs.

hooch *n* alcohol, particularly illicitly produced alcoholic drink. The word originally referred to strong liquor made by the Hoochino Indians of Alaska.

hood *n American* neighbourhood. This abbreviation, heard in the argot of black street gangs, was popularized by the title of the 1991 US movie, *Boyz'N the Hood*.

hood, hoodlum *n American* a criminal, (small-time) gangster. The longer form of the word was in use in the USA by the end of the 19th century; hood became widespread from the 1940s. Many suggestions have been offered as to the origin of the terms. The least unlikely are: a deformation of an Irish surname such as Hoolahan; an altered backslang version of Muldoon; a corruption of 'huddle-'em', supposedly the cry of a gang of muggers; and *hodalem* or *hudilump*, respectively Bavarian and Swiss dialect terms for wretch or naughty boy.

♭*'Go tell your hoodlum friends outside/ you ain't got time to take a ride.'*
(Lyrics to 'Yakety-Yak, by The Coasters, 1958).

hood-top *n Jamaican* the tip of the penis. A vulgarism used as the title of a ragga song by Shabba Ranks in 1993; a female singer riposted with a song entitled *Hood Top Flop*.

hoof *n See* **iron** (hoof) and **horse's hoof**.

hoofer *n* a dancer, particularly a chorus girl, tap dancer, or other hard-working professional dancer.

hoof it *vb*

a to go on foot, walk. In this sense the term has been used since the 17th century.

b to leave, walk away. This sense of the verb dates from the 19th century and enjoyed a vogue in Britain in the late 1980s as a fashionable synonym for **leg it** or **hook it**.

c to dance. A usage popularized in the context of pre-World War II Hollywood musicals. The predictable use of hoof (animals' foot) is probably reinforced by the word's echoing of the panting of hard-working chorus dancers.

hook *vb* **1** *British* to steal. This euphemism, which is still in use in London working-class speech, is at least 200 years old. The 'h' is almost invariably dropped.

♭*'Barry's been out hookin' again.'*
(Recorded, street trader, Islington, London, 1986).

♭*'She managed to hook a few video-tapes.'*

2 hook someone (one) to hit, punch.

3 *Australian* to 'pick up' (a romantic partner). Unsurprisingly, the word has been used in this sense before, e.g., in 19th century England, where it referred to obtaining a potential marriage partner.

♭*'When you hooked Darcy last night, did you sleep with her?'*
(*A Country Practice*, Australian TV series, August 1994).

hooker *n* a prostitute (invariably female). This American term has been imported into British and Australian usage since the mid-1970s, possibly finding a niche since it is less offensive (and therefore broadcast-able) than alternatives such as **whore**, pro, **tart**, etc. The origin of the word is stated authoritatively by many works of reference. However, they disagree. The most popular version cites the Civil War commander, General Hooker, who supposedly encouraged his men to frequent brothels. Another source gives Corlear's Hook, the name of a New York red-light district, as the inspiration for the term. In fact hooker seems to have been in use with its current meaning as early as 1845 (which invalidates the Civil War explanation) and may simply be a figurative use of the literal meaning as 'enticer', 'ensnarer', a sense which it has in Dutch slang (*hoeker* would be known to the large Dutch-American population of New York as meaning 'huckster', for instance). Hooker was obsolescent by the 1920s, but was revived in the late 1960s.

♭*'A high class hooker.'*

♭*'Down on the strip where the hookers hang out.'*

hook it *vb British* to leave, run away. A current London working-class expression popularized by the TV series *Minder* among others. London users almost invariably drop the 'h'. The phrase, a variant of '*hook off*', an earlier and now obsolescent cockney expression, is over 100 years old and is also heard occasionally in the USA. The origin of the hook reference is obscure but may be related to its use to mean anchor (whence the expression to **sling one's hook**: to weigh anchor, although this etymology is disputed).

hooks *n pl* hands. For obvious reasons this metaphorical usage, associated with the images of 'getting one's hooks into' someone or something, and to **hook** meaning to steal, has existed for several hundred years.

hooky *n* truancy, especially from school. Almost always found in the expression **play hooky**.

hooky *adj British* stolen, of dubious provenance, **hot**. A London working-class and underworld term from **hook**, to steal. Hooky is often pronounced with a dropped aspirate.

✎ *'Last time I saw John 'e was sellin' 'ooky watches out of a suitcase down Brick Lane.'*
(Recorded, young male, London, 1988).

hoolie *n* a wild, noisy party or celebration. The word is Irish in origin and is probably an anglicization of the Irish Gaelic term *ceilidh*, meaning an informal gathering for folk music and dance.

hoon *n Australian* a lout, hooligan or disreputable youth. Originally this word (of unknown etymology) signified a man 'living on immoral earnings'; its meaning has now been generalized to denote, for instance, a member of a gang of ne'er-do-wells.

hoop out *vb American* to play basketball. A high-school and campus term. To '*hoop down*' is to play particularly earnestly or dynamically.

hooray, Hooray Henry *n British* a young upper-class male, particularly one who indulges in offensive, rowdy, hearty, and/or vacuous behaviour. This pejorative term arose in the late 1960s to describe the more exhibitionist members of a social subgroup which was later anatomized under the name **Sloane Rangers**. Hooray is a later shortening. A version of this epithet first appeared in Damon Runyon's story *Tight Shoes*, in which a young man called Calvin Colby was described as '*without doubt, strictly a Hooray Henry*'. In March 1990 Viscount Linley won libel damages from *Today* newspaper, which had, among more serious allegations, referred to him as a Hooray.

✎ *'Hooray Henrys sometimes cruise down here just looking for an old codger to beat up. The last time they did it, we smashed up their flashy car.'*
(Homeless dosser, *Observer,* 6 August 1987).

hootch *n* an alternative spelling of **hooch**.

hootchie, hoochie *n American* a female, particularly a promiscuous or sexually active female. This term, derived from hoo(t)chie-coo(t)chie, was part of black street slang of the 1990s. Compare **coo(t)chie**.

✎ *'She sure is one hot hootchie.'*

hootchie cootchie *n American* sexual caresses or erotic dancing. A phrase familiar to blues music enthusiasts, from black slang of the early 20th century. A '*hootchie cootchie man*' is a lover or **stud**. The phrase hootchie cootchie first appeared in the USA in the 1880s, when it denoted a sort of belly-dance. The words may be a pseudo-exotic invention or a distortion of a now-forgotten foreign term.

hooted *adj American* drunk. Although the term, recorded among adolescents, usually describes intoxication by alcohol, it may be influenced by the noun form 'hooter', denoting a **joint**. Alternatively, it may be inspired by the hooting of inebriated celebrants.

hooter *n* **1** *British* nose. A common term of the 1950s and 1960s which is still heard. A synonym less widespread on the same lines is **bugle**.

✎ *'The doc says the 30-year-old vain singer* [Michael Jackson]*'s hooter is collapsing after being broken so often in four operations to change his looks.'*
(*News of the World*, 7 May 1989).

2 *American* a **joint** (marihuana cigarette). A college and high-school term.

hooters *n American* breasts. A favourite term of college boys reminiscent of **bumpers**, **headlamps** and other automotive similes. The usage also plays on the supposed similarity in action between pressing a rubber bulb and manipulating and fondling a breast.

hoover (up) *vb* to devour, eat or drink rapidly or greedily. A popular use of the vacuum cleaner's household name since the late 1960s. The expression is most common in Britain but is known in the USA. During World War II hoovering was the name given to an airborne mopping-up operation by the RAF.

↳'*We laid out a spread and they hoovered it up in minutes.*'
(Recorded, hostess, Weybridge, England, May 1986).

↳'*He hoovered up five pints and got poleaxed.*'
(*The Crack: a Belfast Year*, Sally Belfrage, 1987).

hop a babe, hop on a babe

vb American to have sex (with a woman). A gauche **preppie** term from the 1970s.

hophead

n American a narcotics user. Hop was a late 19th-century term for opium, later extended to any 'stupefying' drug including marihuana. Hophead, dating from the 1940s, was one of the first words for a category of drug-users to use the -head suffix. By the 1960s the word was used mainly by law enforcers and other disapproving adults. It is now rare.

hopped-up

adj under the influence of narcotics. 'Hop' was a late 19th-century term for opium in the USA, later generalized to refer to any intoxicating drug. Hopped-up is a phrase from the early 1960s which does not however usually refer to opiates or other stupefying drugs but rather to stimulating **uppers**. It is characteristically used disapprovingly by non-drug users of abusers.

hopper

n American a toilet (bowl). A term favoured by **hard-hats** and **jocks** among others. (A hopper is a large metal feeder container in grain silos.) Coincidentally or not, 'the hopper' is also in American usage the place where schemes are hatched and ideas nurtured. In business jargon or office slang to '*put something in the hopper*' is to 'feed it into the system' or to 'put it on file'.

↳'*It's all in danger of going down the hopper.*'

horizontal dancing

n phrase sexual intercourse, a jocular euphemism typically used by American college students, etc. from the early 1980s. The term probably originated as a joke among middle-class adult sophisticates.

horlicks

n British a mess, an unpalatable or confused mixture. The trade name of a bedtime drink has here been appropriated as a euphemism for **bollocks**. The word is used by all social classes and began to appear in print in the late 1980s.

↳'*How to make a total horlicks of it in five easy stages.*'

hormone

n a promiscuous, sexually active or successful person. This term, usually applied to males, was popular among adolescents and younger schoolchildren in Britain and Australia in the 1990s.

↳'*He's what we call a raging hormone.*'
(Australian surfer in Biarritz, *Passengers*, Channel 4 TV programme, September 1995).

the horn

n **1 a** the penis, particularly when erect. This obvious metaphor has been commonly employed in English for at least 200 years. Prior to that horn more often referred to the cuckold's emblem.

b an erection. Usually found in phrases such as to '*have the horn*', to **get the horn** or **on the horn**.

2 a telephone. In this sense the word usually occurs in the form '*(get) on the horn*'. This usage is encountered more often in the USA than in Britain.

horny

adj sexually aroused, lustful. Although the **horn** in question is the penis (in an image which dates from the 18th century, if not earlier), the expression is now used by and about both sexes, sometimes in colourful phrases such as '*horny as a hoot-owl*'. It is a 1960s successor of longer phrases such as **get the horn**, to be **on the horn**, etc.

↳'*The total absurdity of it all; seven or eight able bodied policemen keeping 24 hour watch on this horny endomorphic Jewish intellectual.*'
(Bill Levy, *Oz* magazine, February 1970).

horrorball

n a repellent or unpleasant person. A children's term of abuse or joky disapproval of the 1980s. It is a pun on the adjective horrible, influenced by **sleazeball**, **slimeball**, etc.

the horrors

n **1** a bout of terror or fit of existential despair. The term applies especially to the sudden uncontrollable feelings of dread and horror experienced as a result of drug or alcohol abuse (as for example in cases of delirium tremens, heroin withdrawal, amphetamine **comedown**, **acid flashes** or the fits of paranoia associated with over-indulgence in strong cannabis). The expression was used in the 19th century to refer to the effects of alcoholism.

2 menstruation, monthly periods. A rare schoolgirl alternative to **(the) curse**.

horrorshow *adj, n*

a (something) shocking or horrifying.

b (something) sensational, impressive or excellent.

Like **bad**, **creepshow**, **hellacious** and other similar teenage terms of the 1980s horrorshow has undergone the process (technically known as 'amelioration') whereby a pejorative or negative term acquires a positive meaning. This word, inspired by horror films and comics, has the dual implication of awful and thrilling, the intended meaning apparent only in the tone of voice or context.

horse *n* heroin. A word used by drug addicts and **beatniks** in the 1950s, it was already dated by the late 1960s and was generally supplanted, first by **H**, and subsequently by **smack**, **scag**, etc.

horse's ass *n American* a fool, especially an annoying or contemptible one. A common folksy phrase among adults. Like other expressions based on 'horse', the term has not spread to British usage.

horseshit *n* nonsense, foolish or empty talk. A popular term in the USA where it is similar in meaning to **bullshit**, with perhaps the suggestion that horseshit is more transparently ludicrous or frivolous. The British apparently still view the horse with more respect or affection; neither horseshit, **horse's ass** or **horse feathers** have caught on in British English.

↳ *'You see, there's got to be some respite from the horseshit. And cars give you that. They're primitive.'*
(Paul Newman, *Elle* magazine, May 1989).

horseshoe *n South African* a hand-rolled cigarette, especially one containing strong tobacco.

hose *vb American* to have sex with. A mainly male vulgarism.

↳ *'There must be someone here that I could hose ... Better get some more sherry to smooth out my brain.'*
(S. Clay Wilson cartoon, *Head Comix*, 1968).

hose-hound *n American* a promiscuous or sexually active person, usually female. A later coinage based on the verb 'to hose' and the noun '**hoser 2**'.

↳ *'Look at the fun-bags on that hose-hound!'*
(*Dumb and Dumber*, US film, 1994).

hose monster *n American* an extremely promiscuous and/or sexually active person. The term, which may be used pejoratively or appreciatively, is particularly applied to heterosexual females. Compare **shag-monster**.

hoser *n American* **1** a fraud, deceitful person, cheat.

2 a promiscuous person, usually female. Both senses of the term are found in the vocabulary of high-school and college students. The etymology of the word is not certain, but probably derives from **hose** as a noun meaning penis and a verb meaning copulate or **screw** in the figurative sense of defraud.

hospitals *n pl See* **play hospitals**.

ho stroll *n American*

a a prostitute's patrolling of her area, streetwalking.

↳ *'I'm on the ho stroll, honey.'*
(Hispanic New York prostitute, Channel 4 TV documentary, October 1994).

b a provocative gait, as used by prostitutes looking for customers.

hot *adj* **1** stolen, from the image of something 'too hot to handle'. The word was used in this sense in *The Eustace Diamonds* by Trollope in 1875.

↳ *'D'you reckon that video is hot?'*

2 exciting, fashionable. A slang usage (from the language of jazz musicians in which 'hot', frenzied and fast, is contrasted with 'cool', relaxed and slow) which by the mid-1970s had become a common colloquialism.

3 sexually excited or aroused. The adjective has always been used in this sense both literally and figuratively.

↳ *'She's hot for him.'*

↳ *'Talk dirty to me. You know it gets me hot.'*

4 provocative, obstreperous. In this sense the word was defined by one of its users as 'acting too obvious' and denotes a transgression of the unwritten codes of behaviour of adolescent gangs. The term was recorded in use among north London schoolboys in 1993 and 1994.

↳ *'Acting hot.'*

hot-dog *vb American* to perform spectacularly and brilliantly and/or to show

off. The term is applied especially in sports' contexts (the sport of stunt skiing, for example, is known as 'hot-dogging'), or to high-achieving students.

hot-dog, hot-dogger *n, adj*

American (someone or something) outstanding, spectacular and/or successful. The term is used as an exclamation, showing amazement and approval, but when applied to people may often indicate envy or disapproval.

✎'*Hot dog! we're havin' a great time here!*'

hot pants *n* 1 a sexually aroused

state; lustfulness, particularly in a woman.

2 brief shorts as worn by women in a fashion of 1970 and 1971.

hot poop *n* the very latest news, most

up-to-date information. An American term of the early 1960s which had spread to Britain, especially in the armed services and in journalistic speech, by the early 1970s. **Poop** is a nursery term and adult euphemism for **shit**.

hot rocks *n British* the glowing em-

bers at the tip of a lit cigarette or **joint**. An expression from school-playground slang. **Cherry** is a synonym.

hot roller *n American* a stolen car, in

the language of car thieves and police alike. A term of uncertain age, heard in the early 1980s.

the hots *n pl See* have the hots.

hot shit *n, adj* (something) impres-

sive, exciting, superlative. The common colloquial terms 'hot stuff' and 'hotshot' are in fact euphemisms for hot shit, a term both of contempt and approbation common since the beginning of the 20th century in the USA (still heard more often there than in Britain or Australia).

✎'*Some hot-shit record producer.*'

hotshot *vb, n American* (to adminis-

ter) a lethal injection of a narcotic, usually heroin. This term from the vocabulary of addicts and the underworld refers particularly to a deliberate lethal dose, either self-administered or as a gangland method of punishment and murder. Sometimes the hotshot is a high-strength overdose, sometimes a normal dose of the drug mixed with a toxic substance.

✎'*The guys put him away with a Drano hotshot.*'

hot tamale *n American* a sexually

arousing or provocative woman. A male expression of admiration or approval first coined by adults but now probably more popular among enthusiastic if unsophisticated high-school and college students. A *tamale* is a Mexican speciality, a spicy rolled pancake.

hottie, hottie-tottie *n* 1 a hot

water bottle. A short form used in Britain, particularly by children, and in Australia, where it often characterizes an elderly, suburban cosiness.

2 also **hottie-tottie** an alternative form of **tottie**.

hotting *n British* the stealing of cars

for displays of fast driving and subsequent destruction. An organized criminal adolescent hobby which became a vogue in 1991. Hot here combines the slang senses of 'powerful' and 'stolen'.

hot to trot *adj* eager and enthusias-

tic for sex, and by extension for any activity. A jocular rhyming phrase probably deriving from black American usage in the late 1950s, it was adopted by **hippies** and subsequently enjoyed a vogue in the language of disco dancers, devotees of nightclubs, etc. in the late 1970s, when it usually had the innocuous sense of ready to dance.

✎'*Honey get ready – I'm hot to trot.*'

hotty, hottie *n American* an attrac-

tive female. This appreciative term, which probably originated in black street slang, became widespread in campus and high-school speech in the 1990s.

hot-wire *vb* to start (a car) by tam-

pering with the ignition electrics rather than using the key. A thieves' and law enforcers' term.

hound *n British* 1 a reprehensible per-

son. The word is typically used as mild criticism or affectionate disapproval. 2 *See* **brownie-hound**.

house *n* a type of disco music typically

played in amateur or impromptu club sessions in the late 1980s. House music is electronically enhanced versions of black and European dance records, growing out of the **rap** and **scratch** embellishments of 1970s disco. This style of music coupled with the taking of **ecstasy** and other stimulants and hallucinogens produced the **acid house** cult of 1988 and 1989. The word house itself refers to the

Warehouse club in Chicago where this form of music was pioneered.

house moss *n American* another term for **dust bunny**.

house nigger *n American* a sub-servient or deferential black person, a black menial or an 'Uncle Tom'. The old designation, applied originally to slaves and servants, contrasts with the now ob-solete expression 'field nigger' for a black estate worker or poor farmer.

⬧'*He's gonna have to realize that he can't treat me like some house nigger.*'

howler *n British* a child or baby. An item of middle-class and family slang of the later 1980s and 1990s. **Wowler** is an alternative version. Apart from the obvi-ous reference to a baby's crying, the word might also recall the howler monkey.

⬧'*We're going to have to get a sitter for the howler.*'
(Recorded, middle-class working mother, London 1994).

howling *adj Scottish* smelling offen-sively. This is one of many synonyms for stinking, such as **minging**, **bowfing**, **honking**.

hoy *vb British* to throw, discard. An item of **Geordie** speech (it originated ei-ther as a dialect cognate of 'haul' or as an invention influenced by haul and/or hoist) which became more widely used in the 1990s. The same word occurs in Aus-tralian slang.

⬧'*Finish your fag and just hoy it.*'
(*Away the Lads*, BBC 2 TV documentary, February 1993).

huff *n See* **take the huff**.

huff *vb* 1 to sniff, **snort** (an illicit drug). A late 1970s alternative to the more com-mon **snort** in connection with cocaine. The term has a more specific relation to solvent and glue abuse. It is American in origin.
2 *British* to fart. A schoolchildren's term. **Guff** is a synonym.

huffy *adj* irritable, indignant, angry. The word (a colloquialism rather than slang since the 1960s) is inspired by the 'huffing and blowing' of a furious adult. It has been in use at least since the middle of the 19th century.

hum *vb, n* (to) **fart**. Especially popular in Australia, this jocular term probably

relates to the surreptitious sound rather than the colloquial meaning of hum as 'stink'.

humdinger *n Australian* a spectac-ular **fart**. This vulgarism is a specific usage of the well-known colloquialism denoting anything resounding or impres-sive.

hum-hole *n* mouth. An American high-school word, usually employed as part of an insult or challenge. It appears to date from the early 1980s.

⬧'*Tell him to shut his hum-hole.*'

hummer *n* 1 the anus. The vulgar-ism, probably formed from the verb hum, has been recorded in Australia and the UK.
2 *American* an act of fellatio.

hump *vb* 1 to have sex (with). 'Once a fashionable word for copulation', ac-cording to the *Dictionary of the Vulgar Tongue* by Grose, 1785, hump is now scarcely fashionable but still a wide-spread vulgarism, often in the form '*humping*'. *See* **dry-hump**.
2 to carry. This now common informal sense of the word was considered un-orthodox in the 1950s.

hump *n* 1 the hump a feeling of an-noyance, resentment or depression. To '*have the hump*' or '*get the hump*' has meant to be bad-tempered or to take of-fence since the 18th century. It comes from the notion of a hunchback's burden.

⬧'*"I've got the 'ump today!" he told us cheerfully.*'
(Security guard, *Evening Standard*, 12 June 1989).

2 *American* a nickname for a Camel cigar-ette.
3 a despicable or contemptible person. This insult may be based on the old term for a hunchback or may derive from the sexual meaning of the verb 'to hump'.

humpty *adj British* 1 having the **hump**, annoyed, resentful.

⬧'*He's a bit humpty this morning.*'

2 wanting to **hump** someone, priapic, **horny** or sexually aroused. Both senses of the word were current in London work-ing-class usage in the late 1980s. The 'h' is usually silent.

humpty-dumpty *n South African* a foolish and/or fat person. The mocking or insulting epithet derived from the children's rhyme was recorded as an item of Sowetan slang in the *Cape Sunday Times*, 29 January 1995.

humpy *adj* 1 *British* having the hump, annoyed, resentful.

2 *American* sexually aroused. The term, a more recent synonym for **horny**, is used particularly among American adolescents and can refer to either sex.

humpy *n Australian* an aboriginal's shack. This 19th-century term from a native word *oompi* is now sometimes extended to refer to any makeshift cabin or shelter.

humungous, humongous *adj* enormous, terrifying, tremendous. A popular word among schoolchildren and teenagers since the late 1970s, this is an invention combining elements of huge, tremendous and enormous, on the lines of **ginormous**, 'sponditious', etc. It seems to have originated in the USA.

✎*'Darlene and I just killed a huge spider – we hadda use a whole can, it was humungous.'*
(Roseanne, US TV comedy series, 1989).

✎*'Man, I got a humungous thirst on me.'*

hung *adj* 1 a sexually endowed (referring to men). A coarse euphemism which is probably Victorian, perhaps older. The word is often part of colourful comparisons such as '*hung like a horse/bull/jack donkey*' or, alternatively, '*hung like a fieldmouse*'.

✎*'Her opener had a certain showgirl candor: "Is it true what all the girls say – that you're hung like a horse?"'*
(Kenneth Anger, *Hollywood Babylon*, 1975).

b sexually well-endowed, having large genitals. This shortening of **well-hung** has been part of male **gay** jargon since the early 1970s.

✎*'Wow, he's really hung.'*

2 a variation of **hung-up**.

✎*'You got me to/ Fall in love with you/ Though I'm not free to/ Fall in love with you/ Oh, why/ Did I/ Have to get so hung on you?'*
(The Righteous Brothers, 'Hung on You', written by Spector/King/Goffin, 1965).

✎*'Nothing to get hung about.'*
(The Beatles, 'Strawberry Fields Forever', 1967).

hung-up *adj*

a suffering from a complex; neurotic, in-
hibited. A popular **putdown** used by **hippies** to categorize socially or sexually repressed, **uptight** behaviour, especially on the part of **straights**.

b hung up on (someone) obsessed with, in love with (someone). A hippy usage which persisted into the 1980s, and is still heard occasionally.

hunk *n* a well-built sexually attractive male.

Hunkie *n American* a Hungarian. A term applied (with pejorative connotations) to immigrants.

hunky-dory *adj* fine, in good order, perfect. A well-established colloquialism, adopted in Britain some time after World War I. The phrase arose in the USA in the mid-19th century. The 'hunk' component is from the Dutch *honk* meaning a post used as a 'home' in a game of tag; 'dory' is probably a meaningless elaboration.

huntley *n British* karma (personal destiny). An ephemeral and unusual collision between the worlds and concerns of the **hippy** and rhyming slang, this humorous coinage is from Huntley and Palmer, a well-known British biscuit manufacturer.

✎*'Hello love, how's your huntley?'*
(Recorded, social worker, London, 1987).

hurl *vb* to vomit. A usage common in Australia and to a lesser extent in Britain.

hurting *adj American* suffering from the lack of a necessity, usually a drug. The term, previously used in a romantic context, by the 1990s almost invariably referred to narcotics withdrawal.

✎*'I was on the street and hurtin' with nothing to cop with and no-one to cop from.'*

hustle *vb*

a to work as a prostitute, solicit sexual clients.

b to importune, pressurize, take advantage of.

c to make great efforts (often selfishly). All senses of the word (introduced from the USA into other areas in the mid-1960s) derive from its origin in the Dutch *husselen* or *hutseln* meaning to shake up or jostle. This gave rise to an American version of the word meaning hurry or shove, later used in the specific senses above.

hustle *n*

a a high-pressure scheme, an attempt to obtain money, bully or browbeat someone.

b a rush, energetic action. The noun forms derive from the earlier verb form.

hustler *n*

a a prostitute (of either sex). This specific and euphemistic sense of the word remains exclusively North American.

b any intrusive, importunate or over-assertive person. A word which entered world English in the late 1960s, from American usage. Both senses of the word post-date the verb form **hustle**.

hymie, heimie *n* a Jew. An unaffectionate, if not strongly offensive term inspired by the short form of the Jewish male forename Hyman. The word has been used in British English since the 1950s.

hype *vb, n* (to create) excessive, overblown or misleading publicity. A term applied first to the activities of the pop music industry in the early 1970s, hype is a shortening of hyperbole. The word was apparently in use in the USA for many years among swindlers and tricksters before becoming part of commercial jargon (where it is now widespread).

↳ *'If hyping is the pursuit of profit over performance, and anticipation over delivery, then there is a mystical link between the garish posters of the Ringling Brothers ("Giant Two-Storey Elephant") and all those trailers for movies you slept through or ran screaming from into the night.'*
(*Time Out*, March 1989).

hype, hypo *n* a hypodermic syringe. This short form was used by drug abusers in the 1950s and early 1960s, but was always rarer than the more colourful alternatives such as **harpoon**, **works**, **artillery**, etc. It persists in the vocabulary of doctors, paramedics, etc., particularly in the USA.

hyped-up *adj* 1 exaggerated, inflated, overpublicized. From the verb to **hype** (itself from hyperbole).

2 excited, over-stimulated, tense. This sense of the word probably originates in hypersensitive, hyperactive or hyperventilate rather than in hyperbole.

hyper *adj* an abbreviation of hyperactive and/or hyperventilating. The word, which was especially popular among American devotees of group therapy, 'consciousness-raising', etc., has now taken on a generalized sense of agitated or keyed up.

i...

ice *n* 1 diamonds or other jewellery. An underworld term in all English-speaking areas, this word has also been heard in everyday speech.
2 an illicit drug which appeared in Hawaii in 1989 and for a time seemed poised to replace **crack** as a major social scourge in the USA. Ice is a highly synthesized version of methamphetamine (the archetypal **speed** as abused in the 1960s and 1970s under the name of methedrine).

ice *vb* to kill. An American underworld term which may initially have been a shortened form of '*put someone on ice*'. The word has been popularized by its use in crime films and TV series.
↳'*Maybe he saw the Hellinger killing go down – they iced him to keep him quiet.*'
(*The Rockford Files*, US TV series, 1978).

ice cold *n* a beer. An American and Australian term of the 1970s adopted by some British lager drinkers.
↳'*Set up some ice colds, will you.*'

ice cream *n British* 1 a man. This piece of now obsolete low-life and demi-monde slang of the 1950s derives from 'ice-cream freezer', rhyming slang for **geezer**. See also **fridge-freezer**.
2 a white person. This is a quite separate coinage from sense 1 and is mainly used by black and Asian schoolchildren to refer dismissively to whites. The term is not widespread or well-established. There is as yet no universal offensive epithet with which to refer to whites; **honkie** and **whitey** are probably the most common, 'pinky' is a less well-known alternative.

ice man *n American* 1 a jewel thief. From **ice** in the sense of diamonds or other games or jewellery.
2 a **hit-man**, professional killer. From the verb **ice** meaning to kill.

ick *n* an unpleasant substance. The term is probably a back-formation from **icky**, itself a colloquial description or exclamation of distaste possibly influenced by sticky.

icky (poo) *adj* a distasteful, unpleasant. b sickly sentimental, cloying. The word originated as a baby-talk version of 'sticky'. It is now used by adults and particularly by teenagers to refer to something either literally or metaphorically viscous.

iddy, iddy-boy *n British* a Jew. A London working-class term of disparagement and abuse which is a distortion of **yid**.

idiot box *n* a television set. A less common alternative to **gogglebox**, dating from around 1960, by which time the mind-numbing effects of TV-viewing were attracting critical comment.
↳'*An entertaining and salutary study of the tangled, dishonest and sometimes demented relationships our premiers have had with the idiot box.*'
(*Sunday Correspondent*, 13 September 1989).

idiot dancing *n British* a style of frenzied, abandoned dancing on the spot (invariably consisting of writhing hand and arm movements and shaking of the head) to rock music, particularly the **psychedelic** style (a precursor of heavy metal) of the late 1960s. It was influenced by a notion of Indian and oriental religious ecstatic dancing and, more prosaically, by the limited space for any more expressive movement allowed by the packed concert halls and festival sites that were the natural habitat of the idiot dancer. By the mid-1970s it had mutated into the less picturesque **headbanging**.

iffy *adj* a questionable, doubtful or suspicious. In the 1960s this was a slang term heard predominantly in London working-class usage. It enjoyed a vogue among the fashionable in the late 1970s, by which time it was also widespread in the USA. The term is now a common colloquialism.
↳'*Paid-for lessons at some professional club in Romford; and the use of such iffy stimulants as "Matchroom" aftershave.*'
(*GQ* magazine, August 1989).
b *British* (of a person) dishonest, probably

criminal or (of a thing) probably stolen. A milder version of **bent** or **moody**.

ikey (mo) *n British* a Jew. A derogatory term dating from the 19th century. Ikey is a diminutive form of Isaac and Mo (Moses). Ikey Mo was a character in the *Ally Sloper* cartoons at the turn of the century.

illin' *adj* **1 a** unhealthy, sick. This conversion of the adjective ill has been a feature of many English dialects, particularly black and rural ones, since the 18th century.
b stupid, crazy, unbalanced.
2 bad, **uncool**. This sense results from the appropriation of the older expression by black youth and later white emulators in the USA in the early 1980s. The word enjoyed a vogue in Britain in 1987 and 1988, having been imported as one of the buzz-words of the **rap** and **hip-hop** cultures. The word was particularly common in the lyrics used by the band The Beastie Boys.

imbo *n Australian* an imbecile. A characteristic Australian shortening.

imshi *exclamation vb* to go away. An Arabic imperative adopted by members of the armed forces, particularly in Egypt, and imported to Britain where it is still heard occasionally among the older generation.

in *adj* fashionable, modish, in vogue. This well-known expression was considered jargon or slang in the early 1960s. It subsequently became emblematic of the successive fads of the 1960s and passed into common speech. By the mid-1970s the word was no longer used by those who consider themselves fashionable. It remains a rather dated colloquialism.

in-and-out *n* a version of **in-out**.

in-and-out man *n British* an opportunist thief. An underworld and police term describing an offender who takes advantage of an open door, unprotected premises etc. to steal on impulse.

in bother *adj British* in trouble, endangered. From **bother**.
↳ '*I thought you was in bother.*'
(*Only Fools and Horses*, British TV comedy series, 1989).

in costume *adj American* in uniform. Police jargon of the 1980s.

in deep shit *adj* a later elaboration

of '*in the shit*', meaning in trouble. This version of the expression became fashionable in the late 1980s.

Indian hemp *n* cannabis; marihuana or hashish. Very little illegally imported cannabis originates in India, but the potent, smokable strain of the hemp plant has the botanical name *cannabis sativa indica*. **Indian hemp** was a term employed by official and quasi-scientific authorities in the early 20th century (*The Charms of Indian Hemp* was the title of a 1907 publication). In the 1950s smokers of the drug also used the expression, but by the 1960s it was confined to judicial or journalese usage. The word cannabis largely supplanted the term in the 1970s.

indie *n British* **a** an independent record label (i.e. one not affiliated to one of the big business conglomerates known as 'the majors'), or a record issued on one of these. The expression and the phenomenon date from the mid-1970s when small-scale record companies, boosted by the advent of punk rock, with its do-it-yourself ethic, began to threaten the virtual monopoly of the majors. Indie had previously referred to independent films produced in the USA.
↳ '*Apologists for the "indie ghetto", forever championing obscure and unlistenable bands with silly names.*'
(*Independent*, 1 December 1989).
b the youth subculture coalescing around Indie bands from the late 1980s to the mid-1990s.

indijaggers *n British* indigestion, a stomach upset. A public-school term which perhaps originated as a nursery word in the early years of the century.
↳ '*I've got frightful indijaggers!*'
(*Guardian*, Posy Simmonds cartoon, 1981).

in Dutch *adj* in trouble, in a vulnerable condition or delicate situation. This expression is a surviving example of the tendency (dating from the Anglo-Dutch wars of the 17th century) to use Dutch as a pejorative, as in 'Dutch courage', 'Dutch treat' or 'Dutch Uncle'. In Dutch appears to date from the beginning of the 20th century. An alternative etymology would derive the expression from American English in which Dutch refers to the habits of Dutch settlers and indicates peculiarity rather than any more negative qualities.

in effect *adj, adv British* in action, at

large or happening. A black euphemism used particularly by street gangs in the 1980s. The expression has been picked up by black and white schoolchildren.

♭*'Posse in effect.'*
(Graffito on wall, Clapham, London, 1988).

in hock *adj* a pawned.

♭*'I'm living on a Chinese rock/All my best things are in hock ... Everything is in the pawn shop.'*
(Lyrics to 'Chinese Rock', The Ramones, 1980).

b in debt.

♭*'They're in hock to the tune of £2,000.'*
♭*'He's in hock up to his eyes.'*
The term comes from **hock** meaning to pawn.

inked, inky *adj* drunk. These terms,
although rare, are not yet obsolete and are common to Britain, Australia and the USA. The origin of the expressions is unclear. They may be humorous parallels to blotto, or perhaps (and more probably) derive from the fact that cheap red wine was in the early years of the 20th century referred to as 'ink'.

in like Flynn *adj* successful, in a
very comfortable or advantageous position. A phrase which originated in the late 1940s and which shows no signs of disappearing despite the death of Errol Flynn, its inspiration. Flynn, the Australian hero of swashbuckling adventure films, was turned, especially in Australia and Britain, into a folk symbol of male sexual prowess by the press coverage of his trial on trumped-up statutory rape charges. The expression originally referred to success in seduction, but is now generalized to any impressive achievement, piece of opportunism or stroke of luck.

innit? *question tag, exclamation*
British a a question tag used to precede or to follow a statement.

♭*'"Innit?" has now found its way to the beginning of sentences: "Innit we're going to McDonalds today?" '*
(Roy Kerridge writing in the *Evening Standard*, 20 August 1993).

b an exclamation of agreement.

♭*'We should split up and meet back here later.'*
'Innit!'

Unlike some languages, English requires many different question phrases (aren't they?, can't we?, don't you?, etc.) instead

of one (as in French *n'est-ce pas?*). Indian and Pakistani English has for many years used *'isn't it?'* in this way, but in the early 1980s black British speakers appropriated the London working-class *'innit?'* to serve as an all-purpose tag. The usage was imitated by white schoolchildren (leading black speakers to adopt *'in't it?'*, *'an't it?'* and *'don't it?'* as alternatives) and the word became detached from its context as a catchphrase.

in-out *n* sexual intercourse. A eu-
phemism heard among English speakers everywhere since before World War II. In British usage it is often part of expressions such as '(a bit of) the old in-out'. An earlier version was 'in-and-out'.

in power *adj* American successful,
enjoying respect. An item of street-gang jargon in the 1990s, which parallels the British in effect.

in shtuk/shtook/stook/schtuk *adj British* in trouble. A very
widespread expression which moved from a restricted demi-monde and theatrical usage to common currency in the mid-1960s, partly through its use in the entertainment media. *Shtuk* in its various spellings is Yiddish for difficulties. 'In shtuk' often refers to financial difficulties.

inside *adj, adv* in prison. Formerly a
piece of euphemistic underworld slang dating from the 19th century, this word has become so widely known since the late 1950s as to be a colloquialism rather than true slang.

in stir *adj See* stir.

intense *adj American* good, positive.
This all-purpose term of approval, with overtones of exciting, energetic, vital, etc., has been in vogue, particularly among teenagers, since the late 1970s. *See also* **camping**.

intercourse *vb* From 'sexual inter-
course', this term has been used as a humorous euphemism for **fuck** since the late 1970s. It is largely confined to middle- and upper-class speakers such as **yuppies, Sloane Rangers** and university students. The word is employed in various forms according to the usages of **fuck**; *'Oh, intercourse!'* as an exclamation, or *'(I'm totally) intercoursed'*, meaning exhausted, for instance.

interfacing *n* communicating or
getting on well. A piece of jargon from the

world of computing, transposed by **yuppies** and others into a humorous (or straightforward) synonym for communicating (with) or relating to others.

interior decorating *n British* sexual intercourse. A jocular euphemism heard in the 1970s and 1980s.

in the bag *adj American* 1 drunk. A popular expression in American usage.
2 a ruined, botched. The original image evoked is either of a corpse zipped up in a body bag or a gamebird in a poacher's sack. b demoted, in American police jargon. This is probably an extension of sense 2a.

in the club *adj British* pregnant. This very common expression is in origin a shortening of 'in the **pudding club**', which dates from the 17th century, and is one of many folk expressions using baking metaphors in a sexual context. Pudding is an obsolete euphemism for semen and, more rarely, for the female sex organs.

in the frame *adj* identified as a suspect in a crime. This example of police jargon, in use both in Britain and the USA, is derived either from the simple image of a portrait in a frame or from horse-racing parlance, in which it refers to the practice of displaying the numbers of the winning and placed horses in a metal frame at the end of the race.

in the groove *adj, adv* a proceeding smoothly, working well.
b in harmony with others or with one's surroundings, *au fait* with what is going on. Both terms come from the jargon of pre-World War II jazz musicians.

in the nuddie *adj British* a coy or facetious deformation of 'in the nude'.

in the shit *adj* in trouble. This common expression has been in use since the mid-19th century if not earlier. It is a vulgar version of '*in the soup*'.

in your eye, in a pig's eye, in a pig's arse *exclamation* an all-purpose expression of violent negation; usually denial, refusal or dismissal. The first two versions are euphemistic alternatives to the third.

irish *n British* a wig. Rhyming slang from 'Irish jig'. Wigs and toupees, which attract much notice and derision in cockney circles are also known as **syrup of figs**, **rugs**, 'mops' or **dogs**.

Irish apricot/apple/plum *n* a potato. These predictable witticisms have been heard since the 19th century in both Britain and the USA.

Irish confetti *n* stones, rocks and other debris thrown during riots and demonstrations.
↳'*The "Irish confetti" was dancing off upraised shields and bouncing and ricocheting all around in the courtyard.*'
(P. J. O'Rourke, *Holidays in Hell*, 1988).

iron *n* a pistol or revolver. A slang term of the 19th and early 20th century (short for the American 'shooting iron') which survives in the pages of 'Westerns' and crime fiction. Iron was revived in the 1990s by members of US street gangs.

iron (hoof) *n British* a male homosexual. London rhyming slang for **poof**, the expression is an authentic cockney folk term which is still very much in currency.

iron lung *n British* a bribe or gratuity. The term is rhyming slang for **bung**, and occurs in the speech of criminals, the police, sports promoters and journalists.

Irving *n American* a boring person, nonentity. The Christian name was thought in the 1950s to be mundane, personifying an urban dullard.

item *n* 1 a current (sexual) relationship, a couple. An Americanism of the 1970s which became widespread in the 1980s in expressions such as '*they're an item*'. This use of the word began as journalese or jargon of the sort practised by *Variety* magazine, it then passed into showbusiness, 'society' and subsequently teenage usage.
2 an actual or potential sexual partner. A de-personalizing reference, like **unit**, heard typically in the context of US singles' bars since the 1970s.

ixnay *adj, adv, n* no, not, none. An all-purpose negative formed by the principle of **pig Latin** from the word **nix**, itself derived from the Yiddish and German for not or nothing. Ixnay was heard, particularly in the USA, in the 1950s and 1960s, but is now virtually obsolete apart from the phrase '*ixnay ofay*', meaning no white people allowed. Like **nix** it can also function as a verb.

j...

j *n* a **joint** (a cigarette containing cannabis). An abbreviation from the jargon of drug users, dating from the mid-1960s.

↳'*I rolled a couple of js for the concert.*'

jack *n* **1** nothing. This fairly widespread sense of the word may derive from an earlier and now obsolete sense of jack meaning very little or a small or insignificant amount. (A synonymous expression is '*jack shit*'.)

↳'*We didn't get jack.*'

2 a a police officer.

b an informer. These British and Australian senses of the word have existed at least since the 19th century.

3 meths (methylated spirits) as drunk by tramps, **dossers**, etc.

4 money. A common term in the USA which is also found in Britain and Australia.

↳'*Listen, I just need some jack – in a hurry.*'

5 a heroin. In the argot of prison inmates and addicts in the 1960s.

b a single dose of a narcotic, specifically a tablet of prescribed heroin or heroin substitute. A term from the jargon of addicts since the mid-1960s, probably originating in **Jack-and-Jill**, rhyming slang for pill, reinforced by the verb **jack (oneself) up**, to inject.

↳'*I just scored ten jacks of H.*'

c an injection (of an illicit drug). From the verb **jack (oneself) up**.

↳'*Give me a jack of that shit you're banging.*'

6 *British* the anus or buttocks. A rarer euphemism than **jacksie**, typically used in provincial working-class speech.

↳'*A kick up the jack.*'

7 venereal disease. In this sense the word is common in Australia, although it is also heard in Britain. The origin of this usage is either in archaic rhyming-slang, jack in the box: **pox**, or from the archaic use of jack to mean penis or semen.

8 *British* 'on one's jack', on one's own, from the rhyming slang 'Jack Jones', alone. As a racier version of John, the most common Christian name, Jack has long been used as an all-purpose nickname, usually with overtones of raffishness.

jack *vb American* to steal, rob, **mug** or hold up. The term, which became widespread in black street gang jargon in the late 1980s, was probably a shortening of car-jack (itself modelled on hi-jack) describing armed holdups carried out on passing vehicles, a criminal fashion of the time.

↳'*You come down here, you goin' get jacked for sure.*'
(Recorded, black youth, New York City, May 1995).

jack *adj Australian* fed up, tired, weary. To be jack of something or someone has been heard in Australian speech since the early years of the 20th century. It is probably not directly related to the more recent near synonym **jacked off**.

jack (and jill) *n British* the female contraceptive pill. An item of rhyming slang heard since the 1980s.

Jack-and-Jill *n British* a pill, tablet of an illicit or prescribed drug. A rhyming-slang phrase used by drug abusers since the 1960s.

jacked off/out *adj* annoyed, angry. These 1980s expressions (the first international English, the second primarily North American) are typically used by teenagers and young adults as milder synonyms for **hacked-off** and **pissed-off**.

jacked-up *adj* excited, agitated, **hyper**. This usage, encountered in all anglophone areas, is perhaps related to the verb **jack up** by (probably false) analogy with **hyped up**.

jacker *n American* a thief, robber. The term, from the early 1990s, probably originated as car-jacker.

jacket *n American* a personal file, record; particularly a police file or prisoner's dossier. A law enforcer's term, from the jargon of office-workers.

↳'*Let's take a peek at his jacket.*'

jacking *n* **1** *British* talking, gossiping. A version of 'yakking' heard particularly in the north of England.

2 *American* a robbery, theft.

jack off, jackoff *vb, n American* to masturbate. This phrase may be a euphemistic version of **jerk off**, or may be based on 'ejaculate' or on the archaic meaning of **jack** as semen. *See also* **jill off**.

jack roll *n South African* a **gang-bang**. Recorded as an item of Sowetan slang in the *Cape Sunday Times*, 29 January 1995, the expression was previously heard in North American slang where it signified a **mugging**.

jacks *adj, adv British* alone. The word, used for instance by students in the 1990s, is taken from the cockney rhyming slang expression **on one's jack (jones)**.

⋈'*While Kevin was out kicking back somewhere, I was at home, jacks as usual.*'
(Recorded, female university student, London, March 1996).

jack shit *n American* nothing. A dismissive or contemptuous term, originally with folksy southern overtones, but now common.

⋈'*Man, I worked hard all my life and ended up with jack shit.*'

jacksie, jacksy *n*
arse, anus, buttocks. A fairly inoffensive working-class word, particularly popular in the north of England, jacksie (the form jaxy has also been recorded) dates from the 19th century. It is probably an affectionate diminutive form of the commoner nickname **jack**. Instances of the word in American speech point to a recent borrowing from British usage.

⋈'*The jewel in the jacksie of South London, this place is.*'
(*My Beautiful Laundrette*, British film, 1985).

⋈'*I've got ten minutes to spare. If you like I can redecorate the front room. A better idea still, why don't we shove a broom up my jacksie and I could sweep the floor at the same time.*'
(*Moonlighting*, US TV series, 1989).

Jack-the-lad *n British* an individual who is cleverer, more successful, more attractive than the rest. Originating in the working-class language of Liverpool and the surrounding area, the phrase had spread to the rest of Britain by the mid-1980s, probably due to the influence of television drama, films, fiction, etc. It can be used to express either approbation or contempt and is a modern example of the coining of male epithets with 'Jack' since medieval times.

⋈'*He's Jack-the-lad now, but he'll get his come-uppance.*'

⋈'*"Nobody in England today seems to like a jack-the-lad," said Mr King – but when did they ever?*'
(Kate Saunders, TV review, *Evening Standard*, 17 May 1989).

jack up *vb British* to arrange, organize (especially at short notice). This sense of the phrase, used typically by working-class speakers such as police and gang members, suggests mounting an improvised operation or rigging up a contraption. It is presumably an extension of the specific use of the term as employed by car mechanics.

jack (oneself) up *vb* to inject (oneself), usually with heroin, but possibly with amphetamines, etc. Apart from **shoot up**, this was probably the most common expression for the practice in the 1960s.

jag *n* **1** a binge, as in a crying jag, cocaine jag, etc. This sense of the word derives from a 17th-century English dialect-term originally meaning a burden, later extended to mean a bout (of drunkenness). The word virtually disappeared from British usage in the 19th century, but survived in American slang, whence it was re-imported.

2 a an injection.

b an inhalation of glue or another solvent. These invented terms are probably influenced by 'jab', **jack**, **jack (oneself) up** and **jagged**, as well as the first and more widespread sense of jag itself. The first sub-sense dates from the early years of the century, the second from the 1950s.

3 a Jaguar car.

jag *vb* **1** to inject. A prisoners' and addicts' term influenced by the verb **jack (oneself) up** and the noun **jack**, as well as 'jab'.

2 *Australian* to acquire by devious, illegal methods or by pure luck. The term, defined on the Internet, appears to be a recent coinage.

jagged *adj* drunk. This predominantly American term (used by **preppies** among others) can be pronounced either as 'jag-gid' or, more often, as 'jagg'd'. It derived from **jag** in the sense of a drinking bout.

jailbait *n* a sexual partner or potential sexual partner under the legal age of consent. The expression is typically used to refer to sexually attractive young girls; it is also part of the gay vocabulary. Jailbait (also '*gaol-bait*') has been heard in Britain since the 1950s, but has only been in widespread use since the period of sexual liberation in the late 1960s.

↳'*Look again, Billy, this is jailbait – could get you into a lot of trouble.*' (*Hardcore*, US film, 1979).

jake *n British*
meths, methylated spirits as drunk by tramps, **dossers**, etc. It is also known as **jack**.

jake *adj* excellent, satisfactory, correct. A word of unknown origin, used since the turn of the century in Canada and the USA, where it is now rare, and subsequently in Australia, where it is still heard. The word has not appeared in British usage.

jakey, jakie *n British* a tramp, homeless person, particularly one who is a user of alcohol or **jake**.

jalopy, jalloppy *n* an old car. A word which has passed from slang of the 1950s into widespread colloquial use. The word was first used in the USA before World War II and could also refer to an aeroplane. It is of uncertain origin.

jam, jam it *vb* 1 a to play music informally, to improvise. The phrase originally referred to loose aggregations of jazz musicians, typically playing 'after hours', later to rock and blues.
b to make up an improvised **rap** chant. The word and the practice arose in New York in the late 1970s. Rapping, like the original jazz improvisation, took place in informally composed groups, often competing among themselves.
2 *American* to take part in a wild celebration, to 'party'. An extension of the original musical sense of the word.
3 *American* to have sex (with). This vulgarism usually occurs in the form '*jamming*', and is heard typically among adolescents. Slang uses of the word jam as verb or noun play on its standard sense of crush(ed) or wedge(d) together. The additional sense of sweet confection also in-

fluences the use of the word in sexual euphemisms.
4 also **jam it** *American* to move quickly, leave hurriedly. This sense is of uncertain origin, but may refer to jamming the foot on the accelerator.
5 *American* to sniff cocaine. This use of the word presumably refers to jamming the substance up one's nose. It may alternatively refer to jam as something sweet.

jam *n* 1 a a shortening of jam session, meaning a group improvisation or informal performance. The term was originally applied to jazz, and later to rock.
b a **rap** session.
2 *American* a party (usually a wild, crowded affair).
3 a a sex act.
b a sexual partner (of either gender).
c the vagina.
The many sexual sub-senses of jam are based on the two standard meanings of squeeze or wedge and something sweet.

Jamaica talk *n* the local patois or slang of Jamaica, heard in Britain among immigrants and their descendants. Black schoolchildren brought up in London for instance switch from cockney to Jamaica talk to assert their identity or to converse in secret. Words such as **duppy**, **dread**, **illin'** etc., have emerged from Jamaica talk into more widespread and non-black usage.

jamas *n pl See* **jarmies**.

jamboree bags *n pl British* breasts, a vulgarism mainly heard among males in their thirties and forties (in the 1980s), who remember the lucky-dip sweet and toy packets of the same name.

James *n British* a 'first' (first-class honours degree). Students' rhyming slang from 'James the First'.

↳'*We all expected Penny to get a James but she ended up with a Desmond.*' (*Evening Standard*, June 1988).

jam jar *n British* a motor-car. A piece of rhyming slang which dates from the 1920s and is still in use in working-class London speech. An alternative is 'la-di (dah)'.

↳'*He had to blag a jam jar for the get-away.*' (Recorded, petty criminal, Vauxhall, London, 1976).

jammed *adj American* intoxicated by alcohol or drugs. The standard word in its sense of incapacitated/out of order has predictably been appropriated for slang usage.

jammer *n Jamaican* penis. The Caribbean version of the North American **jammy** or **jemmy**.

✎ '*... how must women feel to hear that "the girls dem want the jammer"?*'
(*Sunday Times*, 2 May 1993).

jammies *n pl British* pyjamas. A nursery term. Alternatives are **jarmies** and **jim-jams**.

jammy *adj British* enviably lucky, very fortunate. This common expression, which is particularly popular among schoolchildren (typically expressed in such phrases as '*jammy dodger*', '*jammy bugger*', '*jammy sod*' or '*jammy bastard*') marvelling at a fellow pupil's luck in escaping punishment, derives from the 19th- and early 20th-century colloquial sense of jam as reward, luxury, indulgence, etc.

jammy, jemmy *n American* penis. In its first form the word has been used by **rappers**, including Ice T. The derivation is unclear, but **jam** as verb and noun has been used to mean both 'penetrate' and 'semen' in earlier black street slang.

jamoke *n American* a dupe, 'sucker'. The word, of unknown etymology, has recently been used in this more specialized sense in US east coast and Chicago police slang but dates from the early years of the 20th century: it previously meant simply a man and probably passed through an intermediate stage of specialization during which it signified a hapless or unimportant male.

jam rag *n British* a sanitary towel. A schoolchildren's term in use since the 1950s. It may also refer to a tampon. (A variant form is **tam rag**.)

jam raid *n British* a menstrual period. A schoolchildren's word from the late 1950s and 1960s.

✎ '*She's excused swimming because she's having a jam raid.*'
(Recorded, schoolboy, 1960).

jam roll *n British* parole. A rhyming-slang term from the vocabulary of prison inmates and the underworld.

✎ '*He's out on jam roll/up for his jam roll.*'

jam sandwich *n British* a police car, in the argot of schoolchildren, tramps, **dossers** and the homeless.

✎ '*I'm not going to be moved. The jam sandwiches [police cars] will have to cart me off.*'
(Homeless man, *Observer*, 16 Aug 1987).

jam tart *n* 1 *Australian* a girl or woman. This is a 19th-century British rhyming-slang expression formed to rhyme with sweetheart and influenced by the well-known sense of **tart** as woman.

2 *Australian* a **fart**.

3 *British* heart. A fairly rare item of London rhyming slang.

jane *n* 1 a women's toilet. A feminine version of a **john**. A term probably coined separately by feminists and humorists of both sexes in the 1970s.

2 a a woman.

b a female prostitute. Both senses of the words are counterparts of **john**.

jang *n* 1 *American* penis. A rare version of **yang** or **whang**.

2 a fight. The word occurs in black British speech and may have originated in Caribbean or black American usage, possibly as a shortened form of 'jangle'.

jangle *vb British* to gossip, chat. A word which is popular in northern England, particularly in the Liverpool area where jangling describes the working-class ritual or pastime of gossiping over the back fence or front gate.

janky *adj* unlucky. The word is of uncertain origin but may be an alteration of jinx(ed). It has been used in Britain by adherents of **rave** and dancefloor cultures in the 1990s.

jangle *n British* a gossip, chat. The noun post-dates the verb form.

jangled *adj* disturbed, nervous, tense or irritated. A 1980s usage, from the colloquialism 'jangled nerves'. (Jangle is not related to jingle but is from a Middle English word meaning grumble.)

✎ '*I'm feeling a big jangled today.*'

jankers *n British* military punishment, punishment detail. An army, navy and RAF term heard particularly in the 1950s, when national service was still in force in Britain. The origin of the term is obscure, but it may be related to **jangle**, which had an archaic sense of 'to grumble', hence jankers were either the grumbling servicemen or the punishments which caused them to complain.

JAP *n American* a young Jewish girl, especially a wealthy or spoilt one. An acronym of 'Jewish American Princess'. A member of a social sub-group supposedly characterized by behaving in a comically spoilt, acquisitive and/or self-indulgent way. The mildly derogatory term is pronounced identically to the abbreviation of Japanese, which caused some confusion when the word achieved popularity in the mid-1970s. Originally used humorously by Jewish speakers themselves, there were signs of its derogatory racist and sexist undertones becoming more overt in the late 1980s. Princess here recalls the indulgent term of (usually paternal) affection, and the haughtiness of the subject. Following the *Preppie Handbook*, a *Jap Handbook* was published in 1983, analysing every aspect of the phenomenon.

↝'*What does a JAP make for dinner? Reservations.*'
(*Evening Standard*, 9 May 1988).

jar *n British* a pint of beer. A pub habitués' term which has been widespread since the 1950s. At the turn of the century, ale was served in china mugs, known as jars, as well as glasses.

↝'*Hey Tom I fancy a bit of lunch. Let's stop at that pub for a few jars.*'
(*Roger Mellie*, cartoon in *Viz* magazine, 1989).

jarmies, jarmas, jamas *n pl British* pyjamas. Alternative nursery terms to **jammies** and **jim-jams**.

jarred (up) *adj British* drunk. The term was used of the Irish writer Brendan Behan by his wife.

J Arthur *n British* an act of masturbation. Rhyming slang from J. Arthur Rank (the British cinema magnate): **wank**. A very popular word in the 1960s, used almost invariably by and about men. (In the 1940s the same phrase was used to refer to a bank.)

↝'*He was having a J Arthur behind the bike shed.*'

java *n* coffee. An Americanism that spread worldwide through the influence of Hollywood and pulp-fiction writers.

Coffee was imported from Java in the 19th century.

↝'*Fancy a cup of java?*'

jaxy *n See* **jacksie**.

jay *n* **1** a **joint**. An alternative rendering of J.
2 *American* a dupe, victim, in the language of criminals, gamblers and confidence tricksters. The reference is to the jay-bird, popularly supposed to be garrulous and dim-witted.

jazz *vb* **1 a** to talk deceitfully, bamboozle, **bullshit**.
b to tease or provoke.
Both sub-senses originated in black American slang and have, since the 1970s, become established in general American colloquial speech. In these meanings, **jive** is a synonym.
2 *American* to have sex with.
A black slang term from the early 20th century, jazz is still used, albeit rarely, in this sense. The word jazz is said to be a New Orleans Creole patois term for sex, or erotic dancing or music.

jazz *n* **1 a** empty, pretentious or deceitful talk.
b provocation, obfuscation, nuisance.
2 a stuff, unspecified things. Often heard in the dismissive phrase '*all that jazz*'.
b ornamentation, decoration, showiness. The precise origin of the word jazz is uncertain. It was first used in New Orleans in the early years of the 20th century in the form 'jass', referring to music and dances inspired by African rhythms. The word also had sexual overtones in its Creole origin. It was later applied to improvised music and, later still, to other forms of exciting display.

JB *n British See* **Jodrell (Bank)**.

jeeter *n American* a slovenly male. Jeeter Lester was a quintessentially uncouth rustic character in Erskine Caldwell's 1932 novel *Tobacco Road*; his first name became part of New York slang in the 1940s and subsequently spread to other areas. In the 1990s the term is still used, often as part of domestic slang.

jeez *exclamation* a less offensive form of Jesus, originally American, but now heard elsewhere.

jeff *n American* a white person. This sometimes perjorative black term is applied invariably to white males and is inspired by Jefferson Davis, the American president portrayed on banknotes, seen as a quintessential Caucasian.

Jeffrey *n British* £2,000. A probably ephemeral invention by an anonymous wit in the tradition of a **monkey**, a 'pony', etc. It refers to the sum paid by the author and politician Geoffrey Archer to Miss Monica Coughlan, a prostitute, to enable her to go abroad. Her return in 1987 resulted in Mr Archer bringing a case for libel against the *News of the World*, which he won. This figure has also been referred to as an **Archer**.

jekyll *adj British* snide. An item of rhyming slang from '(Dr) Jekyll and (Mr) Hyde', recorded among middle-class, middle-aged speakers.

jekylls *n pl British* trousers. The word is rhyming slang – Jekyll and Hydes: **strides**.

⋄'*That's a fancy pair of jekylls you've got there.'*

jellies *n pl British* cheap sandals made of brightly coloured transparent plastic as worn by art students, etc. since the early 1980s. The footwear resembled confectionery of the same name.

jelly *n British* gelignite. This is an underworld term for the explosive favoured by safebreakers and other criminals throughout the 1950s and 1960s.

jellybaby *n British* a weak or irresolute person. This item of criminal slang was defined by *FHM* magazine in April 1996, as 'a slithering disgrace to the profession, one who crumbles under interrogation'.

jelly-belly *n* a fat, overweight or paunchy person.

jelly-roll *n American*
a a woman's sex organs.
b sexual intercourse.
c a woman seen as a sexual partner, sex object or sweetheart.
d a male lover or seducer.

All these terms, popularized by their use in jazz, blues and rock music, derive from black American argot of the late 19th century. A jelly roll is literally a jam or Swiss roll. The triple metaphor implied in the first three senses derives from the rolling motion, the supposed resemblance of the

cake to the vulva, and the notion of 'sweet reward'. In the case of the fourth sense, which is less common but may historically antedate the others, the word represents the sweet element of 'sweetheart'.

jerk *n* a foolish, despicable or obnoxious person. This American term crossed over into limited British usage during and after World War II. It is usually pejorative, although it is sometimes used with pitying or even affectionate connotations in American speech. The word seems to derive from **jerk off**, meaning to masturbate, and was probably originally a rural term for an idle or immature boy.

⋄'*Poor Michael Reagan. As if it weren't bad enough being the son of Ronald Reagan, the guy happens to be a complete jerk as well.'*
(Nigella Lawson, book review, *The Sunday Times*, April 1989).

jerkin' the gherkin *n* male masturbation. A rhyming witticism from around 1960, it replaced other rarer phrases employing the word jerk which had been in use since the mid-19th century, such as '*jerk the turkey*', '*jerk the jelly*', etc.

jerk off *vb* to masturbate. An Americanism which has gained currency throughout the English-speaking world since the late 1960s when it became a **hippy** and student vogue term. The phrase existed in British English in the 19th century but was never widespread.

⋄'*Plus the exhibitionist jerk off fantasia of "let's do it in the road".'*
(*Oz* magazine, 1970). *See also* **jerkoff**.

jerkoff *n American* a despicable or obnoxious (male) person. The American equivalent of **wanker** (to **jerk off** is to masturbate). A word which became particularly popular in the USA in the late 1960s and which had spread to other English-speaking areas by the end of the **hippy** era.

⋄'*The guy turned out to be a complete jerkoff.'*

jerk someone around, jerk someone's chain *vb American* to irritate, harass, subject to minor humiliations. The image evoked is of an animal on a rope or lead being tugged at the whim of its owner.

jerkwad *n American* a term of abuse meaning literally a (male) masturbator, a **jerkoff**. ('Wad' figures in many expressions involving male sexuality and may denote penis or semen, or more recently, tissue or toilet paper.)

jerkwater *adj American* remote, insignificant. This expression does not, as is often thought, have any implication of urination or masturbation. It derives from the rural American practice of stopping trains in remote country areas to take on water, by pulling across a connection and sluice, or ladling from a trough.

↳ *'When you work for a jerkwater* [TV] *station like this you learn to do everything.'*
(*Prime Suspect*, US film, 1982).

jessie *n British* a weak or effeminate man. A Scottish and northern English term of ridicule which has become widespread since the mid-1970s, partly due to the influence of comics such as the Scot, Billy Connolly. It is synonymous with **nellie** and **big girl's blouse**. There are two proposed derivations for the word; the first is simply a borrowing of the female name as a term of endearment, the second is a Biblical reference to '*a rod out of the stem of Jesse*' giving rise to jokes on the subject of masturbation, etc.

↳ *'Oaw, come on you big soft jessie.'*
↳ *'Peelie* [John Peel] *blubbed throughout, the big jessie, and before long we all joined in.'*
(*Evening Standard*, 31 August 1989).

Jesus *n See* **creeping Jesus**.

Jesus boots *n pl British* sandals, particularly thong-type sandals which were characteristic of the **beatniks** of the late 1950s and early 1960s. The jocular term was used by students, **mods** and other teenagers, particularly at the time (between 1962 and 1966) when 'chelsea boots' or 'beatle boots' were also fashionable.

jesus freak *n* a born-again Christian, particularly a member of a Christian evangelical or mystical cult of the **hippy** era. A disparaging term, also applied by students in the late 1960s and early 1970s to members of university Christian Unions, etc.

jesus-screamer *n American* a Christian, particularly one considered to be excessively devout or prone to evangelizing.

jet *vb American* to depart, leave. A vogue term in black street argot and

white campus slang in the 1990s. The word has been used figuratively to mean 'run fast' since the 1950s. A variety of euphemisms (like its contemporaries **bail**, **bill**, **book**, and **jam**) for 'run away' are essential to the argot of gang members and their playground imitators.

jewels *n pl British See* **family jewels**.

jewie louie *adj British* in bad taste, showy, flashy, ostentatiously expensive. A term used by **Sloane Rangers** among others to express distaste at nouveau-riche accoutrements and décor.

jewish *adj British* mean, avaricious, penny-pinching. An offensive term which is, however, typically used by schoolchildren who are only dimly aware of the racist implications.

↳ *'Come on, don't be Jewish, lend us some.'*
(Recorded, schoolgirl, Battersea, London, 1973).

Jewish *n, adj South African* (clothing or accessories considered) fashionable and/or expensive.

↳ *'Natty dressers are described as Jewish – because members of that community are considered to be stylish.'*
(*Johannesburg Sunday Times*, 18 June 1995).

Jewish American Princess *n American See* **JAP**.

Jewish flag *n American* a dollar bill or other banknote.

Jewish lightning *n American* arson, the deliberate burning of insured property. A type of fraud supposed to be typically perpetuated by Jewish businessmen or landlords.

Jewish typewriter/piano/pianola/joanna *n* a cash register. Supposedly jocular racist terms, referring to Jews' presumed love of money. Jewish piano has also been used in Britain for a taxi-meter.

Jew's canoe, Jew's Rolls Royce *n British* a Jaguar or other large car. A racist epithet heard in the late 1960s, particularly in provincial cities.

jewy louie *adj See* **jewie louie**.

jig *n British* a black person. A racist term (probably a shortening of **jigaboo**) employed by police officers, among others. It was used in the G. F. Newman TV play, *Black and Blue*, September 1992.

jigaboo, jiggaboo *n American* a black person. This was originally a racist epithet used by whites since the early years of the 20th century and later adopted in a gesture of defiance like **nigger** by blacks to refer to themselves. The black American author and academic Clarence Major derives the expression from the Bantu word *tshikabo*, meaning 'servile', and dates its adoption to the 17th century. In *School Daze*, a 1988 film by the black director Spike Lee, a fictional all-black southern US campus is riven between the 'jigaboo' faction who want the college authorities to sever links with South Africa, and the **wannabes** who are ambitious and apolitical and ape white pastimes and rituals.

jig-a-jig, jiggy-jig *n* sexual intercourse. Since at least the 18th century there have been various slang terms for copulation using versions of the word jig. 'Jiggle' and 'jigger', for instance, are now archaic, but jig-a-jig has survived, probably because of its use by non-English speakers and those imitating lewd invitations in broken English.

jigger *n* a penis. An 18th-century word which is still heard, albeit rarely, and mainly in the north of England.

jiggered *adj*

a *British* exhausted.

b nonplussed, astonished. The usual form of words employed is '*I'll be jiggered*' as an exclamation of surprise on the pattern of '*I'll be blowed*' or '*I'll be damned*'. Jiggered in both the above senses probably originates as a 19th-century euphemism for **buggered**.

jill *n British* a policewoman. A term used predominantly in the north of England, particularly in the Liverpool area. It is coined by analogy with **jack**; a policeman (itself usually in the plural form).

jillion *n American* an almost inexpressibly large number or amount. A teenagers' coinage to refer to uncountable figures in excess of millions and billions. Other similar terms are 'trillion' (in fact a real number) **squillion** and **zillion**.

jillock *n British* a foolish person, buffoon. A variant form of **pillock**, heard since the late 1970s.

jill off *vb* (of a woman) to masturbate. A term coined by women in the 1970s by analogy with the male **jack off**. The term is not widespread but is used both jocularly and seriously, by gay women in particular.

jim-dandy *adj American* excellent, fine. An elaboration of the popular American colloquialism, dandy (jim, like john and jack, was a widespread prefix conferring familiarity). This expression is often used ironically in modern speech.

jim-jams *n pl* 1 pyjamas. A nursery word, especially popular in Britain and Australia.

↳ '*They knew that he* [Ronald Reagan] *was really an old man in his jim-jams, playing with his dog. Why tell him anything? What would be the point?*' (*Observer*, 22 November 1987).

↳ '*A coat that can double as a dressing-gown, nice stripy jim-jams – such are the staples of male Anglo-Saxon sartoria.*' (*Tatler*, November 1985).

2 an attack of nerves, the **heebie-jeebies**. This expression has been applied to delirium tremens (the **DTs**) and to drug-induced terror as well as more mundane jitters. It was first recorded in the mid-19th century.

↳ '*When the smack begins to flow/ I really don't care any more/ About all the jim-jams in this town/ And all the politicians making crazy sounds.*' ('Heroin', written by Lou Reed and recorded by the Velvet Underground, 1967).

the jimmies *n pl Australian* 1 an attack of nerves; a variant form of the second sense of **jim-jams**.

2 an attack of diarrhoea; a variant form of the **Jimmy Brits**.

jimmy *n British* 1 an injection of a narcotic, especially heroin. A word from the lexicon of prison inmates and drug addicts.

2 a shortening of **Jimmy Riddle**, an act of urination.

↳ '*Hang on to me pint for a minute, I've got to go for a jimmy.*' (Recorded, young drinker, London, 1987).

Jimmy Brits, the Jimmy Brits *n pl Australian* an attack of diarrhoea. Australian rhyming slang for **the**

shits, inspired by the name of a British boxer who toured Australia in 1918. (The surname is sometimes spelt Britt.)

jimmy-hat *n* a condom. The term, common in the United States since the 1970s, also occurs in the form '*jim-hat*' and was used by the black comedian Lenny Henry in a televised monologue in November 1993.

Jimmy Hill(s) *n British* pill(s). The term borrows the name of a TV sports commentator to refer to tablets of illicit narcotics.

Jimmy Riddle *n British* an act of urination. A childish and jocular term derived from rhyming slang for **piddle**.

jingle *n* 1 *British* cash, money, coins. A term used in raffish circles since the 1930s, if not earlier. It has also been recorded in Australian speech.

↳'*I'm a bit short of jingle.*'

2 *American* a telephone call. An American version of the British **bell** or **tinkle**, as in '*give me a jingle*'.

jissom, jiss, jizz, jism, jissum, gism *n* semen. A word of unknown origin, dating from the 19th century in the USA and by the early 1970s in use all over the English-speaking world.

jive *n* 1 deceitful or pretentious talk or behaviour, nonsense.

2 a style of fast dancing to accompany swing music or rock 'n' roll.

Both senses of the term originate in black American slang of unknown etymology (it may be from jibe in the sense of change tack, manoeuvre – in conversation or dance – but is more probably derived from a West African dialect term).

3 *American* marihuana. A now obsolete term. *See also* **jive talk**.

jive *vb* 1 to deceive, tease, browbeat. A black American term from the early 20th century which has enjoyed a vogue among black and white speakers in the late 1980s. For the possible origins of the word, see the noun form.

↳'*It was always about the man, how they were going to jive the man into giving them a million dollars.*'
(*The Switch*, Elmore Leonard, 1978).

2 to dance in a fast energetic style which corresponded in the 1940s to swing music and from the 1950s to rock 'n' roll.

jive-ass *adj American* deceitful, pretentious, worthless. A black expression combining **jive** (worthless or deceitful talk or behaviour) and the suffix **-ass**.

↳'*I don't want no jive-ass honky lawyer jerkin' me around.*'

jive talk *n* a style of speech using black musicians' slang and picturesque rhythmic phraseology, originally developed to accompany swing music of the 1930s and 1940s. The vocabulary and cadences of jive talk were adopted by American teenagers in the early 1950s. Jive talk was combined with **bop** talk to influence much of the vocabulary of the later **hipsters** and **beatniks**.

jizz-ball *n American* an obnoxious, repellent, despicable person. A teenage insult based on the variant form of **jissom** and coined by analogy with earlier terms such as **scuzz-ball**.

joanie, joany *adj American* old-fashioned, boringly outdated. A term from the **Valley Girl** lexicon of the 1970s. Its origins are obscure; it may reflect an original antipathy to an individual such as Joan Crawford or Joni Mitchell or may simply be a choice of Joan as a quintessentially older-generation first-name.

joanna *n British* a piano. A rhyme on the cockney pronunciation of the instrument. *See also* **Jewish typewriter/joanna**.

↳'*Give us a tune on the old joanna.*'

Joan of Arc *n Australian* a shark. A piece of native Australian rhyming slang. An alternative is Noah's Ark.

job *n* 1 a crime. This widespread term occurs in expressions such as '*pull a job*' and in specific forms such as '*bank-job*', '*safe-job*', etc. The word was first used in this sense in the 17th century, usually in the context of theft.

2 a person, thing or action. An all-purpose term for a contraption, specimen or piece of handwork.

↳'*Who's the little blonde job by the door?*'

↳'*A six-cylinder job.*'

job (someone) *vb* 1 to hit or beat up. Job is an old dialect variant of jab which has been preserved in this working-class Australianism. The word was used in the same sense in Britain in the 1950s, by street-gangs for instance.

2 *American* to deceive, cheat or ruin. A rare late 1980s usage which is a shortening of '*do a job on (someone)*'.

jobbed *adj*

framed, **fitted-up**, informed upon, deceived, victimized or otherwise taken advantage of. An item from the vocabulary of the underworld.

jobbie, jobbies *n British* **1** an act

of defecation, excrement. A mock nursery word which is used euphemistically by adults, deriving from expressions such as **big jobs**.

2 an all-purpose word for 'thing'. This variation of the colloquial **job** may also be used as a replacement for a forgotten word or name. The term was defined on the Internet by *Bodge World* in 1997.

↳'*Hand me that big jobbie on the top there …*'

jobbie-jabber *n British* a male

homosexual. The term was one of many synonyms denoting 'active' or 'predatory' homosexuality heard in the 1990s. **Fudge-nudger** and **turd-burglar** are synonyms based on the same supposed association with excrement.

jobsworth *n British* an obstinate

petty official, especially a doorman, bouncer or car park attendant, from their turning down of reasonable requests on the grounds that '*It's more than my job's worth*'. The term was popularized in the rock-music press in the early 1970s when it referred to the officials (often ex-servicemen) who prevented music fans from expressing their enthusiasm or meeting their idols.

↳'*There's always some jobsworth between you and the action.*'
(Recorded, amateur musician, London, 1987).

jock *n* **1** *British* a Scot. Since the 19th

century this has been the universal nickname for Scottish males, derived from the northern diminutive for John.

b an un-named male. The word is used, sometimes dismissively, either as a term of address or as a description.

↳'*Ask jock over there what he's drinking.*'

2 a disc jockey. A piece of American radio jargon adopted in other English-speaking areas in the 1970s.

3 *American* an athlete or sportsman. This campus term can now also apply in some cases to sportswomen, in spite of its origin as a shortening of jock strap. Although it can be said affectionately and is a term used by sportsmen about themselves, the word often has overtones of excessive heartiness, brawn, aggression or lack of intelligence.

↳'*And the jock shall dwell with the nerd and the cheerleader lie down with the wimp and there will be peace upon the campus.*'
(*Observer*, 29 May 1988).

jockey *vb South African* to help, par-

ticularly by a temporary loan of money. Recorded as an item of Sowetan slang in the *Cape Sunday Times*, 29 January 1995.

jocks *n pl Australian* underpants, usu-

ally male. The word is a shortening of 'jockey-pants' or 'jockey-shorts'.

Jodrell (Bank) *n British* an act of

masturbation. The term, invariably applying to male masturbation, is rhyming slang for **wank**, using the name of the space research station famous during the 1950s and 1960s. It is sometimes abbreviated and disguised as **J.B.**

joe *n* **1** an ordinary man, chap, **bloke**.

Originally an Americanism, this use of the name spread to other English-speaking areas in World War II.

2 a victim, dupe or weakling. In this sense the word is used by tricksters, prostitutes and prison inmates, among others, and probably derives from the cockney **joey**, itself short for **Joe Hunt**, rhyming slang for **cunt**. (Cunt previously meant a foolish, unfortunate or pitiable person, rather than a despicable one.)

3 coffee.

↳'*I'm not just some kind of machine you can turn on. I need a cup of joe, a trip to the little boys' room, a glance at the sports pages. Then we'll talk.*'
(*Moonlighting*, American TV series, 1988).

Joe Blake *n Australian* a snake. An

item of native Australian rhyming slang. The eponymous Joe Blake is probably fictitious.

the Joe Blakes *n Australian* the

DTs (delirium tremens) as a result of alcoholism, a fit of uncontrolled trembling. Australian rhyming slang for the **shakes**. *See also* **Joe Blake**.

Joe Blow *n* an average man, ordi-

nary person. A rhymed elaboration of **joe**.

Joe Shmo *n American* **1** an average man.

2 a victim, dupe, a simpleton. This Americanism is a personification of '*schmo*' which has also been recorded in British usage.

Joe Soap *n British*

a an average, ordinary man. The equivalent of a **joe** or **Joe Blow**.

b a dim-witted male drudge or victim. This is the original sense of the name, which is rhyming slang for dope.

joey *n* **1** *British* a fool, dupe, victim or weakling. The word is from London working-class usage, deriving from **Joe** or **Joey Hunt**, rhyming slang for **cunt**, which in cockney speech until the 1950s, referred to a foolish or unfortunate, rather than despicable person. Joey is currently used by teenagers to refer to a timid or unpopular fellow-pupil or gang member.

2 *Australian* an effeminate man, fop, hermaphrodite or sodomite. It is uncertain whether this usage is derived from the previous sense or the following one.

3 a *Australian* a young kangaroo. The origin of this term is not the English Christian name but an identical Aboriginal name.

b *Australian* a baby.

4 *British* a package smuggled in or out of a prison, in the jargon of prison inmates.

john, the john *n* **1** a prostitute's customer. John was a 19th-century term for a male sweetheart which was adopted by prostitutes as an all-purpose form of address and later as a synonym for client.

↳'*He liked it during the day, the cute ladies sitting around playing music, laughing at things he said. But he didn't care for the white Johns any, their attitude.*'
(*The Switch*, Elmore Leonard, 1978).

2 the john a toilet. Originally a more genteel American version of the archaic 'jack' or 'jock' and the almost obsolete **jakes**, all euphemisms for privy.

3 *British* an arrest. A rare example of police and criminal jargon of the 1960s from the rhyming slang 'John Bull': **pull**.

4 penis. A fairly rare but recurring usage. Other personifications, such as **John Thomas**, **Willie**, **Peter**, **Percy**, etc., are much more common.

5 *British* a condom. A shortening of 'johnnie (bag)' or **rubber johnny**.

John *n British* an all-purpose term of address, used typically by a male to another male to express overfamiliarity and/or menace. This working-class usage, common in Greater London, was publicized in connection with the quoted threats by **skinheads** in the early 1970s.

↳'*Who you screwing* [looking at] *John?*' (Skinhead challenge used in picking fights).

↳'*'Ello John, got a new motor?*' (Song title, Alexei Sayle, 1984).

John Bull *adj Australian* drunk. This witticism is a rhyme on **full** in its euphemistic sense of intoxicated.

↳'*He was totally John Bull by three-thirty in the arvo.*'

johnnie, johnny *n British* a condom, contraceptive sheath. This is the most widespread slang term in British use since the 1940s, although in the 1960s and 1970s it was more usually in the phrases 'johnnie bag' or **rubber johnny**. John or Johnny is, among many other appellations, a 19th-century personification of the penis.

Johnny Cash *n Australian* cannabis. An item of native Australian rhyming slang for **hash**, appropriating the name of the American country music star.

johnson *n American*

a penis.

b backside, buttocks. Both senses are personifications used humorously or straightforwardly, especially in black speech. They date from the late 19th century and are elaborations of the use of **john** to designate anything male.

↳'*He can kiss my johnson.*'
(*The Bosses' Wife*, US film, 1986).

John Thomas *n British* penis. A hearty and/or affectionate personification in use since the mid-19th century. It was used by D. H. Lawrence in *Lady Chatterley's Lover*, written in 1928 and first published in an unabridged edition in Britain in 1959. The phrase now seems to be used particularly by women.

joint, the joint *n* **1** a marihuana cigarette or a cigarette containing a mix of hashish and tobacco. Joint supplanted **reefer** as the universal term for a cannabis cigarette in the early 1960s. The precise dating and etymology of the word are obscure.

↦'*Several large joints passed along the room before someone suggested it was time to go outside and play with the Kalashnikovs.*'
(*Tatler*, April 1990).

2 the joint *American* prison. A specialization of the colloquial sense of 'joint' as a place, building or premises.

3 *American* penis. A metaphor based on images of meat and (an imaginary) bone.

jollies *n* gratification. The expression can cover indulgences ranging from innocent enjoyment, through thrills, to more sinister and/or sexual stimulation. The word usually occurs in the phrase **get one's jollies**.

jollop *n* **1** medicine, especially a liquid laxative. The word is either a blend of juice and dollop or, more probably, derives from '*jalap*', a Mexican root formerly used in laxative powders.

2 a large portion, lump or serving. A variant form of dollop.

jolly *n British* a **joint**, marihuana cigarette. A term used, mainly by middle-class smokers, in the 1970s and 1980s.

↦'*We were stuck in the queue, so we just decided to sit back and roll a jolly.*'
(Recorded, ex-hippy, London, December, 1988).

jolly d. *adj British* 'jolly decent'. A public-school or upper-class term of approbation, often used ironically or sarcastically. It is usually an interjection, rather than a description.

jonah *n Australian* a shark. This is not a reference to the whale but a contracted form of the rhyming slang **Joan of Arc**.

jones *n American* **1** penis. Now predominantly a term used by black speakers and their imitators. It may derive from a 19th-century personification of the male member as 'Mr. Jones'.

2 a drug habit.

↦'*They said they had to knock over a couple of stores for money to support their scag jones.*'

josser *n British* a foolish or obnoxious person. Used as a less offensive version of **tosser**, the term was heard particularly in the north of England in the 1980s. The word in fact has had a separate existence since the 19th century during which time it has designated a simpleton, a codger, a

fop and a parasite among other senses. Its ultimate origins are obscure, although joss is said to have been a dialect term for bump or jostle.

journo *n Australian* a journalist. A characteristic Australian shortening which showed signs of catching on in Britain in the late 1980s.

joy pop *vb*
a to take illicit drugs on an infrequent and casual, rather than habitual, basis.

b to inject a drug intramuscularly, to **skin-pop**. *See also* **joy bang**.

joy popper *n*
a an occasional drug user, specifically a user of hard drugs who injects infrequently for pleasure rather than regularly to satisfy an addiction.

b a user of heroin, morphine, etc., who injects the drug into the flesh or intramuscularly rather than directly into a vein. An addicts' term of the late 1950s. The activity is also known as **skin popping**.

joystick *n* **1** penis. A pun on the name of the steering control column of aeroplanes, although some authorities claim that the slang euphemism for the male member actually preceded the aeronautic usage (which may in fact derive ultimately from joist).

2 a cannabis cigarette, a **joint**. A fairly rare euphemism.

jub *n British* a menial or junior worker, **gofer**. The word, of uncertain origin, is used in the City of London financial markets in the late 1990s to refer, often dismissively, to messengers and 'back-office' underlings.

↦'*Get a jub to do it.*'

jubbies *n pl British* a woman's breasts. This childish-sounding term was used by (predominantly middle-class) teenagers and adults from the 1980s and is probably a blend of **jugs** and **bubbies**.

jubbly *n British* money, wealth. The word is used in London working-class speech, especially in the phrase '*(lots of) lovely jubbly*'. Jubbly was the trade name of an orange drink sold in a triangular carton. Especially when frozen, it was popular with schoolchildren in the 1950s and 1960s. *Lovely Jubbly!* was its advertising slogan. In the late 1980s the term was particularly popular with the nouveau riche, **yuppies** and criminals.

jubnuts *n pl British* a southern English rural term for **dags** (fragments of dung clinging to the rear of sheep and other shaggy animals).

judy *n British* a girl or woman. A very common word in working-class use in the north of England in the 1950s and 1960s. Judy was a popular 19th-century Christian name, seen as typical of common women (as in Punch and Judy, for example). The word is also used in Australia as an alternative to **Sheila**.

jug *n* prison. This term from the beginning of the 19th century is usually part of the phrases '*in jug*' or '*in the jug*'. It probably derives from 18th-century dialect 'jougs' meaning stocks or pillory (from the French *joug*, yoke) rather than from jug as a container of liquid. In modern usage the term is jocular.

jug, jug up *vb British* 1 to imprison. From the noun **jug**.

2 *vb American* also **jug out.** to drink, usually to excess. The phrases are probably influenced by the categorization 'jug wine', denoting cheap wine bought in large containers, e.g., by students and other drinkers of modest means.

jugged *adj* 1 imprisoned. From the noun **jug**.

2 drunk. A rare but recurrent term.

jug handles *n pl British* ears, particularly large prominent ears. The term is used by all ages and social classes in poking fun.

jugs *n pl* 1 a woman's breasts. Originally an Australian vulgarism, inspired by milk-jugs, and probably influenced by the much older term **dugs**. This expression has also been used in Britain and the USA.

2 ears, particularly large prominent ears. The word used in this sense, primarily in Britain, is a shortening of 'jug-ears' or **jug handles**.

juice *n American* 1 alcohol, **booze**. A pre-World War II American term still in widespread use.

2 electricity, power.

↳'*Give it some more juice.*'

3 *American* gossip, interesting news. A teenage term of the late 1970s and 1980s which is probably a back-formation from 'juicy'.

juiced, juiced-up *adj* drunk. Unlike other slang terms deriving from **juice**, this is not exclusively American.

↳'*Howard you never used to talk to me that way.*'

'*I'm just juiced, that's all.*'
(S. Clay Wilson cartoon in *Head Comix*, 1968).

juicer, juice head/freak *n American* an alcoholic, drunkard or habitual heavy drinker. These terms probably originated in black slang of the 1940s.

J.U.L.F. *n British* an arrogant and/or presumptuous person. The initials stand for '*jumped up little fucker*'. The phrase was identified by Salman Rushdie, describing the slang used by his Special Branch bodyguards, in the *Independent* newspaper, 11 February 1993.

jumbly, jumblie *n British* a jumble sale. A word used particularly by students and teenagers.

jumbo 1 *British* a fool, a slow, large and/or dimwitted person. A mainly working-class term, used for instance by the CID to refer to uniformed police officers. (Jumbo as applied to elephants derives from the African word *jamba*, anglicized as a name for P. T. Barnum's famous animal exhibit.) In this case the image of a slow, ponderous person is probably also influenced by **dumbo**.

2 *British* backside, buttocks.

3 **crack** this is one of many ephemeral nicknames used on the American streets for this powerful drug. Jumbo in this sense was recorded in 1986.

jump *vb* to have sex with. This term implying male assertion, domination or assault has been in use in English since the 17th century. It is paralleled in many other languages (the French equivalent is *sauter*). The word is now often used by street-gang members, etc. to refer to indecent assault, influenced by the term's colloquial meaning of attack unexpectedly.

jump *n* an act of sexual intercourse. This term has been in use since the 17th century. It is almost invariably said by men, implying as it does an active, possessive male and a submissive or victimized female.

jump in (someone's) face *vb*

American to harass, aggress, criticize. The phrase has been recorded in black street parlance since the 1970s. It is probably based on the earlier imperative '*get out of my face!*'.

jump off *vb American*

a (a person) to become aggressive, lose one's temper.

b (of a situation) to happen or escalate suddenly. The phrase probably arose in black slang where jump was a component in a number of obsolete expressions evoking rapidity and/or violence and the contemporary **jump salty**. **Step off** has similar meanings.

jump salty *vb American* to become angry. A well-known item of black argot which was included in so-called **Ebonics**, recognized as a legitimate language variety by school officials in Oakland, California, in late 1996. The phrase, which seems to date from pre-World War II **jive-talk** (it was listed in Cal Calloway's famous Hepster's lexicon in 1938), became part of street slang in the 1970s. It is now in widespread use and is sometimes heard among younger white speakers describing a key behaviour pattern also expressed by **jump off** and **step off** and the British **kick off**.

jump someone's bones *vb American* to have sex with someone. The expression, first heard in the 1960s, has rough-and-ready, crass overtones. It invariably refers to the sex act from the male point of view.

↘'*I guess she realized I just wanted to jump her bones.*'

june-july *vb South African* to tremble or express fear. The European midsummer months occur in midwinter in the southern hemisphere, hence their association with shivering. The expression was recorded as an item of Sowetan slang in the *Cape Sunday Times*, 29 January 1995.

jungle *n South African* a large knife. Recorded as an item of Sowetan slang in the *Cape Sunday Times*, 29 January 1995.

jungle bunny *n* a negro or other dark-skinned person. A racist epithet which is usually applied to Afro-Caribbeans, and is also used by Australians to refer to Aborigines and South Sea Islanders. It has been heard from at least the 1950s.

jungle juice *n* strong, low-quality alcoholic drink. This was the term applied in the armed services during World War II to various home-made alcoholic concoctions. (It was previously a nickname for African rum.) The phrase is now used to refer to any cheap, potent drink.

jungly *adj British* disorganized, messy, primitive or unsophisticated. An upper-class term of disapproval, employed by **Sloane Rangers** among others. It is in fact an Anglo-Indian word from the colonial era. It was then spelled *jungli* (from Urdu).

junk *n* narcotics, hard drugs. The word (originally a Middle English term for nautical paraphernalia and detritus) was applied to opium in American underworld argot in the late 19th century. It was used to designate heroin by the first decade of the 20th century and has remained one of the most widespread synonyms for this and other addictive drugs. The word spread as the drug-taking habit spread in other English-speaking areas, becoming well-known in Britain during the 1950s.

↘'*Fuzz against junk.*'
(Title of book by the pseudonymous Akbar del Piombo, 1965).

junker *n American* **1** a dilapidated car, **banger**.

2 an alternative (and rarer) version of **junkie**.

junkie, junky *n* a drug addict, a habitual user of 'hard' drugs such as heroin or morphine. The term, derived from the word **junk**, became popular in the USA in the 1920s and spread to Britain and Australia in the 1950s.

↘'*When we think of a junkie we picture the reckless youth, squatting in the rubble of his life, a hypodermic in his hand.*'
(*Independent*, 17 July 1989).

jupe, juped *adj British* shamed, humiliated. One of many terms in the lexicon of teenage gangs which refers to respect or the lack/loss of it. The origin of the term is obscure, but it may be a deformation of the standard dupe, duped. It can also be used as an exclamation of triumph or derision. The term was recorded in use among north London schoolboys in 1993 and 1994.

k...

K *n* **1** one thousand. This abbreviation existed in limited slang usage in the 1970s (based on the k of kilo), but it was its use in computer jargon (to mean a storage capacity of 1,024 bytes) which was first transposed to express sums of money when discussing fees or salaries. It then entered general colloquial use in the 1980s.

✎*'He's on 35K a year.'*

2 *British* a knighthood, from the initial letter, or that of KBE, KCMG, etc.

✎*'Brenda has now let it be known to Downing Street that Milne should be given a "K" in the birthday honours list. Surprisingly enough Thatcher seems to approve.'*
(*Private Eye* magazine, April 1989).

kaffir *n* a black person. A racist term used initially (and still) in South Africa to refer to indigenous blacks. (Kaffir was one 19th-century name for Bantu-speaking South African tribespeople, originating in the arabic *kafir*: infidel.) The word is sometimes used, mainly by middle-aged or elderly speakers, in other English-speaking areas.

kahsi *n British* an alternative spelling of **khazi**.

kaifa *n British* an alternative spelling of **kife**.

kalied *adj British* drunk. A fairly popular word in the north of England (usually pronounced 'kay-lide') which has been used in the long-running TV soap opera *Coronation Street*. Some authorities claim that kay- is a dialect prefix meaning askew or awry; Paul Beale in Partridge's *Dictionary of Slang and Unconventional English* derives kalied from 'kali', a children's sherbet dip.

✎*'And all he could do was go out and get kalied.'*

kanga *n Australian* **1** a pneumatic drill. The term compares the pounding, up-and-down motion of the drill (and its operator) to the bounding of a kangaroo. *See also* **kango**.

2 a prison warder. This expression is derived from rhyming slang, 'kangaroo': **screw**. The same usage has been recorded in Britain in the 1980s, both by prisoners and by schoolchildren referring to teachers.

3 money. An alternative piece of rhyming slang gives **screw** in the sense of money earned.

kangaroo (it) *vb Australian* to squat, particularly in order to defecate; from the kangaroo's habit of sitting back on its rear legs, supported by its tail.

✎*'Not wanting to contract any trendy venereal fauna, I kangaroo-ed it.'*
(Kathy Lette, *Girls' Night Out*, 1989).

kangaroos in the top paddock *adj Australian* crazy, eccentric or deranged. A picturesque coinage, probably based on the colloquial 'bats in the belfry'.

kango, kanga *n British* a pneumatic drill. A road labourers' nickname inspired by the kangaroo-like bouncing of the tool.

kaplonker *n British* a crowbar, in the late 1980s jargon of the London Flying Squad. The word is probably in origin a nursery term for any unnamed heavy object.

✎*'Another funny moment came during a Sweeney raid. The cops use an iron bar nicknamed a "kaplonker" to lever open doors.'*
(*News of the World*, 5 February 1987).

kark (it) *vb Australian* an alternative spelling of **cark it**.

karma *n*

a one's personal destiny, fate.

b an aura, impression or influence, **vibes**. Both senses of the word are inaccurate borrowings, dating from the **hippy** era, from Hindu and Buddhist writings in which the Sanskrit word denotes actions determining one's future state of incarnation. *See also* **instant karma**, **huntley**.

karzi *n British* an alternative spelling of **khazi**.

Kate and Sidney *n British* steak

and kidney. A witticism heard in canteens and homes when steak and kidney pie or pudding was a staple dish. The phrase was recorded in 1914 and is still heard.

kayf, kafe *n British* an alternative rendering of **caff** (café), imitating the jocular or unwitting mispronunciation of the original French.

kaylied *adj British* an alternative spelling of **kalied**.

kazi *n British* an alternative spelling of **khazi**.

kazoo *n American* the backside, buttocks. A word of unknown origin (it is probably unconnected with the musical instrument, the name of which imitates its sound); other jocular terms using the same median sounds include **mazoomas**, **gazungas**, etc. (all synonyms for breasts).

kecks *n pl British* trousers. This word is the northern English version of the archaic 'kicks', heard in other parts of the country from the 17th century until the 1940s but now obsolete. Liverpool **mods** of the mid-1960s used to refer contemptuously to 'half-mast kecks', that is unfashionably short trousers which flap around the lower calves or above the ankles. **Strides** was the slang synonym usually preferred further south. **Underkecks** are, of course, underpants, worn by either sex.

keek *n British* an alternative form of **cack**.

keen *adj* excellent, great. A teenage vogue word in North America in the late 1950s and 1960s. The enthusiastic term now sounds dated but is still heard, usually said by ingenuous and ironic adults, although there are some signs of a revival among younger speakers both as a description and exclamation (**neato-keeno** was an elaborated version).

keeno *n British* a keen, enthusiastic person. A schoolchildren's word, usually said scathingly of a **swot** or excessively hearty fellow pupil.

↳'*We just sat at the back and let the keenos volunteer.*'
(Recorded, London schoolgirl, 1987).

keep cave *vb British* to keep quiet, be wary and/or keep a look out. A schoolboy term of the 1950s from the Latin imperative *cave*: beware. In English the word is pronounced 'kay-vee'.

↳'*They asked me to keep cave in case old Goatman came along.*'
(Recorded, former grammar-school boy, 1986).

keep on trucking *vb* carry on, keep going. A black dancers' slogan used as a catchphrase exhortation by American and later British **hippies** from about 1970. **Trucking** has various associated meanings including an exaggerated sauntering stride or simply 'soldiering on', all deriving from jitterbug dance contests of the 1930s and 1940s in which trucking was a dance step.

keester *n American* an alternative spelling of **keister**.

keflumix *vb* an alternative spelling of **kerflummox**.

kegged *adj* drunk. A fairly rare word used typically by college and high-school students in the USA and occasionally by their counterparts in Britain. The British usage may be a separate coinage, also from keg beer.

kegger *n* **1** *American* a beer party. An adolescents' term.

2 a snowboarder.

kegs *n pl British* a variant form of **kecks**.

keister, keester *n American* backside, buttocks, anus. This fairly common term is from Yiddish *kiste*, in turn deriving from Middle and Old Germanic *Kista* and from the Latin *cista*, a chest. The Yiddish word denoted a portable chest and was adapted by English speakers to mean anything used as a travelling container, including a hawker's display cabinet, a satchel and a trouser pocket. The transition from these senses to a part of the human body is not completely clear; it has been suggested that it became an underworld synonym for the anus as used to smuggle contraband across borders or into prison. The term is now rather old-fashioned but was used by Ronald Reagan in the late 1980s.

kelper *n British* an inhabitant of the Falkland Islands. This nickname became known during and after the Falklands War of 1982 and by 1989 was established enough to be used without explanation (but with comic intent) in the press. It derives from kelp, the seaweed gathered for fuel and fertilizer by the inhabitants of many rocky island outposts.

Ken *American* a male dullard, (clean-cut) bland conformist youth or man. Ken is the name given to the male counterpart of the **Barbie Doll**.

Kensington Gore *n British* artificial blood. This expression, which is an elaboration of the literary 'gore', has been theatrical slang since before World War II and is still heard. It is a pun on the name of the road connecting Kensington and Knightsbridge in London.

kerflummox, kerflumix *vb* to baffle, confuse, bamboozle. A humorous embellishment of the colloquial 'flummox'. Ker- is a prefix indicating force, effort or impulse, reminiscent of Anglo-Saxon and modern German *ge-*: 'made'.

✎'*After all their explanations I've got to say I'm totally kerflummoxed.*'
(Recorded, US diplomat's wife, London, 1988).

kermit *n British* a French person. A jocular nickname used by students in the 1980s. It is inspired by the character 'Kermit the Frog' in the 1970s US television series, *The Muppet Show*.

✎'*Don't forget to send invitations to the kermits.*'
(Recorded, student, London, 1988).

kettle *n British* a watch. This old term, still used particularly among police and criminals, is said to be from the rhyming slang '*kettle and hob*', meaning fob.

Kevin *n British* a common, vulgar or boorish young man. This disparaging term of the 1970s and 1980s is typically used by snobs or wags to designate a working-class or lower-middle-class youth without taste or sophistication. The Christian name supposedly epitomizes this social sub-group (the female equivalent of a Kevin is a **Sharon**). **Wayne** is sometimes suggested as an alternative for Kevin.

✎'*That pub's full of Kevins, we never go in there.*'
Compare **Brian**.

kevinish *adj British* common, uncouth, and/or vacuous. From the noun form **Kevin**. A disparaging term used by middle-class speakers since the late 1970s.

✎'*Other schools just can't understand*

why they look so "Kevin-ish" – a term describing the white socks and footballers' haircuts (long at the back) which are so popular there.'
(*Tatler* March 1987).

kewpie doll *n* an excessively cute and/or overdressed or over made-up girl or woman. The original American Kewpie Doll (a trademark name based on Cupid) is a fairy-like baby. In Australia the name is used as rhyming slang for **moll** in the sense of prostitute.

key *n American* a kilo of an illicit drug, typically marihuana, which could be bought by street dealers in this quantity (in Britain the standard quantity is the non-metric **weight**).

✎'*He scored a couple of keys and brought it across the border.*'
See also **church key**.

key *adj* essential, emblematic or supreme. A **preppie** term of approval or endorsement.

✎'*Those shoes are key.*'
✎'*A pair of real key shoes.*'

khazi, kharzie *n British* a toilet. A term dating from the 19th century which has been in widespread use in working-class speech and in the armed services. There are many alternative spellings of this word, which is often assumed to be of African or Far Eastern colonial origin, perhaps by analogy with khaki. In fact it derives from the Latin word for house and its derivatives, such as *casa* in Spanish and Italian or *case* (meaning 'hut') in French. The word entered working-class speech in **parlyaree**, the latinate jargon of tramps, peddlers and show-people. Khazi was first thought suitable for broadcasting in the late 1960s and was popularized by such TV comedies as *Till Death us do Part* (written by Johnny Speight).

khyber *n British* the anus. From the rhyming slang 'Khyber Pass': **arse**. This London working-class expression was used in TV comedies of the late 1960s, trading on the fact that most viewers were only vaguely aware of its vulgar provenance. The word appeared in working-class speech after the Khyber Pass was introduced into the public perception by the Afghan wars of the later 19th century.

✎'*A kick up the Khyber.*'

khyfer *n British* an alternative spelling of **kife**.

kibble *n American* food, meal. Kibble is a word of unknown origin which literally means coarse-ground dogfood.

> ⮑'*OK I've got it, we'll chloroform her kibble!*'
> (*M*A*S*H*, US TV comedy, 1981).

kibitz, kibbitz *vb American* to pass comment on or offer (normally unwelcome) advice. The verb, which typically applies to an annoying onlooker at a card game or sports performance, comes from the Yiddish *kibitsen*, which in turn derives from *Kiebitz*, the German name for a lapwing, a supposedly raucous, insistent bird. The term is sometimes used to mean simply spectate without the pejorative overtones.

kibosh *n British See* **put the kibosh on**.

kick *vb* **1** give up (a habit). A piece of drug addicts' jargon which entered general currency in the 1950s.
2 *American* to be exciting, successful, impressive. This is a shortened form of **kick ass** in its secondary meaning of 'make a strong impression'.

> ⮑'*That suit really kicks.*'

kick *n* **1** a sudden sensation of excitement, thrill. This Americanism spread to the rest of the English-speaking world in the 1940s, helped by Cole Porter's song, 'I get a kick out of you'. The plural form **kicks** was a vogue term of the early 1960s.
2 *American* a particular activity or period of involvement. In the language of **hipsters**, **beatniks**, etc.

> ⮑'*She's on a health kick.*'

kick ass *vb American* to punish or forcibly restore order, make trouble or behave aggressively. An expression used typically of an authority figure such as an army officer or sports coach. 'Kick ass and take names' is an elaborated form of the expression (meaning identify and chastise). By extension, kick ass can simply mean to express oneself or enjoy oneself boisterously.

> ⮑'*That band really kick ass!*'

kickass *adj American* aggressive, rousing and forceful, tough. A word usually indicating admiration or approval (although sometimes grudgingly).

> ⮑'*I think they kind of appreciate his kickass attitude.*'

kickback *n* money returned or paid as part of an illegal or covert agreement. This term, which is no longer slang, originated in the pre-World War II American underworld, in which to kick back meant to pay a fixed part of one's income, or a fixed commission, in return for favour or protection. (The original image evoked was probably that of kicking back a portion of booty across a floor.)

kick back *vb American* to relax. A vogue term (sometimes occurring in the tautological phrase '*kick back and relax/chill out*') from the lexicon of black street gangs, **rappers**, and subsequently surfers, skaters, etc., and adopted by British adolescents in the mid-1990s. It may be based on the notion of a motorcyclist 'throttling back' or on the image of kicking away furniture in order to stretch out.

kicker, the kicker *n* **1a** the 'final straw', clincher.
b a hidden catch.
2a something exciting or stimulating.
b a dynamic person. In the last two senses the word is probably a shortened form of the earlier term **shit-kicker** and was in vogue among UK adolescents in the later 1990s.

kickers *n pl* shoes, boots. This slang term from the 1950s and 1960s (heard mainly in the USA) was appropriated by the French manufacturers of casual sports boots in the 1970s.

kick in *vb* to contribute, subscribe or pay up. The phrase is more popular in the USA than in Britain. It is presumably based on the image of a circle of gang members each kicking a portion of their booty into a central pile. It usually has overtones of illegal or at least unofficial activity, such as bribery or a 'whip-round' to buy liquor.

> ⮑'*If everyone kicks in we should be able to afford to give her a decent sendoff.*'

Compare **kick on**.

kicking *adj* excellent, exciting, powerful. A vogue term of approbation of the later 1990s, probably deriving from the phrase (it) **kicks the shit**.

> ⮑'*The band was kickin' and Christian was the hottest guy there.*'
> (*Clueless*, US film, 1995).

kicking it *n* enjoying oneself, celebrating or relaxing. A vogue term, like the adjective **kicking** derived from the earlier American expression to **kick the shit**. The phrase was recorded in use among north London schoolboys in 1993 and 1994.

kick it *vb* to die. A shortened version of **kick the bucket**.

kick off *vb* 1 *American* to die. A later variation of **kick the bucket**, the equivalent of the British and Australian **kick it**.
2 *American* to leave, go away.
3 *British* to lose one's temper, start to fight. First heard in the speech of the north of England, the phrase became popularized by TV soap operas and became generalized by the mid-1990s.
↳'I'd like to go and see my Dad but only when he retires, we'd just kick off at each other if I went back now.'
(Bez of rock group The Happy Mondays, quoted in the *News of the World*, 21 October 1990).
↳'Every time I try and make a go of something, you kick off.'
(*Brookside*, Channel 4 TV soap opera, December 1995).

kick on *vb Australian* to continue (resolutely). The phrase almost invariably refers to drinkers finding a 'second wind' or a further source of finance for their current drinking session.

kick out the jams *vb American* to 'let rip', get rid of all inhibitions and restrictions. A catch phrase in the rock-music world of the late 1960s, to which it was introduced by the rock group the MC5, who were allied to the anarchistic White Panther movement in Detroit. The phrase probably comes originally from an instruction to remove the chocks or wedges restraining a dragster car or aircraft.

kicks *n pl* 1 *British* trousers. An alternative and now archaic form of **kecks**, dating from the 18th century.
2a *American* sports shoes. A rarer version of **kickers**, used particularly by school and college students.
b *American* shoes. The term is used in black street argot and campus slang.
3 thrills. The plural form of **kick**. A usage which became popular in the late 1950s and notorious for its adoption by juvenile delinquents and other nihilists to explain their motives.
↳'They killed for kicks.'
(Headline in *True Detective* magazine, 1963).

kicksies *n* trousers. A diminutive form of **kicks**, heard since the 19th century, although now rare.

kickstart *vb, n* (to urge into) sudden action. A metaphor taken from motorcycling and applied to a variety of contexts in both literal and figurative senses. **Bump-start** is a synonym.
↳'The chick really had to kickstart the old goat.'
↳'We need to give the project a quick kickstart.'

kick the bucket *vb* to die. The phrase dates from the 17th or 18th century and the bucket in question may be either a suicide's prop or more probably a British dialect word (also in the form 'bucker') for the beam from which slaughtered animals were hung.
↳'Ches hasn't been the same since his old lady kicked the bucket.'
(Recorded, barman, London, 1988).

kick the shit *vb American* to succeed, perform powerfully and/or admirably. The image is one of dancing or other frenzied activity in a rustic setting; the phrase itself may be a back-formation from the adjective **shit-kicking**.

kicky, kicksy *adj American* exciting, stimulating, spirited. From the noun **kick** or **kicks** in the sense of excitement. In the 1970s and 1980s the word has taken on an extra nuance of up-to-date or modish. (The comparative and superlative forms are kickier and kickiest.)
↳'That kicky little red sportscar of yours.'

kiddo *n* a (usually patronizing or provocative) form of address to a younger person. An elaboration of the colloquial kid.

kidlet *n British* a small child. A middle-class term employing the otherwise archaic diminutive suffix '-let' (also seen in **quidlet**).

kif, kief *n* marihuana or hashish. The word, pronounced 'keef', is North African Arabic slang for the cannabis (usually in herbal form) smoked there. More specifically, kif may designate refined powdered hemp plants mixed with powdered tobacco or, as in the Berber stories of Mohammed Mrabet, to uncleaned **grass**. The word's literal meaning is 'pleasure'. Many British drug users of the late 1950s and 1960s had their formative experiences of cannabis in Morocco.

kife, kifer, kyf, kyfer, kaifa, khyfer *n British*

a a woman or women as a sexual partner or sex object.

b sexual activity (invariably heterosexual). This word in its various spellings is now rarely used. It was nearly always restricted to working-class, underworld or armed-services slang, with an area of meaning now more often catered for by words such as **crumpet**, **tottie** or **rumpo**. The exact etymology of the term is obscure; it may be a 19th-century alteration of an Arabic word *keyif*, meaning sensual consolation. As the definition implies, the word is used exclusively by men.

 ✎ *'Bangkok was OK – plenty of kifer.'*
 (Recorded, petroleum engineer, London, 1987).

kifer, kyfer *vb British* to have sex (with). A rare and now virtually obsolete derivation of the nouns **kife**, **kifer**, etc. (meaning women or sex). The word was exclusively used by males.

kike *n, adj* a jew. An old-fashioned racist term which some authorites derive from diminutives of the name Isaac (see **ikey (mo)**). Others, including the Yiddish expert and humorist, Leo Rosten, ascribe to the practice of illiterate Jewish immigrants signing their names with a circle (*kikel* in Yiddish) on arrival in the USA. The word was adopted by British and Australian speakers and is still occasionally heard.

 ✎ *'Take her, kike, she's all yours … a wop whore and a kike fag in a one-room office on the strip should go a long way together.'*
 (*Platinum Logic*, Tony Parsons, 1981).

kiki *n, adj American*

a (a) bisexual.

b (a) male homosexual. A fairly rare descriptive term of uncertain origin. It may be a corruption of an Hispanic word, or of he/she.

killer, killer-diller *n, adj* (something) superlative. Killer-diller was an Americanism of the 1940s which was briefly in vogue in Britain in the late

1950s among **teddy boys** and bohemians. Killer was a popular teenage term in the USA, particularly among black youth in the 1960s and 1970s, spreading to Britain and Australia in the 1980s with disco and hip hop music, break dancing, etc.

 ✎ *'That band's a killer.'*
 ✎ *'Man, that's a killer-diller car.'*

killfile *n* a computer program that allows Internet users to discard unwanted messages and exclude unpopular communicators, in the patois of **cyberpunks** and **net-heads**.

killing floor *n American* a place where sexual intercourse takes place. A phrase which figures in the lyrics of many blues and rock songs until the 1970s. The expression may originally refer to an abattoir in which case the transposition to a sexual context is evoking brutal carnality. Alternatively the sexual usage may arise via a sense of a place where punishing work or effort takes place. The phrase was used as the title of a Howling Wolf record of the early 1960s.

kilt *n British*

a a girl or woman.

b women as sex objects or sexual activity in general.

In both senses the word is usually found as part of a phrase such as *'a bit of kilt'*. It is part of non-regional working-class slang and is occasionally used self-consciously or facetiously by speakers from other backgrounds. In origin it is a humorous substitute for the more widespread but now dated **skirt**.

kimshi, kim'chee *n American* trouble, difficulties. The origin of the term is uncertain.

 ✎ *'You're in deep kimshi, buddy, better have it all in one sock for this one.'*
 (*Under Siege*, US film, 1995).

king hit *n Australian*

a a hit from behind, stab in the back.

b a knockout blow.

King Lear *n British* cannabis. The term is rhyming slang for **gear**, and was in use among London students in 1996 and 1997.

kink *n*

a a sexual deviant.

b a sexual perversion or perverse idiosyncrancy, an unhealthy trait.

Kinky has been used since the 1920s for deviant, becoming a vogue word of the early 1960s. The noun form (borrowed as the name of the pop group, the Kinks) is a later adaptation, usually used to express mild disapproval. In colloquial speech the word has now acquired an innocent sense of 'minor problem', flaw or irregularity.

kinky *adj* perverted or perverse, unorthodox. In Britain in the early 1960s kinky became so widespread a vogue word that its meaning became diluted to denote merely fashionable/interesting. The term began in the 1920s or earlier as an underground euphemism for sexually deviant, and later as an ironic **gay** term of approbation. In spite of its suggestion of perversities such as fetishism the word was inoffensive enough to be used in 'polite' company, hence its popularity in the first flush of sexual liberalism in the 1960s.

✎ *'He looks at me like that, at least he's not kinky. That's a relief. He's too fat to be kinky, too fat and forty guineas at least.'*
(*About Town* magazine, June 1962).

✎ *'Kinky? Kinky is British for weird, you know what I mean?'*
(*Harper*, US film, 1966).

kip *n*

a a period of sleep.
✎ *'If I don't get my full eight hours' kip I'm ratty all day.'*
(Recorded, teacher, Bristol, 1989).
✎ *'I pulled into the layby for a quick kip in the back of the van.'*

b a bed or place to sleep.
✎ *'A kip for the night.'*

The word kippe meant a brothel in 18th-century English, probably deriving from a similar Danish word signifying a low-class inn. In the 19th century the word was extended to denote a **doss house**, and by the early 20th century was acquiring its modern meanings. The word is not unknown in the USA but is much more commonly used in Britain.

kip, kip down *vb* to (lie down to) sleep. The verb comes from the noun **kip**, ultimately deriving from a Danish word for a tavern or hovel.

kipe, kype *vb* to steal.

Kipling *adj British* a term of approval among schoolchildren in 1989. The term

is explained by the following elaborate pun:

✎ *'If training-shoes provoke an excited exclamation of "Hey, man, they're Kipling!" the wearer can rest assured that their street-credibility is intact. Slur "ruddy hard" into Rudyard, and there you have it.'*
(*Guardian*, 26 September 1989).

kipper *n British* the vagina. A vulgarism in use among adolescents in the 1990s and listed in *Viz* comic in 1994.

kippered *adj British* devastated, trounced, **stitched up** or **gutted**. A working-class term which is currently in vogue among the fashionable young in London. The metaphor is 'dead, gutted, skinned and cooked', in the sense of thoroughly humiliated or taken advantage of, and is probably inspired by the earlier '*done up like a kipper*'.

✎ *'I wouldn't advise you to try doing business with them. I tell you, I was kippered …'*
(Recorded, advertising executive, London, 1988).

kiss *n See* **French kiss, soul kiss**.

K.I.S.S. *exclamation* 'keep it simple, stupid!', avoid unnecessary complications. A business catchphrase pronounced like the word 'kiss', when giving an instruction or citing a principle. The expression originated in American computer jargon.

kiss ass *vb American* to abase oneself, flatter or curry favour. A contemptuous description of obsequious or toadying behaviour.

✎ *'You wouldn't like it* [working in a large corporation]; *the first thing you'd have to do is to learn to kiss ass.'*
(Recorded, American female executive, London, 1984).

kiss-ass *n American* a sycophantic person, 'crawler'. This term of contempt can also be employed as an adjective as in a '*kiss-ass speech*', for instance.

kisser *n* mouth. A now rather dated word which probably originated among boxers and their entourages in the mid-19th century. Its meaning is occasionally extended to 'face', particularly as part of an expression such as '*a punch/smack in the kisser*'.

✆'*Wipe that silly expression off your kisser.*'

kissing tackle *n British* mouth, lips. A joky euphemism coined in the late 1980s on the lines of **wedding tackle** and **laughing gear**. The phrase is used by teenagers and young adults.

✆'*There's a Fosters; get your kissing tackle round that.*'

kiss-off *n* a dismissal. Originally an Americanism, the term has entered international English with the connotations of off-handedness, abrupt thoughtlessness or condescending rejection.

kiss the porcelain god *vb* to vomit. A picturesque euphemism which is particularly popular among American college students; an alternative form is 'kneel to the porcelain god' or **drive the porcelain bus**. The image is one of bending over to kiss the feet of an idol. An attack of diarrhoea involves **riding the porcelain Honda**.

kiss up *vb American* to behave as a sycophant (towards), 'crawl' to or flatter. A rarer version of **kiss ass** or the British suck up.

kissy, kissy-kissy *adj* affectionate, sentimental. The words may be applied good-humouredly or pejoratively, suggesting cloying or exaggerated affection.

kit *n British* clothes. A working-class expression typically used by ex-servicemen which enjoyed a vogue in the late 1980s among working-class speakers and their imitators. It is synonymous with **gear** or **clobber**.

✆'"*People have really put some kit on*", remarked a taxi driver as a stream of Philip Somerville hats filed out of St Martin-in-the-Fields.*'
(*Tatler* magazine, June 1985).

✆'*His idea of romantic chat was to say "get your kit off and come over here".*'
(Recorded, female social worker, London, 1987).

kite *vb* to pass a worthless cheque.

✆'*You wouldn't try to kite a cheque on me, would you?*'
(*Budgie*, TV series, 1971).

kite man/dropper/flyer *n* an issuer of worthless cheques. **Kite** has meant a dud cheque or other financial document for the past century. These terms, heard in all anglophone areas, usually refer to professional criminals who specialize in **kiting**.

kiting *n* passing dud cheques. In the 1980s the term invariably described a deliberate criminal activity, although it could formerly refer also to issuing a cheque in the hope, possibly ill-founded, of finding the funds to support it. The word is international English.

kit-kat shuffle *n* an act of female masturbation. The phase was explained in her 1995 TV show by the female standup comedienne Jo Brand. It occurs in the forms '*have a kit-kat shuffle*' or '*do the kit-kat shuffle*'.

kitty *n See* **dust kitty**.

kludge *n* a cumbersome, overcomplicated system or situation. A piece of computer jargon, originating in the USA, blending 'clumsy' and 'sludge'.

klutz *n American* a foolish, clumsy person. The word is from the Yiddish *klots* which literally means lump or block. (It comes from the German *Klotz* with the same meaning, which is related to the English 'clot' and 'clod'.) In the 1980s the word has passed from being an Americanism into world English, particularly among adolescents.

✆'*As the incidents repeated themselves, Ms Reagan told her fellow workers and friends that she was a "klutz" who kept banging into doors and falling down stairs.*'
(*Guardian*, 4 April 1989).

klutzy *adj American* foolish and/or clumsy. A back-formation from the more common noun **klutz**.

knack *vb British* to destroy, damage, mess up. This back-formation from **knacker(ed)** is common in middle-class and armed forces usage, often in the form **knack it**.

knacked *adj British* a variant form of **knackered** in all its senses. The term is heard particularly in the Scottish Lowlands and the north of England.

✆'*She's feeling knacked.*'

✆'*The motor's totally knacked.*'

knacker *vb British* to tire or exhaust. A back-formation from **knackered**.

✆'*I knacker myself at my job to keep her*

nice and warm in my house, with my
kids and my dog.'
(Divorced husband in cartoon by Posy
Simmonds, *Guardian*, 1981).

knackered *adj British* exhausted.
This is not strictly speaking a slang word,
as it derives from 'knacker', a worn-out
horse or a slaughterer of horses, but has
come to be seen as slang because of confusion with **knackers**, in the sense of testicles. The ultimate origin of the word is
probably a dialect word meaning saddle-
maker and based on a version of the word
knock.

↳'*That washing machine's about knackered, gel, and we ain't even finished
payin' for it yet!*'
(*Biff* cartoon, *Guardian*, 1986).

knackers *n pl British* testicles. Originally a dialect or rustic pronunciation of
knockers (with the sense of 'clappers'),
this is the form of the word which has
predominated. In the 1950s and 1960s
the word was often used in the form of an
exclamation on the lines of the now more
widespread **balls**, **bollocks** and **cobblers**,
expressing defiance or contempt.

↳'*Your boyfriend burned his jacket
his ticket expired
his tyres are knackered
his knackers are tired.*'
(*Psycle sluts*, poem by John Cooper
Clarke, 1978).

knee-jerk *n, adj* (a person displaying) a reflex action, an unthinking, automatic reaction. This piece of American
slang of the early 1970s has passed into
general colloquial use since its adoption
as part of disparaging descriptions such
as '*knee-jerk liberal*' or '*knee-jerk reactionary*'. The expression of course derives
from the doctors' testing of the patellar
reflex, featured in cartoons and situation
comedies since the mid-1950s.

knees-up *n British* a boisterous
party, celebration and/or sing-song. The
popular cockney song 'Knees up, Mother
Brown' probably produced the expression.

**kneetrembler, knee-trem-
ble** *n British* an act of sexual intercourse
while standing up. A popular term in the
1960s, when furtive assignations out-
doors were perforce more prevalent. The
word was used in TV comedies such as
The Likely Lads; it originated in the 19th
century and is still heard.

↳'*Lugged their possessions from one
digs to another in a cardboard suitcase, and, by way of recreation, enjoyed a quick "knee-trembler" up
against a tree in a twilit local park.*'
(*The Sunday Times*, book review, 18
March 1990).

knicker-bandit *n British* a
fetishistic thief who steals women's un-
derclothes from washing lines, laun-
derettes, etc. Also known as a **snowdropper**.

knickers! *exclamation British* a cry
of dismissal, defiance or contempt. This
primary and junior schoolchildren's rude
word has been adopted for humorous use
by adults since the early 1970s. Some authorities claim that it was originally a euphemism for the more offensive **knackers**
but this seems unlikely in that underwear
in itself is a favourite subject of prurient
interest in pre-pubescent children.
(Knickers is in origin a shortening of
knickerbockers, meaning baggy knee-
length trousers as worn in 19th-century
Holland.)

knob *vb British* to have sex (with). This
is a variant of **nob**, and is said by users of
the word to be the incorrect spelling, in
spite of the derivation.

↳'*If you were in with the Royal Family
and you were a girl, you'd definitely
want to knob Prince Andrew or someone.*'
(Boy George, *NME*, 4 June 1988).

knob *n British* penis. The word has
been in use with this sense since the 19th
century and was the most common vulgar
synonym in Britain and Australia in the
1950s and 1960s, since when such words
as **dick** and **prick** have increased in popularity.

knobbo *n British* a fool, contemptible
person. The expression, probably based
on **knob-head**, was heard in the 1990s
and quoted in the *NME*, a music paper.

knob-cheese *n British* smegma. A
term from the 1980s, which is a recent
variation on the theme of cheese being
used to describe distasteful by-products of
bodily functions.

knob-end *n British* a stupid, unfortunate or unpleasant person. A fashionable term of adolescent abuse in the late
1980s. (There are no sexual connotations,
in spite of the word's provenance.)

knob-head *n British* a stupid and/or contemptible person. A common insult or term of disapproval recorded since the 1970s.

knob job *n* an act of (male) masturbation or fellatio. A vulgarism in use since the 1960s, **knob** being one of the commonest terms for penis in Britain and Australia. Although **knob** alone is rare in this sense in the USA, 'knob job' is commonly heard there.

knob-jockey *n British* a male masturbator. The phrase itself is invariably used by male speakers.

knock *vb British* 1 to kill. A recent, racier variant of **knock off** or **hit**.
⋄'*I've never spoken to anyone I'm going to knock.*'
(Hit-man quoted in the *Observer*, 31 May 1987).

2 to have sex (with). A 300-year-old usage which has been rare since the early 1960s. It now survives mainly in variations such as **knock off**, **knocked up** or **knocking shop**.

3 to criticize, disparage. The use of knock to mean deprecate is no longer strictly speaking slang; it has been employed in this sense since the 19th century.

4 to cheat. An item of underworld slang.
⋄'*They tried to convince her it was a fair deal, but she definitely got knocked.*'

5 to steal. The term is heard particularly in the Scottish Lowlands and the north of England.
⋄'*Willie and Andy knocked a couple of videos from out the flats.*'

knock *n British* an act of sexual intercourse. A word which is now heard less often than in the 1950s and 1960s.
⋄'*All I wanted was a bit of a knock with Clive, I'm not interested in futile relationships.*'
(Joe Orton's diary, 2 May 1967).

the knock *n British* 1 stolen goods, criminal booty. A police and underworld term derived from **knock off** in the sense of to steal.

2 **a** credit, hire purchase. This meaning is usually expressed by the phrase to buy something '*on the knock*'.

b a loss or bad debt (a **knocker** is a debtor or **welsher**). The phrase usually forms part of a longer expression such as '*take the knock*' or '*get the knock*'. Knock here may originally refer to 'financial damage' or to the rapping of the table by a player who cannot take his or her turn in cards or dominoes.

3 the arrival of the police at one's home, or of a summons to appear in court. From the ominous knock at the door.
⋄'*Charlie got the knock last night.*' *See also* **knocker**, **on the knock**.

knockback *n British*
a a rejection of an application for parole.
⋄'*Jacky's hopeful but if you ask me he's going to get a knockback.*'
b a rejection of sexual advances.
⋄'*Don't worry about it Jane. I was expecting a knockback anyway.*' These terms are specific instances of the more general colloquial sense of knockback as any type of disappointment or rebuff.

knock boots *vb American* to have sex. An expression (also rendered as **get boots**) which was popular among black street gangs from the early 1990s.

knocked out *adj* bowled over, very impressed. Now a fairly widespread colloquial expression, this was considered both an Americanism and slang until the late 1970s. *See also* **knockout**.

knocked up *adj, vb* 1 *American* made pregnant. Amateur lexicologists never tire of pointing out the possibility of confusion between the American sense and the innocently colloquial British sense of waken (someone) up.
⋄'*Garp? My daughter got knocked up by a goddam fish?*'
(*The World According to Garp*, US film, 1982).

2 *Australian* exhausted.

knocker *n British* 1 a borrower of money, debtor, defaulter. The word is used to refer to personal debtors, those reneging on hire purchase agreements or, by prisoners in particular, to those who **welsh** on a bet – a sense in which the word was used in sporting circles before World War II. The origin of this use of knock is not completely clear; it may simply have the sense of to damage (financially), come from an obsolete word meaning to borrow, or may refer to some more specific practice such as rapping on a table to indicate one's inability to continue in a card game.

2 **a** a door-to-door salesperson.

b a door-to-door tout for an antiques dealer, hoping either to trick the gullible into parting with valuables or occasionally to identify items for later theft. *See also* **on the knocker**.

3 a breast. A rarely heard singular form of **knockers**.

knockers *n pl* **1** breasts. A widespread usage which seems to have arisen as recently as the 1940s. It has been suggested, but not convincingly demonstrated, that the word comes from **norks** and was first coined in Australia, whence it spread to the USA and Britain.

↳ '*Aliens have enormous knockers, according to the Sunday Sport.*'
(Recorded, sub-editor, London, July 1989).

2 testicles. This usage is rare. **Knackers** is the usual term.

knockie(-knockie) *n British* sex. A humorous euphemism heard since the early 1980s. It derives from the sexual connotations of the verb to **knock** and is probably also influenced by **nookie**. The expression is sometimes in the form 'play knockie(-knockie)'.

knocking shop *n British* a brothel. A popular light-hearted term now used to refer to a seducer's lair or any scene of promiscuity, as well as to a genuine bordello. The euphemism was recorded with the latter meaning in the mid-19th century.

↳ '*Life here was hell with that girl. We thought she was running a knocking shop and it drove us all mad.*'
(Resident of block of flats, *News of the World*, 19 February 1989).

knock off *vb British* **1** to kill.

2 to steal or rob.

↳ '*They knocked off a lorryload of antiques.*'

↳ '*The boys tried to knock off a bank.*'
See also **knock over**.

3 to have sex with, succeed in seducing. In American English to '*knock off a piece*' is a depersonalizing description of a sexual conquest.

↳ '*The 18-year-old he had been knocking off since she was 14.*'
(*Daily Mirror*, 11 May 1989).

All these uses of the phrase are variations of the underlying meaning of 'to account for' or 'accomplish hurriedly'.

knock one on *vb British* to have

sex. A vulgar euphemism reported as being in use in the London area in *City Limits* magazine in May 1992. *Compare* **knock one out**.

knock one out *vb British* to masturbate. The term is used by and of males in the slang of prison/hospital inmates. *Compare* **knock one on**.

knock out *vb British* to sell or distribute. In this sense the phrase probably originates in illegal auctions where the apportioning of the (usually stolen) goods was accompanied by the rap of a gavel. The term is now typically used by or of street traders.

↳ '*We've been knocking out over a hundred of those every week.*'

knockout *adj* wonderful, impressive, first-rate. Originally an Americanism, deriving from the noun form meaning something stunning, the word was introduced to Britain and Australia in the hippy era and by the mid-1970s sounded somewhat dated. It was often used in the form of an exclamation of (over)enthusiasm.

↳ '*I met this knockout chick.*'

knock over *vb* to rob. A racier euphemism than **knock off**, this American underworld expression was picked up by British speakers in the early 1980s.

↳ '*Willis is suspected of knocking over a bank in Oregon.*'

knot-head *n* a fool or dim-witted person. A term heard all over the English-speaking world. The knot in question is probably that normally found in pieces of timber (recalling 'wooden-headed') rather than in string.

knuckle *vb* to hit, beat up. A word used in Britain by street-gangs and other 'toughs'.

↳ '*He knuckled the geezer.*'

knuckle, knuckle-up *n British* a brawl, fistfight.

knucklehead *n* an idiot. A variation of the older **bonehead**, the term originated as a folksy Americanism, entering world English in the 1950s.

↳ '*The most startling language occurs on a thing called "Bob George", which features a monologue from some knuckle-head having it out with his lady.*'
(*Independent*, 26 February 1988).

knuckle sandwich *n* a blow from a fist, a punch in the mouth or face. A humorous phrase which is often used in unfunny situations in all English-speaking countries. The expression dates from before World War II when it probably originated in a euphemism such as *'feed someone a knuckle sandwich.'*

knucks *n pl* a knuckleduster, brass knuckles. Like the device, the word is part of the repertoire of street-gangs, thugs, etc., especially in the USA.

kode *n* the complex system of language and signals used by **gays** in order to secretly communicate with one another, particularly about their sexual proclivities or preferences. This includes the wearing of key rings, chains and specific colours of handkerchiefs in specific pockets, etc. The language is literally code in that it takes terms from standard English such as **straight, clone, boystown**, etc. and uses them ironically. The alternative spelling of code is an example of the use of K to render English words more Germanic or Slavonic and thus lend them totalitarian overtones, as in 'Amerika' or 'klan'.

kong *n American*
a strong alcoholic drink.
b a strong narcotic.
Both senses derive from the celebrated fictional giant gorilla *'King Kong'* as a symbol of potency.

konk *n* an alternative spelling of **conk** in its sense of hairstyle.

kook *n American* an eccentric, quirky or crazy person. This word is an alteration of cuckoo which has been popular in the USA since the 1950s. It has spread to Australia, but although understood in Britain is rarely used there.

kooky *adj American* eccentric, quirky, crazy. This adjective probably post-dates the noun **kook**.

kopacetic *adj American* another spelling of **copacetic**.

kosher *adj* correct, proper, aboveboard. This Yiddish term (usually referring to food prepared according to Talmudic law) is originally from the Hebrew *kasher*, meaning fitting or proper. The word was adopted in the late 19th century by non-Jewish speakers, particularly in the underworld, market trading or other raffish contexts. By the 1970s kosher was generally understood and used by speakers from a wide variety of backgrounds.
ᛦ*'Don't worry, it's quite kosher.'*
ᛦ*'Let's check out his so-called company and see if its a kosher set-up.'*

kraut *n* a German. The word, which originated in the USA, has supplanted hun and later **Jerry** in British slang usage. It is a shortening of *sauerkraut*, thin-cut cabbage pickled in brine, which is a popular German food.

kron(z) *n American* an alternative spelling of **cronz**.

kugel *n South African* a spoilt young female. The term, which is derived from Yiddish, has a male counterpart, which is **baigel**. Kugel has been defined by users of the word as 'a superficial and indulged young adult girl from a Jewish family'.

kuri, koorie *n New Zealand*
a a Maori.
b an unpleasant or unpopular person.
c *Australian* an aborigine. This racist epithet is the Maori word for mongrel.

kushti *adj British* an alternative spelling of **cushdy**.

Kuwaiti tanker *n British* rhyming slang for **wanker**. The probably ephemeral phrase arose during the Gulf crisis of 1986 and 1987 when Kuwaiti tankers among other craft were escorted through the straights of Hormuz to prevent attack by Iran. A contemporary synonym was **merchant banker**.

kvetch *vb* to complain, whine, **whinge**. An Americanism that has been adopted by fashionable and literary sectors of British and Australian society. It is the Yiddish verb meaning to squeeze or press.

kvetch *n* a person who complains constantly, a whiner or **whinger**. The word comes via the USA from the Yiddish verb meaning to squeeze or press.

kweef *n American* a vaginal **fart**.

kybosh *n See* **put the kibosh on**.

kyf, kyfer *n British* an alternative spelling of **kife**.

kyfer *vb British* an alternative spelling of **kifer**.

l...

labonza *n American*

a belly or paunch.

↳'*A punch in the labonza.*'

b backside, buttocks. A word used particularly by pugilists, criminals and working-class speakers. It is mock-Italian or Spanish, probably based on *la pancia* or *la panza*, both related to the English paunch. The second sense referring to the posterior is rarer.

lace curtain *n* a foreskin. A term from the homosexual lexicon, punning on a symbol of coy respectability which predates **gay** emancipation.

laced *adj American* intoxicated by drugs or drink. The term usually refers to a mild intoxication by, e.g., marihuana.

↳'*It's OK to get laced at a party but not to get fried all on your own.*'

laced up *adj British*

a (of a person) fully occupied, obligated, embroiled.

b (of a thing) completed, accomplished, 'in the bag'. Both senses are variant forms of standard metaphorical meanings of tied up.

c repressed, inhibited. In this sense the phrase is influenced by strait-laced.

↳'*She's a bit laced up isn't she?*'

Compare **laced**.

laddish *adj British* boisterous, uncouth and **macho**. The word, which appeared in the late 1970s, refers to the typical behaviour of adolescent males in groups. It is inspired by 'male-bonding' expressions such as '*one of the lads*' and the **geordie** battle cry, '*howay the lads!*' but is more often used disparagingly or dismissively by women or more mature males. The term took on greater significance when it was applied to a social tendency among young adult males in the second half of the 1990s, which involved celebrating rather than disguising hedonistic excess, love of sport/cars/hardware, socializing in male groups, etc. The new 'laddishness' was celebrated in publications such as *Loaded* magazine and TV comedies such as *Men Behaving Badly*.

Lady Godiva *n British*

a a £5 note, a sum of £5. London rhyming slang for 'fiver'. The phrase is still heard although alternatives such as **deep sea diver** are now probably more popular.

b £5 million, in the slang of city traders of the 1990s. In this sense the word is usually shortened to **Lady**.

Lady Muck *n British* a woman thought to be 'putting on airs' or behaving high-handedly. The female equivalent of **Lord Muck**.

↳'*Who does she think she is, carrying on like Lady Muck?*'

laff *n* a source or occasion of amusement. A jocular, ironic or journalese form of laugh. When said by southern British speakers it is distinguished by a pronunciation rhyming with 'chaff'.

lag *n*

a a convict or former convict or recidivist. In non-criminal circles the word is usually heard only in the phrase **old lag**.

b a term of imprisonment. At different times in different areas the term has denoted specific periods. **Lagging** is now the more usual form of the word.

lag, lag up *vb British*

a also **lag up**, to send to prison.

b to arrest. Both words, which are now rare, date from the beginning of the 19th century, when lag meant specifically to transport to a penal colony. (An archaic meaning of the word was 'to carry away'.)

lag, lag on *vb Australian* to inform (on someone), to tell tales. A prisoners' and schoolchildren's word, this was British slang of the 19th century with the meaning of 'betray to the authorities'. It has survived in Australia but has not been heard in the UK since the turn of the century. Its frequent use in Australian TV soap operas of the late 1980s may result in the reintroduction of the term.

↳'*Don't worry – 'e won't go laggin' on us.*'

(*Prisoner: Cell Block H*, Australian TV series, 1985).

lagging *n British* a period of imprisonment. The word has sometimes had the specific sense of a term of three years or more.

lah-di *n British* a motor car. Rhyming slang from 'la-di-dah'. An alternative 'cockney' term to **jam-jar**.

laid *See* lay.

laid back *adj* relaxed, easy-going. This expression was first widely propagated in the USA in the **hippy** period and was particularly appropriate to self-consciously relaxed attitudes prevalent in the Californian counter-culture and later alternative therapy circles. It may simply derive from the notion of lying back and relaxing or perhaps be influenced by a more specific jargon such as that of American **bikers** for whom laid back was the driving position when cruising.

⌇'*The President and Nancy like to change into pyjamas at 6 pm. This method – not laid back so much as lying down – didn't matter when things were going well....*'
(*Observer*, 22 November 1987).

laid out *adj American*

a drunk. Another synonym for inebriated. Although the original metaphor is of someone knocked unconscious (or placed in a mortuary), the use of the phrase does not necessarily indicate intoxication to the point of stupefaction.

b under the influence of drugs. This sense of the term, deriving from the previous one, is most commonly used by teenagers.

lair, lare *n Australian* a layabout, flashy young tough. This modern usage post-dates an earlier sense of the word denoting an over-dressed, showy or beautiful man. Since the 1940s the term has been identified specifically with delinquent or disreputable young males. It forms the basis of many combinations such as '*come the lair*', '*lair it up*' or '*ten-cent lair*'. Lair is based on a variant form of older British words such as **leery**, **leary**, etc.

lairy *adj*

a flashy, showy, especially in an ostentatious, provocative or vulgar way. This term is especially popular in Australia but was also in use among British youth in the late 1980s.

⌇'*Wow, Ches's got a really lairy T-shirt.*'
(Recorded, youth, Portobello Road, London, 1986).

b vain, presumptuous or boastful. This sense of the term was in use among working-class speakers, particularly **teddy boys**, in Britain in the 1950s and early 1960s.

Both sub-senses of the word come from the earlier **leary** or **leery**.

la-la-land *n* a state of drugged or drunken euphoria. An expression usually used disparagingly by abstainers.

⌇'*Cameraman Gerry McGough, who snapped these shots, said "She was completely in la-la land".*'
(Caption to pictures of drunken celebrity, *Daily Mirror*, 9 February 1989).

lallies *n pl British* legs. A word used in theatrical circles and by dancers, art students, etc. in the 1960s. Lallies was given exposure in the radio comedy shows *Beyond our Ken* and *Round the Horne* in the exchanges between Kenneth Horne and the **camp** characters 'Julian' and 'Sandy', played by Kenneth Williams and Hugh Paddick. The word, of unknown origin, is still in limited use.

lam *vb* **1** to run away or escape from prison. The verb form is probably a back formation from the phrase '*on the lam*', although 'lam' originates in a verb, lambaste, meaning to hit or beat.

2 *Australian* to have sex. Like many synonyms (**boff**, **biff**, **bonk**, etc.) the term uses the notion of striking in evoking sex from the male perspective. Lam in its earlier colloquial sense derives from the Old Norse *lemja*, to thrash.

lamb chop *vb British* to inject (e.g., heroin). The phrase is rhyming slang for **pop**.

lame *adj*

a poor quality, disappointing, bad. The common colloquialism was adopted as an all-purpose teenage vogue word in the late 1980s.

b unfortunate, unfair. Based either on the colloquial sense of lame meaning poor (as in 'lame excuse'), or on the image of a lame person who is unable to keep pace, the term has been generalized and intensified in the fashionable speech of adolescents in the 1990s.

lame-arse *n, adj British* (a person who is) unpleasant, unfair, obnoxious. A vogue term from the language of adolescents in the late 1990s, probably adopted from the following American usage.

lame-ass *n, adj American* (a) feeble, disappointing, unconvincing (person). An embellishment of the colloquial 'lame'.

↳'*Another lame-ass excuse.*'

lamebrain *n, adj* (a) dim-witted (person). Lame has been used to mean feeble or weak in colloquial speech throughout the Anglophone community. This compound form was coined in the 1960s in the USA, whence it spread in the 1970s.

↳'"*English people don't expect high standards because they don't know how to go out and eat in restaurants,*" scolds Payton. "*We're also lamebrains when it comes to going to the cinema*".'
(*Evening Standard Magazine*, May 1989).

lamp *vb* 1 to look (at), to eye. The term, (currently in vogue among fashionable adolescents in Britain), comes from a now archaic three-hundred-year-old use of lamp as a slang synonym for eye.
2 *British* to hit, beat up or attack. A now dated usage perhaps combining elements of 'lam', in the sense of beat, and lump. The word was frequently used with this meaning in the 1950s.
3 *Australian* to have sex (with). A synonym for **lam/slam**.

laney, lany, lani, lainie *adj* inferior, worthless. These recent vogue terms are probably deformations of the obsolescent American slang 'lane', which signified unsophisticated, provincial or naïve, and which was said to derive from the notion of a rustic living on a country lane. Originating in American adolescent speech in the 1980s, these variants were adopted by young British speakers in the 1990s.

langered *adj British* extremely drunk. A vogue term in the adolescent drinkers' lexicon since the mid-1990s.

lani *n South African* a white person. Recorded as an item of Sowetan slang in the *Cape Sunday Times*, 29 January 1995.

lard *n American* a police officer, or the police. The usage is derived from the earlier **bacon** and **pig**.

lard-ass, lard-bucket *n American* a fat person. The American equivalents of the British 'tub of lard'.

lard-head *n* a stupid or slow-witted person. An expression used in Australia and the USA.

lardo *n* a fat person. An innocuous variant of **lard-ass**.

↳'*Apart from being a congenital lardo,* [Clive] *James has a further hurdle before he can reasonably take part in the pro-celeb car chase: he can't drive.*'
(*Independent*, 23 December 1988).

lare *n Australian* an alternative spelling of **lair**.

large *n, n pl British* one thousand, a grand. A shortening of 'large one(s)', used typically by criminals, market traders, gamblers, etc.

↳'*I give him five large and asked him to get hold of some gear for me.*'

large *adj British* excellent, powerful, exciting. A vogue term of approbation among devotees of **rave**, techno, and **indie** subcultures in the 1990s. This usage also occurs in North American adolescent speech.

large it *vb British* to enjoy oneself, behave boisterously. Together with **large** and **give it large**, this was a vogue term among devotees of **rave** and **indie** culture in 1994, although it had been recorded in London usage in 1991 and may originally have been adopted from black American speech.

larrikin *n Australian* a ruffian, ne'er-do-well. The word has been in use in Australia since the mid-19th century and may be a native coinage or an imported British dialect term based on 'lark'. It is not usually strongly pejorative, having the sense of (fairly harmlessly) rowdy and cheeky.

larrup *vb* to beat, spank, thrash. A word used by toughs in Australia but mainly by parents to children in Britain, where it now sounds rather dated. The term may be a blend of 'leather' and wallop or may be an attempt to imitate the sound of blows landing.

lary *adj* an alternative form of **lairy** or **leery**.

lash *n Australian* 1 a rampage, bout of wild behaviour.

↳'*To go on a lash/have a bit of a lash.*'
2 an attempt, try. A variant of bash as in 'have a bash (at)'.

lash it *vb British* to keep quiet, restrain oneself. The expression from provincial rather than London speech often occurs as an imperative.

↳*'Just lash it, will you!'*

later(s) *exclamation*

a an all-purpose farewell, an abbreviation of the standard *'see you/catch you later'*, probably originating in US speech but heard among UK teenagers in the 1990s.

b a threat to be carried out in future, as implied by statements such as *'I'll see you/deal with you/get you later'*. These terms, from code employed among adolescent gang members, were adopted as fashionable expressions among adolescents in general from the mid-1990s.

lathered *adj British* drunk. The word may suggest the image of beer froth or saliva on the face of the drinker, or may, like many similar terms, be based on the notion of beating/punishment as conveyed by the colloquial sense of lather, meaning to thrash.

↳*'... topics that might appear unrelated to those not pleasantly lathered at this comfortably indecent hour.'*
(*Q* magazine, March 1997).

lattie *n British* a flat, home. This item of **parlyaree** originated as 'lettie' (from the Italian *letto*), denoting a bed. Most recently it has occurred in **gay** and theatrical speech.

laughing boy *n British*

a a morose, grumbling, sullen or excessively serious-looking person. The phrase is used with heavy irony to deride or provoke someone thought to be unnecessarily grumpy, stern or self-pitying.

↳*'Why don't you go and ask laughing boy over there.'*

b someone who is smirking or offensively cheerful. A less common sub-sense of the term.

laughing gear *n British* mouth. A joky euphemism playing on the notion of body parts as equipment on the lines of **kissing tackle** or **wedding tackle**. It probably dates from the 1970s.

↳*'Get your laughing gear around this!'*
(Dialogue in TV advertisement for Heineken beer, 1988).

laughing soup/water/juice *n* alcohol. These are middle-class witticisms applied particularly to champagne or gin. Laughing water also recalls the Indian princess in Longfellow's long narrative poem *Hiawatha*. Similar terms still in use are **giggle water** and **electric** or **lunatic soup**.

launch lunch *vb American* to vomit.

↳*'He looked like he was into it, but she looked like she was going to launch lunch over Mr Jurgen.'*
(*Things To Do In Denver When You're Dead*, US film, 1996).

lavender *adj* homosexual (male), **gay**. A facetious term appropriated from the vocabulary of heterosexual mockers for use by the gay community itself; the colour and scent of lavender being thought as quintessentially feminine and 'old-maidish', respectively.

lay *n*

a a person viewed or evaluated as a sexual partner.

b an act of sexual intercourse.

↳*'He's not interested in her, he's just looking for a lay.'* These uses of the word spread to British English from the USA with the verb form during the 1950s and 1960s, becoming established by the early 1970s. In the first sense the word is nearly always used in combinations such as 'a good lay' or 'an easy lay'.

lay *vb* to have sex with. The verb was absorbed into British English gradually during the 1950s and 1960s from the USA, where it had been current since the turn of the century. The term implies sex from the male viewpoint but during the **hippy** era began to be used by women. The word is a development of the literal sense of to lay someone down, and of the euphemistic 'lie with', meaning to copulate with, well known from its use in the King James translation of the Bible.

↳*'One time I thought she was trying to make me come lay her – flirting to herself at the sink – lay back on huge bed that filled most of the room, dress up round her hips.'*
(*Kaddish*, poem by Allen Ginsberg, 1958).

lay an egg *vb* **1** *American* to fail, to be responsible for a dismal or disappointing performance. This expression comes from the Victorian British 'lay a duck's egg' meaning to score zero (now extinct in British speech).

2 *Australian* to behave in an agitated,

over-excited way. One of many farmyard metaphors in Australian use.

lay down *vb See* **lie down**.

lay (someone) down *vb American* to kill. A euphemism used among black street gangs in the late 1980s.

lay (something) on (someone) *vb* to inflict or impose on. This is one of many expressions originating in black speech which were disseminated during the **hippy** era, often in the form '*lay a (heavy) trip on*', for example.

lay one on someone *vb* to hit, punch. A euphemistic expression on the same lines as '*stick one on*', **put one on someone, hang one on**.
⋄'*If that joker doesn't stop mouthing off I'm going to be forced to lay one on him.*'

lay rubber *vb American* to drive very fast, especially from a standing start, in a car or on a motorcycle. The phrase is inspired by the shedding of tyre rubber when spinning the wheels at speed, a technique used in **drag** racing to ensure good road adhesion at the beginning of a race.

lay some on *vb British* to acquire illicit drugs. The term usually applies to **scoring** for personal use and was in currency among aficionados of dancefloor culture in the 1990s.

Lazy Y *n See* **lunching at the Lazy Y**.

leaf *n* marihuana. A predictable nickname for herbal cannabis.
⋄'*We blew some leaf and mellowed out.*'

leak *n* an act of urination. Usually in the expressions '*have a leak*' or '*take a leak*'. The origin of this predictable usage may be nautical.

leak air *vb American* to talk nonsense, jabber crazily. The image evoked is that of a collapsing inflatable or punctured balloon or tyre.
⋄'*Take no notice – the guy's just leaking air.*'

lean *adj British* under the influence of illicit drugs. The usage which appeared in the later 1990s is possibly related to the American **laney**.
⋄'*Nowadays lean in youth parlance has less to do with slim and healthy than spaced and out. It is the consequence*

of indulging in untold quantities of unspecified substances.'
(*Sunday Telegraph Magazine*, 15 December 1996).

leaper *n* a stimulant drug such as an amphetamine; a **pep pill** or **upper**. This term was briefly adopted by (mainly middle-class) British drug users in the late 1960s, giving way to more widespread terms such as uppers or **speed**. It was probably coined by analogy with sleeper in the sense of sedative or tranquillizer.

leary *adj* an alternative spelling of leery or **lairy**.

the least *n, adj American* (something) very bad, disappointing, of the worst quality. This term, which is popular especially with teenagers, was probably coined in the 1970s as a humorous complement to the older **hip** expression **the most** (meaning superlative). 'The very least' is a stronger term.
⋄'*Boy, that movie was the least.*'

leather *n British* 1 a middle-aged male jet-setter, an ageing sun-tanned playboy. This term was coined by the upper-class young and their imitators in the late 1970s to refer disparagingly to the more prominent members of the international **white trash** frequenting ski resorts, yacht basins, etc. The word could occasionally be extended to apply to women, too. Leather refers to the skin texture of the sub-group in question (perhaps compounded by their characteristic wearing of expensive leather clothes in the period in question).
2 a wallet or purse. A long established item from the underworld lexicon.

leatherboy *n*
a a motorcycle enthusiast, **rocker** or **biker**. A word popular with parents and journalists in the early 1960s.
⋄'*The mean and moody leatherboy on a thundering bike is the strongest image of pop culture.*'
(Johnny Stuart, *Rockers*, 1987).
b a young male homosexual, male prostitute or androgynous youth wearing leather.
⋄'*A faggy little leatherboy with a smaller piece of stick.*'
(Lyrics to 'Memo from Turner', by Mick Jagger, 1969).

lech, letch *n British*
a a carnal desire, brief sexual infatua-

tion. This word, often used by women, was particularly popular in the 1960s and early 1970s in upper- or middle-class speech. It was often (and sometimes is still) used in the form '*letch, letch!*' as a jocular or coyly prurient exclamation (although this more probably refers to the verb form to **lech after** or **lech for**).

✎'*Leched over by managers, stitched up by agents, girls in the music biz have traditionally paid a high price for succumbing to the lure of lurex.*' (*Ms London* magazine, 4 September 1989).

b a lecherous person, usually male. A word expressing attitudes ranging from light mockery to angry rejection.

✎'*He's nothing but a boring old lech.*'

lech/letch after/for/over/on

vb British to nurse or exhibit a carnal desire for, to behave lecherously towards (someone). A back formation from the adjective lecherous.

✎'*He's always letching after young girls.*'

lechy, letchy *adj British* lecherous.
A popular form of word heard particularly from the 1960s to the mid-1970s.

lecky, the lecky *n British* the Electricity Board. The electricity supply, electricity. A Liverpudlian contraction which seems to be gaining popularity elsewhere.

✎'*We had the lecky round to check the meter yesterday.*'

leech off (someone) *vb* to behave as a parasite. An extension of the colloquial use of the noun form.

leery, leary *adj*

a wary, suspicious, shy, cautious. This sense of the word is standard in all English-speaking areas.

b *British* alert, clever, cheeky. This sense of leery is related to **lairy**, meaning both flashy and conceited.

c *British* bad-tempered, 'sour'.

d *British* untrustworthy, devious, cunning. These nuances of meaning within the same term are difficult to disentangle, given that modern usage is probably derived from two originally separate words: the archaic 'leer', from an Anglo-Saxon word meaning face or cheek, and the obsolete dialect term 'lere', related to learn and lore and similar in meaning to know-how.

left field *n, adj* (something) unorthodox, bizarre, unexpected. An American usage which was picked up by British journalists, musicians etc. in the mid-1970s. The term arises from an earlier colloquial expression '*out of left field*', used to describe something startling or totally unexpected coming from an improbable source. The field in question is the baseball field and left field, (the area to the batter's left and beyond third base), is an area of the park which sees little action and from which the ball rarely arrives. The same thing can be said of right field, however, and the choice of left perhaps has something to do with the overtones of unorthodoxy and radicalism inherent in 'left' in its political context, or simply by analogy with left-handed.

left-footer *n* **1** a Catholic.

2 a homosexual. Both uses of the term have been heard since the 1960s and are derived from the notion of abnormality associated with left-handed/footedness.

leg-biter *n* a small child, a toddler or baby. A less common alternative to **ankle-biter**, heard in the 1980s.

legged over *adj British* the phrase from the jargon of City of London financial traders is a euphemism for **shagged** or **fucked** in the sense of having lost money (and perhaps been humiliated) in a failed transaction. It is based on the verb to **get one's leg over**.

leggner *n British* a twelve-month sentence in the jargon of prisoners, recorded in Brixton and Wandsworth prisons in the 1990s. The term is of obscure origin, although the lexicographer Paul Beale suggests that it is cognate with **lag** or **lagging**. The word was recorded in *The Lag's Lexicon*, published in 1950.

leg it *vb British* to run away, escape or leave. A working-class expression, formerly popular with police and criminals, which has become fashionable in middle-class circles in the later 1980s in keeping with a tendency among **yuppies**, students and those in the media, among others, to affect 'cockney' styles of speech.

✎'*His pals sprang him by blowing a hole in the wall. He then legged it to Amsterdam, where he changed his name.*' (Charles Catchpole, *News of the World*, 5 February 1989).

legless *adj* drunk. The word originally denoted someone who was helplessly or

falling-down drunk; nowadays 'getting legless' can simply mean getting drunk. It has moved from being a raffish slang term to a common colloquialism over the last 25 years.

↳*'LEGLESS BUT LOVELY: Blonde beauty Sam Brown admits she became a big time boozer when she was a schoolgirl.'*
(Picture caption in the *People*, 23 April 1989).

leg-man *n* a male whose preferred part of the female body is the legs, as opposed to an **arse-man** or **tit-man**.

legover *n British* an act of sexual intercourse (usually from a male perspective). The term originates in the expression **get one's leg over**, one of many 18th- and 19th-century phrases in which leg is meant both literally and as a euphemism for the parts of the lower body ('leg-business' is one archaic example). In the 1980s the satirical magazine *Private Eye* has regularly referred to a 'legover situation', a supposed middle-class code for copulation.

lemon *n* **1** something substandard, useless or worthless. The word is used, particularly in the USA, to apply particularly to cars which are unsaleable. It may also denote any 'dud', from an unattractive woman to a badly-performing share in the stock exchange. This negative sense of the name of a fairly popular fruit derives from the unavoidably sour taste.

2 a fool, embarrassed or discomfited person. To 'feel a lemon' is to be put in an uncomfortable or humiliating situation.

3 the penis. In black American slang the word has been used in this sense which, although no longer common, is immortalized in the lyrics of many blues songs.

↳*'Squeeze my lemon, baby/ 'till the juice runs down my leg.'*

4 *American* a quaalude, **'lude** (a hypnotic tranquillizing drug, the equivalent of the British Mandrax or **mandy**).

See **lemons**.

lemons *n pl* the breasts. Another image of fruitfulness and rotundity on the lines of **melons**, **cantaloupes**, **apples**, etc. The term is probably most widespread in Australian speech.

lemon-squeezer *n British* a man. This phrase, rhyming slang for **geezer**, occurs in anthologies of such expressions

but is rarely actually heard in everyday speech. **Ice cream** is a synonym.

lend *n Australian See* **have a lend (of someone)**.

length *n British* **1** a six-month prison sentence.

2 the penis. The word is almost invariably used in the phrase **slip someone a length**.

lerg(h)i, lurg(h)i *British* an unspecified disease, a mysterious infection or illness. An invented word (the 'g' is hard) in imitation of exotic or tropical complaints, much used by schoolchildren in the 1950s and still heard today, often in the phrase 'the dreaded lergi'.

↳*'Hilary was supposed to come but she's gone down with the lergi.'*
(Recorded, housewife, London suburbs, 1986).

les, lez, lezzie, lesbo *n* a lesbian. Shortened forms of the word in use throughout the English-speaking community.

letch *n, vb British* an alternative spelling of **lech**.

letchy *adj British* an alternative spelling of **lechy**.

let it all hang out *vb exclamation* to express oneself or otherwise behave without inhibitions, act without restraint. This euphemism became a catchphrase of the late 1960s 'counter-culture', spreading with it from the USA to other English-speaking areas. The phrase survived mainly among **straight** commentators who employed it disapprovingly or ironically. (The nature of the unspecific 'it' is not recorded: sexual characteristics or hair are likely candidates.)

let off, let one off *vb British* to fart. The first variant is a common schoolchildren's term, the other forms tend to be used by adults. **Blow off** is one synonym among many.

let one go *vb British*
a to fire a shot from a gun. An East End gangland euphemism from the 1960s quoted by Albert Donaghue, former Kray brothers' associate in an ITV interview, March 1994.
b to fart.

lettuce *n* money. Another term like **long green**, **cabbage**, etc. that makes the connection between green banknotes and succulent vegetation. The word was probably first heard in raffish use in the USA, where banknotes of all denominations are and were predominantly green.

Lewis *n British* a barrel. This instance of educated rhyming slang, using the name of the author Lewis Carroll, has only been recorded in the probably ephemeral phrase '*you've got me over a Lewis*'.

lez *n* an alternative spelling of **les**.

lezz, lezzie, lezzo *n* a lesbian.

lick *vb American* to smoke **crack**, by sucking the smoke from a burning pellet of the drug through a glass pipe or tube. The term is from the users' own jargon.

lick *n American* an illicit drug, particularly cocaine.

the lick *n* a superlative person, thing or situation. This term, meaning 'the (very) best', probably originated in black American speech but by the mid-1990s was in use among adolescents in Britain, too. It may be related to **lickin' stick**.

licker *n British* a **swot**, sycophant. This abbreviated form of **arse-licker** is in use among schoolchildren together with its synonym, **boff**.

✎ *"Licker", says Jonathon Angel, 13. "That's what you get called if you have your hand up all the time; licker or swot."'*
(*Independent*, 17 October 1996).

lickin' stick *n American* a sweetheart, favourite friend. This item of black slang (the item referred to is a licorice-stick or popsicle) was used by the feminist writer Mtozke Shange.

licks *n pl* plangent sequences of notes played on the electric guitar, short improvised musical solos. The term was adopted by rock guitarists from earlier jazz musicians who had adapted the colloquial 'lick', meaning both a stroke or hit and an attempt. The word is part of the terminology which includes **chops** and **riff**.

✎ *'Jimi [Hendrix] has got some licks that none of us can match.'*
(Eric Clapton, speaking in 1970).

lid *n* **1** *American* a measure of marihuana (about one ounce), so called because it is approximately the amount which can be held on the lid of a beer can or tobacco tin.

2 a military or motorcyclist's helmet.

liddy *adj American* crazy, eccentric. A term deriving from the expression to flip one's lid. **Wiggy** is a word of similar provenance.

lie down, lay down *vb* to surrender, abase oneself. A fashionable euphemism in the late 1980s, particularly in the contexts of business and politics. It normally has the sense of giving up without a struggle in an adversarial situation. **Sit down** and **bend over** are used similarly.

✎ *'I'm damned if I'm going to lie down for them.'*

Liffey water *n Irish & British* Guinness. The Liffey is the river flowing through Dublin, where Guinness is brewed, and Liffey water is an archaic rhyming-term for porter, of which Guinness is an example.

lift *vb* **1** to arrest or capture, in police jargon and a 'sanitized' euphemism of Vietnam-era military parlance.

2 to steal. Lift has been used euphemistically in this sense since the 16th century.

3 to drink (alcohol). A beer-drinkers' euphemism inspired by the raising of glasses; **hoist** is an American synonym.

✎ *'What say we go and lift a few?'*

lift-off *n American* an erection.

✎ *'She doesn't give you a boner? – because I definitely have lift-off.'*
(*Disclosure*, US film, 1995).

lig *vb British* to freeload, enjoy oneself at someone else's expense. The word, coined in Britain in the early 1970s, refers to the activities of hangers-on, **groupies**, music journalists, etc., who attend receptions, parties, concerts, and other functions, usually financed by record companies. The origin of the word is obscure, it has been suggested that it is made up of the initials of 'least important guest' or is a blend of linger and **gig**. Alternatively it may be an obscure vagrants' term from a dialect survival of Anglo-Saxon liegan, to lie.

lig *n British* an opportunity for free-loading, a party, reception or other occasion when it is possible to enjoy oneself at someone else's expense. The word refers to the rock and pop-music world, and probably postdates the verb form **lig** and the noun **ligger**.

ligeratti *n British* a journalese blend of **ligger** and '**glitteratti**'.

♦'*"The club animals" own Johnny Morris, Caris Davis, who wrote about clubland's scenestealers, wimp-bods and ligeratti in his novel, "Stealth".*'
(*Observer*, Section 5 magazine, 7 May 1989).

ligger *n British* a freeloader, hanger-on or gatecrasher at concerts, receptions, parties, etc., in the rock and pop-music milieus. The word is part of rock music's jargon and was adopted enthusiastically by journalists in such publications as *New Musical Express* in the 1970s to describe those enjoying themselves at the expense of record companies.

♦'*Julia Riddiough, 27 "going on 180", is a world-class ligger who could club for Britain.*'
(*Observer*, Section 5 magazine, 7 May 1989).

lighten up *vb* to relax or take things less seriously, calm down and/or cheer up. This expression moved from US parlance into the rest of the English-speaking world in the early 1980s.

♦'*Lighten up will ya – do you have to take the fun out of everything?*'
(*Cheers*, US TV comedy series, 1985).

lightning *n American* 1 another name for the drug **crack**.
2 *see* **white lightning**.

lightweight *adj British* insufficiently daring, outrageous, excessive. In the fashionable adolescent vocabulary of the late 1990s this is the opposite of **hardcore**.

likely lad *n British* an alert, smart and/or cheeky youth. A colloquial working-class phrase used particularly in the north of England to describe a young man who shows promise or self-confidence. The expression was adopted as the title of a popular Newcastle-based TV comedy series in the 1960s.

lilac *adj* (male) homosexual or effeminate. A rarer synonym for **lavender**.

Lillian Gish *n British* (a) fish. This old item of cockney slang, borrowing the name of the silent film star and used, e.g., by the Great Train Robber, Ronnie Biggs, in interview, was still heard in the late 1990s.

lils *n pl British* breasts. A vulgar schoolchildren's word of the 1950s and 1960s, which may be a shortening of an earlier 'lily-whites' or an invention, possibly influenced by 'loll' and 'spill'.

limer *n Caribbean* a hanger-on. A back-formed verb, to lime, is also heard. Both are inspired by the adhesive qualities of birdlime or quicklime. The word was adopted by some white speakers in London in the later 1980s.

limey *n, adj* (an) English (person). The word, used mostly in North America, is a shortening of 'lime-juicer', a usually pejorative term applied originally to British sailors who were issued with rations of lime juice as a protection against scurvy. The word limey is now rather dated; Brit is increasingly taking its place.

limo *n* a limousine, luxury car. An American abbreviation, employed by chauffeurs, then showbiz journalists among others, in the early 1970s and now widely used.

limp-dick *n, adj* (someone who is) weak, ineffectual, irresolute. The metaphor is one of impotence, but the term is invariably used to express generalized rather than sexual contempt. The phrase probably originated in the USA as a harsher version of **limp-wristed**.

limp-wristed *adj* effete, effeminate, **camp**, ineffectual. A pejorative term applied especially by men to those considered less masculine or less resolute than themselves. The phrase is sufficiently established to count as a colloquialism, rather than slang.

line *n* a portion of cocaine, amphetamine or other drug ready for **snorting**. The powdered crystals of the drug are scraped into a strip (quite literally 'a line of coke/speed'), typically on a mirror, tile or similar surface, so that they can be sniffed through a straw, rolled banknote, or any other improvised tube.

♦'*We had dinner at 192 and then I went back to Sophie's place to do a few lines.*'
(Recorded, record company executive, London, 1983).

line (up/out) *vb* to sniff **lines** of cocaine or amphetamine. A drug users' euphemism of the 1980s.

linen *n British* a newspaper. This old

item of London rhyming slang (from '*linen draper*', meaning paper) is still in use in the 1990s.

꘎'... *although she does not know much about rhyming slang, it is good to see that she reads a good "linen" on Sunday.*'
(Reader's letter to the *Sunday Times*, 13 September 1992).

lingo *n* a language, jargon or way of speaking. The word, which often indicates puzzlement, amusement or xenophobia on the part of the speaker, obviously derives ultimately from the Latin word *lingua*, meaning tongue and language. The question as to which romance language inspired the modern slang word is difficult to resolve; it may be a corruption of the Latin word itself, or of Italian, Spanish (*lengua*), or Portuguese (*lingoa*). Provençal is the only modern language in which the correct form of the word is *lingo*.

꘎'[Oxford University] *aristocrats disguise themselves with lingo like: "It's wicked, guy."*'
(*Evening Standard*, 16 June 1988).

lint-brain, lint-head *n American* a dim-witted or foolish person. This adolescent term of abuse draws on the American use of lint to denote fluff, particularly that lodged in the 'belly-button'.

Lionel Blairs, Lionels *n pl British* flared trousers. This item of rhyming slang, using the name of a celebrity dancer, replaced the earlier **Grosvenor Squares**, and was itself supplanted by **Tony Blairs** in the late 1990s.

lip *n* cheek, back-chat. The expression dates to at least 1818, and is typically used by authority figures to characterize the utterances of unruly subordinates. It is a common usage in Britain and Australia, but less so in the USA.

꘎'*Lesson number one: learn to give less lip and do more work.*'
(*Neighbours*, Australian TV soap opera, 1987).

lip *vb* 1 to cheek, speak insolently (to). 2 to play a wind instrument, blow. A jazz musicians' term.

꘎'*Lip that thing.*'
꘎'*Cool lipping.*'

lippy *adj* cheeky, insolent. This usage comes from the noun form **lip**, which was first recorded in 1818.

꘎'*He's a bit too lippy for his own good.*'

lip service *n* fellatio. A humorous euphemism from the professional jargon of prostitution and pornography (punning on the standard idiom 'to pay lip service to').

lipstick *n American* a lesbian interested in high-fashion, a 'feminine' lesbian. A Yale University term of the 1970s. Lipsticks are contrasted in this setting with the more aggressive or 'masculine' **crunchies**. The word lipstick has subsequently entered the **gay** female lexicon.

liquid cosh *n British* a heavy tranquillizer or sedative. In the jargon of prison inmates the phrase has been used to describe substances such as Largactil, Paraldehyde, etc.

liquid laugh *n* a bout of vomiting. The term probably originated in Australia. It is now heard in Britain (where it was part of the vocabulary of the influential late 1960s cartoon character Barry McKenzie, the Australian boor and ingénu) and, especially on campus, in the USA.

liquid lunch *n* a lunchtime session of alcoholic drinking (usually as an alternative rather than an accompaniment to eating).

liquored up/out *adj American* drunk. The same phrase was in use in Britain in the 19th century.

little boy's room, the little boys' room *n* a gentlemen's toilet. Originally a coy euphemism, used by some Americans in all seriousness, this expression has come to be used facetiously all over the English-speaking world.

꘎'*I'm not just some kind of machine you can turn on. I need a cup of joe, a trip to the little boys' room, a glance at the sports' pages. Then we'll talk.*'
(*Moonlighting*, American TV series, 1989).

little girl's room, the little girls' room *n* a ladies' toilet. A coy euphemism now almost always used humorously, but originally (in the USA in the late 1940s) used to spare the blushes of the speaker and audience.

little jobs *n British* an act of urination, as opposed to **big jobs** (defecation), in the now rather dated euphemistic language of the middle-class nursery.

little man/boy in the boat *n*

the clitoris. So-called because of a supposed resemblance, though it is unclear why the pilot of this particular craft is invariably male. In the 19th century the same phrase referred to the navel.

little number *n See* number.

lit up, lit *adj* drunk.

Originally an American expression, this phrase derives from the visible effects of alcohol (a 'glow', red nose, etc.) as well as the sensation of heat and the notion of alcohol as firewater or fuel. Embellishments of this usage are '*lit up like a Christmas tree*' and '*lit up like a dime-store window*'. The shorter form, lit, often signifies tipsy or merry rather than thoroughly inebriated.

↳'*As a whiskey salesman … I'm often lit up by elevenses, loop-legged by luncheon and totally schnockered by 6.*'
(Cartoon by Posy Simmonds, *Guardian*, 1979).

livener *n British* a strong alcoholic drink.

Liverbird *n British* a girl or young woman from Liverpool, specifically a working-class or lower-middle-class girl like those portrayed in Carla Lane's TV comedy series of the same name. The term (the first part of which is pronounced as in 'alive') puns on the use of bird to mean young woman. It also refers to the statues of fanciful birds on the roof of the Liver building on the Liverpool waterfront, which have become emblematic of the city.

the living *n British* a superlative thing, person or situation. A vogue term from the vocabulary of adolescents in the later 1990s, it is probably a shortening of 'the living end'.

lizards *n pl* snakeskin, crocodile-skin or iguana-hide footwear. Part of the sartorial repertoire of many social subgroups including cowboys, pimps, street gangs, etc., lizards are also known as reptiles.

load *vb Australian* to plant (someone) with illicit drugs or stolen goods, or to frame by manufacturing evidence. A term from the Australian criminal milieu which was first recorded in the 1930s and is still in use. The noun form is occasionally used to mean either an act of framing or the supposed evidence used.

load *n* nonsense, something worthless or unpleasant. In this sense the word is a shortening of the colloquial vulgarism 'a load of shit'.

↳'*… academic electronic music – what a load!*'
(*Vivisect*, Australian fanzine, July 1994).

loaded *adj* 1 a drunk. An Americanism in use since the turn of the century, now heard elsewhere in the English-speaking world. The original metaphor may refer to a burden or a large quantity being imbibed or, more dramatically, to the person being charged like a firearm.

↳'*Dropped into a tavern/ Saw some friends of mine./ Party was gettin' under way/ And the juice was really flyin' and I got loaded.*'
('I Got Loaded', song recorded by Peppermint Harris, 1957).

b intoxicated by illicit drugs. An American term popular in the late 1960s and early 1970s. It was this sense that inspired the title of the fourth LP by the seminal New York rock group The Velvet Underground in 1970.

2 rich. This term, formerly slang, is now a common colloquialism.

3 *British* in the mood for sex or sexually aroused. The term, which refers to males only, is part of the language of adolescents in use in the later 1990s and was included in *Just Seventeen* magazine's 'lingo of lurve' in August 1996.

↳'*I can tell he's loaded/feeling loaded.*'

loadie *n American* a drunkard or habitual drug user; someone who is often or permanently loaded. A teenage and campus expression of the late 1970s, usually indicating disapproval.

loadsamoney *n British* (someone flaunting) excessive wealth; vulgar, conspicuous consumption. The eponymous comedy character Loadsamoney, created by Harry Enfield in 1987, was based on observation of a specific social group. This group comprises bumptious and philistine skilled and semi-skilled working-class young people from south-eastern England, who use their comparative wealth – often gained as part of the black economy – to taunt and provoke those worse off than themselves.

The catchphrase 'loadsamoney!' was seized upon by journalists and by the leader of the Labour opposition, Neil Kinnock, who in May 1988 accused the Thatcher administration of fostering an uncaring 'loadsamoney mentality'. In journalese 'loadsa-' was a vogue prefix in 1988 and 1989.

✆'*Singer Mike Rivers has vowed never again to work for the Hooray Henry set – "I hate those loadsamoney thugs," he declared.'*
(*News of the World*, 29 May 1988).

load up *vb American* to take illicit drugs. A campus and high-school term of the late 1970s.

✆'*Listen, if you're loading up, that's it between us.'*

loaf *n British*
a head. The shortening of the cockney rhyming-slang phrase 'loaf of bread' is now more a colloquialism than slang. Since the late 1950s, it has largely been confined to the phrase '*use your loaf!*'.
b life. The more common sense of 'head' and the word 'life' itself are blended in the cockney oath '*on my mother's loaf*'.

lob *vb British* to throw away, dispose of. A fashionable narrowing of the standard English meaning of the word, heard, particularly in the London area, since the beginning of the 1980s. A near-synonym to **bin**.

✆'*It's no use any more – just lob it.'*

lob (in) *vb Australian* to arrive unexpectedly, drop in.

✆'*You'd better get home right away; the rellos have lobbed.'*

lobe *n British* a dull, conformist person. This word, used typically by schoolchildren of a tedious or unpopular fellow pupil is a shortening of 'earlobe', itself inspired by the long established working-class **ear'ole**.

loc *n, adj American* (a person who is) crazy. This abbreviated form of **loco** (pronounced to rhyme with 'poke') became a vogue term among devotees of **rap** and hip hop culture in the late 1990s. The word could be used either pejoratively or with admiration for a fanatical individual.

lock *n American* 1 a certainty, usually heard in the teenagers' phrase '*it's a lock*'. This sense of the word is an adaptation of the colloquial phrase to '*have (the situation) all locked up*'.
2 a person of Polish origin or descent.

The racist term heard in the US is supposedly a corruption of **polack**.

loco *adj* mad, crazy. This word, popularized worldwide by its use in Western movies and cowboy fiction, is the standard informal Spanish word for crazy, deriving from the Latin *ulucus*: owl (which is incidentally related to the English ululate).

lodge (someone) *vb British* to reject or eject a person, especially a partner. This item of London working-class speech was recorded in the BBC documentary *Forty Minutes* on 30 November 1993.

✆'*He was taken completely by surprise when Debbie lodged him.'*

log *n* 1 *Australian* a lazy, inert person.
2 a piece of excrement, a **turd**.
3 a surfboard. The term was defined in *Just Seventeen* magazine in January 1994.

log-rolling *n* unofficial or dubious collaboration for mutual advantage, especially in the word of politics. This expression has been in use since the 19th century when it referred to lumberjacking, where pioneer neighbours would help each other move the timber required for building by physically rolling the logs to their destination before cutting them up; it has recently become popular in British journalistic circles under American influence.

loid, lloid *vb* to open a door by moving a strip of celluloid or piece of plastic, (e.g. a credit card), up and down in the gap between the door and its frame, slipping the lock. A police and underworld term, like the practice in use since before World War II.

lollapalooza, lolapaloosa *n American* something wonderful, outstanding, enormous and/or spectacular. This invented term is a synonym for words like whopper, **lulu** or **humdinger**, depending on the context. (Like whopper it can sometimes refer to an outrageous lie.) The word is used in particular by schoolchildren and parents.

lollies *n Australian* sweets, candy. Australasia has retained the more general meaning of the word, narrowed in Britain to refer only to lollipops. (Lolly originated as a rural British dialect term for tongue, related historically to the verb to loll.)

lollipop *vb British* to inform on someone, betray (to the police). This is London
rhyming slang for the term to **shop**. It is
sometimes shortened to **lolly**.

ᛃ*'It wouldn't be like Smoky to lollipop
his mates.'*

ᛃ*'If you ask me they were lollied.'*

lolly *n British* money. A well-established, light-hearted word, popular in the
1950s and 1960s and enjoyed a revival,
significantly, in the 'Thatcher years' (the
mid- and late 1980s), when many obsolescent euphemisms for money had received a new lease of life. It is said to
originate in the Romany word *loli*, meaning red, used by gypsies to mean copper
coins, and hence money in general. It is
perhaps easier to derive the word from
lolly, meaning sweet or candy which itself
originated in dialect with the meaning of
tongue. (The sense of lollipop is later.)

ᛃ*'Lots of lovely lolly – that's what we
want.'*

lolly *vb British* a short form of the
rhyming slang **lollipop**.

lolly water *n Australian* soft
drink(s). The expression, from the Australian sense of **lollies** as sweets, is often
used scathingly by committed drinkers of
alcohol referring to non-alcoholic bever-
ages, or even by **macho** drinkers to refer
to alcoholic drinks considered unmanly.

lombard *n British* a wealthy but stupid and/or unpleasant person. A late
1980s acronym from '*loads of money but
a real dickhead*', coined by **yuppies** to
refer particularly to young moneymak-
ers in the City of London, on the lines of
expressions such as **dinky**, **nimby**,
homey, etc. The word's resonance is enhanced by the role of London's Lombard
Street as the home of banking and insurance companies. (The historical Lombards were incidentally a 6th-century
Germanic people who invaded northern
Italy and became known as money-
lenders.)

ᛃ*'If they were not Sloanes or yuppies
they had to be dinkies (dual income no
kids), lombards (lots of money but a
real dickhead) or even swells (single
women earning lots of lolly).'*
(*Evening Standard Magazine*, May
1988).

longbeard *n* an old person. A quasi-
folksy term from science or fantasy fiction
adopted facetiously by rock-music jour-

nalists to describe members of the older
generation (or themselves when reminiscing). **Greybeard** is a slightly more
widespread alternative.

long green *n American* money (dollar bills of all denominations in America
are coloured green). The euphemism is
old, dating from the turn of the century,
and is still in use.

ᛃ*'We'll soon have enough of that long
green to choke a horse.'*
(*Knight Rider*, US TV series, 1981).

long streak of misery *n British*
a tall, thin person who may or may not be
morose, gloomy or habitually pessimistic.
This expression, like the less common
'long drink of water' and the more vulgar
long streak of piss is normally part of
the working-class catchphrase announcement '*here he comes again – the
long streak of misery!*' which may indicate
affectionate recognition or genuine dislike. The phrase can refer to women as
well as men.

long streak of piss *n British* a
tall, thin person. An expression of contempt or dismissiveness, usually implying weakness or insignificance as well as
an ectomorphic body shape. The expression is almost always applied to males.

loo *n British* a toilet. The most widespread and socially acceptable euphemism for lavatory, privy, etc. This
word, which became firmly established
in the mid-1960s, is a favourite of amateur etymologists who derive it variously
from *lieu* ('place', as in the French euphemism *lieu d'aisance*, 'place of ease');
from *l'eau* (water) or *gardez l'eau* (mock-
French for 'watch out for water', said to
be the cry of someone emptying a chamber-pot from an upstairs window into the
street below in 17th-century British
cities); from 'bordalou', a type of travellers' chamber-pot; from an abbreviation of the name of Lady Louis Hamilton
(apparently affixed to a lavatory door) in
Dublin in 1870; or, least convincingly of
all, from leeward (the side of a boat from
which one would logically urinate). It may
be significant, however, that this rather
refined euphemism for water-closet was
not recorded until well after the battle of
Waterloo and the naming of the London
railway station.

ᛃ*'And a bit about doing up the loo in
chintz is sure to do the trick.'*
(*About Town* magazine, June 1962).

looka(h) *n See* luka.

looker *n* an attractive person. The word can now be applied to either sex; formerly it was invariably used appreciatively (if sometimes patronizingly) by men of women. It originated as a truncated form of good-looker.

loon *n*

a a crazy, eccentric or silly person. This word is in its modern usage a convergence of three sources. It is both a shortening of lunatic and the name of an American diving bird with a cry like a demented laugh. In addition, it probably also recalls an archaic Middle English and later Scottish dialect word, 'loun', meaning a rogue. Keith Moon, drummer with the English rock group The Who, who was notorious for his wild and outrageous behaviour, was dubbed 'Moon the loon' in the late 1960s by acquaintances and the press.

b *British* a bout of uninhibited and eccentric behaviour. In this sense the noun is derived from the following verb.

loon, loon about, loon out *vb*
British to behave in an uninhibited, lighthearted and/or outrageous manner. The expression was coined at the end of the 1960s to describe a bout of high-spirited, anarchic play typical of those liberated from convention by drug use and/or progressive ideas.

↪*'Gone is the rampaging looner of old, the very sight of whom would strike fear into the hearts of publicans and club owners throughout the land.'*
(*Record Mirror*, 26 August 1967).

loon pants *n pl British* flared trousers in cotton, canvas or velvet, sold in London around 1970s and emblematic of the **hippy** style of the time. Loon pants, which began as cut-down naval bell-bottoms, were so-called by sellers and wearers under the influence of the verb **to loon**. This apparel, especially the once-ubiquitous purple cotton variety, was singled out for particular derision by later, post-**punk** disparagers of the hippies.

loony, looney *adj* crazy. An adaptation of lunatic (see the noun **loon** for other influences) which is now a common colloquialism.

loony bin *n* a hospital for the insane or mentally subnormal, an 'insane asylum'. The most common slang expression

for such an institution in the English-speaking world since the end of the 19th century. In modern British parlance it is usually shortened to **the bin**.

loony tune/tunes/toons *n, adj*
(a) mad or eccentric (person). Originally an Americanism derived from *Looney Tunes*, the name of a series of cinema cartoon comedies in the 1940s, the term has become fashionable since the 1980s in Britain and Australia.

↪*'I've been hit twice in the face this morning and now some loony tune is breaking up my aircraft.'*
(*The Flying Doctors*, Australian TV series, 1987).

↪*'That is it, Mork! He's got to go, or I'll end up as loony-tunes as he is.'*
(*Mork and Mindy*, US TV series, 1979).

loop-the-loop *n British* **1** soup. An example of London working-class rhyming slang heard since the 1970s. It was used in a TV commercial for Heinz in 1988.

2 **soixante-neuf** or 69, in the professional jargon of prostitution and pornography.

loopy *adj*

a crazy, eccentric, silly.

b illogical, out of control. A fairly mild pejorative, often said in bemusement or disbelief rather than disapproval. The word has been in use since the early years of the 20th century, but its origin is obscure.

loose cannon *n American* a dangerously uncontrolled ally or associate; a member of one's team who is liable to run amok or cause havoc. This piece of political and journalistic jargon has become fashionable since the late 1980s. It continues the nautical image evoked by such vogue clichés as 'take on board'. In this case the person in question is seen as an unsecured cannon careering unpredictably and dangerously across a deck with the pitching of a ship. The phrase was used of General Haig during the Nixon administration and of Colonel Oliver North under the Reagan administration.

↪*'Danko is the perfect weapon Charlie – a loose cannon. If he helps us find Victor Rosla, great. If he screws up, breaks rules ... he's a Russian.'*
(*Red Heat*, US film, 1988).

loot *n* money. A predictable extension of the standard English sense of booty. The

word is an Anglicized spelling of the Hindi word *lut* which sounds and means the same as the English derivation.

↳ *'I tell you what though, Zackerman can recruit the very best because he's got the loot.'*
(*Serious Money*, play by Caryl Churchill, 1987).

Lord Muck *n British* a man thought to be 'putting on airs' or behaving high-handedly. This expression from the turn of the century is now probably less prevalent than the female equivalent, **Lady Muck**.

↳ *'Well, won't you just look at them – Lord and Lady Muck.'*

lorg *n American* a foolish, clumsy person. The word is probably a deformation of **log**, as used to denote an inert individual.

lose it *vb* 1 to lose one's temper or control over oneself.
2 *See* **lose the plot**.

lose one's bottle *vb British* to lose one's nerve, have one's courage desert one. A vogue term of the late 1970s, when it crossed from the jargon of marginals, criminals and the lower working-class into general currency. (For the origins of the expression see **bottle**.)

lose one's cool *vb* to lose one's composure or one's temper. A phrase from the 1950s American **hip** vocabulary, usually heard in the form of an admonition. It was adopted in Britain, first by jazz fans and **beatniks**, in the late 1950s.

↳ *'Try not to lose your cool even if the guy provokes you.'*

lose one's lunch/dough-nuts/pizza *vb American* to vomit. Hearty, jocular high-school and college terms.

lose one's marbles *vb* to become deranged or feeble-minded, go crazy. **Marbles** when referring to male faculties usually refers to testicles, but in this case one's wits or intelligence are in question. The origin of this phrase is uncertain, in spite of many attempts to clarify the choice of words (marbles have been seen as a synonym for the bearings which allow a machine to operate or as part of a catchphrase based on a story in which a monkey steals a boy's marbles). What is undisputed is that the expression originated in the USA.

lose one's rag *vb British* to lose one's temper, lose control of oneself. This mainly working-class expression is of obscure origin; the word rag has meant variously one's tongue, a flag, to tease, to bluster or rage, but none of these senses can be definitively linked to the modern phrase.

↳ *'Don't you go losing your rag – stay cool.'*
(*Eastenders*, British TV series, July 1988).

lose the plot, lose it *vb* these vogue terms of the later 1990s probably originated in references to, e.g., a film director whose work became incoherent after an auspicious beginning.

lotion *n British* an alcoholic drink. A now dated middle-class term with the implications of the soothing medicinal effects of (strong) liquor. The word can be countable ('a lotion') or uncountable ('some lotion').

louie *n American See* **hang a louie**.

lousy *adj Australian* ill, under the weather. A local synonym for **crook**.

love blobs *n pl British* testicles. A jocular schoolboy or armed-forces coinage briefly popular in the early 1980s and broadcast in the BBC alternative comedy series *The Young Ones*. Similar phrases such as **love bumps** or **love handles** are also in use. 'Love bubbles' is an archaic euphemism for breasts.

love bumps *n pl British* breasts. A 'schoolboyish' euphemism of the 1970s. 'Love bubbles' was a pre-World War II synonym. **Love lumps** is an alternative form.

love handles *n pl* folds of flesh at the waist or paunch. An affectionate, joky, reassuring or polite euphemism usually applied to the male body by women or by the person himself.

↳ *'The love handles of Jonathan Ross are no strangers to this column, but news reaches us that they are shrinking by the hour.'*
(*Time Out* magazine, July 1989).

love-in *n* a gathering involving displays of mutual affection and/or ecstatic 'one-ness'. An ephemeral phenomenon and term from the early **hippy** era, seized upon by the press.

love-in-a-punt *n British* weak beer or watered-down alcohol. The expression is a pun playing pseudo-romantically on the plant love-in-a-mist and on the notion that the drink in question is 'fucking near water'. Paul Beale in Eric Partridge's *Dictionary of Slang and Unconventional English* (1984) specifies 'a brew sold in the Portsmouth area in the 1950s'.

love lumps *n pl British* breasts. A jocular term used by university students and teenagers in the mid- to late 1980s in keeping with the trend to coin childishly coy expressions as alternatives to established or taboo terms. **Love bumps** is an alternative form.

love sausage *n American* the penis.

love-truncheon *n British* the penis. This joke euphemism was employed by the comedians Rik Mayall and Ade Edmonson in the stage performance of their TV comedy *Bottom* and subsequently occurred in student slang in the later 1990s.

love-tunnel *n British* the vagina. A vulgarism in use among adolescents in the 1990s and listed in *Viz* comic in 1994.

low budget *adj British* sleazy, sordid, shabby, poor. This phrase, inspired by its earlier application to feature films, has been adopted in the 1980s, typically by **yuppies** or **Sloane Rangers**, as a British version of the American **low rent**.

‣ *'She lives in an awfully low budget sort of place.'*

low-flyer *n British* a liar. An item of rhyming slang heard in the 1990s.

low-heel, low-wheel *n Australian* a prostitute. The term refers to someone who is literally down at heel from walking the streets. The second form of the expression is based on a mishearing of the true phrase.

lowlife *n American* a disreputable and/or contemptible person. A fashionable term of the 1970s which was adopted by some British speakers to refer to those considered socially unacceptable.

‣ *'Jesus, Katy, what are you doing with this lowlife?'*

low rent *adj American* shabby, sordid, inferior. A phrase referring to lodgings, extended first to denote a poor district, then to signify anything or anyone considered distasteful or third-rate. **Low budget** is a near-synonym in British English.

low rider *n American*

a a devotee of customized cars with lowered suspension characteristic of Chicano or Hispanic youth gangs in Los Angeles and elsewhere during the 1970s. The term low rider (the fashion was still in evidence at the end of the 1980s) can also be applied to the car itself. Low riding involves (contrary to raising suspension for road racing or rallying) driving very slowly in convoys for display.

b an obnoxious or disreputable youth. This pejorative use of the word is an extension of the original sense, probably influenced also by standard terms such as low.

L7 *n, adj American* (a person who is) conformist, dull reactionary. The term is a synonym for **square** and is based on the square made by the two symbols. It was adopted as the name of a *rriot grrrl* band of the early 1990s.

lubricated *adj* drunk. A politely jocular euphemism on the same lines as **well-oiled**.

luck out *vb American*

a to 'strike it lucky'.

b to have bad luck. This term with its contrary senses is occasionally used by British speakers.

lucoddy *n British* body. Part of the **parlyaree** lexicon used, e.g., by the **gay** and theatrical community in the 1960s. The precise derivation of the term is unclear, apart from the obvious rhyme.

Lucy Locket *n British* a pocket. A piece of London rhyming slang inspired by a nursery rhyme character. **Sky-rocket** and **Davy Crockett** are alternative versions.

'lude *n American* a Quaalude (pronounced 'kway-lood') tablet. A widely prescribed and misused methaqualone (hypnotic sleeping pill), equivalent to the British Mandrax or **mandy**. The drug was taken, particularly in the 1970s, for its relaxing and disinhibiting effects and to mitigate the after- and side-effects of other drugs.

lug *British* an inhalation of smoke, **drag**. The term is used in this sense in British and Irish speech.

↧*'Didn't any of them enjoy a lug on the herbals?'*
(*Q* magazine, March 1997).

lughole, lug'ole *n British* ear. A common term of the 1950s and 1960s which now sounds folksy or dated, although the comedian Frankie Howerd employed 'pin back your lugholes' as one of his catchphrases. Lug has been the commonest colloquialism for 'ear' outside London since the 16th century. It originated in Middle English meaning flap or ear-cover, from an older Scandinavian word *lugga*, to pull.

luka, lookah *n British* money, wealth. This word, spelled in a variety of ways, which was recorded among London schoolchildren in the mid-1990s, is in fact the much older ('filthy) lucre' adopted as a vogue term, probably in ignorance of its origin. (Lucre is Middle English from the Latin *lucrum*, meaning reward or booty.) In American slang **ducats** is another archaism which has been revived in a similar context.

lulu *n* 1 something spectacular, impressive, exceptional. This word was originally an Americanism, in use since the mid-19th century: many attempts have been made to explain its etymology, which remains obscure. (It is almost certainly unconnected with the female nickname.)
2 *British* an elaboration of **loo**.

lumber *n British*

a trouble, burdensome difficulties. This sense of the word is usually expressed by the 'cockney' phrases '*in lumber*' or '*in dead lumber*'.

b a fight or struggle. A word which in working-class, particularly northern, usage is often in the form of an exclamation to signal the start of a street or playground brawl, and is another sense of lumber as 'trouble'.

↧*'Tables flew, bottles broke, the bouncers shouted lumber/ the dummy got too chummy in a Bing Crosby number.'*
(*Salome Maloney the Sweetheart of the Ritz*, poem by John Cooper Clarke, 1980).

lumber *vb, n British* (to pick up) a partner of the opposite sex. The usage probably originated in the Lowlands of Scotland but is now heard in other parts of Britain, employed as a synonym for 'get off with' or **pull**.

lummock, lummox *n* a large, clumsy and/or stupid person. The word is used in the USA and Australia as well as in Britain, but is originally a rural British dialect form of 'lump', in the same way as hummock is a diminutive form of hump.

↧*'The awkward lummox of a kid who, though only ten years old, was almost as big as his fifth grade teacher.'*
(*Wild Town*, Jim Thompson, 1957).

the lump *n British* the casual work system in the British building trade, or the casual non-union work force, exploited by employers in the 1960s and 1970s.

lunatic soup *n* alcoholic drink. A humorous expression on the lines of **electric soup**, **giggle water** and **laughing soup**.

lunchbox *n* 1 the stomach, belly or abdomen. A jocular euphemism, used particularly in the context of fighting.
↧*'A kick/punch in the lunchbox.'*
2 the male genitals as visible through tight clothing. The term, an elaboration of the earlier **box**, was applied by the *Sun* newspaper to the athlete Linford Christie in a number of headlines in the mid-1990s and the stand-up comedian Ben Elton drew attention to the usage at the Montreal Comedy Festival in 1992. Synonyms are **packet** and **basket**.
↧*'Gym bans a big boys' lunchbox'*
(Headline in the *News of the World*, August 1994)

lunching at the Lazy Y *n phrase* engaging in oral sex, particularly cunnilingus. A humorous expression playing on the shape of a reclining person with their legs spread and a famous cattle brand from the American Wild West. (A 'lazy' letter in a brand was one lying on its side.) An alternative form is 'dining at the Y'.

lunchy, lunchie *adj*

a crazy, eccentric, deviant. From the colloquialism 'out to lunch', this became a vogue term of the 1990s, originating among American adolescents.
↧*'I knew the kid was lunchie, but not this fuckin' lunchie!'*
(*Things To Do In Denver When You're Dead*, US film, 1996).

b inferior, unacceptable, unpleasant. This generalization of the original sense of the term was adopted by British adolescents as a vogue term in the mid-1990s.

lundy *n British* a collaborator, traitor. A Northern Irish term derived from the name of the governor of Londonderry in the 18th century, Lieutenant Colonel Robert Lundy, who was suspected of Catholic sympathies by the Protestant community.

lunk, lunkhead *n American* a slow-witted person, dullard. The term originated in the USA in the 19th century. It usually evokes a large, clumsy, ungainly person of low intelligence and/or slow reactions. It is a blend of lump and hunk.

lurgi, lurghi *n* alternative spellings of **lerg(h)i**.

lurk *n Australian* a dodge, shady scheme, clever and/or disreputable trick. The word is now used in these senses mainly- by middle-aged and elderly speakers.

lurker *n* 1 *British* a a disreputable, suspicious, unwholesome person. A word often used by disaffected youth ironically of themselves, it was adopted as a name by a suburban London **punk**-rock group in 1977.
b a fly-by-night or unlicensed street trader.
2 *Australian* a petty criminal, fraudster or cardsharp. All these senses are variations on the standard English meaning of lurk which comes from the Middle English lurken, to lie in wait.
3 a market stallholder who simply waits for customers without attempting to attract them. *Compare* **rorter**, **pitcher**.
4 an Internet user who observes communications without participating, in the patois of **cyberpunks** and **net-heads**.
✎'[Lurkers] *are invisible unless you run a roll call command and see how many voyeuristic weazels* [sic] *there actually are.'*
(*Surfing on the Internet* by J. C. Herz, 1994).

lurk off *vb British* to leave, go away. The verb often, but not invariably, suggests slinking away. It can also be employed as a euphemism for the imperative **fuck off** as in the 1995 BBC 2 TV comedy *Game On*.

lush *n* an alcoholic, habitual drunkard or heavy drinker. This is an American term, adopted by British speakers in the 1960s, which derived from an earlier British usage which had fallen into desuetude; from at least the 18th century until the early 20th century lush had been used to mean alcoholic drink.

lush *adj British*
a very attractive and/or desirable.
✎'*A lush bird.'*
✎'*I love your ski pants, Tray Nice aren't they! £12.99. You want to get some. You'll look lush.'*
(*The Fat Slags*, cartoon in *Viz* magazine, 1989).
b delicious.
✎'*Well, how was it?'*
'*Lush.'*
This British colloquialism, heard especially in the 1960s among schoolchildren, young people and unsophisticated adults, is a short form of luscious rather than the standard adjective (as in 'lush vegetation', for example).

lushed *adj* drunk. This is probably a recent coinage inspired by **lush** meaning a heavy drinker. In fact lush as a verb, and lushed as a past participle, had existed in English slang and dialect since the early 19th century, but had fallen out of use in most areas before World War II. The renewed use of the term is mainly confined to teenagers and students.

lyin' and testifyin' *n American* misleading and/or persuasive badinage, 'smooth talk'. In black speech the phrase is not necessarily pejorative – 'lyin' denotes the skilful telling of stories. An item of black street talk which was included in so-called **Ebonics**, recognized as a legitimate language variety by school officials in Oakland, California, in late 1996.
✎'*It was precisely the danger that lyin' and testifyin' homeys (smooth talking blacks) would be classified as stupid that Oakland wanted federal funds for its teachers to learn Ebonics.'*
(*Sunday Times*, 29 December 1996).

M *n* morphine. A drug users' abbreviation.

mac *n* **1** *American* a term of address to a male stranger. The word often conveys a hint of provocation rather than straightforward friendliness.
2 *British* a mackintosh, raincoat. *See* **the dirty mac brigade**.

machine gun *n* a hypodermic syringe, in the language of drug addicts and prison inmates of the late 1950s and 1960s. This is one of many self-dramatizing terms (**shooting gallery**, **harpoon**, etc.) in the vocabulary of hard-drug users.

machismo *n* assertive maleness, overt masculinity. The word evokes virility, supremacism, etc. It is not strictly speaking slang but a direct borrowing from the Spanish (and as such should be pronounced as in 'match' not 'mack').

macho *adj* assertively male, aggressively masculine. The word is a direct borrowing from Spanish in which it means male, particularly in an animal context, hence virile.
↳'*Her experience among women rappers trying to cut it in the macho world of Hip Hop, led Charlotte to look again at the girl groups from the Seventies she'd always loved.*'
(*Ms London* magazine, 4 September 1989).

macho up *vb* an alternative form of **butch up** (to behave more assertively, courageously or to show more masculine characteristics). **Macho** is Spanish for male in the assertive or dominant sense of the word.

mack *n British* the penis. The word, of uncertain origin, was reported in *Loaded* magazine in October 1994.

macker *n British* a black person. An item of racist rhyming slang based on

'*macaroon*: **coon**' heard in London working-class circles in the early 1990s and reported in the London *Evening Standard* newspaper, 9 September 1991.

Madchester *n British* the music and fashion subculture emanating from Manchester in the early 1990s and centred round bands such as the Happy Mondays and the Stone Roses. The 'mad' element not only evoked the unrestrained **Ecstasy**-driven hedonism of the movement, but was a vogue word constantly used by its devotees.

made-in *n British* a 'two-one' honours degree. A students' jocularism based on 'made-in-Taiwan'. An alternative form is a **draw**: 'two won'.

made-up *adj British* content, satisfied. This regional term from the Merseyside area became widespread in the 1990s, following its use in TV soap operas such as *Brookside* and *Coronation Street* and reports such as that of the London *Evening Standard*, 25 November 1993, regarding the James Bulger murder case.

mad for it *adj British* enthusiastic, unrestrained. The phrase was popular in Manchester during the mid- to late 1990s and was a favourite expression of Liam Gallagher of the Britpop band Oasis.
↳'*Everyone's going, oh you're splitting up, but we're not splitting up. 'Cos we're mad for it.*'
(Liam Gallagher quoted in the *NME*, 30 September 1995).

madhead *n British* a crazy, unrestrained person.
↳'*The majority of the press we've had makes us out to be these madheads who only appeal to dickheads who'd stick a bottle over your head.*'
(Liam Gallagher of Oasis quoted in the *NME*, 30 September 1995).

mad money *n American*
a money set aside by a girl or woman in case she is abandoned or offended by her date. In this sense of the word mad signifies anger (on the part of the girl or her escort).
b money set aside for frivolous, impulsive or self-indulgent purposes. In this version the sense of mad is the British 'crazy'. Both uses of the phrase date from before World War II. They are now dated but not quite obsolete.

mad-up *adj British* annoyed. An item of black British slang.

mady *n South African* sweetheart or wife. Recorded as an item of Sowetan slang in the *Cape Sunday Times*, 29 January 1995.

mag *n Australian* a conversation, chat. Usually heard in the phrase to '*have a mag with someone*'. This sense of the word was first recorded in England in the 18th century and is said to be derived from 'magpie' as a synonym for or an evocation of chatter.

ma-gent, amagent *n South African* a young male, particularly one considered dapper, alert, aware, etc. Recorded as an item of Sowetan slang in the *Cape Sunday Times*, 29 January 1995.

maggot *n* 1 a despicable, dirty and/or insignificant person. In British use, the predominant idea is usually 'beneath contempt', whereas in Australia maggot is a generalized term of abuse.
2 *British* money. A rare usage, heard among petty criminals or their imitators among others. Like many obscure synonyms for money it has been rehabilitated in the late 1980s.
᭬'*I've got to get hold of some maggot in a hurry.*'

maggoted *adj Australian* drunk. One of many synonyms evoking low, despicable behaviour and/or impaired movement.

magic *adj British* superlative, excellent. An over-used colloquialism since the late 1970s which is characteristic of garrulous or over-enthusiastic lower-middle-class and working-class speech. It is often heard in the context of sports such as football or darts.
᭬'*Belfast is "magic" – local demotic for "super" or "marvellous" or whatever high superlative leaps instinctively off the tongue.*'
(*The Crack: a Belfast Year*, Sally Belfrage, 1987).

magic, magic dust/mist *n American* the drug PCP (also known as **angel dust**).

magic mushrooms *n pl* any hallucinogenic mushrooms such as psilocybin or the native British 'liberty caps'. In the later 1980s users began to refer to them as 'shrooms'. *Compare* **rooms**.

make babies *vb* to have sex, make love. A coy or jocular euphemism used by adults.

main drag *n* the main or central street. An American phrase from the early years of the century, heard elsewhere since the 1970s. (**Drag** was also used to mean street in Victorian cockney speech.)

mainline *vb* to inject (an illicit drug) directly into a vein. The term is one of the most persistent pieces of addicts' jargon, contrasted with **skin-popping** (injecting subcutaneously or intramuscularly). The meaning is sometimes extended to denote the regular ingestion of anything in large quantities.

main man *n American*
a a boss, leader.
᭬'*He's the main man around here.*'
b (a woman's) partner, boyfriend, husband or protector.
᭬'*He's my main man.*'
c one's best friend, **buddy**, bosom pal.
᭬'*Yo, Billy, my main man! How're they hanging?*'

main squeeze *n American*
a (one's) boyfriend or girlfriend, sweetheart.
b most important person, boss, leader.

major *adj* excellent, exceptional, admirable. A vogue adjective in adolescent usage in the 1990s. The appropriation of the standard term probably occurred first in American speech. Like **mega** and **totally** it was initially used to qualify another word before being allowed to stand alone.
᭬'*... the sixties were mega, the seventies were major, and what you are going to see now is going to be totally massive!*'
(*Scratchy & Co.*, children's TV show, 8 March 1997).

make *n American* 1 a an identification or instance of recognition (of a suspect).
b a check in official records on the identity of a suspect or on another piece of evidence.
᭬'*Run a make on this guy, will you?*'
᭬'*Can we have a make on the license number?*'
2 a sex partner. The term is a back-for-

mation from the sexual sense of the verb **make**, on the same principle as **lay**.

make *vb American* **1** to identify, recognize (a suspect or adversary). A piece of police and criminal jargon well-known from its use in fiction, TV and films.

↳ *'Can you make him?'*
(*The French Connection*, US film, 1971).
2 to have sex with, seduce. This turn-of-the-century euphemism, although understood, has never caught on in Britain or Australia. It has occasionally been adopted by individuals, including the philosopher Bertrand Russell.

make out *vb American*

a to indulge in **necking** or heavy petting. **b** to succeed in having sex. Both are teenagers' extensions of the colloquial sense of the phrase; to be successful. The usage is probably influenced by the verb **make** as a euphemism for seduce or have sex with. *See also* **make-out artist**.

make-out artist *n American* a successful seducer, **stud**. The term is invariably applied to males. It is from the verb **make out**, meaning achieve sexual satisfaction or success.

make the scene *vb* to be present (in a particular milieu), to arrive, in the literal sense or in the sense of achieving a desired position or level of recognition. The phrase is from the talk of jazz musicians, **hipsters** and **beatniks** of the late 1950s. It was briefly and self-consciously adopted in the same circles in Britain but did not survive the derision its use often occasioned.

mallie, mall rat *n American* a (usually female) teenager who hangs around shopping malls in order to meet friends, misbehave and/or otherwise have a 'good time'. A phenomenon, and expression, in existence since the early 1980s.

malteser *n* **1** an old or middle-aged male. This item of rhyming slang for **geezer** was quoted in *Private Eye* magazine, 6 May 1994, ascribed to Essex girls at Tramp nightclub who were referring derisively to the newspaper editor Andrew Neil.
2 a black person who adopts or accepts white culture.

↳ *'What's wrong? This one's a racist and this one's a malteser.'*

(*Grange Hill*, BBC TV series, February 1997).

mampy, manpy *adj British* ugly. This term, originating in black usage, was adopted as a vogue word by London schoolchildren in the 1990s, along with near-synonyms **mash-up**, **bruck(ers)** and **uggers**. Its precise etymology is uncertain.

the Man *n American* **1 a** the police, the government, the (white) establishment or any other authority, or person in authority. A usage coined by underdogs which was taken up by the black power and **hippy** movements of the late 1960s.

↳ *'Looking for a job in the city/ Working for the Man ev'ry night and day.'*
('Proud Mary' by John Fogerty, recorded by Creedence Clearwater Revival, 1969).
b a sports champion, pop singer, etc. considered by the speaker to be the top practitioner of his craft.

↳ *'There were a lot of good heavyweights around in the '60s, but Ali was the Man.'*
2 a supplier of illicit drugs, a **pusher**, **dealer** or **connection**.

↳ *'I'm waiting for my man/ Twenty-six dollars in my hand.'*
('I'm Waiting for my Man' written by Lou Reed, recorded by The Velvet Underground, 1967).

mandie, mandy *n British* a tablet of Mandrax (the British trademark name of methaqualone, a potentially addictive 'hypnotic' sleeping preparation). These drugs, like their American counterparts, Quaaludes or **'ludes**, were taken by drug abusers for their relaxant, disinhibiting and supposedly aphrodisiac effects (mandies were, according to users' slogans, certain to make one **bandy** or **randy**), particularly in the 1970s.

↳ *'The staff and editors of Oz wish to protest against the flippant attitude of our art director towards Mandrax in the caption above ['Mandies make you randy']. Mandies are both addictive and dangerous.'*
(*Oz* magazine, July 1972).

mangoes *n pl American* breasts. One of many terms employing the metaphor of round fruit.

manicure *vb American* to remove the stalks and seeds from herbal marihuana in order to purify it before selling or smoking.

man in the boat *n See* **little man in the boat**.

manky *adj British*
grotty, disgusting or distasteful. A 1960s vogue word, mainly in middle-class usage. The word had existed previously in working-class speech: it may be an invention influenced by mangy, cranky, 'wonky', etc., or a corruption of the French *manqué* (lacking, failed). It is still used in northern England where its usual sense is naughty or spoilt.

man-like ... *combining form British*
in the fashionable language of teenage gangs of the mid-1990s, the phrase is affixed to a proper name, for example, '*man-like Toby*', when addressing or referring to a friend. The term was recorded in use among north London schoolboys in 1993 and 1994.

manners *n pl West Indian* situation, moral ambience. Usually heard in the phrase **under heavy manners**, meaning oppressed, behaving under the threat of discipline. The term was employed in the context of the Rastafarian and reggae subculture in the early 1970s and was briefly adopted by young whites, especially in the world of rock music.

mano-a-mano *adj, adv, n American* (engaged in) a physical confrontation or face-to-face encounter. The term, which refers literally to grappling or wrestling, is the Spanish for 'hand to hand'.
↳'*He remembered his mano-a-mano with Palma.*'

manor *n British* one's own district or area of jurisdiction. A word used by both police and criminals since before World War II.

man up! *exclamation American* a cry of alarm, signalling the arrival of the police. A 1980s street-slang usage based either on **the Man**, meaning authority, or from military jargon meaning 'target identified and moving'.
↳'*"Man up!" the lookouts shout as plainclothes officers Jeff Ziernicki and Harold Braxton creep up Susquehanna Avenue in their boxy blue Plymouth.*'
(*The Sunday Times*, 10 September 1989).

the man upstairs *n* a humorous euphemism for God.

map of France/Ireland/America/etc. *n* **a** a stain on a sheet. **b** a patch of vomit.
The use of the phrase map of Ireland to describe semen stains on bedsheets is said to originate among chambermaids, many of whom were themselves Irish.

mapping *n British* tracing the contours of a partner's body with the fingers. The term is usually heard among adolescents describing petting, and was included in *Just Seventeen* magazine's 'lingo of lurve' in August 1996.

maracas *n pl* **a** breasts. A mainly American usage. **b** testicles. In British speech the (rare) term is reinforced by the rhyme with **knackers**.

maratata *n South African* a gun.

marbles *n pl* **1** testicles. A predictable drawing of a literal parallel (rather than, as some have claimed, an example of rhyming slang on 'marble halls'). **Pills**, **balls**, **stones** and **nuts** are similar metaphors. **2** common sense, sanity, mental faculties. This use of the word was originally American, perhaps deriving from a folk tale. *See also* **lose one's marbles**. **3** money, wealth. This sense of the word, which exists principally in British and Australian usages, probably derives from the children's wish to amass a collection of marbles, influenced by the luxury implied by the use of the substance marble.

mardarse, mardie *n British* a 'softie', a weak person. A schoolchildren's word heard from the 1930s onwards, particularly in the north of England. It is now rare, but not quite archaic, and comes from a dialect form of 'marred' which has the specific sense of spoilt or sulky. Anthony Burgess mentions that the word was used of him by tormentors during his childhood. Mardie has also been heard in use as an adjective.
↳'*Go out with your Dad. Don't be such a bloody mardie.*'
(Recorded, Leicester, 1990).

mare *n British* a woman. A derogatory working-class usage on the lines of **cow**, **bitch** or **sow**. Mare usually has overtones of 'nag' in both its senses and hence denotes a drab, wearisome woman. The word was given a wider currency by its use as a strong but acceptable term of abuse in TV comedies.

✧'*It was a mare of a game.*'
(Comedian Bob Mills in ITV *Heroes and Villains*, 1994).

mark *n* a dupe or target chosen by a conman, pickpocket, etc. An old term, recorded as long ago as 1885 and still in use all over the English-speaking world.

✧'[She] *is drawn into an underworld of cons, scams, "marks" (suckers) and "tells" (their involuntary give-away gestures).*'
(Review of David Mamet's US film, *House of Games*, *Independent*, 19 November 1987).

mark someone's card *vb* *British* to tip someone off, give someone a warning. This phrase from the jargon of horse-racing has been adopted by London working-class speakers, in particular in police and underworld circles. The usual implication is a firm but gentle (or menacing) taking aside and 'putting in the picture'.

✧'*You can leave it to me, I'll mark his card for him.*'

marmalize, marmelise *vb* *British* to destroy, utterly defeat. This invented word, suggesting like **spifflicate** some unspecified but comprehensive punishment, is probably a children's invention, perhaps based on marmalade. It has been used by adults for comic effect, particularly on radio and television (by Ken Dodd's 'Diddymen' and the scriptwriters of *Coronation Street* among others).

✧'*I'll marmalize you!*'

marmite-driller *n British* a male homosexual. The term, one of a set of synonyms including **chutney-ferret**, **fudge-nudger**, and **turd-burglar**, was used, e.g., by the British stand-up comedian Ben Elton in a monologue in January 1994. The reference is to contact with excrement in the course of sodomy.

marmite motorway *n British* the anus. A synonym is **Bourneville Boulevard**; the US equivalent is **Hershey highway**.

marvie *adj American* marvellous. A teenagers' term typically used either with gushing enthusiasm or irony.

mary ann *n British* a male homosexual, effeminate man. One of several usages of common Victorian or Edwardian female forenames (Nancy, as part of **nancy boy**, and **jessie** are others which have survived) to refer derisively to effeminate men.

Mary Jane, Mary Warner, Mary Jane Warner *n* marihuana. These are English puns or **hobson-jobson** versions of the Spanish name for cannabis. One spelling of the word, *marijuana*, is a literal translation of Mary-Jane, although the original Mexican form, *marihuana*, is a familiarizing prefix (from 'Maria') added to a native Amerindian word meaning something like 'herbal substance'.

the Marzipan set *n British* a probably ephemeral **yuppie** coinage from 1987, defined by George Pitcher in the *Observer* as 'Those city flyers who are above the rich cake but below the icing'.

mash, mash-up, mashed (-up) *adj British* 1 **a** destroyed or damaged. **b** ugly

2 **a** exhausted, worn out.

b intoxicated by drugs, **high**.

✧'*After secretly munching her pills my mates watched in confusion as I sweated my way through lasers and flame-throwers. I was totally mashed; Christmas had definitely come early.*'
(*Independent*, 24 January 1995).

c extremely drunk.

All the senses of the words arose in black speech and derive from the image of destruction and damage. In the later 1990s the expression crossed over into the fashionable slang of white teenagers and young adults.

mash *n, vb British* (to make) tea. From the use of the term in the beer-brewing process.

mass *n British* a gang or group of friends. A fashionable synonym for **crew**, **set**, **posse** in the mid-1990s. The term was recorded in use among north London schoolboys in 1993 and 1994.

massive *adj* excellent. This sense of the word probably arose from its use in the music and film industries in such formulations as 'massive hit' extended to 'this band are going to be massive'.

✧'*... the sixties were mega, the seventies were major, and what you are going to see now is going to be totally massive!*' (*Scratchy & Co.*, children's TV show, 8 March 1997).

Masters of the Universe *n pl*

American **yuppies**, 'high-fliers', senior or influential figures. In the early 1990s the phrase was adopted from video games and children's toys to refer only partly ironically to the most successful Wall Street traders, brokers, etc.

matelot *n British*

a a sailor, referred to patronisingly by soldiers, policemen, etc.
b a member of the river police, as referred to by other sections of the police force. The word *matelot* is French for sailor.

mattress-muncher *n Australian*

a (passive) male homosexual. A rarer and probably later version of **pillow-biter**.

maulers *n pl British* hands.

A mainly middle-class schoolchildren's usage, popular in the 1950s and early 1960s.
↳'*Keep your maulers off my things, will you.*'

mau-mau *vb American* to harass,

bully or coerce. The phrase was briefly in vogue, mainly in literary and journalistic circles, in the early 1970s. It was the name of a Kenyan guerilla group which fought for independence in the 1950s and gained a reputation in the west for carrying out atrocities.
↳'*Radical Chic and mau-mauing the flak-catchers and other stories.*'
(Title of book, Tom Wolfe, 1970).

mau-mau *n*

a *American* a 'black power' supporter or black activist.
b *American* a black street-gang member.
c *British* a black person. The first two senses are not necessarily pejorative, the British usage invariably is.

MAW *n American* a glamorous and/or

idle woman of uncertain profession. An abbreviation of '*model, actress, whatever ...*', it was an ironic social categorization originating in the later 1980s and heard in showbusiness and media circles. (It is pronounced as a word rather than letter by letter.)

max *adv* at most, to the maximum ex-

tent. *See also* **to the max**.
↳'*I swear he only earns £25k, max.*'

mazooma, mazuma *n* money.

An American term heard since the early years of the 20th century. Like many other picturesque but dated synonyms it

was revived in British speech in the late 1980s. The word is originally Hebrew, entering American slang via Yiddish.

mezoomas *n pl* breasts.

One of many similar invented terms probably based on the archaic **bazumas**, a corruption of bosom.

McDonald *n British* the sum of £250

or, more usually, £250,000 in the argot of City of London financial traders in the 1990s. The reference is to the McDonald's 'quarter-pounder' hamburger.

McJob *n American* a menial and/or

temporary job. The term arose in connection with the **slacker** generation/**Generation X** and was based on the notion of educated middle-class youngsters taking temporary jobs at, e.g., McDonalds burger restaurants.
↳'*He ... works as a bartender (X-ers have low pay, low prestige, ersatz "McJobs") and suffers from paralyzing millenial gloom.*'
(*Sunday Times*, 26 April 1992).
↳'*People with short attention spans and no work ethic ... barely surviving in ... low status, short-term McJobs.*'
(*Independent*, 24 April 1997).

MCP *n* a sexist man.

An abbreviation of 'male chauvinist pig', a feminist vogue term which appeared in 1970. It was often used in this shortened form both in writing and, less often, in speech. If used, the expression is now usually truncated to chauvinist or even chauve.
↳'*He'd ordered a Heineken from a waitress who was a real throwback, an MCP's delight.*'
(*The Serial*, Cyra McFadden, 1976).

MDA *n* methyldiamphetamine, a syn-

thetic drug which is chemically related to the stimulant amphetamines, but which in some users elicits hallucinogenic experiences supposedly similar to those associated with LSD. The drug was first popular in the early 1970s in the USA, and came once again into vogue in the late 1980s in the UK, where it was known as **adam** or, more usually, **ecstasy**, and became the drug of choice among young club-goers and dancers. MDA has also been designated by the initials MDMA and MMDA.

mean *adj* wonderful, impressive, ex-

cellent. A typical reversal of the standard (American) meaning in black code and later teenage usage, like the more recent **bad** and **wicked**.

mean machine *n* any (supposedly) impressive, spectacular contraption such as a motorcycle or car, or figuratively a male or the male sex organ. A black American all-purpose euphemism of the late 1960s.

meat and two veg *n British* the male genitals. A working-class vulgarism dating from the days when these components constituted the standard British meal, as advertised in cafés, boarding houses, etc. (Veg is short for vegetables and is spoken with a soft 'g'.) Meat has been a slang synonym for penis, as well as for human sexuality in general, since at least the 16th century.

meatball *n* a clod or fool; a brawny but unintelligent male. The word may be used as a variation of **meathead**, or less pejoratively to denote an attractive male, **hunk** (albeit patronizingly).

↳'*My Swedish Meatball.*'
(Title of an American softcore movie).

meathead, meat head *n* a stupid person, dullard. This word was first popularized in the USA. The image evoked is either based on meat signifying solid muscle (instead of brains) or perhaps on the sexual sense of **meat** as penis, in which case the expression is a precursor of the popular term **dickhead**.

↳'*A man of patient indulgence, apparently capable of putting up with every bozo and meathead who comes his way.*'
(Jonathan Keates reviewing Malcolm Bradbury's *Unsent Letter*, *Observer*, 5 June 1988).

meat injection *n British* an act of sexual intercourse. The vulgar euphemism is invariably used by male speakers.

meat market *n* a place where people congregate in the search for sexual partners; a singles bar. The phrase is usually used dismissively of dance halls, clubs, etc. by non-participants or ex-participants.

meat puppet *n American* 1 a prostitute. A short-lived black Los Angeles term, adopted as the name of a **hardcore** group of the 1980s.
2 penis.

meat rack *n* a place where, or oc-

casion when available sexual partners are on display. The phrase is specifically used in a **gay** context to describe public places and events such as bars, discos, parties, etc. at which homosexuals gather.

meat wagon *n*
a a police van, **black maria**.
b an ambulance.
c a hearse. All the senses of the phrase were first heard between the World Wars.

mega *adj* enormous, hugely successful, great, wonderful. A popular teenage buzzword since the mid-1980s, by the end of the decade mega had penetrated adult speech, in particular journalese. In origin it was an adaptation by black American youth of the fashionable late-1970s prefix 'mega' into an independent adjective.

↳'*We had this real mega thrash.*'

megabucks *n* an enormous amount of money. An Americanism of the 1970s which is now heard elsewhere, including Britain, where 'bucks' remains the suffix although not strictly appropriate. (Mega was a fashionable prefix of the late 1970s.)

↳'*He's making megabucks in the City.*'

mellow out *vb* to become relaxed, serene; to free oneself from tension and inhibition. The phrase is a cliché of the **hippy** era, taken from the jargon of jazz and, later, rock musicians. It is still heard, largely in American speech.

melon *n American* head. The humorous usage featured in the cult 1992 film, *Wayne's World*.

↳'*Use your melon, guy!*'

melon(-head) *n British* a stupid person. The word was recorded in use among younger teenagers in the late 1980s.

melons *n pl* breasts. An obvious metaphor which exists in other languages, notably Spanish. The word was employed as a nickname by the British tabloid press in 1986 to refer to the supposedly buxom figure of Lady Helen Windsor.

Melvin *n American* a boring person, nonentity. The Christian name was thought in the 1950s to be quintessentially mundane, personifying a suburban dullard. More recently it has been a term of abuse among college students.

melvin *vb American* to grab by the testicles.

✧'*I don't believe we just melvined death.*'
(*Bill and Ted's Bogus Journey*, US comedy film, 1991).

memsahib *n British* **a** one's wife.
b a dignified, domineering or redoubtable woman.

The word, now usually employed facetiously, is a form of madame-sahib (*sahib* is Hindi for master or lord), a form of address used by Indian servants in the colonial era. (The usual pronunciation is 'memsaab'.)

meneer *n South African* a teacher. The term is Afrikaans for 'sir'. Recorded as an item of Sowetan slang in the *Cape Sunday Times*, 29 January 1995.

mensch, mensh *n*
a a reputable, admirable or dependable person (usually, but not invariably, a male). An approving term from Yiddish and German in which its literal meaning is man, woman, person or humankind.
b an exclamation of surprise or alarm from Yiddish or German.

mental *n See* **throw/chuck a mental**.

mental *adj British* mentally ill, subnormal or deranged, crazy. A widespread colloquialism which showed signs of losing popularity in the 1970s, perhaps due to increased sensitivity; this tendency was reversed by **punks**, fans of heavy-metal and others who enthusiastically adopted the term to refer to their characteristic frenzies, **headbanging**, etc. In these circles the word may be used to express admiration. *See also* **radio rentals**.

me 'n' you *n* a menu. A time-honoured pun heard in all English-speaking areas.

merchant banker *n British* a contemptible person, a **wanker**. This rhyming slang, coined in the late 1980s like its synonym **Kuwaiti tanker**, highlights a contemporary concern (in this case the spectacular mid-1980s developments in the financial centres of the City of London) to revitalize a familiar epithet.

mereng *n South African* money.

merkin *n* **a** the female pubic area or female sex organs.
b an artificial vagina, used as a sex aid.

Merkin is a late medieval word for a wig designed to be worn on the female pubis, usually in order to disguise the effects of syphilis. It probably originates as an affectionate diminutive form of Mary. In the 1960s the word was better known in the USA than Britain. A well-known Californian **groupie** of the late 1960s adopted the pseudonym, Trixie Merkin, and Anthony Newley used the fictitious names 'Hieronymous Merkin' and 'Mercy Humppe' in the title of a semi-autobiographical fantasy film.

mersh *adj* commercial. A word used in the 1980s in fashionable youth circles and rock journalism, usually at least slightly pejoratively.
✧'*Mersh tendencies.*'

mestern *n South African* fashionable clothing. Recorded as an item of Sowetan slang in the *Cape Sunday Times*, 29 January 1995.

the Met *n British* the London Metropolitan Police force. The abbreviation by which they refer both to themselves and their district or area of jurisdiction (which covers most of central and suburban London but excludes the City).

meth *n* Methedrine (the trademark name for methamphetamine). A drug user's abbreviation for the powerful amphetamine-based stimulant (**speed**), which has been widely abused, particularly in the mid and late 1960s.

meths *n British* methylated spirits, as drunk for its intoxicating effects by alcoholics, vagrants, etc.

Mexican breakfast *n* a cigarette and a glass of water. A witticism originating in the USA, where the Mexican reference is supposed to evoke poverty and lack of sophistication or competence. There have been other, probably later, variations on this pattern, among which are **dingo's breakfast** and 'pelican's breakfast' (a glass of water).

Michael Jackson *n British* an amount or quantity under ten. The term was used by City of London financial traders in the 1990s and the reference was to the celebrity singer's supposed attachments to young children.

mick *n*
a an Irish person. This shortening of one of the most common Irish Christian names (along with Patrick or **Paddy**) was

first used in the USA and Australia to personify the Irishman or person of Irish descent. The usage had spread to Britain by the early years of this century.

b a Roman Catholic, by extension from the first sense. In both senses, the word is usually used unaffectionately or pejoratively.

Mickey (Bliss) *See* take the mickey.

mickey (finn) *n* a soporific or stupefying drug administered to a person without their knowledge. The word was first recorded in the USA in the early 20th century. It may derive from the name of a real individual or from a generic (probably seafarers') term for a cudgel or thug.

Mickey Mouse *adj* amateurish, unworthy of consideration or respect. A contemptuous description beloved of the business world in the 1970s and 1980s, Mickey Mouse has in fact been used in this way since before World War II when the phrase was applied for instance to childish or simplistic music or the bands which played it. It subsequently denoted any institution or venture which did not deserve to be taken seriously.

 ⍦*'It's strictly a Mickey Mouse operation they're running there.'*

middle leg *n* the penis. **Third leg** is an alternative form of the euphemism.

middy *n* **1** *Australian* a medium-sized beer glass.
2 *British* a toilet. A form of the archaic standard English 'midden'.

mighty greens *n South African* dagga. The term, referring to the colour of the herbal cannabis, was recorded as an item of Sowetan slang in the *Cape Sunday Times*, 29 January 1995.

militant *adj* an all-purpose term of approval. A usage originating in Jamaican **yardie** speech, which has now been taken up by adolescents in the US and Britain.

milko *n* a milkman. The Australian abbreviation is now in use in Britain, too, largely replacing the dated milkie.

milned-up *adj British* incarcerated. The term, from the jargon of prisoners, now often refers to temporary imprisonment in, e.g., an observation cell. In the form '*milned-in*' the phrase dates back

at least to the 1940s: Milne were the makers of door-locks used in prisons.

milquetoast, milktoast *n American* an un-macho, meek man, a **wimp**. Reminiscent of the food given to invalids, Milquetoast derives from the name of the fictional character Caspar Milquetoast, created by the American cartoonist H. T. Webster. Zsa Zsa Gabor used the term, to the puzzlement of many British viewers, when interviewed during her trial for assault in California in 1989.

 ⍦*'Asked why she resisted, she said: "I'm a Hungarian woman … not a milquetoast".'*
(Agency report on Zsa Zsa Gabor during trial).

minces *n pl British* eyes. From the cockney rhyming phrase, **mince pies**. The expression is still used today by working-class Londoners; it is now invariably heard in the shortened, one-word form.

 ⍦*'OK then, feast your minces on this!'*

minder *n* a bodyguard. A word which emerged from the obscurity of working-class and criminal slang into general usage in the early 1970s, mainly due to the fashion for quasi-realist crime drama on British television. This trend culminated in the later, gentler television series of the same name, starring Dennis Waterman and George Cole.

mindfuck *n* a disorienting experience, a manipulation of or interference with one's mind, a staggering idea or event. A **hippy** expression which has lingered on into post-hippy usage. It has been used approvingly to describe a particularly strong drug.

minge *n British* the female pudenda. A taboo word which was particularly prevalent in working-class speech of the 1950s. It originated in late 19th-century country dialect and may be from Romany.

 ⍦*'Minge is one of the assortment of words for the sexual bits that people think should keep him* [Chubby Brown] *off television because some viewers would not understand him anyway.'*
(*Independent*, 31 July 1989).

minger *n British* an unattractive person, particularly a promiscuous woman. A vogue term among adolescents in the later 1990s. The term comes from the verb 'to ming', originally a Scottish dialect synonym for stink.

mingy *adj British* a term of childish criticism or abuse which is a blend of mean and stingy with which it rhymes rather than an adaptation of the taboo word **minge**.

mink *n* 1 *American* **a** a woman, particularly a provocative, spirited and/or sexually attractive or active woman.
b the female sex organs, female sexuality.
↳'*We gotta get us some mink.*'
2 *Irish* a gypsy. The word is used by Romany travellers to refer to themselves, presumably evoking the fast-moving and alert animal and perhaps reflecting the irony that the mink is considered both valuable and vermin.

mint *adj British* excellent, fashionable. A vogue term of approbation used by adolescents in the 1990s. Synonyms are **fit** and **top**.

miraculous *adj Scottish* drunk. The humorous and ironic usage may derive from the word's resemblance to **ridiculous**, which is used in the same sense or, as Eric Partridge suggests, may be a mocking adaptation of a 19th-century euphemism such as '*(in) miraculous high spirits*'.

mish *n British* a journey or task. This abbreviated term for 'mission' was a popular term among adolescents in the later 1990s, and can probably be considered as a new coinage, although the same word was recorded in public school slang as early as 1913.

Miss Brown *n British* (a cup of) coffee. A code term from the slang of medical staff.
↳'*If ever your doctor is asked, "Would you like to see Miss Brown after this patient?" he or she is being offered a cup of coffee.*'
(*Sunday Times*, 6 October 1996).

Mister Nice-guy *n* a paragon of kindness, friendliness, tolerance, etc. This American expression has become international mainly in the form of the catchphrase '*No more Mr Nice-guy!*', expressing exasperation.

mither *vb British* to complain, nag, bother or prevaricate. A northern English dialect word which is now widely known due to its use by comics such as Jasper Carrot and in the soap opera *Coronation Street*. It is a variant form of 'moither' or 'moider', words first recorded in the 17th century and meaning both to babble and to baffle or bewilder.
↳'*His endless mithering about what he's going to do and how he's going to afford it.*'

mitt, mit *n* hand. A shortening of mitten, first used to mean glove (particularly in boxing and baseball) and later hand. This American slang term, popular among pugilists and underworld 'tough guys', crossed the Atlantic in the early 20th century. Mitten itself is from an old French word (*mitain(e)*) which was either a pet name for a cat or a corruption of the Latin *media*; half (-fingered).
↳'*He started with a cartwheel/finished in the splits/leaving Salome with his toupee in her mits.*'
(*Salome Maloney, the Sweetheart of the Ritz*, poem by John Cooper Clarke, 1980).

mo 1 *vb, n American* (to behave like) a homosexual, particularly in over-familiar or over-affectionate behaviour or inadvertent toucher, etc. A high-school and college shortening of **homo**.
2 *n Australian* a moustache.

the mob *n American* organized crime, the mafia. Mob was used to refer to gangster syndicates from the 1930s onwards, in underworld and police jargon and subsequently in journalese. The term is now standard. It has produced derivatives such as mobster and mobbed-up (involved with the mob).

moby *adj American* **a** huge.
↳'*A moby truck.*'
b overweight.
↳'*Getting/going moby.*'
Both terms derive from the fictional whale *Moby Dick* as a symbol of enormity. The first sense may be appreciative or neutral, the second usually pejorative.

mockers *n British* misfortune, curse, frustration. An expression which is used by schoolchildren as an exclamation, sometimes of defiance, more usually in an attempt to put off or jinx an opponent in sports or games. The word mocker or mockers, meaning jinx or curse, has been widespread in Australian and British working-class slang since around the 1920s. Mockers probably derives via the Yiddish *makeh* from Hebrew *makah*, meaning plague or wound, reinforced by the English words mock and muck (up). In adult usage the word normally appears in the phrase **put the mockers on**, meaning to ruin, thwart or jinx.

mockie *n American* a Jew. A pejorative term of uncertain etymology; it may be related to the British **mockers**, but this cannot be demonstrated conclusively.

mockney *n British* (a person) affecting a quasi-proletarian accent. The term arose in theatrical circles and was picked up by media in the late 1980s to refer to attempts by upper- and middle-class speakers to modify their accents in order to render them more stylish and 'streetwise'.

mod *n British* a member of a 1960s youth cult characterized by an obsessive interest in fashionable clothing, in the riding of motor-scooters and in listening and dancing to soul and ska music. The first mods, who began to gain prominence in 1962, referred to themselves as modernists, whence the more lasting epithet. The intention behind the word at this time was to distinguish these style-conscious, mainly working-class young people from the parochial or traditional appearance and attitudes then prevalent in Britain. The mods were influenced sartorially by Italy, France and the American 'Ivy League' look. Musical influences included American rhythm-and-blues and soul and Jamaican blue beat and ska, as well as native rock music represented by such groups as the Who and the Small Faces. The mod culture later expanded to encompass a much larger group of fashion-conscious young, in opposition to the **teddy boys**, **beats** and **rockers** of the time. So-called mod fashions were revived self-consciously in the late 1970s, one of the first attempts to find an 'acceptable' youth culture to replace **punk**.

↳'*When we found out that mods were just as conformist and reactionary as anyone else, we moved on from that phase too.*'
(Pete Townshend, *Rave* magazine, February 1966).

mode *adj British* affectedly fashionable, pretentious. A deliberate mispronunciation of **mod**, heard in the 1960s and used to express derision.

↳'*Oh yes, get a load of that gear, very mode!*'

MoFo *n American* a disguised form of **motherfucker**, used in conversation and in journalese in the 1990s.

moggy, moggie, mog *n British* a cat. Moggy was originally a term of endearment/familiarity for any animal. In northern English dialect it was used to designate mouse, calf or cat for example. The exact etymology of the word is uncertain; it may be from the Norse *magi*, meaning stomach or from the use of 'Maggie' as a name for a pet.

↳'*Can I just inform you that in South Lancashire a moggy is not a cat, it is a mouse or a small insect. When will the rest of the country learn this?*'
(Reader's letter to the *Independent*, 4 September 1992).

mojo *n* **a** a magic charm, spell or influence. A black American concept, popularized elsewhere by its use in blues and rhythm-and-blues records of the 1950s and early 1960s. The word's origin is thought to be West African, but no specific source has been identified.
b any un-named object; thingummy. The word can be used as a euphemism for anything, but is characteristically employed for sex organs or drugs.

moll *n* *Australian* a prostitute. Moll, a short form of Molly (itself a familiar version of Mary) has been used to denote a woman of 'easy virtue' since at least the time of *Moll Flanders* by Daniel Defoe, published in 1722. This sense has survived in Australia, where a band moll, for instance, is a **groupie**.
b *American* a woman, specifically a female companion. This sense of the word, familiar from its use in crime fiction as gun moll or gangster's moll, is now outdated.

mollo *adj Australian* drunk. The word is an abbreviation of the rhyming slang, **Molly the Monk**.

Molly the Monk *adj Australian* drunk. A piece of rhyming slang first recorded in the 1960s. The name appears to be a nonsense coinage.

momma *n* a female adherent to a Hell's Angels chapter. The momma is a sort of unattached member of the entourage; steady girlfriends are usually known as 'old ladies'.

↳'*We've got a few mommas so they get passed around.*'
(London Hell's Angel, *Oz* magazine, April 1969).

momser, momzer *n*

a a contemptible person, particularly a cadger or sponger.

b a cheeky, enterprising or self-willed person. The term, which is most often heard in American speech and applied to males, is the Hebrew word for 'bastard'.

mondo- *combining form American* an

all-purpose combining word which in Italian and Spanish means world (of) and in American English means 'a situation of... or 'a state of affairs characterized by...' The word is then followed by the defining word, usually with a mock-Latin 'o' ending as in mondo-sleazo, mondo-bozo or mondo-cheapo. This pattern derives from the 1963 Italian documentary film *Mondo Cane* (translated as 'A Dog's Life') which acquired cult status and inspired first intellectual wits and later college students and **Valley Girls** to coin similar phrases. (The affixing of pseudo-Italian or Hispanic endings is paralleled in the suffix '-ola'; an Anglo-Saxon equivalent is '-city'.)

mondo *adj British* excellent, ad-

mirable. The American combining form was adopted as a synonym for such vogue terms of approbation as **top** in around 1991.

✎ '*That new video-game is mega-mondo.*'

Monet *adj American* attractive at a

distance but not when seen at close quarters. This vogue pejorative term from the language of Californian high-school girls in the 1990s (it features in the 1994 US film *Clueless*) is applied to the appearance of persons and occasionally objects. It is based on the notion of Impressionist paintings.

✎ '*To her character Cher Silverstone would have therefore been a 'Monet' – which means OK from a distance but a mess close up.*'
(*Sunday Times* 'Style' magazine, 22 October 1995).

mong *n British* an idiot, clumsy fool. A

shortened form of 'mongol', itself a term (for those suffering from Down's syndrome) now considered offensive. Mong was a vogue term of abuse among London schoolchildren in the early 1970s.

mong'd, monged *adj British* in-

toxicated and incapacitated by drugs. The words, fashionable in 1990s **rave** culture, are based on 'mongol(oid)'. **Gurning** and **sledgied** are similar terms.

mongie, mongy *adj British* (of a

person) stupid, dull-witted, slow and clumsy. A 1970s derivation from **mong**, itself short for the pejorative mongol. Both spellings of the word are pronounced with a hard 'g'. Like the noun, the adjective was mainly heard among schoolchildren.

mongrel *n* **a** a despicable person.

This use of the standard word dates from the 1700s. It is now particularly prevalent in Australia and New Zealand.

✎ '*When they bring that mongrel back we'll make sure he gets what he deserves.*'
(*Home and Away*, Australian TV series, 1987).

b *Australian* a person of mixed race. A racist term of abuse since the 18th century.

moniker, monniker, monicker *n* a name, nickname or alias. No

definitive history of this word has been established. What is known is that it has existed in various spellings since the mid-19th century and that it was first used by tramps, vagrants and other 'marginals'. The three most likely derivations are from monarch, monk or monogram, but none of these is provable nor is there any clear connection with the (Saint's) name Monica.

✎ '*Christened by his father – a heavy duty John Wayne and Cowboy fan – with the name WAYNE WANG. Would this split-cultural, cartoon moniker destine the baby to grow up, leave Hong Kong and end up in California directing an all-American film ... and a violent one at that?*'
(*I-D* magazine, November 1987).

monkey *n British* **1** £500. A raffish

term in use among gamblers, street traders, **spivs**, etc. The origin of the term is obscure; it has been in use since at least the early 19th century and, confusingly, is also used to refer to sums of £50 or on occasion, £50,000.

✎ '*My client is not the kind of man to be satisfied with a mere monkey for his services.*'
('Arthur Daley' in *Minder*, British TV series, 1987).

2 an inferior or menial. Inspired by such images as the organ grinder and his monkey, the word is used to refer dismissively or contemptuously to underlings or errand-runners, etc.

✎ '*I'll deal with this myself; the monkeys downstairs can take care of the calculations.*'
(Recorded, accountant, London, 1986).

monkey run/walk/parade *n*
British a teenagers' promenade, a ritual
parade of courting couples or hopeful
'singles'. This dated term was used particularly before World War II to describe
both the location and the practice. The
expression continued to be used by older
speakers until the 1960s.

monkey's *n British* a damn. A word
invariably heard as part of the dismissive or defiant expressions 'don't
give/care a monkey's'. The term is an abbreviated form of an undefined but presumably offensive phrase such as monkey's **fart, fuck** or **balls**.
↳*'What do they* [the police] *think of us?
I haven't got a clue … and I couldn't
give a monkey's.'*
(Actor from TV series *The Bill, One Day
in the Life of Television*, November
1989).

monkey suit *n* a uniform, particularly one which is thought to demean the
wearer. Typically applied to bellboys,
doormen etc. dressed in absurd or confining outfits, the term derives from the
practice of dressing monkeys in such
clothing for carnival displays.

monniker *n* an alternative spelling of
moniker.

-monster *combining form*
a *American* a personification of a threat
or irritation as in *'rack-monster'* (exhaustion), *'pavement monster'* (bumps or
holes in a road surface).
b an epitome or outstanding example as
in *'beer monster'*, **shag-monster**.

monster! *exclamation British* excellent. A popular expression of enthusiasm
or admiration, mostly heard among middle-aged speakers in the 1990s.

monstering *n British* (a) chastisement, 'dressing-down' or harangue. A
word which occurs predominantly in middle-aged usage in a professional context
and among members of the armed forces.
↳*'In one confrontation, Montgomery, the
group's chief executive, delivered such
a "Hitlerian monstering" to a senior
executive that she was reduced to
tears.'*
(*Sunday Times*, 30 March 1995).

Montezuma's revenge *n* diarrhoea. Heard all over the English-speaking world, this jocular expression is the
American equivalent of **Delhi belly** or

gyppy tummy. In Mexico Montezuma
(spelled Moctezuma locally and by many
academics), the 16th-century Aztec emperor, is a national hero. Facetious references such as this are not appreciated.
However, American Presidents Carter and
Reagan both referred to this condition in
the presence of Mexican dignitaries during their terms of office.

monty *See* the **full monty**.

moo *n British* a woman, particularly a
stupid or unpleasant woman. It has been
claimed that the comedy script-writer
Johnny Speight invented this abusive
term for his 1960s television series *Till
Death do us Part* to avoid the BBC ban, in
force at that time, on the use of the word
cow. In fact the word already existed in
London working-class vocabulary from
at least the 1950s.

mooch *vb*
a to hang around, linger aimlessly, idle.
b to 'sponge', cadge, take advantage of
(one's friends). The word has been in use
since the 19th century in both senses and
has formed part of the lexicons of tramps,
criminals, **beatniks** and the fashionable
young of the 1980s in both Britain and the
USA. Its origin is uncertain.

moody *n British*
a a sulk, fit of bad temper or sullenness.
A popular working-class expression of
the late 1970s, usually in the form 'throw
a moody'. Moody was a popular all-purpose cockney term for negative, fake or
false in the earlier 20th century and
'doing a moody' used to mean acting sus-
piciously. Later, a moody signified a sim-
ulated fight or quarrel.
b a lie. A word which usually occurs in
criminal or police usage, sometimes in
the form *'old moody'*.
↳*'Listen we don't need old moody, give
us the names.'*

moody *adj British* illegal, counterfeit,
of dubious value, quality or provenance.
A London working-class term which
began from the late 1980s to spread into
fashionable youth parlance.
↳*'They accused him of selling moody
gear off his stall in the market.'*

mooey *adj British* rotten. A word used
by market traders, greengrocers and others in the 1980s to describe over-ripe fruit
and vegetables. It is presumably a blend
of mushy and gooey.

mook *n American* a term of abuse of uncertain meaning and unknown origin. It may be a variant form of **mooch** or even **mug**.

↳ *'It's very nasty to call a person a honky mook.'*
(Steve Martin, *All of Me*, US film, 1984).

moolah, moola *n* money. A humorous word imported into Britain from the USA before World War II. It is an invented term, probably in imitation of Amerindian, African or other foreign languages as is the more recent British synonym, **womba**. Like most slang terms for money, moolah underwent something of a revival in the late 1980s.

↳ *'Many congressmen arrive in Washington expecting to get rich – if not quick, at least before they leave. The art is in finding ways to get the moolah without contravening the various laws and rules of ethics.'*
(*Observer*, 12 June 1989).

moon *vb* to exhibit the buttocks publically, typically from the window of a moving car. A term and practice popular with American teenagers since the 1950s. It has been a common practice among young male students in Britain from at least the late 1970s. (Moon refers to the white globes on display.)

↳ *'And it's hard not to warm to Panic's bare-faced nerve – mooning in discos, lifting a wallet and rifling through it insolently in full view of the impotent owner.'*
(*Independent*, 12 January 1988).

moonrock *n American* a mixture of **crack** and heroin.

moose *n* an ugly or unattractive female. A vogue term among British adolescents in the later 1990s.

moreish, morish *adj British* appetizing, tempting. This predominantly middle-class colloquialism, applied to anything edible, is a pun on moorish (as in architecture), dating surprisingly from the 18th century.

moriarty *n British* a party. A fairly rare item of rhyming slang employing the name of the arch enemy of Sherlock Holmes, later reinvented as a dastardly villain in the BBC radio comedy show *The Goons* in the 1950s, from when this usage dates.

mortal, mortalled *adj Scottish* drunk. The expression *'mortal* (i.e., hopelessly or dangerously) *drunk'* was in use from the early 19th century.

moshing *n British* dancing in a packed scrimmage to heavy metal, **hardcore** or any other fast, loud rock music. This activity, which is more a form of energetic communal writhing than dancing, was adopted by fans of hard rock during the late 1980s as a successor to **slam dancing**, **headbanging** or the characteristic playing of imaginary guitars ('air guitar'). Often, part of the experience is for members of the audience to climb on to the stage then hurl themselves bodily into the crush at the front, a practice known as 'stage-diving'. The word mosh is an invention influenced by such words as jostle, mash, mass, squash, crush and thrust.

moss-back *n American* an elderly person. The term is often applied affectionately in family slang to an older relative. A synonym is **frost-top**.

the most *n* something superlative, the very best. A well-known item from the vocabulary of **hipsters**, **beatniks**, etc. of the 1950s. (A later jocular coinage by analogy is **the least**.)

mother *n American* **1** an abbreviated and euphemistic version of **motherfucker**. This version, more commonly than the full form, is often used appreciatively rather than pejoratively. In imitation of black or Southern pronunciation it is sometimes spelled **muthah**. The word is probably used to refer to objects and animals as often as humans.

↳ *'Man, that was some big mother.'*
2 a male homosexual, particularly a man in a dominant, protective or influential relation to younger males.

motherfucker *n American*
a a despicable person. The most common term of strong abuse in the American vocabulary. (Euphemistic forms such as mother-raper, mother-jumper or just **mother** are sometimes substituted.) The expression, naming the ultimate in degeneracy, originated among poor blacks.

↳ *'Oedipus was a motherfucker.'*
(Graffito, Euston station, London, 1972).
b an awesome or appalling thing, situation, etc.

↳ *'One motherfucker of a mess.'*

mother's ruin *n* gin. A late 19th-century nickname which refers to the widespread effects of cheap gin on the working class (of both sexes); to the later supposed predilection of women for the drink; and to its long-lived reputation as an abortifacient.

motor *n British* a car. A word which has moved between working-class and middle-class colloquial speech, becoming prevalent since the early 1970s in working-class circles. It is characteristic of London speech, usually pronounced 'mo'or', that is, with a glottal stop in place of the 't'.

↳'*Reggie Kray decided that Dickson should have a new motor and so took him to a car showroom in Walthamstow.*'
(*Evening Standard*, 9 May 1988).

motoring *n British* making good progress, performing well. A driver's expression of the 1970s (meaning moving at speed) which has become generalized in the 1980s to mean roughly the same as the American **cooking**.

↳'*OK, great, now we're motoring!*'

motormouth *n American* a person who talks excessively, a 'fast-talker'. A popular term from the mid-1970s, it originated in black ghetto slang. The word was later applied to amphetamine users, disc jockeys, comics and **rap** artists.

mott *n British* the female sex organs. A vulgarism still widely used (by men) in the 1960s, but now rare. It is from the French *motte*, meaning mound, used by 19th-century pornographers among others.

motzer, motza *n* (an instance of) good fortune, surprising luck. The words heard in British and Australian speech, are versions of the Yiddish name for an outsize cookie, itself related to *mazel*: good luck.

mousetrap *n British* a Japanese person. An item of cockney rhyming slang (for 'Jap') which probably originated during World War II, but is still heard, for instance, among City financial traders in London.

mouth-breather *n* a primitive, brutish person. The phrase is used contemptuously for those considered thuggish and/or moronic, evoking the image of a shambling, open-mouthed, slack-jawed creature, invariably male.

mouth down *vb American* to keep quiet, shut up.

mouthpiece *n* a lawyer, specifically one's defence counsel or legal representative. A term used, particularly by the underworld, since the mid-19th century. The word is sometimes extended to refer to any spokesperson.

↳'*A deliberate slip of the tongue gets a laugh. A sergeant begins a question: "When a defendant has got a mouthpiece – sorry, I mean solicitor...".*'
(*Inside the British Police*, Simon Holdaway, 1983).

mouthy *adj British* talkative, boastful or verbose. A pejorative working-class term.

moxie *n American* spirit, vim, courage, enterprise. Moxie was the trade name of a soft drink on sale in the USA in the 19th century (probably based on a local Amerindian place name). The drinks company used the advertising slogan: '*What this country needs is plenty of Moxie!*'

Mozart *adj Australian* drunk. The word is one half of the rhyming-slang phrase 'Mozart and Liszt': **pissed**. The British equivalent is **Brahms (and Liszt)**.

mozzer, mozza *n* luck, good fortune. This seems to be the main surviving variant among many words (mozz, mozzle, mozzy) deriving from the Yiddish *mazel*: a cookie blessing the consumer with good luck. The words have existed in British working-class speech since at least the 1880s and later became part of Australian usage, usually in the forms **motzer** or **motza**.

↳'*That was a bit of mozzer – all six at one stall.*'
(Recorded, Newbury, 1989).

mozzie, mozzy *n* a mosquito. A short form of the word in use in Britain and Australia.

Mr/Mister Sausage *n* the penis. An adults' imitation nursery-word of the sort which has enjoyed a vogue since the mid-1980s, particularly in middle-class British usage. The playwright Mike Leigh used the term in dialogue ascribed to a **yuppie** couple in his 1988 feature film, *High Hopes*.

Mr/Mister Whippy *n British* flagellation. A code term from the argot and repertoire of prostitutes. The light hearted euphemism is from the name of a brand of ice cream displayed on vans.

MTF *n British* a sexually importunate male. The initials stand for 'must touch flesh'. An ephemeral early 1980s **Sloane Ranger** term of feminine disapproval.

muckamuck, (high) mucky-muck *n American* a person in authority or a VIP, especially a self-important one. The term originated in the 19th century and apparently derives from an Amerindian phrase meaning plenty-to-eat.

⍦'*Fuck you. It* [a concealed gun]*'s in Mr Chancellor's name. He got it okayed by the muckamucks.*'
(Jonathan Kellerman, *Over the Edge*, 1987).

mucker *n* a friend, mate, pal. The term is said to have originated in armed-service usage as a longer expression; 'mucking-in pal' or 'mucking-in spud' soon shortened to mucker. The word survives mainly in the speech of hearty males.

⍦'*There you are, Keith, me old mucker.*'

mudsucker *n American* an unpleasant or despicable person. A term of abuse coined to echo the syllables of the more offensive **motherfucker**.

muff *n* the female sex organs and/or the female pubic hair. This euphemistic use of the standard word for an enveloping hand- or ear-warmer of fur (deriving ultimately from the mediaeval Latin for mitten, *muffula*) originated in the 17th century and is still current, although less common than in the 1950s and early 1960s.

muff-diving *n* cunnilingus. A jocular coinage based on the long established use of **muff** to denote the female genitals.

muffin *n* the female genitals. An elaboration on the older muff, used singularly or generically. The term is heard in Britain and Australia. In the USA the plural form is occasionally used to denote breasts.

muffins *n pl American* the female breasts. **Baps** are a British synonym.

mug *n* 1 face. The word has had this meaning since the early 1700s; it derived from the practice of making china drinking-mugs decorated with grotesque human faces.

2 a fool, dupe. This use of the word was inspired by the image of the victim as an open-mouthed receptacle.

muggins *n British* a victim, dupe or 'loser', especially when referring to oneself. The word is an embellishment of **mug** (and is also an authentic, if comic-sounding, surname). It is now so common as to be an innocent colloquialism rather than true slang.

muggy *adj British* stupid, naïve. An adjectival form of the colloquial 'mug', which was heard in working-class speech from the 1960s.

⍦'*These blokes were just muggy bone-heads.*'

mug (someone) off *vb British* to make a fool of, take advantage of. An item of London working-class speech dating from the 1950s.

⍦'*She's taken the mickey and mugged me right off.*'
(Gangster Ronnie Kray, quoted in the *Sun*, 5 October 1993).

mugwump *n American* an important, powerful person. This now rather dated word is invariably used facetiously or pejoratively and is especially applied to someone who has power and influence but is a maverick or unreliable. It is from the Algonquin Indian *mugquamp*, a chief.

mule *n* a carrier of illicit drugs across frontiers and/or through customs, a transporter of contraband; someone hired to do this rather than the owner of the drugs. The term was first used by smugglers, later by law enforcers.

⍦'*He used to go over and buy the stuff, then pack it, but it was always brought in by mules.*'
(Recorded, London, 1989).

mulga *n Australian* an unpleasant situation, experience etc. Mulga is a native Australian synonym for acacia and originally denoted an inhospitable or deserted region of bush. '*Mulga-madness*' is an archaic term for the mental disorientation experienced by outbackers.

mulled *adj British* drunk. An inoffensive term heard predominantly outside the London area.

mullered *adj British* intoxicated by drink or drugs. A popular term among adolescents in the 1990s, it is an elaboration of the earlier **mulled**.

mum *n British* a homely female. The term is one of a set of (mainly unflattering) categorizations applied by young males such as City of London financial traders to female colleagues in the 1990s. Others include **Nora**, **oof**, **dragon**. A mum is not necessarily motherly, but benevolent and sexually irrelevant. *See also* **Mumsy**.

mumblefucker *n British* an irritatingly clumsy, inept or fastidious person. A term heard in the early 1970s. There have been other invented terms, with a similar lack of meaning, playing on the comical overtones of the syllables employed; **fucknuckle** is an example.

mummerset *n British* the (often grotesque and usually inaccurate) imitation of rustic West-Country speech used by actors. The theatrical term is a blend of mumble and Somerset.

↳ '*And what about that Mummerset accent? Even them Archers-folk don't speak like that no more.*'
(Charles Catchpole, *News of the World*, 26 June 1988).

mumping *adj British* scrounging, soliciting favours, begging. A word dating from the 17th century which survives in police and underworld argot. It used to refer to the activities of beggars and vagabonds; it is now often applied to the reciprocal favours encouraged by police officers in contact with local people. The word is descended from the Dutch *mompen*, to cheat.

mumsy *adj British* the older generation's colloquialism to describe a woman who is unglamorous and 'motherly' has become a fashionable categorization for a younger generation for whom the maternal aspect is probably less important than the suggestion of fussiness, unfashionable appearance, asexuality, etc.

munch *n British* food. A recent usage posted on the Internet by *Bodge World* in February 1997.

(the) munchies *n* hunger, especially a craving for food brought on by the lowering of blood-sugar levels that is a side-effect of smoking cannabis. The word was a children's synonym for snacks which was adopted by **hippy**-era smokers of hashish and marihuana.

↳ '*Those smug, stupid hippies, who thought it so cool to be comatose called that post-smoke famished feeling "the munchies", and for once they were right.*'
(*Platinum Logic*, Tony Parsons, 1981).

munchkin *n* a cute small child, dwarf, underling. An American expression taken from the name of the little people in the musical, *The Wizard of Oz*; the word is used affectionately or condescendingly. (A low-level munchkin is an employee near or at the bottom of a hierarchy.)

mung *n* dirt, muck. A term that encompasses everything filthy or distasteful, used particularly by teenagers or students since the late 1970s.

munt *n South African* a black person. A highly offensive term used by white racists. The word is Afrikaans slang deriving from the Bantu *umuntu*, a person.

muppet *n British* a retarded, incapacitated or grotesque person. A word usually used with none of the affection or humour that its innocent source (the American TV puppet show of the 1970s) might suggest. The term has been applied to hospital inmates, mentally deranged prisoners or simply to unattractive teenagers by their peers.

murphies *n pl American* the female breasts. The word 'murphy' is adapted from its use (since the 19th century) as a nickname for potato.

murphy, the murphy *n* **1** *British* a potato. The Irish surname has been used as a joky synonym since the early 19th century.
2 the murphy *American* a confidence trick whereby valuables lodged for safekeeping are stolen or substituted by worthless goods.

murphy *vb American* to subject (someone) to **the murphy** (a term denoting various forms of a simple confidence trick).

mush, moosh *n British* **1** face. A word which has been in use since the 19th century, when it often referred specifically to the mouth. Mush is nearly always used in connection with fisticuffs and may have originated as pugilists' slang. The precise etymology of the word is uncertain, but it has obvious connotations of softness and mastication.
2 a an all-purpose term of address to a stranger (invariably used by men to other men). A working-class, mainly London,

usage which was common in the 1950s and 1960s but is now rarely used. The word is not particularly friendly and is quite often used provocatively. It comes from the Romany word for man, *moosh*.

ᕦ'*Are you asking for a punch up the faghole, mush?*'
(*Hancock's Half Hour*, BBC TV comedy, 6 November 1959).

b a man, unnamed person. The derivation for this usage is as for the previous sense. The word has rarely been used thus (rather than as a term of address) since the 1950s.

musical veg *n British* baked beans. The humorous term, referring to flatulence, is in use in the armed forces and among schoolchildren.

musha, musher *n British* an owner of a new taxi. In the jargon of cabbies this designation refers to a driver in debt for the cost of his new vehicle; he will have to 'mush' like the driver of a sleigh team in order to earn back the sum in question. The nickname was recorded in the London *Evening Standard*, 22 April 1996.

mushroom *n* an innocent bystander caught in the crossfire of a gunfight. This term, from the jargon of the Jamaican **yardie** 'Shower Posse', was reported in the *Sunday Times*, 14 November 1993.

muso *n* **a** a musician, player of rock music with real technical expertise.
b a rock or progressive music fan who displays a pedantic or obsessive interest in his or her favourite music and/or musicians. The term, coined by musicians and used by journalists and fans, is sometimes pejorative (implying that the technical expertise does not compensate for or hide a basic lack of something to express) but can also be applied neutrally or appreciatively.

ᕦ'*Melody Maker was at last shaking off the "muso" tag that it had been lumbered with during the punk period.*'
(*Independent*, 1 December 1989).

mutant *n* a clumsy, foolish or otherwise unpopular individual. A term used by adolescents to refer to unpopular or despised fellow-students or other contemporaries. The same word is used with the opposite connotations in the form **mutie**.

muthah *n* an alternative spelling of **mother** (in its slang or euphemistic

sense), particularly used by fans of heavy-metal music to refer appreciatively to each other or their heroes.

mutie *n British* a daring exponent, devotee. A word used by skateboarders and some surfers and rock-music fans to refer to themselves and their fellows. The word is a diminutive form of **mutant** which itself is usually employed with negative connotations. Mutant has been used to evoke a science-fiction sense of extremism, exoticism and unpredictability when referring to designs, insignia or performance in the subcultures in question.

mutton, Mutt 'n' Jeff *adj British* deaf. Rhyming slang, from the cartoon figures created by Bud Fischer, which were popular before World War II. The slang expression has been heard in London from the late 1940s to the present day. It was spread further afield by its use by the character of Albert in the popular 1960s television comedy series *Steptoe and Son*.

ᕦ'*I'm sorry, love, you'll have to speak up. I'm a bit mutton in my old age.*'
(Recorded, London, 1988).

mutton dagger *n* the penis. A joky euphemism on the lines of **pork sword** and **beef bayonet**.

muttonhead *n* a variation of **meathead**.

my bad! *exclamation American See* **bad**.

mystery *n British* a runaway person, vunerable minor. A term from the language of pimps, paedophiles, the homeless and police, referring to someone of uncertain origin or identity.

mystery bags *n pl Australian* sausages. The term is influenced by the name of a children's lucky dip sweet packet and is both a rhyming slang term for **snags** (another slang term for sausages) and an ironical comment on the dubious contents of some sausages. Often thought to be a native Australian coinage, mystery bags is another example of British slang of the 19th century which seems to have died out in the country of origin but has survived among the emigrant population; it was recorded in 1889 in this form; previously occurring simply as 'mystery' or 'bag of mystery'.

ᕦ'*What's for dinner?*'
'*Mystery bags ... snags ... sausages.*'
(*Razorback*, Australian film, 1984).

n...

nabe *n American*
a neighbourhood.

✎'*A new guy in the nabe.*'

b neighbour.

✎'*The nabes are acting up again.*' A shortening of the sort popularized by *Variety* magazine and perpetuated in teenage speech. (Merch, mersh and burbs are other examples of this trend which enjoyed a particular vogue in 1988 and 1989.)

nack *vb British See* **knack**.

nadgered *adj British* a middle-class alternative of **knackered** in all its senses.

✎'*By the time I got home I was feeling pretty nadgered.*'
(Recorded, 15-year-old boy, Horsham, England, October 1995).

nadgers, the nadgers *n pl British* **1 the nadgers** signified a state of nervous agitation, irritation, distress or unhealthiness in such phrases as '*he's got the nadgers*' or '*it gives me the nadgers*'. The word could also be used to describe a curse or jinx in the same way as **mockers**. This humorous nonsense term of the 1950s (popularized in broadcast comedies such as *Hancock's Half Hour*) is now virtually obsolete.

2 testicles. The word was probably used in this sense merely due to the resemblance to **knackers**. It has not been widely used since the 1960s.

✎'*A kick in the nadgers.*'

nads *n pl American* testicles. An abbreviated form of gonads used jocularly by teenagers in the 1980s.

naff *adj* tasteless, inferior, shoddy and unappealing. Naff had existed in working-class slang for at least 40 years by the time it became a vogue word in the later 1970s. It had been used in the jargon of prostitutes to mean nothing or negligible. In the theatrical, criminal and street-trading milieus it meant third-rate or poor quality. The word's sudden popularity occurred probably because it was seized upon by TV scriptwriters (particularly Dick Clement and Ian La Frenais in the comedy series *Porridge*) as an acceptable euphemism for **fuck** in such forms as 'naff-all' (meaning **fuck-all**), **naffing** and **naff off**. Naff's ultimate origin, which seems to be 19th century, is nonetheless obscure. It has been claimed that it is a backslang form of **fan(ny)** (in the sense of female sex organs) or an acronym or alteration of a phrase involving the word **fuck** (such as 'not a fucking fart' or similar). Neither etymology is attested (or particularly convincing), and the similarity to NAAFI is probably coincidental.

✎'*To be naff is to be unstylish, whatever that may mean.*'
(*The Complete Naff Guide*, Bryson *et al.*, 1983).

✎'*Lancing is a healthy, wealthy school. So why do the boys look so naff? The school photo could be an advert for Top Man's summer collection.*'
(*Tatler*, March 1987).

naffing *adj British* an all-purpose intensifying adjective used as a euphemism for **fucking**.

naff off *vb British* to leave, go away. The expression is usually in the form of a dismissive exclamation or instruction synonymous with **fuck off**. First used in the TV series *Porridge* in the mid-1970s, the phrase was given great prominence in 1982 when Princess Anne told reporters who were pestering her to naff off.

nag *n* a horse. The well-known term is used particularly by horse-racing enthusiasts. It was first recorded in 1400 when it was paralleled by the Dutch *negge*, meaning a small horse.

nail (someone) *vb* to identify, catch, punish or defeat (or any combination of these). This common term, which can now also by extension (and by analogy with **screw**) refer to the sexual conquest of a woman by a male, has been heard since at least the 18th century.

nailed-up *adj British* arrested, imprisoned. An item of police and underworld slang.

✎'*I used to shift cars, but I'm telling you that there's more money and less*

hassle in this. I don't know anyone
who's been nailed-up for shifting
spares.'
(Car thief, quoted in the *AA Magazine*,
1995).

namby *n British* **1** a weak, cowardly
person, a **wimp**. A schoolchildren's word
of the late 1980s which is a shortening of
the standard English adjective 'namby-
pamby'.

٭*'Him? He's a fucking namby.'*
(Recorded, teenage schoolgirl, London,
1988).

2 a committed opponent of a controversial environmental policy (such as nuclear power). This journalistic quasi-
acronym of 'not in anyone's backyard'
was coined in imitation of the more common **nimby** ('not in *my* backyard') in the
USA in the mid-1980s.

nana *n British* a silly fool. This word
was very popular among children from
the 1950s to the early 1970s and is still
sometimes revived; adults, too, used the
term in the late 1950s and early 1960s. It
is a nursery shortening of banana, a
meaning it still retains in post-colonial
nurseries in areas such as India and the
Caribbean.

nanana *n South African* a small car.
Recorded as an item of Sowetan slang in
the *Cape Sunday Times*, 29 January 1995.

nanny (goat) *n British* a quote. An
item of journalistic rhyming slang of the
1990s.

nancy boy, nance *n British* an
effeminate man, a male homosexual. This
term seems to have originated in the late
19th century, when the name Nancy, a
diminutive form of Ann or Agnes, was applied indiscriminately to women as a term
of affection and familiarity. The echoes
of 'nice' and 'mince' in the rather prissy
sound of the word probably went toward
reinforcing its derogatory use for men.
There was a vogue in the East End of
London in the 1930s for male street-
dancers in women's clothing who were
known as nancy boys. The phrase was
widespread in all social classes throughout Britain in the 1950s and 1960s, but is
now somewhat dated.

٭*'See the nancy boys do their dance.'*
(Poster in satirical illustration of decadent England, *Private Eye* magazine,
1963).

nanty, nanti, nants *adj British*

no, none, nothing. The word was in use in
London working-class and theatrical
slang from the early 19th century until
the 1960s; this is an example of **parlyaree**, the Italian-inspired patois of actors,
showmen and circus workers. Nanty originates in the Italian *niente*, meaning nothing. The last recorded instance of its use
was in the radio comedy *Round the Horne*,
in which the effeminate characters Julian and Sandy referred to Kenneth
Horne's having *nanty* **riah** (no hair).

nappy-valley *n Australian* a suburban housing development populated
mainly by young families. It is a pun on
'Happy Valley', a name often chosen, at
least in fiction, for such places.

narc, narco *n American* a narcotics
investigator or member of a police drug-
squad. The word is particularly heard
among drug users referring to undercover agents. It may be influenced by, but
is not directly related to, the British **nark**.

nards *n pl American* testicles. A distorted pronunciation of **nads**, itself an abbreviation of gonads. The word is heard
among pubescent and adolescent males.

narg *n British* a tediously or offensively
hard-working and/or socially inept individual. The term was first recorded as
part of Oxbridge student slang in the
1960s and is invariably applied to males
who are typically unattractive and badly
dressed. It may derive from an imitation
of the drawling nasal speech seen as typical of such students.

nark *vb British* **1** to inform on, betray.
From the noun, **nark**.

2 to stop, or to keep quiet. This cockney
usage invariably occurred in the command '*nark it!*'.

3 to annoy or affront, **needle**. This expression, which was particularly popular
in the 1950s and which is also heard in
Australia, is derived ultimately from the
Romany word *nak*, meaning nose. Nark in
its modern sense is semantically related
to such expressions as '*to have one's nose
put out of joint*', '*to get up one's nose*', or
'*poke one's nose in*'. It is often heard in
the form of its past participle, **narked**,
meaning annoyed or affronted.

٭*'The trouble is, many people today
they won't do anything. I got a very
poor opinion of my fellow creatures, a
very poor opinion. So I nark them
whenever I can. I like narking people.'*

(82-year-old Ted Bosley, quoted in the *Independent*, 18 May 1989).

nark *n British*

a an informer. The expression originated in the 19th century as 'copper's nark', meaning a police spy or **grass**, nark being an alteration of the Romany (gypsy) word *nak*, nose.

b a spoilsport, teacher's pet, nuisance or toady. This more generalized usage, deriving from the previous sense, was fairly widespread in the 1950s in working-class circles and is still heard among schoolchildren.

c a policeman. In underworld, prison and tramp's jargon.

narked *adj British* irritated, annoyed,
affronted. For the derivation of the word see the verb **nark**.

narky *adj British* irritable, upset. A
working-class term used principally in the north of England.

↳'*She's been a bit narky all morning.*'

↳'*He's feeling narky.*'

narly *adj American* an alternative
spelling of **gnarly**.

narr *exclamation British* a synonym
for or alteration of 'no'. The fashionable usage was posted on the Internet in February 1997 by *Bodge World*.

nasties *n pl British* nursery slang for
(old and dirty) underwear or swimming trunks. A narrowing of a general notion of 'offensive objects'.

↳'*Don't forget to pack some nasties if we're going anywhere near a beach.*'
(Recorded, social worker, London, 1986).

nasty *n* 1 a sex organ, genitals. A child-
ish word used humorously by adults in phrases such as '*as dry as a nun's nasty*': thirsty.

2 a sexual act. A synonym of the coy or euphemistic **naughty**.

natch *adv* naturally. A shortening used
in **hip** talk.

nathan *n American* nothing. The
name is substituted in black street slang and campus usage.

natty *adj* impressive, admirable, **cool**.
A vogue term in Jamaican youth patois, particularly in the phrase '*natty dread*', but usable as an all-purpose term of approval. It derives from a shortening of

'natural', referring in Rastafarian terms to someone following the laws of God and nature, perhaps influenced by the standard English adjective meaning trim or smartly-dressed (which itself is probably a variation of neat).

naughty *n* an illicit act, usually re-
ferring to sex and typically occurring in phrases such as '*have a (quick) naughty*'. The coy expression, which sometimes also refers to a crime, is heard in both British and Australian speech.

naughty *adj British*

a criminal, corrupt. A typical piece of understatement from the argot of police and the underworld. This tendency is characteristic of London working-class speech, (**spanking**, meaning a (severe) beating-up, would be another instance).

b impressive, daring. A fashionable usage in working-class speech, generally among adults, in the late 1980s; the word is used to indicate admiration or approval as in '*That's a well-naughty looking bird*'.

nause *n British*

a a nauseatingly unpleasant person. A middle-class term popular in the mid-1960s and now very rarely heard. It has been suggested that this word is in fact a variation of **Noah's**, short for 'Noah's Ark', 1950s underworld rhyming slang for **nark**. As nauseate and nauseous were both fashionable terms in middle-class British and American use in the early 1960s, they would seem more likely origins.

↳'*She was going out with a policeman; God, he was a real nause.*'
(Recorded, student teacher, London, 1965).

b a nuisance, unpleasant situation or task. Nauseate had a (now obsolete) slang sense of bother, irritate or infuriate in the 1950s, whence this usage. The concept is rendered in modern speech by the colloquial expression to **get up one's nose**.

nause (someone) out *vb* to dis-
gust, nauseate. The term is used by adolescents on both sides of the Atlantic, although often in Britain minus the 'out' component.

nauticals *n pl British* haemorrhoids,
piles. An item of jocular rhyming slang (on 'nautical miles') used in *Viz* comic in the 1990s.

↳'*Ooh, me nauticals!*'

navvy *n British* a manual labourer, unskilled construction worker or road digger. Navvy is a shortening of navigator, which was a nickname given to open-air construction workers engaged in building roads, canals and railways in the late 18th and early 19th centuries. Canals in England were often built by navigation companies, hence the nickname of their employees.

neat *adj American* an all-purpose term of approval which became popular among teenagers in the mid-1960s and has survived. It is often ridiculed by sophisticates as evidence of naïve or gushing enthusiasm. The word occurred with this sense in the slang of jazz musicians, the 'smart set' and adolescents as long ago as the early 1920s.

♣*'You're a neat girl.'*
'So are you – I mean ... you're a neat guy.'
(*Blue Velvet*, US film, 1986).

nebbish, nebesh, nebech *n* a fool, an ineffectual, clumsy or pathetic person. The word entered English speech from Yiddish in which one of its meanings is a pitiful nonentity or 'loser'. The ultimate origin of the word is the Czech adjective *nebohy*, meaning unhappy, unfortunate or diseased.

♣*'A nebech is more to be pitied than a shlemiel. You feel sorry for a nebech; you can dislike a shlemiel.'*
(*The Joys of Yiddish*, Leo Rosten, 1970).

neck *n* cheek, impudence, daring, **chutzpah**. This sense of the word is at least 100 years old, originating in rustic northern English speech. It survives principally in the form **brass neck**, a synonym for bare-faced cheek.

♣*'I tell you, she's got plenty of neck: she walked out* [on her husband] *and then told him to move out.'*
(Recorded, housewife, London, 1988).

neck *vb* 1 to kiss, embrace and pet. An American euphemism dating from the early years of the century.
2 *British* to drink, ingest. The raffish verb, probably a back-formation from the drinkers' catchphrase-injunction '*Get this down your neck!*', became fashionable from the early 1990s. It was adopted by members of the **acid-house** and **rave** subcultures who referred to '*necking E's*' (swallowing tablets of **Ecstasy**).

neck-oil *n* alcohol. Drink thought of as a physical and social lubricant by (usually hearty) drinkers.

ned *n Scottish* a hooligan. The word has been in use since the 1960s: it may be related to **ted(dy) boy**.

neddy *n British* a horse, **gee-gee**. A children's pet name appropriated by adults, particularly in the context of betting and horse-racing.

need it! *exclamation British* an all-purpose cry of provocation, defiance, solidarity, used by schoolchildren in the 1970s.

the needle *n* 1 *British* irritation, resentment, provocation. The word has been used in expressions such as '*take the needle*' (take offence), '*give someone the needle*' and **get the (dead) needle** since the late 19th century. 2 *See* **on the needle**.

needle-dick *n* (someone with) a small penis. This expression (usually heard in the USA) is also sometimes used as a non-specific term of abuse.

nellie, nelly *n British* 1 an ineffectual, weak, effete or sentimental person. Often given more emphasis by phrases like '*big soft nellie*' or '*great wet nellie*'. Nellie was used until the late 1940s in the USA and Britain as a humorous or contemptuous appellation for a male homosexual.
2 in **not on your nellie**, the word was originally Nelly Duff, an invented name providing a rhyme for **puff** in the sense of breath, hence life.

nellie, nelly *adj American* effeminate. The adjective, based on the earlier noun form, has become fairly widespread in the late 1990s.

nerd *n* a gormless, vacuous, tedious and/or ineffectual person. Since the later 1970s this has been a vogue term, particularly among adolescents. It was coined in the USA in the late 1960s or early 1970s by members of surfing and hot-rodding cliques to refer to outsiders considered feeble or conformist. The word was then taken up on student campuses and by **hippies**. (An underground cartoon strip of the early 1970s portrayed nerds as a sub-species of suburban dullards.) The word nerd itself (**nurd** was an earlier alternative spelling) is of uncertain origin, but may be influenced by **turd**.

✎ *'And the jock shall dwell with the nerd and the cheerleader lie down with the wimp and there will be peace upon the campus.'*
(*Observer*, 29 May 1988).

✎ *'Simon Templar is a nerd. What sensible human being, on the run from the police, continues to drive around at 100 mph in a car bearing his initials (ST 1) on the registration plate?'*
(TV review by Jaci Stephen, *Evening Standard*, 4 September 1989).

✎ *'"Being a nerd is chic these days," proclaimed the tediously Teutonic Britta Hoffner from Frankfurt, Germany. "I am a nerd and proud of it."'*
(*Sunday Express*, 27 February 1994).

nerdling *n British* performing devious financial manoeuvres, 'massaging the figures'. The word was used by City financial traders in London in the 1990s. It is a technical term from the game of Tiddlywinks, in which it means to execute a clever move that confounds one's opponents.

nerd pack *n*

a a set of coloured pens (normally held together with an elastic band and worn ostentatiously in a breast pocket). The item in question is held to characterize an eager but vacuous office employee. This item of business slang was quoted in the column 'Business Buzzwords' in *International Management Magazine*, March 1989.

b the same term was also used in the USA by high-school and college students to describe a plastic shield worn on a shirt breastpocket to prevent ink stains from pens.

nerdy *adj* gormless, ineffectual, characteristic of a **nerd**. The adjective postdates the noun.

✎ *'He favoured dark business suits, dark ties that hung straight down against his white shirts, and a short nerdy Afro.'*
(*Where Did Our Love Go?*, Nelson George, 1985).

nerk *n British* a fool. An invented, mainly middle-class term which predates the (probably unrelated) American **nerd**. **Fred Nerk** was a fictitious personifica-

tion of idiocy or small-mindedness in the 1950s.

nerts *n American* a polite alteration of **nuts**.

net-head *n* an enthusiastic user of the computer Internet. This phrase, using the component **head** in the sense of aficionado (as in, e.g., **petrol-head**), moved in the 1990s from being an obscure item of American jargon to being a widespread and fairly respectable designation.

✎ *'A net-head's adventures online.'*
(Subtitle to *Surfing on the Internet* by J. C. Herz, 1994).

never-never *n British See* on the never-never.

newbie *n* a newcomer or new user on the Internet, in the patois of **cyberpunks** and **net-heads**.

✎ *'Depending on where they show up or on how they behave, newbies are either patiently tolerated or mercilessly hazed.'*
(*Surfing on the Internet* by J. C. Herz, 1994).

newted *adj British* drunk. A term based on the vulgar expression 'as **pissed** as a newt'.

N.F.A. *adj British* a homeless person in the jargon of the police and representatives of other authorities. The term is based on the official designation of 'no fixed abode'.

N.F.N. *adj British* unintelligent and/or unsophisticated. An item of medical slang (reported in the *Sunday Times* 'Style' section, 6 October 1996) which can be written on case notes in front of patients without their understanding. It is an abbreviation of *'normal for Norwich'*, based on the supposition that inhabitants of that city are characteristically slow-witted and provincial.

niagaras *n pl* testicles, **balls**. Rhyming slang from 'Niagara Falls'. A word heard in Britain and Australia, where it has been adopted especially by students, rock journalists, etc., from the original 1950s working-class usage.

✎ *'She kicked him in the niagaras.'*

nibhead *n British* a gormless or comical young person, especially a young man with the characteristic short hair and baggy trousers of the later 1980s (hence the supposed resemblance to a pen). The word was often used as a synonym for **pinhead** in London club-going circles.

nice guy *n See* **Mister Nice-guy**.

nick *vb British* **1** to steal. The word has been used in this sense since at least the 1820s. The word is rare in the USA, but has been recorded in the sense of rob.

↳'*The doctor's had his bike nicked and his place turned over, and the only time we see the Old Bill is when they're in here getting legless.*'
(*Biff* cartoon, 1986).

2 to arrest. Nick was a colloquial term for catch from the 16th century. By the early 19th century it had also acquired this specific meaning.

nick, the *n British* a prison or police station. This common expression dates from before World War II and post-dates the verb form **nick**, meaning to arrest.

↳'*I think you'd better come down the nick and explain yourself.*'

↳'*He's been in nick on and off all his life.*'

See also **nick-bent**.

nick-bent *adj British* temporarily or expediently homosexual because incarcerated. A prisoners' term mentioned by the upper-middle-class former prisoner Rosie Johnston in 1989. **Nick** is a well-established slang synonym for prison, **bent** for homosexual.

nickel-and-dime *adj American* trifling, cheap, petty. Nickels and dimes (five and ten cent coins) constitute small change.

nicker *n British* £1, one pound (sterling). This common term has been in use since about the turn of the century (when it also denoted a sovereign). Nicker was the name given to pieces of metal thrown down in a game and later applied, in racing, to flinging down a sovereign bet on a horse.

↳'*I made about fifty nicker on the deal, didn't I?*'

nick off *vb British* to play truant. A synonym of **bunk off**, **wag it** or **wag off**.

niff *vb, n British* (to give off) a bad smell. Originally an Eastern English dialect version of sniff.

↳'*There's a terrible niff in here.*'

↳'*I wouldn't get too near to that dog; he niffs a bit.*'
(Recorded, editor, London, 1988).

nifty *n British* a sum of £50. This old rhyme was revived among City traders and subsequently adolescents in general during the 1990s.

↳'*Bung him a nifty and he'll probably come across.*'

Nigel *n British* an upper-middle-class or upper-class male. A pejorative term since the 1960s, Nigel is thought to epitomize ostentatious young men who drive sports cars and wear flat caps and tweed jackets.

↳'*Naff causes of death: … racing a right Nigel from Oxford to Cambridge in a silly sports car.*'
(*The Complete Naff Guide*, Bryson et al., 1983).

↳'*Each writer discusses sex and alcohol, scorns anyone "bespectacled" and uses the name Nigel for further derision.*'
(Laura Cumming reviewing *The Oxford Myth*, edited by Rachel Johnson, in the *Evening Standard*, 16 June 1988).

Nigerian lager *n British* Guinness beer, stout. A witticism inspired by the black colour of the brew. **African lager** is a synonym.

nigger *n* a black person. This word has been in use since the late 18th century. It is now a term of racist abuse when used by white speakers, although it can be used affectionately or sardonically between black speakers. The word is derived from *niger*, the Latin word for the colour black, via Spanish (*negro*), French (*nègre*) and the archaic English neger.

nigra *n American* a representation of a southern American pronunciation of negro or **nigger**.

nimby *n* an opponent of controversial legislation (typically on environmental issues) only so long as he or she is directly affected. The word is an acronym for the slogan or catchphrase '*not in my back yard*', coined in the United States (where 'yard' is garden) in the 1980s to describe a syndrome whereby a person supports a potentially harmful move or policy in principle but opposes it for selfish reasons. The American expression entered common currency in Britain around

1986. (An unqualified opponent to the same issues is a **namby**.)

 ✎ '*He thinks working motherhood is a jolly good thing, but he's also a nimby ("by all means let mothers work, so long as it's not in my office").*'
(Sarah Jane Evans, *Sunday Times*, 18 March 1989).

nine-bob note *n British*

a a homosexual, sexual deviant.

b something false, obviously counterfeit or crooked.

Both senses are usually expressed in the phrase '*bent as a nine-bob note*', a surviving example of many expressions using comparisons beginning '**queer** as–' or '**bent** as–'.

ning-nong *n Australian* a fool. A

now-dated but not altogether obsolete word inspired by **nig-nog** (in the earlier non-racist sense) and nincompoop. It may be unrelated to the synonymous **nong**.

nip, Nip *n* 1 a Japanese person. (*Nip-pon* is the Japanese word for Japan.) **Jap** has been the preferred term among British speakers, but nip has made headway since the mid-1970s. This term is largely pejorative.

2 a computer microchip.

nit *n* 1 *British* a foolish person. A contraction of **nitwit** which was popular in the 1950s, especially among radio comedians, but is now almost obsolete.

2 *American* nothing. A variant form of **nix**.

nitso, nitto *n British* nothing. British

alternative forms of **nix**, in working-class London usage.

the nitty-gritty *n* the essentials,

small details. This now common phrase was adopted in Britain from American speech in the second half of the 1960s. The expression originated in black slang in which nitty-gritty referred to the scalp in the context of grooming.

nitwit *n British* a foolish and stupid

person. Literally, someone with the brains of a head louse. An inoffensive colloquialism in modern speech, nitwit entered the language in the 1920s.

nix *n* no, nothing, none. One of very

few German words to enter the thieves' and low-life cant of the early 19th century and remain in occasional use. *Nichts* is the standard German for nothing or not, *nix* being a colloquial version.

nix *vb* to forbid, veto. This form of the

word is predominantly American, its brevity recommending it to journalese usage.

 ✎ '*The governor nixed the proposals.*'

nixon, Nixon *n American* a spuri-

ous or fraudulent deal, especially one involving illicit drugs. An Americanism inspired by the reputation of the former president.

 ✎ '*They pulled a nixon on me.*'
 ✎ '*He got stuck with a nixon.*'

Noah, Noah's *n*

a *Australian* a shark.

b *British* a park.

c *British* a **nark** (informer). All the senses of the word are examples of rhyming slang, from 'Noah's ark'. The two British instances are now rare if not obsolete.

nob *vb British* to copulate. A working-

class usage which became fashionable in the 1970s and early 1980s. It derives from the use of **(k)nob** to mean penis, and as such is usually, but not invariably, used by and about men.

 ✎ '*We ate your food and nobbed your tarts.*'
(Jools Holland, of the pop group Squeeze, at the end of a tour of Venezuela, 1980).

nob *n British* 1 head. This now old-

fashioned usage dates from the 17th century or earlier and is a form of archaic words which survive as napper, nape and knob.

2 an aristocrat or VIP. Nob in this sense may derive from sense **1** (by way of the notion of a famous, prominent or swollen-headed personage) from the use of nob to designate the head on the Jack card in cribbage or, more straightforwardly, as a shortening of noble or nobility.

 ✎ '*A second battle between the nobs and the yobs was a slice of real life, as filmed by BBC2's new documentary series, "Enterprise Culture". A builder named Ken King has bought Avebury Manor.*'
(Kate Saunders, TV review, *Evening Standard*, 17 May 1989).

3 penis. In this sense the spelling **knob** is usually preferred.

nobble *n British* 1 an act of dishon-

estly interfering with a process, such as

by bribing a member of a jury or drugging a racehorse. From the verb.

2 a trick, a devious scheme or clever way of doing things.

↳'*I said, look, the nobble is to give me some money and I'll get you some [drugs]. It's just a bit of a nobble really.*'
(Rockstars' minder, *Guardian*, August 1987).

nobble *vb British* to incapacitate or subvert. The term applies specifically to drugging or otherwise distressing a racehorse in order to adversely affect its performance, or to suborning or threatening members of a jury. The word probably originated in rustic use with the meaning '*knock on the head*', perhaps influenced by **nob**, and hobble.

nobbo *See* **knobbo**.

noddy *n British* a buffoon, simpleton, clumsy or ungainly person. In modern usage the term has been specifically applied to low-ranking police officers by members of the CID and public. Noddy is an archaic rustic term for a simpleminded or cloddish individual, inspired by such a person's inadvertent head movements. The use of the word for the famous children's storybook character created by Enid Blyton reinforced the image evoked.

Noddy *n British* a folder. This piece of student rhyming slang borrows the name – Noddy Holder – of the singer from the 1970s band Slade.

noddy bike *n British* a Velocette motor cycle, as used by police patrolmen until the end of the 1960s. The ungainly, inelegant motorbikes were derided by professional police motorcyclists, motorbike enthusiasts, **rockers**, etc. **Noddy** is a nickname applied to low-ranking police officers reinforced by identification with the children's storybook character created by Enid Blyton.

nod out *vb* to become unconscious or fall asleep. This racier version of the standard 'nod off' is used especially in connection with drug-induced somnolence or stupor.

noggin *n British*

a a drink. The word of unknown origin may designate a measure of a quarter

pint or simply an alcoholic drink of any size or type.

b one's head.

noid *n* a paranoid person. The clipped form, typical of adolescent slang since the late 1980s, is popular among students in Britain in the late 1990s.

↳'*Don't be such a noid, no one's getting at you.*'

nonce, nonse *n British* a prisoner found guilty of sexual offences against children or other acts against the pale of prison morality. Short for 'nonsense boy', 'nonsense case'.

↳'*Nonce meaning nothing, a non-sense, a no one, a non-thing, a phenomenon existing somewhere between noun and verb, between the most terrible acts and the dreadful word for them: pervert, child molester, sex offender, monster, beast … The nonce is the game in an open season.*'
(Ken Smith, *Inside Time*, 1988).

↳'*I was very happy to note a black face hunched up in the corner of the van, but when I saw who it was, a nonce who had raped several girls, the happiness soon subsided and I sunk down into my seat.*'
(Trevor Hercules, *Labelled a Black Villain*, 1989).

noncey *adj British* affected, pretentious, overly respectable. The word is probably an alteration of **ponc(e)y**, perhaps influenced by **nancy boy** or **nonce**.

↳'*There was a time in my life when this sort of noncey Robert Robertson thing would have made me puke, but I must be getting old or something.*'
(Zoë Heller, *Sunday Times Magazine*, 12 November 1995).

nondie *n British* an unmarked police vehicle. The term derives from the official designation 'nondescript'. An item of police slang recorded by the *Evening Standard* magazine in February 1993.

nong *n Australian* a fool. The word is of obscure origin; it may originate in an Aboriginal word or as a corruption of *non compos mentis* (meaning 'not of sound mind'). It is probably unrelated to the synonymous **ning-nong**.

non-linear *adj* upset, agitated, anxious. In this sense the term arose in the language of computer specialists in the 1990s.

no-no *n* something forbidden, impossible, unwelcome, inadvisable, etc. An American slang term which, since the early 1970s, has become a common colloquialism in all English-speaking countries.

non-trivial *adj* important and/or demanding. A usage originating in the jargon of computer specialists.

noodle *n* 1 head. In this sense the word is a variant form of **noddle**.
2 a fool or simpleton. This sense of the word is probably inspired by the notion of softness.

noodling *n* behaving in an aimless and/or unhurried manner. This use of the word is variously explained as being inspired by the length and consistency of noodles, or as an alteration of 'nodules' – the object apparently of leisurely 'fossicking' by Australian miners.
⤷'*The Dead would crank up an old standard … and zone off into extended soloing and noodling as their LSD trips unfurled.*'
(*Q* magazine, March 1997).

noogie, nuggy *n American*
a a kiss or hug.
b petting or other sexual activity.
This Americanism, which may possibly be distantly related to the British **nookie**, is a survival of an archaic British dialect term nug, which is itself related to the verb nudge, and which meant to fondle.

nookie *n British* sexual intercourse or sex in general. This coy term became popular in the late 1970s and 1980s, probably due to its use in the media in place of more offensive synonyms. (Nookie also occurs, albeit rarely, in American usage.) The etymology of the word is uncertain. It may be a form of the archaic British dialect verb nug (which has survived in American speech in the form **noogie**: kiss or hug), or it may alternatively be an alteration of an older euphemism for the female pudenda as a 'shady nook'.

noov, noovo *n, adj British* (a) nouveau riche (person). A dismissive term employed by upper-class and public-school speakers and pseudo-intellectu-

als. Etonian schoolboys applied the term to Harrovians in the late 1980s.

Nora *n British* a drab or unattractive woman. The phrase '*a right Nora*' has been used in the 1990s by students and other adolescents to condemn any female thought to be frumpy, unattractive or shrewish. The term is inspired by the character of Nora Batty in the TV comedy *Last of the Summer Wine*.

norks *n pl Australian* breasts. This word is said to be inspired by the wrapper design for butter produced in the 1950s by the Norco Co-operative Dairy Company, which showed a cow with a full udder. The word was introduced to British speakers by the *Barry McKenzie* cartoon series, running in *Private Eye* magazine in the 1960s. 'Norkers' and 'norgs' were earlier forms.

norm *n British*
a a heterosexual. A derogatory term employed by homosexuals in the 1960s. In the era of **gay** liberation **straight** supplanted this abbreviation of 'normal'.
⤷'*We went to Malaga. Not a hotel room to be had. All these old norms darling. All norming about.*'
(Kenneth Williams, quoted in Joe Orton's diaries, 11 March 1967).
b an abbreviated form of **Norman Normal**.

Norman Normal *n British* a very conventional, conformist person. The mythical Norman (supposedly an especially dull, typically bourgeois or petit bourgeois, Christian name as well as resembling 'normal') was invoked by the last **beatniks** and, after them, the **hippies** as a term of light-hearted contempt.

north and south *n British* mouth. A piece of Victorian London working-class rhyming slang that is still heard, always in the full form.
⤷'*What a mouth, what a mouth/ What a north and south/ Blimey what a mouth he's got!*'
(Lyrics to 'What a Mouth', recorded by Tommy Steele, 1960).

nosebleed *n American* an obnoxious person.

nose candy *n American* cocaine. Another euphemistic use of **candy** in particular and sweet imagery in general to describe drugs. This term was widespread among users following the adoption of cocaine as a middle-class fashion in the late 1970s.

nosh *n British* food. In Yiddish, the noun (deriving from the verb form, itself from German *naschen*) signifies a snack or tidbit eaten between meals. In English usage it has been generalized to encompass all sizes of meal.

✤'*Hey look at all that lovely nosh going to waste.*'
(*Biff* cartoon, 1986).

nosh *vb* to eat. The word is a later alteration of *nashn*, a Yiddish version of the German word *naschen*, to snack or eat surreptitiously.

✤'*After he'd noshed everything on the table, he started in on the fridge.*'

nosh (someone) off *vb British* to have oral sex with someone, perform fellatio or cunnilingus. A 1980s invention in self-conscious imitation of cockney forms of the 1950s.

not(!) *exclamation* a contradiction of the previous statement. The usage, which some linguists claim to have originated in Celtic languages, was popularized by the cult US movie *Wayne's World* in 1992 and the comedy sketches on the US TV programme, *Saturday Night Live*, on which it was based. It neatly replaces the older mechanism whereby the phrase 'I don't think!' was appended.

✤'*She's my favourite person. Not!*'

notch *n American* the female sex organs.

not many! *exclamation British* an all-purpose term of dismissal, derision, etc., in London working-class speech. Its precise derivation is unclear, but it may be a replacement for the earlier use of 'not much!' as an ironic riposte to a statement of the obvious.

nouve, nouveau *n, adj British* alternative renderings of **noov, noovo**.

nowhere *adj* worthless, inferior, hopeless, uninteresting. A dismissive term which formed part of the **beatnik** vocabulary in the USA in the 1950s and later in Britain. When the Beatles recorded *Nowhere Man* in 1965, the word was in vogue in very limited circles; it was subsequently heard among **hippies**, particularly in the USA.

nowt *n British* nothing. A northern English dialect version of the archaic or literary naught. The word is sometimes appropriated by southern speakers for emphasis, irony or familiarity.

nozzer *n British* a new naval recruit. This nickname, which has been used for some time in naval training establishments, was given wider currency in a TV documentary broadcast in 1987.

N.T.D. *adj British* an abbreviation of 'not top-drawer'; a code term of snobbish disapproval sometimes used in all seriousness by **Sloane Rangers** or would-be members of the upper classes.

nubian *n American* a black person, particularly one who is a promoter of African culture. The word is heard on college campuses and is used by blacks and whites, sometimes with differing nuances (Nubian culture, based on an 800-year empire in Northern Africa, is a vital component of recent Afrocentrism).

nuddy, nuddie *adj British* nude, naked. A schoolchildren's humorous or coy mispronunciation of the standard English term, usually in the phrase **in the nuddie**.

nudger *n* a gay male. This pejorative term is a shortened form of **fudge-nudger**.

nudnik, noodnik *n American* an irritating, boring or stupid person. This Yiddish word is derived from the Czech adjective *nudny*, meaning tiresome, boring.

'nuff *n* a humorous rendering of enough reflecting its pronunciation in rapid or childish speech. The word is usually seen in this form in the cliché '*nuff said*'. Vogue expressions also employing the word were '*nuff-tuff*', meaning bold or daring and '*nuff earn*', enough money, both used by teenagers in the late 1980s.

nug *n American* a girl(friend). The term is probably a shortening of the word **nuggy** which is equivalent to the British **nookie**.

nuggets *n pl American* testicles.

✤'*Man, it was so cold my nuggets nearly froze off.*'

nuggy *n American* an alternative spelling of **noogie**.

nuke *vb*

a to attack with nuclear weapons. The verb was coined by 'hawks' in the USA in the early 1970s. During the Falklands War of 1981 T-shirts and car stickers were produced in Britain with the exhortation *'Nuke Buenos Aires!'*.

b to devastate, defeat, overwhelm. By extension the verb is now used with this general meaning, particularly by teenagers and students.
▷*'We nuked them in the inter-college playoff.'*

c to cook in a microwave oven. The colloquial verb for a nuclear attack has been used in this sense throughout the English-speaking world.

nukes *n pl*

nuclear weapons. An abbreviated form first seen in the USA in the 1970s, especially in the disarmament slogan *'no nukes!'*.

number *n*

1 a marihuana cigarette, **joint**. A vogue term of the late 1960s originating in the USA and deriving from the use of number to mean item, piece or unit. The word remains in use among cannabis smokers.
▷*'Roll another number for the road.'*
(Song title, the Holy Modal Rounders, 1969).

2 an act of betrayal, a confidence trick, a scam. Most often heard in the phrase **do a number on (someone)**: make a dupe of someone. Related is the phrase *'to get someone's number'*: to see through someone's deception.

3 a sexual partner. An unromantic term of the 1970s and 1980s denoting a casual or anonymous pick-up. (American author John Rechy published a novel with the title *Numbers*, dealing with gay liaisons, in 1970.)
▷*'She goes to singles bars to pick up what she calls "numbers".'*
(Recorded, London, 1986).

number (someone) *vb*

to identify, single out, denounce.
▷*'They numbered him as a prime suspect.'*
▷*'I got numbered.'*

number-cruncher *n*

a (human or mechanical) calculator, handler or manipulator of (usually large) numbers. This light-hearted phrase evoking a mill or grinding mechanism fed with figures has become a standard item of business jargon.

number-crunching *n*

the activity or practice of handling complex calculations and large quantities (see **number-cruncher**).

number one(s) *n, vb*

urination. A nursery term dating from the Victorian concept of personal hygiene as a drill. The idea is usually expressed in the form *'do number ones'*. In the USA it is occasionally a verb, 'to number one'. *See also* **number two(s)**.

number two(s) *n*

defecation. A children's term often used humorously by adults. It occurs in both British and American speech. *See also* **number one(s)**.

numb-nuts *n*

an ineffectual, stupid or contemptible person, invariably male. A term of abuse popular for instance with college students in the USA; since the mid-1980s it has been heard in other English-speaking areas. (Nuts refers to testicles, although the epithet has no sexual connotations.)

numero uno *n, adj*

American (something or someone considered) superlative or supreme. A borrowing, from Hispanic American speech, of the Spanish for 'number one'.

numptie, numbty, numshie *n*

British a fool, buffoon. This Scottish term became more widespread from the early 1990s. It has been derived from the unfortunate children's character Humpty-Dumpty, but is equally likely to be based on 'numb(-skull)'.

nunnie, noonie *n*

American backside, **butt**, **ass**. An invented inoffensive euphemism.
▷*'You're gonna freeze your nunnie.'*
(*M*A*S*H*, US TV comedy series, 1981).

nurd *n*

an alternative spelling of **nerd**.

nurk *n*

an alternative spelling of **nerk**.

nut *n*

1 head. A predictable metaphor which had become established slang by the mid-19th century (see the verb form).

2 a a crazy, eccentric person. The word was used in this sense in the USA for about thirty years before its adoption by British speakers in the late 1940s, from **nut-case**.

b a devotee, fan(atic) or **buff**. The word is used, particularly in American English, as a combining form or suffix, as in 'health-nut'.

nut *vb British* to butt someone with one's head, usually in the face, a common form of assault among street fighters and practised brawlers. The concept is also expressed by phrases such as **stick the nut on someone** or 'give someone the nut'; **Gorbals kiss** and **Glasgow kiss/handshake** are colourful alternatives.

↳ '*Millions of TV viewers ... saw the Wimbledon wildman nut Everton skipper Kevin Ratcliffe.*'
(*News of the World*, 12 February 1989).

nut-case *n* a crazy person. A slang version of 'mental case' which spread from American speech into British usage at the end of the 1950s. It is now a fairly mild term, usually denoting harmless eccentricity. A racier, more modern version is **headcase**.

nut-house *n* a psychiatric hospital, mental home. The phrase has been in use since the 1920s.

nut-job *n American* a more recent variation of **nut-case**.

nut out/up *vb* to go crazy, lose control of oneself, run amok. A recent teenagers' and college students' term.

nuts *adj* **1a** crazy, absurd, insane. An Americanism of the turn of the century, adopted elsewhere before World War II, it derives ultimately from the 19th-century notion of '*off one's nut*', a slang version of the colloquial '*off one's head*'.
b extremely enthusiastic or enamoured.
↳ '*He's nuts about her!*'

nuts *n pl* testicles. A metaphorical use of the word which serves as a more acceptable euphemism for **balls**.

nuts! *exclamation* an exclamation of defiance which may be used without offence unlike the synonymous **balls**. The most famous instance of this (typically American) expression was General McAuliffe's one-word riposte to the German army's request for surrender at Bastogne in World War II.

nutter *n British* a maniacal, unrestrained, unpredictable person. Often said in awe or grudging admiration of the subject's energy and capabilities.

↳ '*He then began saying I would get into trouble. "That boy of yours looks a nutter to me!" *'
(Joe Orton's diary, 12 May 1967).

nutty *adj* **1** crazy, absurd, eccentric. A usage which slightly pre-dates the almost synonymous **nuts**. By the 1960s it was considered a well-established colloquialism.

2 *Jamaican* **natty** (in the standard and patois senses), smart and spirited. Caribbean English has retained the 19th-century British sense of dandified. The word was applied by the white British pop group, Madness to themselves in a punning reference to their 'craziness' and the inspiration they gained from black music.

nyaff *n Scottish* an irritating or obnoxious person. The term is supposed to be echoic in origin, and is based on the irritating sound of a dog or a small child.

nyam (up) *vb British* to eat. The term was heard in black British speech in the early 1990s. It was thought to be echoic but possibly originates from a west African language.

nympho *n* a promiscuous woman. The word is a shortening of nymphomaniac. The word has often been used by schoolchildren since the 1950s.

O...

O *n* 1 opium, in the jargon of drug users. 2 *See* **the big O**.

081 *n, adj British* a person who is 'suburban', unsophisticated. Following the redesignation of outer-London telephone numbers by the prefix 081 in 1990 (as opposed to 071 for the central area) this jocular piece of snobbery was recorded by Christa De Souza in the *Sunday Times*, 19 September 1993. By the time 081 was replaced by 0181 the expression seemed to have fallen into disuse.

oats *n pl See* **feel one's oats** and **get one's oats**.

oatsy *adj* spirited, assertive, restive or feisty. A coinage derived from the earlier phrase to **feel one's oats**.

obbo *n British* observation by police officers, surveillance. An item of police slang recorded by the *Evening Standard* magazine, February 1993, and popularized by its use in the many TV dramas based on police work broadcast in the later 1990s.

ocean-going *combining form British* an all-purpose intensifier used to prefix nouns, as in '*an ocean-going shit*' (an extremely obnoxious person). The usage is inspired by such terms as 'ocean-going yacht', denoting a larger and more powerful version of the thing in question. **Born-again** is used in a similar way.

ocker *n Australian* a working-class male, especially one epitomizing the more boorish Australian attributes. This word, which seems to be related to the British **oik** by an unrecorded process, has a resonance beyond its simple definition. It has overtones of the American 'good ole boy'. 'Ockerism' and 'ockerdom' describe the cult or syndrome of male comradeship, beer-drinking and lack of refinement embodied in such cultural icons as the comedian Paul Hogan's 'Hoag' character and the Test cricketer Merv Hughes. (**Alf** is a less well-known synonym for ocker.)

⮑'*Paul Hogan …the archetypal Aussie Ocker.*'
(Photo caption, *Southern Cross* magazine, July 1989).

ockerina, ocarina *n Australian* a female **ocker**. A play on words heard occasionally.

octopus *n British* a bus. An item of rhyming slang from the Merseyside area, given exposure by its use in the TV soap opera *Brookside*.

O.D., o.d. *n, vb* (to) overdose. The abbreviation replaced the full form in the 1960s among 'counterculture' and street drug users. It is still in use and is sometimes extended to refer to a surfeit of something innocuous.

⮑'*Billy O.D'd on Drano on the night that he was wed.*'
('People Who Died', written and recorded by Jim Carroll, 1981).

⮑'*Oh God, I've completely o.d.'d on those chocolates.*'

oddball *n, adj* (an) eccentric (person), nonconformist or outsider. An Americanism which has been established in British and American speech since the 1950s. The origin of the expression probably lies in pool playing or another sport.

⮑'*She's a bit of an oddball.*'
⮑'*That's thoroughly oddball behaviour.*'

odds *vb British* to risk, take a chance on. A gamblers' term which occurred in working-class London speech from the 1950s to the late 1970s. The phrase **odds it** is the more durable alternative form.

odds and sods *n pl British* a rhyming vulgarization of 'odds and ends'.

odds it *vb British* to 'play the odds', take a risk or chance. A piece of London working-class terminology, used particularly by police officers and members of the underworld.

⮑'*You're oddsin' it a bit, aren't you?*'
⮑'*I can't be sure, we'll just have to odds it.*'

ofay *n American* a white person. The word is said to be a **backslang** version of 'foe' in black American slang of the late 1960s. Another proposed etymology is the

Yoruba word *ofé*, meaning a ju-ju or charm. The word probably originated earlier in the century in the immigrant underworld as a code reference to the police and other authority figures. It is sometimes encountered in the phrase 'ixnay ofay(s)', meaning 'no whites'.

↳ *'Nice integrated neighbourhood, ofays, Arabs, Chaldeans, a few colored folks. Ethnic, man.'*
(*The Switch*, Elmore Leonard, 1978).

O.F.D.s *n pl British* police patrol officers. The initials stand for '*only fucking drivers*'. An item of police slang recorded by the London *Evening Standard* magazine, February 1993.

off *vb American* to kill. A word popular at the time of the Vietnam War when '*off the pigs*' was a slogan much chanted by militant protesters. The term, possibly derived from **bump off**, was picked up by British speakers and enjoyed a brief vogue in the early 1970s. It is still heard occasionally, especially in the verb form 'off oneself' (to commit suicide).

↳ *'Isn't he the dude on trial for offing the undercover cop?'*
(*The Last Innocent Man*, US film, 1987).

off *n British* a fight. A playground term also used by teenage gangs.

↳ *'Quick, there's going to be an off.'*

offie *n British* an off-licence. An abbreviated form of the word which has become increasingly popular through the 1980s.

off one's block/chump/ crust/head/nut/onion *adj* mad, crazy. These phrases are all elaborations of the well-established colloquialism, 'off one's head' (heard since the mid-19th century). The terms are sometimes extended to mean intoxicated by drugs or drink, more usually denoted by phrases beginning with 'out of', such as **out of one's head**.

off one's face *adj* completely drunk or under the influence of drugs. A variant of 'off one's head'. The usage arose in Australian speech, but by the mid-1990s was in common use in Britain among younger speakers. The variant *off one's case* is also used by prison inmates in the UK.

↳ *'"I went high at university!" he said reasonably. "Used to really get on my face in fact …"'*

↳ *'"Off! Off! Dad, it's off your face," Mouche screeched from the bed.'*
(*Girls' Night Out*, Kathy Lette, 1989).

↳ *'… inside, we were buzzing nicely … I was off my face: 1995 had come early.'*
(*Independent*, 24 January 1995).

off one's trolley *adj British* deranged, unstable, crazy. A variation on the **off one's block** phrase, which has been popular in British speech since the 1970s. The original image evoked may be of a child losing control of a cart or scooter, or of a patient falling from a mobile stretcher or frame.

off-side *adj British* unfair, improper behaviour. An upper- and middle-class term of disapproval, deriving from various field sports.

off the wall *adj American* eccentric, unusual, **way-out**. A phrase (possibly inspired by the unpredictable trajectory of a ball or an ice-hockey puck rebounding from a wall) which has been adopted outside the USA, usually in connection with zany and/or creatively original ideas or behaviour.

O.G. *n American* 'original gangster'; an older and respected gang member. A term from the code of the Los Angeles street gangs of the 1980s.

ogens *n pl American* female breasts. The name of the small spherical variety of melons is used figuratively, sometimes altered to **Hogans**.

oggie, oggy *n British* a Cornish pasty. A term of uncertain origin heard in the West of England. It more usually occurs in the form **tiddy oggie**.

oggle *vb British* a humorous, or simply mispronounced version of the verb to ogle, usually in the sense of 'eye lasciviously'. A middle-class colloquialism.

oggle-rye *n British*
a eye.
b eyelash.
c eyebrow.
A **parlyaree** term recorded since the 1960s, in use particularly among London **gays** and transvestites. It combines the verb '*oggle*' (a deformation of ogle) and a nonsense syllable to provide the rhyme.

-oid *suffix* the suffix, seen in slang since the late 1960s, confers a sense of the pseudo-scientific or pathological on the preceding word or part of a word. It is invariably also pejorative, and as such performs as a negative version of the neutral '-ish' or '-esque'. Examples are **Ramboid**, 'bozoid' (from **bozo**), **trendoid** and **zomboid**.

oik *n British* 1 a vulgar, coarse, boorish or socially inferior person. This term was, and still is, applied by public schoolboys (rarely by girls) to local children or those attending state schools. It is also sometimes used self-effacingly or ironically by working-class males to refer to themselves. The word's origin is obscure, (one suggestion is that it was an imitation of the sound of unsophisticated speech), but seems to lie in the 19th century; it is almost certainly cognate with the 20th-century Australian **ocker**, also denoting a working-class male. Evelyn Waugh used the word, referring in his diary entry of 7 January 1920, to his host as a '*wizened, pleasant little oik*'.

↪ '*I'm constantly amazed that a couple of oiks like me and Gray have managed to make it.*'
(Recorded, advertising executive, London, 1986).

2 a person with 'one income and kids'. An acronym in **yuppie** use in the late 1980s. Similar coinages are **dinky** and **oink**.

oiler *n* 1 *British* a sycophant. The *Sunday Times*, 16 October 1994 reported that Princess Diana had used the term in reference to Prince Charles's entourage.

2 *American* a synonym for **greaser** in the sense of a Hispanic person.

oily *n British* a stupid, unsophisticated or unfortunate person. This derogatory term heard among black teenagers in the late 1980s, is probably a blend of **oik** and **wally**, rather than a specialized use of the standard English adjective.

↪ '*I don't want to walk down the street and have them shout, "Hey, oily" because of how I look.*'
(Recorded, black youth, London, 1989).

oily rag *n British* 1 this disparaging term is applied to inexperienced or incompetent motor mechanics who are assigned menial jobs such as wiping away grease.

2 a cigarette. This piece of rhyming slang, from **fag**, was common in the 1950s but is now rarely heard.

oink *n* a person with 'one income and

no kids'. An acronym characterizing one type of worker in the **yuppie** milieu of the late 1980s. Similar coinages are **dinky** and **oik**.

oinker *n American* a vulgar, obnoxious or greedy person. A young person's euphemism for 'pig'. The term was and is, predictably, applied to police officers.

OK, O.K., okay *interjection* all right, correct. The term is no longer thought to be slang, but its origins are frequently debated by amateur and professional etymologists. The first recorded use was in the Boston *Morning Post* of 23 March 1839 by C. G. Greene, who used OK as a facetious abbreviation of a misspelled 'Orl Korrect'. This novelty, possibly reinforced by the Scottish phrase 'Och, aye', which has the same meaning and an almost identical pronunciation, was imitated by other comic writers and taken as the title of a Democratic political club in 1840; this last example was also probably a pun on 'Old Kinderhook', the nickname of the politician Martin van Buren. The several other proposed sources for the word, including a posited cry in French, *au quai!* ('to or on the quayside') are probably spurious. By the end of the 19th century OK was in use in Britain.

OK-yah *n British* a **Sloane Ranger** or **hooray**. The term was popularized by the Steve Wright radio show in the early 1990s, from the supposedly characteristic braying cry of this social group. The phrase was shortened to **yah** in Edinburgh slang.

OK yah-die *n British* a young white middle-class person who affects black Caribbean mannerisms. The mocking phrase, heard in London in the 1990s, is a pun combining the supposedly typical cry of the **Sloane Ranger** or **hooray** of the later 1980s, 'OK ya!' with **yardie**. Compare **wigga**. *See also* **yah**.

-ola *suffix* this word ending has been appropriated from Spanish where it signifies large and negative. It is added to standard terms and slang terms (as in **payola** and **boffola**) to convey the notion of outrageous, excessive or 'super-'. The usage arose in the USA in the 1950s.

Old Bill, the Old Bill *n British* *See* **the Bill**.

old cheese *n Australian* a mother or

matriarch. An affectionate epithet used principally by males.

old Dutch, my old Dutch *n British* wife. This cockney phrase has been in use since the late 19th century. There is disagreement about its origin, which may be in the rhyming slang 'Dutch plate': mate, or the use of 'duchess' as a term of endearment or affection. Old Dutch, usually preceded by 'my', is now rarely heard except among elderly Londoners.

old fellow *n* penis. An affectionate euphemism used by hearty males.

old lady *n* one's mother, wife or sweetheart. The term was notably adopted by **hippies** in Britain in the late 1960s, not from local working-class usage, but in imitation of American **bikers**, etc.

old lag *n British* a recidivist, habitual offender or former prisoner. **Lag** is an elastic term which since the early 19th century has encompassed imprisonment, sentencing, a notion of transportation, or simply convict.

old man *n* one's father, husband or sweetheart. *See also* **old lady**.

old moody *n British See* **moody**.

old trout *n British* a middle-aged or elderly woman, especially one who is frumpish or short-tempered. This expression has been used as a mild pejorative (very occasionally even affectionately) since the 19th century.

↳ '*Here's what's coming up for you; two old trouts and a man who should be in the army.*'
(Victoria Wood, *As Seen on TV*, BBC comedy series, April 1988).

Oliver (Reed), Olly *n British* amphetamine, **speed**. A rhyming-slang term coined by middle-class drug users in the 1970s, ironically taking the name of a film actor notorious for his liking for alcohol.

Oliver (Twist) *adj British* drunk. An item of rhyming slang for **pissed**. Unlike many similar multi-word examples, it invariably occurs in its full form, rather than being abbreviated to 'Oliver'. Compare **Oliver (Reed)**.

ollie *n British* a marble, in the literal sense of the children's plaything (which is

probably a variant form of **allie**), and in the figurative sense, as in the expression to **lose one's marbles**.

↳ '*Another few days with those dozy gob-shites and I'd have lost me ollies.*' (Alexei Sayle, *Great Bus Journeys of the World*, 1988).

olly *n See* **Oliver (Reed)**.

omi, omee *n British* a man. A **parlyaree** word which survived into the modern era, omi is a corruption of the Italian *uomo*, man. The term featured in the language of the theatre and among street traders and vagrants among others.

omipolone, omipoloni *n British* a male homosexual. This now dated form has survived in theatrical and film usage from more widespread earlier currency in the argot of the underworld, tramps, tinkers, etc. It is a portmanteau comprising **omi** (man) and **polone** (woman). The word was used as a euphemism in the radio comedy series *Round the Horne* during the 1960s.

on a mish *See* **mish**.

on canvas *adj, adv British* in solitary confinement, in prison. The phrase derives from the fact that prisoners in solitary confinement are issued with canvas mattresses and nightshirts.

oncer *n British* an alternative spelling of **oneser**.

one-eyed trouser snake *n* penis. A colourful metaphor which probably originated in Australia in the 1950s. The word has spread to Britain and the United States and is nowadays generally truncated to **trouser snake**, which has developed further connotations.

oneser *n British* a one-pound note or pound coin.
↳ '*All I got on me is a oneser.*'

one-up someone *vb* to (try to) out-do, better or snub someone. The common adjectival form is occasionally employed as a verb in all English-speaking areas.
↳ '*She tries one-upping me at every chance she gets.*'

on holiday *adj British* in prison (temporarily), in the argot of tramps and the homeless.

on one *adj British*
a under the influence of (a tablet of) **MDA** or **ecstasy**. An expression from the jargon of **acid house** club habitués.
↳*'Are you on one, matey?'*
b in the know, *au fait* or *au courant*. In both senses, this is an adolescent vogue phrase of the late 1980s.

on one's Jack, Jack Jones
adj, adv, British alone, on one's own. Rhyming slang from the name of the American singer.

on one's tod *adj, adv British* alone, on one's own. The phrase is rhyming slang from 'Tod Sloan', the name of an American jockey active at the turn of the century.

on one's way *adv British* intoxicated by drugs. The phrase, heard from the mid-1990s, refers usually to the effects of **ecstasy**, occasionally to those of **speed**.

on the arm *adj British* bribed, corrupted. An instance of police and criminal slang.
↳*'Don't worry, we've got a prison officer on the arm.'*

on the batter *vb British* engaged in prostitution and soliciting. An item of working-class slang heard throughout the UK since the 1960s, deriving from a more generalized 19th-century sense of the phrase as signifying 'engaged in a violent debauch.'

on the blob *adj* menstruating. The expression, which seems to be used mainly by males, is heard in many English-speaking communities. **Blob** has also been used in several sexually related contexts. **On the rag** is an older synonym.

on the brew *adj phrase British* on the dole, unemployed. The sense of 'brew' in this phrase, which was heard in the 1980s, especially in the north of England, is unclear.

on the bum *adj, adv* **1 a** on the road. Leading the life of a hobo or tramp.
↳*'Just about a year ago I took off on the bum.'*
(Lyrics from 'Lodi', written by John Fogerty and recorded by Creedence Clearwater Revival, 1968).
b engaged in cadging or begging. From the verb to **bum**.

2 malfunctioning, out of order. A less common synonym of **on the blink**, **bum** here meaning dud or useless.

on the bung *adj Australian* out of order, broken down.

on the creep *adj, adv* in search of a sexual partner. The term, heard in the Lowlands of Scotland and the north of England, usually refers to male behaviour. Contemporary synonyms include **on the sniff** and **out trouting**.

on the drip *adv, adj British* on hire purchase, by instalments. One of many synonyms (including **on the knock, on the never-never,** and **on the strap, on the lay-by**) in use since the 1950s.

on the earhole/ear'ole *adj, adv British* cadging, trying to borrow money. An old London working-class expression still heard in the 1980s. For the etymology, *see* **ear'ole**.

on the elbow *adv British* engaged in cadging, borrowing money or scrounging. A London working-class expression. The elbow reference may evoke literal nudging or figurative barging, pushing.

on the floor *adj British* rhyming slang for poor.

on the fritz *adj, adv American* malfunctioning, out of order. A synonym of the colloquial on the blink. Fritz here may be the German nickname, probably alluding to imported German goods, thought by Americans in the 1930s to be shoddy. It may alternatively echo the sound of a short circuit, a buzzing in electrical equipment.
↳*'We're thinking about getting a doberman since the alarm system went on the fritz.'*
(*Hart to Hart*, US TV series, 1981).

on the heavy bevvie *adv* engaged in heavy drinking. The term is heard particularly in the Scottish Lowlands and the north of England.

on the (h)orn *n British* having an erection. A very common working-class and schoolboy vulgarism of the 1950s and early 1960s, now somewhat dated. 'Horn' has been a synonym for penis since at least the 18th century.

on the hot cross (bun) *adj, adv British* on the run. An item of rhyming slang used and possibly coined by the crime novelist Ruth Rendell.

on the hurry-up *adv British* at full speed. An item of London police jargon.

on the job *adj, adv British* engaged in sexual intercourse. An unromantic euphemistic phrase which has been used increasingly in 'polite' company in Britain and Australia since the 1960s.

on the knock *adj, adv British* **1** on credit or hire purchase, by instalments. *See* **knock**.
2 engaged in selling or canvassing door to door. An alternative form of **on the knocker**.

on the knocker *adj, adv British* going from door to door. Typically to sell something of dubious worth or to persuade the gullible to part with items such as antiques for less than their true value. A non-regional working-class term.

on the money *adj* correct, accurate. The phrase, which probably originated in the US in gambling circles, is usually heard among middle-class speakers.
✎ *'It's good when the band's on the money.'*
(UK TV documentary on the band Status Quo, 18 June 1993).

on the needle *adj* habitually injecting heroin or another narcotic.
✎ *'She finally admitted she was back on the needle.'*

on the nest *adj, adv Australian* having sex.

on the never-never *adj, adv British* on hire purchase, on credit, by instalments. One of many such phrases originating in the 1950s; this one ruefully reflects on the impossibility of ever getting out of debt once enmeshed.

on the nose *adj Australian* stinking, smelly, rank. The expression is either a shortening of a phrase such as *'heavy on the nose'* or an inversion of an earlier expression *'to have a nose on (someone or something)'*, meaning to dislike.

on the piss *adj, adv British* engaged in a drinking bout or habitual heavy drinking.

on the pull *adv, adj British* looking for a sexual partner, hoping to pick up a member of the opposite sex. A working-class term in use since the late 1960s from **pull**; its predatory overtones mean that it is usually applied to males.
✎ *'Don't bother asking – those two are out on the pull again.'*
(Recorded, adolescent girl, London, 1987).

on the q.t. *adv* discreetly, secretly. A version of 'on the quiet', first recorded in 1870.

on the rag *adj British* menstruating. **Rag** is a common slang-synonym for sanitary towel.

on the salmon *adj British* (of a male) having an erection. The phrase is a shortened form of the rhyming slang '*on the salmon and prawn*', meaning **(on the) horn**. The phrase was used as the title of an art exhibition in the East End of London by the young artist Sarah Lucas in 1995.

on the sniff *adj, adv* looking for a sexual partner. This more obscure synonym of **on the pull**, **out trouting**, etc., was used by the Scottish comic character Rab C. Nesbitt in the BBC comedy of the same name, 18 November 1993.

on the square *adj British* belonging to a Masonic lodge. A term from the code of freemasons themselves. (The square is a Masonic symbol.)
✎ *'Three Crown witnesses were themselves "on the square".'*
(Former detective quoted in *Inside the Brotherhood*, Martin Short, 1989).

on the strap *adj, adv British* on credit or hire purchase, by paying instalments. A less common alternative form of **on the drip**, **on the never-never**, etc. The exact significance of the strap in question is unknown, but there may be a connection with the colloquial '*strapped for cash*'. The phrase is old; strap has been used to mean credit since the 1830s.
✎ *'Don't buy a second-hand car, buy a new one. Get it on the strap.'*
(Recorded, publisher, London, 1989).

on the team *adj British* belonging to the **gay** community. This euphemism is adapted from the generalized, colloquial sense of the phrase.

on the thumb *adj, adv British* hitch-hiking.

on the up-and-up *adj, adv* above board, bona fide. Originally an Americanism of uncertain derivation (perhaps an intensification of upright), the term is now widely used in Britain, especially in London working-class speech.

↪'*No it's OK: he finally convinced me that the deal was on the up-and-up.*'

on tilt *adj, adv American* unsteady, unbalanced. The phrase comes from the light flashed on a pintable to say that the game has been curtailed because the machine has been forced out of alignment by overenthusiastic play. It often refers to a person who is behaving uncharacteristically or eccentrically.

on top *adj, adv British* (caught) in the act, (caught) red-handed. A criminal and police expression evoking the image of, for example, a burglar on a roof, i.e. exposed.

oof *n British* a promiscuous or sexually willing female. One of a set of terms in use among male City traders, recorded by psychologist Belinda Brookes in the *Independent on Sunday*, 9 July 1995. Others included **mum** and **dragon**. The word may imitate a gasp of desire, like its 1920s' predecessor, 'oomph' (an archaic term for sex-appeal).

oojamaflip *n British* an unspecified or unnameable thing. A nonsense word used particularly by middle-class speakers in the same way as thingummybob, thingy, etc.

OPP *n American* an abbreviation for '*other people's property*', sometimes redefined as '*other people's pussy*'.

oppo *n British* **1** opposite number, partner. A military abbreviation used in police, underworld and more general contexts. Most users assume understandably (and probably correctly) that this is based on 'opposite'. A more fanciful suggestion is that it is in fact a corruption of '*hop o' my thumb*', rhyming slang for chum.
2 an operation, particularly a military operation (a surgical operation is simply an op).

oracle *n See* **work the oracle**.

orbital, orbital rave *n British* an **acid house** party. In 1989 there was a vogue for large-scale gatherings of adolescent party goers, usually paying to attend clandestine dance celebrations which often ended in confrontations with the police. The practice was part of the **acid-house** cult in which the drug **ecstasy** played an integral part. The parties in question revived the dated term **rave** and were held within reach of the London orbital motorway, the M25, hence the names.

orchestras *n pl British* testicles. The word is late 19th- or early 20th-century rhyming slang from 'orchestra stalls' (a category of theatre seating): **balls**. It is invariably used literally rather than figuratively.

the order of the boot *n British* (notice of) rejection, dismissal or refusal. The humorous expression, based on the more exalted Order of the Bath, Order of the Garter, etc., is normally employed in the context of a sacking or a rejection by a lover. This form of words has largely supplanted the earlier 'order of the push'.

original *adj British* excellent, acceptable. A vogue word of approval first used among black British gangs and later adopted by schoolchildren in the mid-1990s.

original gangster *n American See* **O.G.**

O.S. *adv Australian* overseas.
↪'*Charlene's gone O.S.*'

oscar *adj British* unrestrained, out of control, wild. This pun on the name of the writer Oscar Wilde was in use among commune dwellers and **hippies** in the late 1970s in such phrases as to 'go completely Oscar'. (In archaic slang in both Britain and Australia an oscar was a male homosexual.)

ossifer *n* a police officer. A facetious and/or provocative deformation of the standard word, often said in imitation of the slurred speech of a drunk. It occurs all over the English-speaking world.

O.T.F. *adj British Jewish.* The initials stand for '*of the faith*'. The phrase is used euphemistically by Jews and non-Jews and is also occasionally used by other users in the London area to mean 'one of us'.

the other *n* sexual intercourse or other sexual misbehaviour. A common euphemism probably deriving from the phrase '*this, that and the other*', coyly referring, like 'hanky-panky', to unnameable activities. Until the late 1950s the other often signified homosexual activity as opposed to orthodox sex. Nowadays phrases such as '*a bit of the other*' are usually heard in a heterosexual context.

✎'*He asked me if I fancied a bit of the other, so I told him yes, but only if the bit belonged to some other bloke.*'
(Recorded, London, 1965).

O.T.S. *adv British See* **go over the side**.

O.T.T. *adj British* outrageous, wild and uncontrolled. A shortening of the late 1970s catchphrase **over the top**, given wider currency by its adoption as the title of an anarchic TV comedy show in the early 1980s. It often occurs in phrases such as 'go (completely) O.T.T.'.

out *adj* living or behaving openly as a homosexual. The result of having **come out** (of the **closet**). A term from the gay lexicon.

✎'*Bruce is out.*'
✎'*She's been out for some time now.*'

out *vb* **1** to reveal or denounce as being a homosexual. The term, originally an obscure item of gay jargon, became famous in the 1980s as the practice of public naming of **closet cases** gathered momentum.
2 to knock unconscious, beat up. A term from the lexicon of **teddy boys** and **mods**.

outasight *adj* superlative, excellent, sensational. The phrase 'out of sight' was probably used first in this sense by jazz musicians and their **beatnik** imitators in the late 1950s in the USA. Outasight, like the earlier **way-out** and the coeval **far-out**, used the image of something far from the ordinary or far outdistancing its rivals. The expression was popular among the **hippies** of the late 1960s and in the jargon of soul music. It is now rarely heard outside the USA and is mainly confined there to black American speech.

outfit *n See* **fit**.

outlaw *n* a gang member. The word has been adopted by gangs in many different milieus, including the American **biker** gangs of the 1950s and more recently the black street-gangs of the USA and urban Britain.

outlaw *adj American* exceptional, outstanding. A teenage expression, originally a term of approbation from the street,

where outlaw is a term used of gang members by themselves.

✎'*Outlaw dress.*'
(*Broadcast News*, US film, 1987).

out of it *adj* euphoric and/or semi-conscious after ingesting drink or drugs. A fashionable shortened version of **out of one's head/skull/box** which spread from the USA to other English-speaking areas around 1971.

✎'*Her main hobby these days seems to be getting out of it as often as possible.*'
(Recorded, female rock singer, Devon, 1986).

✎'*1969 ... got really out of it last night at the roundhouse.*'
(*Biff* cartoon, 1986).

out of one's head/skull/box *adj*
a mentally deranged.
b intoxicated by drugs or drink. These terms became widespread in the mid-1960s, before which synonymous phrases (with the exception of '*out of one's mind*') usually began with 'off'. When the Rolling Stones called their 1965 album *Out of Our Heads* the phrase was still a little-known Americanism. The 'box' version has been fashionable in Britain since the mid-1970s.

out of one's pram *adj British* out of control, crazy. An alternative form of **off one's trolley**, the term has overtones of a childish tantrum or loss of temper rather than true insanity.

out of one's tree *adj*
a crazy, deranged.
b intoxicated with drugs or drink. A colourful variation on **out of one's head** that is typically American and Australian. The implication is of someone volubly or energetically crazy or **high** and chattering like a monkey.

out of order *adj British* **1** transgressing, beyond the pale.

✎'*"I think you're well out of order," he said. Apparently he had been waiting for seven years to see Grace [Jones] again, and was peeved about the extra four hours standing around.*'
(*Independent*, 30 March 1990).

2 incapacitated, particularly by drink or illicit drugs. These extensions of the standard sense of the phrase became fashionable in raffish speech in the early

1970s. The first sense is more often heard in working-class speech, the second, predictably, in the drug-using subcultures.

out to lunch *adj*

a crazy, deranged.

ᗌ'*The second most out-to-lunch politburo in the north of England.*'
(*Private Eye* magazine, 27 October 1989).

b unconscious, incapacitated by drink or drugs. A usage which was particularly popular in Britain around 1975.

out trouting *n British* looking for a sexual partner. A vogue term of the mid-1990s heard in raffish usage, particularly among young adults in the advertising industry, journalism and city financial circles. It is based on the derogatory **old trout**, meaning woman.

over the top *adj, adv British* outrageous, bizarre, beyond the bounds of normal behaviour or decorum. The expression equally describes fury, extraordinary generosity or simple bad taste. It derives from the general idea of going 'off the scale', of being beyond measurable or acceptable limits, reinforced perhaps by the use of the phrase in World War I to describe troops climbing out of the trenches to go into battle, hence throwing caution to the winds. Often abbreviated to **O.T.T.**, the phrase was a vogue term in 1979.

ᗌ'*There's no point in going over the top about someone like that.*'

ᗌ'*Wearing that dress with those shoes is really over the top.*'

own goal *n British* a suicide. An unsentimental item of police jargon since the 1970s.

Oz *n* Australia.

Ozzie and Harriet *n pl American* a particularly stuffy, middle-class, middle-aged couple. The term is taken from the title of a long-running American TV show of the 1950s and 1960s, in which Ozzie and Harriet Nelson (incidentally the parents of the singer Ricky Nelson) played just such a couple. The names have become a by-word for respectability and domesticity.

p...

packed *adj*
well-hung. The term was used by the comedienne Dawn French in January 1994.

packet *n* the male genitals. A term from the **gay** lexicon, usually referring to the crotch as it appears clothed.

pad *n* a home. The word now invariably refers to a room, apartment or house. In 17th-century Britain pad was used by peasants and poor travellers to designate a bed made of straw or rags, while in American slang before 1950 it designated a pallet or couch on which opium smokers or other drug takers reclined; this sense was later extended to encompass any room or place in which drug users gathered, or the beds on which they slept. The dissemination of **beatnik**-related jargon introduced the word to a wider audience, as did its adoption by the **hippy** generation. In Britain the word pad now tends to be identified negatively with the outdated hippy subculture and native slang terms such as **gaff** and **drum** are often preferred, although the term is still in use, often in a jocular context.
ᗒ'*Drop-out pads for the large numbers of people hitting London at the moment looking for the mythical beautiful dreamboat.*'
(*International Times*, April 1968).

paddle *vb* to hit, beat, thrash. This synonym of wallop probably derives from the archaic use of the noun paddle to mean both hand, and more rarely, foot. Long before signifying a bat, paddle also denoted a small spade.

Paddy *n* an Irish person. A nickname derived from the short form of Patrick, the most common male Christian name in Ireland. It has been used since at least the 18th century. Although the term can be used as an epithet, it may be used de-

scriptively and is also heard among the Irish themselves, where it is usually a personification of a typical rustic Irishman. An alternative, usually with a slightly more pejorative emphasis, is **mick**.
ᗒ'*We Import More Paddies Every Year.*'
(Joke acronym for Wimpey, British construction and civil engineering firm).

paddywaggon *n* a secure police van, a **black maria** or a police car. This term was introduced into Britain and Australia from the United States at the end of the 19th century. The reference to paddy reflects the importance of the Irish population of New York and other northern cities in providing police officers at the time, rather than to the number of Irishmen arrested. **Meat wagon** is a racier, more modern alternative.

pail *n American* An unfortunate person. An item of possibly ersatz slang from the lexicon of the cult 1992 film, *Wayne's World*. **Bucket** is a synonym.

pain in the arse/ass *n* a nuisance, irritation or source of problems. A vulgar version of '*pain in the neck*'; an expression in use since the early 20th century. (**Arse** may be substituted by any synonym or **balls**, etc.)
ᗒ'*A few drinks and respectable family men, dads, became lecherous pains in the ass.*'
(*The Switch*, Elmore Leonard, 1978).

paint *vb British* to beat up, thrash. A fairly uncommon working-class term, coined on the same lines as **paste** and the colloquial 'lather'.

painters *n pl See* **have the decorators/painters in.**

paki *n British*
a a Pakistani. The abbreviation, invariably in a racist context, began to be heard in the later 1960s.
ᗒ'*Paki scum go home.*'
(Racist graffito, Whitechapel, London, 1980).
b a shop, usually a supermarket or general store, operated by a Pakistani or other South Asian.
ᗒ'*I'm just off down the paki for a can of beans.*'
(Recorded, housewife, London, 1987).
The simple shortening is used, in the first sense, as an offensive racial epithet and in the second sense as a simple descriptive

term for the many independent corner stores owned and run by immigrant families. In both senses the word is often applied, loosely, to any immigrant from the subcontinent, including those of Bengali, Indian or Sri Lankan origin.

paki-bashing *n British* the attacking, intimidation and harassment of Asians by white thugs or racists. The phenomenon began on a large scale in the **skinhead** era (around 1969) and has not abated.

paladic, palatic *adj British* drunk, a light-hearted term of uncertain origin; it may be a corruption of **paralytic**.

palari *n British* speech, talk, particularly in **camp** and theatrical circles. It is a corruption of the Italian *parlare* or of **parlyaree**.

palatic *adj See* **paladic**.

palooka *n American* a large, clumsy and/or slow-witted male. Before World War II the word was usually employed to describe a third-rate prizefighter. It was apparently coined by Jack Conway, an ex-baseball player and sports writer. The resemblance to *peluca*, Spanish for wig, may be coincidental.

&'*This big palooka has been trying to get me pregnant every which way but lop-sided.*'
(*The Boss's Wife*, US film, 1986).

palookaville *n American*
a an out-of-the-way, slow, rustic town, **the boondocks**. The expression describes the kind of town popularly supposed to be inhabited by **palookas**.
b oblivion, ignominy. A metaphorical use, describing the state of mind characteristic of washed-up, punch-drunk prizefighters.

&'*You keep on fighting out of your class, you're buying a one-way ticket to palookaville.*'

pan-handle *n British* an erection. The term probably dates back to the 1950s, but was popularized in the late 1980s by *Viz* comic.

pansy *n*
a male homosexual or an effeminate, effete or weak male. A word first used in this context in the 1920s and well-established until the late 1960s. It survives mainly in the speech of the middle-aged and elderly.

pants *n, exclamation, adj British* this all-purpose term of disapproval was a vogue word of 1995 and 1996 among adolescents. (Under)pants had long been a subject for pubescent children's jokes, a tradition reinforced when the word was picked up by disc-jockeys and comedians, e.g. on the children's TV programme *Alive and Kicking*.

&'*Pants, said Tom, pants, pants ... I'm afraid I think this pants is a very silly word. I must go, I've a book to read.*'
(*Independent*, 9 October 1996).

pants man *n Australian* a promiscuous male, seducer or **stud**.

pantywaist *adj American* an effete person, sissy or weakling. The term comes from the image of a male wearing women's underwear or a type of toddler's one-piece garment of the same name.

paper bag job *n* an ugly or unattractive person. The image is of a person who could only be considered as a sexual partner if his or her face were covered. The expression, first heard in the 1960s, probably originated in US high-school or campus usage; it enjoyed a vogue among schoolboys in Britain in 1968–9. *Compare* **bag one's face**.

paper-hanger *n American* a passer of dud cheques and/or counterfeit money in the jargon of the underworld and police.

paraffin lamp *n British* a tramp. This rhyming-slang expression was recorded in the Merseyside area in the early 1990s, although it is presumably much older. **Penny stamp** is a synonym.

parallel parking *n American* sexual intercourse. A popular euphemism since the 1970s among high-school students and **preppies**. (The phrase is displayed on car park notices to remind drivers of parking discipline.)

paralytic, paralysed *adj* (extremely) drunk. A very common expression in Britain (but less so in the USA, where **paralysed** is probably more prevalent) since the first decade of the twentieth century.

paraphernalia *n* the apparatus and equipment (pipes, cigarette papers, scales, etc.) accompanying the taking of illicit drugs. A euphemism popularized by its use in 'head shops' from the late

1960s, paraphernalia there refers to the soft-drug culture of cannabis and hallucinogens. The same term is used, especially by law enforcers, to describe the equipment used by hard-drug addicts and users.

park a custard/tiger *vb British*
to vomit. The chosen words are intended to suggest consistency or colour. The first version was said by Eric Partridge to be in use in the Royal Navy in the 1930s.

⤷ *'People … were actually* trying *to park a custard after eating something they had only identified after swallowing and didn't want to digest.'*
(*Love it or Shove it*, Julie Burchill, 1985).

parental units *n pl American* parents, a rarer form of **units** or **rents**.

parking *n American*
necking and petting in cars. A teenage euphemism of the 1950s which is still in limited use. (In the early 1960s this activity – especially, though not exclusively, when done on the coast – was known as 'watching the submarine races'.)

park one's arse/bum/carcass *vb* to seat oneself, position oneself.

parky *adj British* cold. A word of obscure origin dating from at least before World War II and still in use. Among middle- and upper-class speakers the term is occasionally altered to parquet (as in 'parquet flooring').

⤷ *'It's a bit parky in here – mind if I close this window?'*
(Recorded, teacher, London, 1987).

parlyaree, parliari *n British* The
strong Italian influence on the theatre, dance, music and the humbler entertainments of the streets from the late 17th to the late 19th centuries gave rise to an Italianate jargon. This terminology was adopted by English speakers (including vagabonds, street traders and the like), with resulting deformation of the original Italian words. This code, later known as parlyaree or parliari (itself a corruption of the Italian, *parlare*, to speak), has died out slowly during the 20th century. Certain terms remain in limited use, among them **nanty**, **omi**, **khazi** and **bona**.

parni *n See* pawnee.

paro, parro *adj British* paranoid, in the popular sense of nervous or suspicious. These short forms were in use

among schoolchildren at the end of the 1980s. *Compare* **noid**.

parquet *adj British*
See **parky**.

party down *vb American* to let oneself go, to enjoy oneself to the full. A later embellishment of the colloquial verb to party, with overtones of dedicated involvement or application.

party-hat *n American* a condom.
Synonyms are **hat**, **jim(my)-hat**.

party pooper *n* a spoilsport, 'wet blanket'. This expression (see **poop** for the probable origin) was introduced to Britain from the United States in the early 1960s. It originally referred to adults interfering in teenagers' activities, but was later generalized to describe any morose or unconvivial person.

pash *n British* a teenage 'crush', an infatuation; especially a young girl's feelings towards an older girl or teacher. A shortening of 'passion' still heard in public schools.

⤷ *'Amanda has a pash on Miss.'*

passion pit *n American* a cinema (not necessarily a **fleapit**) or other location as a venue for seduction.

passion wagon *n* a car or van used for purposes of dating and/or seduction. The word was probably first used in armed-services slang during World War II, describing buses used to transport female personnel. **Draggin' wagon** and **shaggin' wagon** are later, racier alternatives.

paste (someone), paste one on (someone) *vb British* to hit, beat up, 'thrash' or defeat. This use of the word paste, perhaps inspired by the slapping of paste on walls, posters, etc., or from baste or lambaste, arose in the 19th century and was popular in colloquial speech until the late 1950s. Paste one on (someone) was then an alternative version; 'give someone a (good) pasting' survives.

pasting *n* a beating or resounding defeat. From the verb to **paste (someone)**.

patch *n* one's territory, area of jurisdiction. A designation used by streetgangs, drug dealers and law enforcers.

patootie *n American* 1 backside, but-

tocks. An inoffensive term which may be an invention or a deformation of 'potato'.

↳*'She fell flat on her patootie.'*

↳*'You can bet your sweet patootie I will!'*

2 a girlfriend or boyfriend, sweetheart. In this (now obsolescent) sense the word is almost certainly a jocular alteration of (sweet) potato.

patsy *n* a dupe. The term dates from the early years of the century but its original significance is lost. (Robert L. Chapman's *New Dictionary of American Slang* tentatively derives it from *pasqualino*, Italian for scapegoat or loser.)

pattie *n British* a 'first' (first-class degree). A student pun (rhyming slang on Pattie Hearst) on the pattern of **Desmond**, etc. A set of nicknames of this sort was coined in 1987 and 1988.

pavement pizza *n* a patch of vomit in the street. A drinkers' term from the 1980s which forms part of a set of terms such as **road pizza**, **road apple** etc. as supposedly humorous euphemisms for distasteful discoveries.

paw *n* hand.

pawnee *n British*

a a body of water; lake, pond, sea.

↳*'Two ducks on the pawnee.'*

(Bingo callers' code for the number 22).

b water in any form (such as rain, tears, etc.). The word, now very rarely heard but not extinct, is a corruption of the Hindi *pani*, entering English through colonial slang, Romany, or both.

pax *exclamation British* a request for a truce, usually heard in the course of children's games. The word is Latin for peace and was formerly used by public-school masters as well as boys to appeal for calm or silence. Non-public-school children usually employed the word **faynits**.

paydirt *n* profit, reward, success. A mining metaphor originating in the USA.

payola *n* bribery or extortion. This underworld term achieved prominence in the 1960s in the USA when it was applied to a scandal involving illicit payment to disc jockeys in return for airplays. It is the word pay with the Spanish suffix **-ola** (big, grandiose or outrageous).

P.C.P. *n*

angel dust. The initials are from phencyclidine, an animal tranquillizer that was abused (and manufactured in home laboratories), particularly in the USA in the 1970s, for its disorienting effects.

P.D.A. *n American* a 'public display of affection'. A **preppie** code term for overt kissing, hugging, etc., usually said in a disapproving tone.

P.D.Q. *adj, adv* 'pretty damn quick'. A middle-class adults' expression often used in issuing commands or instructions. The term was recorded in Britain in 1900 and may be earlier.

pea-brain(ed) *n, adj* (someone who is) stupid.

peace, peace out! *exclamation American* goodbye. A term from the lexicon of **rap** and hip-hop aficionados which was adopted by some white speakers, particularly on university campuses in the 1990s.

peach *n British* a foolish person. A less common synonym of **plum** and **pear**, used by schoolchildren in the 1990s.

peach (on someone) *vb* to inform upon someone. This term originated in the 15th century as a shortening of the archaic term 'apeach' (related to impeach) and has yet to be adopted into orthodox usage. It was commonly used as late as the 1960s but is now rare, except in the speech of an older generation.

peachy *adj American* wonderful, excellent. The term, now often used ironically, is based on the earlier noun peach, meaning someone or something delectable. Peachy-keen is an intensive form of the word.

peaky *adj American* producing euphoria. This appreciative term formed from 'peaking' (i.e. achieving a maximum **high**) refers to the enjoyable effects of drugs.

↳*'We managed to get hold of some peaky shit.'*

pearler *n Australian* an excellent, exceptional person or object. From the notion of a pearl as a peerless example.

↳*'She's a little pearler. I don't know what I'd do without her.'*

pears *n pl Australian* breasts. Another example of the tendency for any vaguely rounded fruit to be used to symbolize breasts. Compare **apples**, **melons**, etc.

pear-shaped *adj British* awry, faulty, inadequate. This increasingly common adult colloquialism is usually heard in the phrase to 'go pear-shaped', presumably from the image of a balloon or football losing its spherical shape after puncturing.

✎ *'Things were OK until Christine left and then within a short time it all started to go pear-shaped.'*
(Recorded, London schoolteacher, February 1996).

pecker *n American* penis. The term may originate as a rural shortening of woodpecker, or as a euphemism for **cock**, or simply as a metaphor for an importunate member.

✎ *'When I told him to get a-hold of himself I didn't mean for him to get his pecker out.'*
(Recorded, US oilman, Norway, 1982).

peckerhead *n American* a fool, slow-witted or clumsy person. Originally used by country people, now a favourite term of abuse among college students and others. The British and Australian equivalent is **dickhead**.

peckerwood *n American* a white person. This derogatory term has been used by black and white alike and uses the southern American name for the red-headed woodpecker (the link is the reference to that bird's red neck). The term is sometimes abbreviated to 'wood' and is often thought wrongly to be a synonym for **peckerhead**.

✎ *'Selective breeding in the good-old-boy peckerwood, white-sheet, lynch-mob states has brought about a monster ... a dog that is auditioning for the apocalypse ...'*
(*Lights Out for the Territory* by Iain Sinclair, 1997).

pecs *n pl American* pectoral muscles. A word used particularly by body builders and by women admiring (or disparaging) the male physique. The shortening became widespread in the 1970s.

✎ *'The guys there [California] all have great pecs, but I guess that's not the only thing.'*
(Recorded, American female executive, London, 1986).

pedigree chum *n British* an upper-class girl's escort or boyfriend. A witticism inspired by **debs' delight** punning on the brand name of a dogfood. The phrase arose in the 1980s.

pee, pee-pee *n* urine or an act of urination. The word is probably in origin a euphemistic form of the more onomatopoeic **piss**, but is reinforced by being the initial sound of **piddle** and a cognate of other European forms (such as the French *pipi*). It was not recorded before the 18th century.

pee, pee-pee *vb* to urinate.
(For the origins of the word see the noun form.)

pee'd *adj British* a more polite version of **pissed**.

pee'd off *adj* a less offensive version of **pissed-off**.

peek *n British* an observation cell in a prison, in the jargon of prisoners recorded in the 1990s. (The verb 'peek' itself is not slang, being a direct descendant from Middle English 'piken'.)

peeler *n British* a policeman. From Robert Peel, the 19th-century statesman responsible for Britain's first coherently organized police force. The term is now archaic in most parts of the British Isles but is still used by Republicans and their sympathizers in Northern Ireland to refer disparagingly to the British security forces.

peely-wally *adj British* wan, ailing. The phrase is heard particularly in the Scottish Lowlands and the north of England, but is also sometimes used by Jamaican and black British speakers. The expression may be an elaboration of 'pale' or derive from a personal nickname.

✎ *'Feeling/looking a bit peely-wally.'*

peepers *n pl* eyes. A humorous euphemism.

peeps *n pl* people. The term occurs in American slang, in which it may refer to one's fellow gang members or one's friends and family, and in British, where it is often a plural term of address, probably inspired by its use in the comic monologues delivered by the comedian Harry Enfield in the character of Stavros the kebab-shop owner in the 1980s.

peg it, peg out *vb* to die. The first

version of the phrase is currently more fashionable than the earlier peg out, which appeared in the USA in the mid-19th century, inspired by the use of pegs in the game of cribbage ('pegging-out' was finishing the game). The form peg out may also mean to collapse exhausted or fail in one's efforts.

pelf *n British* money. An old term, like many others (**rhino**, **spondulicks**, etc.) revived in the money-conscious environment of the later 1980s. Pelf is from the Middle English pelfre, related to 'pilfer' and meaning loot.

↳'*Miss Smith ... Cold as the Ice itself; She admires nought but Pelf.*'
(*List of Covent Garden Ladies, or the New Atlantis*, pamphlet, 1773).

pen-and-ink *n, vb British* (a) stink. An early 20th-century cockney rhyming-slang term which has survived to the present. It can be used as a noun phrase, as in '*there's a real pen-and-ink in here!*' or as a verb, normally in a form such as '*it don't half pen-and-ink in here!*'.

pencil-dick *n American* a vulgar alternative of **pencil-neck** and **pencil geek**.

pencil geek *n American* a tediously studious person, **swot**. One of many high-school and campus categorizations of fellow students; **grind** and **conch** are synonymous. *See* **geek**.

pencil-neck *n American* an earnest, unattractive, excessively studious male. A derogatory term, suggesting the appearance of a scrawny individual, which has been used as a synonym for **nerd**, **grind**, etc. **Pencil geek** is an alternative form.

penguin suit *n* formal male evening dress; a dinner suit.

penny stamp *n British* a tramp. This old example of London rhyming slang was still in use in the 1990s, now referring to homeless persons in general. **Paraffin lamp** is an alternative.

pep pill *n* a tablet of amphetamine or a similar drug. This term was used in the 1940s when stimulant drugs such as caffeine and benzedrine were taken to combat fatigue and sleep. The expression was used by illicit drug takers until the early 1960s when it was appropriated by spokesmen for the anti-drug establishment and the media. **Speed** and **uppers** became the generic slang terms for this class of drugs from the mid-1960s.

percy *n* the penis. One of a number of personifications of the male member which include **peter, dick, willie, John Thomas**, etc. The word principally functions as part of the phrase **point percy at the porcelain**.

perk *vb Australian* to vomit. A variant of **puke**, perhaps influenced by the phrase 'to perk up' or the word 'percolate'.

perp *n American* a wrongdoer, felon. An abbreviation of 'perpetrator' used by law enforcers.

↳'*All three bridges raise and the perp can't get off the island.*'
(*The Dancer's Touch*, US film, 1989).

personals *n Australian* lingerie, (ladies') underwear. An adult euphemism used both facetiously and seriously.

↳'*I wouldn't hang your personals out here in full view.*'

Peruvian marching powder
n cocaine. A jocular middle-class American euphemism of the mid- to late 1970s which was probably too long and unwieldy to gain a wider currency.

perve, perv *n* a lascivious or perverted person, a 'dirty old man'. A shortening of pervert heard since the 1960s.

perve, perv *vb Australian* to behave lasciviously. From the noun form.

pervy *adj* perverted or lascivious.

peter *n* 1 penis. A personification and predictable euphemism dating from the 19th century (if not earlier) and mainly used by adults.

↳'*Absence makes the peter fonda.*'
(Caption to nude photograph of Peter Fonda, *OZ* magazine, 1969).

2 a safe. In the jargon of the underworld peter originally meant a trunk or strongbox, later a safe. The word was being used with this sense as early as the 17th century, perhaps inspired by some sort of biblical pun, now lost.

peter-man *n British* a safecracker. An underworld and police term in use for the last few decades or so. Peter is an old word for safe or strongbox.

Peter Tosh
n British a wash. An item of rhyming slang recorded in the 1980s employing the name of the late Jamaican reggae star.

petrified *adj American* intoxicated by alcohol or drugs. The term has no connection with the colloquial sense of 'terrified' but is a pun on the more common **stoned**.

petrol-head *n* a car enthusiast. The term is heard both in Britain and Australia and has been given wider currency in Britain in the 1990s by its usage in motoring magazines and such television programmes as BBC TV's *Top Gear*.

pew *n British* a chair. A colloquialism usually heard in the verb form 'take a pew': sit down. This humorously elevated version of chair arose around the turn of the century.

phat *adj* excellent, **hip**. The re-spelling of **fat** (itself alternatively derived from its use in the phrase **fat-city** or from the fat tyres favoured by **low-riders**, etc.) was an emblematic term first in hip-hop and **rap** circles and then in other youth subcultures such as surfers, skateboarders and skaters, etc. (A magazine named *Phat* catering for rollerbladers and computer-game fans was briefly published in Britain in 1994.) In this spelling the word, which some authorities claimed was actually based on 'emphatically', had no comparative or superlative forms to compare with **fattier, fattiest**.
꙳'*Phat garms.*'

phreak *vb* to hack into a telephone, telecommunications or computer system, in the patois of **cyberpunks** and **netheads**. The term is a later back-formation from '*phreaker*', the designation for the first hackers who interfered with the US telephone system for fun, in search of knowledge or for profit.

piano *adj British* faint, delicate, 'under the weather' or indisposed. This upper-class expression derives from the Italian musical term *piano*, which is an instruction to play or sing softly. The British speaker's pronunciation, in imitation of the original Italian, is 'pee-aah-no'.
꙳'*Please don't disturb her, she seems to be feeling a little piano today.*'
(Recorded, hostess, Dorset, 1974).

pickled *adj* drunk. A fairly inoffensive term, usually heard in the speech of the middle-aged or elderly.
꙳'*I sat next to Pat Collins who is a very intelligent and delightful woman. I felt sorry that she had George Brown,*

completely pickled, on the other side of her.'
(Tony Benn's Diaries, 14 October 1969).

piddle *vb British* to urinate. A childish or humorous-sounding word, this is nonetheless one of Britain's oldest 'non-respectable' words in current use. (*See also* the noun form **piddle**.)

piddle *n British* urine or an act of urination. Piddle is etymologically related to puddle and to piddling meaning insignificant or trifling. It has been used as the name of small rivers in county districts and seems to have had a colloquial meaning of 'small water' or 'insignificant scrap' before its narrowing to the modern sense during the 18th and 19th centuries.
꙳'*Piddles were done out of the back window last night, standing on the bed.*'
(Spike Milligan, *Adolf Hitler; My Part in His Downfall*, 1971).

piece *n* 1 *American* a gun. An underworld euphemism.
2 a graffiti artist's *oeuvre*. A shortening of 'piece of work' or 'masterpiece' and forming part of the graffiti sub-culture lexicon of the 1980s.
꙳'*Kids do it mainly for the clothes – jeans or trainers, or to buy cans of spray paint to do pieces (graffiti).*'
(Teenage mugger, *Observer*, 22 May 1988).

piece (of ass) *n American* a woman (or, less often, a man) considered as a sexual object. Piece has been employed in a similar sexual context, invariably referring unromantically to a woman, since the 15th century. The various phrases such as piece of ass, **piece of tail**, etc. are probably more recent, arising, like **bit of fluff**, in the 19th century.

piece of piss/pudding *n British* something easy to accomplish, presenting no problems, a 'pushover'. Both terms are variants on the common colloquialism 'a piece of cake'.

piece of tail *n* an alternative form of **piece of ass**.

pieces *n pl British See* **do one's nut/pieces**.

pie-eater *n Australian*
a a poor, unimpressive or unfortunate person.
b a stupid or unsophisticated person.

Both usages are based on the notion of (meat) pies as the staple diet of the poorest **ockers**.

pie-face *n American* a general term of endearment.

pie-hole *n American* mouth. A humorous usage heard among adolescents and featured in the US movie, *Sleepwalkers*, 1992. **Hum-hole** and the earlier British **cakehole** are synonyms.

piff *n British* nonsense. A 1980s shortening of the colloquial 'piffle', heard among adolescents.
↳'*A load of piff.*'

piffy *adj British* dubious, doubtful, suspect. A middle-class usage, often said disdainfully or superciliously. Its origin is obscure; it does not appear to be related to piffling, in the sense of insignificant, but may be influenced by 'iffy' or 'piffle'.

pig *n* 1 a policeman or -woman. An offensive term that gained its greatest currency in the 1960s in the USA whence it was reimported into Britain. (It was used in the same sense in the late Victorian underworld.)
↳'*Today's pig is tomorrow's bacon.*'
(Anti-war protestors' and demonstrators' slogan of the 1960s).
2 **a** a girl. A usage from the argot of street-gangs, **beatniks**, etc. since the 1950s. Surprisingly in these contexts the word is not necessarily pejorative.
b *American* an ugly, repellent girl. A term current in the late 1980s at US colleges, where 'Pig of the Year (or Week)' contests took place and the unwitting winner was presented with a prize.
3 a sexist male, as characterized by feminists. A shortening of the catchphrase 'male chauvinist pig' (also rendered as MCP).
4 a segment of an orange.
These sub-senses evoke the familiar images of the pig as gluttonous and disgusting or round and chubby.

pigfucker *n* a despicable, disgusting and/or unpleasant person. An all-purpose term of strong abuse, usually applied to males. This version of the insult is probably more prevalent in the USA; **fuckpig** is a British synonym.

pig in a blanket *n British* a sausage roll or hot-dog. The nickname is used by caterers.

pigging *adj British* an intensifying adjective used as a milder substitute for **fucking**. Pigging has the merit of being able to be broadcast. It is used, often with vehemence, by both men and, particularly, women.
↳'*I told him to take his pigging "peace offering" and get lost.*'

pig it *vb British* to behave in a disgusting manner. The expression may apply to living in filthy surroundings, acting in a slovenly way or 'slumming'.

pig Latin *n* a synonym for **backslang**, or a means of coining slang terms by the rearranging of syllables. **Ixnay** is an example.

piglet *n Australian* an unattractive teenage girl. See **pig**.

pigmobile *n* a police car. A term used by adolescents and **hippies** since the early 1970s.

pig off *vb* to leave, go away. A euphemism for more offensive terms such as **piss off**, etc., usually heard in the form of an imperative. It is often used by women who wish to express themselves forcefully without obscenity.
↳'*I finally got fed up and told him to pig off.*'
(Recorded, female teacher, London, 1989).

pig out *vb* to eat excessively and/or messily, to behave in an outrageous or obsessive way. This racier version of the colloquial 'pig (oneself)', meaning to overindulge, probably originated in the USA, and was established in Britain during the later 1960s.

pig's, pig's ear *n British* 1 beer. A London rhyming-slang term that is still heard. (The dismissive exclamatory phrase '*in a pig's ear!*' is unconnected, being a euphemism for '*in a pig's arse!*'.)
↳'*I'll have a pint of pig's.*'
2 another version of **pig's breakfast**.

pig's breakfast/arse/ear *n British* a mess, an outrageous failure, a complete disaster. Most often heard in forms such as '*you've made a right pig's breakfast of that!*'.

piker *n American* a mean, 'tightfisted' person; a welsher on a bet or a shirker. A now obsolescent word, related distantly to the British **pikey**, or from an abbreviation of 'turnpike', piker occurred in the writings of Raymond Chandler in the 1940s. It originally referred to the unreliability of vagrants or itinerants.

pikey, pikie *n British* a gypsy or vagrant. The term now properly denotes one of the travelling people who lives in a settlement, such as a member of a family of hop-pickers. It is now fairly rare, but was still common in the 1950s. The precise origins of these terms (and the American **piker**) are unclear because of the convergence of two similar senses of pike; the first is a toll road as in turnpike, the second is an archaic British verb meaning to depart or travel.

pill *n British* 1 a ball. A schoolboy term of the 1950s.

↳ '*If I pla there is dead silence becos i never hit the pill at all they are all air shots chiz.*'
(Geoffrey Willans and Ronald Searle, *Back in the Jug Agane*, 1959).

2 **pills** testicles; by extension from the above.

3 a foolish or stupid, annoying person. A shortening of **pillock**.

4 *South African* a **joint**. Recorded as an item of Sowetan slang in the *Cape Sunday Times*, 29 January 1995.

pill-head *n* an amphetamine user or addict.

pillock *n British* a foolish or stupid, annoying person. A vulgar but not taboo term of abuse which had existed in British slang usage since the 1950s (its exact date of origin is undetermined), coming into vogue in the mid-1970s; various etymologies have been proposed for the word; 'pillicock' was a late medieval term for penis, sometimes used as an expression of endearment or affectionate abuse; pillocks has also been explained as a rural term for rabbit droppings, or as a synonym for testicles (**pills**) employing the diminutive or affectionate suffix '-ocks' (as in the case of **balls** and **bollocks**).

pillow-biter *n* a male homosexual, particularly a passive partner in sodomy. This expression probably originated in Australia, where it is common. It was introduced to the British public during the trial of Jeremy Thorpe (accused of plotting the murder of a male model, Norman Scott, in 1974) by the satirical magazine *Private Eye*.

pill-popper *n* a user of amphetamines or tranquillizers.

pimp (someone) (over) *vb American* to deceive, cheat.

↳ '*Man. I got pimped that time.*'
↳ '*He pimped us over good.*'

pimps *n, adj British* (something) very easy, a 'pushover'. A word used by young schoolchildren in the late 1980s, particularly when showing off or boasting. The word is usually used in an exclamation such as 'that's pimps!' or 'it's pimps!', meaning 'there's nothing to it'. There seems to be no relation between this term and the standard English word for a procurer or the archaic use of pimp to mean sneak or inform upon.

pimpsy, pipsy *adj British* easily accomplished, no trouble. A variant of **pimps** used typically by middle-class schoolchildren.

pinch *vb, n* (to make) an arrest. An underworld and police term on both sides of the Atlantic.

pinch a loaf, pinch one off *vb American* to defecate. The phrases are part of male **toilet-talk**.

pineapple *n Australian See* **rough end of the pineapple**.

ping *vb British* to shoot, or wound by shooting. An item of underworld slang from the early 1990s, the word is echoic, imitating the sound of a small-calibre gunshot or a ricochet. *Compare* **plinking**.

pinhead *n*
a a fool, idiot.
b a person with a small head and a (proportionately) large body. *See* **nibhead**.

pink *adj* a code or facetious term for gay adopted from the heterosexual lexicon by the male homosexual community for ironic or semi-ironic self-reference. (The Nazis affixed pink triangles to homosexuals.) **Lavender** is a similar usage.

pink *n American* the female genitals. This term, which arose in the language of pornographers, prostitutes, etc., was picked up in show-business jargon in such phrases as '*surrender the pink*' (the title of a book by the actress Carrie Fisher) and the name '*Kissing the Pink*' adopted by an early 1990s rock band.

pinkie *n* 1 a white person. A term of mild racist abuse used by black speakers in London in the mid-1970s. A more accurate and less flattering version of **whitey**.

2 the little finger. An American term now generally understood in Britain and Australia.

pinko *n, adj American* someone with liberal or left-of-centre politics or ideas. The image is of a watered-down 'red' (someone with extreme left-wing beliefs).

pinko *adj, n Australian* (intoxicated by) methylated spirits, which are often dyed pink.

pinned-up *adj British* under the influence of heroin. An addicts' or users' term of the 1980s referring to the way the pupils of the eye contract to pinpoints after an injection of the narcotic.

pipe *n* 1 *American* a gun. An item of street jargon used especially by adolescent criminals in the 1990s.

↳*'Teachers report that teenagers talk about "packing a barrel" or "chilling someone with a pipe".'*
(*Sunday Times*, 31 August 1992)

2 *British* a telephone, particularly a mobile telephone, in the jargon of truck-drivers and rescue services.

3 *American* a very easy task, programme of study, etc. This usage is probably based on the earlier phrase '*pipe course*', used on campuses to describe an undemanding study option. The relationship to the standard sense of the word is unclear.

pipe *vb British* to look at, watch. The origin of this use of the word is obscure; it seems to have come to Britain at the end of the 19th century from the United States, where it was used in underworld circles to mean spy on or keep an eye on. The word now sounds dated in British slang speech, but is still occasionally heard.

↳*'Pipe the widow ginger!'*
(Recorded, bookie's runner, London, 1958).

pipe one's eye *vb* to weep. This phrase is now almost obsolete, except in self-consciously fanciful speech. Although 'pipe your eye' has been interpreted as cockney rhyming slang for cry, the expression had been recorded as early as the beginning of the 19th century (before either cockney rhyming slang or the use

of the word cry to mean weep were widespread). Connections have been drawn with plaintive, tear-provoking pipe music or the more prosaic image of waterworks, but the precise origins of the term remain uncertain.

piper *n American* a **crack** smoker. A term of the late 1980s.

↳*'Clocking means getting a pack of cocaine from somebody like Felix, then standing on a street corner to hand off caps of crack to the pipers and users who drift by.'*
(*Sunday Times*, 10 September 1989).

piss, the piss *n* 1 urine or urination. An echoic word with cognates in other European languages (*pisser* is the French verb), which has been in use since the Middle English period. Its level of respectability has varied; originally it was a generally acceptable term, by the 18th century a vulgarism, and by the mid-19th century virtually taboo. Since the 1960s it has been possible to use the word in public although **pee** is preferred in polite company.

2 *British* **the piss**. Alcoholic drink. In this sense the term usually occurs in the phrase **on the piss**.

3 weak beer.

4 nonsense. *See* **take the piss**.

piss about/around *vb* a vulgar version of 'mess about'.

piss all over (someone) *vb* to thoroughly defeat, humiliate or overwhelm. The image is taken from the literal behaviour of animals or humans ritually signalling victory.

piss and wind *n See* **all piss and wind**.

piss-ant, pissant *adj American* trifling, paltry, insignificant. Although a fairly strong indicator of contempt or dismissal, this word is not treated as a taboo item in the same way as other compounds containing **piss**. The word is originally a rustic noun (also rendered 'piss-mire') meaning an ant. The piss element refers to formic acid.

piss-artist *n British* an habitual or accomplished heavy drinker, drunkard. A term used sometimes with contempt, sometimes with admiration.

pissed *adj* 1 *British* drunk. This usage came into the language at some unrecorded date early in the 20th century. It presumably originally referred to the incontinence of a helpless inebriate, or else to the equation of alcohol itself with urine. This sense of the word is rare in American English, but is encountered for example in the 1980s parlance of East coast sophisticates.

⬦ *'He served in Northern Ireland, but mainly he played sport and got pissed. Then he was sent off to the Falklands, where he found himself at the centre of the biggest British cockup of the war, the bombing of the Sir Galahad, which killed 48 men.'*
(*Observer*, 9 April 1989).

2 *American* upset, angry, **pissed-off**.
⬦ *'When I told him to go he got really pissed.'*
⬦ *'I was pissed at her for making me go through all that grief.'*

pissed-off *adj* angry, irritated, disappointed, upset. Like the verb to **piss (someone) off**, this usage emerged at the time of World War II.
⬦ *'Well … people who bought from our competitors are probably pretty pissed off. The plastic should be worn through just about now!'*
(Record bootlegger, *Oz* magazine, February 1970).

piss-elegant *adj American* smart, refined or fashionable. This (fairly mild) vulgarism implies either that the elegance in question is excessive or pretentious or simply that the speaker is envious or disapproving.

pisser *n* **1** something annoying or disappointing. Originally an Americanism the term spread to Britain in the mid-1970s.
⬦ *'Living in a world where nothing boring ever happens is a real pisser.'*
(*The Young Ones*, BBC TV comedy, 1982).

2 a toilet. *See* **wicked pisser**.

pisshead *n* **1** *British* a habitual drunkard, **piss-artist**.
2 *American* an unpleasant person, **shit-head**.

pissing-match, pissing contest *n American* a competitive display, especially a futile one. The term, inspired by the common male pastime of competing to urinate farthest or highest, is used typically to describe displays of masculine aggression or rivalry.

⬦ *'Look sister, I don't want to get into a pissing contest with you, just tell me where the command bunker is.'*
(*Screamers*, US film, 1996).

piss in someone's pool *vb American* a vulgar alternative to **rain on someone's parade**.

piss in the wind *vb* to do something futile, make a doomed attempt. A vulgar version of such colloquialisms as 'whistle in the wind/dark'.

piss it *vb British* to succeed effortlessly. A term probably deriving from **piece of piss**: a ridiculously easy task. The expression piss it was widespread in the 1980s throughout all social classes.
⬦ *'They told Sophie the entrance exam would be a bugger, but she absolutely pissed it.'*
(Recorded, personal assistant, London, 1989).

piss off *vb* to leave, go away. This vulgarism has been in use throughout the 20th century, particularly in British speech. The word piss has no specific significance, but adds intensity and often overtones of exasperation both where used descriptively and as an instruction.
⬦ *'I feel like pissing off and spending the night in some Arab doss house.'*
(Joe Orton's Diary, 14 May 1967).

piss (someone) off *vb* to irritate, anger, annoy or provoke. This phrase entered the English slang lexicon around the time of World War II and was probably more prevalent in American speech than British until the 1970s.
⬦ *'It really pisses me off the way she just assumes I'm going to pick up the pieces.'*

piss on someone's chips/ sandwiches *vb British* more vulgar synonyms for the American phrase **rain on someone's parade**. The latter version was used by the standup comedienne Jo Brand in 1994.

piss-poor *adj* dreadfully bad. Piss is used here as an intensifying addition. The phrase was earlier used to mean destitute; since the late 1970s it has enjoyed something of a vogue, particularly in journalistic circles to denote 'of miserable quality', pitiful.

piss pot *n* a chamber-pot, potty.

piss-take *n British* an act of mockery, parody. A common back formation from the phrase to **take the piss (out of)**.

piss-up *n British* a drinking bout, drunken celebration. A vulgarism generally used neutrally or with cheerful overtones rather than disapprovingly.

✎ '*Bob Bee, for Hawkhead Productions, has secured the ultimate television commission: to organise a piss-up in a brewery.*'
(*Independent on Sunday*, 1 April 1990).

pissy *adj* insignificant, trivial, inferior.

pistol *n American* an attractive, active or powerful person. Used of and by both sexes as a term of admiration, the word need not have sexual connotations, but in modern usage often does.

✎ '*Isn't she a pistol?*'

pit *n* 1 a bed. A popular word in the armed services since before World War II, now in general use.
2 any dirty, sordid or unpleasant place. A more recent alternative to dump, a synonym for **tip**. *See also* **the pits**, **throttle pit**.

pitcher *n British* a market trader who sells his or her wares by way of an ostentatious performance. *Compare* **lurker**, **rorter**.

the pits *n* an unpleasant, disgusting and/or unbearable place, situation or person; the worst place, situation or state of affairs imaginable. This Americanism has become widely used throughout the English-speaking world. It is in origin said to be a shortening of armpits.

✎ '*You are the pits of the world!*'
(John McEnroe characterizing an umpire, Wimbledon Lawn Tennis Championship, 1981).

✎ '*This review has nothing to do with the world of mountaineering and in a sport where there is a wealth of first-rate literature, this "offering" can only be regarded as the pits.*'
(Reader's letter, *Sunday Times* Books supplement, October 1989).

pit stop *n*
a a pause in a drinking bout in order to visit the toilet.
b a pause in a journey or other activity for alcoholic refreshment.
Both senses are humorous adaptations of the pit stops made by racing drivers in order to undergo refuelling, a change of tyres or running repairs.

plank *n* 1 *British* a dull-witted person, someone who is as '*thick as two short planks*'.
2 a solid-bodied electric guitar. A musician's term of the 1980s; playing such a guitar is known as **spanking the plank**.

plank *vb American* to have sex (with). A fairly rare usage inspired by the image of lying flat.

plastic *adj* (usually of a person) artificial, shallow, insincere. A **hippy** buzz-word of the 1960s, borrowed from **beatnik** usage to castigate the conformist and materialist world of the **straights** as well as the legions of 'weekend' **hippy** imitators. The word submerged during the 1970s, but by 1990 was back in use in British playground slang.

plat *n Australian* a stupid person. The word's origin is uncertain (Eric Partridge derives it from the French *plat*: flat), but the resemblance to **prat** may not be fortuitous.

plate *vb* to perform fellatio. A term from the 1960s, now dated, which was part of the jargon of rock-music **groupies**. Conflicting etymologies cite the rhyming slang 'plate of ham' for **gam** (a synonym for fellatio), or simply the image of licking a plate.

plate-face *n Australian* someone of oriental origin. A derogatory racist term referring to the supposedly wide, flat, round faces of the Mongoloid racial type.

plates (of meat) *n pl British* feet. A well-known example of cockney rhyming slang which is actually still used, although almost always in the shortened form, by working-class Londoners.

✎ '*I've got to sit down – I've been on me plates all day.*'

plating *n* fellatio. A term from the jargon of prostitutes and pornographers which was adopted by **groupies** in the late 1960s. *See* **plate**.

platter *n* a phonograph record. The term dates back to the era of 78 r.p.m. records; it does not seem to have been transferred to apply to CDs.

play footsie *vb*
a to indulge in amorous or flirtatious ca-

resses with the feet, typically covertly under a table.

b to flirt with or toy with in a general sense; often in the context of business and commercial relationships.

play gooseberry *vb British* to be the unwanted third person present at a romantic assignation, as a chaperone, uninvited guest or unwitting intruder. The expression dates from the 19th century: in the language of parents and children 'gooseberry' then as now denoted a buffoon or figure of fun, possibly from the supposedly comic appearance of the fruit or its sour taste.

play hardball *vb American* to behave in a tough, unrelenting or uncompromising way. A phrase used for instance among business people, politicians, sportsmen, etc. from the 1960s, and now heard outside the United States. A metaphor taken from baseball, where a hard ball is used by professionals and a soft one by juniors and amateurs.

play hooky *vb American* to play truant. Hooky (or 'hookey') is related to the cockney **hook it**: 'to take to one's heels', escape.

play hospitals/doctor/doctors and nurses *vb* to engage in sexual play or activity. The reference can refer literally to children's exploratory play or, coyly, to adult sexual activity. **Doctors and nurses** is a variant.

play the whale *vb Australian* to vomit. The image is of a whale spouting.

pleb *n* a plebeian, member of the lower classes. A fashionable term in Britain in the early 1960s when class-consciousness preceded 'consciousness-expanding' among the educated young.

plinking *n American* shooting a firearm for pleasure and competition rather than criminal intent. The word imitates the sound of small-calibre gunfire. *Compare* **ping**.

plod, the plod *n British* the police force or a uniformed policeman. From 'P.C. Plod', a character from the popular children's stories featuring Noddy, written by Enid Blyton in the 1950s. The term additionally evokes a slow-witted, literal and figurative plodder in a civilian context.

plonk *n British* **1** wine, especially cheap wine. The word usually refers to red wine, although it was originally a corruption of *vin blanc* coined by British soldiers in France during World War I.
2 a woman police officer. An item of derogatory police slang (from **plonker**) recorded by the *Evening Standard* magazine, February 1993.

plonker *n British* **1** penis. A term probably influenced by 'plonk (down)' in the sense of place down heavily or present defiantly. The word has been in use since early in the 20th century. It was rarely heard during the 1960s and 1970s but was revived during the 1980s vogue for 'schoolboy' vulgarity.

↳ *'If she's game and wants your plonker wear a Jiffi so you can bonk her.'*
(Promotion slogan for *Jiffi* condoms, 1988).

2 a **dickhead**. Inspired by the previous sense of the word and by the suggestion in 'plonk' of ponderous or clumsy movement, this usage has become a vogue term of the late 1980s. Unlike its synonym **dickhead**, it can be broadcast, and has gained popular appeal, particularly when applied to the character 'Rodney' in the British TV comedy series *Only Fools and Horses*.

↳ *'You end up shouting at the people who care about yer, not to the plonkers who treat you like dirt.'*
(*EastEnders*, British TV drama series, 1989).

3 a gaffe or blunder.

4 a kiss, particularly a heavy **smacker**.

plook, pluke *n Scottish* a spot or pimple on the skin, **zit**. The etymology of the word is obscure.

ploughed, plowed *adj American* drunk. One of many terms evoking an image of laid low, crushed or destroyed. **Blitzed**, **smashed**, **legless**, etc. are others on this theme.

plow *vb American* to have (aggressive) sex (with someone). The vulgarism, which refers to sex from the male perspective, is in use among both adolescents and adults. The verb has been used figuratively in this way at various periods over the last few centuries.

p.l.u. *n, adj British* 'people like us'. An upper-class code term of approbation and social discrimination.

↳ *'I'm afraid they're not really quite p.l.u.'*

plum *n British* a foolish person. Synonyms are the less common **pear** and **peach**. The widespread term was recorded in use by junior-school children in the 1980s and among teenage north London schoolboys in 1993 and 1994.

plums *n pl* testicles. One of many examples of fruit as a sexual metaphor.

plunker *n American* a condom.

po *n British* a chamber-pot, potty, toilet. Now a dated nursery word, po was used by adults until the 1960s. The word is an imitation of the French pronunciation of *pot (de chambre)*.

pocket billiards/pool *n* (of a man) manipulation of one's genitals through the trouser pockets. The first phrase is British, the second the American version.

pod *n American* marihuana. A dated term derived from the seedheads found in herbal cannabis.

podger *n British* an act of sex. The humorous vulgarism was used, e.g., in the British TV comedy *Absolutely* in 1991. It is perhaps influenced by **roger** and the many sexually related terms beginning with p-, or could be a hitherto unrecorded term for an erection based on the colloquial 'podgy'.

�ℵ '*A swift podger.*'

pogie, pogey, pogy *n American* the female sex organs. The word is probably derived from the obsolete 'pogie' or 'pogue', which denoted a male homosexual, hence sexual activity in general.

point percy at the porcelain *vb* to urinate. An expression invented by Barry Humphries, which via the comic strip *The Wonderful World of Barry McKenzie* has passed into common currency in Britain as well as Australia. **Percy** is one of many common personifications of the male member.

pointy-head *n American* an intellectual or person of excessive refinement. The expression has been used in the USA since the late 1960s by the self-consciously philistine or genuinely uncultured in expressing contempt for political or social pundits, artists, academics, etc.

poison dwarf *n British* an obnoxious small person, brutish individual. The epithet was coined by Germans referring to Scottish members of the British Rhine army. The phrase lodged itself in the British lexicon of abuse (whence it was borrowed by Terry Wogan to refer to the character of 'Lucy Ewing' in the US TV series *Dallas*, for instance).

poke *n* 1 an act of sexual intercourse. Poke shares this sexual sense with **bang**, **boff**, **knock**, etc., which are all synonyms for strike.
2 a punch, blow. A specialized sense of the standard English word poke meaning to prod (having the same meaning as the Middle Dutch *poken*).

polack *n* a Polish person. The slang term, often pejorative in American usage, is, minus the e, the word for Pole in the Polish language.

polisher *n* a toady, ingratiating person, obsequious flatterer. A London working-class term also briefly in vogue in the media in the early 1980s. It is a truncated form of the (originally American) **apple-polisher** (from the image of a schoolchild presenting an apple to a teacher in order to curry favour).

Polish fire drill *n American* a chaotic situation, bungled operation, mess. A supposedly jocular expression heard in adult speech since the 1970s. (Polish may in US slang play the part that Irish or Egyptian have traditionally played in British racist jokes.)

poll *adj British* an archaic upper-class term meaning roughly 'non-u' or **naff**. The word is of obscure origin, but may be derived from the Greek *polloi* (common people). Poll was recorded as a verb, meaning to snub, in late Victorian speech.

polluted *adj American* drunk. A probably ephemeral campus and **preppie** term.

polone, poloni *n British* a woman, female. A near-obsolete term of theatrical and showman's slang, dating from the 19th century. The word is an example of non-Italian **parlyaree**, ultimately derived from *beluñi*, a Spanish gypsy term for an (immoral) woman. *See* **omipolone**.

pom *n Australian* a native of Britain, especially an Englishman. The word is a shortening of the earlier **pommy**.

pomgolia *n* an alternative form of **pongolia**.

pommy, pommie *n, adj Australian* (a) British (person). The standard and usually derogatory slang term for natives of or immigrants from the British Isles, pommy is probably a corruption of 'pomegranate', chanted as a humorous semi-rhyme for 'immigrant'. The epithet has been in use since the first decade of the 20th century. The noun is now probably more common in the form **pom**.

pom-pom *n Jamaican* the vagina. The word was used in the lyrics to ragga music.

ponce *n British* 1 a pimp, procurer. This sense of the word was first recorded in the late 19th century.
2 a an ostentatious, effeminate male.
b a parasite, 'sponger', idler.
Ponce derives either from the standard English pounce, or possibly from the French *pensionnaire*, in the sense of non-paying guest. In its first and literal sense, ponce is virtually standard English (used by the police force among others). The following senses are terms of contempt directed at individuals thought to be showy, smugly idle or parasitic.

ponce (off someone) *vb British* to take advantage (of), borrow or cadge (from). A widespread usage derived from the noun.
↳'Can I ponce a fag off you?'

ponce around/about *vb British* to behave in a showy and/or irresponsible manner. A usage based on the noun, **ponce**.

ponced-up *adj British* smartly dressed or overdressed. From the noun **ponce** (pimp, idler or show-off).

pond scum, pond life *n* a contemptible, worthless person or people. Originating in American usage in the 1980s, this more colourful rendering of the colloquial 'low-life' became widespread in all English-speaking areas in the 1990s.

pondo *n British* £1. The term was used by **Sloane Rangers** in the 1970s to refer to a £1 note, and has subsequently been applied to £1 coins.

pong *vb, n British* (to) stink. The word is of uncertain origin but may derive from a similar Romany (gypsy) verb.

pong *n Australian* an oriental. A racist epithet, either based on **pongo**, or imitating the sound of oriental speech.

pongo *n* 1 a black man, a coloured person, a foreigner. A patronizingly derogatory middle-class term used, for example, in public-school and army speech.
2 an English person; an Australian and New Zealand slang term derived from the previous sense of the word.

pongolia, pomgolia *n Australia and New Zealand* the UK, Britain. Jocular terms based on **pom** and **pongo** and punning on Mongolia (evoking the notion of a distant and barbaric country).

the ponies *n pl British* horses, in the context of horseracing and betting.
↳'I lost it all on the ponies.'

pony *n British* the sum of £25 or, more recently, £25,000, in the jargon of the racetrack, underworld, market traders, etc. In its traditional sense the word was probably adopted to reflect the small size of a £25 bet.

pony up *vb American* to pay. A synonym for 'pay up' or 'fork out', the phrase was first recorded in the early 19th century and was said to derive from the earlier British use of the Latin form *pone*, meaning put (money down or forward).
↳'At 100,000 tax dollars a pop the American people ponied up for one reason; it was the future.'
(*Philadelphia Project*, US film, 1993).

poo *n British*
a nursery term for excrement that has passed into standard colloquial English.
2 champagne. A **yuppie** and **Sloane Ranger** abbreviation of **shampoo**.
↳'You're getting good at this. Extra poo tonight.'
(*Serious Money*, play by Caryl Churchill, 1987).

pooch *n* a dog. This well-known term, particularly well-established in the USA, is of mysterious origin. Possible etymologies are from a dialect version of pouch (alluding to a dog's insatiable desire to 'tuck away' food) or from a term of endearment, possibly the German *putzi*.
↳'Podgy Chas Clark, son of ex-Chancellor Nigel Lawson's financial guru Sir William Clark, called his pooch Charlie – a nickname for cocaine.'
(*News of the World*, 29 October 1989).

poodle-faker an effete, over-re-fined or offensively genteel young man, specifically a young man in attendance on older ladies. Faker here implies insin-cerity and poodle the attitude or appear-ance of a lapdog. The word appeared in Britain in the second decade of the 20th century.

poof, pouff, poove, poofter, pooftah, puff *n* a male homosex-ual. The most common slang term in Britain and Australia. The variations of the word go in and out of fashion. Poof and poove were popular in the 1960s, poofter in the 1970s. The origin of the epithet is obscure and the subject of ar-gument. Possibilities include 'pouff!' as a supposedly affected exclamation of dis-dain, or a northern English pronuncia-tion of 'puff', which itself could be a di-alect exclamation of disgust, a reference to puffed-up with pride, or a Victorian term for a sodomite. It might equally be inspired by the 'puff' of 'powder puff', or the French words *pouffe*: a stuffed seat and *pouffer (de rire)*: giggle.

poon, poontang *n American* 1 the female pudenda.

2 women in general, seen as sexual ob-jects. The word is from Louisiana French in which it is a corruption of *putain* (the standard French term for **whore**), first applied to black women.

✎'*I guess this means my poon days are over.*'
(Remark widely attributed to John F. Kennedy following his inauguration as US president, 1960).

poona *n American* marihuana or hashish. A word of uncertain origin (Poona is an Indian city but is not renowned as a source of narcotics) recorded in adolescent usage in the 1990s.

poop *n, vb* excrement, **crap**. A nursery word used humorously by adults and in the phrases poop-scoop, a small lidded shovel used to clear up dog-droppings, and **hot poop**, the latest news or gossip, the newest fashion. Poop is heard all over the anglophone community but is partic-ularly prevalent in the USA. It has ex-isted since the time of Middle English and the same word has been used with the same meaning in Dutch. Poo-poo is a syn-onym.

poop catchers *n pl See* **cack-catchers**.

poop-chute *n* the anus.

pooped, pooped out *adj* ex-hausted, out of breath. The word is prob-ably an imitation of the sound of puffing and blowing, although there is a theory that it derives from British sailors' slang for a ship being swamped by a 'poop' wave. In its current sense originally a North American term, it spread to Aus-tralia and Britain in the 1960s.

✎'*Too pooped to pop.*'

pooper *n See* **party pooper**.

poo-poo *See* **poop**.

poot *n, vb* (to) **fart**. Originally an echoic nursery word, probably originating in the USA, poot has achieved prominence in the vogue for references to flatulence in adolescent humour of the late 1980s (epitomized by *Viz* magazine). In Ameri-can usage poot may also mean excre-ment.

poove *n British* a version of **poof** which was current in the early 1960s.

pop *vb* 1 *British* to pawn. The word has had this meaning since the 18th century. *See* **pop one's clogs**.

2 **a** to take (an illicit drug) orally. The ex-pression refers particularly to amphet-a-mines or barbiturates rather than hallu-cinogenics such as LSD or hard drugs such as heroin.

b to inject a narcotic. The word is used more often in connection with intramus-cular than intravenous injection, often in the specific forms **skin-pop** and **joy pop**.

3 to hit, punch.

✎'*He popped him one in the eye.*'

4 to give birth.

✎'*Has she popped yet?*'

5 to have sex with or to achieve orgasm. This usage of the word is long-estab-lished, pre-dating for instance **pop one's rocks**.

6 **a** to shoot

b to kill. An underworld euphemism.

pop a chubby *See* **chubby**.

pop a vein *vb American* to become apoplectic with anger. A children's equiv-alent of 'burst a blood vessel', applied to and about furious adults.

pop it *vb* to die. The phrase is heard in Britain and Australia.

pop one's clogs *vb British* to die. A humorous, sometimes incongruously light-hearted phrase popular for example with TV presenters, disc jockeys and other entertainers. 'Pop' here is probably the old slang word for pawn, the suggestion being that when the family member dies, his or her clogs are sold.

pop one's rocks *vb* to achieve orgasm, ejaculate. A version of **get one's rocks off** which was briefly a vogue expression in the early 1970s. Pop has been used in a sexual sense at least since the 19th century. (An American synonym is 'pop one's cookies'.)

popper *n American* a gun. In this sense the word was first recorded (referring to a revolver) in the 1940s and was still in use among street gangs in the 1990s.

poppers *n pl* amyl nitrite capsules. This strong stimulant drug, prescribed to relieve angina pectoris, comes in glass phials which are broken under the nose and sniffed. The drug was taken for pleasure in the 1960s and 1970s and later specifically for its supposed effects as an enhancer of sexual pleasure by the **gay** community in the 1970s and 1980s.

poppy *n British* money. A word from the working-class speech of London. It may refer either to the 'gaudy' attractiveness of cash or banknotes or to **pop** in the sense of pawn. The term is in only limited circulation and has not as yet featured in the revival of archaic synonyms for money which began in the late 1980s.

porcelain *n See* **point percy at the porcelain, pray to the porcelain god**.

porch monkey *n* a black person. The racist phrase, adopted by some adolescents in the 1990s from their elders, is intended to evoke a slave or child asleep on a porch or ministering to its white superiors.

pork *vb American* to have sexual intercourse (with someone). A college students' word that has been widely used in films in the 1980s. It probably derives from the earlier **pork sword** and **dork**.
⸙'*He claims to be porking her.*'

porker *n* 1 a fat person. From the use of **pig** to mean glutton.
2 a police officer. This is a later development from **pig**, used for instance by anarchists, squatters and late-1980s **hippies**.

pork out *vb* to eat to excess. A variant form of the colloquial **pig out**, recorded since the early 1980s.

pork pie, porky-pie, porky *n British* a lie, untruth. A piece of rhyming slang from London working-class speech that surfaced suddenly in the playground and the media and became widely popular at the end of the 1970s.
⸙'*I think you'll be finding that William's been telling porky-pies again.*'
(Recorded, secretary, London, 1986).
⸙'*You wouldn't be tellin' me porkies would you, son?*'
(*Minder*, British TV series, 1987).

pork sword *n* penis. A term used particularly by American college students on the same lines as **mutton dagger** or **beef bayonet**.

porridge *n British* a term of imprisonment. Leaden, grey, institutional porridge is evoked as an image of the general deprivations of prison life, but is probably in origin a pun on **stir**. This underworld term was given wider currency by its use as the title of a BBC TV comedy series, starring Ronnie Barker.

portion *n British See* **give someone a portion**.

posho *n, adj British* (a person who is) snobbish and/or from a privileged background. This elaboration of the colloquial 'posh' was used by students in the mid-1990s.
⸙'*King's College is full of poshos.*'
(Recorded, London student, March 1996).
⸙'*A posho restaurant.*'

posse *n*
a *Jamaican* a criminal gang or secret society. The self-dramatizing term, from western movies, was adopted in the 1970s to describe **yardies**. It became known through their overseas activities in Britain and the USA in the 1980s.
b a youth gang. The word was adopted in urban Britain by teenagers in the late 1980s.

postal *adj American* uncontrollable, irrational, disoriented. This vogue term among Californian adolescents was popularized by the 1994 US film *Clueless*. It often occurs in the form '*go postal*'. The term is derived from the image of deranged postal workers who embark on a shooting spree before committing suicide.

↘'*By the time I got home, dad was, like, totally postal.*'

postie *n* 1 a postman, mailman. A shortening that is heard in Britain and Australia.

2 a postgraduate student.

pot *n* 1 cannabis. This 1950s term was considered old-fashioned by drug users by the early 1960s, but was adopted by critics and commentators in the press to refer to hashish and marihuana. This use of the word originated in North America in the early years of the 20th century but its etymology is unknown. Some authorities claim a derivation from an obscure Mexican term for the drug (*potiguaya* or *potaguaya*), others that there is a connection with the use of **tea** as a nickname for marihuana, or that it is a deformation of **pod**, an attested synonym.

↘'*I do not advocate legislation of pot, merely because I dread the inevitable hassle of commercialism.*'
(Letter to *Oz* magazine, June 1969).

2 a pot belly.

↘'*He's got a bit of a pot on him.*'

potatoes *n British* money. In armed-service slang during World War II '*(big) potatoes*' denoted both great wealth and the possessor thereof. The use of the same word in the 1990s may be a separate coinage.

↘'*Oh where are those potatoes? Tell me about those potatoes because I can't eat, I can't eat.*'
(Sarah Ferguson, Duchess of York, in conversation with her psychic, Madame Vasso, reported in 1996).

potato-head *n*

a a person with coarse or indistinct features.

b a stupid person. 'Mr Potato-head' was a children's toy popular during the 1970s. It consisted of a set of plastic parts to stick into a potato.

pothead *n* an habitual smoker of cannabis (hashish or marihuana). An early 1960s term which was out of fashion by the late 1960s, save in whimsical or ironical usage.

potless *adj* destitute, 'broke'. This use of the word is probably from the vulgar colloquialism 'without a pot to piss in', or may simply refer to the pot of money for a gambling session.

potter *n British* a Jew. A piece of London rhyming slang from 'pot o' glue', rarely heard, but always occurring in the shortened form.

potty-mouth *n American* a user of obscene language, 'foul-mouth'. This jocular middle-aged colloquialism was adopted by adolescents in the 1990s, including the **rriot grrrl** band Bratmobile who used it as an album title in 1993.

pouff *n* an alternative spelling of **poof**.

poultice *n* a wager. This use of the word, which usually refers to a significant bet, seems to have originated in pre-World War II Australia, either evoking the idea of a quantity of money 'stuck' on a horse (race) or a wad of banknotes resembling a medicated dressing.

pound, the pound *n Australian* a solitary-confinement cell or wing in a prison. A term employed in the Australian television cult drama series, *Prisoner: Cell Block H*.

pound one's pork/pudding/meat/weenie, etc. *vb* (of a male) to masturbate.

pox, the pox *n* venereal disease. Originally referring to syphilis, pox is a variant form of 'pocks' (as in pock-marks) meaning pustules and itself related to pocket.

poxy *adj British* very bad, worthless, inferior. Originally signifying diseased, from the use of **pox** to mean syphilis, poxy is now a fairly strong (mainly working-class) term of contempt.

PP9 *vb British* to cosh someone with an improvised weapon made from a PP9 radio battery inside a prison sock. An item of prison slang.

↘'*One remark can start a ruck, and before you know it someone has been PP9'd.*'
(*Ms London* magazine, 20 September 1993).

P.R. *n American* a Puerto Rican. The

abbreviation is usually heard in a derogatory context.

prairie-fairy *n American* an environmentalist, green activist. A derogatory term which featured in the 1992 Montana State Election debate. Synonyms are **tree-hugger**, **eagle-freak**, etc.

pram *n See* **out of one's pram**.

prang *vb, n British* (to) crash. A word, used in the context of motoring, which moved from echoic air-force slang of the 1940s to become a common colloquialism of the 1970s and 1980s.

prannet *n British* a fool. A term which enjoyed a vogue in the late 1970s. Prannet looks like a blend of **prat** and **gannet**, both widespread terms of mild abuse. However, it is probably a form of a much earlier word (also seen in the form **pranny**) denoting buttocks and the female pudenda.

pranny, prannie *n British* a fool. Variant (and possibly earlier) forms of **prannet**.

prat, pratt *n British* **1 a** backside, buttocks. A word dating from the 16th century or earlier which is currently an inoffensive if rare synonym for **bum**, etc. (encountered in the compound 'pratfall'). **b** the vagina. This sense of the term is an extension of the preceding, it has been rare since the 1960s.
2 a fool, idiot, buffoon. A sharp, but not obscene term of criticism or abuse, in vogue in the 1980s. The word denotes extreme foolishness and is derived in the same way as the synonymous **arse** or **twat** from the previous senses of the term.

> ✎'*Anyone who bought a futon from the Nagasaki Futon Company should return this to the shop immediately as a serious design fault could result in the owner looking like a stupid prat.*'
> (*Great Bus Journeys of the World*, Alexei Sayle, 1988).

prat about *vb British* to behave stupidly or irresponsibly, to do things in a disorganized, messy way. From the noun, **prat**.

prawn *n See* **come the raw prawn**.

pray to the porcelain god *vb* to vomit.

preggers *adj* pregnant. Originally an upper- or middle-class expression using the Oxbridge and public school termination '-ers'.

preppie, preppy *n American*
a a student or ex-student of an American preparatory school. The term was popularized by Erich Segal in his best-selling novel *Love Story*. American prep schools (as opposed to the British version which educates boys from 8 to 13) prepare teenage boys for higher education.
b a young person embodying the values, manners and dress of upper-class America. The preppy is roughly the equivalent of the British **Sloane Ranger**.

> ✎'*He is variously described as "Ivy League" or "preppy" and he is instantly recognizable by his blue button-down Oxford cloth shirt, navy blazer, club tie and penny loafers. He might be viewed as an American Hooray Henry, except that he is quietly-spoken, excessively polite and never throws muffins.*'
> (*Independent*, 12 March 1988).

presh *n, adj British* a vogue term of endearment based on 'precious' and used both straightforwardly and ironically in London **parlyaree**, since the 1960s. '*Presh-bag*' is an elaborated form used often teasingly to a loved one or acquaintance.

previous *adj British* premature, impetuous, presumptuous. A term of mild disapproval favoured by London working-class speakers and members of the police force, usually in the phrase '*a bit previous*'.

previous *n British* a criminal record, previous convictions. A shortening adopted by police officers and the underworld, usually in the phrase '*has he/she got any previous?*'.

prick *n* **1** penis. The Oxford English Dictionary records the first use of the term in 1592; it was probably extant in the spoken language for some time before. Prick was probably coined with the image of a thorn in mind, from the shape and the image of penetration evoked. In the 20th century while it is in 'polite company' the least acceptable of the many terms (**cock**, **tool**, etc.) for the male member, it is nevertheless commonly used, together with **dick**, by women in preference to those alternatives.

2 a fool, obnoxious or contemptible male.

᧬ '*"He's a rude prick who's suing Val Hennessy for libel," I said. "That's a bloody scandal," he said, and told everyone to shut up. "Do any of you layabouts know a rude prick called Bolloms?" he shouted. No one did.'* (William Donaldson writing in the *Independent*, 26 August 1989).

prick-tease, prick-teaser *n* a potential sex partner who excites sexual arousal without allowing consummation. This phenomenon, usually in the context of male-female encounters, is paralleled by the French *chauffe-cul* and the synonymous **cock-tease, cock-teaser** in English.

primo *adj* first class. (From the Spanish for first.) **El primo** is an alternative version.

Pringle *n British* a young male working-class member of a late 1970s and early 1980s social sub-group characterized by wearing designer-label sports clothing and including so-called 'football hooligans' and **casuals**. (Pringle is the brand name of a variety of expensive and typically pastel-coloured woollen sweaters.)

privates *n pl* genitals, 'private parts'. A euphemistic or humorous term.

pro *n* a prostitute.

prod *n British* a Protestant. **Prot** is an Australian alternative version.

profiling *n American* behaving ostentatiously, 'posing'. A term from the black lexicon, often denoting ritual showing-off within a group. *Compare* **styling, vogueing.**

prole *n British* a proletarian, member of the 'lower' classes. A contemptuous term employed by overt snobs or, ironically or self-deprecatingly, by the 'proles' themselves.

prong *n* penis.

proper! *exclamation American* a general cry of appreciation, approval, etc., in use among adolescents on the west coast in the 1990s. The term was also heard among middle-class youth in London as reported by the *Evening Standard* magazine, July 1994. *Compare* **proper job.**

proper job *n, exclamation British* an all-purpose term of approbation often used as an exclamation, particularly in the speech of the West Country and Devon and Cornwall.

props *n American* respect. An item of black street talk (a shortening of '*[pay/show] proper respect*') which was included in so-called **Ebonics**, recognized as a legitimate language variety by school officials in Oakland, California, in late 1996.

prot *See* **prod.**

prune *n British* a foolish person. A mild term of childish abuse, employing one of the less appetizing elements on the typical family and/or school-dinner menus of the 1950s and 1960s.

pseud *n British* a pseudo-intellectual, pretentious or 'bogus' individual. A buzzword of 1962 and 1963, largely because of its frequent use in *Private Eye* magazine. The word, originating among public-school (it was current at Shrewsbury around 1960, where some of the founders of *Private Eye* were educated) and Oxbridge speakers, epitomized the focus of contempt of hearty sportsmen, 'establishment' conformists and genuine intellectuals alike. *Pseud's Corner* in *Private Eye* is a long-running column, reprinting instances of pretentiousness.

psych (oneself) up *vb* to work oneself into a state of mental alertness, aggression, intensity. The phrase originated in the USA (probably in the context of self-expression or therapy groups) in the early 1970s.

᧬ '*In fact his* [the footballer Vinny Jones] *disturbing habit of psyching himself up before a game by screaming, kicking doors and head-butting dressing-room walls is causing team-mates increasing concern.*' (*News of the World*, 12 February 1989).

psych (someone) out *vb* to unnerve, outmanoeuvre or overwhelm. An Americanism which has spread to other areas, psych out originally meant to use psychology to gauge an opponent's weakness.

P.T. *n British* 1 **prick-tease**. A pun on the school subject physical-training. 2 *See* **Egyptian PT.**

pud *n American* 1 penis. The word is a clipped form of '*pudding*' which has denoted both the male member and semen in earlier slang usage.

2 a worthless, contemptible or obnoxious person. This term of adolescent abuse may be a shortened version of **pud-w(h)apper**.

pudding *See* **pull one's pud/pudding**.

pudding club *n See* **in the club**.

pud-w(h)apper *n American* an obnoxious or comptemptible person. One of many synonyms in use among young adolescents employing the notion of male masturbation. Here it combines **whap**, meaning beat or thrash, with **pud**, meaning penis.

ᔐ*'That little pud-whapper just trod on my foot.'*
(*Heathers*, US film, 1986).

puff *n* **1** an alternative spelling of **poof**.
2 *British* life. In humorous working-class speech the notion of 'breath of life' has given rise to this usage. It is probably most prevalent in northern English conversation.

ᔐ*'Budgie never had a winner in his puff.'*
(*Budgie*, British TV series, 1971).
ᔐ*'Never in all my born puff.'*
(*Coronation Street*, British TV series, 1989).

puff *vb British* to smoke cannabis. A usage appearing in the 1990s.

puff-bucket *n American* a braggart or 'wind-bag'. A mild term of abuse denoting a loquacious or pompous individual.

puffy *n British* cannabis. This innocent-sounding nursery term, playing upon puffs of smoke, is used typically as a code word by users and dealers.

ᔐ*'There's no news on the puffy front – my friend's friend is still out in Morocco.'*
(Recorded, drug dealer, London, 1987).

puggled *adj British* drunk. The term usually denotes disoriented or 'merry' rather than extremely inebriated. It is heard particularly in the Scottish Lowlands and the north of England, but may ultimately derive from an Indian term meaning a madman, brought to Britain by colonial soldiers.

puggy *n Scottish*

a monkey.
b an unnamed object, animal, or person. This old nickname is thought to derive from 'pog', a dialect term for hobgoblin or puck-figure.

puke *vb* to vomit. An echoic expression pre-dating Shakespeare's reference to '*an infant mewling and puking*'.

pukka *adj British*
a authentic, first-rate. A word adopted from the Hindi *pakka* (meaning substantial) for use in the Anglo-Indian speech of the colonial era.
b excellent, admirable. The earlier term was adopted as an adolescent vogue word in the 1990s, often used by those who were ignorant of its provenance and longevity.

ᔐ*'Well pukka shoes.'*
ᔐ*'A pukka geezer.'*

puky, pukey *adj* disgusting, sickening, awful. An adolescent usage based on the ancient verb to **puke**.

pull *vb British* **1** to 'pick up' a member of the opposite sex. A common term applied to males searching for sexual partners, since the late 1960s when it was usually part of a phrase such as 'pull a bird' or 'pull a chick'. In current working-class usage predatory males are said to be **on the pull**. (Pull is now part of the homosexual as well as heterosexual lexicon and women also use the expression.)
2 to arrest or take into custody. A police jargon usage.

pull a stroke *vb British* to succeed in a clever manoeuvre, effect a trick or deception. 'Stroke' is a common colloquialism for move, ploy or action.

pullet *n British* a young male who is a passive homosexual partner or victim of an older man. A version of **chicken**, the more widespread term for an underage sexual partner.

pull finger *vb New Zealand* to get a move on, stop dawdling, increase efficiency. A brusque shortening of the colloquial 'pull one's finger out'.

ᔐ*'OK, it's time to pull finger and get moving.'*

pulling power *n British* sexual attraction, the ability to attract and/or 'pick up' members of the opposite sex. The term, from the verb **pull**, is usually applied to males.

pull (oneself/someone) off
vb to masturbate oneself or someone else. A term used invariably of men, now dated.

pull one's pud/pudding *vb*
British (of a man) to masturbate. The word pudding has been used with various connotations in a sexual context (penis, semen, pregnancy, etc.) since the 16th century.

pull the plug *vb* to commit suicide.
An unsentimental euphemism, from the colloquial sense of the phrase meaning to abort (a venture).

ᗌ'*Kathy was eleven when she pulled the plug, on 26 reds and a bottle of wine.*'
(Lyrics to 'People who died', Jim Carrol, 1981).

pump *vb* 1 *British* to **fart**. A children's
term adopted by adults and now appearing in print in such publications as *Viz* magazine.
2 *American* to have sex (with). A vulgarism usually heard in the catchphrase '*pump 'em and dump 'em*', a male expression of the late 1980s.

pump *n American* the heart. The pre-
dictable usage occurs in the language of prizefighters and street-gangs etc.

ᗌ'*He got it right in the pump.*'

pumps *n pl British* tennis shoes, train-
ers. Like **daps** and **bumpers**, this is typically a schoolchildren's term.

punch deck *vb* to type on a com-
puter keyboard. This item of **net-head** slang was employed in interviews, perhaps partly ironically, by the **cyberpunk** author, William Gibson, in 1995.

pung *n South African* trash. Recorded
as an item of Sowetan slang in the *Cape Sunday Times*, 29 January 1995.

punk *n* 1 a bumptious but insignifi-
cant or contemptible person. This sense of the word has been well-established in American English since the 19th century referring typically to a youth, particularly a presumptuous or irritating one, or to a petty criminal or gangster. The word originated in British slang around the end of the 17th century when it was used to denote a **whore** and later a precursor of the modern **rent boy**. In the 20th century the

term punk fell out of use in Britain, being reintroduced via the American media and later by way of the punk rock phenomenon of 1976 and 1977.

ᗌ'*The play-house Puncks, who in a loose undress*
Each night receive some Cullie's soft address...'
(*Poor Pensive Punck*, poem by John Dryden, 1691).

2 an adherent of a youth sub-culture first coalescing in 1976 around punk rock music. Punk rock was so called because of the callow, defiant poses and amateurish musicianship of its proponents. Led by American groups such as the Ramones and the British band the Sex Pistols, punk rock became the musical vogue of 1977, accompanied by a self-consciously nihilistic and pessimist attitude and imagery, spikey and mohican hairstyles, safety pins and chains, etc. While the first wave of the phenomenon metamorphosed into other sub-cults (neo-**mods**, **goths** and **grebos**, etc.), later imitators perpetuated punk in a frozen iconography. It now forms part of modern British folklore, much in the same way as the **teddy boy** image persists.

punkette *n* a young female **punk**
(rocker).

punk out *vb American* to behave in a
cowardly manner. An item of street-gang argot, deriving from the sense of **punk** as weakling. **Wimp out** is a slightly milder version.

punter *n British*
a a gambler, speculator. Coming from the terminology of card games, punt was transferred to the context of horseracing, then to betting in general in the 19th century. In the late 1980s it was used for example of small investors or share purchasers. The term enjoys continuing popularity.

b a customer or client. The sense of punter as gambler was extended to refer to anyone paying money for a service or item. First specifically applied to prostitutes, and street-trader's customers, punter became a key word in the market-oriented 1980s.

punting *n British* engaged in prosti-
tution. An item of police slang (from the idea of looking for **punters**).

purple hearts *n pl* amphetamine
tablets. The phrase referred to purple or

blue coloured tablets of amphetamines, barbiturate or a mixture of the two as prescribed and abused in the USA in the late 1950s. (The 'purple heart' was a medal awarded for bravery.) In Britain the word was adopted in the early 1960s as a generic term for **pep pills**, **speed**.

push *n Australian* a gang of **larrikins**. The word was recorded in the 1880s and evokes the image of a band of street toughs shouldering people out of the way as they walk down the street.

push *vb* to sell illegal drugs, especially when the sale involves coercion.

pusher *n* a supplier of illicit drugs, especially addictive drugs. The word implies that the seller uses coercion or tries to lead people into addiction in order to profit from them (if this is not the case, **dealer** is the alternative). The term is now used by police, journalists, parents, etc. and only rarely by drug users or sellers.

puss *n* 1 *American* face, mouth. A word often used in compounds such as 'sour puss' and 'glamour-puss', puss was a favourite word of pugilists and 'tough guys' in the earlier 20th century. It derives from the Irish Gaelic *pus*, mouth.

✎ *'He told her if she didn't shut up he'd give her a sock in the puss.'*

2 pussy (in all its senses).

puss-weed *n American* a variant form of **pussy** in the sense of **wimp**, heard among US adolescents since the late 1980s.

pussy *n* 1 the female genitals. A cause of many double entendres and minor embarrassments, this usage of the word derives from the resemblance of pubic hair to fur, perhaps reinforced by male notions of affection. (The French equivalent is *chatte*, virtually a literal translation.) Pussy or **puss** was first recorded in the sexual sense in the 16th century.

2 women viewed as sex objects. An unromantic male term used in the same indiscriminate manner as **tail**, **ass**, etc. In this generic sense, the term may be expressed as pussy, 'some pussy' or occasionally 'a piece of pussy'.

✎ *'I hate to say it but I understand in London there's a lot of pussy over there.'*
(US police officer, *Sunday Times* colour supplement, 1 January 1967).

3 *also* **pussycat** a weak, harmless male, a timid person. A word which probably originated in the boxers' lexicon to describe the feeble, patting punches of a loser.

✎ *'He's a pussy, Frank.'*
'Yeah, but he's our pussy.'
(*Blue Velvet*, US film, 1986).

4 furs, in the jargon of criminals and police. This example of the jargon of cat burglars was recorded in *FHM* magazine in April 1996.

5 a coquettish or 'kittenish' female, in lesbian parlance.

pussy *adj British* unpleasant, execrable. This use of the word in the late 1990s is probably inspired by the noun sense of female pudenda, rather than that of a weak, ineffectual person and reflects a distaste for female sexuality on the part of male adolescent gang members, its first users.

pussy-whipped *adj* 'hen-pecked'. An American vulgarism probably inspired by the western cliché 'pistol-whipped'. **Pussy** is a long-established term for the female genitals or women in general.

put (someone) down *vb* to snub, humiliate or belittle. A vogue term among British **beatniks** in the early 1960s, adopted from American street slang.

✎ *'Evil hearted you, you always try to put me down, with the things you do and the words you spread around ...'*
(Lyrics to 'Evil-hearted You', the Yardbirds, 1965).

putdown *n* a snub or humiliation. A back-formation from the verb to **put (someone) down**.

✎ *'Being left off the guest list was the ultimate putdown.'*

put-in *adj Australian* imprisoned. An item of police and criminal jargon recorded in the 1990s.

put in the fix, put the fix in *vb American* to bribe, suborn, or corrupt (in order to resolve a problem).

put-on *n* a deception, fraud, cheat. A back-formation (with slightly changed emphasis) from the verb to **put someone on** (although Partridge cites instances of the expression in Victorian use).

put one on someone *vb* to hit, punch. An aggressive euphemism which is also rendered by **lay**, or **hang one on someone**.

✎*'One of my colleagues said that he felt like "putting one on" the attendant for the way he treated the child.'*
(*Inside the British Police*, Simon Holdaway, 1983).

put one's hands up *vb* to surrender, give in, confess. A euphemism popular among the British police and underworld.

✎*'It was brilliant. He couldn't believe it. He had to put his hands up. Yes I did that one by subterfuge.'*
(Police officer quoted in *Inside the British Police*, Simon Holdaway, 1983).

put someone away *vb British* to kill. A euphemism employed by underworld or would-be underworld figures.

✎*'When I told him he went spare – he threatened to put the guy away.'*

put someone on *vb* to tease, mock or deceive (someone). This American usage spread to Britain in the later 1960s as a synonym for kid, fool or **con**. It is now usually heard in the phrase *'you're putting me on!'*.

put the bite on *vb* to pressurize someone, especially for a loan or repayment of money owed, or as part of a campaign of intimidation. This expression seems to have originated in North American usage early in the 20th century.

put the boot in *vb British*
a to kick (someone). An expression used by **skinheads** of the late 1960s as part of their repertoire (along with **aggro**, **bother** and **put the nut on**).
b to attack someone figuratively, particularly when they are already under attack, vulnerable or incapacitated.

put the frighteners on (someone) *vb British* to menace, threaten or intimidate. An underworld and police expression employing a familiar form of words (as in **put the bite/kybosh/mockers on**).

put the hammer on (someone) *vb* to bully, oppress, extort. This phrase is heard throughout the English-speaking world, particularly in Scotland, meaning to pressurize someone for a loan, gift, etc., and in the US, where it commonly denotes bullying or menacing.

✎*'Every time we go near a pub one of you guys puts the hammer on me.'*

✎*'As soon as he starts to put the hammer on, let me know.'*

put the kybosh/kibosh on *vb* to frustrate, ruin, prevent, jeopardize. Many conflicting and often far-fetched etymologies have been suggested for this phrase, first recorded in the 1830s meaning to defeat. Its ultimate origin remains obscure.

put the mockers on *vb British* to frustrate or jeopardize (someone's plans), to curse with bad luck. This old phrase was last popular in the 1960s, but is still heard occasionally. It almost certainly originates in the Yiddish *mockers*, curse or bad luck, from the Hebrew *maches*, plague.

put the moves on (someone) *vb American* to menace, oppress, cheat. An item of street slang also heard among adolescents and featured in the US film, *The Sandlot Kids*, 1994.

putz *n American* a foolish, clumsy or unfortunate person. The word is the Yiddish for 'ornament' used as a synonym for the male member, hence **prick**. Despite its (little-known) origin, putz is a relatively mild term of abuse in English; in Yiddish it still carries more pejorative overtones.

p.w.t. *n American* an abbreviation of '*poor* **white trash**'.

Q *n*

a a geriatric person.

b a hospital patient.

c a corpse.

All senses of the term are based on the image of the capital letter Q as representing an open mouth with lolling tongue and seem to have originated in the slang of North American health carers. The letter may be written (in notes, on charts, etc.) or pronounced by medical staff.

Q.T., q.t. *n See* on the q.t.

quack *n, adj* a doctor. This usually lightheartedly pejorative term originated in the 17th century when it referred to a peddler of spurious cures. It is a shortening of 'quacksalver' which is composed of quack (give one's verbal 'patter'), and salve (save, soothe or cure), and is a pun on quicksilver.

quad, quod *n American* a clumsy or unfortunate person, misfit. The word, used by high school and college students in the 1990s, is probably a shortening of 'quadriplegic' (disabled in all four limbs), although some users derive it from 'quadrilateral' as a version of **square**.

quail *n* a girl, young woman, or females viewed as sex objects. This equating of the female with the game bird is approximately three hundred years old, surviving in the language of American high-school and college students, where predatory males also talk of going out 'loaded for quail' (ready or equipped for seduction).

quandong *n Australian* a woman. The quandong fruit (*santalum acuminatus*) is fleshy with a hard seed centre; the word has thus been appropriated to refer to women with supposedly similar quali-

ties – either prostitutes or friendly females who refuse to be seduced.

quean *n British* the earlier spelling of **queen**, meaning an effeminate homosexual. This spelling coexisted with queen until the early 1960s when it virtually disappeared. Quean was a descendant of Old and Middle English words related to (but not derived from) queen, stemming ultimately from an Indo-European ancestor, *gwena*, meaning woman. Over 1,000 years the senses of quean shifted from 'woman' to 'wanton', before being transferred to a male context.

queef *n American* an alternative spelling of **kweef**.

queen *n, vb* an (effeminate) homosexual. The word **quean** signified a **whore** in early 19th-century slang. This appellation was transferred to male prostitutes (often transvestite) and thence to male homosexuals in general. The use of the word is obviously reinforced by its colloquial use to mean an imperious or ostentatious (older) woman. In the **gay** environment of the 1970s and 1980s queen has been used to refer specifically to individuals who are affected in manner, elderly and/or consciously effeminate.

꜀'*And he's just a go-getting queen. He's interested in you purely because of your plays.*'
(Kenneth Halliwell, quoted in Joe Orton's Diary, 2 May 1967, 1986).

queer *n, adj* (a) homosexual. Until the 19th century queer denoted odd or curious, as it still does in standard English. Its use as first a euphemism, then a slang synonym for homosexual arose between the World Wars, probably first in the USA. Since the advent of the neutral term **gay** and pejorative terms such as **bent**, queer has been relegated to the role of a somewhat dated term of disapproval. (The 1980 pop song 'Johnny are you queer?' by Josie Cotton was banned by several US radio stations under pressure from gay groups.) Queer ultimately derives from *quer*, a German word meaning crooked or awry.

꜀'*You can't expect to pick up a young post-office worker and his middle-aged keeper, and burst into tears because the keeper is queer.*'
(Joe Orton's Diary, 2 May 1967, 1986).

In the mid-1980s gay activists began to use the term to refer to themselves, in keeping with the trend among 'transgressive' minorities to appropriate the language of their oppressors (as in the earlier case of **nigger**).

queer-bashing *n British* the attacking, intimidation or **mugging** of male homosexuals. A practice indulged in by **teddy boys** and later **skinheads**, among others. The term has more recently been extended to denote verbal aggression or prejudice against **gays**.

queer-rolling *n British* the robbing of homosexual males. A practice which was particularly prevalent in the late 1950s and early 1960s when homosexuality itself was illegal and **gay** victims rarely dared to report the crime.

quiche out *vb British* **1** to eat very greedily or to excess. A **Sloane Ranger** and **yuppie** version of **pig out**, which was later adopted by university students.

2 *vb* to behave in a weak, irresolute, cowardly way, **wimp out**. In this sense the term has been used in Oxbridge student slang, sometimes shortened to 'quiche'.

quickie *n* a hurried or short-lived sex act.

quid *n* a pound sterling. The word was first used to refer to a guinea, then a sovereign, later to the sum of one pound. The origin of the word (it arose in the 17th century) is obscure. Partridge suggests 'what' (*quid* in Latin) as a synonym for 'wherewithal'. An equally plausible derivation is from *quid pro quo*, alluding to the words on older banknotes, '*I promise to pay the bearer the sum of...*'

quidlets *n pl British* money, pounds

sterling. A humorous version of **quid** using the diminutive suffix -let.

quiff *n* **1** *British* a pompadour hairstyle, kiss-curl or backcombed fringe. The quiff was fashionable among **teddy boys** and **rockers** among others.

2 *British* a male homosexual or effeminate male. The usage is probably influenced by the words **queer** and **poof**.

3 a **fart**.

4 *American* **a** a prostitute or promiscuous woman.

b a woman or women as sex object(s). A term used invariably by males.

᠐'*I'm going to get me some quiff.*'

quim *n British* the female sex organs. A taboo term featuring in 19th-century pornography and the 20th-century lexicon of obscenity. The word has probably lost popularity since the 1950s, although it remains in use, invariably among males, particularly outside the southeast of the country. The exact origin of quim is unclear. It may be related to the Chaucerian queynte (vagina) or the Welsh *cwm* (valley or crevice).

quince *n Australian* a male homosexual or effeminate male. The word is probably a blend of **queen** and 'mince'. It may also be derived from the Asian fruit of the same name.

quoit *n Australian* anus. A coinage inspired by the earlier **ring**.

quoted *adj American* initiated into full gang membership. A code term reported in the Channel 4 TV documentary *Gang War*, August 1995.

r...

raas *n Jamaican* an all-purpose term of abuse or exclamation of anger or contempt. A version of (up) (your) **arse** or a short form of **raasclat**. *Compare* **yass**.

raasclat, rassclaat *n Jamaican* a term of strong abuse used as an insult or as an exclamation. The word literally means a rag for wiping the backside, the equivalent of the later American insult **ass-wipe**, **raas** being a patois version of (your) **arse** and clat, cloth. *Compare* **bloodclat**.

rabbit *vb, n* (to) talk, gossip, (have a) conversation. The term is cockney rhyming slang, from 'rabbit and pork': talk. The word gained widespread currency through TV comedies of the 1970s and the soundtrack to a 1980s advertisement for Courage Best beer. Rabbit (or 'rabbit on') is now often used by middle-class speakers unaware of its rhyming provenance. Genuine cockneys often prefer the derivation **bunny**.

race off, race *vb American* to seduce. A common term in the 1960s. The original image evoked is that of sweeping a victim off her feet and away.

rack *n American* **1** a bed. This use of the word is probably of armed-service origin.
2 the female breasts.
✎ *'She's attractive – great rack, nipples like pencil erasers...'*
(*Disclosure*, US film, 1995).

rack attack *n American* a bout of extreme laziness, a period spent in bed. A campus witticism (other rhyming compounds are **snack attack** and **tack attack**) based on the use of **rack** to mean bed.

racked *adj American* **1** ruined, defeated, disabled. The term referred orig-

inally to being kicked or struck in the **rack** or male genital area.
2 intoxicated by drugs or alcohol. The adolescent usage is probably a borrowing of the standard term as it occurs in phrases such as 'racked with pain', although it may be based on the preceding sense or be an alteration of **wrecked**.
✎ *'I was racked by 9 p.m.'*

racked-off *adj Australian* irritated, disgruntled. An expression ranking in vehemence somewhere between 'cheesed-off' and **pissed-off**.

racked-up *adj American* tense, stressed, **strung up**. An expression heard occasionally since the 1970s.
✎ *'I remember my first shoot. You know I was really racked-up but the lieutenant was there for me.'*
(*Miami Vice*, US TV series, 1988).

rack off *vb Australian* to go away, leave. A brusque, but less offensive alternative to **piss off**, **fuck off**, etc. The phrase, usually in the form of an admonition, has been introduced to a British audience via Australian soap operas of the late 1980s, such as *Neighbours*.

rack (out) *vb American* to lie down and/or go to sleep. An expression now used principally by teenagers and college students, but which originates in the armed-service slang noun **rack**, meaning bed.

rad *adj American* excellent, outstanding, admirable. A shortening of **radical**, used as a term of great approbation by school and college children in the late 1970s. It is also heard in the UK and Australia since the 1980s where it has become a vogue term especially among the subcultures of surfers and skateboarders.
✎ *'But the really rad word is still to be had from the skater/authors themselves ...'*
(*Mail on Sunday 'Biz'* magazine, June 1987).

radical *adj* excellent. The word has moved from its political sense, via 'radical chic' to a generalized meaning in adolescent speech of admirable. It is sometimes shortened to **rad**.
✎ *'The word "radical", which no longer has rebellious or left-wing connotations but means simply wonderful or remarkable.'*

(*Independent* magazine, 24 December 1988).

radio rentals *adj British* crazy, deranged, **mental**. A humorous expression recorded in 1988, employing an approximate rhyme using the name of a television hire chain.

✧'*If you ask me, she's completely radio rentals.*'

rag (on) (someone) *vb American* criticize, denigrate, nag. This usage dates back to the 19th century when 'ragging' was also employed in British slang to mean teasing or provoking. In black American slang of the 1990s rag is often used synonymously with **diss**.

rage *n Australian* a wild party or celebration. A 1960s expression which is the equivalent of the British **rave-up** and, like that term, undergoing a revival in the late 1980s.

ragged out/up *adj American* **1** dressed or dressed up. Since the 19th century this term has been used colloquially like 'dolled up' or 'in one's glad rags'. **Ragged up** is an alternative version.
2 distasteful, unpleasant. A teenage and **Valley Girl** expression of the late 1970s.

raggedy-ass, ragged-ass *adj American* unkempt, uncouth, disorganized. An elaboration of ragged.

rag-head *n* an arab. A pejorative term inspired by the headdress worn particularly by gulf arab males. The term is occasionally applied to turban-wearers, too. An alternative is **towel head**.

raging *n British* a 'first'(-class honours degree). Students' rhyming slang of the late 1980s, on 'raging thirst'. **James** and **Pattie** are alternative versions.

✧'*He was tipped for a raging, but he ended up with a Desmond.*'

See also **Douglas, Hawaii, Made-in, Richard, Taiwan.**

rags *n pl American* clothes. Heard in the speech of black Americans since the 1960s (**threads** and **vines** were contemporary synonyms) and later elsewhere, the word has more recently been supplanted to some extent by **garms**.

✧'*Where d'you get them cool rags?*'

rag-top *n* a convertible car. The Americanism has also occasionally been heard in Britain as an alternative for soft-top or the earlier drop-head.

rain on someone's parade *vb American* to spoil someone's enjoyment, frustrate someone's efforts etc. A colloquial phrase which gave rise to many more vulgar synonyms such as **piss in someone's pool/on someone's chips**.

rally *vb American* to behave outrageously, indulge in wild activity. A **preppie** term, used invariably by and about males.

✧'*Come on, let's rally!*'
✧'*They were really rallying.*'

ralph *vb* **1** to vomit. One of many echoic terms for the activity, ralph is typically heard among students in all English-speaking areas. 'Call (for) Ralph' is another version.
2 also **hang a ralph** *American* to take a right turn.

ralph *n* a right turn. The word is usually part of the phrase **hang a ralph** (as opposed to **hang a louie**).

ram *n* a sexually promiscuous or successful male. A rare synonym for **stud**.

ram *vb* to have sex (with). A term normally used by or of males with the implication of animal forcefulness or brutish assertiveness.

Ramboid *adj* brutally excessive, aggressive and mindlessly **gung-ho**. A pejorative term inspired by the character 'Rambo' interpreted by Sylvester Stallone in the films of the same name.

rambunctious *adj* lively, troublesome, loud. A facetious invention elaborated from rumbustious. The term has been in use since the early 19th century and is probably Irish or American in origin, although the invention of such jocularities (as in the 19th-century 'obstrepalous' and the recent 'spondicious') was paralleled in Britain.

✧'*This is a lullaby my mother used to play when I'd get rambunctious. It always seemed to calm me down.*'
(*Kindred*, US film, 1987).

ram-job *n American* an act of sex. The term generally refers unromantically to heterosexual intercourse and is usually used by, and of, males.

ramp up *vb British* to organize or

arrange. The phrase presumably comes from the terminology of car mechanics whence it has been extended in working-class usage (by police officers among others) to mean mounting any sort of operation.

ranch *vb American* to ejaculate. The slang usage, heard among adolescents, seems to be unconnected to the standard sense of the word.

Randolph (Scott) *n British* a spot (on the skin). An item of rhyming slang (featured in the TV comedy *Only Fools and Horses*) borrowing the name of the Hollywood cowboy star of the 1940s and 50s.

random *n, adj American* (a person who is) unfashionable, unattractive, mediocre, or excluded from fashionable circles. The term has been popular among adolescents, particularly female, on college and high-school campuses in the US during the 1990s.

♭'*There's no getting round the style question. If you want to be "do-able" …you cannot afford to dress "random".'*
(*Sunday Times* 'Style' magazine, 22 October 1995).

R and R *n* 1 relaxation. A piece of armed-services shorthand (for 'rest and recreation') now used by civilians.
2 rock 'n' roll. A short form used by aficionados and the record industry.

randy *adj British* sexually aroused, lecherous. A word which was formerly considered unsuitable for normal use, but which since the 1960s has been used in the media and in 'respectable' conversation. (Mickey Dolenz of the pop group The Monkees heard the phrase '*randy Scouse git*' on the British TV comedy series 'Till death us do part' and used it as the title of a single in 1967. This was deemed too offensive for radio and in Britain the song title was changed.) Randy is of uncertain origin. It was first recorded at the end of the 18th century. Two suggested etymologies for the word are: a dialect verb meaning to behave in a wild or wanton manner, and a Hindi word meaning lustful. Of these, the first (the rarely recorded word was related to 'rant' and 'random') is the more likely. The use of randy is rare in American English except as a short form of Randolph.

♭'*Girls…showing their arms in thin,*

thin frocks (good luck to randy grandfathers).'
(*About Town* magazine, June 1962).

♭'*Randy banker's wife Marilyn Divall revealed last night how an evil conman turned her into his sex slave. The bonking brunette admitted to having an orgy with EIGHT men.'*
(*News of the World*, 7 May 1989).

rang(e)y *adj American* aggressive, oppressive. The term (which rhymes with 'tangy') is of uncertain origin.

rank *adj* 1 unpleasant. The standard adjective (its original meaning was overbearing or excessively strong) has been adopted as an all-purpose vogue term of disapproval by teenagers in the USA and in Britain, where it probably originated in black usage.

♭'*This health-drink stuff is just so rank!'*
(Recorded, teenage schoolboy, London, 1994)

2 excellent, admirable. A term of approbation originating, it is said, in the 1960s 'pachuco' (Hispanic street-)culture of the USA.

rank, rank out, rank on (someone) *vb American* to insult, taunt or provoke. The terms, which occur in adolescent speech, probably originated in black street slang.

ranting *n British* a style of stand-up poetry recital which became popular in the post-**punk** milieu of the late 1970s. The poems were characterized in content and delivery by anger and aggression: the principal exponents of the style were Steven 'Seething' Wells and Attila the Stockbroker. The word ranting accurately describes the performance style as well as recalling the name of the sect of 17th-century dissident preachers.

rap *n* 1 a a conversation, especially an earnest and/or lengthy discussion. A word which became an important part of the counterculture lexicon at the end of the 1960s, rap was originally used by blacks and **beatniks**, deriving from the verb form.

b a rhythmic spoken chant, often to a musical background. This form of (originally) improvised delivery became a vogue first among young blacks in New York and other eastern American cities (inspired by Jamaican **toasting**), and then a worldwide pop phenomenon in the 1980s.

2 an accusation or charge, blame or punishment. An 18th-century British use of the verb rap was to denote swearing an oath against, accusing of, or charging (with a crime). This sense survives, via American English, in the phrase 'take the rap' and 'beat the rap' and the term **rap sheet**.

rap *vb*

a to talk, converse or discuss. A key term from the **hippy** era which usually denoted an earnest or communal exchange of ideas. The word was first heard in this sense in black American speech; it was subsequently adopted by white **hipsters**, **beatniks** and **hippies** in turn. (Rap was in use in Britain in the late 1960s but in its original sense is now confined to the remnants of **hippy** culture.) The exact origin of this use of the word is not at all clear; possible etymologies include a shortening of rapid (speech), rapport or repartee. The term might come simply from the similarity between talking and tapping ('rapping') on a drum or other surface; this might fit an origin among jazz musicians. Alternatively, in archaic slang a rapper was someone who 'talked' to the authorities (see the noun form) and this notion may have become generalized in black argot into 'talk'.

b to deliver an (originally improvised) monologue to a musical backing; to perform **rap** music. This musical form of the 1980s originated as a street phenomenon among black youth in American cities in the 1970s.

rapper *n* a practitioner or devotee of **rap** music.

rap session *n American* a conversation or discussion. A phrase first used in the 1950s by black Americans, **hipsters** and **beatniks**, later taken up by **hippies**, alternative therapists and teenagers.

rap sheet *n American* (documentary evidence of) a person's criminal record. The expression has been in use since World War II and derives from the underworld slang noun-form **rap**, meaning arrest or arraignment.

rapt *adj* delighted. A vogue term of the late 1980s which seems to have spread from Australia to both Britain and the USA in the **hip** parlance of adolescents. The word is the standard (literary) English term meaning enraptured.

↳'*She wasn't exactly rapt when I told her, I can tell you.*'

rare *adj British* an all-purpose term of approbation, often employed as an exclamation by schoolchildren since the 1980s especially in the north of England and Scotland. This sense of the word probably originated in black youth-culture in the USA and was transmitted via **rap**, skateboarding terminology, etc. Rare was previously used as a generalized vogue term in this way by **mods** briefly in 1966. It was used as long ago as the 16th century, with sporadic examples in between.

rash *adj* wonderful. A term of high appreciation among American teenagers and aficionados of hip-hop in the 1980s. It is nearly always expressed as 'totally rash' and was coined on the lines of **wild**, **bad**, **wicked**, etc.

raspberry *n* a farting sound made by blowing through the lips, a **Bronx cheer**. Now an innocent colloquialism heard all over the English-speaking world, it derives from the late 19th-century London rhyming-slang, 'raspberry tart': **fart**.

raspberry (ripple) *n British* a cripple. A piece of London rhyming-slang playing on the name of a type of ice cream.

rasta *n* a Rastafarian. The word is a shortening of the name of the devotees of Ras Tafari (one of the titles of the late emperor of Ethiopia, Haile Selassie) whose sacrament is **ganja** and who wear **dreadlocks**. The language of the Jamaican movement has influenced English slang mainly via reggae music.

rat-arsed *adj* drunk. The terms rat-arsed, **rat-faced** and the milder **ratted** enjoyed a vogue among adolescents and young adults (particularly those from middle- and upper-class backgrounds) from the mid-1980s. Terms employing rat- as a prefix evoking disgust were heard throughout the English-speaking community in the 1980s (see **rat-boy**, **rathole**, **ratshit**, etc.) particularly in Australia and the USA.

ratbag *n Australian* a despicable, disreputable or obnoxious person. This term of abuse originated in Australia where it derived either literally from a bag used by a rat-catcher or from the notion of a bag full of rats as the epitome of obnoxious-

ness. The word became popular in Britain in the early 1960s (helped in no small part by its frequent use in the popular radio comedy-series *Hancock's Half Hour*) and is now often used with a degree of affection. In Australia it often denotes an eccentric.

↳'*She's a total ratbag – I don't want to have anything more to do with her.*' (*Neighbours*, Australian TV soap opera, 1987).

rated *adj British* excellent, admirable. A vogue term of approbation heard among adolescents in the later 1990s, which began as an abbreviated form of 'A-rated' or 'highly-rated'.

rat-faced *adj* drunk. A vogue term of the late 1980s among all social classes in Britain (particularly heard among **Sloane Rangers** and **yuppies**).

ratfink *n American* a treacherous, despicable person. The word is a combination of rat (traitor) and **fink** (informer) and was first used to refer to union blacklegs or **scabs**. It enjoyed a vogue in the 1960s in its more generalized sense and is still used, albeit less widely. *See also* **fink**.

rathole, rat-hole *n* a disgusting, squalid place. A fashionable expression of distaste in the later 1980s. In 1987 the college lecturers' union NATFHE condemned 'Thatcher's rathole Britain' in a press handout.

Ratners *n pl British* rubbish, worthless goods. The jocular term refers to the jewellery retailer Gerald Ratner's remark made in 1991 that some of his own goods were **crap**. The word often occurred in the phrase '*a load of old Ratners*'.

rat (on) *vb* to inform on or betray (someone). An Americanism employing the familiar identification of a rat with treachery or spite. The phrase was imported into Britain and Australia before World War II.

↳'*Rule number one is you don't rat on your friends.*'

rat out *vb* to abandon, betray, cravenly withdraw. An Americanism which is also heard in Australia and, to a lesser extent, in Britain. Usages involving the 'rat' components were in vogue during the 1980s.

↳'*She ratted out at the last minute.*'

↳'*They ratted out on us.*'

rat-run *n British* a side street used for fast commuter traffic. A phrase and phenomenon of the late 1980s.

ratshit *adj Australian* worthless, inferior, utterly disappointing. The word (pronounced like 'ratchet') usually expresses bitter disapproval or disillusion.

ratted *adj British* drunk. A more polite version of **rat-faced** or **rat-arsed**. All three terms were in vogue in the second half of the 1980s.

↳'*When we were looking for the personification of the Kentucky face, we got so ratted, so drunk ... for an entire week.*' (Ralph Steadman, *I-D* magazine, November 1987).

rattlehead *n British* someone listening to a personal stereo in a public place, or on public transport. The term refers to the noise leaking from the headphones to the discomfort of fellow passengers. Rattlehead was heard among adolescents in the later 1980s.

rattler *n* **1** a surface or underground train. The word has been used in Britain and the USA (where travelling hobos referred to 'hopping a rattler') since the 19th century. Until the late 1950s the London underground system was sometimes known to workmen as the Rattler.
2 *British* a womanizer, seducer. It derives from the verb form **rattle (someone)**, meaning to have sex with, and like that term is heard mainly in Scotland.

rattle someone's cage *vb* to provoke, disturb, rouse. A phrase in mainly working-class usage, like others ('drop off the perch', 'sick as a parrot') using the imagery of a caged bird or animal. The expression usually forms part of a provocative rhetorical question '*who rattled your cage?*' addressed to someone suddenly roused to anger or indignation. **Yank (someone around/someone's chain)** is an American alternative.

raunchy *adj* sexually provocative, earthy, risqué; lustful or lust-inducing. The word probably took one of its original meanings, 'ripe' or over-ripe in the metaphorical sense, from the Italian *rancio*, rank or rotten, although a British dialect origin has also been posited. Until the late 1960s raunchy was mainly in American usage. It is now a fairly common colloquialism in all English-speaking areas.

rave, rave-up *n British* a wild party, dance or occasion of abandoned behaviour. A usage originating in bohemian circles in the late 1950s. In the early 1960s the word was taken up by **mods** and shortly thereafter by the media and the older generation, who still employ the term. More recently still the **acid house** youth cult adopted the word to refer to their (typically large-scale and movable) celebrations, sometimes specified as **orbital raves** (those within reach of the M25 motorway). By 1990 schoolchildren were also using the word as a synonym for party.

raver *n British* an unrestrained, hedonistic person. An archetypal 1960s term which originated in the 1950s among bohemians and **beatniks**, when it was applied to frequent attenders of all-night parties and jazz clubs, etc. In the later 1960s the already slightly dated word epitomized **hippy** abandonment to euphoria. Subsequently the word has survived mainly in working-class male usage to refer, rather like **goer**, to wild or promiscuous (usually young) women in expressions such as '*right little raver*'.

raw meat *n* a euphemism for sex organs or sexual activity, heard in the late 1960s and 1970s.

razoo *n Australian* a very small sum of money, 'a brass farthing'. A word said to be of Maori origin, used in negative phrases such as '*I haven't got a brass razoo*' or '*without a razoo*'.

razorblade *n British* a black person. An unaffectionate rhyming-slang term (based on **spade**) used by police officers among others in the 1970s and 1980s.

razz *vb* to tease or deride. A word which is currently more popular in Australia and the USA than Britain (although it features in British public-school argot). Razz was originally a theatrical shortening of **raspberry** and the verb is still used in theatrical parlance to mean jeer. In modern usage it often appears to have overtones common to 'rag', rouse and **roust**.

readies *n* cash, banknotes, money. A shorter and racier version of the phrases 'ready cash' or 'ready money'.

↳'*It was always the same old story. "I've no money on me. Have you any readies, Al?" They must think we're a bit daft up North.*'

(*Guardian*, 12 December 1987).

ready, the ready *n* money, cash. This is currently a less common form (except in the USA) of the plural **readies**. Ready or the ready was in fact probably the original form of the term, first recorded in the 17th century.

rear-end *vb* to ruin, damage. The figurative use of the phrase probably derives from the colloquialism referring to a car collision, with possible suggestions also of sexual activity.

↳'*The guys upstairs rear-ended him good.*'
(Reported, New York office worker, September 1995).

rear-gunner *n British* a male homosexual. One of many pejorative synonyms in use among heterosexuals since the 1980s. The phrase was used on more than one occasion in interviews by the **punk** singer John 'Johnnie Rotten' Lydon.

recce *n British* a reconnaissance or reconnoitring. An armed-service shortening (pronounced 'reckie'), which has been generalized in civilian usage to mean a preliminary check or look around.

recco *n Australian* recognition, peer-group respect. An abbreviation heard among young adults and adolescents.

red-arse *n British* a new army recruit. In the early 20th century the term referred specifically to a Guardsman (whose jacket was red).

red-assed *adj American* furious, irate.

red biddy *n British* cheap red wine or methylated spirits as drunk by tramps or derelicts. Biddy, originally a diminutive of Bridget, was an affectionate name for a woman, preserved in the colloquial term 'old biddy'.

the red-eye *n* an early-morning or overnight flight or train service. The expression, which refers to the tired appearance of the passengers, originated in the USA where it was a nickname given to coast-to-coast flights.

red-high *adj British* delighted, ecstatic. The term was recorded in use among north London schoolboys in 1993 and 1994.

red-inker *n British* a recorded arrest. A 'score' in the tally of arrests for a particular officer or police station, in the jargon of the police force.

redneck *n American* a rustic bigot or boor. This now familiar expression became well known in the late 1960s when it was extended from the original sense of a rural white Southern farmer (with a neck red from being bent to the sun, or from anger) to include all opponents of liberation or the counterculture.

red Ned *n Australian* cheap red wine. The Australian version of **red biddy**.

reds, red devils *n pl American* capsules of Seconal, a barbiturate used by drug abusers, from the colour of the capsules.
⬧'The use of "reds" or barbiturates for highs (lows would be more descriptive) seems to be increasing again.'
(*Dr Hip Pocrates* (Eugene Schoenfeld), 1969).

red sails in the sunset *adj* menstruating. A phrase, taken from the title of a popular song, which has been used (almost invariably by men) since the 1960s.
⬧'Looks as if she's red sails in the sunset.'

reeb *n British* beer in **backslang**. A word which was heard in the 1950s and which survives in limited use (among young market-workers for instance).

reefer, reef *n*
a a marihuana cigarette, an earlier term for **joint**. A word which fell out of favour with cannabis smokers in the late 1950s but which was perpetuated by the media and law enforcement agencies.
b marihuana. A famous and risible American anti-drug firm of 1936 was entitled *Reefer Madness*. In origin the word is a corruption of *grifa*, the Spanish slang for marihuana.

reek *vb American* to be repellent, inferior or worthless. A vogue term of disparagement or denigration among American adolescents in the 1990s. It is a synonym for **suck**, 'stink', and **wipe**.
⬧'Like it totally reeks!'

reen *n British* an alternative spelling of **rene**.

re-entry *n American* in the parlance of LSD users, the return to normality after

the effects of an LSD **trip** have worn off. A term briefly popular in the mid- and late 1960s, derived from the jargon of space exploration.

reestie *adj American* unpleasant, obnoxious. The word can be applied to persons or objects and is characteristically used by adolescents. It is probable a blend of **reek** and **beasty**.

reffo *n Australian* a refugee. An unaffectionate term for an immigrant (typically a European fleeing Nazi or Soviet repression).

reject *n* a term of abuse popular among British schoolchildren in the 1980s.

rello *n Australian* a relative, relation.
⬧'We're having the rellos over.'

remmy, remmie *n British* a fool. This item of schoolchildren's slang was reported in the 1990 publication *Bad Language* by the sociolinguist Peter Trudgill. It may derive from the designation 'remedial (pupil/lesson)'.

rene, reen, renee *n British* a young female working-class Londoner. The term was used (and perhaps coined) by the south London female group the Gymslips to epitomize people like themselves. Rene is the christian name Renée in its anglicized form and pronunciation. According to the group, renes characteristically wear monkey boots and have short cropped hair, drink beer and enjoy pie and mash.
⬧'Rocking with the Renes.'
(LP title, the Gymslips, 1980).

rentacop *n* a hired security guard. A term generally used disapprovingly or derisively, particularly in the era of student unrest when US campus authorities frequently called on such personnel for assistance.

rentals *n pl American* parents. A version of **parental unit(s)**, also rendered as **rents** or **units**. The expressions became fairly well known from the later 1980s.
⬧'I'm going to be in deep doodoo when the rentals see this.'

rent boy *n British* a young male prostitute. A **gay** slang term of the later 1960s that moved into common currency following press revelations of scandals in the 1980s. Young, sometimes homeless (and often heterosexual) rent boys frequented the Piccadilly area of London from at least the 1970s.

rents *n pl* parents. Originally a term in use among American teenagers, this clipping, typical of youth slang of the late 1980s and early 1990s, was adopted by other English-speaking adolescents in the 1990s. A synonym is **unit(s)**.

♥'*The rents are away for the weekend.*'

rep *n* a shortening of 'reputation', used especially to denote (appreciatively) a reputation for violence or sexual prowess or (pejoratively) promiscuity. The word, typical of the clippings popularized first by American adolescents from the late 1970s, has moved from the language of streetgangs and **rappers** into school-children's usage in the late 1990s.

♥'*He's gotta protect his rep.*'
♥'*If she goes on like this she's going to get a rep for skeezing.*'

reptiles *n pl* **1** shoes or boots, particularly those made of alligator, lizard or snakeskin. This footwear, favoured by American pimps, for instance, is also referred to as **lizards** or **alligator shoes** (which also ironically denotes old, open-toed shoes).

♥'*I wanted to wear the silk suits, wear the reptiles on my feet.*'
(Washington DC drug dealer, *World in Action*, British TV documentary, 10 April 1989).
2 journalists, reporters, the press in general, especially those from the gutter press. A usage popularized by its use in the *Dear Bill* letters featured in *Private Eye* magazine.

respect *n American* a key term from the rituals of street-based black subcultures of the late 1970s and early 1980s, 'respect' was both an exclamation of greeting and acknowledgement and an essential concept in peer-group relationships.
See also **touch-respect**.
♥'*He didn't give me no respect.*'

result, a result *n British*
a an outcome in one's favour, what is due, a good result. The term originated in football jargon where to 'get a result' means not to lose.

♥'*He owes me money. He's not ill – it's just a ploy to stop me getting a result!*'

(*Minder*, British TV series, 1982).
b an arrest and/or conviction. A specialized use of the above among members of the police force.

retard *n* a term of abuse among schoolchildren in the UK and the USA (where it is more fashionably shortened to **tard**) since the 1970s.

rettes *n pl American* cigarettes. A shortening fashionable among **preppies** in the late 1970s.

rhino *n British* money. A raffish term which seemed obsolescent until its revival along with synonyms such as **pelf**, **dosh**, **moolah**, etc. during the glamorizing of finance and commerce in the mid-1980s. The word has had this meaning since the end of the 17th century, perhaps because of the value of the (supposedly aphrodisiac) rhinoceros horn or simply because the animal was at that time a fabulous symbol of wealth and exoticism.

rhubarb *n British* meaningless babble, nonsense, empty talk. The theatrical term for background mumbling or hubbub has been adopted by London working-class users as a contemptuous or dismissive term for rubbish of all sorts.
♥'*He gave me a load of old rhubarb.*'

riah, riach *n British* hair, head of hair. One of the few instances of **back-slang** to escape from a very restricted milieu. The word, usually pronounced to rhyme with 'fire', was used in the 1950s and early 1960s by actors, dressmakers, hairdressers, etc.

rice-burner *n American*
a a Japanese motorcycle. A contemptuous term used by US **bikers** and particularly by police motorcyclists who were forced to exchange their Harley Davidsons for Japanese motorcycles in the 1970s.
♥'*Once these rice-burners start to go [wrong], there's no stopping them.*'
(*Midnight Witness*, US film, 1994).
b any vehicle made or designed in the Pacific rim.

rice-queen *n* a **gay** male who is attracted to oriental partners. *Compare* **curry-queen**.

Richard *n British* a third-class university degree. Like **Desmond**, **Pattie**, **Taiwan** and **made-in**, it is a student witticism, based on 'Richard the Third'. A

Douglas (Hurd) is a more recent and fashionable version.

Richard (Gere) *n British* (a glass of) beer. An item of rhyming slang using the name of the Hollywood star, heard amongst students from the early 1990s.

richard-mary *n British* a **gay** male. The rhyming slang phrase is for **fairy** and was recorded in Wales and elsewhere in the 1980s.

Richard the Third *n British* 1 a bird (in the literal sense or as slang for a woman).

2 a **turd**. The phrase has two senses in cockney rhyming slang; the first is now dated whereas the second has achieved limited currency among non-cockneys in the 1970s and 1980s.

3 the longer (rarely used) form of a **Richard**.

ricket *n British* an error, blunder. This slightly dated term is still heard among older speakers. It may be related to 'rickety' or the disease rickets, but the etymology is obscure.

riddle *n See* **Jimmy Riddle**.

ride *vb* to copulate (with). A metaphorical usage which has been in evidence since at least the 16th century, when it was a standard synonym or euphemism in the same way as mount. Ride is still heard in this sexual sense, albeit rarely, whereas the noun form is still fairly widespread.

ride *n* an act of sexual intercourse or a sex partner. This is a later derivation of the (now less common) verb form of the word.

ride the baloney-pony *vb*
a to have sex.
b (of a male) to masturbate. This adolescent witticism is inspired by the American name for the Bologna sausage.

ride someone's ass *vb American* to nag, harass. The phrase is a pun on 'ass' as donkey, as well as evoking an image of driving or urging from behind.
&'*Quit riding his ass over this, will you?*'

ride the porcelain Honda/bus *vb American* to suffer from diarrhoea, sit on the toilet. A **preppie** witticism on the pattern of **kiss the porcelain god** (to vomit).

ridgy-didge, ridgy-didgy *adj Australian* truthful, reliable, honest, authentic. This phrase, which is still heard in Australian speech, has been derived from 'rigid digger', meaning an upstanding, honest Australian. Alternatively it may be based on the archaic English 'ridge', meaning gold.

ridiculous *adj British* drunk. The term is particularly heard in Glaswegian speech. **Miraculous** is a synonym.

riffed *adj American* intoxicated by drugs or alcohol. The word 'riff' has had several slang senses, but it is not clear which, if any, gave rise to this usage.

riffing *n American* behaving in a provocative or obstreperous manner. The term, heard in black slang of the 1990s, covers a number of meanings related to earlier use of the word 'riff' in **jive talk**, including provoking, complaining and boasting, but the logic of the connection is unclear.

rift *n See* **get a rift on**.

rift *vb British* (to emit) a belch. The term, which imitates the sound of the eructation, is heard particularly in the Scottish Lowlands and the north of England.

rig *n American* 1 the male sex organs. A word used, especially by women, in the **hippy** era, although the word is older.
&'*I got this cute little pendant in the form of a flying rig.*'
(*Groupies*, US film, 1973).
2 a truck, large van or bus.
3 a heroin user's syringe, ligature, etc.
&'*I remember saying to the guy I was with "Don't fill the rig up. Don't put too much coke in it".*'
(*Q* magazine, March 1997).

righteous *adj American*
a good, admirable.
&'*A righteous dude.*'
b large or excessive.
&'*A righteous mess.*'
Both senses are originally black adaptations of the standard English term, influenced by religious jargon. The terms are now also used, sometimes ironically, by white speakers.

right-on *adj American* admirable, thoroughgoing, authentic. A term of approval from the late 1970s which derives from 'right on!', the 1960s exclamation of enthusiasm, support, agreement or solidarity (itself originally from black American speech). The phrase is increasingly used ironically to mean **gung-ho** or self-righteous.

↳'*A right-on guy.*'

↳'*She was right-on.*'

right-on *n British* an endorser of radical, liberal or leftist opinion. The invariably pejorative usage is based on 'right on!', the catchphrase supposedly characteristic of fashionable leftists of the 1960s.

↳'*She comes across as a bit of a right-on, unfortunately.*'

rigid *adj* drunk. The term often (but not necessarily) refers to someone helplessly drunk.

rim *vb*

a to lick the anus as part of sexual stimulation.

b to sodomize.

ring *n* the anus. A common vulgarism in all English-speaking communities. The word has also occasionally been used for the vagina.

ringburner *n British* a hot curry, or the condition following its digestion and excretion. An expression used typically among males for whom a hot curry is a test of **machismo** and/or a natural adjunct to drinking. (The ring in question is the anus and the word is a pun on a designation of a stove or cooking hob.)

ringer *n* **1 a** something, such as a stolen or defective car, a racehorse or greyhound, which has been tampered with or doctored in order to deceive.

b a person who alters the appearance of a car, racehorse, antique, etc., in order to deceive.

2 *American* a substitute introduced by subterfuge into a game or race to gain an unfair advantage.

ring-piece *n British* the anus. An elaboration of **ring** popularized by its constant appearance in *Viz* comic.

ring someone's bell *vb* to bring to a sexual climax. A euphemistic phrase which appears in the lyrics of several soul and disco records of the 1970s, also sometimes meaning simply 'catch someone's eye' or 'strike a chord'.

rinky-dink *adj British* **1** cute, neat, smart. This fairly rare sense of the phrase may be based on a misunderstanding of the American usage, or a separate coinage influenced by **dinky**.

2 *American* shoddy, makeshift, meretricious. The phrase probably originated as an imitation of the sound of fairground music, evoking gaudiness and kitsch.

rip off *vb* to cheat, steal (from) or take advantage (of). A raffish black street euphemism for steal or rob, in the mid-1960s rip off passed quickly via **hippy** jargon into popular currency all over the English-speaking world.

↳'*Well, just about everyone in the music business has been ripped off, financially speaking. That's Entertainment!*'

(*Ms London* magazine, 4 September 1989).

rip-off *n* an instance of theft, deception or unfair appropriation. It is now used in fairly mundane contexts, such as overcharging or plagiarism. The noun, like the verb, is from 1960s black argot in which it meant a robbery or a fraud.

rip-off *adj* (of goods) overpriced; (of people) grasping; and (of financial arrangements) crooked.

ripoff artist *n* a practitioner of **rip-offs**, fraudster or thief. The late 1960s **-artist** suffix does not denote expertise, but merely habitual involvement.

ripped *adj* **1 stoned** on marihuana or a similar drug. The word is occasionally also used to mean drunk and is often elaborated into 'ripped to the gills' or 'ripped to the tits'.

↳'*We're just sitting around getting ripped and listening to records.*'

(*IT* magazine, July 1972).

2 *American* killed. A 'tough guy' euphemism of the 1970s and 1980s.

↳'*He just got ripped.*'

ripper *adj Australian* excellent, first-rate. A word which goes in and out of vogue, ripper was a British term of admiration, probably originating in the sports world (it has denoted a well-bowled cricket ball or a devastating punch in boxing) in the mid-19th century.

ripple *n British See* **raspberry (ripple)**.

rippy *adj British* excellent, thrilling. A late 1980s version of the archaic 'ripping' (Australian **ripper**), heard among middle-class teenagers, for instance.

rivets *n American* money, dollars. The term was recorded in British speech from the early 1800s but is now rare.

rizzer *n British* a candidate for student office whose chances are 'risible'. A probably ephemeral term employed by Oxford University students in 1988.

roach *n* **1 a** the butt of a **joint** (marihuana cigarette). An American term adopted elsewhere in the late 1960s; this use of the word arose before World War II and is probably simply a borrowing of cockroach. (Some authorities have suggested a connection with 'to roach', i.e. to clip a horse's mane.) In Britain roach may apply to the cardboard filter inserted into joints made of hashish mixed with tobacco. In the USA the lack of these necessitates the use of roach clips; metal tweezers that allow the stub of a marihuana cigarette to be held and smoked to the end without burning the fingers.
b a marihuana cigarette, **joint**. A US teenage usage, probably derived from the first, more widespread sense of the word.
2 *American* **a** a despicable or contemptible person.
b an unattached girl.

road apple *n* a piece of horse manure on the highway. In the USA where the term probably originated the synonym **alley apple** also exists.

road brew, road sauce *n American* beer. A college-students' term. The significance of the 'road' component is unclear; **brew** and **sauce** are both slang terms for alcohol in their own rights.

roader *n British* a long and lucrative cab ride. An item of taxi drivers' jargon, recorded in the *Evening Standard*, 22 April 1996.

roadie *n* **1** a rock group's assistant, responsible for handling equipment and general tasks. The word is a short form of the portentous official title 'road manager'.
2 *American* beer. A shortened version of **road brew** or **road sauce** in **preppie** jargon. It is usually in the plural form.

✎'*Let's grab some roadies.*'

road pizza *n American* any small creature that has been run over and flattened by a car. The sardonic witticism of the late 1980s. *Compare* **pavement pizza** and **street pizza**.

roarer *n British* a male homosexual, especially one who is actually or supposedly flagrant. This alternative form of 'roaring **pouff/queen**', etc., is a heterosexual term of abuse of the 1970s and 1980s.

robobabe *n American* an overwhelmingly attractive female. An item of invented slang from the cult 1992 US movie, *Wayne's World*. The prefix is adopted from the earlier cult film *Robocop*. *Compare* **babia majora**.

robot *n South African* a set of traffic lights.

rock *n* **1** a gem, diamond.
2 crack, cocaine. The term has been used for many years by dealers and users to denote any crystalline preparation of a narcotic. In the USA in the late 1980s, rock is the most widespread generic term for crack among law-enforcers and breakers.

✎'*Mr Wardle said the* [black British] *girls didn't call it crack. "They'd heard of crack from the media, knew it was a very bad thing and some of them thought that crack and heroin are the same drug." However, they were alarmingly familiar with "rock".*'
(*Guardian*, 5 September 1989).

✎'*A $15 "rock" – costing about the same as two cinema tickets – contains six "hits", enough to keep two people high for 90 minutes.*'
(*Independent*, 24 July 1989).

3 the Rock.
a Gibraltar.
b Alcatraz, the escape-proof island prison (now closed) in San Francisco Bay, USA.

rocker *n British* a member of a youth cult of the early 1960s, characterized by the wearing of black leather jackets and enthusiasm for motorcycles and 1950s rock 'n' roll music. These mainly working-class teenagers and young adults were the successors to the **ton-up boys** and coevals of the self-consciously 'progressive' **mods**, who despised them for their adherence to 1950s American fashions and music. Mods and rockers fought each other sporadically until the late 1960s, when each group metamorphosed; rockers into **greasers** and subsequent anonymity, or into **bikers**.

৬'*Rockers' hard-wearing clothes were of the type worn out of doors. Mods on the other hand were recruited in the main from the forum of office juniors and shop assistants.*'
(Johnny Stuart, *Rockers*, 1987).

rockets *n pl* breasts, particularly when prominent or 'jutting'.

rock-head *n American* a stupid person. Like its later derivative **rubblehead**, rock-head is based on the uniquely North American notion of having rocks in one's head instead of brains.

rock house *n American* premises where **crack** (also known as **rock**) is processed and/or sold.

৬'*In the depressed inner-city areas of Los Angeles or New York, crack is frequently consumed in "crack houses" or "rock houses" – derelict buildings, often occupied by squatters, where addicts can buy and consume the drug.*'
(*Sunday Times*, 10 September 1989).

the rock 'n' roll *n British* the dole, or a dole office (the term is extended to cover Social Security payments and offices). A piece of recent rhyming slang.

৬'*On the rock 'n' roll again.*'
৬'*I'm going down the rock 'n' roll.*'
See also **rocky**.

rocks *n pl* testicles. An American version of the archaic British 'stones', rocks is now in limited use elsewhere in the English-speaking world. *See* **get one's rocks off**.

rod *n* 1 *American* a gun, particularly a pistol or revolver.
2 the penis.
3 a short form of hot rod.

Rodney *n British* a foolish or stupid person. This use of the name (by schoolchildren since the 1980s) is inspired by the character of Rodney in the long-running British TV comedy *Only Fools and Horses*.

rod-walloper *n* a male masturbator. **Rod** is an occasional slang synonym for penis.

Rogan (Josh) *n British* money. The term (the name of a popular curry dish) is rhyming slang for **dosh**.

৬'*By the look of them they're not short of a bit of the old Rogan Josh.*'
(Recorded, musician, London, August 1994).

roger *vb British* to copulate with (a woman). First recorded in 1711, the term is probably older. Roger, like **dick**, **peter**, **willie**, etc., has been used in the past as a nickname for the penis. It was also frequently given as a name to bulls and rams. In modern British middle-class use it is often employed as an 'acceptable' alternative to taboo synonyms. Roger has also been employed to denote buggery (in a homosexual context).

৬'*Should not a Half-pay Officer roger for sixpence?*'
(James Boswell, writing in his *London Journal*, 1762).

roll *vb* 1 to rob or mug (someone). Originally the term referred to robbing someone who was dead drunk or asleep, hence literally rolling over an inert body in order to rifle pockets.
2 to have sex with. The verb form is much rarer than the noun in this sense.

roll *n* 1 an act of sexual intercourse. Usually heard in a fairly light-hearted context, particularly in the cliché 'a roll in the hay'.
2 a wad of banknotes, a bankroll.
3 an act of mugging or robbing, particularly of an already unconscious person. A rare noun form of the verb sense.

roller *n British* a Rolls-Royce car. A working-class and underworld nickname that entered general colloquial use in the later 1970s.

rollick, rollock *vb British* to dress (someone) down, upbraid or chastise. A mainly middle- and upper-class euphemism for **bollock** which has been heard since before World War II. Its use is probably reinforced by the jocular use of 'rowlocks' as a noun synonym for **bollocks**. *See also* **rollocking**.

rolling *adj British* rich. A middle-class colloquial shortening of 'rolling in it', which is itself based on the image of a pig, horse or other animal rolling in manure.
৬'*She's absolutely rolling.*'

rollocking *n British* a severe dressing-down, an angry and pointed tirade. The word is a euphemism for **bollocking**.

↳*'Though Dad gave me a real rollock-ing, in the end I won. I just fluttered my eyelids at him and promised I wouldn't be seeing Josh again.'*
(Jade Jagger, quoted in the *News of the World*, 29 March 1989).

ronk *vb British* to stink. An invented word probably combining 'stink' and 'rot-ten'. **Honk** is a synonym. Ronk is a popu-lar word in Liverpool and elsewhere in the north of England, though its use is not restricted to this area.

↳*'God, it doesn't half ronk in here.'*

rookie *n* a learner, neophyte or new-comer, particularly to a job or a sports team. The term originated in Britain in the armed forces of the late 19th century, but more recently rookie has been in more widespread use in the USA. The word is said to be a deformation of 're-cruit', perhaps influenced by the noisy chattering of rooks.

↳*'Are you crazy? You're just a rookie. I've been on night patrol for years.'*
(*Night Patrol*, US film, 1984).

rooms *n pl American* mushrooms. This abbreviation refers to innocuous mushrooms as eaten on pizzas rather than **magic mushrooms**, which are known as **shrooms**.

rooster *n* a male homosexual, partic-ularly a predatory prison inmate who dominates or victimizes younger fellow prisoners. In **gay** and prison jargon, roosters or **chickenhawks** prey upon **chickens**. Rooster is American for cock in the sense of male chicken.

root *vb* to have sex (with). A vulgar eu-phemism which occurs in working-class English speech and which is common in Australia. It derives from the archaic use of root to mean penis and from 'root/ rootle around', in the sense of searching in crevices. The term, first recorded in the 19th century but probably older, is hardly ever used in a homosexual context or by women.

root *n* 1 a an act of sexual intercourse.
b a sexual partner or available 'sex ob-ject'. The noun senses post-date the verb, and are widespread in British and Aus-tralian usage.
2 *American* a cigarette or **joint**. A rare term which may originate in 'cheroot'.

rooted *adj Australian*
a ruined, destroyed, broken. Used in the same way as the more offensive **fucked** and **buggered**, this expression derives from the verb **to root**.
↳*'Christ, now the engine's rooted!'*
b exhausted.

root-faced *adj Australian* humour-less-looking, having a morose expression. A phrase known in Britain mainly through the writing and performances of the Melbourne satirist, Barry Humphries, it is inspired by the wooden, knotted ap-pearance of an old root.

rope *n* 1 a *American* a cigar.
b tobacco.
c marihuana. The connection and re-semblance between tobacco, hemp and rope has given rise to these usages.
2 *American* a decorative metal chain, es-pecially a heavy golden chain as worn by males. This item of hip-hop regalia dates from the early 1980s. A synonym is **cable**.

ropeable *adj Australian* furious or berserk. A slang interpretation of the no-tion contained in the colloquial expression 'fit to be tied'.
↳*'Well when we broke the news to her – I tell you, she was ropeable.'*

rort *n Australian* 1 a swindle, a small-time confidence trick. This term of un-certain origin, until recently used mainly by people over 40 years of age, is under-going something of a revival in media circles.
2 a noisy, riotous and wild party or cele-bration. In this sense the noun is probably a back-formation from the adjective **rorty**. See **rorter**.

rort *vb Australian* to cheat, manipulate or bamboozle.
↳*'The Federal Government is to crack down on abuse of English language courses to rort the migrant selection system following examination of an inter-departmental submission to Cab-inet.'*
(*LAW* [*London Australasian Weekly*] magazine, 4 September 1989).

rorter *n* 1 *Australian* a swindler, small-time confidence trickster or cheat. The origin of the Australian terms based on the word **rort** is unclear; one sugges-tion is that they are in fact based on 'wrought(er)', an archaic British term for trick(ster).

2 *British* a market trader who shouts his or her wares. This category, like the **lurker** and the **pitcher**, was defined in a Channel 4 TV documentary, 28 July 1994.

rory *n British* **1** the floor.
2 a door.

Both senses are examples of rhyming slang which still belongs to a restricted working-class London milieu. The rhyme is 'Rory O'Moore', a fictional personage invoked since the 19th century.

rory *adj* flat broke. The word is from the rhyming slang for '(on) the floor': 'Rory O'Moore'. 'On the floor' is itself rhyming slang for poor. The Rory O'Moore in question is a probably fictional Scots/Irish personification of the 19th century.

rosie, Rosie Lee *n British* tea. A genuine example of cockney rhyming slang which has been adopted for light-hearted use by non-cockneys. The term seems to have originated at the turn of the century, from a common proper name, and was reinforced by the later fame of the American striptease artist Gypsy Rose Lee.
↳ '*A nice cup of rosie should do the trick.*'

rot-gut *adj, n* low quality alcoholic drink. A four-hundred-year-old term which was applied formerly to weak beer, but which more recently has usually denoted inferior spirits or wine.

rotten *adj* very drunk. A euphemism in British and Australian usage.

rough *adj British* **1** unpleasant, distasteful, disgusting. The standard term became an all-purpose pejorative in working-class speech and then a vogue word among adolescents and then younger schoolchildren in the mid-1990s.
↳ '*That girlfriend of his is well rough if you ask me.*'
2 excellent. The process whereby negative becomes positive operated particularly rapidly in the case of rough, which by the late 1990s was being used appreciatively.
↳ '*... "wicked" (for good) has vanished, replaced by the new term of high praise, "rough" invariably accompanied by a jerky wave of the right hand at shoulder level.*'

(*Guardian*, 19 October 1996).

the rough end of the pineapple *n Australian* a disadvantageous position, the worst of a deal. A colourful alternative to such phrases as 'the sharp end of the stick' or 'the shitty end of the stick'.

roughneck, ruff-neck *n British* a youth, especially a tough, admirable male. A 1990s synonym for **rude boy** or **bad-boy** first used by black gang-members before being adopted by other schoolchildren and teenagers. Like those terms, it is typical of the tendency by transgressive subcultures to adopt for the purpose of irony and bravado the pejorative language of their critics (as in **bad**, **wicked**, etc.).

rough trade *n British*
a a homosexual lover (usually a casual pick-up) considered to be lower class, uncouth and/or violent. From the homosexual underground slang of the 1950s, used for instance by male prostitutes about their customers. The phrase was later used to characterize a stereotypical homosexual icon, i.e. the muscular, aggressively masculine 'working man'.
b an uncouth or violent client of a heterosexual prostitute.
↳ '*Behind the throat-level peep-holes eyes took in the body swathed in Ralph Lauren finery trailing after her piece of rough trade.*'
(*Platinum Logic*, Tony Parsons, 1981).

roundeye *n* **1** a white person. The term, used originally by orientals as an opposite of 'slit-eyed', is also used by blacks.
2 *American* the anus, especially as a focus of sexual attention.

roundhead *n British* (a male with) a circumcized penis. A schoolboy counterpart to cavalier.

round the houses *adv British*
a on a (long and) futile mission.
b all over the body. The phrase is prostitutes' and pornographers' code for all-over sexual stimulation.

round the twist *adj, adv British* crazy, deranged. A racier version of the colloquial 'round the bend', this phrase moved from limited working-class usage to general currency in the 1960s.

roust *vb American* to disturb, harass and/or arrest. The word is usually used to describe the actions of police against suspects. Roust was first used by criminals or street-frequenters in the early 20th century, later by the law-enforcers themselves; it is from the noun 'rouster', a version of 'roustabout', employing a strong form of rouse.

rozzer *n British* a police officer. This word originated in the 19th century and is still in limited use. The standard derivations offered by reference sources (Romany *roozlo*, meaning strong, or 'roosher', a supposed corruption of 'rusher') are not entirely convincing.

rriot-grrrl *n American* a member or devotee of a neo-**punk** movement organized by various all-girl rock bands, including Bratmobile and L7 in 1992 and 1993.

rub-a-dub, rubbidy *n* a public house. These rhyming-slang phrases (with pub) are heard in both Britain and Australia. Rub-a-dub(dub) has also been used in Britain, especially in underworld circles, as rhyming slang for club.

rubber, rubber johnny *n* a condom. The first version is international English, the second British. Johnnie, Johnny and Johnny-bag are synonyms.

rubbish *vb* to deride, condemn, tease. Originally Australian, the expression has established itself in British English since the early 1970s.

rubblehead *n American* an idiot. A term, like **rock-head**, which evokes the notion of having rocks rather than brains in one's head. This version was popular among teenagers and college students in the late 1980s.

rube *n American* a yokel or rustic simpleton. A short form of the male Christian name Reuben.

rub off *vb* (of a female) to masturbate.

rub out *vb* to kill, murder. A euphemism from the language of the American underworld of the 1920s and 1930s, enthusiastically adopted by crime novelists. In modern street parlance the phrase is often shortened to rub.

Ruby (Murray) *n British* a curry. This item of rhyming slang comes from the name of an Irish-born popular singer of the 1950s. The word or phrase is perpetuated by some speakers too young to be familiar with its inspiration.

ruck *n British* an undisciplined brawl, gang fight. A characteristic London working-class use of a mild-sounding term (from 'ruckus') to denote something often involving extreme violence. (**Bother** and **aggro** are examples of the same tendency.) The word is an important element in the football hooligan and **skinhead** vocabulary.

⌖'*He* [a hooligan] *brags about his "rucks" with Millwall's notorious F troop.'*
(*News of the World*, 17 July 1988).

⌖'*One remark can start a ruck, and before you know it someone has been PP9'd.'*
(*Ms London* magazine, 20 September 1993).

rucking, ruck-up *n British* a brawl, row or dressing-down. These are variant forms of **ruck**.

ruddy *adj British* an inoffensive intensifying adjective, now dated, but used extensively from the turn of the century until the mid-1960s as a milder euphemism for **bloody**.

rude *adj* excellent. In this sense the term probably adapted from or imitating black speech was used by Californian adolescents in the mid-1990s often in the form '*totally rude*'.

rude bits *n pl British* the breasts and/or genitals. A coy quasi-nursery term in middle-class use.

rude boy *n*

a *Jamaican* a gangster, gang member.

⌖'*Interestingly, there is a theory that the word "reggae" was originally derived from its Kingston rude boy exponents being derided as "ragamuffin men".'*
(*Independent*, 1 September 1989).

b *British* a would-be tough and/or fashionable youth.

rug *n* **1a** a toupee, wig. A predictable pre-World War II jocularism which probably originated in theatrical slang.
b female pubic hair. **2** *see* **cut a rug**.

rug bug *n* an alternative form of **rug rat**.

rugged *adj Australian* suffering from bad luck.

rugger bugger *n British* a hearty (usually boorish) sportsman. The expression became popular from the 1960s primarily to denote the stereotypical rugby-club mentality.

rug-muncher *n American* a lesbian. **Carpet-muncher** is an alternative version of the pejorative term as used by males.

rug rat *n* a child. A phrase which, like the synonymous **ankle-biter**, has become popular, especially in young middle-class families, in the 1980s. **Rug bug** and **carpet rat** are alternative forms. The phrase was popularized by its adoption as the title of a US TV cartoon in the mid-1990s.

the ruler *n British* an impressive admirable individual. A key term in the adolescent language of status since the late 1980s. 'The boss' and 'the man' were earlier colloquial synonyms.

ᚼ'*Chris Evans is the ruler, seriously he is so rad, totally funny, he knows what's up (nice shirts) and when he is not presenting the show, it sucks.*'
(*Phat* magazine, 1993).

rum *adj British* strange, puzzling, mysterious. The term, which is a rather obsolescent colloquialism, usually has an added sense of 'disreputable' or 'suspicious' implied by its origin in the Romany word for a man, *rom*, used by and about gypsies, the traditional outsiders or non-conformists.

ᚼ'*Protheroe is a rum cove who used to be a colonel in the Territorial Army while running the Beeb.*'
(*Private Eye* magazine, April 1989).

rumble *n* a fight, especially a planned streetfight or brawl involving gangs. An American expression used by teenage neighbourhood gangs since the 1950s, the word has subsequently been picked up in other English-speaking areas.

rumble *vb* 1 to fight. The word like the noun form originated in the slang of American urban gangs of the 1950s. It has since been appropriated and generalized by other adolescents in the USA, UK and Australia.

ᚼ'*If you wanna stop us then you'll have to come and rumble us.*'
(*The Firm*, British TV play, 1989).

2 *British* to uncover (a deception), to be disabused. Now a fairly widespread colloquialism, rumble, like tumble, in this sense originated in the 19th century. Rumble probably derives from the archaic 'romboyle', to search for a wanted fugitive or suspect (a 17th-century term of unknown origin).

ᚼ'*We better get out of here – we've been rumbled.*'

rummage *vb British* to raid and/or search (premises). The specialized sense deriving from the standard colloquialism is used by police and criminals in the 1990s.

ᚼ'*It's going to be rummaged tomorrow.*'
(*River Police*, ITV documentary, 15 September 1995).

rumpo *n British* sex. A 'smutty' euphemism first popularized by the fictitious folksinger and specialist in innuendo, 'Rambling Sid Rumpo', played by Kenneth Williams in the Kenneth Horne radio comedies of the 1960s. In the 1980s the term is seen as an acceptable suggestive euphemism. It derives from rump as an archaic verb meaning to copulate and from the noun as a synonym for **tail**, **arse**, etc. **Rumpty-tumpty** and **rumpy-pumpy** are elaborated forms.

ᚼ'*Susannah Hoffs is writing a "steamy" romance novel. Packed with intrigue and rumpo, it will, she claims "put Jackie Collins in the shade".*'
(*Smash Hits* magazine, November 1989).

rump-ranger *n American* a male homosexual. A pejorative term used by (invariably male) heterosexuals.

ᚼ'*That old Greek rump-ranger just saw me knocking on the fuckin' door.*'
(*Sketch Artist*, US film, 1993).

rumpty-tumpty, rumpy-pumpy *n British* sex, or sexually related 'naughtiness'. Quasi-nursery elaborations of **rumpo**, used typically by disc jockeys, TV comedians and tabloid journalists in the 1980s.

ᚼ'*And if they were to temporarily stray from marital fidelity, where would they turn for a bit of royal rumpy pumpy?*'
(*Viz* magazine, May 1989).

run *n* 1 *American* a rally by Hell's Angels, usually involving a lengthy mobile debauch.

2 an initial euphoric sensation following

the ingestion or injection of a narcotic, particularly heroin; a **rush**.

↳ *'When I'm rushing, on my run/And I feel just like Jesus's son.'*
('Heroin', the Velvet Underground, 1967).

run *vb British* to denigrate, humiliate. A term reflecting the ritualistic status games of adolescent gangs, it is probably an abbreviated form of the colloquial meaning of 'run down'. The term was recorded in use among north London schoolboys in 1993 and 1994.

run-in *n British* police station. An item of police slang recorded by the *Evening Standard* magazine, February 1993. It is a back-formation from the colloquial verb which has meant 'take into custody' since the 19th century.

runner *n British*

a an escapee. The word is thus used in police jargon.

b an escape, disappearance, unauthorized departure. A usage well known in the form **do a runner**.

running *adj* intoxicated by drugs. The term, coined by analogy with **buzzing** and **rushing**, particularly applied to those under the effects of amphetamines, **crack**, or later **ecstasy**.

run off at the mouth *vb American* to talk excessively, to say more than one should. Usually used in an accusatory way, for instance to someone who betrays secrets.

the runs *n British* an attack of diarrhoea. The expression is based on both the notion of runniness and running to a place of relief. A more sedate alternative is **the trots**.

rush *n* the initial heady or euphoric sensation consequent on taking a mind-altering drug. The word is used especially, and most literally, of stimulant drugs such as cocaine and amphetamines; it generally refers to the sudden effects of a drug injected intravenously or taken through the mucous membranes rather than the more gradual onset attendant upon smoking or swallowing. The term is sometimes extended to refer to any exciting or stimulating action or situation.

↳ *'When you inhale real hard, even before you exhale you're starting to feel the rush. It just goes straight to your head quicker than any other drug, and a better rush than any other drug.'*
(Crack smoker, *Independent*, 24 July 1989).

rust-bucket *n* an old dilapidated or shoddily manufactured car. The term was earlier applied to ships and aeroplanes.

S...

S.A. *n American* sex appeal. A coy abbreviation used typically by female high-school and college students.

sabbing *n British* an act of sabotage. A word used by animal-rights activists and hunt saboteurs in the 1980s.
✎'*Meeting to discuss sabbing tactics.*' (Campus announcement, Essex University, 1986).

sack *vb British* to discard or reject. Used in this sense and generalized from the colloquial meaning of dismissal from one's job, the term was popular in adolescent slang of the 1990s, often in reference to 'dumping' a partner.
✎'*I think we should sack the whole idea.*'
✎'*Tina's planning to sack Martin, but she won't admit it if you ask her.*'

sack *n* bed. The word was probably first used of hammocks in the 19th century. *See also* **sad sack**.

sack artist *n* a womanizer, seducer, lothario. In the *Literary Review*, June 1987, in a review of *Intercourse* by Andrea Dworkin, Jane Ellison attributed this to Martin Amis. She was wrong. It is North American in origin, in common with other formulations such as 'con artist', spreading to Britain in the 1980s. Sack artist started life with the quite different meaning of a lazy person or idler (who spent most of their time in the **sack**).

sack out *vb American* to go to bed, (lie down and) sleep. A colloquialism based on the long-established use of **sack** to mean bed.

sack time *n*
a bed time. An armed forces and prison usage, carried over into civilian colloquialism.
✎'*Lift that weight drag that woodbine/*
lights out mate sackarooni time/ lights out sack time.'
('36 Hours', poem by John Cooper Clarke, 1980).
b time spent sleeping.

sad *adj British* unfortunate, unattractive, unexciting. This standard word was appropriated as an all-purpose vogue term of dismissal, disapproval, etc., among adolescents and younger children in the early 1990s, shortly afterwards crossing over into adult speech. (The bouffanted Tory minister Michael Portillo, for instance, was said to have 'sad hair'.)
✎'*I hate myself when I find myself using "sad" in all its repulsively contemporary glory ... basically it's no more than the latest linguistic expression of the bullying, teasing ways of school – it refers to kids with glasses, trainspotters, slow learners ...*'
(Paul Stump, *Guardian*, 8 November 1992).

saddo *n British* a pitiable, contemptible or unfortunate individual. An elaborated form of the fashionable adjective **sad** in adolescent usage throughout the 1990s.
'*What sort of chronic saddo really believes that the best days of his life were spent in the mud at Woodstock or fighting on Brighton beach.*'
(Julie Burchill, *Sunday Times* magazine, 28 November 1993).

sad sack *n American* an unfortunate or characteristically depressed or confused individual. This term originated before World War II and was subsequently widespread in armed service slang to discribe a misfit or pitiable person (normally male). The name was given to a popular cartoon character of the 1950s.

safe *adj British* good, fine. The standard meaning was extended in schoolchildren's slang at the end of the 1980s to encompass anything positive. The word is thus used as an all-purpose term of approbation, often as an exclamation. 'Safe' in this generalized sense probably derives from its over-use by petty criminals and gang members.

safe *n Canadian* a short form of **French safe**.

sag (off) *vb British* to play truant. The verb, which can be used transitively or intransitively, became well known after reports of the abduction and murder of the toddler James Bulger by truanting boys in 1993. Partridge dates 'sag' in the sense of absenting oneself from work to the 19th century, and in the sense of truancy to the Merseyside of the 1930s.

> *In the first interview child A admitted "sagging off" school with B and going to the Strand precinct, but denied taking James.'*
> (London *Evening Standard*, 2 November 1993).

salami, salam' *n American* **1** penis. A teenagers' term almost always heard in the phrase **hide the salami** (a euphemism for sexual intercourse).

2 a fool. A high-school and campus term.

salamite *n British* a male homosexual. Part of the language of teenage London schoolchildren in the 1990s, this term, usually used derogatively, is probably a deformation or misunderstanding of 'sodomite', perhaps blended with 'catamite'.

> *'Kayleigh said Keith was a salamite and he completely lost it.'*
> (Recorded, London schoolgirl, May 1995).

salmon *n British* **1** a cigarette. This usage, which is probably older rhyming slang '*salmon and trout*', meaning **snout**, was popular among London schoolchildren in the mid-1990s and was featured in the Shamen's controversial 1995 hit *Ebenezer Goode*. **Biff** was a contemporary synonym.

2 *See* **on the salmon**.

salt *n* **1** *British* a girl. A term used by London **mods** in the 1960s. They adopted the usage from the argot of working-class and marginal milieus where it had been heard since at least the 19th century. Since the 16th century 'salt' had been used as an adjective meaning lecherous or lewd, and as a noun meaning a sex act or (female) sexual partner. These now archaic terms are derived from the French *assaut* (whence 'assault') in its literal sense of 'on the jump'. Salt meaning girl is pronounced in London speech as 'sort' for which it is often mistaken.

> *'I had a game of soccer this afternoon and afterwards popped a bit into my salt – she don't take none of your tablets either.'*
> (Letter to *Oz* magazine, June 1969).

2 *American* heroin. From the resemblance.

salty *adj American See* **jump salty**.

sambo *n* a black person (usually male). This derogatory racist term comes from *zambo*, the Spanish American designation of those (slaves) with three-quarters negro and one-quarter Amerindian or European blood. The word was picked up by English speakers in the early 18th century and its use was reinforced by the 19th-century children's storybook character, 'Little Black Sambo'. The term has fallen out of use in the USA since the 1950s but is heard in Britain and Australia.

sandbag *vb American* **1 a** to attack unexpectedly, stop (someone) dead, incapacitate or thwart. A sand-filled bag was formerly used as an improvised cosh or blackjack. The word has been taken up into business jargon in the 1980s. (**Handbag** has been coined as a feminine counterpart.)

> *'You sandbagged me on Blue Star!'*
> (*Wall Street*, US film, 1987).

b to obstruct or outmanoeuvre, especially by feigning weakness. The word is a gambling term now extended to other contexts.

2 to drive at full speed, in the jargon of 'hotrodders'.

S. and M. *n* sado-masochistic practices, in the code of pornographers and prostitutes.

sap *n American* **1** a fool, simpleton or dupe. Originally a British term, the word is now more often heard in the USA. It was in origin a shortening of the word 'sapskull', meaning wooden-head, dating from the late 17th century. In the 19th century schoolboy **swots** were known as 'saps' from the Latin *sapiens* (wise or knowledgeable) and this meaning applied ironically may have converged with the older sense of the word.

2 a blackjack, cosh. This sense of the word is probably based on sap meaning hoe or shovel in archaic speech.

saphead *n American* a fool, simpleton or dupe. A version of **sap**.

sarnie *n British* a sandwich. A diminutive form which has spread from the north of England.

sashay *vb* to walk proudly, stride, flounce or 'mince'. Sashay originated as an Americanization of the French *chassé* (in this case a rapid, gliding movement; a term used in square dancing).

꙳'*She sashayed up to the bar and ordered a daiquiri.*'

sass *vb American* to speak or behave irreverently or insolently (towards), to cheek (someone). The verb is from the earlier, but now rarer, noun form.

꙳'*Don't you sass me, boy.*'

sass *n American* impudence, insolence. Sass is a folksy or dialect form of 'sauce', in the sense of sauciness. It is now rare in the noun form although the verb is still used.

꙳'*I don't need none of your sass.*'

sauce *n* alcoholic drink. In Britain this is a mainly middle-class euphemism employed particularly by heavy drinkers; the implication is that alcohol is liberally dispensed. There may also be a subconscious identification with **soused**.

꙳'*I couldn't stop – I got on the sauce real good.*'
(*The Dancer's Touch*, US film, 1989)

sauce *vb* to have sex with, seduce. A humorous coinage employed by alternative comedians Ben Elton and Rik Mayall in the early 1990s.

꙳'*They accused me of having sauced his wife.*'

sauced (out) *adj* drunk. A usage based on **sauce** as a slang term for alcoholic drink (and influenced by **soused**). The '-out' version is a racier modern variant.

saucepan lids *n pl British See* **dustbin lids**.

sausage grappler *n Australian* a male masturbator. One of many synonymous vulgarisms (**rod-walloper**, etc.) heard since the 1960s.

sausage jockey *n American* a **gay** male. A pejorative term used by heterosexuals in the 1990s. The British equivalent is **sausage-rider**.

sausage-rider *n British* a male homosexual. The term was one of many supposedly comic synonyms in use among heterosexuals in the 1990s.

savage *adj* excellent. Like many similar terms (**brutal, evil, tough,** etc) the standard word has been appropriated for

use in adolescent slang in both Britain and the US.

sawbuck *n American* a ten dollar bill. The Latin X for ten was thought to recall the wooden cross-struts of a saw horse.

sawn-off, sawed-off *n American* a person of restricted stature, 'runt'.

saying! *exclamation British* a synonym of **safe** and **seen** heard among adolescents in the late 1990s.

say uncle *vb American See* **uncle**.

scads, scad *n American* a great deal, large quantity (particularly of money). This colloquialism is of uncertain origin; it probably derives from a British dialect form of 'shed(full)' or from a dialect word 'scald', meaning multitude.

scaffer, scuffer *n British* a homeless person, beggar, or tramp. The term is heard in Scotland and the north of England. It is probably a version of the archaic dialect word 'scaff', related to 'shuffle' and denoting a vagabond or idler.

scag, skag *n* heroin. This word entered American usage in the later 1960s, probably from black street slang in which skag and **skank** were used to refer to anything inferior or unpleasant. The word presumably first referred to low-quality narcotics.

꙳'*The ladies kept a couple of grams* [of cocaine] *in the refrigerator. Ordell said he would not tolerate any scag, though.*'
(*The Switch*, Elmore Leonard, 1978).

scag nod *n American* a state of stupor or drowsiness from taking heroin.

꙳'*He told them if he saw any lady in a scag nod he'd throw her ass out the window.*'
(*The Switch*, Elmore Leonard, 1978).

scally *n British*
a a young man, lad.
b a criminal, delinquent or hooligan.
c a male inhabitant of the Liverpool area.

The word has overtones of 'cheeky', 'smart' and 'one of the boys'; it is a regional shortening of 'scallywag', a word meaning reprobate or rascal first used abusively in the USA before the Civil War. Scallywag itself is probably a form of an older expression from English or Scottish dialect meaning something like 'scurvy wretch'.

scallywag *n American* penis. The standard colloquial term for a rascal (which dates from the 19th century but is of unknown origin) has been appropriated by older teenagers and young adults for facetious use.

scalper *n* a ticket tout or other form of ruthless (though small-scale) profiteer. The term comes from the verb to scalp which was 19th-century stock-exchange jargon for buying cheap and selling at an exaggerated price (from the notion of 'taking a cut off the top').

scalping *n* profiteering, particularly by re-selling tickets at an inflated price.

⌁'*This is a shrewd and practised Londoner trading in what the Americans call "scalping". We call the business "touting", and this summer ticket touts are set for a final beano.'*
(*Evening Standard*, 9 May 1988).

scam *n* a deception, fraud, swindle or confidence trick. This Americanism entered fashionable British usage around 1977, subsequently becoming fairly widespread, particularly in business parlance. 'Scampery' was British slang for highway robbery in the 18th century, a word later used by vagrants, showmen etc. This, via American adoption, may explain the modern term (the similarity with 'scheme' is probably fortuitous). By the late 1980s scam had come sometimes to be used to mean merely 'dubious scheme or display'.

⌁'*"You know, I think there are a million people running scams out there," said Suzanne McGuire, the tournament's director of corporate marketing. "But what can you do? This is New York." '*
(*Sunday Times*, 10 September 1989).

scam *vb American* to perpetrate a fraud, deception or devious scheme. The verb is derived from the noun.

scan *vb British* to be vigilant, watch out. The standard term has been appropriated for the language of adolescent gangs. It was recorded in use among north London schoolboys in 1993 and 1994. 'Scan out' is a variant heard in black American speech in the 1990s.

⌁'*You stay here and scan while we check out the shop.'*

scangey *adj American* unpleasant, squalid, disreputable. A term of unknown

origin (it is pronounced to rhyme with 'mangy') which became fashionable in adolescent speech at the beginning of the **grunge** era around 1992.

scarf (up/down) *vb* devour greedily and completely, eat and/or drink voraciously. Perhaps a humorous alternative, tinged with onomatopoeia, of **scoff**, the term originated in the USA where it was adopted by adolescents from 'low-life' milieus in the 1960s. ('Scarf out' is another derivative; a synonym of 'pig-out'.)

⌁'*Harvey watched Joan scarfing down Milanos, biting them in half with her even teeth.'*
(*The Serial*, Cyra McFadden, 1976).

scarfing *n British* practising auto-asphyxiation as sexual stimulus. The term came to prominence after the death of Conservative MP Stephen Milligan in 1994. Practitioners are known as **gaspers**.

scarper *vb* to leave hurriedly, run away. The word was adopted by cockneys at the turn of the century, from **parlyaree**, the Italianate pidgin used by peddlars, showmen, actors, etc. *Scappare* (to escape) is the original Italian. Since World War I many have assumed that the word is rhyming slang: 'Scapa flow': go.

scene *n British* a promiscuous woman or prostitute. In this sense the word is used by young black speakers in the late 1990s.

scene, the scene *n* **1** the fashionable, **hip** or currently favoured milieu. A favourite word from the **beatnik** and later **hippy** vocabularies, often used in such phrases as **make the scene** (to be present or active in the currently hip environment) and 'on the scene'. 'It's not my scene' was a common dismissal of an undesirable activity or place. In colloquial usage the word simply means environment or 'world', as in 'the music scene'. The word is now dated but is still used by some journalists and, self-consciously or ironically, by the fashionable young.
2 a state of affairs, situation. In this generalized sense the word is now dated.

⌁'*"It was a very emotional time, a lot of yelling and screaming, a really bad scene," Bolker remembered.'*
(*Sunday Times*, 24 September 1989).

3 *See* **have a scene (with)**.

sch- *prefix* Many slang words of Yiddish origin may be spelled with these initial letters, but 'Sch' is the standard *German* form and, as such, is not employed in this dictionary, except for words which have been specifically recorded in this form. The alternative spelling **sh-** is used in writing by most Yiddish speakers and writers in English-speaking countries and is therefore preferred here.

Schindlers *adj Australian* drunk. The word, reported by *Good Weekend* magazine as still widely used in 1995, is an abbreviation form of the rhyming slang, '*Schindler's List*' (the title of the 1993 US movie), meaning **pissed**.

schizzed-out *adj American*
a deranged, uncontrolled.
b drunk. The term is an elaboration of 'schizophrenic' or 'schizoid'. In fashionable slang of the early 1970s, schizzed-out was used in the same way as the more common **flipped out** or **freaked out**. The sense of drunk was an adaptation by high-school and **preppie** speakers.

schlemiel *n* a fool, clumsy unfortunate, loser. A Yiddish word (pronounced 'shler-*meal*') used with a mixture of pity and contempt. In 1813 von Chamisso wrote *Peter Schlemihl's Wunderbare Geschlichte*; a parable describing a man selling his shadow and his soul. The author probably took the name from Schlumiel, a biblical general notorious for losing battles.
֍*'I've never been able to stand Woody Allen – he's such a schlemiel.'*
(Recorded, antiquarist, London, 1986).

schlong *n American* penis. A Yiddish word (meaning 'snake') which has entered the mainstream of American slang since the 1960s. It has been used in the novels of Elmore Leonard, Philip Roth's *Portnoy's Complaint* and the film *Sophie's Choice*, among other instances. In the late 1980s wits coined an alternative form; 'schlort'.

schlub, schlob *n American* alternative or earlier forms of **slob**.

schmaltz *n* sickly sentimentality. The word is Yiddish, from the German for cooking fat or dripping. The word was used in the New York Jewish community to describe what Leo Rosten in *The Joys of Yiddish* (1970) defines as 'corn, pathos, maudlin and mawkish substance; excessive sentimentality, overly emotional mush, sugary banality'.
֍*'With chapter headings such as "I'm in love with a dishwasher", "I love you too, Mommy", "I love you, Michael", and "We all love each other", On the Outside Looking In has more schmaltz than a New York deli.'*
(Book review by Nigella Lawson, *Sunday Times*, April 1989).

schmeck *n American* **1** a sniff or taste (in Yiddish from German).
2 heroin. It is this second sense which is the origin of the more recent **smack**.

schmendrick, shmendrik *n American* a foolish or clumsy nonentity. A Yiddish word which is used by Jews and non-Jews alike in American speech. Shmendrik was a character in an operetta by Abraham Goldfaden.

schmock, schmuck *n* heroin. A variant form of **schmeck** and an earlier form of **smack** used by addicts and prisoners in the USA and Britain until the early 1960s.

schmuck *n American* a pitiful, foolish or obnoxious person, usually male. Schmuck is from the Yiddish word *shmok*, itself from the German *Schmuck*, meaning ornament. In Yiddish usage the word was used first as a euphemism for the male member, then becoming a synonym for the English **prick**, figuratively as well as literally. As employed especially by non-Jewish speakers today schmuck is a fairly mild term of abuse, often used ruefully, despairingly or affectionately. It was perceived as an obscenity in the USA for many years with the result that the euphemism **shmo** was invented in the 1940s.
֍*'He gave his small son a gun and taught him how to shoot all God's little creatures ... and called him "his little schmuck", giving Mike a nice warm glow, until he finds out what it means.'*
(Nigella Lawson, *Sunday Times*, April 1989).

schmutter *n* clothing. The word is Yiddish, deriving from the Polish *szmata*, meaning rag. Schmutter was popularized in Britain by its use in the tailoring trade.
֍*'A nice bit of schmutter if you ask me.'*
֍*'They used to be in the schmutter business.'*

schnockered *adj* drunk. The word is probably not Yiddish or German, despite its most usual spelling, but may derive from an archaic dialect term 'snock', to hit. Schnockered, also spelled **snockered**, is encountered more often in American speech than British.

ᗍ*'As a whiskey salesman ... I'm often lit up by elevenses, loop-legged by luncheon and totally schnockered by 6.'*
(Posy Simmonds cartoon, *Guardian*, 1979).

schnook *n American* an unfortunate, timid or pathetic person. The word is Yiddish, but apparently coined in the USA. It is probably related to the German *Schnucki*: darling, or *Schnuck*: a small sheep.

schnozzle, schnozz *n* nose. The word is Yiddish, from German, in which *Schnauze* is the translation of 'snout'. The comedian Jimmy 'Schnozzle' Durante (named for his large nose) introduced the word to non-Americans.

schooling *n American*
a learning.
b teaching.
Both senses of the term occur in black American usage, in which they have a special resonance, whether describing success in orthodox education or learning from (bitter) experience.

schwing! *exclamation American* an expression of male delight at the sight of an attractive female. The word is a mock-Yiddish alteration of 'swing' and probably refers to an erection. It originated in the ersatz slang of the cult 1992 movie, *Wayne's World*, and was subsequently adopted by high-school and college students in the US.

scoff *n British* food. A noun formed from the colloquial verb (itself probably from an imitative dialect word) and used, particularly by young people, as a more fashionable synonym for **grub**. In fact this use of scoff dates from the 19th century.

ᗍ*'What I've got my eye on is all that lovely scoff.'*
(Recorded, student, London 1987).

scooby *adj*
a excellent, attractive.
b delicious. A vogue term among adolescents in the 1990s, the word was also used by adults, particularly women. It is

part of the nonsense phrase '*scooby-doo*', which was used as the name of a cartoon character in the 1970s and of a plastic swatch used in children's games in the 1960s (then in the French form *scoubidou*).

scooby *n British* a treat, enjoyable experience. The noun derives from the adjective **scooby**, which itself derives from the earlier '*scooby-doo*'.

scoop *n American* the latest news, information, gossip. The phrase has been in use since at least the later 1970s and is often used in the phrase '*have the scoop on something/someone*' or '*give me the scoop*'.

scoots *n pl American* dollars. A word of unknown origin used mainly by adolescent speakers.

scope *vb American* to look at, examine. A vogue term among adolescents since the 1980s, it is heard on college campuses and is in use among the neo-**Valley Girls** featured in the 1995 US film, *Clueless*. In black speech '*scope on (something/someone)*' is a common variant.

ᗍ*'We're going to scope the betties in the park.'*

scope out *vb American* to explore, investigate, evaluate.

score *n* **1** *British* £20. The word has been particularly popular in underworld and police usage since before World War II.

ᗍ*'I thought it was worth at least a hundred, but I only got a score for it.'*

2 a success or coup, especially a successful crime, seduction or arrest.

ᗍ*'Shaft's Big Score!'*
(Title of US film, 1972).

3 a drug purchase. From the verb form.

ᗍ*'They set up a score downtown.'*

score *vb* **1 a** to buy (illicit drugs). An Americanism that became the standard term world-wide in the late 1960s.

ᗍ*'Addicts devote all their money to feeding their habit, not their body. They spend their time "scoring", and become unhealthy, malnutritioned.'*
(Tam Stewart, *Independent*, 4 April 1988).

b to obtain. This is a young person's generalization of the previous raffish usage.

ᗍ*'Look on the bright side – you may not*

have got the job, but at least you
scored a free lunch.'
2 to succeed in gaining sexual satisfaction.

↪'*I saw you leaving the pub with that
redhead – did you score?*'

scorf *n, vb British*
a a variant form of **scoff**.
b a variant form of to **scarf**.

scouse *adj British* of or from Liverpool. The word is derived from 'lobscouse', a stew traditionally containing vegetables, hard-tack or ship's biscuit, and sometimes meat. Lobscouse was eaten by sailors and was popular in the Liverpool area.

scouse *n British* the accent and speech of the Liverpool area.

scouser *n British* a Liverpudlian. From **scouse**.

scrag *vb* **1** *British* to torment, tease, attack, beat up. A schoolboy term dating from the 19th century.
2 *American* **a** to kill, destroy. An underworld term adopted by black street gangs in the 1980s. In 18th- and 19th-century British slang scrag was used to mean 'execute by hanging', strangle or grab by the neck. The word is originally a Scottish dialect term for neck and is related to 'crag'.
b to copulate (with).

scram *vb* to leave quickly, go away. Nearly always heard in the form of a brusque dismissal, the word is a shortening of 'scramble', first used in the USA at the turn of the century. (The **pig Latin** version of the term is **amscray**.)

scran *n British* food. The word is used throughout the armed services and by some civilians, particularly public schoolchildren and students. It comes originally from Romany and has been employed since the 18th century to mean victuals, scraps or leftovers.

↪'*All we want to know is where we can
get some decent scran in a hurry.*'

scratch *n* cash, ready money. This sense of the word has been in use since the end of the 19th century. It is either derived from the notion of 'scratching a living' or of banknotes which are 'up to scratch', i.e. genuine.

↪'*What about you Charlie; why don't*

you try to come up with some scratch
for a change.'
(*The Late Show*, US film, 1977).

scratcher *n British* a match, in the jargon of prisoners since the early years of the 20th century.

scratchy *adj* irritable or bad-tempered and over-sensitive. Predominantly American with rustic overtones, the word is a synonym for prickly or tetchy.

scream *n American* ice cream. A conflated form heard among adolescents.

screamer *n* a flagrant homosexual. A derogatory term used typically by flagrant heterosexuals, derived from 'screaming queen/nancy,' etc. The word is heard in Britain and Australia.
See also **Jesus screamer**.

screaming (h)abdabs *n pl British* a state of mental agitation bordering on hysteria. Usually heard in the phrase '*It gives me (a case of) the screaming abdabs*': it makes me extremely irritated, agitated. *See* **'abdabs**.

screw *vb* **1** to have sex (with). This use of the word was recorded in Grose's *Dictionary of the Vulgar Tongue* in 1785. It may be a direct metaphor or may be influenced by the archaic use of screw to mean a key (turning in a lock). Since the late 1960s the verb can refer to the sexual act from the woman's point of view as well as the man's. The word owed much of its popularity to the fact that it is a synonym for **fuck** which is nevertheless acceptable in the media and what used to be referred to as 'mixed company'.
2 a to take advantage of, defraud, cheat or treat unfairly.
b to ruin or spoil. An extension of the previous sense paralleled by **fuck**, **bugger** etc.
3 *British* to stare (at). In working class London speech, especially among **skinheads** of the late 1960s, the question '*Who're you screwin'?*' was often the prelude to violence. It has been suggested that this use of the word is in origin a shortening of scrutinize, but this seems hard to credit. Screwing up one's eyes or metaphorically boring a hole into someone are other possibilities.

↪'*Villains call it clocking in Leeds, eyeballing in Manchester and screwing in London's East End ... It came as a*

shock: juries can be intimidated by a stare.'
(*Sunday Times*, 5 June 1988).

4 *British* to rob, in the argot of the underworld.

screw *n* **1 a** an act of sexual intercourse.

b a sexual partner. Both usages derive from the verb form.

2 *British* a prison guard. This is the standard term applied to prison officers by inmates since the 19th century. It derives from the archaic use of the same word to mean key. Thus 'turnscrew', later shortened to screw, was a synonym for turnkey.

↳'A banner was draped from the cell windows reading: Support the screws – Old Bill out.'
(*Guardian*, 31 January 1989).

3 an income, wage or salary. In this sense, first recorded in the mid-19th century, the word almost invariably occurs as part of the common phrase '(on) a good screw'.

screw around *vb* **1** to 'mess about', behave clumsily, irresponsibly or irresolutely. The phrase, which is particularly popular in the USA, is a milder form of **fuck around/about**.

2 to behave in a sexually promiscuous way. A brusquer version of 'sleep around'.

↳'The strongest possible piece of advice I would give to any young woman is: Don't screw around, and don't smoke.'
(Edwina Currie, government minister, *Observer*, 3 April 1988).

screw the pooch *vb American* to waste time. A phrase heard typically in the slang of the armed services, it is a slightly politer version of 'fuck the dog', meaning to engage in idle or futile activity.

screw up *vb*

a to make a mess, or mistake, perform ineptly, fail, ruin. This phrase was in predominantly American currency until the late 1960s.

b to traumatize, render maladjusted.

↳'She claims she's been screwed up by her upbringing.'

script *n* a drug prescription. The word has been used since the 1950s by drug

users and by the police and some doctors.

↳'I got him to give me a script for methadone.'

↳'They were trying to sell some stolen blank scripts.'

scrote *n British*

a a non-specific term of abuse used, and perhaps invented by Clement and la Frenais in their 1970s TV comedy *Porridge* (set in a prison). It is presumably inspired by scrotum.

↳'One man in the West Belfast area said they (British paratroopers) had a nickname for us – it was scrotes … they were young guys and aggressive.'
(*Sunday Times*, 29 January 1995).

b a synonym for **crustie** or **smellie**, in use among the homeless, travellers, etc.

scrubber *n British* a coarse, vulgar and/or promiscuous female. This now common term was first heard in the 1920s. 'Scrub' had been used to mean a shabby or seedy person, or prostitute since the 18th century. Scrubber, like scrub, derives from the notion of having to scrape and forage for food or money, rather than to scrub floors, etc.

scrumming *n British* eating. The word (as a transitive verb 'scrum' is rare), which is typically used by middle- or upper-class speakers, often denotes voracious or exuberant feeding and is probably inspired by 'scrumptious'.

↳'As far as I can tell, he's been scrumming non-stop all day.'

scrummy *adj British* atractive, delectable, excellent. A blend of 'scrumptious' and 'yummy', used particularly by middle-class speakers.

↳'Actually, I thought he was rather scrummy really.'
(Recorded, female public relations consultant, London, 1994).

scrump *vb American* to have sex. The verb, which in slang is usually intransitive or in the form 'scrumping', is inspired by the old term for stealing apples (itself British dialect related to scrounge and scrimp) perhaps also influenced by other words such as **screw** and 'rump'.

scuffer *n British* a police officer. This word (more often heard in the plural) originated in the Liverpool area. It derives from dialect terms associated with 'shuffle', 'scuff' and 'cuff' (in the sense of a blow).

scumbag *n American* a despicable person. This term of abuse is now widespread and is permitted in the broadcast media, in spite of the fact that its origin, unknown to many of its users, is as an obscene euphemism for condom, 'scum' being an obsolescent American term for semen. The word was adopted by British speakers around 1985.
❧'*Even scumbags have rights here in the USA.*'
(*Red Heat*, US film, 1988).

scum-sucker *n American* a despicable, contemptible or degenerate person. This word, originally synonymous with **cocksucker**, in that 'scum' is an obsolescent American slang term for semen, is now often used as if it were a milder, euphemistic epithet.

scum-sucking *adj American* disgusting, contemptible. The word is usually employed as a meaningless intensifier in longer terms of abuse. (For the original sense see **scum-sucker**).
❧'*This scum-sucking low-life deserves to die!*'

scumwad *n American* an alternative version of **scumbag**, heard in the late 1980s. (**Wad** is a common component of vulgar compounds, having as it does several sexual connotations.)

scungy *adj Australian* dirty, messy, unkempt or sordid. The word is probably a coinage blending the sounds and connotations of such words as 'scurvy', 'mangy' and **gunge**. It may alternatively be influenced by **scunner**.

scunner *n British* a despicable, traitorous, or devious person. This unusual word has spread beyond its origins in Scottish dialect and is occasionally heard throughout the north and Midlands of England.

scuttlebutt *n American* gossip or rumour. The scuttlebutt was a cask or fountain of drinking water on board naval ships, around which news was exchanged.
❧'*I hear some scuttlebutt says he likes to kick the ladies around.*'
(*Night Game*, US film, 1988).

scuzz *n American*
a dirt, seediness, anything distasteful. The

word has been widely used since the late 1960s and probably post-dates the adjective form **scuzzy**. The word had been picked up by some British speakers by the 1980s.
❧'*Foul-mouthed critics and their lairs – Old Compton St, the Coach and Horses,* Private Eye, The Spectator, Fleet Street Freelancer – *the whole scuzz world of journalism is here in black and white (albeit seen through the bottom of a glass).*'
(*I-D* magazine, November 1987).
b also **scuzzball, scuzzbag, scuzzo;** a disreputable, unpleasant, unattractive or worthless person. A derivative of **scuzzy** which has been popular since the early 1970s.
❧'*He's upstairs smoking dope with some scuzz.*'
(*The Last Innocent Man*, US film, 1987).

scuzzed out *adj* disgusted. A more recent synonym of **grossed out**, based on **scuzzy** and **scuzz**.

scuzzy *adj American* dirty, unpleasant, distasteful, shabby and disreputable. This word, which is used particularly by young people, may be a nursery version of 'disgusting' or an invention influenced by 'scum' and 'fuzz'. Scuzzy has been heard in North America since the late 1960s but to date has not been adopted elsewhere, except by a handful of journalists.

seeing-to *n British*
a a beating-up, an assault. A typically understated, hence menacing euphemism in working-class, police and criminal usage.
❧'*He's asking for a seeing-to.*'
b a sexual act; specifically the sexual 'possession' of a woman by a man. The word has simultaneous and revealing overtones of brusque, no-nonsense domination, of a duty accomplished and of an unaffectionate resolution.
❧'*Well, I gave her a good seeing-to, didn't I.*'

Selwyn *n British* an unpleasant and/or disappointing experience. The name is part of the rhyming slang phrase '*John Selwyn Gummer*', meaning **bummer**, borrowing the name of an unpopular and unprepossessing Tory minister. It was recorded in middle-class usage in 1994.

send *vb* to transport emotionally or intellectually. This supposed **beatnik** term of the late 1950s (originating among US jazz musicians in the 1940s) was used to characterize **hip** youth in various unhip media.

꘎'*I just love Elvis. He sends me!'*

sender *n See* **solid sender**.

sent down *adj British* sentenced to imprisonment, imprisoned. This euphemism, also used to mean expelled from university, has been in currency since the 19th century. The phrase may originate in the image of the convict descending the steps from the dock.

sent up *adj American* imprisoned. The American version of **sent down**. Sent up has been in use since the late 19th century; it may be derived from **upriver**. In Britain, to be 'sent up' is to be imitated in a parodic manner.

septic *n Australian* an American. A piece of native Australian rhyming slang, from septic tank: **Yank**. The word was first recorded being applied to visiting American servicemen during World War II. It is still in use among older speakers and shows signs of being in continued currency among the younger generation. (**Sherman (tank)** is a British equivalent.)

sesh *n British* a drinking bout. A shortening of '(drinking) session' used typically by middle-class youths in Britain in the late 1980s.

꘎'*We had a good sesh last night.'*

set *n* the fashionable word for gang in the early 1990s argot of the Los Angeles **rap** and street-gang subcultures.

꘎'*I ain't nothing without my set. They the only ones who care.'*
(*Grand Canyon*, US film, 1991).

severe *adj* impressive, excellent. An all-purpose vogue term of approval used first by British **mods** in 1963 and 1964 and later by American teenagers and their British imitators in the 1970s and 1980s.

꘎'*That's a really severe shirt.'*
꘎'*How did she look? – severe, man!'*

sexing *vb British* having sex. A term used by young children.

꘎'*Fraser said he saw someone in a car sexing.'*
(Recorded, 8-year-old, London, 1988).

sexy *adj* attractive or enticing, particularly in commercial or financial terms. A

jargon use of the common colloquialism, heard sporadically from the late 1970s. The usage became well established in **Yuppie** parlance of the 1980s.

sh- *prefix* This form is generally preferred in this dictionary for the many words of Yiddish origin which exist in modern English slang. Certain terms are recorded under the alternative (German) **sch-** when there is evidence of their prevalence in that form.

shabba *n British* an act of masturbation. An item of 1990s rhyming slang from '*Shabba Ranks*', meaning **wank(s)**, using the name of a ragga music star known for his salacious lyrics.

꘎'*He was having a quick shabba.'*

shack *vb American* to stab (someone). The word was used by prison inmates and members of the underworld.

shack up *vb* to live with someone in a sexual relationship outside marriage. Such a relationship is sometimes known as a 'shack-up'. The term was an Americanism first used by itinerants and marginals between the World Wars; it was adopted into World English during the 1960s.

shade *n American* a receiver of stolen goods, **fence**. The word, an item of slang from the police and underworld lexicon, in use since the 1920s, may be derived from 'shady' (dealing).

shades *n pl* sunglasses. The word was first used in this sense in the USA in the 1940s. (Shades are blinds in American English.)

shaft *n* **1** penis. A predictable but rare use of the standard term.

2 a an act of sexual intercourse.
꘎'*A quick shaft.'*
b a sex partner.
꘎'*A good shaft.'*
These usages are back-formations from the verb.

3 the shaft an alternative form of a **shafting**. It usually occurs in the form 'get the shaft'.

shaft *vb* **1** to have sex with, to penetrate. From **shaft**: penis.

2 to ruin, damage, destroy (someone). Most often heard in the form of the past participle 'shafted', this term is another example of a slang word literally meaning to have sex with someone used metaphorically to mean humiliate or abase.

Compare **fuck**, **bugger**, **roger**, **screw**.

↳'*I tell you, we were well and truly shafted over that Abco deal.*'

shafting *n.* an instance of extremely harsh, ruinous and/or unfair treatment. The term derives from the sexual senses of the verb to **shaft**.

shag *vb* 1 to have sex (with). A common vulgarism in Britain and Australia which is unknown in this sense in the USA. The word is an archaic relative of 'shake', which was used in a sexual sense from at least the 16th century. In Britain shag took over the taboo role in the 18th century. In modern usage the word is considered less offensive than **fuck** in male company, but more vulgar than other synonyms. Like fuck it occurs in other forms, such as the noun **shag**, the intensifying adjective 'shagging' and phrases such as 'shag off'.

↳'*When I was 17 I was obsessively in love with a girl who only liked me. It blighted my adolescence. I would have given anything to shag her.*'
(Ben Elton, quoted in *NME*, March 1989).

2 *American* to depart, leave. The 1990s use of the term, which may be related to earlier uses of the word to denote a fast jitterbug-style dance or later a reluctant, shuffling walk, also occurs in the phrase '*shag off/out*'. By the 18th century *shag* had come to mean 'move quickly' in American speech.

shag *n* 1 *British* a sexual act or a sexual partner. See the verb form for origins.

2 *American* **a** a boyfriend, girlfriend or escort. This now obsolete term has none of the overtly sexual and vulgar overtones of the British and Australian usages.

b the Shag a teenage dance craze of the 1960s. When a film of this name was released in Britain in 1988, press hand-outs were necessary in order to reassure the public as to the innocence of the term.

3 *British* a term of endearment used primarily between males which became fashionable particularly among City of London financial traders from the mid-1990s.

shagged out, shagged *adj British* exhausted, worn out. The vulgar origin of the phrase (tired out from sexual activity) is partially forgotten in the modern usage wherein the expression serves as a more robust version of **knackered**.

↳'*Listen. I really can't make it, I'm feeling absolutely shagged.*'

shaggin' wagon, shag-wagon *n* a more vulgar term for **passion wagon** or **draggin' wagon**. This form of the expression is heard in Britain and Australia.

↳'*Old Gregory turned up in a brand new shaggin' wagon.*'

shag-monster *n British* a promiscuous or sexually active person. The term can be used either pejoratively or appreciatively.

↳'*Lyrics like "We should both go to bed until we make each other sore"... have seen* [singer Louise Wener] *labelled a "sluttish shag-monster"...*'
(*The Big Issue*, 6 March 1995).

shake *vb* 1 *British* to alert, rouse, summon. This use of the word, obviously deriving from the literal shaking of someone to wake them, is now employed as part of police, underworld and working-class jargon.

↳'*The solicitors ... We'll shake them for you.*'
(*Flying Squad*, British TV documentary, March 1989).

2 *American* to search, or stop and harass (a suspect). The word, used by police and criminals, is a shortening of the more familiar **shake down**.

shake down *vb American* 1 to extort money from (someone) either face-to-face (usually by threats), or by blackmail.

2 to search a person or premises. The phrase usually refers to an official search by police officers which may involve a degree of harassment or force.

shakedown *n American* 1 an act of extortion or blackmail.

2 a search of a person or place, usually by police.

shamed-up *adj British* humiliated, shamed. A 'buzz-term' among teenagers in the 1980s, from the admonitory catchphrase 'take the shame!'. This playground phrase is from black slang.

shampoo *n* champagne. A **Sloane Ranger** and **yuppie** witticism of the 1980s. The word is often abbreviated to poo. In the USA **preppies** and others also use the terms.

shank *n American* a homemade knife. A term used in prisons and by the members of street gangs since the 1950s. In standard English shank denotes the shaft or connecting rod of a tool or instrument.

sharking *n British* pursuing members of the opposite sex. This item of Oxbridge slang of the 1990s often denotes aggressive or devious attempts at seduction, usually on the part of males.

Sharon *n British* the female equivalent of a **Kevin** or **Wayne**. The name is used to designate a supposedly typical (and by implication uncultured) working-class young woman. These generic epithets were coined in the 1970s for the purpose of social stereotyping. (In 1965 Sharon was the tenth most popular Christian name for new-born girls in Britain.)

⍾'*A thousand slavish Sharons copied Diana's wedding look, as they did her flicked 'n' sprayed hairstyle.*'
(Judy Rumbold, *Guardian*, 11 December 1989).

⍾'*The male models in leopard-skin-print Gaultier jackets getting eye-balled by Sharons with Bucks Fizz haircuts and pound signs in their eyes at the Limelight.*'
(*Observer*, section 5, 7 May 1989).

sharpies *n pl Australian* members of a short-lived teenage youth movement of the 1950s who were contemporaries of the **bodgies** and **widgies**. Sharpies were short-haired, aggressive and less flamboyant than the **teddy boy**-like bodgies.

shat upon *adj* humiliated, slighted, victimized or punished. Shat is a past tense of the verb to **shit**.

shedloads *n British* a disguised version of the more vulgar **shitloads**, meaning a large quantity. The expression was popular among City of London traders in the late 1990s.

⍾'*... how can a T & G sponsored prime minister break it to the union which gives his party shedloads of money that the marriage is over?*'
(*Private Eye*, 11 July 1997).

sheeny *n* a Jew. The term appeared in Britain in the early 19th century when it did not necessarily have the offensive racist overtones it has acquired in the 20th century. Many possible etymologies have been proposed for sheeny: the three most plausible are the German word *schön* (beautiful) as applied either to their children or to merchandise by Jews; the 'sheen' of dark hair or skin as perceived by Anglo-Saxons, or the Yiddish phrase *a miesse meshina* ('an ugly fate or death'), a phrase supposedly common among Jews.

sheep-dip *n* low-quality alcoholic drink.

sheepdog *n Australian* a brassière. The jocular usage, invariably heard in male speech, is based on the notion that, like the bra, the dog 'rounds them up and keeps them together'.

sheepshagger *n British* a rustic, bumpkin or primitive. A vulgarism heard since the 19th century.

sheet *n British* an official report. An item of prison jargon recorded in the 1990s, in Brixton and Wandsworth prisons.

sheila *n Australian* a woman. This well-known Australianism, although old-fashioned, is still heard. It is an alteration of an earlier word 'shaler' (meaning 'young woman'), of Gaelic origin, which was used by Irish immigrants. The word became a generic term for females, the feminine counterpart of **paddy**, and was altered to coincide with the female Christian name.

⍾'*Cripes! I was nearly up shit creek that time. Now I'm stuck with this po-faced Sheila!*'
(Barry Humphries and Nicholas Garland, *The Wonderful World of Barry McKenzie*, 1988).

shell *n American* 1 a dollar. This usage may recall the use of cowries and other sea shells as currency, or come from the verb 'shell out' (in which shell refers to the shell or pod containing seeds). **Clams** is a synonym.

2 a beer, beercan. This rare sense of the word may conceivably draw a comparison between empty beer cans and discarded (ammunition) shell cases.

shellacked *adj* drunk. A term originating in the USA in the 1920s; shellack (its standard meaning being to apply varnish) first meant to beat or punish; this was then extended to denote the effects of alcohol.

shellacking *n* a beating, defeat. A humorous borrowing of the standard term meaning to slap on shellac, a resin used for varnishing and insulation. The slang sense arose in the USA where it is still heard; it is not unknown in British speech.

Sherman (tank) *n British* an act of masturbation, a **wank**. A probably ephemeral piece of rhyming slang of the late 1980s, quoted for instance in Steve Bell's *If* comic strip in the *Guardian* newspaper, it replaces the 1950s use of the same phrase for **yank**.

sherrif *n British* a fifty-pence coin. The nickname comes from the supposed resemblance to a western sheriff's star.

shickered, shikkered, shicker *adj* drunk. The word is used primarily in the USA and Australia. It is from *shikker*, the Yiddish word for inebriated, which itself is from Hebrew *shikor*.

♭ '*You're stoned, Bazza!*'
Come off it – just a bit shicker.'
(*Bazza Comes into His Own*, cartoon by Barry Humphries and Nicholas Garland, 1988).

shift *vb Irish* (to have) sexual intercourse. The usage was explained to a British audience by the stand-up comedienne Jo Brand in her 1995 TV show.

shikse, shiksa *n American* a non-jewish female. A Yiddish term used by Jews of gentiles often, but nowadays not always, pejoratively.

shill *n* a con-man's accomplice. The word has been used since the 19th century to denote a decoy or agent planted in a crowd to stimulate trade or encourage spending. Nowadays it usually refers to a participant in a rigged card game or other fraud. The origin of the term is unclear; it is said to be based either on a proper name such as Shillibeer or on an archaic dialect form of 'skill'.

shine *n American* a black person. This now dated, usually pejorative term from the early 20th century (used by Raymond Chandler among others when describing the Los Angeles low-life of the 1940s) is still occasionally heard. The origin of this usage is obscure; it may be inspired by the appearance of black skin or contrast-ing white teeth, or may even be a shortening of shoe-shine.

shine *vb American* to snub, reject. The term is probably a back-formation of the earlier **shined-on**.

♭ '*Let's face it, she shined you.*'
(*California Man*, US film, 1992).

shined-on *adj American* ignored, disregarded. Its origin may be by analogy with **mooning** (showing one's buttocks as a gesture of contempt) or connected with **shine** meaning black person, hence social inferior; or more poetically may derive from the image of the moon shining down with cold indifference.

♭ '*I'm not going to be shined on! I think I deserve some attention.*'

shiny-ass *n American* an office-worker, bureaucrat. The dismissive phrase refers to the trousers or skirt of a desk-bound 'pen-pusher' polished by long contact with a chair.

shirt-lifter *n* a male homosexual. An Australian euphemism used pejoratively but usually humorously. The phrase originated in the 1960s and had been adopted by some British speakers by the late 1970s. (The Melbourne satirist Barry Humphries has frequently used the term, and has coined 'chemise-lifter' as a lesbian counterpart.)

shit *n*

a excrement. This word of Anglo-Saxon origin has parallels in other Germanic languages (in modern German *Scheisse*, for example). It derives from an ancient common verb, imitative of the sound of defecation. In English shit is now a mild vulgarism, although in rustic speech it has been the standard term for centuries.
b an act of defecation, usually in phrases such as have or take a shit.
c a contemptible person. This usage conveys real dislike or disapproval and has been common, particularly in upper and middle class speech in Britain since the 1920s.

♭ '*Tiny 19-year-old Mark Aldrich beat up two youths who called him "a little shit" – but the comment "could be appropriate" a judge said yesterday.*'
(*Daily Mirror*, 10 September 1988).

d an illicit drug, especially hashish. In the 1950s heroin users referred to their drug as shit; by the mid-1960s the word usually designated hashish (which is characteristically brown) or marihuana. When used in this context the word is synonymous with 'stuff' and carries virtually no pejorative overtones.

↳ *'Hey, this is excellent shit, man.'*

↳ *'P.S. I cannot get any shit, my friends have split to other lands, they are free.'*
(Reader's letter in *Oz* magazine, February 1970).

e rubbish, something worthless or inferior.

f nonsense, lies or deceitful talk. This is a specific use of shit as something worthless, or simply a shortening of **bullshit**.

↳ *'Come on, don't give me that shit, I wasn't born yesterday.'*

g unnecessarily hostile behaviour or ill-treatment.

↳ *'I've put up with a lot of shit from them over the years.'*
(Recorded, disgruntled employee, London, 1987).

shit *vb* 1 to defecate. The verb probably predates the noun form. Both seem to have existed in Old English, deriving from a common Germanic ancestor, itself cognate with the Greek *skat-* (later giving 'scatological'). Used intransitively the verb is now probably rarer than phrases such as have a shit. (The usual past form in British English is shat, in American shit.)

2 a to deceive, bamboozle, confuse (someone).

b to browbeat or annoy (someone). These transitive usages may originate as short forms of the verb **bullshit**, but have taken on separate identities as a designation, usually in American speech, of time-wasting or harassment by lies or deceit.

3 shit oneself to be overcome with fear or panic.

shit *adj* 1 awful, inferior. A simple transference of the noun form, popular especially in British youth parlance of the 1980s.

↳ *'a shit record.'*

2 *American* excellent, admirable. In the **hip** language of the street, of **rap** and hip-hop practitioners and their teenage imitators, shit has been used with this unexpected sense. The probable explanation is that it is a shortening of **shit-hot**.

shit a brick, shit bricks *vb* to panic, be in a state of nervous apprehen-

sion. *'Shit a brick!'* is sometimes used as an exclamation of surprise or irritation.

shit and derision *n British* a terrible state of affairs, confusion, mess. A mainly middle-class term typically used ruefully or humorously.

shit-ass *adj American* very unpleasant, worthless, contemptible. Used especially in Canadian English, in much the same way as **shithouse** in Australia.

shitbag *n British* an obnoxious or unpleasant person. A term which was widespread in the 1960s but is now less common.

shitcan *vb*

a *Australian* to denigrate, to **rubbish**. The word is used to signify the upbraiding or insulting of someone who deserves to be humiliated.

b *American* to throw away, reject.

Both senses derive from the noun shitcan as a toilet receptacle or rubbish bin.

shite *n British* a variant form of **shit**, heard particularly in northern English speech.

shit-eating grin *n* a facial expression showing extreme (usually malicious) satisfaction. Originally an Americanism, the expression is now also heard elsewhere.

↳ *'I didn't want to see the shit-eating grins on the cozzers' faces.'*
(Jimmy Robinson, released prisoner speaking on the BBC TV programme *Panorama*, 24 February 1997).

shitfaced *adj American* drunk, helplessly or squalidly intoxicated. The term was particularly in vogue in the mid-1970s.

↳ *'She was totally shitfaced.'*

↳ *'Let's get shitfaced.'*

shit-fit *n* a bout of anger or intense irritation etc. The term probably originated in the US but by the mid-1990s was common throughout the English-speaking world.

↳ *'Look at this mess! Lloyd is going to have a shit-fit.'*
(*A Passion for Murder*, US film, 1993).

shit-for-brains *n* a very stupid person. This term of abuse, deriving from an earlier rustic expression on the line of *he/she must have shit for brains*, has been widespread in the USA and Australia since the 1970s. It is now sometimes used adjectivally as in *a shit-for-brains idea*.

shithead *n* **1 a** a despicably unpleasant or unfriendly person. This sense of the word has been predominant since the 1970s.

b a stupid or foolish person.

2 a hashish smoker. This sense of the word was briefly current from the mid-1960s, before being replaced by synonyms such as **doper**, etc. (**Pothead** was a less contentious or ambiguous synonym.)

shitheel *n American* an unpleasant or obnoxious person. An embellished form of the milder and more common 'heel'.

shit-hot *adj*

a first-rate, excellent, powerful or dynamic.

b very keen, enthusiastic or punctilious. Shit here is used as an intensifier rather than a metaphor.

shithouse *n*

a a toilet.

b a dirty or untidy place.

shithouse *adj* terrible, inferior, worthless. This elaboration of **shit** or **shitty** is particularly common in Australian speech.

shit-kicker *n* **1** a lowly menial, humble worker or rustic. An alternative to 'shit-shoveller' heard particularly in the USA and Australia.

2 a dynamic or energetic person.

shit-kicking *adj* wild, earthy, primitive. The word is used especially in the context of country or rock music and signals approval rather than criticism.

↳'*Some stomping, howling, shit-kicking rhythm 'n' blues*'.

shit-list *n American* a real or imaginary black list; either as kept by organizations or individuals.

↳'*Jerry's top of my shit-list this week.*'

↳'*I think I'm on the shit list of every bar in town.*'

shit-load, shitloads *n* an enormous amount or quantity. The term originated in US speech but by the mid-1990s was heard throughout the English-speak-

ing world. **Shedloads** is a British euphemism.

↳'*What about the Mets? I bet you won a shit-load of money!*'
(*Bad Lieutenant*, US film, 1994).

↳'*We're in shitloads of trouble here.*'

shit on one's own doorstep *vb British* to do something damaging or unpardonable which will rebound upon oneself or one's friends; ruin one's own environment. This expression, like the politer 'foul the nest', has equivalents in most European languages (normally involving beds rather than doorsteps).

shit on wheels *n American* an extremely adept, adroit person. The phrase is based on the notion of 'a slippery customer'.

shit-parade *n American* an alternative form of **shit-list**.

the shits *n*

a diarrhoea.

b a feeling of annoyance, disgust or bitter resentment. This figurative sense of the preceding vulgarism seems to be acquiring a separate identity, usually in the form it/he/she gives me the shits.

shit-scared *adj British* terrified. An intensive form of the standard adjective.

shit-sheet *n American* a police file (recording criminal activity) or school report (particularly one recording poor results).

shit-storm *n American* a spectacular fuss and/or mess.

the shitter *n* **1** a toilet.

2 the anus.

shitty *adj*

a unpleasant, unfair. The word may mean merely bad or nasty, but usually carries overtones of resentment on the part of the speaker.

↳'*That was a really shitty thing to do.*'

b inferior, poor quality.

↳'*That cassette machine's got shitty sound.*'

shiv *n* a knife. An alternative rendering of **chiv**, a Romany word used in British underworld and low-life milieus since the 17th century. In the 20th century the word has been used (also in the USA) to mean any bladed weapon, including homemade knives and razors. **Shiv** was also used as a verb, particularly in the argot of street gangs of the 1950s and early 1960s.

shivoo *n Australian* a party, particularly a lively gathering. Attempts have been made to derive the word from the 18th-century use of the French *chevaux* ('horses') to denote a display or social gathering, but it is more likely to be derived ultimately from *charivari* (a celebration or serenade) anglicized in the USA in the late 1800s as 'shivaree'.

shlemiel *n See* **schlemiel**.

shlep, schlepp *vb*

a to drag, haul pull or carry.

b to drag oneself, move or travel with difficulty. This is the Yiddish version of the German verb *schleppen*, to drag. It has entered English slang via the American underworld and entertainment industry.

♭'*I don't want to shlep all the way down there.*'
(*Budgie*, British TV series, 1971).

shlep, schlepp *n* **1** a long, tedious, or tiring journey or burdensome task. The noun form is based on the verb.

♭'*I hate having to go there – it's a real shlep up that hill.*'

2 *American* a tedious, feeble or irritating person. This sense of the term is inspired by the notion of burden and drag (literally and metaphorically) in the verb to **shlep**.

shlepper, schlepper *n* **1** a clumsy, inept and/or irritating person.

2 *American* a cadger, scrounger or hustler.

3 a sluttish, slovenly and/or immoral person. All the sub-senses of shlepper, which encompass a number of nuances and connotations, derive ultimately from the verb **shlep** with its suggestions of burdensome activity. In British English sense 3 has been extended to denote a prostitute in London slang.

shlock *n* anything shoddy, inferior or meretricious. The word is Yiddish from German (either *schlacke*: dregs, or *schlagen*: slap or knock, in the sense of jacking up prices or damaged goods). The main application of shlock in American and later British slang has been to the products of the entertainment industry, particularly films and television.

shlong *n See* **schlong**.

shlub *n See* **schlub**.

shm- *prefix* this is the spelling representing the initial sound of many slang terms of Yiddish origin (see also **sch-** and **sh-**). Jewish wits and their emulators substitute these letters for the standard beginnings of English words to indicate mockery or negation.

♭'*Revolution; Shmevolution.*'
(Headline in *Wall Street Journal*, January 1968).

♭'*It's not the season for beagling.*'
'*Season shmeason!*'
(*Ticket to Ride*, British TV series, 1988).

shmarmy *adj British* smarmy, offensively ingratiating or smug. This new pronunciation of the common colloquialism represents a late 1980s, phenomenon in fashionable and youth circles whereby certain words are altered to resemble the many words of Yiddish origin beginning with **sh-**.

♭'*That shmarmy man in the coffee advert.*'
(Interview, *Making the Break*, British TV documentary about advertising, 1989).

shmear *n* a term of Yiddish origin literally meaning a smear or spreading-out but now denoting a complete state of affairs, situation, 'scenario'.

♭'*The Goldmark Gallery, in the person of the friendly and efficient greeter, Sally Jones, demystifies the whole shmear.*'
(*Lights Out for the Territory*, Iain Sinclair, 1997).

shmeg *n British* an idiot. A schoolchildren's term, fashionable from the 1980s, which is a variant form of **smeg** or **smeggy** (from smegma), a word popular among young males in the **punk** era. The altered pronunciation is influenced by Yiddish words such as **schmock**, **schmuck**, **schmendrick**, etc.

shmegegge, shmegeggy *n American* a contemptible or foolish person. The word is Yiddish, but seems to have been an American coinage, often heard in showbusiness circles. It does not appear to derive from any older term.

Shmendrik *n See* **Schmendrick**.

shmo, shmoe *n* a fool, 'sucker' or jerk. The word was invented in the USA as an acceptable euphemism for the Yiddish **schmuck** in the late 1940s when the latter term was understood in its literal and obscene sense. Shmo, like shmuck, has been heard in Britain in Jewish and non-Jewish circles since the 1950s.

ॐ'*She seems to like him but the guy's a bit of a shmo if you ask me.*'

shmooze, shmoose *vb American* to chat or gossip at length, to have a heart-to-heart talk. This American Yiddish word comes from the Hebrew *shmous*, meaning 'things heard'. The word, with a hard or soft final 's', has overtones of intimacy and affection rather than malicious gossip.

shmuck *n* an alternative spelling of **schmuck**.

shmutter *See* **schmutter**.

shnide *adj British*
snide (in both its standard sense of sneering and its slang sense of counterfeit). This quasi-Yiddish pronunciation has been popular with the **hip** young and some working-class speakers since the 1950s; other words are having their pronunciation altered in similar fashion (*see* **shmarmy** and **shmeg**, for instance). In this case the speakers may be reproducing the original pronunciation (*see* **snide** for the origins of the word). *See also* **jekyll**.

shnorrer *n* a cadger, scrounger or hustler. This is a Yiddish word occasionally used by non-Jewish speakers, particularly in the USA, to refer to a sponger or parasite. It derives from the German verb *schnorren*, to beg (itself from *schnurren*, purr or whirr – the sound of a beggar's entreaties or their musical accompaniment).

shoe *adj American* excellent, admirable, fashionable or acceptable. A **preppie** term of approval, of uncertain derivation.

shonk, shonker *n British* 1 a nose, especially a large and prominent one. A synonym of **conk**, this is derived from the following sense.

2 a Jew. An offensive, racist term dating from the 19th century, when *shonniker* was a Yiddish word denoting a small-time trader or pedlar.

shonkie, shonky *n, adj* 1 (a) Jew(ish). Like **shonk** and **shonker**, these words derive from *shonniker*, an archaic

Yiddish term for a pedlar or small-time tradesperson. 2 (a) mean, grasping (person).

shoo-in *n American* a certainty; a candidate or contestant who is certain to win. The term is inspired by the idea of a horse which merely has to be ushered across the finishing line. The phrase is a common colloquialism in the USA which was picked up by some British journalists in the second half of the 1980s.

shoomers *n pl British* patrons of clubs playing **acid house** music. *Shoom* was the name of one such club in London in 1988 when the cult was at its height (and before the **orbital raves** of 1989 became established). The word probably evokes the rush of euphoria experienced by users of the drug **ecstasy**.

shoot *n American* an inoffensive euphemism for **shit** used as an exclamation since the 19th century.

shoot *vb* 1 also **shoot off** to ejaculate. The word has been used in this sense since the 19th century.

2 also **shoot up** to inject. A drug user's term, widespread since the late 1950s.

3 to leave hurriedly. A word used in Britain mainly by young people since the 1970s. It is probably a shortening of 'shoot off'.

ॐ'*I've got to shoot, I'll see you later.*'

shoot a cat *vb British* to vomit. A mainly middle and upper class phrase, since the 1970s largely replacing 'shoot the cat' which has been heard since the early 19th century. 'Cat' itself is an archaic verb for vomit, either from the sound of the word or from the cat's habit of deliberate regurgitating.

shooter *n British* a gun. Neither a colourful nor particularly imaginative piece of slang, but the only term with any real currency, as opposed to the inventions of crime fiction.

ॐ'*Standing over two corpses with a hot shooter in your hand.*'
(*Twinkle, Twinkle Little Spy*, Len Deighton, 1976).

shooting gallery *n* a place where drug users gather to inject themselves. The word has been applied to open spaces, pubs and communal flats for instance. It is an addict's pun which the police have also adopted both in Britain and the USA.

↳ '*Sam got his leg broken recently in some mysterious street-corner dispute – heading for the shooting gallery they call the Chateau Luzerne.*'
(*Sunday Times*, 10 September 1989).

shoot one's bolt/load/wad

vb to ejaculate. These terms for the male orgasm have been in use since the 19th century.

shoot one's cookies *vb American*

an alternative form of **toss one's cookies/tacos**.

shoot the breeze/bull *vb* to

chat inconsequentially.

↳ '[Stephen King] *A regular guy who just happens to have 70 million copies of his books in print; a literary mechanic who has stepped off the production line to shoot the breeze for an hour or two.*'
(*Sunday Times* magazine, 15 October 1989).

shoot the shit *vb American* to talk,

gossip. A vulgarization of **shoot the breeze**.

shoot through *vb Australian*

a to die. An expression probably first introduced to an English audience via the lyrics of Rolf Harris's hit record 'Tie Me Kangaroo Down, Sport'.

b to leave, depart. The phrase has been in use in Australia since before World War II and is still heard.

shoot up *vb* to inject (a narcotic).

shootzie *adj British* fashionable, chic.

This item of 1960s London **parlyaree**, recorded in the TV documentary *Out* in July 1992, is of uncertain origin. It may derive from **chutzpah**.

shop *vb British* to inform on (some-

one). The noun shop meant prison in 16th-century British underworld parlance. The verb form was first used to mean imprison, then (since the first decades of the 19th century) to cause to be imprisoned. The word has become a well-known colloquialism since the 1960s; in school and prison slang it has largely been overtaken by the synonymous **grass**.

the-short-and-curlies *n pl*

British pubic hair(s). The expressions

'got/grabbed/caught by the short-and-curlies', meaning rendered helpless or vulnerable, is a common vulgarism.

short arm *n* the penis. A euphemism

heard especially in the armed services; short arm is an archaic variation of 'small arm' in the sense of handgun. 'Arm' also reflects the common notion of the penis as a limb. 'Short-arm inspection' was the medical examination for symptoms of venereal disease.

shortarse *n* a small person. A con-

temptuous term heard particularly in London working class speech and in Australia since the early years of the century.

short-eyes *n American* the under-

world and prisoners' term for a child molester. The equivalent of the British **nonce**. The exact significance of the words is unclear; the phrase may be related to 'shut-eyes', an archaic term for sex offender.

short hairs *n pl* pubic hair(s). A eu-

phemism in use since the 19th century. It is most often heard figuratively in phrases such as '*they've got us by the short hairs*' (i.e. at their mercy, rendered helpless).

short out *vb American* to lose control

of oneself, lose one's temper, 'blow a fuse'. The image is of an electrical system developing a short circuit.

↳ '*He tries to keep his cool, but every now and again he shorts out.*'

short-stuff *n American* a small per-

son. An affectionate or condescending form of address almost invariably said to a child by an adult.

shot *n* an injection. *See* **hotshot**.

shout *n British* 1 a round of drinks or

the ordering thereof.

↳ '*It's my shout.*'

2 a message indicating an emergency, request for help, etc. (usually by radio). A piece of jargon used by police and emergency services.

shout *vb Australian* 1 also 'shout at the

floor' to vomit.

2 to buy (someone) (a drink), to treat someone to something.

↳ '*Real generous...like giving me a job when I was stoney and shouting me all them chilled stubbies the other day.*'

(*The Adventures of Barry McKenzie*, cartoon strip by Barry Humphries and Nicholas Garland, 1988).

show *n British* an accidental display of a woman's underwear or naked body. A schoolboy word used especially in the later 1960s when 'revealing' skirts, blouses, etc. were in fashion.

shrapnel *n British* small change, coins. A vogue term among adolescents in the later 1990s. Unsurprisingly, the term may have come from the armed forces. Partridge has recorded that New Zealand soldiers used the word to refer to tattered banknotes in World War I. **Smash** is a synonym from the same period.

shreddies *n British* revolting, tattered (shredded) underwear. A mainly middle class usage among students and schoolchildren, punning on the name of a popular breakfast cereal. The term has been heard since the 1960s. The term may possibly derive from the British rugby players' practice of 'shredding'. This involves an attempt to remove a pair of underpants from a male victim by pulling them upwards rather than downwards.

shrimping *n American* sucking someone's toes for the purposes of sexual gratification, a jargon term among pornographers, prostitutes, etc.

shrink *n* a psychiatrist, psychoanalyst. Shrink is a shortening of the earlier **headshrinker**, which was imported from America to Britain and Australia in the 1960s.

↳ '*We called in a consultant, a psychiatrist.*'
'*A shrink?*'
'*A highly respected doctor.*'
(*The Dancer's Touch*, US film, 1989).

shrooms *n pl*
magic mushrooms. This abbreviated form describing hallucinogenic mushrooms probably originated in British adolescent slang in the 1990s. *Compare* **rooms**.

shtenkie *n, adj British* (a person considered) obnoxious, contemptible. The term is a quasi-Yiddish deformation of 'stink(y)' and was popular among **acid house** aficionados and **ravers** in the 1990s.

shtick *n*
a a performance, term, act or routine, in the context of the entertainment business.
b a piece of (repeated) behaviour characteristic of a particular person.
c a gimmick, trick or ruse.
The Yiddish word *shtik* from Middle German *stücke*: piece, was passed via American showbiz slang into fashionable speech and journalese in the 1980s.

shtum *adj* silent, unspeaking. Most often heard in the phrase 'keep' or 'stay shtum': be quiet. A Yiddish term from the German *stumm*: dumb, which entered London working-class slang via Jewish influence in the East End.

shtup *vb* to have sex (with). This Yiddish word meaning press or push (oneself) is from the German *stupsen* (push). In American slang it has come to mean copulate in which sense it was occasionally heard in fashionable British speech in the 1980s.

↳ '*As any regular reader of* Marie Claire *magazine knows, some four out of five young French women would rather shop than shtup.*'
(Julie Burchill, *Elle* magazine, December 1987).

shufti *n British* a look, glance. The word is Arabic and was imported by armed service personnel before World War II.

shutzie *adj British See* **shootzie**.

shyster *n* a dishonest, avaricious, contemptible person. The term is usually applied to unscrupulous professionals, particularly lawyers, who were the original subjects of the epithet in the USA in the mid-19th century. The etymology of shyster is open to several interpretations; 'shicer' was a 19th-century anglicization of the German *scheisser* (literally 'shitter'); 'shy' was used in the 19th century colloquially to mean disreputable. In addition there is a historical record of a lawyer named Scheuster who was officially reprimanded in New York courtrooms for obstructive and unprofessional behaviour.

sick *adj American* amusing, funny. An item of black street talk which was included in so-called **Ebonics**, recognized as a legitimate language variety by school officials in Oakland, California, in late 1996.

✎'*He's such a sick dude when he's tellin' all those stories!*'

✎'*That's so sick!*'

sicko *n* a pervert or mentally disturbed person. The word generally denotes a sexual deviant and is now heard in Britain as well as the USA, where it originated.

sidley, siddly *adj British* stealthy, furtive, but in an elegant, even arrogant way. This rare word could possibly be a variant of 'sidity', an Edwardian word meaning affectedly insincere, which itself may be related to the notion of 'side', meaning duplicity or hypocrisy.

✎'*You've got to admire those sidley spades.*'
(Recorded, art student, London, 1986).

(the) siff *n* an alternative spelling of (the) syph.

sighted! *exclamation British* an all-purpose exclamation of solidarity which ranges in meaning from 'thank you' to 'beware'. Synonyms from the same period are **seen** and **safe**. The term, which probably originated as a warning or shout of recognition by a gang lookout, was recorded in use among north London schoolboys in 1993 and 1994.

silk *n American* a white person. The term may be used by black speakers neutrally or pejoratively, rarely nowadays appreciatively. In the 1950s and 1960s it often occurred in the form '*silk broad*' and referred to a white woman. It is said to derive from the supposed texture of white female hair rather than white silk cloth.

simoleons *n American* coins, cash, dollars, money. This archaic term (a blend of 'Simon': obsolete slang for dollar, and 'Napoleon': a 20 franc gold coin) is occasionally revived in the same way as similar British words such as **rhino** or **pelf**.

simp *n* a dim-witted individual. The word, originating in the USA early in the 20th century, was a shortening of 'simpleton'. More recently it has sometimes acquired connotations suggested by 'simper' and **wimp**.

✎'*Some guest and some employer – the simp and the blimp.*'
(*Honeymooners*, US TV comedy series, 1951).

simpatico *adj* agreeable, pleasant, friendly. The Spanish and Italian word has been adopted by certain English speakers.

sin bin *n British* a place to which difficult or 'hopeless' cases are consigned. The term is applied particularly to schools or other educational or correctional institutions. It is derived from ice hockey, where the sin bin is the rinkside area where transgressing players serve out time penalties.

sing *vb* to inform, confess, give information to the authorities. This underworld term, originating in the USA before World War II, is often embellished as 'sing like a bird' or 'sing like a canary'.

✎'*Last month the alleged cocaine importer from America was driven north to a secure house where he is said by detectives to be "singing like a bird".*'
(*Observer*, 16 August 1987).

sink *vb* to drink, down (alcohol). This drinkers' euphemism usually occurs in such phrases as the invitation to 'sink a few (jars)'.

sink the sausage *vb Australian* a version of **hide the sausage**.

siphon/syphon the python *vb* to urinate. A humorous vulgarism introduced to a British audience via the Australian character Barry McKenzie in Barry Humphries' and Nicholas Garland's cartoon strip in *Private Eye* magazine in the late 1960s. **Drain the lizard/dragon/snake** is an alternative.

✎'*Hang on a jiff, though, will you? I've just got to nip into the dunnee to syphon the python.*'
(*Bazza Pulls It Off*, cartoon strip by Barry Humphries and Nicholas Garland, 1988).

sitch *n American* situation. An abbreviated form of the word in use in adolescent speech.

✎'*So what's the latest sitch?*'

sit down *vb* to acquiesce, submit or suffer in silence. The opposite to 'standing up for oneself', sit down is a synonym for the (probably more widespread) **lie down**. The phrase has become a vogue term and a business-jargon expression rather than a mere metaphor.

✎'*There's no way I'm going to sit down for this one. We've taken enough!*'

six-pack *n*

a the male abdomen showing the stomach muscles.

✎ *'He's got a great six-pack.'*

b a powerful and/or attractive male.

✎ *'The beach was covered with six-packs.'*

These uses of the term based on a comparison with a row of beer cans arose in the US in the early 1990s and by the end of the decade were also heard (especially in the second sense) in the UK.

sixteen-valve *n South African* an attractive female. The designation is that as applied to a powerful car. **Spoilers** and **hatchback** are other automotive images used in the same context in the late 1990s.

sixty-nine *n* simultaneous and mutual oral sex. The term, originating in the French *soixante-neuf* (suggested by the shape of bodies engaged in cunnilingus and fellatio) is from the jargon of pornography and prostitution. The expression also occurs as a verb.

size queen *n* a male homosexual who favours sexual partners according to the size of their genitals. The expression is part of the post-1960s **gay** lexicon and is generally used to indicate disapproval. The term is occasionally applied to women adopting the same criterion.

skag *n* another spelling of **scag**.

skangey *adj American* an alternative spelling of **scangey**.

skank *n* a trick, neat manoeuvre. An item of jargon originating in Nintendo *Game Boy* usage.

skank *n, adj American* something or someone unpleasant or disgusting. The word seems to have arisen in black speech, but its etymology is uncertain. Skank is sometimes used specifically to denote an immoral woman or prostitute.

skanking *n* a swinging and jerking style of dancing characteristic of reggae and the 'two-tone' music of 1977 to 1980. The word originally means stealing, and hence behaving disreputably, moving stealthily, in Jamaican patois.

skat *adj* fashionable. A short-lived vogue word from 1985 and 1986, of unknown origin. The word was used by ado-

lescents in the fashion, music and club milieus of New York and London.

skate *n American* a pushover, easy task, a 'smooth ride'. A 1980s usage, from the image of skating across a surface or between obstacles.

✎ *'Relax, it's going to be a skate.'*

skate it *vb British* to succeed easily or effortlessly. The term is heard particularly in the Scottish Lowlands and the north of England.

skattie *n*

a *South African* a girlfriend.

b *British* a promiscuous woman or prostitute. The term, of obscure origin, was in use among young adult and teenage black males in the late 1990s.

skeet *vb American* to achieve male orgasm, **come**. This item of black slang is of uncertain provenance but is presumably related to **skeeze**.

skeeze *vb American* to have sex. The word has been common in black speech since the late 1980s, but its exact etymology is unknown.

skeezer, skeeze *n American*

a a promiscuous female. The term is almost invariably pejorative.

b a **groupie** or ardent fan of hip-hop or **rap** performers.

The words appeared in the 1980s.

skell *n American* a homeless person. The origin of the term, heard in the 1990s, is uncertain.

-ski, -sky *suffix American* a humorous ending added, usually to slang terms, by teenagers and students. Examples are **finski**, **buttinsky**. The termination indicates friendship, respect, acceptance into the group when attached to a proper name, e.g., 'Normski' (a black UK TV presenter). When terminating the name of an object, e.g., **brewski**, it denotes affectionate familiarity. The suffix occurs in Slavonic languages and in many Yiddish surnames.

skid *vb* **1** to leave, go away. A usage which was fashionable among adolescents in Britain in the late 1980s.

2 *British* to 'slum', make do with little money, secondhand clothes, etc. This student term of the 1980s is probably inspired by 'skid row'.

skid-lid *n British* a crash helmet.

skid-marks *n pl* traces of excrement on underwear.

↬'*Hand-me downs – me first nappy had your skid-marks on it!*'
(*Birds of a Feather*, British TV comedy series, October 1989).

skidoo, skiddoo *vb* a version of **skedaddle**.

skids *n pl Australian* the fortunes of fate, hard luck, the 'breaks'. An encapsulation of the philosophy of the young and callously indifferent, most often heard in the shrug-off sentence 'them's the skids': 'that's the breaks'.

↬'*"Them's the skids", as the young fry say.*'
(Peter Corris, *The Greenwich Apartments*, 1986).

skill *n British* a younger schoolchildren's exclamation of admiration, appreciation or approval, heard in the late 1980s. The word has been extended from its original literal sense to become an all purpose vogue word, sometimes in the phrase 'skill and brill'.

skimming *n* taking money illegally (for example before declaring it for tax purposes, or to defraud the eventual recipients) from income or profits, especially in casinos. The word is part of underworld jargon as used by organized crime in the USA. 'Skim' was used to mean money or profit in both Britain and the USA in the 19th century, the image being evoked being that of taking the cream off the top of the milk.

skin *n* 1 *British* a **skinhead**.
2 *British* a cigarette rolling paper, as part of the makings of a **joint**. A word from the lexicon of drug users since the 1960s, now occasionally heard to describe cigarette papers put to more legitimate use. *See also* **skin up**.
3 *American* a dollar bill.

skin *vb* to rob or defraud, **rip off** or 'fleece' someone. The word implies comprehensive and efficient removal of wealth.

↬'*He thought he was pretty smart but those guys skinned him.*'
↬'*We got skinned in that deal.*'

skin and blister *n British* sister. A cockney rhyming-slang phrase which is still known if not used by many Londoners.

skinflick *n* a pornographic or semi-pornographic film. The skin element of the phrase refers to nudity; **flick** has been a slang term for film since the days of the silent movie. Skinflick is an Americanism which has been understood albeit not widely used in other English-speaking areas since the early 1970s.

skinful *n* an excess of alcohol. The word dates from the 18th century and evokes a distended belly or bladder.

↬'*We'd better get him home, he's had a skinful.*'

skinhead *n* 1 a bald person or someone with close-cropped hair. (**Chromedome** is a more recent synonym.)
2 a member of a working class youth cult originating in the late 1960s. the skinheads (the term was applied scornfully by longer-haired contemporaries, particularly **hippies**) mutated from the **mods** and **tickets** of the mid-1960s. They dressed in a functional uniform of American shirts, jeans and, often, **bovver boots** and espoused soul music and gang violence. The style survived with only minor changes into the 1980s and 90s; in the 1970s skinheads became firmly identified with racism, right-wing extremism and football hooliganism.

skin it *vb* to shake or slap hands as a greeting and gesture of solidarity. The term, like the action itself (which is sometimes accompanied by the cry '*give me some skin!*' or '*skin me!*') is part of 1990s youth culture throughout the English-speaking world.

skinny *n American* news, information, gossip. A vogue term among adolescents in the 1980s. This use of the word is said to have originated in the armed forces in the 1940s and might be jocularly based on 'the naked truth'.

↬'*These guys've got the skinny on what's going on after hours.*'

skin-pop *vb* to inject (an illicit drug) intramuscularly or into flesh, rather than into a vein. An addicts' term.

skins *n pl* 1 drums, in the jargon of jazz and rock musicians.

2 car or motorcycle tyres in the jargon of racers, bikers, etc.

3 *British* **skinheads**.

skin up *vb* to roll a **joint**. From **skin**; a cigarette rolling paper.

skip *n* **1** *British* an escape or an instance of jumping bail. This specialized use of the common colloquialism for 'avoid' is part of underworld jargon.

2 *American* a person who fails to answer a bail bond, an escapee.

3 *British* boss, **guvnor**. A shortening of **skipper**, used typically by police officers in familiar address to a superior, or, in sports, by team-members to their captain.

4 *British* a place to sleep or shelter. A shortened form of the tramps' **skipper**.

5 *British* a dilapidated, old or cheap vehicle, particularly a car. The name of the common large metal refuse containers has been appropriated as a vogue term among schoolchildren since around 1988. (One of a series of popular jokes at the expense of Skoda, likening the Czechoslovak car to a rubbish skip.)

skipper *n British* **1** a captain of a ship or a team. Skipper in this sense is not, strictly speaking, slang, although it is considered to be so by some. The word has been in use since it was anglicized from the Middle Dutch *schipper* (from *schip*, ship).

2 *British* a rough shelter, place to sleep for the night, typically in a derelict building. The word, which may describe no more than a patch of rough ground, is now a near-synonym for **doss house** or **derry**. It is part of the vocabulary of tramps, **dossers** and other down-and-outs, and originated in Celtic words for barn (rendered as *ysgubor* in Welsh, *sciber* in Old Cornish).

✎ *'When you're drunk and face-down in some skipper you just don't think there's much future in it.'*
(Recorded, vagrant, Waterloo, London 1987).

3 *British* friend, **mate**. A friendly term of address between males, now rarely used except by vagrants.

skipper *vb British* to sleep rough, be homeless. From the noun.

✎ *'I tell you, I was forced to skipper. I never had any choice.'*
(Recorded, vagrant, Waterloo, London, 1987).

skippering *n British* sleeping rough, living in derelict buildings or improvised or makeshift shelters. From the second sense of the noun **skipper**.

skippy *n American* a male homosexual, particularly an effeminate or affected one. the word was previously used to refer to female prostitutes by the US army in the Pacific. 'Skibby' was an earlier form of the word, the derivation of which is obscure: some relation to 'skivvy' looks possible, but there is no proof of this.

skirt *n* a woman or girl, or females in general. A depersonalizing term as used by males in the 20th century. The usage is much older, probably originating in the 1500s.

skite *vb Australian* to boast. The word is a shortened form of **blatherskite**.

skive, skive off *vb British* to avoid work or duty, malinger. Skive is either from the obscure verb in standard English meaning to shave off (pieces of leather), from Old Norse *skifa*, to slice, or from another unrecorded dialect term. It has been heard in the sense of shirk since the early 20th century.

skivvies *n pl American* men's underwear. The origin of the word is not known.

✎ *'Ordell looked over at Louis Gara having his morning coffee in his skivvies, his bare feet up on the coffee table.'*
(*The Switch*, Elmore Leonard, 1978).

skrag *vb* a variant spelling of **scrag**.

skull *n American* **1** a synonym for 'head' in racy speech or **hip** talk. The word most usually occurs in the phrase **out of one's skull** (intoxicated or crazy) or in the following extended specialized sense.

2 oral sex, especially fellatio. This term, popular among college students since the late 1970s, is either derived from, or an imitation of black street slang; a racier version of **head**, in its sexual context. It is usually used as part of the parodic exhortation '**whip some skull on me baby!**'.

skull *vb Australian* to drink (alcohol).

skulled *adj* drunk or **stoned** on drugs. the term is a shorter form of **out of one's skull** (although when used by Australian speakers the verb skull meaning to drink may also come into play).

skull-fuck *vb, n American* (to perform) an act of fellatio.

skunk *n British* marihuana, cannabis. Originally referring to '*skunk-weed*', a hydroponically grown and extra-strong strain of **grass**, the term became generalized to refer to other marihuana in the 1990s.

sky pilot *n*
a priest, particularly a naval or military chaplain. The phrase dates from the later 19th century.

sky rocket *n British* a pocket. A piece of London rhyming slang which is still used unselfconsciously by some older speakers. **Davy Crockett** and **Lucy Locket** are alternative forms.

slack *n See* **cut (someone) a little/slack**.

slack *adj Caribbean* immoral, particularly in a sexual context. This use of the word is archaic in Britain (although it was probably the origin of **slack**) but survives in **Jamaica talk**.
ᛪ'*The spurned wife of Tessa Sanderson's lover called the Olympic athlete "slack" – Jamaican slang for promiscuous.*'
(*Guardian*, February 1990).

slacker *n American* a disaffected, apathetic middle-class young person, a member of **Generation X**. '*Slacker-culture*' was promoted as a significant youth movement (supposedly a reaction against **yuppie** materialism and ambition) for a brief period in the early to mid-1990s on the USA's west coast.

slackness *n Jamaican* immoral behaviour, speech, etc., obscenity. The term was picked up by devotees of hip-hop and **rap** culture in the US during the 1990s.
ᛪ'*... not all black women take slackness lying down ... Rasheda Ashanti ... says; we don't want to continually hear explicit details about our anatomy ...*'
(*Sunday Times*, 2 May 1993).

slag *n British*
a a (supposedly) promiscuous woman. A derogatory word used mainly by working-

class men and women which often carries overtones of slovenliness and coarseness.
ᛪ'*Self-conscious and self-adoring parodists of slagdom, such as Madonna and Samantha Fox, understand this; that a man who calls a woman a slag isn't saying anything about her, but a lot about his condom size.*'
(Julie Burchill, *Elle* magazine, December 1987).
b a despicable male. The word conveys real contempt and distaste; it is now generally heard in London working-class or criminal usage. Slag has been used since the 18th century to convey notions of moral laxity and worthlessness. The ultimate source of the word is probably in 'slack' rather than 'slag' meaning mining or smelting residue.

slag *vb See* **slag off**.

a slagging *n British* a bout of criticism, denigration or abuse, a serious dressing-down. The noun comes from the verb to **slag** or **slag off**.
ᛪ'*This time at The Marquee, they provoked a review in Melody Maker – "a slagging, but still worth it".*'
(*Independent*, 27 January 1989).

slaggy *adj British* criminal, reprehensible, coarse and drab. An adjective applied to individuals, derived from the noun **slag**.

slag off, slag *vb British* to denigrate, criticize bitterly or insult. This working class term probably derives from the dialect slag, meaning to smear, or from the standard English noun slag, meaning refuse or waste material. In the form 'slag' the modern expression occurs in American speech. US authorities cite the German verb *schlagen* (to beat or lash), but this is an unlikely source for the British usage.
ᛪ'*We get slagged off something chronic by a lot of people.*'
(Recorded, telephone engineer, London, May 1989).

slaister *n British* a messy eater, dribbler, a dirty, slovenly person. A Scottish dialect term used especially of children and occasionally heard south of the border.

slam *vb* to have sex. The term, heard particularly in New Zealand and the USA, like its synonyms **lam** and **lamp**, invariably refers to male sexual activity. It can be used both transitively and intransitively.

§ *'Drew's been hoping to slam her for weeks.'*

slam-hound *n American* a promiscuous and/or sluttish female.

slammed *adj British* drunk. A mainly middle- and upper-class term of the 1980s. (Certain cocktails are known as 'slammers'; both words evoke the sudden and stunning effect of strong alcohol.)

slammer *n* prison. An Americanism used in Britain and Australia since the early 1960s, it was originally a 1930s slang word for door, hence cell door and, since World War II, jail.

§ *'You're consortin' with a criminal, so when he goes to the slammer, you go, too!'*
(*Smokey and the Bandit III*, US film, 1983).

slamming *n American* injecting heroin, **shooting up**. An item of police and underworld slang which is interchangeable in addicts' parlance with **geezing**.

slamming *adj British* excellent, exciting. Like its synonyms **banging** and **kicking**, it is a vogue term of approbation in use among adolescents since the early 1990s.

slanging *n American* selling illicit drugs, usually on the street. This usage from black American street argot in the 1990s is found in the phrase *'slangin' and bangin' '* (banging here is **gangbanging**) to describe the typical behaviour of gang members and devotees of drug subcultures. The word is almost certainly a deformation of **slinging**, which has also been used with the same meaning.

slant *n* an oriental person. A shortening of 'slant-eyed', used in the United States and Australia since the 1960s and now heard among young Londoners; for example, young city businessmen referring disparagingly to the Japanese.

slap *n British* 1 make-up, face-paint. A piece of theatrical slang which Partridge's *Dictionary of Slang and Unconventional English* dates to 1860 and claims to be obsolete by 1930. In fact the term is still in common currency in the theatre in the late 1980s.

§ *'We're going to need some more slap on here.'*

2 a meal, feast. Derived from 'slap-up' (meal), the term was recorded among bohemians and students in the late 1950s and early 1960s.

§ *'A good slap.'*

slap-and-tickle *n British* petting, kissing and caressing. A joky and innocuous euphemism for love-play of various degrees of intensity. The phrase dates from the Edwardian era but was most popular in the late 1950s, usually in the form 'a bit of slap-and-tickle'.

slaphead *n British* a bald person. A vogue term among adolescents from the early 1990s. The phrase may have been inspired by the comedian Benny Hill slapping the bald head of his diminutive assistant in his TV comedy shows of the 1980s.

slapper *n British* a prostitute or slut. This working class term from East London and Essex is probably a corruption of **shlepper** or **schlepper**, a word of Yiddish origin, one of whose meanings is a slovenly or immoral woman.

slash *n British* an act of urination. A vulgar term, used generally by males. The word came into use in this sense sometime before the 1950s, but was not recorded in writing until recently. The word usually occurs in phrases such as 'have a slash' or 'take a slash'. Slash may be echoic (as 'slosh' or 'slush') or may be inspired by the standard use of the word to refer to rain driving obliquely.

slash *vb British* to urinate. The verb form is less common than the noun.

slats *n pl* 1 ribs. A now obsolete slang term from the argot of boxers, bruisers, brawlers, etc., usually in the form of 'a punch/kick in the slats'.
2 *Australian* the vulval labia.

slaughter *n British* a place where stolen goods are hidden and/or shared out. This example of the jargon of cat burglars was recorded in *FHM* magazine in April 1996. It probably originated in underworld argot as 'slaughterhouse' or 'slaughter-yard', but the exact significance is unclear.

slaughtered *adj British* extremely

drunk. A fashionable item from the adolescent drinkers' lexicon of the 1990s.

✎ *'They [a convention of "nerds"] crammed the hotel to get slaughtered on non-alcoholic wines and beers.'* (*Sunday Express*, 27 February 1994).

sleaze *n* 1 shabbiness, sordidness, immorality. This term is a back formation from the earlier sleazy. Like the adjective, the noun form was adopted from American slang in the early 1970s.
2 a squalid, disreputable or reprehensible person. A term indicating great distaste and disapproval, based on the earlier adjective, sleazy. *See also* **sleazo**.

sleazeball, sleaze-bag, sleaze-bucket *n American* a very unpleasant person. A socially acceptable alternative to terms such as **shit-bag**, etc., popular in the late 1970s and 1980s.

sleazo, sleazoid *n* a 'sleazy' person; a disreputable, immoral or otherwise repellent individual. These Americanisms are now heard elsewhere.

sleeping policeman *n British* a ridge across a road or driveway in order to slow down traffic. These were known as speed-bumps or speed-ramps in official jargon and as sleeping policemen in popular speech since the 1970s when they were introduced. The phrase is said to come from Caribbean English.

sledgied *adj British* intoxicated by drugs or drink. A vogue term among devotees of **rave** culture since the early 1990s and subsequently among students, it is probably based on the notion of being suddenly struck as with a sledgehammer.

sleighride *n American* 1 a smooth or easy passage, the easy achievement of a task.
2 a bout of cocaine intoxication. A witticism inspired by the exhilaration resulting from ingestion of **snow**.

slewed *adj* drunk. The word (formerly sometimes spelled 'slued') has been used in this sense since the mid-19th century.

slice *vb American* to harass, oppress, criticize. A piece of adolescent and teenage slang of the early 1990s, almost always referring to parents or teachers.

✎ *'I sure wish the rents would quit slicing me.'*

slide *b American* to leave, depart. A vogue term, like **jam, jet, bail,** etc., probably originating among street gangs and subsequently in use among adolescents on high-school and college campuses.

✎ *'It's time to slide.'*

slider *n British* a shirker, idler. Probably a clipped form of the word 'backslider', this late-1990s usage was defined on the Internet by *Bodge World* in February 1997 as 'someone who manages to get out of doing work'.

slime *vb* 1 to behave in a devious, sycophantic or ingratiating way. A usage popular among adolescents and young adults in the 1980s.
2 *Australian* to ejaculate.

slime, slimeball, slimebucket, slimebag *a* despicable person; popular terms of abuse or distaste in the 1980s.

sling off *vb Australian* to denigrate, criticize.

sling one's hook *vb British* to leave, go away. This term which originated and largely survives in working-class speech is either of nautical or mining origin. It dates from the second half of the 19th century. **Hook it** is a racier alternative.

✎ *'We don't want you here. Go on, sling your 'ook!'*

slip it to someone *vb British* to have sex with someone. A version of the more common vulgar euphemism, **slip someone a length**. The phrase is generally employed by men and usually implies a casual and surreptitious coupling.

slip someone a length *vb* to have sex with someone (from the male point of view). A euphemism originating in the 19th century.

slit *n*
a the vagina.

✎ *'A vagina indeed! Admittedly, some people did call it a slit sometimes.'* (*Nice Work* by David Lodge, 1988).

b a female. The word in the plural was adopted as the name of a British all-girl **punk** group in 1977.

Sloane Ranger, sloane *n British* a young upper-middle or upper-class person, educated at a public school and affecting certain well defined modes of dress and behaviour. The phrase was applied to a recognizable sub-category of British youth displaying characteristics of what used to be known as the 'county set'. The equivalent of the American **preppies** and the French '*B.C.B.G.'s* (for '*bon chic, bon genre*'), Sloane Rangers were defined and described by the journalists Peter York and later Ann Barr in articles in *Harpers and Queen* magazine and publications such as *The Official Sloane Ranger's Handbook* (1982). The first time the words appeared in print was in October 1975, but Peter York was not the originator of the expression. It was used by bar-room wits of the early 1970s to refer to would-be 'men about town' frequenting Chelsea pubs, only some of whom were the upper-class youths (then known solely as **Hooray Henrys**) later so described. The source of the pun, the Lone Ranger, was the dashing cowboy hero of a 1950s TV series; Sloane Square is in Chelsea.

➣'*The appalling Sloane Ranger look. Worn by strapping, horsey girls aged 20 going on 53. Other components: striped shirts, a tame string of pearls, impenetrable pleated skirt, blue tights and prissy shoes. Printed headscarves optional. Thick ankles mandatory.*'
(Description of female Sloane Ranger, Judy Rumbold, *Guardian*, 11 December 1989).

slob *n* a coarse, slovenly and/or lazy individual. This word had existed for many years in Anglo-Irish speech where it denoted a fat, slow child (probably from *slab*, Irish Gaelic for mud). Coincidentally a similar word, apparently of Slavonic origin and rendered as *zhlub* or *shlub*, exists in Yiddish. It means an uncouth person, but is probably derived from a root form related to the Czech *zlobit*, to get angry.

slope *n* an oriental person, especially a Vietnamese. This derogatory term, deriving from 'slope-eyed', moved from the US to Australia in the 1970s.

➣'*The newest "new Australians", as anyone who looks foreign is called, are the Lebanese and the Vietnamese, the "slopes".*'
(*Observer* magazine, 13 December 1987).

Compare **slant**.

slope off *vb* to leave, depart surreptitiously. This colloquialism derives from the 19th-century slang use of 'slope' alone to mean decamp or sneak away. The term

originated in the USA. It is either from the Dutch *sloop*, to steal away, or from the standard verb.

sloppy joe *n* a large baggy sweater as worn by students, **bobby-soxers** and especially **beatniks**. The term originated in the USA in the 1940s.

sloshed *adj* drunk. One of the most common and least offensive terms in British usage since the late 19th century. It is also heard in the USA.

slot *n*
a the anus. In **gay** parlance.
b the vagina.

sly *adj British* an all-purpose term of disapproval fashionable in the later 1990s. It was defined on the Internet by *Bodge World* in March 1997.

smack *n* heroin. Originally an American term, the word spread to Britain and Australia at the time of the Vietnam War. It is derived from the Yiddish *shmek*, meaning a sniff, whiff or taste, reinforced by the English word's suggestion of a sudden, violent effect.

➣'*I don't think Jimmy Hendrix was on smack 'cos I was with him last Saturday night and I know when a man's on smack and he wasn't.*'
(Murray Roman, quoted in *Oz* magazine, June 1969).

➣'*Two days later I was in All Saints Road, Notting Hill, with a knife being held against my neck after I tried to score some smack.*'
(Former addict quoted in the *Observer* Magazine, December 1987).

smacked-out *adj* addicted to, or under the influence of heroin (**smack**).

➣'*Nathan had staked everything he had ever worked for on this loser who was too smacked out to worry about taking MOM Records into the bankruptcy court.*'
(*Platinum Logic*, Tony Parsons, 1981).

smacker *n British* an active or potential sexual partner. In this sense, the term was used by aficionados of London dancefloor culture in the early 1990s.

smackers *n pl* pounds or dollars. Like **smacker** in the sense of kiss, this lighthearted term is often embellished to give 'smackeroos' or 'smackeroonies'. The original word probably refers to the slapping of coins or notes onto a table or

counter or into the palm of an out-
stretched hand.

> ⚭'*Do you wanna take the thousand
> smackers or try for the sensational
> bathroom suite?*'
> (*Biff* cartoon, 1986).

smack-head *n adj* a heroin addict,
a junkie. A combining of **smack** with the
'-head' suffix meaning habitué. ('Smack-
freak' was a synonymous term of the late
1960s and early 1970s, subsequently
yielding to smack-head in popularity.)

> ⚭'*If a smack-head tries to chat you up,
> what's he really after?*'
> (UK Government anti-heroin advertise-
> ment, 1986).

smartarse, smartass *n, adj* (a)
know-all, smug or insolent (person). The
word describes someone whose display of
real or supposed cleverness renders them
obnoxious. 'Smart alec' or 'wise-guy' are
politer synonyms.

> ⚭'*If she felt like giving them a smartass
> answer, why didn't she? Because she
> couldn't think of a smartass answer
> fast enough.*'
> (*The Switch*, Elmore Leonard, 1978).

smartmouth *vb American* to cheek,
speak disrespectfully or insolently (of
someone).

smarts *n* intelligence, wits. A coinage
inspired by the word wits itself and/or
'brains'. The word is American, but is occasionally heard in Britain.

> ⚭'*She's got more than her share of
> smarts.*'

smash *n British* small change, money
in the form of coins. The term is heard
particularly in the Scottish Lowlands and
the north of England. **Shrapnel** is a southern equivalent.

smashed *adj* drunk or intoxicated by
drugs.

> ⚭'*Having discovered that it is possible
> to be smashed, keep on the stereo
> headphones AND read, I have man-
> aged to ... get through ... several
> books.*'
> (Jim Anderson in *Oz* magazine, February
> 1970).

> ⚭'*Her husband Russ added: "She [Joan
> Kennedy] looked smashed and I do
> mean smashed. She was goo-goo-
> eyed."*'
> (*News of the World*, 10 July 1988).

smash mouth *vb American* to kiss.
A humorous equivalent to the better
known 'chew face' among adolescents.

smeg, smeggy *n British* a foolish
and/or dirty person. These terms, deriving from smegma, are vulgarisms which
have been popular with schoolboys, students, **punks** and other youths since the
mid-1970s. Despite their origin the words
do not usually indicate great distaste but
rather mild contempt or even affection.
Smeg and various derivatives such as
'smeg-head' were used in the cult British
TV comedy series of the late 1980s *Red
Dwarf* as an all-purpose swearword, a
euphemism for **fuck**.

smellie *n British* a beggar or homeless
person, **crustie**.

**smidgin, smidgeon, smid-
geon, smidge** *n* a small amount,
soupçon, touch. The word is a mid-19th
century American variant form of
'smitch', an English dialect word (for stain
or smut), itself a form of 'smudge'.
Smidgin is now common throughout the
anglophone world.

> ⚭'*If the House is sitting, I tend to smug-
> gle a smidgin of High Tea – perhaps a
> toasted cheese and baked bean sand-
> wich, or some of Mr Matthews's excel-
> lent Turkey Drumsticks – into the
> Chamber in a trouser pocket.*'
> (*Private Eye*, 27 October 1989).

smok *n South African* a flirtatious or
unconventional female. Recorded as an
item of Sowetan slang in the *Cape Sunday
Times*, 29 January 1995. In 19th-century
British slang 'smock' could be used to denote a 'loose woman'.

smoke *vb American*
a to kill. A euphemism in underworld and
police usage since the 1940s, this unsentimental term was fashionable in teenage
speech and crime fiction in the 1980s.
b also **smoke out, smoke off** to defeat or
to better (someone) in the **hip** jargon of
the rock music business since the 1970s.

> ⚭'*Out-playing the headliner is known in
> the trade as "smoking"...Thin Lizzy
> were notorious for smoking their su-
> periors – and consequently for being
> mysteriously removed from bills.*'
> (*Independent*, 27 January 1989).

smoke *n*
a tobacco.

b hashish or marihuana.

the smoke, the big smoke *n*
London or any large town or city (in British and Australian usage). The word was first recorded in this sense in 1864 referring to London. It usually evokes the city as seen by those who are not native to it or are in temporary exile from it.

↳'*This is one of the things they have come for – an escape from the Smoke and a whiff of the sea.*'
(*Town* magazine, September 1963).

smoker *n British* 1 an old, worn-out or mechanically unsound motor-car. A piece of jargon from the vocabulary of second-hand car dealers and enthusiasts. 2 a cannabis smoker.

smokey, smoky *n American* a police officer. The term derives from 'Smokey the Bear', a cartoon character wearing the hat of a Forest Ranger, who issued warnings against careless behaviour that could cause forest fires; it was then applied, jocularly at first, to any uniformed authority figure. Smokey became the CB (Citizens' Band) radio code word for highway patrol officer in the 1970s.

smoodge *vb Australian* a variant form of **schmooze** in the sense of ingratiate oneself or flatter.

↳'*Don't try and smoodge me, it won't work.*'

smudger *n British* 1 a friend, 'mate'.
↳'*All right me old smudger?*'
2 a a photographer. A jocular reference to inept developing and printing.
b also **smudge** a photograph. This old item of press slang came in the 1990s to refer specifically to an illicit paparazzi snap of, e.g., a star *en déshabille*.
3 a flatulent person. All three sense of the word are from working class speech; the first and third specific to the London area. All are now dated but not obsolete.

smurf *n*
a *British* a black person. A racist pejorative.
b *British* an unfortunate, contemptible person or misfit, in working-class and schoolchildren's usage.
c a smuggler of drugs, specifically a lowly courier or dupe.
d *British* another word for **jub**. The Smurfs were ugly, plump, gnome-like cartoon creatures marketed as a children's craze in the early 1970s and revived in the late 1990s.

smurf *vb*
a to transport illicit narcotics.
b to 'launder' money. Both terms are from underworld usage, probably originating in North America.

smut *n Irish* a photograph. The word is probably related to the British **smudge(r)**, or else derived from 'smutty' in the sense of 'dirty' photos.

smuts *n Irish* the cinema. By analogy with the colloquial 'pictures'. The expression uses the plural of the regional 'smut'.

snack attack *n* a bout of compulsive eating, **(the) munchies**. A late 1980s vogue term, in limited circulation (as is its contemporary, **tack attack**).
↳'*I'm afraid in the middle of the night I had a snack attack.*'

snafu *n* an impossible situation, a foul-up, a labyrinth of incompetence. The expression, from 'Situation Normal, All Fucked Up' was developed in the US army in World War II (in imitation of that institution's passion for acronyms) to describe the quotidian effects of bureaucratic stupidity.
↳'*I tell you, its been snafu after bloody snafu here.*'
(Recorded, businessman, London, 1987).

snag *vb American* steal, appropriate. A term from street slang that was adopted by middle-class adolescents during the 1990s, often to describe the seduction of another's partner.

snags *n pl Australian* sausages. A word in use since the 1940s and still heard, particularly at **barbies**.

snake *n South African* an unfaithful female. Recorded as an item of Sowetan slang in the *Cape Sunday Times*, 29 January 1995.

snake *vb American* to seduce and/or have sex with. The term's recent usage may have originated in black slang, but the same word was employed with the sense of 'steal surreptitiously' in British slang of the 19th century.
↳'*He goddam tried to snake my old lady.*'
(Recorded, Californian male, September 1995).

snakes *n Australian*

a urine or an act of urination. The word is native Australian rhyming slang from 'snake's hiss': **piss**.

b a toilet.

snap one's gums *vb American* to talk. An alternative form of **bat/flap one's gums**.

snapper *n Irish, British* a child. The term, popularized by the Irish writer Roddy Doyle's story and 1993 film of the same name, may have originated as a shortening of 'whippersnapper'.

snarf *vb*

a to eat, devour.

b to appropriate, adopt wholesale. In the language of **cyberpunks** and **net-heads**, the term refers to incorporating information from elsewhere into one's own documents and files, etc. It is probably a blend of 'snort' or **snag** and **scarf (up)**.

snart *vb, n British*

a (to) snigger or snort (with derision).

b (to) sniff or inhale. (In the latter sense, 'snart up' is an alternative form.)

c to sneeze.

A rare expression heard among students and others since the early 1970s. It is a humorous corruption of **snort** in both its standard and slang senses.

snatch *n* 1 **a** the vagina.

b women in general. In the 16th century this word was used to denote an impromptu and/or hasty ('snatched') sexual encounter. The meaning was transferred to the female pudenda, and in the 20th century extended to refer to females as sex objects. The use of snatch in these senses has never been common but enjoyed a brief vogue in the late 1960s and early 1970s, first in the US and Canada, subsequently in Britain.

2 *British* an instance of bag-snatching, in the argot of teenage muggers.

↪ *'The child muggers told with chilling frankness how and why they resorted to muggings or "snatches" as they are sometimes called.'*
(*Observer*, 22 May 1988).

3 a kidnap or abduction, in underworld jargon.

snazz *n* elegance, smart showiness, élan. The noun, most commonly encoun-

tered in American speech, is a back-formation from the adjective **snazzy**.

snazzed-up *adj* smart, elegant, dressed-up, embellished or enhanced. A more recent derivation of **snazzy**.

snazzy *adj* smart, elegant, stylishly impressive. The word (and its connotations) are a blend of 'snappy' and 'jazzy'. It originated in the USA in the 1940s.

↪ *'They'd toy with their goddamn transistor radios, and admire their snazzy new clothes in front of a full-length mirror.'*
(Len Deighton, *Twinkle, Twinkle Little Spy*, 1976).

sneaks *n pl American* trainers, sneakers. A teenage abbreviation heard in the 1990s.

sneeze *n* cocaine. A term used by **yuppies** in the late 1980s.

snide *adj British* illegal, counterfeit, dishonest or unacceptable. The word's exact origins are obscure but it is related to the German *schneiden* (or its Dutch or Yiddish equivalent), meaning clip, and was used in the context both of coin-cutting and of cutting remarks. The former sense gives rise to the modern slang usage and the latter to the standard English meaning. Snide was first heard in Britain in the mid-19th century. Interestingly, young speakers have begun to revert to a Yiddish or Germanic pronunciation of the word as **shnide**.

↪ *'Are you accusing me of selling snide gear?'*
(Recorded, street trader, Portobello Road, London, 1986).

snip *n* a small, insignificant and/or irritating person. The word usually implies aggression and pettiness. It is derived from the notion of snip meaning to cut.

↪ *'Some little snip throwing her weight around.'*

snippy *adj* irritatingly critical, brusque or presumptuous. Snippy is a dialect word for 'cutting' in origin.

↪ *'She struck me as a little snippy snitch.'*

sniptious *adj American* stylish, well-dressed, dapper. The term was first recorded in the 19th century but remains slang, never having achieved the status of orthodox speech. Its precise etymology is uncertain, but it may be related to the word 'snip(s)', associated with the attentions of a tailor or dressmaker.

snit *n* **1 a** a small, obnoxious or devious person. The term is typically used of a smug or devious child.
b an insignificant person. The word is an invention influenced by **snip**, **snitch** and possibly **snot**.
2 a fit of irritation, tantrum.

snitch *vb* to inform (on someone). Snitch was originally a slang term for nose which was itself used to signify a police spy or **grass** in the 18th century (as was **nark**). Snitch began to be used in the verb form in the 19th century and is still in use in the USA, although in Britain it survives mainly in children's speech, meaning 'tell tales'.

snitch *n* an informer. The word (like **nark** originally meaning 'nose') was first used in this sense in the 18th century. It is still used in the USA to mean a paid police informer, whereas in Britain it is largely confined to the language of children, in which it denotes a 'tell-tale'.

snockered *adj* **1** an alternative form of **schnockered**.
2 *American* completed, finalized, solved. A term heard particularly among schoolchildren, students and parents.

snog *vb* to kiss ('snog up', used transitively, is a racier late 1980s version). This lighthearted word, used typically by children and adolescents, first appeared in Britain before World War II. It is probably a variant of 'snug' and 'snuggle (up)'. In the 1950s particularly in the USA, snog took on a more general sense of flirt. It retains its specific sense in Britain.
↳'*And I expect she's seen you walking out with Dolly Clackett, and snogging on the front porch.*'
(*Hancock's Half-hour*, BBC radio comedy, May 1960).

snog *n British* a kissing session. (For the origin of the term, see the verb form.)
↳'*They were having a quick snog while the lights were out.*'

snoot *n* **1** nose. A humorous variant form of 'snout'. (In Middle English snout was written *snute* and pronounced 'snooter'.)
↳'*A punch on the snoot.*'

2 a snooty person.

snooze *n* something boring or tedious. A synonym of **yawn**.
↳'*I must admit that last Tuesday's board meeting was a bit of a snooze.*' (*Maid to Order*, US film, 1987).

snore *n* a boring experience. A synonym of **snooze** and **yawn**, typically used by adolescents.
↳'*A three hour talk on the EU; God what a snore!*'

snork *n Australian* **1** a baby or immature person. The word is said to be a distortion of 'stork', but may also be influenced by such words as 'snort', 'snicker', 'snit', 'snot' and the following sense of the word.
2 a sausage. This rare use of the word may be related to the synonymous **snag**.

snorker *n Australian*
a a sausage.
b penis.
The words are obviously related to the Australian **snork**, and perhaps to **snag**, but the exact origin of all of these terms is obscure.

snort *vb* to sniff or inhale (illicit drugs such as heroin, cocaine, amphetamines, etc.). An Americanism which spread to Britain and Australia in the 1960s. The word supplanted the more sedate 'sniff', used previously.
↳'*And am I dreary if I think that showing someone snorting coke on the telly is not such a great idea?*'
(Janet Street-Porter, *Today*, 19 March 1988).

snot *n* **1** mucus from the nose. The word is from Middle English *snotte*, itself from old English *gesnot*, variant forms of which existed in all Germanic languages. These terms are related either to 'snout' or to an Indo-European root meaning to flow. Snot is a widespread term but because of its distasteful context is considered a vulgarism.
↳'*Wipe the snot off your face and cheer up.*'
2 an obnoxious person, usually a young or diminutive and self-important individual.
↳'*That little snot.*'

snot-nosed, snotty-nose(d)

adj obnoxious and immature; young and over-confident.

✧*'I'm not letting some snot-nosed kid tell me what to do!'*

snot-rag *n British* a handkerchief.

snotted *adj American* intoxicated, drunk.

snotty *adj* 1 suffering from catarrh, afflicted with a runny nose.
2 obnoxious, self-important, snooty.

snout *n British* 1 nose.
2 a paid police informer. 'Nose' was used to denote a police spy or informer and so were slang synonyms such as **nark**, **snitch** and snout. Snout is of more recent origin than the other terms, dating from between the World Wars.
3 tobacco, a cigarette. The use of snout to mean tobacco dates from the end of the 19th century when it originated among prison inmates. It was inspired by convicts touching their noses, either while cupping a surreptitious smoke or as a silent sign requesting tobacco. (The explanations are not mutually exclusive, one may have given rise to the other.) In the 1950s the use of 'a snout' for a cigarette became widespread in working-class speech.

snout *vb British* to inform, especially regularly in return for pay. The verb is derived from the earlier noun form.

✧*'Naff ways of making money – snouting for a gossip columnist (esp. Nigel Dempster).'*
(*The Complete Naff Guide*, Bryson et al, 1983).

snow *n* 1 cocaine. The white crystalline drug resembles snow and its anaesthetic effect numbs like cold. The slang term dates from the turn of the century. ('Snowbird' and 'snowball' were elaborations used in some circles.)

✧*'A little snow at Christmas never did anyone any harm.'*
(Legend on a 1969 Christmas card sent out by the record producer Phil Spector, featuring a still from the film *Easy Rider*, in which he had a cameo role as a cocaine dealer).
2 a **snow job**.
3 *Australian* a nickname for a blond male, usually used pejoratively.

snow *vb* to fool, cheat, bamboozle, especially by overloading someone with in-

formation. This Americanism (now occasionally heard in Britain) is based on the notion of 'snowing someone under' in order to deceive or manipulate them. It may also have originally evoked a 'snowstorm' of documentation.

✧*'When you go into town on a false pass who do you think you're snowing?'*
(*Battle Cry*, US film, 1954).

snowdrop *vb* to steal clothes, typically underwear, from a clothes line. The underworld and police term may refer to a fetishistic practice or the actions of vagrants.

✧*'We busked on street corners and snowdropped clothes from the backyard Hills Hoists of trendy Paddington.'*
(*Girls' Night Out*, Kathy Lette, 1989).

snowdropper *n British* someone who steals clothing, usually lingerie from washing lines, in the language of vagrants, police and prisoners. The term first referred (in the early 19th century) to the theft of clothes due to poverty; it now often denotes the act of a fetishist.

snow job *n American* a case of deceit, browbeating or manipulation, particularly by means of glib or overwhelming persuasion or flattery. The phrase has been common since World War II.

snow out *vb* to lose one's bearings or consciousness, 'blank out'. The term evokes the sensation of being lost in a snowstorm or the 'snowstorm effect' of a blank TV screen. Snow out has been heard, typically but not exclusively among drug users in the 1980s.

Snow White *n American* a white female or the personification of white womanhood. A black term almost always used pejoratively or facetiously.

snuff *vb* 1 to kill. An old term, derived from the notion of extinguishing a candle. The curt 'tough guy' use of the word remains popular in street slang and crime fiction, particularly in the USA. See **snuff movie**.
2 to sniff cocaine. An item from the drug user's vocabulary.

snuff *n* cocaine.

snuff it *vb British* to die. Inspired by the snuffing out of a candle, this expression has been heard in British English, particularly in working class usage, since the turn of the century.

༒'*If geology has taught me one thing, Stuart, it's that we are on the earth for only a short time. I am 50 next week. In 10 years I could snuff it. I have to get out there and make things happen.*'
(Professional fossil-hunter Stanley Wood, quoted in the *Sunday Times*, 17 December 1989).

snuff movie *n* a violent, **hardcore** pornographic film supposedly featuring the actual death of one of the actors. Rumoured to have been made in the early 1970s, the actual existence of such a movie has never been proved. In the 1980s the term began to be applied to **splatter movies**, where the death and mayhem is indisputably faked.

snufty *n British* an individual who derives sexual excitement from sniffing (clothing, bicycle saddles, etc.).

snyster *n British* a snack. A dialect term from Lowlands Scots occasionally heard in other parts of the country.

soap-dodger *n British* a dirty, unkempt or smelly person, a 'scruffbag' or **dosser**. **Bath-dodger** is a synonym. An expression of disapproval among adults.

S.O.B., s.o.b. *n American* **son of a bitch**. The initial letters are often used in order to moderate the strength of the phrase, which is highly offensive in American usage.

༒'*Some S.O.B. walked off with her purse.*'

sod *n British* **1 a** an unpleasant person (of either sex, but more often male). The word often implies unfair or cruel behaviour on the part of the person described.

༒'*I'm sorry I was such a sod to you.*'

b an individual. Like **bugger**, the term is used when referring to someone with pity, irony or mild contempt.

༒'*And that was another coincidence because he was the bloke I'd met earlier in the boozer, so I gave him my last £20 note because I thought, poor sod, he'll soon be dead.*'
(William Donaldson, *Independent*, 26 August 1989).

c a nuisance or annoyance.

༒'*That lid's a real sod to get off.*'

2 a sodomite. The original sense of the word is almost never heard in current English, it was last used in this way in the early 1960s. (The inhabitants of Sodom were according to the book of Genesis guilty of unnatural sexual practices.)

sod *vb British* the verb usually occurs as part of expletives such as 'sod you!' (indicating indifference, rejection, etc.) or 'sod it!' (indicating irritation or anger). Unlike its synonym **bugger**, the word is not used to mean sodomize.

soda *n American* cocaine or **crack**. A term current among police and drug users in the late 1980s. From the resemblance and volatile effects of the drug(s).

sod-all *n British* nothing, **bugger-all**.

༒'*He got the profit and I got sod-all.*'

sodding *adj British* an intensifying adjective like **bloody**, **bleeding**, etc. Sodding usually carries overtones of extreme irritation, impatience, etc.

sod off *vb British* to leave, go away. The phrase is almost always an imperative, sometimes conveying only mild annoyance or aggression.

༒'*I told them to sod off and leave me alone.*'

sofa spud *n American* a lazy, inert person. The term is a jocular variant of **couch potato**.

soft boy *n Jamaican* a male homosexual or an effete or effeminate man. This phrase from Jamaican patois was adopted ironically as a name by the Soft Boys, a London rock group of the 1970s.

softshoe *vb* to move or behave surreptitiously or in a manner both cautious and devious. Like **tap-dance** the metaphor is applied in raffish or **hip** talk to someone manoeuvring cleverly in social or professional situations. The expression is of course from the 'softshoe shuffle' dance step.

༒'*The guy managed to softshoe his way out of trouble again.*'

soggies *n British* breakfast cereal. A middle and upper class term of the late 1970s and early 1980s inspired by the trademark names of cereals such as *Shreddies* and *Frosties* and their eventual consistency.

soixante-neuf *n See* **sixty-nine**.

soldier *See* **dead soldier**.

solid sender *n American* an exciting musician. The expression originated among pre-World War II American jazz musicians; solid is a surviving **hip** term for excellent, 'sender' implies generating and communicating excitement.

something else *n* (something or someone) outstanding, excellent, exceptional. An enduring phrase from the **hip** lexicon of the 1950s.

✧'*She goes with all the guys from out of my class*
But that can't stop me from thinking to myself,
"She's sure fine looking, man, she's something else."'
('Something Else', written by Sharon Sheeley and Eddie Cochran, recorded by Eddie Cochran, 1959).

son of a bitch, sonofabitch *n American* an unpleasant, obnoxious or despicable person. The expression is roughly the equivalent of the British **bastard** or **sod**, and often implies active nastiness, although it may be used with pity ('*poor son of a bitch*') or annoyance ('*that engine's a son of a bitch!*'). The epithet fell out of use in British speech around the middle of the 19th century. (The British Reverend Benjamin Newton records in his diary for 1818, a wealthy fellow clergyman who had two sons, calling the one born out of wedlock 'son of a whore' and the one born within 'son of a bitch'.) In American speech the phrase son of a bitch was until recently considered too offensive for 'polite company' or broadcasting and would often be reduced to S.O.B.

✧'*Wherever he went, Andy would have to be the nice guy and I had to be the sonofabitch.*'
(Fred Hughes on Andy Warhol, *Observer* magazine, March 1988).

✧'*He* [Patrick McGoohan] *has been called everything from a difficult son of a bitch to a genius.*'
(*Evening Standard*, 17 March 1988)

sook, sooky *n Australian* a 'crybaby'. The noun probably post-dates the adjective **sooky**, but the origins of both forms are uncertain.

sooky *adj Australian*

a sulky, sullen.

b sentimental, 'soft' or 'unmanly'. The word may be a corruption or nursery version of 'sulky' itself, but the etymology is obscure. It has been suggested that it may derive from an archaic diminutive of Susan.

sooty *n British* a black or coloured person, an arab. The racist epithet is derived from the colour of soot and the name of a glove puppet of a yellow bear, a popular figure in children's entertainment, especially television, since the 1950s. Although sooty does not sound unaffectionate, in actuality it is often used highly offensively. (In 1745 Henry Fielding referred to Jews as 'the Sooty Tribe' in his *Covent Garden Tragedy*.)

✧'*We're pretty liberal really, we've only got one rule: no sooties.*'
(Recorded, proprietor of Sloane Rangers' nightclub, 1986).

soppo *adj British* fashionable, exciting. This term of unknown origin, recorded among London's schoolchildren in the early 1990s, was defined by one user as '**funky** or **groovy**'. It is unlikely to be related to the negative 'soppy', but might be an alteration of 'sophisticated'.

sort *n* a girl or woman. This specific sense of the word as used in working-class British and Australian speech is probably a version of **salt**.

sorted *adj British*

a in a satisfactory situation, comfortable and content.

✧'*I reckon if you've got a girl, a car and a few bob, you're sorted.*'

✧'*Sorted for E's and Whizz.*'
(Title of song by Pulp, 1995).

b excellent.

✧'*Let's finish up and get going*'
'*Sorted.*'

This use of the word (a clipping of the phrase 'sorted out'), which originated in criminal circles, meaning 'safely arranged' or 'adequately supplied', became one of the most popular vogue terms of the 1990s, beginning as a catchphrase among drug-dealers and eventually finding its way into the colloquial speech of middle-class adults.

sort (out) *vb British* 1 to beat up. An innocuous euphemism describing a brutal reality, in keeping with a tendency of London working-class slang toward menacing understatement (see **bother, see-ing-to**, etc.).

✧*'I'll go and sort this Daley geezer.'*
(*Minder*, British TV series, 1987).

2 to have sex with. A masculine vulgarism with overtones of de-personalization and brusqueness.

soul kiss *n American* a late 1960s synonym for **French kiss**, now dated.

sound *adj British* excellent. A vogue term of approbation, generalized from the standard sense of 'reliable' for use among adolescents from the early 1990s. The word was particularly popular in the speech of the Merseyside area and often used as an exclamation.

soused *adj* drunk, from the standard use of the word to mean soaked or drenched.

sov *n British* one pound. The word is a shortening of 'sovereign' and was used to designate that gold coin (worth one pound) until its discontinuance in 1914. Sov has been popularized by its copious use in the popular TV series *Minder*, set among the working-class and criminal population of London.

✧*'[Eric] Idle sounds as though he might just have relieved a punter of 500 sovs for a second-hand motor.'*
(*Independent*, 17 March 1989).

sow *n British* an unpleasant woman. The (fairly rare) term of abuse usually implies real distaste or bitter recrimination.

S.P. *n British* starting price, the odds on a horse. Hence essential information, a basis for judgement, the known form. A term fashionable in working-class and raffish circles in the later 1980s. It has been in underworld and gambling use since the 1950s.

✧*'What's the S.P. on Murphy? Dead from the neck up!'*
('Arthur Daley' in *Minder*, British TV series, 1984).

space *vb American* to daydream, lose concentration or enter a euphoric state. An adolescents' expression based on the earlier **spaced out** and **spacy**.

✧*'She puts on the headphones and just starts to space.'*

space cadet *n American* an eccentric, mad or **spaced-out** person. A popular expression since the later 1970s,

which has entered British and Australian usage. The term is inspired by the expression **spaced out** and the 1950s science fiction TV series, *Tom Corbett, Space Cadet*. 'Space-case' is a synonymous term.

space-case *n American See* **space cadet**.

spaced out *adj* under the influence of drugs or behaving in an eccentric or insane fashion. A term that originated in America and spread to Britain with the drug-culture of the 1960s. The term is based on the notion of being extremely **high** and disconnected from earthly realities.

spack *adj Australian* an all-purpose term of disapproval or doubt, in use among schoolchildren in the late 1980s. The word, of uncertain origin, is used as an adjective or exclamation.

spacy, spacey *adj*
a producing euphoria or evoking a dream-like state.
✧*'Spacy music.'*
✧*'This is spacy dope.'*
b behaving in a distracted, euphoric or **spaced out** way.

spade *n* **1** a black person. The term comes from the expression 'as black as the ace of spades' and originated sometime before the 1920s. Spade has almost never been used with racist connotations; it was the word used by white devotees of West Indian culture and music in Britain in the 1950s and 1960s, notably in the title of Colin Wilson's landmark novel, *City of Spades*, published in 1959.

✧*'The spades have taken over the city dump.'*
(Caption to Robert Crumb cartoon in *Head Comix*, 1968).

✧*'A constable said to me, as he left the canteen, "I'm going to get a spade now, sarge". He punched a fist in the palm of his hand.'*
(Simon Holdaway, *Inside the British Police*, 1983).

2 *South African* a gun, in particular an AK-47 rifle.

spaghetti-eater, spaghetti-bender, spag *n* an Italian. These are derogatory terms heard predominantly in Australia, referring to immigrants. The equivalent American term is usually simply 'spaghetti'.

spam! *vb* to flood another's computing system with redundant or meaningless information. The practice is indulged in as a prank or punishment by **cyberpunks** or **net-heads**.

&'*Spamming is often doled out as punishment for behaviour that runs against the grain of net culture – corporate advertising say – or posting a chain letter …*'
(*Surfing on the Internet* by J. C. Herz, 1994).

spam! *exclamation British* an all-purpose exclamation of defiance, rejection, irritation. The word was defined on the Internet in February 1997 by *Bodge World*.

the Spanish archer *n British* a rejection (by an actual or potential lover). The phrase, originating in London speech, popular among students, and chosen as the title of a feature on UK L!VE (cable) TV in 1996, is a strained pun on 'the elbow' ('el bow' being the mock Spanish).

&'*She gave him the Spanish archer.*'

spank, spanking *n British* a beating, usually a severe one. An example of menacing understatement in working-class slang, as used by police and criminals. The term is used only slightly more lightheartedly as a euphemism for sadistic games or flagellation.

&'*D'you want your spankin' now?*'
(*The Firm*, British TV play, 1989).

&'*Taking part in spanking sessions.*'

spank the plank *vb* to play the guitar. A piece of musicians' jargon.

spanner *n British* an unfortunate, weak individual, misfit. The term became a popular phrase among adolescents in the early 1990s following its use on the BBC TV comedy, *The Mary Whitehouse Experience*. It probably originated as a schoolboy variation of **spastic**, **spasmo**, perhaps blended with **prannet** or **prannie**.

spare *n British* an unattached, and presumably available female or females. A condescending, slightly archaic term, usually forming part of a phrase such as 'a bit of spare'.

&'*What's it like down the dancehall? Plenty of spare?*'

spare *adj British* out of control, furious. The word usually in the form 'go spare' has been in use since before World War II. It derives from the notion of excess.

spark *vb British* to incite someone to anger or violence. A vogue term among British adolescents in the 1990s.

&'*It's easy to spark him, but I wouldn't do it if I were you.*'

sparkler *n British* a lie, especially a welcome or helpful lie. A working-class Londoner's expression.

&'*So he wouldn't say the old sparkler?*'
(Simon Holdaway, *Inside the British Police*, 1983).

sparklers *n pl* jewels, gems. A long established term from the lexicon of thieves, counterfeiters, **spivs**, etc.

spark out, sparko *adj, adv British* fast asleep or completely unconscious. The expression is now a mainly working-class colloquialism; it was formerly a rustic expression evoking a dead fire or extinguished candle. Sparko is a variant form heard in the 1980s.

&'*He had three or four drinks and went spark out.*'

&'*She's been sparko for the last hour or so.*'

spark up *vb* to light a cigarette or **joint**. The phrase, becoming widespread in the 1990s, also occurs as a request or demand to '*spark me up*'.

sparrowfart *n* dawn. A jokey euphemism inspired by 'cock-crow'. The phrase became obsolete in Britain in the 1930s but remained in use in Australia, and was revived in Britain in the late 1960s by the cartoon strip *The Adventures of Barry McKenzie*, published in the satirical magazine *Private Eye*. The term originally may have been a vulgarization of 'sparrow-cough', an ironic comment on the air pollution of industrial cities.

spasmo *n British* a variant form of **spastic** or **spazz**.

spastic *adj, n* (behaving like or reminiscent of) a clumsy, unfortunate, feeble, foolish or unpopular individual. A schoolchildren's vogue word in Britain from the early 1960s onwards, prompted by the publicity given to charities and other schemes to aid spastic children. The same word was used in the 1950s by adults, particularly in the armed services, and in the 1960s by schoolchildren and adolescents in the USA. The noun form is frequently shortened to 'spas' or **spazz**; the adjective altered to 'spazzy'.

ↄ'*That's an utterly spastic idea.*'

ↄ'*You can't fancy him! He looks an utter spastic.*'

spazz, spaz *n, adj* (a) foolish, clumsy, incapable (person). A version of **spastic** used by schoolchildren in Britain and the USA.

spazzmobile *n British*

a an invalid car.

b an old, decrepit or (supposedly) ludicrous vehicle.

The word has been used by schoolchildren since the 1960s.

spazz out *vb American* to lose control of oneself; become hysterical or agitated, go berserk. A teenage phrase of the 1970s and 1980s from **spastic**.

spear the bearded clam *vb Australian* to have sex with a woman. A colourful vulgarism dating from the 1960s, possibly originating in **surfie** parlance. Like many similar expressions it was introduced to a British audience via the cartoon strip *The Adventures of Barry McKenzie*, by Barry Humphries and Nicholas Garland running in *Private Eye* magazine in the late 1960s and early 1970s.

specky *adj Australian* neat, clever. The fairly common term has been defined by Internet slang enthusiasts as 'nifty'. 'Specking' was an old term for mining for gold, but the connection is not proven.

spee *n British* a friend, comrade. In an article in the *New Statesman and Society*, Maria Manning reports this word, of unknown origin, as being used in school playgrounds in the UK in February 1990.

speed *n* an amphetamine drug. The word was first applied in the 1960s to methedrine, a powerful stimulant. By 1968 it was becoming the generic term for all amphetamines (which literally 'speed up' the nervous system).

ↄ'*Someone suffering (and they do!) from speed hang-ups and come-downs really drags the whole scene down.*'
(Letter to *Oz* magazine, June 1968).

speedball *n* a combination of stimu-

lant and depressant (for example heroin and cocaine) for injection. The word arose among hard-drug users of the 1940s in the USA. By the 1980s it was also used to designate various other concoctions including those taken orally or by inhalation.

speedfreak *n*

a a user of **speed** (amphetamines).

b by extension, a person who behaves as if over-stimulated.

speeding *adj* under the influence of **speed**.

spencer *n South African* an attractive young female.

spesh *adj British* exceptional, excellent. A characteristic clipping of the standard sense for adolescent usage in the 1990s.

ↄ'*They were hoping for something really spesh.*'

ↄ'*You're my spesh mate.*'

spewing *adj Australian* extremely irritated, agitated, flustered, etc.

spick, spic *n, adj* a person of Latin origin, an Italian or Hispanic. This highly offensive racist term parodies the speech of such people in the catchphrase 'no spick da Inglish'.

spiel *vb, n* (to give) a speech or talk, particularly a glib or persuasive patter. The expression may also encompass hard luck stories or lengthy excuses. The word originated in the 19th century, deriving from the German *Spieler* (player) or *spielen* (to play) as applied to card-sharps, hence hucksters, fast-talkers, etc.

ↄ'*He gave me this long spiel about how he was so overworked he wouldn't have time to help.*'

spiffed, spiffed-up, spiffed out *adj* dressed smartly. These expressions, now popular among American teenagers, are like the British **spiffy**, spiffing and **spiv**, a derivation of the early-19th-century British dialect term 'spiff', meaning dandy. Spiffed itself was heard in British speech until the 1930s and spiffed-up until the 1960s.

spifflicate *vb British* to beat up, thoroughly defeat. A nursery word of the 1950s, spifflicate was coined in the 18th century (the first recorded use was in 1785 meaning to confound). It does not derive directly from any standard or dialect term, but is an invention imitating latinate multisyllabics.

spiffy *adj* smart, dapper, impressive. A word which, since it is in mainly middle- and upper-class use, is generally considered colloquial rather than slang. It derives from the archaic 19th century dialect word 'spiff' (noun and adjective) meaning a dandy or smartly dressed, which is also the origin of **spiffing** and **spiv**.

§'*That's a spiffy little car you've got.*' (Recorded, Sloane Ranger, London, 1982).

§'*You're the best looking cop in the place.*'
'*Well, you look pretty spiffy yourself.*' (*Legwork*, US TV series, 1987).

spike *n* a hypodermic syringe. An item of drug addicts' jargon dating from the 1950s. The word was used to denote an ordinary needle for many years before that.

§'*When I put a spike into my vein, Then I tell you things aren't quite the same.*'
(Lyrics to 'Heroin', written by Lou Reed and recorded by the Velvet Underground, 1967).

spike up *vb* to inject onself (with a narcotic).

spill *vb* to confess, own up or reveal a secret. A racier version of the colloquial 'spill the beans', the term is typically used in an underworld context, often involving informing on associates or otherwise betraying a confidence.

§'*I couldn't get him to spill.*'

spill one's guts *vb* to confess or reveal information. An elaboration of **spill** or 'spill the beans' used particularly by or about criminals.

§'*They put a little pressure on him and the creep spilled his guts.*'

spin *n British* a search (of a home or other premises), typically by police. A derivation of **spin (someone's) drum**.

§'*I think we'd better give their gaff a spin.*'
§'*He's about due for a spin.*'

spin (someone's) drum *vb British* to make an official search of someone's house, in the jargon of the police force. **Drum** is one's home, spin provides

the play on words, referring to the spinning of a drum in a fairground lottery. In 1990 spin has been heard as an expression synonymous with 'up yours', and is accompanied by a one-fingered gesture.

spit *n American*
a rubbish, nonsense, **shit**.
b nothing at all, **zip, zilch**. In both cases spit is a euphemism for **shit**, usable in fairly polite company or in the mass media.

§'*What did he tell me? – he told me spit.*'
(*Macgruder and Loud*, US film, 1985).

spit *n See* **the big spit**.

spit-spot *adj* fine, excellent, as it should be. A euphemistic version of **shit-hot**. (The expression is used by the fictional Mary Poppins in the film of the same name, as a synonym for 'chop-chop'.)

spit the dummy *vb Australian* to lose one's temper, express one's anger. The image is presumably that of a baby expelling its pacifier in a fit of rage.

spitting feathers *n British* exhibiting extreme enthusiasm or agitation. The colourful phrase is heard particularly in armed-forces' usage and probably evokes the squawking of a frantic bird. It is one of many bird-related images in colloquial speech such as **drop off the perch/twig** and 'sick as a parrot'.

spiv *n British* a disreputable, flashy male, typically one who lives by shady dealing rather than orthodox work. This word had existed in the jargon of racetrack habitués and petty criminals since the late 19th century, but came into its own after World War II, when it was adopted by the press and public to designate the touts, black marketeers and 'wide boys' who flourished in the late 1940s and early 1950s. Spiv is an alteration of 'spiff', an archaic dialect word for dandy which also gave rise to the adjectives **spiffy** and **spiffing**.

§'*He* [the marketing manager] *may be a little spiv but he certainly brings in the customers.*'
(Recorded, language-school owner, York, 1981).

§'*Max Kidd was an ex-plumber made good; a total spiv down to the last camel hair in his coat.*'
(TV review by Kate Saunders, *Evening*

Standard, 17 May 1989).

splash the boots *vb* to urinate. A euphemism heard, particularly among drinkers, in Australia and Britain since the 1960s.

ᗌ*'Excuse I, but could you direct me to the bathroom. I've got to splash the boots.'*
(*The Wonderful World of Barry McKenzie*, cartoon strip by Barry Humphries and Nicholas Garland, 1966).

splatter movie *n* a film in which many characters are killed off graphically and bloodily for the entertainment of the audience rather than the furtherance of the plot. The first film to earn the title was *The Texas Chainsaw Massacre*, 1974. It is a journalistic generic term. *See also* **snuff movie**.

splay *n American* marihuana. A word of obscure origin used by schoolchildren and students.

splay *vb American* to have sex. The vulgarism invariably applies to male sexual activity. It has been recorded among Californian pornographers and prostitutes and may have originated as photographers' jargon, *'splay-shot'*, employing the standard word (itself a Middle English clipping of 'display').

splendid *adj British* excellent. The standard word was borrowed as a vogue term of approbation by British teenagers in the early 1990s.

splib *n American* an Afro-Caribbean person. A racist epithet heard since the 1980s, of uncertain origin, although it is claimed unconvincingly to be a blend of **spade** and liberal. It is more likely to be a nonsense **bebop** or **jive-talk** coinage.

splice *vb British* to have sex with.

ᗌ*'I spliced his woman while he was on bar duty downstairs.'*
(*Harry's Kingdom*, British TV film, 1986).

spliff *n* a cannabis cigarette, **joint**. The word which is of uncertain derivation, originated in Britain or the Caribbean in the 1960s. In the USA it designates a joint containing both cannabis and tobacco, in the 'English style'.

split *vb* to leave. A piece of American slang that came to Britain in the **hippy** era, it is a shortening of the earlier beatnik term 'split the scene' (from the notion

of separating oneself from a group or gathering).

split *n British* a female. This highly derogatory term is short for *'split arse'* and was popularized by the comedian Roy 'Chubby' Brown.

ᗌ*'Lesley Morris, 23, said sailors called the WRENS sluts, slags, splits and turtles.'*
(*The Daily Mirror*, 4 February 1997).

splosh *n British* **1 a** a woman, women in general.
b sex.
Both these related uses are vulgarisms popular in London working-class usage since the late 1970s, often in the form 'a bit of splosh'.
2 money. This sense of the word is now almost obsolete, but existed in the vocabularies of cockneys, **spivs** and their upper-class imitators in the 1950s.

spod *n British* **1 a** smegma.
b seminal fluid. A vulgarism in use among adolescents in the 1990s.
2 a clumsy, dimwitted or socially unacceptable person. The term is applied to school misfits by fellow pupils and was reported to be in current use at Eton in the September 1989 issue of the *Tatler*. In the 1990s it has been defined as a synonym for **narg** in Oxbridge student slang.

spod *vb British* to engage in meaningless activities when supposedly doing a job. Posted on the Internet by *Bodge World* in 1997.

spoilers *n pl South African* buttocks. An appreciative term applied to females by males by analogy with the rear of a sports car. **Hatchback** and **sixteen-valve** are other automotive terms applied to females.

spon *n British* **1** money. A clipped form of **spondulicks**, fashionable in certain circles in the late 1980s.

ᗌ*'We're going to have to go round to Bill's to pick up some spon.'*
(Recorded, self-employed decorator, London, 1988).
2 a fool. This childish term of abuse or disparagement has been obsolete since the early 1960s. It was almost certainly a survival of the early 19th century use of **spoon** to mean simpleton (see the verb form of **spoon**).

spondulicks, spondoolicks

n money, wealth. A lighthearted term which was obsolescent by the 1960s (having originated in the USA in the 1850s), but which like other synonyms for money was revived in the 1980s (compare **rhino**, **pelf**, etc.). It originated as a learned witticism, borrowing the Greek term, *spondylikos*; pertaining to the *spondylos*, a seashell used as currency.

spooge *n American* sperm. The word is an invention based on the standard term and used by children and adolescents.

spook *n American* **1** a black person. The reference is either an ironic one to the subjects' black colour (as opposed to the white of spectres) or to their 'haunting' of certain locations.

2 a spy, secret agent. This usage may be a simple reference to unseen 'ghosts' or may derive from the fact that many World War II agents were recruited from the Yale secret society the 'Skull and Bones'.

↳*'In 30 beautifully crafted novels during the past 16 years, he* [Ted Allbeury] *has revealed details from the real world of spooks that have been struck from others' memoirs.'*
(*Sunday Times*, 17 December 1989).

spooky *adj British* eccentric, crazy. An item of youth slang recorded in the 1990s which may have originated in black usage.

↳*'That Linda's well spooky.'*

spoon *n British* a person from a privileged and/or wealthy background. The word became fashionable among young London City financial traders in the early 1990s, used either contemptuously or teasingly by working-class speakers of their upper- (or sometimes middle-)class fellows. It derives from the expression 'born with a silver spoon in one's mouth'.

spot (someone) *vb American* to pay for, lend or advance money to. This usage of spot probably derives from gambling or sports jargon in which it means to specify odds or conditions.

↳*'Spot me a twenty will you?'*

spout off *vb British* to talk volubly, pompously or out of turn. A post-1970 version of the earlier 'spout' or the more literary 'spout forth', suggesting the outpouring of words. Spout off, like 'mouth

off', is usually used intransitively and is more disparaging than the earlier forms.

spring (someone) *vb* to obtain someone's release from captivity or prison, either as a result of a legal manoeuvre or, more commonly, by assisting their escape.

spring for *vb British* to pay for. A raffish expression used typically by working-class speakers indicating willingness or alacrity.

↳*'OK, keep your hand in your pocket, I'll spring for the grub.'*

sprog *n British*
a a child, offspring.
b a novice, new recruit.
The first sense of the word has become widespread in colloquial speech since the mid-1970s, the second is limited to the context of institutions including the armed services. The exact origin of the word is obscure, but it is reasonable to assume that it is a blend of 'sprout' and 'sprig'. Sprog also means head in Australia.

sprout *n British* a child. The word is a middle-class 1990s' alternative to the earlier **sprog** and more recent **howler** and **wowler**.

sprung *adj American* infatuated. An item of teenage slang applied to someone who 'has a crush' on another.

↳*'I could tell she was totally sprung on me.'*

spud *n* **1** a potato. This universal slang term has been recorded since the 1840s. A 'spud' was a small narrow spade (from Middle English *spudde*, dagger, itself from Italian *spada*, sword) of the sort used to dig up potatoes.

2 a stupid person. This use of the word, recorded among schoolchildren, may be an alteration of **spod** rather than a reference to the potato.

spud-bashing *n British* potato-peeling, especially as a punishment.

spunk *n*
a spirit, vim. The word has been recorded in this sense since the 18th century. Most authorities derive it from *spong* a Gaelic word for tinder (itself from Latin *spongia*, sponge), hence 'spark'.
b semen. The idea of life-force, 'vital spark' or spirit in the male context led to

spunk being used in this sense (as was 'mettle' in archaic speech) from the 19th century onwards.

2 *Australian* a **spunk rat**. The shorter form, usually referring to males only, has become increasingly widespread since about 1987.

spunk rat *n Australian* a sexually attractive young person. The phrase is based on **spunky** in the sense of spirited, influenced also by **spunk** in the sexual sense.

↳*'But it's all right for her, she's got a whole smorgasbord selection of classic spunk rats.'*
(Kathy Lette, *Girl's Night Out*, 1989).

spunky *adj* spirited. The adjective is derived from the noun **spunk**.

squaddie *n British* an army private. The word is either from 'squad' or from the archaic 'swaddy', a bumpkin.

square *adj, n* (a) conventional, conservative or unfashionable (person). Since the 17th century square has been used to mean honest, reputable or straightforward. The modern sense of the word dates from the 1930s **jive talk** of black jazz musicians in Harlem, New York. (Cab Calloway's 1938 lexicon defines a square as an 'unhip person'.)

↳*'To be square is to be dull, middle aged, old fashioned. To be square is to be not with it.'*
(*About Town* magazine, June 1962).

squarehead *n* **1** a German. The North and East Germanic peoples supposedly have squarer heads than Anglo-Saxons. This supposition was reinforced in the World Wars by German military hairstyles (and in World War II by helmets).

2 a **square**.

squashed *adj American* drunk. A rare **preppie** term, in the tradition of employing synonyms for 'destroyed' (**smashed**, **wrecked**, etc.) to mean intoxicated.

squat *n American* (a) **shit**. From the action of squatting down to defecate. By extension, squat, a word used typically in country areas of the USA, is also used to mean nothing, or a worthless thing. **Doodly squat** is an elaboration.

↳*'It ain't worth squat.'*

squawk *vb* **1** to complain noisily or raucously.
2 to inform (on someone). A rarer synonym of **squeal**.

squawk *n* a radio message. A term used especially by police or military personnel for a short burst of information coming into a walkie-talkie radio or field telephone.

squawker *n British*
a a walkie-talkie as used by police or security guards.
b a mobile telephone.
Both terms were commonly used from the early 1990s.

squeak *n British* a young naive teenager. A term applied by older adolescents to would-be members of the fashionable circles of London in the late 1980s. The term usually refers to a girl of the sort previously designated as a **teenybopper**.

↳*'The bouncer gets a bit heavy demanding ID from a group of squeaks who look like they have given their babysitter the slip.'*
(*Evening Standard* magazine, May 1989).

squeal *vb* to inform (on someone). The usage arose in early 19th century dialect, spreading to underworld argot first in Britain and subsequently in the USA.

squeegee *n British* an amateur windscreen cleaner. The word is a trademark name for a sponge.

squeeze *n* **1** *American* a girlfriend or boyfriend, sweetheart. The word is inspired by the squeeze of an embrace and is often heard in the form **main squeeze** (which has the added meaning of 'most important person').

2 *British* money, cash. The word often has overtones of hard-earned or reluctantly paid.

squid *n American* a **swot**. A high school and campus term, perhaps suggesting 'oiliness'.

squidgy *n British* an amateur windscreen cleaner. **Squeegee** is an alternative form.

squiff *n Australian*

a a drunkard.

b a drinking bout. Both terms are back formations from the adjective **squiffy**.

squiffy *adj* (slightly) drunk, merry or inebriated. An inoffensive, lighthearted word suggesting slight disorientation, squiffy has been in use since the 19th century.

squiffy doo *adj British* dubious, doubtful, suspect. A middle class expression heard in the 1980s. It derives from the notion of 'askew', 'out of true' expressed by the adjective **squiffy**.

squillion *n British* a hyperbolically huge number. A pseudo-nursery word, typically used by condescending or ingratiating journalists in teenage magazines, that became a teenage vogue term of the 1980s.

✎ *'Last week we got thirteen squillion letters asking which video company brought out Star Trek IV, our fab giveaway. Well it was CIC. So there.'*
(*Just Seventeen*, teenage girls' magazine, December 1987).

squirly *adj American* restless. A word with rustic overtones which is probably a form of 'squirrely' (which itself was not only a metaphor, but formerly a punning synonym for **nuts**).

✎ *'Come on, don't be so squirly.'*
(*The Hunter*, US film, 1980).

✎ *'He [Richard Ford] tends to throw plenty of relish onto his words, especially ones like "squirly" which you do not often hear, even in Bath (it means "restless").'*
(*Independent*, 8 July 1989).

squirt *n* 1 an insignificant, diminutive and/or impudent and annoying individual (usually male). This figurative use of the standard word dates from the mid-19th century. It is not certain whether it originated in British or American speech.

2 *British* money, cash, funds. The term is probably based on the idea of a squirt of oil lubricating the system, or a squirt of spirit igniting a fire or engine.

✎ *'We just need a bit more squirt and we can go ahead with our plans.'*

the squirts *n* a case of diarrhoea. An alternative form of **the squits**.

squit *n British* an insignificant, small and/or irritating person. The word is a variant form of the synonymous **squirt** and has been heard since the 1880s.

✎ *'There are 5 squits, 9 snekes, 19 cribbers, 2 maniaks, 2 swots.'*
(*Back in the Jug Agane*, Geoffrey Willans and Ronald Searle, 1959).

(the) squits, squitters *n* a case of diarrhoea. Both words are onomatopoeic.

✎ *'No thanks, love, olive oil doesn't agree with me.'*
'Gives you the squits, does it, Grandad?'
(*Nice Work*, David Lodge, 1988).

squizz *n New Zealand* a look, glance.

✎ *'Let's take a squizz at the new place.'*
(*Brain Dead*, New Zealand film, 1993).

stabber *n British* a male homosexual. The term was applied to supposedly active **gay** males as opposed to the passive **stooper**. The pejorative, supposedly humorous designations were in use among heterosexual Fleet Street/Wapping journalists in 1990. Stabber is said to be a shortening of **suit-stabber**.

stack *adj* 1 excellent, fantastic. An ephemeral teenage vogue word of 1987, used as an exclamation of approval or delight. The term spread from the language of hip-hop in New York to London aficionados.

✎ *'Just forget about using the word mega to express your delight. The latest expression is stack!'*
(*Daily Mirror*, September 1987).

2 the word like many similar vogue terms is also used to mean its virtual opposite: inferior, negative, 'no way', etc.

✎ *'Stack (meaning: not at all, i.e. Samantha Fox is immensely talented ... STACK!) is now the only logo to be seen with (we know, we invented it).'*
(Advertisement in *I-D* magazine, November 1987).

stack *vb* to crash (a vehicle), destroy. The word is used in this sense throughout the English-speaking world.

stacked *adj* having large breasts (of a woman), 'well-endowed'. A male term of approbation which is now offensive to most women. The expression, first popular in the USA, is a shortening of 'well-stacked'.

✎ *'When one person is important and the other person is stacked and/or well-hung.'*

(Sub-heading in P. J. O'Rourke's *Modern Manners*, 1983).

stacking *n British* ingesting several tablets of **ecstasy** at once. A piece of ravers' jargon from the **acid house** subculture of the early 1990s.

stack some zees/zeds *vb* to sleep. The phrase, originating in the USA, is synonymous with the more common **cop/bag some zees**.

stains *n pl British* unfashionable, tedious individuals or **swots**. The term of contempt was in use among university students in the late 1980s. It is usually a synonym of **anorak**; unbeknown to most users it is short for 'wank-stain', i.e. a despicable nonentity.

ᗷ '"*Stains" are "replete with acne and anoraks".*'
(*Evening Standard*, 16 June 1988).

stalk *n*

a an erection or penis. This British and Australian sense of the word principally survives in the phrases **stalk fever** and **stalk-on**.

b effrontery (in a male), cheek, **bottle**. A rare working-class usage (recorded in *The Signs of Crime, A Field Manual for Police* by Deputy Assistant Commissioner David Powis, 1977).

stalk fever *n Australian* lust (experience by a male), priapism. The expression was in use until the late 1960s but is now rare. It derives from the slang sense of **stalk** as erection or penis.

stalk-on *n* an erection. A vulgarism heard since the 1950s.

stallion *n* a stud. the term has been used figuratively in this way since the 14th century.

stand, stand-on *n* an erection.

stand-up *adj American* honourable, reliable, steadfast. A term of (mainly male) approbation or admiration in such clichés as 'a stand-up guy'. It derives from the notion of 'standing up for someone' or being willing to 'stand up and be counted'.

ᗷ '*It's funny that priest going AWOL. I always thought he was a real standup guy.*'
(*V*, US TV film, 1983).

stanky *n American* an unstylish person. A more recent variation of **skank(y)**, **scang(e)y**.

starkers *adj British* naked. A characteristic public school or Oxbridge version of 'stark naked' which has become a common colloquialism. (It is sometimes elaborated into **harry-starkers**.)

star-spa *n British* a friend, fellow gang member. The term was used as an indicator of solidarity by adolescent gang members and as a term of address. It was recorded in use among north London schoolboys in 1993 and 1994.

stash *vb* to hide, put (away). The word, which spread from America to the rest of the English-speaking world at the turn of the century, was probably originally a blend of 'stow', 'store' and 'cache'. It was formerly often spelled 'stache'.

state *n British* a mess, disaster. This word became an all-purpose vogue term in London working-class speech of the early 1970s. The original notion of 'to be in a (bit of a) state' was transformed so that state (**two-and-eight** in rhyming slang) came to refer to the individual rather than the situation.

ᗷ '*He looks a right old state, doesn't he?*'

static *n American* criticism or hostile interference. A respectable slang term inspired by the standard sense of electrical disturbance or interference. The suggestion is typically of opposition from various quarters that threatens to frustrate a scheme.

ᗷ '*We're getting a lot of static from higher up now that the powers that be have been informed.*'

stay loose *vb American* an alternative version of **hang loose**.

steamboats *adj British* drunk. A lighthearted term of uncertain derivation. It may have something to do with the use of a name such as 'Steamboat Bill', possibly in a lost rhyming-slang expression.

ᗷ '*He was completely steamboats by midday.*'

steamed *adj American* furious. A 1980s variation on the more generalized 'steamed-up'.

steamer *n British* a bout of heavy

drinking. Often heard in the phrase '*on/in a steamer*'.

steamers *n pl British* gangs of muggers who enter a shop, train compartment, etc. en masse and overwhelm their victims with some force. From the colloquial 'steam (in)'; move forcefully and quickly. The term arose in London in 1985 among black street gangs.

steaming *n British* the activity of **steamers**.

↳'*Steaming is very modern, a term for mob-handed theft often by joeys, young criminals.*'
(James Morten, *Independent*, 23 December 1988).

steaming *adj British* **1** an otherwise meaningless intensifying adjective, almost invariably used in the now dated expression '(a) steaming nit' which was briefly popular in the early 1960s.
2 drunk.

↳'*You've only had two cans and you're steaming.*'
(*Red Dwarf IV*, BBC comedy, 1994).

stem *n* a knife, particularly when carried or used for criminal purposes. An item of New York street slang that spread to other English-speaking areas in the early 1990s.

step off *vb American* **1** to opt out, desist, stop.
2 to lose one's temper, become aggressive. Both usages originated in black street slang and may refer to the figurative sense of stepping off the straight and narrow, or the physical sense of leaving a path, sidewalk, escalator, etc., in order to launch an attack.

step on *adj* to adulterate, cut (a drug). The term has been used by drug users and dealers since the end of the 1960s, particularly in reference to cocaine or heroin; occasionally it is used of amphetamines, but not of cannabis or other organic substances.

↳'*You expect a cut at this level, but this stuff has been stepped on by a gang of navvies in hob-nailed boots.*'
(Recorded, cocaine user, London, 1982).

step on one's dick *vb American* to make a blunder. A term used particularly in the context of the workplace or the armed forces.

↳'*Just give those guys some slack and*

pretty soon one of them will step on his dick.'

stepford *adj American* dully conformist, android-like. The term is inspired by the 1975 cult movie *The Stepford Wives*, depicting a suburb in which women are turned by men into placid robot *hausfraus*. **Devo** carries the same connotations.

stick *n* **1** a **joint**, **reefer** (cannabis cigarette). A term which was fairly widespread among smokers of the drug (**beatniks**, prisoners, etc.) until the mid-1960s, when joint and **spliff** largely supplanted it.
2 *British* chastisement, physical or verbal punishment. Originally implying a literal thrashing with a stick or cane, then generalized to any violent assault, the expression is now used, especially by middle-class speakers, to encompass verbal abuse, denigration or nagging.

↳'*You've done nothing but snipe at me since I got home – what have I done to deserve all this stick?*'
3 *British* a police truncheon.

↳'*His trousers weren't done up and his shirt tails were flapping and he had a stick in his hand.*'
(Police officer, *Inside the British Police*, Simon Holdaway, 1983).
4 an excessively serious, dull or repressed person.
From the notions of rigidity, woodeness and chastisement.
5 a pickpocket's associate or decoy. *See* **sticksing**.

sticker *n British* an unsolved crime, case left open in the jargon of the police.

the sticks *n* the countryside, a rural or provincial place, the 'backwoods'. Originally in the USA and Canada a humorous reference to trees, the term had spread to other English-speaking areas by the 1950s.

↳'*He lives way out in the sticks somewhere – Ongar I believe.*'

sticksing *n British* pickpocketing. A term used in black criminal circles.

stick the nut on (someone) *vb British See* to **nut**.

sticky *adj Irish* connected with or frequented by the official, as opposed to Provisional, IRA. The word is used in the

London Irish community, as well as in Ireland, to designate certain pubs.

sticky *n British* a liqueur. The word (like the object in middle-class and 'society' usage) is occasionally extended to refer to sweet wines.

sticky beak *n Australian* a 'nosy parker', an interfering or inquisitive person. The common phrase evokes a bird poking its bill into something viscous.
⬥'*If he hasn't told you … it's certainly not my place.*'
'*And what is your place? Head chook in the sticky beak brigade?*'
(*Neighbours*, Australian TV series, 1988).

sticky-beak *vb Australian* to poke one's nose into other people's affairs. A back-formation from the noun.

stiff *vb* **1 a** to kill. An Americanism based on the noun form of the word (meaning corpse). Since the 1960s the term has been heard in raffish or underworld parlance in Britain.
b *British* to attack physically, trounce.
2 to take financial advantage of (someone); cheat, rob or extort from.
⬥'*She tried to stiff me for the fare.*'
3 to 'stand someone up', snub (someone).
⬥'*I don't like getting stiffed like this.*'
4 to flop, fail. A term used typically in the context of the entertainment business or sports.
⬥'*Their last single stiffed.*'
The first four senses of stiff are related to the noun form denoting a corpse.
5 *American* to aggress, treat harshly. The term is from 'stiff-arm', a version of 'strong-arm'.
6 *British* to have sex with. A working-class vulgarism.

stiff *n*
a a corpse. An unsentimental term inspired by rigor mortis and originating in American slang in the 19th century.
b a rigidly conventional, dull or serious person.
c an individual, particularly one to be pitied.
⬥'*I'm just a poor working stiff.*'
d *American* a hobo, vagrant.
e a drunk.
f a flop or failure.
Most of the many sub-senses of stiff are related to the idea of corpse-like rigidity

or absence of life. The notion of 'stiff-necked' also plays a part in the case of sense **b**.

stiffie *n British* **1** an erection. A jocular term heard principally among middle class males, although women also employ the word.
⬥'*Got a stiffie? Wear a Jiffi!*'
(Promotional T-shirt logo for Jiffi condoms, 1985).
2 an invitation card. The term describes the engraved social missives exchanged in traditional, **Sloane Ranger** and **yuppie** circles.

stikkie *n South African* a sweetheart, girlfriend. Recorded as an item of Sowetan slang in the *Cape Sunday Times*, 29 January 1995.

still *n British* a foolish, clumsy person, misfit. In this sense the word is a jocular substitute for **Benny**. It is explained by the story that British armed-forces personnel stationed on the Falkland Islands were forbidden by their officers to refer to the inhabitants as Bennies, so replaced the offending word with 'still' on the grounds that they were 'still (i.e., nonetheless) Bennies'.

sting *n American*
a a confidence trick, fraud or act of extortion.
b a scheme devised in order to trap or entrap criminals.
Both senses of the word (popularized by the film of the same name released in 1973) imply an elaborate arrangement with a sudden 'pay-off'.

stinking *adj British* **1** a short form of 'stinking rich'.
2 extremely drunk, **stinko**.

stinko *adj* drunk. This word (abbreviation from 'stinking drunk', with the addition of the lighthearted adjectival suffix -o) is almost obsolete in British speech except in upper-class usage.

stinky finger, stink-finger, stinky pinky *n* manual stimulation of a woman's genitals. The phrases are typically used by adolescent males.

stir *n* prison. Various Romany (gypsy) words such as *stardo*, *steripen*, dealing with the concept of imprisonment gave rise to 'start', an 18th-century-British slang term for prison, and later, in the mid-19th century to stir, which has remained one of the most widespread words for jail or imprisonment in all English-speaking areas, particularly in the phrase **in stir**.

stir crazy/happy *adj* psychologically disturbed as a result of confinement in prison (**stir**). The notion is sometimes extended to encompass a sense of frustration or hysteria felt in any institutional surroundings. (The less common form **stir happy** is now dated.)

stitch *n American* something funny, a source of hilarity. A typically middle-class and **preppie** term derived from the expression 'to be in stitches'.

ᖡ'*Oh Jean-Marie, you're a stitch!*'
(*Planes, Trains and Automobiles*, US film, 1987).

stitch (someone) up *vb British*
a to concoct false evidence against someone, to **frame**. A piece of underworld and police jargon from the 1950s which penetrated popular speech in the 1980s.

ᖡ'*Openshaw, 41, allegedly said on his arrest: "I'm being stitched up." The trial goes on.*'
(Court report, *Daily Mirror*, 14 July 1989).

b to outmanoeuvre comprehensively, defeat by devious means, render helpless. This extension of the previous sense of the phrase became a vogue term of the early 1980s.

ᖡ'*Leched over by managers, stitched up by agents, girls in the music biz have traditionally paid a high price for succumbing to the lure of lurex.*'
(*Ms London* magazine, 4 September 1989).

stitch this! *exclamation British* an exclamation of defiance said while hitting someone, particularly when butting them in the face. The phrase is used by 'toughs'.

stoat *n British* the vagina. A vulgarism in use among adolescents in the 1990s and listed in *Viz* comic in 1994.

stodge *n British* suet pudding or dumplings as served (and often loathed) in school canteens. A children's term heard since the 1950s.

stogie *n American* a cigar. An old but surviving nickname which is from Conestoga, Pennsylvania, where covered

wagons were manufactured. The driver of the wagons smoked cheap cigars which became known as stogies.

stoked *adj* excited, thrilled, stimulated. The usage probably arose in the surfing community in the US, whence it spread to other English-speaking areas. It is now popular, particularly in Australian speech. It derives from the image of a furnace being 'stoked up' or perhaps from the words 'stunned' or 'choked'.

ᖡ'*Beth's really stoked you're going to give her away.*'
(*Neighbours*, Australian TV soap opera, 1993).

stomp *vb* to beat up, attack and/or defeat. A usage which was part of the Hells Angels' lexicon, referring to the ritual punishing of enemies. The word was adopted by **hippies** in the USA and Britain in about 1968.

stompers *n pl American*
a the American term for **brothel creepers**, thick-soled shoes as worn by teenagers in the 1950s.
b heavy workboots or cowboy boots.

stomp it *vb British* to hurry, go. The term is used by devotees of dancefloor and **rave** culture.

ᖡ'*On Tuesday we stomped it down to the Limelight.*'

stoned *adj* intoxicated by narcotics or alcohol. In the 1960s stoned proved the most popular of a number of synonyms employing the metaphor of punishment or damage (**wrecked, destroyed, blitzed**, etc.). It became the standard term to describe the effects of cannabis in particular. This use of the word originated in the argot of jazz musicians and bohemians in the USA in the 1940s.

ᖡ'[Richard Neville] *suggesting making love when stoned with stereo headphones on both partners, playing the first Blind Faith album.*'
(*Oz* magazine, February 1970).

stone me! *exclamation British* an exclamation of surprised realization or astonishment. The working-class expression has been heard less often since the late 1960s. It enjoyed a vogue in the late 1950s and early 1960s especially in TV comedy dialogue.

stone the crows! *exclamation British* an exclamation of astonishment, heard particularly in working class speech in the 1950s.

stonewall bonker *n British* a certainty. This raffish phrase has been in use since the 1930s and is still heard in certain underworld and working class circles. Unbeknown to most speakers, the 'bonk' or 'bonker' in question was originally the blow of an auctioneer's gavel in closing a deal. 'Stonewall' is an elaboration of 'stone' in the colloquial sense of absolute(ly).

stonker *n British*

a something stunning, devastating or powerful. This invented word should logically be derived from a verb 'to stonk' which is however unrecorded in modern slang although **stonkered** and **stonking** are. In origin the term is probably influenced by words such as 'stun', 'clunk', 'bonk'.

b *See* **stonkers**.

stonkered *adj*

a drunk.

b destroyed, out of action, devastated or exhausted. (For the probable derivation see **stonker**.)

stonking *adj British* extremely. The word is an all-purpose intensifying adjective, usually in place of more offensive terms. Mainly in working class and armed service usage, stonking was in vogue in the late 1980s. It probably post-dates **stonker** and **stonkered**.

stony, stoney *adj* penniless. A shortened form of 'stony broke', heard especially in Australia.

stooge *n British* an innocent stand-in at an identity parade. A term from the jargon of police, from the standard colloquial senses of menial, dupe, etc. (The word stooge, which appeared in the USA in the 19th century, is said to be a corruption of 'studious' or 'students').

↳ *'They don't think they can get the I.D. parade off the ground. I don't know if there are problems with the stooges, or what.'*
(*Flying Squad*, British TV documentary, March 1985).

stoolie *n* an informer. A shortening of **stool pigeon**.

stool pigeon *n* an informer. In North America in the 19th century pigeons were tied to wooden frames (known as stools) as decoys to lure game birds. The expression was later applied to a cardsharp's human decoy and later still to a police informer or spy. By World War I the use of the phrase had spread to Britain where it was adopted by crime fiction and the real underworld. The term is commonly shortened to **stoolie**.

stooper *n British* a male homosexual. The word is applied to a supposedly 'passive' **gay** male. The pejorative term (its counterpart is **stabber**) was reportedly in use by Wapping journalists in 1990.

stormer *n British* an impressive, admirable thing, person, etc.

storming *adj British* excellent, exciting. One of many vogue terms in adolescent usage, particularly among devotees of dancefloor, techno and jungle music.

stoshious, stotious, stocious, stoshers *adj British*

a drunk.

b silent, tight-lipped, discreet. This mysterious word can be traced to the 19th century and was thought by some authorities to be extinct by the 1930s. It survives however in jocular usage. The term is either a mock-latinate invention or a corruption of a dialect word for waterlogged or muddy.

stouch, stoush, stoosh *adj British* presumptuous, arrogant, overbearing. The fashionable term, recorded among adolescents in the 1990s, was defined by *Touch* magazine in September 1993 as 'acting like your shit don't stink'. The origin of the expression is uncertain.

stoush *n Australian* a brawl. The word is probably a descendant of lost dialect terms for 'uproar' or 'strike'.

S.T.P. *n* a hallucinogenic drug claimed to be much more powerful than L.S.D. which it resembled in its effects. It originated in **hippy** circles in the USA in about 1970 and was named after a well-known engine oil additive.

straight *n* 1 a heterosexual, particularly heard in the language of homosexuals.

2 a conventional person, someone who does not take drugs or ascribe to 'counterculture' values. A term from the language of drug abusers and countercul-

ture members which was a 'buzz word' of the later 1960s.

ᗷ*'Would you say Hunter Thompson was afraid of anything in particular? "Ah … Straights".'*
(Ralph Steadman, *I-D* magazine, November 1987).

3 a cigarette (as opposed to a **joint**). A now dated cannabis users' term in wide currency in the 1960s.

ᗷ*'If you give me a straight I'll roll us something for the journey.'*

4 *South African* a bottle of alcoholic liquor. Recorded as an item of Sowetan slang in the *Cape Sunday Times*, 29 January 1995.

straight *adj* **1 a** honest, not criminal or corrupt.

ᗷ*'You couldn't bribe or compromise him because he was straight. However, he was also naive.'*
(Former detective, *Inside the Brotherhood*, Martin Short, 1989).

b heterosexual. (In the first two subsenses, the slang alternative in British English is **bent**.)

c not under the influence of drugs, not a drug-user.

ᗷ*'I've been straight for three days.'*
ᗷ*'Don't offer her any, she's straight.'*

The word has been used to mean 'upright' or honest, fair, scrupulous, etc. for more than a century. The sub-senses above, not always used approvingly, have been established in the 1950s and 1960s. The following sense is in ironic contrast.

2 restored to one's desired state of drunkenness or drugged euphoria.

ᗷ*'Just one shot and I'll be straight again.'*

straightened-out *adj* bribed, suborned or otherwise corrupted. A euphemism in underworld and police usage.

ᗷ*'Their tip-off was supported by a tape recording of a bugged conversation involving an American criminal, referring to "a top man" who had been "straightened out in Scotland Yard".'*
(*Observer*, 16 August 1987).

straighten (someone) out *vb* *British* to bribe or corrupt. A euphemistic term in use among criminals and police.

ᗷ*'We wanted to straighten out a magistrate, but we couldn't get to any of them in time.'*

strain the potatoes *vb* Aus-

tralian to urinate. The phrase is a survival of a 19th century British euphemism inspired by the resulting colour of water. In Britain, the phrase 'strain the greens' was heard before the 1950s.

stramash *n Scottish* a noisy disturbance. A dialect term first recorded in the 19th century and still in use.

strangler *n British* an enviably lucky person. A shortening of 'jam-strangler' (which gives **jammy**). The term is rare, occurring in armed-service slang in particular.

strap *n American* **1** a gun, in the argot of street gangs and other criminals.

ᗷ*'I'm hoping to hook up with some more straps …'*
(*Gang War*, Channel 4 TV documentary, August 1995).

2 a humorous synonym for **jock**.

strapped *adj* **1** short of money, broke. A short version of the phrase 'strapped for cash'.

2 armed with a gun. In this form the word has crossed the Atlantic eastwards so that by the early 1990s criminals in the UK were referring to '*going strapped*'.

strapping *n American* carrying a firearm.

strawberry *n American* a prostitute who sells sex for drugs.

ᗷ*'All the vice girl victims [of a Los Angeles serial killer] were known as strawberries – American slang for hookers who trade sex for drugs.'*
(*Sunday Mirror*, 3 March 1989).

stray *n British* a heterosexual who associates with **gays**. The probably ephemeral term was defined in the *Modern Review*, June 1994.

streak *vb* to run naked in a public place. The term came to prominence along with the fad in the early 1970s. It began as a form of mass or individual protest and was quickly taken up for the purposes of fun and/or exhibitionism.

ᗷ*'She streaked across the campus for a £5 bet.'*

streak *n* **1** a run through a public place while naked. From the verb.

ᗷ*'Some guy did a streak at the Test Match.'*

2 *British* a person of ectomorphic build. A

mildy pejorative term, sometimes expressed more brutally as **long streak of piss**, invariably said of males. **Long streak of misery** denotes a tall, thin and morose or excessively serious individual.

street *adj American* 'streetwise' or having 'street credibility'. A term of approbation originating in black argot of the 1970s.

ϧ*'She's OK, she's street.'*

street apple *n See* **road apple**.

street pizza *n See* **road pizza**.

stressed-out *adj British*

a unwell, uncomfortable, discontented. In secondary school playground slang this use of the colloquialism is generalized from its normal sense to incorporate almost any negative feeling.

b inferior, inadequate. A further generalization of the original sense of the word, used as a vogue term by teenage gang members in the late 1990s.

stretch *n* 1 *American* a tall, thin person. A term of cheerful mockery. The equivalent of the British **streak**, or rather, the nickname 'Lofty', since stretch is often a term of address.

ϧ*'How're y' keeping, Stretch?'*

2 a period of imprisonment. This underworld term originally referred specifically to one year's incarceration; it is now generalized to mean a term of whatever length.

ϧ*'He did a four-year stretch.'*

strides *n* trousers. The word has existed in raffish usage since the turn of the century; it is now heard in Britain and Australia.

ϧ*'Fair crack of the whip! Lady, I'm not taking me strides off for anyone.'* (*Bazza Pulls it Off*, cartoon by Barry Humphries and Nicholas Garland, *Private Eye*, 1970).

ϧ*'This stupid bloke called me a freak, and kept asking why I was wearing "fucking moody strides". I went home really annoyed and thought right, I'm not having this.'* (*Caron Geary, Time Out*, 26 July 1989).

stripe *n* a scar, especially as the result of a knife or razor slash.

stroke book *n American* a pornographic or semi-pornographic publica-

tion. 'Stroke' in this context refers to male masturbation.

stroll on! *exclamation British* a cry of dismissal or disbelief. The phrase usually conveys indignation.

strong it *vb British* to behave aggressively, presumptuously or excessively. A working class expression heard particularly in the London area in the 1980s. It is a variation on the colloquial phrases 'come on strong', 'come it strong', 'go it strong'.

ϧ*'You been strongin' it again down our boozer?'*

stroppy *adj British* obstreporous, aggressive, uncooperative. The word is an alteration of obstreporous, perhaps via a fanciful deformation of the word such as 'obstropalous'. Stroppy appeared in the 1940s. Various deformations of obstreporous have been recorded since the 18th century.

strumping *n British* promiscuous behaviour (on the part of a female). This back-formation from 'strumpet' was used in the TV comedy *Birds of a Feather*.

strung out *adj*

a tense, nervous and upset.

ϧ*'She was strung-out inside, nibbling there on her lower lip and smoking one cigarette after another'.*

b suffering from the effects of an illicit drug, or from withdrawal.

ϧ*'Strung out on morphine'.*

The first, now widespread, usage derives from the second which is a drug user's slang expression dating from the 1950s.

strung up *adj* a less common variant of **strung out**.

stubbies *n pl Australian* short trousers, as worn by men.

stubby, stubbie *n Australian* a small bottle of lager.

stuck on *adj British* arrested, 'booked' (for instance for a traffic violation) in police and criminal jargon of the 1990s.

stud *n* a sexually active, powerful, potent male. Only slang when applied to men as opposed to (real) animals, the term often indicates a degree of approval or admiration, even if grudgingly. In black American street parlance the word was sometimes used in the 1960s and 1970s simply to mean 'guy'. There seems to be no female equivalent that stresses sexual power rather than degeneracy.

✧ *'The eternal teenage sexual paradox is that boys who "put it about" are called "studs" by their admiring friends but girls who do the same are "slags".'*
(17-year-old public-school pupil, *Harpers and Queen* magazine, August 1978).

stud-muffin *n American*

a an attractive male.

b a male seducer (of females). In both senses this elaboration of **stud** was heard from the early 1990s, first among adolescents and later among adult speakers.

studsley *n American* a smart, dapper or sophisticated male. A term of address between males which seems to have originated as a black elaboration of **stud** in the sense of 'fine fellow'.

stuff *vb* 1 to have sex with. The verb has very seldom been used in the active or transitive form since the 19th century (and it was never common). The abusive exclamation 'get stuffed' is its main legacy.

2 to dismiss, throw away, destroy. This adaptation of the sexual sense of the word, or of the expression 'stuff it up your arse!' has proved useful as a non-taboo means of conveying strong rejection, impatience, etc. It often occurs in the all-purpose exclamation 'stuff it!'

✧ *'Stuff the wedding!'*
(Anti-royal-wedding slogan written on walls and reproduced on badges in Britain 1981).

Stuff is currently fashionable in media, sporting and raffish circles with the sense of defeat or humiliate.

stuffed *adj British* ruined, abandoned, 'kaput'. A brusque but fairly inoffensive derivation of the verb **stuff**.

stuff up *vb Australian* to blunder or fail. A euphemistic version of **screw up**.

✧ *'I really stuffed up, didn't I?'*
'You sure did.'
(*Flying Doctors*, Australian TV series, 1995).

stumblebum *n American* a vagrant or derelict, literally a stumbling, helpless tramp. The word is now usually general-

ized to denote an inept, incompetent or clumsy person.

stunned mullet *n Australian* (the facial expression of) a gormless, slow-witted or stupid person. The phrase is common in Australian speech and was used in Parliament by the Premier Paul Keating, among others, when describing the supposedly vacuous expression of political opponents.

styler *n British* a person who attempts to be stylish and fashionable, a 'trendy'. This vogue term of the later 1990s is invariably used by adolescents to indicate derision or disapproval. It is probably influenced by the black American concept of **styling**.

styling *n American* showing off, behaving ostentatiously. A vogue term in the 1990s in hip-hop and dancefloor culture which originated more than thirty years earlier in black American speech. *Compare* **profiling, vogueing.**

substance *n British* cannabis; hashish or marihuana. A euphemism adopted by users of the drug from the legalistic description (employed particularly in sentences such as *'Certain substances were taken away for analysis'*).

✧ *'Got any substance?'*

suck *vb American* to be repellent, inferior or worthless. An extremely common term of strong disparagement or denigration in American English, suck is both a euphemism for **fuck** and an amalgam of notions contained in words such as 'sucker', **cocksucker**, etc.

✧ *'To say something or someone "sucks" is to use America's most common term of disparagement ... The term suck originally had as its prefix the word for a male hen.'*
(Simon Hoggart, *Observer* magazine, 1989).

sucked in *adj Australian* fooled, duped, 'conned'. A racier version of 'taken in'.

sucker-punch *vb American* to attack from behind or without warning, to land an unfair or surprise blow. From the colloquialism 'sucker'; a dupe or easy victim.

✧ *'You're a witness, Alex. I just came here to talk to you and Fruitfly sucker-punched me.'*
(Jonathon Kellerman, *Over the Edge,*

1987).

suck face *vb American* to kiss. An adolescent euphemism on the lines of **swap spit**.

suck-hole, suck-holer *n Australian* a sycophant, toady or other contemptible person. A more recent variant on the ancient notion expressed by 'bum-sucker', **arse-licker**, etc.

suck off *vb* to perform fellatio (on someone).

sucky *adj American* tasty, sweet.

suds *n American* beer; a 'college-boy' word.

suedehead *n British* a member of the youth subculture of the later 1970s who resembled **skinheads**, but wore their hair slightly longer, hence this epithet.

suffer! *exclamation Australian* a cry of defiance, challenge or contempt as used by schoolchildren and adolescents from at least the late 1970s.

sugar daddy *n* a wealthy older protector and lover of a young woman. Judith S. Neaman and Carole G. Silver in their *Dictionary of Euphemisms* (1983) date this expression to the 1920s and derive it from American rhyming slang 'sugar and honey': money. While this is possible, sugar had been a term of endearment or a metaphor for affection or luxury for many years before.
  ⮑'*I see Natalie's managed to find herself another sugar daddy.*'
  (Recorded, magazine editor, London, 1986).

suit *n* a bureaucratic functionary, *apparatchik*, corporation man. The term appeared in the 1980s and is used contemptuously or dismissively by working people and, especially, the fashionable young. In 1989 and 1990 the elaboration, 'empty suit' was heard, underlining the notion of anonymity. In the jargon of advertising agencies in Britain in the late 1980s the word is applied (neutrally rather than pejoratively) to the account executives who deal face to face with clients as opposed to the creative staff who dress casually.
  ⮑'*What the hell is that?*'
  '*Some suit from the mayor's office.*'
  '*Just in time for the evening news.*'
  (*Cagney and Lacey*, US TV series, 1982).

suit-stabber *n British See* **stabber**.

sunnies *n pl Australian* breasts.

supercharge *n American* one of many nicknames for **crack**.

supersonic *n British* tonic (water). The rhyming slang term was used by bar staff and drinkers in the 1990s sometimes in conjunction with **Vera Lynn**.

surfboard *n* 1 a flat-chested girl. An expression popular among pubescent schoolgirls.
2 a promiscuous girl or woman. From the image of supine acquiescence and the sexual connotations of **ride**.

surfie *n Australian* a member of a 1960s sub-culture based only partly on surfing. They were the contemporaries of British **mods** and contributed (like their American surfer counterparts) many colourful expressions to modern Australian slang.

surf the crimson wave *vb American* to menstruate. The phrase occurs in adolescent speech, and was featured in the 1995 US film *Clueless*, where it may have originated.

suss *adj British* suspect or suspicious.
  ⮑'*I thought it was a bit suss when they offered it to me for nothing.*'

suss *n British* 1 'knowhow', 'savvy'. A usage in currency since the 1970s, based on **suss (out)**.
  ⮑'*I wouldn't worry about her, she's got a lot of suss.*'
2 also **sus** suspicion. The much criticized Vagrancy Act under whose provisions (young) people could be arrested for 'loitering with intent (to commit an arrestable offence)', was known as 'the sus law'. 'On sus(s)' refers to being taken into custody on suspicion.

suss (out) *vb British* to discern, discover, deduce or realize. A vogue expression among **beatniks** of the early 1960s (in the longer form); it had probably been in sporadic use before that. At first the phrase usually meant to perceive someone's true nature or intentions, it is now a fairly common colloquialism, often meaning no more than 'work out'.
  ⮑'*I think I've managed to suss out a way round this.*'
  ⮑'*She sussed him out in five minutes.*'

sussed, sussed out *adj British* (of a person) well-adjusted, adapted to the circumstances, self-aware or self-reliant. This more recent derivation of the verb **suss out** is based on the notion of **suss** in the sense of 'knowhow'. In the 1980s it is often in the form 'well-sussed'.

↳*'This time, man, we've got it all sussed … all the albums gonna be made here, first class jobs.'*
(Record bootlegger, *Oz* magazine, February 1970).

↳*'A post punk skatezine that's aggressive, sussed and caustic about skating UK.'*
(*Mail on Sunday*, *'Biz'* magazine, June 1987).

swag *n* loot, booty, stolen goods. In this sense the word originated among itinerants and thieves in the early 19th century. It had earlier denoted goods or possessions when carried. The word is ultimately related, via dialect, to 'sway' and 'swing'. In modern usage swag is usually used humorously.

swallow *n British* a drink of alcohol.
↳*'Shall we go for a quick swallow?'*

swap spit *vb American* to kiss, particularly referring to **French kissing**, in the jargon of teenagers and students.

swayve *n, adj* (the quality of being) sophisticated, elegant, refined. The word is a mock-affected mispronunciation of 'suave' (along the lines of the earlier British **fabe** and **mode**).
↳*'He's got loads of swayve, hasn't he?'*
↳*'She's très swayve.'*

sweat *vb American* to put pressure on (someone).
↳*'No-one's sweating you to join a gang.'*
(Los Angeles policeman to street-gang member, ITV documentary, August 1989).

sweat *n British* a brutish, unsophisticated individual. The term sometimes denotes someone engaged in menial tasks and is heard in working-class speech in the 1990s.
↳*'No you don't ya dozy sweat!'*
(*Blonde Fist*, UK film, 1994).

sweat-hog *n American* a physically repugnant person. A term of contempt or abuse typically applied by males such as college students to females.

sweaty *n British* a disco, dance or frenetic party, in the 1990s jargon of Oxbridge students.

swedish *n American* (of a male or males) **gay**. A euphemistic or humorous term, inspired by the popularity of Swedish porn and pin-up material.

sweet *adj British* excellent, acceptable. A vogue term of approval among adolescents in the later 1990s.

sweet F.A./Fanny Adams *n British*
a nothing at all, **fuck-all**.
b a pitifully small amount. In 19th century naval slang, 'Fanny Adams' was tinned or cooked meat, a sardonic reference to a girl of the same name who was murdered and dismembered in 1867. The name was later matched with the initials of **fuck-all** and used euphemistically in its place.

swell *n British* a well-off single woman in **yuppie** argot of the late 1980s. An acronym ('single woman earning lots of lolly') also recalling the dated description of a fashionable 'person-about-town'.

swift *vb British* to give false evidence, 'bend' the evidence. A piece of police slang. A police officer who is adept at this practice is known as 'a (bit of a) swifter'. 'Swift it' is another form of the verb.

swift *adj*
a *American* alert, clever. Now heard among various social groups, the word has been used in this sense in black adult speech since before World War II.
↳*'The kid's not too swift.'*
b *British* devious, cunning, deceitful. This usage has occurred in London working-class and underworld speech since the 1950s.
↳*'I thought it was a bit swift when they left me standing holding the gear.'*

swing *vb*
a to behave in an uninhibitedly hedonistic way. This use of the word, originating in jazz and rock music circles, was popular in the 1960s; by the early 1970s it had been narrowed to its current sense (see sense **b**).
b to engage in 'liberated' and/or sophisticated sexual practices, particularly wife-swapping and group sex. The word is a

catch-all euphemism for promiscuity, originating and still mainly heard in the USA.

swing both ways *vb* to engage in sexual relations with both men and women. A euphemism heard in the USA since the later 1960s.

swinger *n*

a a sophisticated hedonist, fashionable pleasure lover. This quintessential 1960s term evolved quickly into sense **b** (see below).

b a euphemism for a practitioner of wife-swapping or other types of sexual adventure. This American term was adopted by 'adult' magazines, contact agencies, etc. in the 1970s as an acceptable designation for adultery and/or promiscuity, etc.

swinging dick *n American* a variant form of **Big Swinging Dick (BSD)**.

↳'*I ain't no swinging dick. I know better than to fuck with the wrong people.*' (*Heaven's Prisoners*, US film, 1995).

swish *n American* a **gay** or effeminate male. A mildly pejorative term, inspired by the actual or supposed flouncing of the individuals in question. It is used by **gay** as well as heterosexual commentators.

switched-on *adj British*

a fashionable, alert. A vogue term of the 1960s equating with **turned-on**.

b excited either sexually or by drugs. A short-lived sense of the phrase, current in the mid to late 1960s.

switch-hitter *n* a bisexual person.

The phrase is used in the USA and Australia; it is from baseball jargon in which it denotes an ambidextrous batter.

sword *n See* **pork sword**.

swot *n* a diligent, hard-working student. A pejorative term which has survived from the mid-19th century into modern usage. It is an alteration of 'sweat' and like that word may be used as noun or verb. In the USA there are many terms used enviously or contemptuously of conscientious fellow-students, among them **grind**, **pencil-geek**, **squid** and **wonk**.

↳'*But finally armed with a baseball bat, he intervenes when a bullying sports-star humiliates a kindly swot, preaching a sermon that converts the whole institution.*' (*Observer*, 29 May 1988).

(the) syph, siff *n* syphilis.

syphon the python *vb See* **siphon the python**.

syrup (of figs) *n British* a wig. A piece of approximate rhyming slang invoking a laxative remedy.

↳'*Got a groovy syrup of figs, Oliver Cromwell make.*' ('Surgery' written and recorded by the Gymslips, 1981).

↳'*That is not a syrup.*' '*I've got a tenner here says that's a syrup.*' (*Only Fools and Horses*, British TV comedy series, 1989).

t...

T *n* marihuana. An alternative form of **tea**.

tab *n* 1 a tablet, specifically a table or dose of the drug LSD, from the jargon of users in the late 1960s and 1970s.

🌿'*A tab a day keeps reality at bay.*'
(Graffito, Canterbury, 1970).

🌿'*Well, the one that stopped me from doing acid forever was when I dropped seven tabs. I completely lost my mind and went to Muppetland – the whole trip lasted for about six months.*'
(Zodiac Mindwarp, *I-D* magazine, November 1987).

2 *British* a cigarette. The word, probably from 'tab-end', appeared in northern British usage before World War II but since its use in *Viz* magazine from the 1980s has been used in other regions, mainly by adolescents.

🌿'*He pulls out the tab ... he's trying to get the packet into his top pocket ...*'
(Jack Docherty's talk show, Channel 4 TV, March 1997).

tache, tash *n British* a moustache.

tack *n* 1 squalor, shabbiness, seediness, bad taste. A back-formation from the earlier Americanism, **tacky**. 'Tackiness' is an alternative noun form. (Very often tackiness refers to the quality, tack to the evidence thereof.)

2 *British* cannabis. A term used by adolescents particularly in the northeast of England during the 1990s. It may be a shortening of 'tackle' as used to mean equipment or heroin.

tack attack *n British* a fit or bout of bad taste. A witticism based on **tack** and **tacky** heard among fashionable 'young professionals' and media circles in London in 1988 and 1989. (**Rack attack** and **snack attack** are other rhyming phrases.)

🌿'*Judging by the décor of his flat, I'd say he'd had a tack attack.*'

tacker *n British* a child. A northern English dialect word of obscure origin but possibly related to thumb(tack). It is occasionally heard in other parts of Britain.

tackle *n British* 1 a short form of the humorous euphemism **wedding tackle** (male genitals). Tackle alone was used in this sense from the 18th century, if not earlier.

2 heroin. An item of prison slang.

tacky *adj* shabby, seedy, inferior, vulgar. An American term which had existed in Southern speech in the USA since the late 19th century, before being understood (in the early 1970s) and partially adopted (in the late 1970s) in Britain. The origin is not in 'tacky': sticky or viscous, but in a dialect word for an inferior horse, hence a shabby yokel. 'Tack-e-e-e' is the last word and final verdict in the main text of Kenneth Anger's *Hollywood Babylon* (1975), an exposé of showbusiness scandal.

taco-bender *n American* a Mexican or other person of Hispanic origin. A derogatory term coined on the lines of **spaghetti-bender** or **bagel-bender**. (A taco is a Mexican fried bread pancake.)

tacos *n pl American See* **toss one's cookies/tacos**.

tad *n, adj, adv* a small or slight amount, a little, slightly. An American expression now fairly widespread in British use, especially in phrases such as 'a tad hungry'. In American English tad has been used to mean a small boy since the late 19th century. It is probably from earlier British dialect, in which it is related to 'toad' or 'tadpole'.

tadger *n British* penis. A vulgarism of unknown origin (probably from a lost dialect verb) used for many years in the north of England and revived by students, alternative comedians, etc. in the 1980s. **Todger** is an alternative modern version.

tag 1 *vb, n* (to spray) a graffiti artist's personalized signature or motif. The word has been a colloquialism for a person's name for many years. It was adopted by teenage graffiti artists in the 1970s in the USA, whence it spread with the craze.

🌿'*If you go to one of the big guys of hip hop art and they have not heard of*

your tag, you are nothing. But if they've seen it and like it then you are bad.'
(15-year-old graffiti artist, *Evening Standard*, 11 November 1987).

2 *vb* **a** *American* to hit/knock out.

b to kill, especially by shooting. In the latter sense the term was used in the cult US 1993 film *Reservoir Dogs*.

tagger *n* a graffiti 'artist'. From the use of **tag** to mean one's name or pictorial signature.

taig, teague *n British* a Roman Catholic. A derogatory term used by Protestants. The nickname used to denote an Irishman in general and derives from an English rendering of the Gaelic proper name *Tadhg*. (It is sometimes further anglicized to **tyke**.)

tail *n*

a a woman, or women, seen as sexual objects. The word usually occurs in phrases such as 'a bit/piece of tail', tail being a euphemism dating from the 14th century for the less polite **arse** or **ass**.

b (particularly in Caribbean or **gay** usage) a man or men as sex objects.

↳*'She spend all her time chasin' tail!'*
(Recorded, Trinidadian student, London, 1988).

tail-end *n British* penis. Confusingly, since the term usually denotes the backside, it may also, particularly in the northeast of England, refer to the male member.

tailpipe *n American* the anus. A US teenagers' term. This predictable use of the word ('exhaust-pipe' in British English) is possibly influenced by the car driver's experience of having another driver 'up one's tailpipe', i.e. driving too close.

Taiwan *n British* an upper second or 2.1 ('two-one') university degree. A student nickname on the lines of **Desmond**, **Pattie**, **Douglas**, etc. coined in the mid-1980s. A **made-in** is a synonym from the same source.

take a bath *vb* to suffer a financial loss or commercial setback. A piece of business jargon that has become fairly widespread. The image evoked seems to be of drenching rather than washing.

take a dive/tumble/fall *vb* to deliberately lose a boxing match or other contest. Expressions in use since the inter-war years, originating in the USA.

take a dump *vb See* **dump**.

take a leak *vb See* **leak**.

take a pill *vb American* to relax, luxuriate. The phrase was popularized by the 1992 US movie, *Wayne's World*.

take a pop (at) *vb* to attack, hit, lash out at. A phrase popular in working-class London speech in the late 1980s.

↳*'Now you're taking a pop at my business partners.'*
(*EastEnders*, British TV soap opera, 1988).

take a powder *vb* to leave (quickly), go away. A now dated expression originating in the USA in the 1920s. The powder in question refers to a laxative or stimulant medicine.

take a raincheck *vb* to accept a postponement, put something off to a future date. An Americanism which has entered international English since the mid-1970s. The raincheck in question was originally a ticket stub entitling the holder to entry to a ball game at some future date if the fixture is rained off.

take berties *vb British* to behave in a presumptuous or intrusive way. The jocular phrase, used by university students in the later 1990s, is a shortening of the colloquial 'take liberties'.

↳*'You can stay but just don't go taking berties.'*

take down *vb American* to kill or immobilize. A 'tough-guy' euphemism.

take names *vb American* act resolutely and/or primitively, chastise. The image evoked is that of an authority figure noting the names of miscreants. The phrase is often placed after **kick ass**.

↳*'Listen you're going to have to go in there and kick ass and take names!'*

take one's lumps *vb American* to suffer misfortune or harsh treatment.

take out *vb* to kill or destroy. A military euphemism which came to public notice in the USA during the Vietnam War. The term was subsequently appropriated for use in the context of crime and law enforcement.

take   the   mick/mickey/

– 385 –

michael *vb British* to mock, deride, poke fun at. These expressions are milder versions of **take the piss**. Unbeknownst to most users, they employ rhyming slang; Mickey is short for a mythical 'Mickey Bliss', providing the rhyme for **piss**. 'Michael' is a humorous variant. The phrases, like their more vulgar counterpart, have been in use since the 1940s.

take the piss (out of someone) *vb British* to mock, deride, poke fun (at). This vulgarism has been in widespread use since the late 1940s. The original idea evoked by the expression was that of deflating someone, recalling the description of a self-important blusterer as **all piss and wind**.

take the shame *vb British* to accept the blame (publicly and/or wholeheartedly) or face the criticism of one's peers. A key phrase in the playground vocabulary of London teenagers since the later 1970s. The concept is from black speech; 'shamed-up' is another derivation from the same source.

talent *n British* attractive potential sexual partners. A generic term first applied before World War II to women and men. Since the mid-1960s female speakers have also applied the word (sometimes ironically) to desirable males.
↳'*Let's check out the local talent.*'

talking-brooch *n British* police-officer's personal radio, also known as a **squawker** and **batphone**. An item of police slang recorded by the London *Evening Standard* magazine, February 1993.

talk on the big white telephone *vb* to vomit in a toilet. This colourful expression probably originated among US college students, like the synonymous 'kneel' or **pray to the porcelain god**.

talk turkey *vb* to perform oral sex. A 1980s pun on the slang usage **gobble** and the well-known colloquial American expression meaning to discuss openly (also perhaps influenced in US usage by **turkey-neck**: penis).

tall poppies *n pl Australian* 'overachievers', persons of prominence. The expression originates in the 1930s when the Lang government threatened to enforce tax laws which would '*cut off the heads of the tall poppies*'.

tamale *n American See* **hot tamale**.

tam rag *n British* a sanitary towel or tampon. A variant of **jam rag** influenced by 'tampon' and the trademark 'Tampax'.

T and A *n American*
'**tits** and **ass**'. The American equivalent of the British **B and T**, a phrase describing a visual or tactile experience of a naked woman or women. The abbreviation and the expression in full probably originated in the jargon of journalists and/or showmen.

tank *n* 1 *American* a firearm, handgun. A hyperbolic term occasionally used by criminals and law enforcers.
2 *British* a police car or van. The word is used in this way by ironic or self-dramatizing police officers. *Compare* **gunship**.

tank *vb British*
a to crush, overwhelm.
↳'*They'd all tank Tyson.*'
(Headline in the *Sun*, 28 February 1989).
b to defeat, trounce.
↳'*England are going to tank Monaco tomorrow!*'
(TV sports trailer, February 1997).
c to move forcefully and powerfully.
↳'*Tanking up and down the motorway all holiday … but Christmas itself was very quiet … very pleasant….*'
(*Biff* cartoon, *Guardian*, December 1987).
All senses of the word became popular in the later 1980s.

tanked, tanked-up *adj* drunk. A common term since the turn of the century; the shorter form is more recent. Tank up evokes the filling of a container or fuelling of a vehicle and parallels such expressions as **loaded** and **canned**.
↳'*I'll do the washing-up tomorrow if I don't get too tanked-up tonight.*'
(*Biff* cartoon, *Guardian*, 1986).

tap, tap up *vb* to borrow, or seek to borrow, from (someone). To tap meant to spend liberally in archaic slang; by the early 20th century it had acquired the second sense of solicit, borrow or obtain. The origin of the term is in the tapping of liquid from a container, reinforced by tapping someone on the shoulder to gain their attention and the later slang sense of 'hitting' someone for a loan. Tap is international English, while the form tap up is in British usage.

tap city *n, adj American* (the condition of being) penniless, broke. A humorous version of **tapped-out**.

↳ *'It's no good asking me. I'm in tap city.'*

↳ *'It's tap city the rest of this month.'*

tap-dance *n* a clever evasion, devious manoeuvre. The term, which is used all over the English-speaking world, recalls a dancer either **busking** or improvising in a difficult situation or merely executing an elegant sequence of steps.

↳ *'That was not an opinion – that was a tap-dance worthy of Fred Astaire.'* (*Hooperman*, US TV series, 1987).

↳ *'On occasions he [Harvey Goldsmith] has done as much tap-dancing, financially speaking, as Lew Grade in his Lordship's first business career.'* (*Sunday Times* magazine, June 1989).

tap-dancer *n* a person who can avoid danger by a combination of clever, if devious or dishonest actions and luck; someone able to talk themselves out of difficult situations.

↳ *'That man's a born tap-dancer; he's always out the back door five minutes before the front door's kicked in.'* (Recorded, drug dealer, London, 1988).

tapioca *adj* broke, penniless (usually temporarily). A **preppie** witticism derived from **tapped-out**.

tapped-out *adj American*

a without money, broke. A term used especially by gamblers, and more recently by adolescents. It is inspired by the very old slang use of the word to **tap**, meaning both to spend, and later to obtain money from another person.

↳ *'I'm tapped-out, Mark. American Express got a hitman out looking for me.'* (*Wall Street*, US film, 1987).

b exhausted. From the idea of being 'drained'.

tapped up *adj British See* **get tapped up**.

tapper *n British* an obnoxious or disreputable person. A vogue term recorded from junior schools from 1991. The origin is obscure but may relate to a sexual sense such as **(get) tapped up**.

tar baby *n American* a derogatory term for a black person. The racist epithet uses the previously innocuous nickname from the children's stories by Mabel Lucy Atwell.

tarbrush *n See* **a touch of the tarbrush**.

tard *n American* a fool, simpleton. A teenagers' shortening of the popular term of contempt, **retard**. The word was adopted by British adolescents in the late 1980s.

tart *n* a promiscuous, vulgar or sexually provocative woman. This modern sense of the word has gradually supplanted the older meaning which was simply a woman or sweetheart. As a term of affection (inspired by the pastry sweetmeat and reinforced by 'sweetheart'), tart was applied to women of all ages from the mid-19th century. By the early years of the 20th century it was more often used of the flighty or immoral and by the interwar years often referred to prostitutes. In modern theatrical, **gay** (where it is often used of men), cockney and Australian speech, tart is still used affectionately.

tart about *vb British* **a** to flounce about, behave archly or flamboyantly.

b to mess about, behave in a disorganized or irresolute way. Many derogatory or vulgar terms (**arse, dick, fanny,** etc.) have been converted to verbs on the same pattern.

tash *n British* an alternative spelling of **tache**.

tassel, tassle *n* a penis. An inoffensive term often used by parents and children and referring particularly to the member of an immature male. In older (pre-1950s) British usage, 'pencil-and-tassle' was a euphemism for a boy's genitals.

tasty *adj British* attractive, desirable, smart. An all-purpose term of approbation, used in working-class London speech for many years and more specifically as a fashionable word among the young in the late 1970s and 1980s.

↳ *'A tasty geezer.'*

↳ *'Love the threads. Really tasty.'*

tasty *n British* an alcoholic drink. A specific application of the wider notion of something desirable, from the popular cockney adjective.

↳ *'I know a pub that does late tasties.'* (*Only Fools and Horses*, British TV comedy series, 1989).

tat *n British* shoddy, cheap or low-quality material. A colloquialism, originally meaning specifically rags or cloth remnants, which is derived from tatter(s) and tatty (themselves ultimately descended from an old Germanic term meaning tuft).

↳ '*Liverpool comprehensive pupils would not be seen dead in "second-hand tat", however grand the previous incumbent.'*
(*Sunday Times* magazine, 30 July 1989).

ta-tas, tatters, tats *n British* a walk. A nursery term, usually used in the form 'go ta-tas', which was especially widespread in the 1950s. Pronounced 'tatters', the word probably, but not provably, derives from 'ta-ta!', meaning goodbye.

taters *n British* 1 potatoes. A short form most often heard in London and the south of England.

2 *see* **do one's nut/taters etc.**

taters (in the mould) *adj British* cold. This authentic cockney rhyming-slang expression has survived in its shortened form to the present day. It is now common in 'respectable' jocular speech and is usually thought by users to be merely a shortening of 'cold potatoes'.

↳ '*It's a bit taters out there, I can tell you.'*

taties *n pl British* potatoes. A variant form of **taters** more often heard in Scotland and the north of England.

tats, tatts *n pl* 1 a *Australian* teeth, especially false teeth.

b *British* dice. Both senses of the word are now rare; the first probably post-dating the second. The origin of the term is obscure but may imitate the clattering of the objects in question.

2 another form of **ta-tas**.

3 tattoos.

tatters *n British See* **ta-tas**.

tax *vb* to **mug** or steal from someone, leaving them with a proportion of their money. A miscreants' jargon term for partial robbery, recorded among street gangs in London and Liverpool since the late 1970s.

taxi-cabs *n pl British* (a case of) **crabs**; an infestation of body lice. The rhyming-slang phrase has fallen from use since the mid-1960s.

t.b. *adj American* loyal, faithful. This abbreviation of 'true blue' was in use among adolescents in the 1990s and was featured in the 1994 US movie *Clueless*.

↳ '*You don't have to worry about her, she's t.b.'*

↳ '*A t.b. buddy.'*

T.B.A. *n, adj American* to be avoided. An item of **preppie** code similar to the British **Sloane Ranger** term N.S.I.T. ('not safe in taxis') but extended to refer to things and situations as well as people.

tea *n* marihuana. Tea has been a nickname for herbal cannabis since the early years of the 20th century. Originally an Americanism, the term derives from the close resemblance in all but colour between the two substances. By the mid-1960s tea was a dated word restricted to older speakers, having been supplanted by such synonyms as **pot**, **charge**, **shit**, etc. **Teaed-up**, in the sense of intoxicated by marihuana, survives in teenage use. *See also* **T** *and* **vitamin T**.

teaed-up, tea'd-up *adj American* high on marihuana. A (mainly middle-class) teenagers' term which preserves the otherwise obsolescent **tea** as a euphemism for cannabis.

teague *n British* an alternative spelling of **taig**.

teahead *n* a marihuana smoker. An outdated and transitory term from the early 1960s, soon supplanted by **pothead**.

tea-leaf *n British* a thief. A well-known item of rhyming slang in use since the end of the 19th century. It also occurs in Australian speech and is occasionally heard as a verb.

team *n* a street gang. Like **firm** and **crew**, the usage evokes the notion of camaraderie and united effort.

tear-arse, tear-arse around/about *vb British* to rush about or otherwise behave hastily and recklessly. The image evoked is of activity so violent that it would tear the bottom out of a vehicle or of one's clothing.

tearaway *n British* a wild, reckless (usually young) person. This previously obscure term, which had referred to a 'tough-guy' or **mugger** since the turn of the 19th century, was popularized as a useful epithet for unruly youths or 'juvenile delinquents' in the early 1960s. It is still heard in colloquial usage.

tear off a piece *vb* to have sex. A phrase denoting seduction or sexual achievement from the male point of view. The expression is American or Australian and dates from the end of the 19th century. (The use of 'tear off a strip' with this sexual sense has been recorded in Britain.) The unromantic image evoked is that of tearing a piece of meat off a carcass for consumption.

tear one off *vb* to succeed in seduction, have sex. A less common version of **tear off a piece**, and like that expression used mostly in the USA and Australia.

technicolour yawn *n* an act of vomiting. An Australian expression of the early 1960s, popularized in Britain by the *Barry McKenzie* comic strip by Barry Humphries and Nicholas Garland.

ted, teddy boy *n British* a member of a youth cult of the 1950s characterized by a particular style of dress (a long drape or waisted jacket worn with **drainpipe** trousers and thick crepe-soled **brothel-creeper** shoes) and music (jitterbug from about 1948, rock 'n' roll from 1956). Teddy boys, mainly working class in origin, combined a rough simulacrum of Edwardian dress (hence their name: they were sometimes jocularly referred to as **Edwardians**) with the adoption of American teenage hairstyles and music. As a living subculture, the ted phenomenon was virtually over by about 1963, but many of the original adherents and younger imitators have perpetuated the style which greatly influenced later fashions.

tee, tee-tee *n American* urine, urination. A nursery term in use among adults. It may be an alteration of **pee**, **pee-pee** or the initial of the term **tinkle**.

teenybopper *n* a lively, fashionable teenager or pre-teenager. The word, originating in the USA sometime in the mid-1960s, has often been used in a condescending or derogatory sense in the 1970s and 1980s. (When used approvingly or neutrally in the 1970s, the term was often shortened to **bopper**.) The expression is composed of a diminutive form of teen(ager) and **bop**, to dance or behave enthusiastically.

↳*'The Doors are a chance for all the little teenyboppers in the States to think they're digging something avant garde.'*
(Mike Ratledge of the Soft Machine, *Oz* magazine, February 1969).

telephone *n See* **talk on the big white telephone, trombone** and **dog (and bone)**.

telly-spud *n British* a jocular synonym for **couch-potato**, heard in the 1990s among adolescent speakers. **Sofa spud** is an alternative form.

tent-pole *n* an erection.

thicko, thickie *n British* an unintelligent, slow witted person. Common terms, especially among children and adolescents, derived from the colloquial use of 'thick' to denote cloddish, 'dense'.

↳*'I'm not some blinkin' thickie, I'm Billericay Dickie and I'm doin' very well.'*
('Billericay Dickie', recorded by Ian Dury, 1977).

thing *n* a synonym for **scene, kick, vibe** or **trip** in the sense of main activity, preferred ambience. This item of raffish or **hip** usage (originating in the USA, probably in the 1940s) has become a well established colloquialism in such phrases as '*it's not really my thing*'.

third leg *n* the penis. A variant of **middle leg**.

thrape *vb British*
a to perform energetically and at full capacity.
b to defeat (an opponent). The word seems to have originated in Midland and East Anglian dialect and is now used predominantly by middle-aged speakers.

thrash *n* **1** a wild celebration, dance or party. In this sense the word has been used since before World War II.
2 a variety of very fast 'heavy metal' music of the late 1980s, in the jargon of rock journalists and aficionados.

threads *n* clothes. A usage which originated in the black-influenced **jive talk** of the 1930s in the USA. Like many similar Americanisms, it was imported into Britain and Australia with the youth culture of the 1960s. If used today the term is generally self-consciously **hip**, humorous or ironic.

↳*'Wide-boy or spiv, personified in Oliver*

Schmitz' film by Panic, an unprivileged South African black in loud threads and two-tone shoes.'
(*Independent*, 12 January 1988).

the threepenny bits *n* diarrhoea. A rhyming expression for **the shits**. **Tray-bits** and **tom tits** are alternative versions; all are especially popular in Australian speech.

throat *n American* a **swot**, in **preppie** jargon. This is one of many synonyms used by US adolescents for a tedious, conscientious and/or unpopular fellow-student; **grind**, **squid** and **pencil geek** are others. This term probably derives from '*cut-throat (competitor)*'.

throne *n* a lavatory, toilet pedestal. A humorous synonym widely heard since before World War II and still in use. (A 'potty throne' was a device formerly used for toilet training.)
✎'*He can't come to the phone right now – he's on the throne.*'

throne room *n* a lavatory, toilet. A humorous pun playing on the euphemism **throne** for toilet pedestal and the room used by a sovereign for giving formal audiences.

throttle pit *n Australian* a toilet. A vulgarism inspired by several expressions using the verb **throttle** as a synonym for defecate.

throw, throw up *n, vb* (to) vomit. Throw is a short form of synonyms such as throw up, **throw one's voice**, etc.

throw a Bennie *vb British* to lose control of oneself, become flustered or furious. The phrase, heard in the late 1990s, employs **Bennie** in the sense of a slow-witted or confused individual.

throw a flaky *vb British* to lose control of oneself, lose one's temper. This phrase has been heard since the 1960s, particularly in Scotland and the north of England.

throw a mental *vb American* to lose control of oneself, lose one's temper. A teenage and **Valley Girl** term of the early 1980s, the phrase with its variant form, **chuck a mental**, has become popular among British and Australian schoolchildren.
✎'*I totalled the car and Mom threw a mental.*'

throw a wobbly/wobbler *vb British* to suddenly behave irrationally or to have a temper tantrum. This phrase has become popular in Britain since the end of the 1970s, but dates from the 1950s. Its exact derivation is unclear, but may reflect simply an attack of shaking or quivering, or alternatively refer to throwing or bowling a ball in an erratic and confusing arc, or to the loss of control when a wobbling wheel comes off a wagon or a bicycle for example.
✎'*She's been very up and down lately. She threw another wobbly a couple of days ago.*'
(Recorded, London, 1988).
See also **wobbler, wobbly**.

throw one's voice *vb Australian* to vomit. One of many colourful synonyms originating in Australia in the late 1950s. Since the 1970s the expression is often shortened simply to **throw**.

thumb *n See* **on the thumb**.

thumbsucker *n British* an immature weakling, baby.
✎'*I ain't followin' a bunch of thumbsuckers – you want to run a national firm, friend, you put your arse in gear behind us.*'
(*The Firm*, British TV play, 1989).

thumper *n Scottish* an erection.

thumping, thump-up *n British* a beating, physical attack. Since the 1950s these have been terms in use in the school playground and among street gangs and thugs: the second version is a more recent and racier alternative.
✎'*Bar-room fights, a thump-up in a dance hall, a vicious war like Vietnam.*'
(Pete Townshend of the Who, *Rave* magazine, February 1966).

thunder-bags *n pl Australian* male underpants. A jocularism drawing the analogy with explosive flatulence or defecation, more often encountered in the expression **thunderbox**.

thunder-bowl *n British* a toilet. A variant of **thunderbox** used by predominantly middle-class speakers.

thunderbox *n* 1 *British* a toilet. The word was originally applied particularly to a commode, in the colonial period. It was later extended, especially in middle-

and upper-class usage, to a small privy and later any lavatory.

2 *American* a **ghettoblaster**.

tick *adj British* excellent, attractive. This all-purpose vogue term, heard especially among young black speakers in the late 1990s, usually indicates admiration of someone's appearance or physique. Although it is the Afro-Caribbean pronunciation of 'thick', the word more probably refers to a tick as a mark of approval.

tick *n British* **1** a smaller, and often younger, school pupil, usually one considered insignificant and irritating. A traditional public-school term which is still heard today, it likens the person to the parasitic insect.

2 hire purchase, short-term credit. Tick meant 'credit' in post-17th-century slang. It has survived mainly in the phrase 'on tick'.

ticked off *adj* annoyed, irritated, angry or resentful. A politer form or euphemism for **pissed-off**, heard especially in the USA.

↳*'Thank you guys, but Mork's not here and I'm too ticked off to go anywhere.'*
(*Mork and Mindy*, US TV comedy series, 1981).

ticker *n* one's heart. Ticker was first slang for a clock or fob-watch then, by analogy, the heart.

↳*'Oh my dicky ticker!'*
(Catchphrase from the British TV comedy, *'Allo 'Allo!*).

ticket *n British* a would-be **mod**. Ticket, like **face**, first denoted a singular person or individual, hence one of the fashionable crowd. In 1964 the term began to be applied derisively to less sophisticated emulators of the mod elite; tickets typically wore parkas, garish T-shirts and cheap sports shoes. The word was last heard in 1966.

tickle *n British*

a a hint.

b an inkling.

c a minor success or sign of future success.

d a mild expression of interest.

All these closely-related sub-senses of the word are well established in working-class speech and commercial jargon. They derive from the use of tickle to de-

note the sensation felt when a fish nibbles at a bait.

tickle the ivories *vb* to play the piano.

tickle the pickle *vb* (of a male) to masturbate. A humorous coinage in imitation of the more widespread **jerkin' the gherkin**, mainly heard in Britain and Australia.

ticky-tacky *n American* shoddy, inferior material(s). This light-hearted expression (related to **tacky**, which has survived and flourished), was popularized by its use in the song 'Little Boxes', written by Malvina Reynolds and sung by Pete Seeger in 1960.

tiddly, tiddlywink *n British* **1** a drink. A piece of rhyming slang dating from the 19th century and still heard in the early 1960s referring invariably to alcohol. The well known adjective tiddly is derived from this.

2 a Chinese person. London rhyming slang for **chink**.

tiddly-dum *adj British* tedious, dull, boring. An imitation of bored humming, synonymous with but rarer than **ho-hum**.

tie off *vb* to bind one's limb in order to raise a vein in which to inject narcotics. An addicts' term.

tie one on *vb* to get drunk. Like its synonym **hang one on**, this phrase was a 1930s Americanism, now heard in other English-speaking areas. The precise etymology of these expressions is not clear, but probably conveys the image of attacking a quantity of liquor or the burden resulting from its ingestion.

tiger's milk/sweat *n* very strong alcoholic drink. These terms date from the colonial era and are not yet quite obsolete. 'Tiger's milk' is also the brand name of a type of white wine.

tight *adj* **1** mean, stingy, miserly. Now a common colloquialism rather than slang, this usage originated in the USA in the early 19th century. The image evoked is of someone who is 'tight-fisted'. A modern elaboration is **tight-arsed**.

2 tipsy or drunk. The word was first used in this sense in the USA in 1843, being adopted almost immediately in Britain. The word evokes someone full of or bulging with alcoholic liquid.

3 *American* very friendly, close.

✎'*Me and Harry been tight since we were kids.*'

4 *American* excellent, skilful. A generalization of the use of the term in musicians' jargon, in which it signifies closely co-ordinated.

tight-arse, tight-ass *n* 1 a mean, miserly person. This sense of the word is more common in British usage than the following sense. The term has existed, mainly in working-class speech, since the early part of the 20th century. Tight alone has had this meaning since the mid-19th century.

2 a repressed, prudish or **uptight** person, an 'anal retentive'. This use of the expression is probably more widespread in American speech. In the 19th century it usually meant specifically sexually repressed, puritanical or chaste.

tight-arsed *adj British* miserly, mean, stingy. This is an elaboration of **tight** (itself used to mean stingy since the 1820s), heard since the early years of the 20th century.

tighten one's face *vb American* to shut up, keep quiet. A teenagers' and **Valley Girl** expression, usually heard in the form of an instruction.

✎'*Aw, come on, you, like tighten your face!*'

tight little unit *n See* t.l.u.

tightwad *n* a miserly, ungenerous person. A pre-World War I Americanism later adopted elsewhere. The **wad** in question is a role of banknotes.

Tijuana bible *n American* a pornographic magazine or book. Just across the US-Mexico border, the town of Tijuana has long been a centre of uncontrolled sexual amenities for visitors from the north.

time *n* a term of imprisonment. This well-known expression, usually in the phrase 'do time', originated in underworld argot in the mid-19th century.

tin *n* money, cash coins. A fairly rare expression.

tin-arse(d) *adj, n*
a lucky, privileged. The expression which is now dated in British usage, but well established in Australia, is a humorous parallel to 'copper-bottomed' in the sense of well protected, solidly based or invulnerable.

b smug. A less common sense of the phrase.

✎'*We knew you were homo and therefore we expected none of that conventional tin-arse filth which one finds in the hetero about man and woman relationships.*'
(Robert Graves in an (undated) letter to Tom Driberg, quoted in Driberg's autobiography).

tincture *n British* 1 an alcoholic drink. An adult male middle-class term, popularized by the fictional Denis Thatcher in the satirical 'Dear Bill' letters in *Private Eye* magazine in the 1980s.

2 tincture of cannabis; hashish in liquid form as legally prescribed to some drug users for a period in the 1960s.

tin-cupping *n* cadging or begging for money. The phrase has become part of business jargon where it refers to approaching a series of companies for loans.

tinker *n British* 1 a nursery term of endearment, used usually by women to little boys in the form 'little tinker'. (Tinkers were formerly thought to be archetypally mischievous.) The expression is often applied ironically to older males.

2 penis. In this sense the word may be a version of or a confusion for **tinkler**, or an extension of the preceding usage.

Tinkerbelle *n British* an effeminate, effete or fey male. A term of derision typically employed by 'tough guys' derived from the famous female fairy in *Peter Pan*.

tinkle *n British* 1 an act of urination. A coy, humorous or childish expression, in common use since the 1920s.

✎'*I'm just off upstairs for a tinkle.*'

2 a telephone call. This colloquial usage was inspired by the thin, slow ringing of early telephones.

3 money, cash, wealth. A working-class term heard especially in the late 1950s and early 1960s.

✎'*Got any tinkle for me?*'

tinkle *vb* to urinate. A childish, coy or humorous euphemism which has been in widespread use since the 1920s, although it probably originated earlier as an echoic nursery term.

tinkler *n British* penis. A nursery term

from **tinkle**, also applied ironically or derisively in reference to older males.

tinkle the ivories *vb* an alternative, less common version of **tickle the ivories** (play the piano).

tinnie, tinny *n Australian* a can of beer. There has been recent argument in Australia as to whether this term is now archaic or not, but as late as 1988 it was recorded in London among young expatriate Australians.

tin-tacked *n British* dismissed from one's job. An item of rhyming slang based on the colloquial 'sacked'.

tiny *n British* a small child, younger fellow-pupil. 'The tinies' is the (usually dismissive or condescending) standard middle-class, prep or public-school designation of children 'lower down' the school.

tip *n British* a dirty, messy or squalid place. The term has become a popular colloquialism in the 1980s, often describing an untidy bedroom. It is a shortening of 'rubbish tip'.

tiswas, tizwoz *n British* a state of confusion and/or flustered excitement. Usually found in the expressions 'all of a tiswas' or 'in a (bit of a) tiswas'. This folksy, light-hearted term probably comes from 'it is – it was', that is, expressing a disorientation in time; or else is an elaborated form of the colloquial 'tizz' and 'tizzy'.

tit *n* 1 a a breast. Various Old Germanic languages and late Latin dialects contained related words formed on the root *tet-* or *tit-* (*teta* in Spanish and *téton* in French are modern cognates). Teat was for many centuries the standard English form; in the 17th century the alternative spelling and pronunciation tit began to be used. It is only in the 20th century that the variant spellings and pronunciation have clearly differentiated vulgar and standard usages.
b any button, knob, nipple or small protuberance.
↳*'You have to attach it to the tit on the end.'*
c the sight or touch of a woman's breast(s). An exclusively male vulgarism.
↳*'I got some tit.'*
d women in general, seen as sexual partners. An exclusively male vulgarism.

↳*'There's loads of tit around.'*
2 a fool, buffoon. The word has been heard in this sense since the early 20th century in British usage.
↳*'There were two outstanding things about Q.E.D.'s "The Battle Of The Sexes" – Faith Brown. Stuart Hall merely made a right tit of himself.'* (Charles Catchpole, *News of the World*, 5 February 1989).

tit about/around *vb British* to mess about or behave in a disorganized or ineffectual manner. One of many synonyms such as **arse about**, **fanny about**, **fart about**, etc.

titfer *n British* a hat. One of the best-known examples of rhyming slang (from the cliché 'tit-for-tat'), the term probably dates from the end of the 19th century and is still heard.

titless wonder *n American* an unfortunate, feeble or clumsy person of either sex. The expression, also recorded in British armed-services slang, formerly referred literally to a 'flat-chested' woman.

tit-man *n* a male whose preferred part of the female anatomy is the breasts: **arse-man** and **leg-man** are alternatives.

tittie, titty *n* 1 a breast. An affectionate or diminutive form of **tit**, in use since the 18th century when it was considered less vulgar than it is today.
2 *see* **tough titty**.

tits *n pl See* **off one's tits**.

tits-up *adj See* **go tits up**.

titty fuck *vb American* to have sex by putting the penis between the breasts. **Dutch (fuck)** is an alternative term for the same practice.

tit-wrench *n British* a stupid, inept or ridiculous individual. The word suggests an imaginary and presumably unnecessary tool.

t.l.u. *n American* a **tight little unit**, i.e. an attractive compact girl. An item of **Valley Girl** slang from earlier surfers' jargon.

toadsucker *n American* a teenage term of abuse which while offensive has the advantage of not being obscene.

toast *adj American* confounded, in trouble. The word nearly always occurs in the form '*I'm toast!*', an admission that one is about to suffer, e.g., punishment or humiliation.

toasted *adj American* drunk or tipsy.

↪*'It's not much* [money]*, just enough to go out and get toasted some time you need it.'*
(*Working Girl*, US film, 1988).

toasting *n* a form of music in which a rhythmic narrative is chanted over a reggae backing. Toasting was the 1970s forerunner of **rap** music.

↪*'Imagine a female Eek-A-Mouse toasting over a Yello track, the lyrics written by Morrissey with a spliff in his mouth, and you'll have a very close approximation.'*
(*Time Out* magazine, 26 July 1989).

ToBo *adj American* worthless, inauthentic, pretentious. A shortening of the **Valley Girls'** standard dismissal 'totally **bogus**'. The formation is based on the pattern of phrases such as **MoFo**, etc., and was first recorded in 1991.

tod *n See* **on one's tod**.

Tod (Sloan) *n British See* **on one's tod**.

todger *n British* penis. A version of the more common **tadger**.

↪*'Orange Y-fronts with a slogan like "my todger is in here".'*
(Alternative-comedy act, Jo Brand ('the Sea-Monster'), Montreal Comedy Festival, 1988).

to die *adj American* utterly excellent, wonderful. A **preppie** term, used typically by female speakers in thrilled approval or admiration. The expression, shortened from the colloquial 'to die for', refers to the notion of dying for something or of love for someone and is probably influenced by a usage such as **killer**.

↪*'Did you see that boy in the cut-off chinos? My god, he was to die!'*
↪*'It was just to die.'*

toe-jam *n* an accretion of dirt between the toes.

toerag *n British* a contemptible person, a scrounger, ne'er-do-well, tramp or thief. Toe-rags were the bindings wound around the feet of convicts or tramps in the 19th century. The word had taken on its present meaning by early in the 20th century in both Britain and Australia. During the 1950s and 1960s toerag was

an obscure cockney term; it was given wider currency in the 1970s by TV programmes such as *The Sweeney* and the pop songs of Ian Dury. From the mid-1980s it has been revived by working-class Londoners. In Britain toerag is often used facetiously or slightly dismissively, in Australia it can sometimes indicate approval of one who acts like a (natural, rather than social) gentleman.

toes *n pl See* **have it (away) on one's toes**.

toey *adj Australian* nervous, agitated.

toff *n British* a socially superior and/or wealthy person. The word dates from the middle of the 19th century and probably derives from 'tuft' (used of a titled undergraduate at Oxford or Cambridge who wore a decoration on his cap) rather than the later **toffee-nosed**. The word had an archaic ring in the 1960s and early 1970s but like other working-class terms relating to money and status has been revived by modern cockneys and their 'upwardly-mobile' emulators.

↪*'Max was trying to build a high-tech laboratory complex, but all kinds of posh people were blocking his path. Basically, nobody loves you if you're common and you presume to take liberties with toffs.'*
(Kate Saunders, *Evening Standard*, 17 May 1989).

toffee *n British* **1** nonsense, empty talk or flattery. This is predominantly a working-class usage, particularly popular in the armed forces and in London. The origin of the image is probably in the idea of something sweet, sticky and attractively wrapped.

↪*'She gave me a load of old toffee as usual about what a reputable organisation they are and how they enjoy doing business with us.'*
(Recorded, advertising executive, London, 1988).

2 gelignite. A term used by criminals and terrorists since the 1950s, from the explosive's appearance.

together *adj* in control of oneself, well organized, adjusted, collected. Derived from the phrase **get it together**, this became a catchword of the late 1960s and early 1970s, designating an approved state of self-possession, inner harmony, etc.; the antonym was **untogether**. The usage is now dated.

togg outs *n British See* **give someone togg outs.**

togs *n pl* clothes. Now a well established informal term which has given rise to expressions such as 'togged up' and 'togged out' (dressed) and 'toggery' (clothes shop or wardrobe); togs originated in the early 19th century from a verb to 'tog', ultimately related to 'toga'.

toilet *n* a disgusting, squalid or depressing place. A usage which has been in vogue since the 1980s.

toilet-talk *n* 'smutty', coarse or obscene conversation. An American euphemism of the 1950s which has since been adopted for ironic or jocular use in Britain and Australia.

♦'*OK I'll go next door and you two can get on with your toilet-talk.*'
(Recorded, Devon, 1986).

toke *vb, n* (to take) an inhalation of a **joint** or pipe of cannabis. This has been a standard term in the marihuana and hashish smokers' vocabulary since the late 1960s. Toke probably comes from the Spanish *tocar* meaning to touch, although, perhaps coincidentally, the word existed for many years in British underworld slang meaning prison bread or a small piece or slice, becoming archaic by the 1930s.

tokus *n American See* **tush.**

tom *n British* 1 jewellery. A piece of underworld rhyming slang, from 'tomfoolery'.
2 a prostitute. In police jargon and in the slang of the underworld and prison this has been a standard term since the 1940s. It derives from a 19th-century use of the nickname Tom to denote a masculine, assertive or aggressive streetwalker.

♦'*...and he says that the tom couldn't have been where the police officer said she was because she was in bed with him. He was transferred the same day.*'
(Police sergeant, *Inside the British Police*, Simon Holdaway, 1989).

3 an act of defecation. Rhyming slang from 'tom-tit' (the bird): **shit.**
4 an injection of a narcotic. A shortened form of the rhyming slang **Tom Mix** (the Hollywood cowboy hero of silent films): **fix.**

tom *vb British* to work as a prostitute. A fairly rare extension of the noun sense.

tombstones *n pl* teeth. A jocular simile often applied to gapped, uneven or partly discoloured teeth.

tomcat, tomcat around *vb American* to prowl, usually at night, in search of sexual activity. A term used disapprovingly, usually by women of men.

tomfoolery *n British* jewellery. A piece of rhyming slang more often heard in the short form **tom.**

Tom Mix *n British* 1 an injection of a narcotic. A piece of drug abusers' terminology from the 1960s, rhyming on **fix.** (Tom Mix was the star of silent western movies.)
2 a predicament, difficult situation, rhyming on the colloquial meaning of 'fix'.

tommy-gun *n* a hypodermic syringe. Like **machine gun** and other words such as **artillery**, this is an item from the self-dramatizing vocabulary of hard-drug addicts of the late 1950s and 1960s. ('Tommy-gun' is the Thompson sub-machine gun favoured by US gangsters of the 1920s and 1930s.)

the toms, the tom-tits *n Australian* an attack of diarrhoea, or feelings of intense discomfort or dislike. A vulgarism based on the rhyme tom-tits: **shits.** The singular form is more prevalent in British rhyming slang.

ton, a ton, the ton *n*
a the ton (or less commonly **a ton**), 100 miles per hour. A term, used typically by British motorcyclists, which has been in use since the early 1950s. It was popularized by the press describing the activities of **ton-up kids.** The word was adopted by American hotrodders in the 1960s.
b a ton £100, in working-class and underworld parlance.
c £1000 in the parlance of City of London financial traders and others in the mid-1990s.

tongue-job, tongue-bath *n*
a a **French kiss.**
b an act of cunnilingus.

Both uses of both terms are from the late 1960s lexicon of **hippies** and pornographers. In the sense of kiss the expression has been supplanted in US teenage and **preppie** usage by **tongue sushi**.

tongue sushi *n American*

French kissing. A **preppie** term inspired by the Japanese raw fish delicacy fashionable from the late 1970s and 1980s.

tonguing *n*

French kissing. A term popular among British teenagers in the 1990s. It was incuded in *Just Seventeen* magazine's article, 'lingo of lurve' (a guide to the slang of dating) in August 1996.

↳ *'We weren't actually doing it, only tonguing in the back of the car.'*
(Recorded, London student, 1995).

tonk, tonker *n Australian*

a a fool.

b an effeminate or homosexual male. Both usages date from before the 1950s and are of unknown origin. ('Tong' is an archaic term for penis but may be quite unrelated.)

tonking *adj British* a euphemism for

fucking in its literal sense, used especially in the armed forces in the late 1970s and 1980s. The noun **tonk** is also increasingly in evidence, although **tonk** as a verb is rare.

tonsil hockey *n American*

a French kissing. '*Tongue-hockey*' is an alternative form of the expression.

b oral sex, usually fellatio. The term was popular among American college students in the late 1990s.

ton-up kid/boy *n British* a teenage

or young adult motorcyclist, precursor of the **rocker**. Ton-up boys were the bugbears of the popular press in the late 1950s. **A ton** or **the ton** was 100 mph, the goal of the leather-jacketed groups who gathered near suburban by-passes and main roads to stage informal speed trials and races or to go for a 'burn-up' (to drive as quickly as possible, simply for the enjoyment of speed).

↳ *'The BBC broadcast of "Morning Service" from Keele University, Staffs, yesterday was interrupted when a record about "ton-up" boys was heard above the hymn singing. A loudspeaker was found hidden behind a stage in the chapel.'*
(*Daily Telegraph*, 25 January 1965).

Tony Blairs, Tonys *n pl British*

flared trousers. A jocular usage by British adolescents in the later 1990s borrowing the name of the leader of the Labour party to replace the earlier rhymes **Lionel Blairs** and **Grosvenor Squares**.

tool *n* 1 the penis. The notion of the

male member as an implement is very ancient. The word tool itself appeared in Middle English and by the 16th century had been recorded as a sexual metaphor. It was at first an acceptable colloquialism, but since the beginning of the 19th century has been considered vulgar.

↳ *'Play it safe*
Play it cool
Wear a Jiffi
On your tool'
(Promotion slogan for *Jiffi* condoms, 1988).

↳ *'He had a thing about his penis. When he was away from me, he was always referring to it as "my noble tool".'*
(Anna Kashfi referring to ex-husband Marlon Brando, *Sunday Mirror*, 3 September 1989).

2 a fool. Like many other words designating the male member, tool has the secondary meaning of a stupid (male) person.

3 a weapon. This usage is now rare, but has given rise to the standard underworld and police jargon expression **tooled-up** (armed with firearms) in British English.

tool *vb British* to attack with a razor. A

slang term used by streetgang members in the 1950s, particularly in London and Glasgow.

tool around/about *vb* to idle or

loaf, mess around at trivial tasks. Originally an upper-class Edwardian phrase, (probably from the sense of tool as meaning to drive (a coach) skilfully and smoothly, hence to perform without effort). In modern speech there may also be a convergence with the sense of **tool** as male member, paralleled in the synonymous usage **dick around**.

tooled-up *adj British*

a armed, issued with firearms. A term used by the underworld and the police since the early 1950s. The noun **tool**, denoting a firearm, is now archaic. The expression tooled-up has become more widely known in the later 1970s and 1980s after reference in the media; it is sometimes extended to denote armed with knives, coshes or other weapons.

↳ *'Some of the briefing scenes could have come straight from a movie*

*thriller as the elite Squad members
get "tooled up" – issued with snub-
nosed revolvers and pump-action
shotguns.'*
(*News of the World*, 5 February 1989).
b equipped with housebreaking implements. A piece of police and underworld
jargon.

tool up *vb British* to arm oneself.
✎ *'We're going to have to tool up if we
take that lot on.'*

too much *exclamation* excellent, exceptional, outstanding. A now dated
usage which originated in the **jive talk** of
pre-World War II jazz musicians in the
USA and became a (sometimes derided)
cliché expression of **hippy** enthusiasm.

toot *vb* to take any inhaled drug, but especially cocaine or amphetamine crystals
(**speed**). This word had existed in the
drug users' lexicon since the mid-1960s,
but became widespread in the late 1970s
with the increased popularity of cocaine
among otherwise 'respectable' people. It
employs the predictable simile (as in
bugle, hooter) of the nose as a musical instrument.

toot *n* **1 a** an inhalation or sniff of a
crystalline drug.
✎ *'D'you want a toot of this?'*
b a drug normally inhaled, particularly
cocaine.
✎ *'This is grade A toot.'*
2 *Australian* a toilet. The word is pronounced to rhyme with foot, and is used
by middle-class speakers.

tootie-fruitie *n See* tutti-frutti.

tootin' *adv, adj American* absolutely
(right). An adjective used to intensify, as
in the cliché expression 'damn' or 'darn
tootin' right', whence the shortened version 'darned tootin'' or simply 'tootin'',
meaning correct. The word is ultimately
derived from 'rootin'-tootin'', meaning
originally cheering and whistling.

toot sweet *adv* immediately. The
phrase is an anglicized version of the
French *tout de suite* ('straightaway') used
jocularly, typically by students.

top *vb* to kill or execute (someone). The
term, which is part of underworld jargon, has existed since the late 18th century when it referred to hanging.

top *adj British* excellent, fashionable. A

vogue term of approbation among adolescents from the late 1980s. In this sense,
the word was probably adopted first in
the north of England, later spreading to
all other regions. **Mint** and **fit** were other
fashionable synonyms from the same period.
✎ *'... do you enjoy being a pop star?'
'I think it's top, me.'*
(Liam Gallagher of Oasis interviewed in
NME, 30 September 1995).

top *n* manual contact with female
breasts. This item of working-class slang
is often heard in the phrase 'a bit of top',
and was used by the London singer/co-
median Richard Digance in his TV show,
20 July 1991.

top bollocks *n pl* female breasts. A
vulgarism used by males in Britain and
Australia since the early 1960s.

top man *n British* a vulgarly or unfashionably dressed male. The ironic
term, heard among adolescents and
young adults, particularly students and
yuppies in the late 1980s, refers to the
Top Man stores which sell low-price fashion clothing.

torch *vb* to set fire to something, usually to get rid of incriminating evidence or
as part of an insurance fraud.
✎ *'But torching the building made little
difference to the neighbourhood.
There are three other crack houses
within easy walking distance.'*
(*Sunday Times*, 10 September 1989).

torch *n* an arsonist, especially one who
is paid to burn down buildings in order to
collect fire insurance. The word, which is
part of police and underworld jargon, is
also used as a verb.

torch job *n* an act or case of arson.

torpedo *n American* a hired gunman,
thug or **hit-man**.
✎ *'What is there to worry about? I have
the protection of Chicago's top
torpedo.'*
(*Murderer's Row*, US film, 1966).

tosh *n British* **1** a term of address to a
stranger, invariably used by a man to another man. This working-class word, now
obsolescent, was a favourite with **spivs**
and young toughs in the 1950s and early
1960s. It can be used with bravado, in
rough comradeship, or provokingly. In
this sense it possibly derives from Scottish

or Cornish dialect, in which it meant smart or well-dressed.

2 nonsense. A 19th-century public-school and university term that was obsolescent, except in affected usage, during the 1960s and 1970s but was revived in the 1980s, it often forms part of phrases such as 'tosh and tarradiddle' or 'tosh and twaddle', equating with 'stuff and nonsense'. The origin of this sense of the word is obscure: it may be an imitation of a snort of derision (as in 'tish' or 'bosh') or derive from 'toshy' meaning over-dressed (see preceding sense).

↳'*He gave me some sort of explanation, but it was basically a load of old tosh.*'
(Recorded, film producer, London, 1986).

toss *n British* **1** something futile, worthless or useless. A word usually found in the phrase 'a load of old toss'. It denotes the semen ejaculated in masturbation, influenced also by **tosh**, meaning nonsense.

2 an obnoxious and/or foolish person. The term is a shortening of **tosser** or **toss-bag**.

toss *vb* **1** to deliberately lose a match, game or contest (usually as part of a gambling conspiracy). A racier version of 'throw'.

2 to search and/or ransack premises in pursuit of evidence of crime or of booty. An underworld and law enforcers' term.

3 *Australian* to defeat. A term used particularly in sport; it probably derives from the image of a wrestler or bull tossing an opponent, or simply from the standard sense of 'toss aside'.

toss-bag *n* an idle, worthless, foolish, and/or obnoxious person.

tossed *adj American* searched and/or ransacked. A law-enforcers' and underworld term meaning the same as the colloquial 'turned-over', as applied to a room, apartment, etc.

tosser *n British* an idle, worthless or foolish person. A mainly working-class term of contempt which enjoyed a particular vogue in the later 1970s. It is a synonym of a **wanker**, from the verb **toss off**.

↳'*Yis wan to be different, isn't tha' it? Yis don't want to end like these tossers here. Amn't I righ'?*'
(*The Commitments*, Roddy Doyle, 1988).

tossing *adj British* an intensifier for use with nouns in the same way as the more vulgar **frigging**, **fucking**, etc. The term is heard in working-class speech especially in northern England.

toss off *vb* to masturbate. This verb, used transitively or intransitively, has been in use since before its first recording in 1735 to refer to male masturbation. In modern English slang the word is restricted to British and Australian speech.

toss one's cookies/tacos *vb American* to vomit. Jocularisms popular among college students in particular.

toss-pot *n* **1** a drunkard or habitual heavy drinker. This term of disapproval or affectionate abuse has been a British colloquialism for hundreds of years. The pot in question is a jar of ale, which is tossed down the throat.

2 a foolish, weak, unpleasant or incompetent person. Users of the term in this sense probably confuse it with **tosser**, falsely identifying the verb with the sense of masturbate. In Australia the expression toss-pot is sometimes used as a meaningless term of hearty address.

total *vb* to destroy completely. A widespread term, especially among teenagers, since the 1960s; it derives from the notion of a 'total wreck' or a 'total loss' in official accident reports. Originally an Americanism, it is now heard elsewhere.

↳'*I was so out of control I totaled the car, crashed it somehow into the side of the road.*'
(John Philips, *Papa John*, 1986).

totally *adj* an all-purpose deliberately ambivalent usage (in the same way as **very**) often heard as an exclamation by female adolescents in the US. It frequently, but not necessarily, indicates approbation.

↳'*It's like totally!*'

to the max *adv American* to the greatest extent, utterly. A **Valley Girl** term typically occurring in exclamations such as '**grody** to the max' (utterly awful), but sometimes used on its own to mean absolutely or completely.

↳'*Was it really awful?*'
'*To the max!*'

totsie *n British* a girl. A now dated version of **tottie**.

tottie, totty, totsie *n British* a girl, or women in general, seen as potential sexual partners. The word meant prostitute or woman of easy virtue in the 19th century and is probably an affectionate diminutive of Dorothy. It is still a fairly common term all over Britain particularly among working-class males and servicemen.

꘎'A nice little tottie.'

toto adj British completely, totally. An item of **parlyaree** recorded in the TV documentary Out in July 1992. It is Italian for 'all'.

꘎'Everyone could see she was toto blotto.'

touch down vb to have sex. The term, which probably originated in black American usage as a sports metaphor, invariably refers to male success in seducing/penetrating females.

touch (someone) for (something) vb to solicit, cadge. This colloquialism, used almost invariably in connection with a loan, has been recorded since 1760. **Touch up** is a less common alternative form, particularly in the USA.

a touch of the tarbrush n (having) a skin colour which suggests a trace of black or coloured ancestry. This euphemism, often heard in a discriminatory context, originated in the mid-19th century, when it was also used to refer to sailors (the tarbrush being used on board ship).

touch-respect exclamation British an all-purpose greeting or indication of approval in use among teenage gangs. The term, an elaboration of the earlier **respect**, was recorded in use among north London schoolboys in 1993 and 1994.

touch up vb 1 British to caress sexually, grope. A phrase (often used derogatively) prevalent among adolescents.
2 touch (in the sense of solicit a loan from).

tough adj 1 excellent. A vogue term (sometimes spelt **tuff**) from the early 1990s applied particularly to music.

꘎'Tough sounds.'

2 unpleasant, disgusting, ugly, etc. A vogue term of disapproval that originated in the language of black street gangs in the early 1990s and was adopted by other adolescents.

꘎'He's well tough.'
(Recorded, London schoolboy, 1994).

tough bounce/buns n hard luck. These are rueful or, alternatively unsympathetic versions of the colloquial 'tough luck'. The expressions originated in American speech.

tough titty n hard luck, a raw deal. The phrase is most often heard as an unsympathetic dismissal of another's complaint.

toup, toop n American a toupée or wig.

touristas n pl American an alternative spelling of **turistas**.

tout n British an informer. A Northern Irish expression, used typically by the IRA or its supporters of a turncoat or **grass**. In mainland British English, the sense of tout as a **spiv** or lookout, from which this usage derives, is now archaic, having been replaced by the sense of cheapjack (ticket) salesman or tipster. All these derive ultimately from the Middle English verb tuten: to peer or peep.

towel head n an arab. A predictable pejorative term. **Rag-head** is a more widespread synonym.

꘎'Some towel-head from Hizbullah marched up and down the street twice.'
(Republican Party Reptile, P. J. O'Rourke, 1987).

town bike/pump n a local woman supposedly available for sex with all and sundry. A form of this masculine term of contempt occurs in all English-speaking countries: the first variant employs **ride** as a sexual metaphor; the second is American.

toyboy n a young male lover of an older woman. A vogue word from 1987 which started as a code term among sophisticates and was eventually popularized by the press. The expression filled a 'lexical gap' in the English language, coinciding with the perceived trend whereby many celebrities of the 1960s were taking up with younger lovers. (The female counterpart was often provided by **bimbo**.)

tracks, trackmarks n pl needle marks or scars on the limbs of addicts of hard drugs resulting from regular injections into the veins.

꘎'You got more tracks on you baby than the tracks of this train.'

(Lyric from 'Been on a Train', Laura Nyro, 1970).

trade *n* a sexual partner or partners, particularly a paying customer of a prostitute. A generic term for custom or customers in the jargon of male and female streetwalkers, the word has sometimes been extended since the late 1960s in the **gay** lexicon to refer to any sex partner.

↳'*He'd been having the trade back and finally his landlady said "You've been bringing people back, haven't you?". She looked disapproving.*'
(Kenneth Williams, quoted in Joe Orton's Diary, 25 April 1967).

tradesmen's entrance *n British* the anus. A vulgar euphemism often used jocularly, dating from the 1940s when even middle-class houses might have a rear or side entrance for hawkers, deliveries, etc.

traf, traff *vb, n British* (to) *fart*. An instance of **backslang** heard in working-class speech in the late 1950s and occasionally since.

trailer-trash *n American* (a member of) the white underclass. The phrase became fashionable in the later 1990s, both to denigrate poor whites of the sort who are characteristically forced to live in trailer-parks and to describe a fashion for cheap, garish and **kitsch** accessories. A synonym for poor **white trash**.

train *n* an act of serial sexual intercourse. The word is usually used as part of a phrase such as **do a train (on someone)**.

trainspotter *n British* an unfashionable, excessively earnest, unattractive individual. The phrase became a vogue term as a synonym for **anorak** and **nerd** in the mid-1990s, before being used as the title of Irving Welsh's cult novel, *Trainspotting*.

train surfing *n* joy-riding on the top or outside of mainline or underground trains. A lethal teenage prank of the 1980s in the USA and, more recently, Britain.

tramp *adj British* inferior, inadequate, shabby. An all-purpose pejorative, formed from the noun, in use particularly amongst younger schoolchildren in the later 1990s.

↳'*... this is a tramp school anyway.*'

(Truanting schoolboy interviewed in the *Sunday Times*, 27 October 1996).

tranks, tranqs, trancs, tranx *n pl* tranquillizers. The abbreviations are employed by drug abusers rather than the estimated three million people in Britain suffering from dependency on prescribed drugs.

tranny, trannie *n British* **1** a transistor radio. An abbreviated form which has survived beyond the dated full phrase from the 1960s.

↳'*Records were less affordable in those days (a "trannie" and Radio Caroline being the nearest thing to free music).*'
(Maureen Nolan and Roma Singleton, *Very Heaven*, 1988).

2 a a transexual.

b a transvestite. Both shortenings were part of the **gay** lexicon of the 1980s.

3 a (photographic) transparency. This is particularly popular in the parlance of designers and publishers.

4 a transport café.

5 a Ford Transit van. The means of transport for many (humbler) pop groups.

trashed *adj American* drunk. A teenage and **preppie** term on the familiar lines of **destroyed**, **smashed**, etc.

trashed out *adj American* exhausted. A popular phrase among teenagers and students since the 1970s. The term recalls synonyms such as 'shattered' or **wrecked**.

tray *See* **très**.

the trays, tray-bits *n Australian* an attack of diarrhoea. A 'tray-bit' is a turn-of-the-century British term for a threepenny piece (from **parlyaree**; '-tray' is from the Italian for three, *tre*). The phrase was adopted in Australia as rhyming slang for **the shits**. Widespread in the 1950s, the expression is now obsolescent.

treach *adj* a hip-hop term of approbation. It is probably, but not certainly, a shortening of 'treacherous', by analogy with **wicked** and **bad**.

↳'*This month's music selections are frightfully def, totally treach and all those other hip hop clichés.*'
(*I-D* magazine, November 1987).

treat *vb American* to seduce. An item of black street slang of the 1990s.

tree *n American* cannabis, marihuana. A predictable borrowing of the word by college students and others, perhaps influenced by the earlier use of **bush**.

tree-hugger *n American* an environmentalist, green activist. A derogatory term which featured in the 1992 Montana State Election debate. Synonyms are **prairie-fairy**, **eagle-freak**, etc.

trembler *n British* a burglar alarm. This example of the jargon of cat burglars was recorded in *FHM* magazine in April 1996.

très *adv* very. The French word is used for comic effect, e.g., *très cool*.

trey, trey-bits *n Australian* an alternative spelling of **the trays, tray-bits**.

trich, trick *n* trichomoniasis, a mild sexually transmitted infection.

trick *n* 1 a a prostitute's client.
⮑'*Sandy had invited two girlfriends to live with them who gave Ordell "rent money", twenty per cent of what they made entertaining tricks, so it wasn't like Ordell was pimping.*'
(Elmore Leonard, *The Switch*, 1978).
b a session or transaction between a prostitute and client. These senses of the word have been current in the USA since the first decade of the 20th century. They derive from the notion of an entertainer's 'turn' or stratagem. Trick has appeared in British English since World War II, often in the phrases 'on a trick' or **turn a trick**.
2 *see* **trich**.

trick *vb American* to sell sexual favours for money. This derivation from the noun form has not crossed the Atlantic.
⮑'*Whenever she runs out of dope she goes out tricking.*'

trick *adj* fancy, attractive and sophisticated. A 1980s term used by enthusiasts in fields where high technology is admired.
⮑'*A legendary homemade speed machine dominated the bike park last summer: a Kawasaki-powered, Harris-framed, turbo-charged, nitrous oxide-assisted rocket. To bikers, this bike is "trick", very trick.*'
(*Independent*, 6 April 1988).

trick cyclist *n* a psychiatrist. A humorous alteration of the standard word, evoking like **shrink** a suspicious contempt

for the profession. The phrase was first heard in the 1930s.
⮑'*They are suspicious of the "trick cyclist" (nearly every policeman I have met uses the phrase to describe psychiatrists).*'
(*Town* magazine, March 1964).

triff *adj British* terrific, wonderful, exciting. This shortening like the more widespread **brill** became a vogue term among teenagers in the 1980s.

trim *n British* a female, especially an attractive girl. A briefly fashionable phrase used in **hip** circles and among medical students etc. in the early 1990s. It was probably adapted from the (somewhat dated) black American use of the word to denote the female genitals or women as sex objects.

trim *vb American* to kill. The term was employed in the US movie, *Plain Clothes*, in 1988.

trimmed *adj* cheated, swindled, in the parlance of gamblers. The word implies the neat removal of a dupe's (excess) money or winnings.

trip *n* 1 a an experience of a **psychedelic** drug such as LSD. A typical LSD trip would last around 6–8 hours, during which time the user would undergo profound sensory and psychological changes. The image evoked is that of an 'inward journey'.
⮑'*Leary himself has been on over 300 trips although he has abstained for nearly a year.*'
(*Sunday Times* colour supplement, 1 January 1967).
⮑'*There follows much discussion of the Floyd and Peel's one and only acid trip – "I hired a boat on The Serpentine in Hyde Park with Marc Bolan and floated about to the strains of 'Interstellar Overdrive".*'
(*New Musical Express*, 7 February 1987).
b a single dose, tablet, or capsule of LSD.
2 a state of mind, state of affairs or personal experience. The original 1960s counterculture sense of LSD experience was soon broadened to encompass these meanings. The word was used in a variety of sub-senses, in expressions such as a guilt trip (a bout of remorse), 'lay a trip on someone' (subject someone to one's own preoccupation, obsession or problem), a heavy trip (a devastating or op-

pressive experience), or 'on one's own trip' (preoccupied with oneself, introverted).

trip (out) *vb* to experience the effects of LSD or a similar hallucinogenic drug. The term was coined in California in the early 1960s to describe the period (often around 8 hours) under the influence of the drug wherein one is 'transported on an inner voyage'.

tripehound *n British* a term of abuse, now often used affectionately but formerly with real venom, particularly in the North and Midlands of England. The image is that of an offal-eating dog.

tripped-out *adj*

a under the influence of LSD or a similar hallucinogenic drug.

b exhibiting signs of euphoria or eccentricity caused by, or typical of, the use of LSD.

tripping *adj British* strange, weird. This adjective, unknown before the 1990s, denotes a generally bizarre situation, thing, person, etc., rather than referring specifically to the simulation of the effects of LSD.

tripping *n American* enjoying oneself, having fun. In the slang of black hip-hop aficionados the 1960s term for LSD usage has been generalized.

trippy *adj* exhibiting or suggesting the euphoric, surrealistic effects of **psychedelic** drugs such as LSD. The word, based on **trip**, was heard from about 1967.

↳'Listen to this – it's got a really trippy guitar solo.'

trog *vb British* to trek, walk energetically or wearily. An armed-services' term which passed into civilian usage in the 1970s. It is probably a blend of trek and slog.

trog, trogg *n British* a simplistic, (literally or figuratively) low-browed person, someone of restricted intelligence or no social graces, a 'Philistine' or 'Neanderthal'. This shortening of 'troglodyte' (cave-dweller) was used in the armed forces in the early 1950s and particularly by jazz enthusiasts, **beatniks** and students in the late 1950s and early 1960s to describe those who were dull, boorish or out of touch. The word had virtually died out in fashionable teenage use by the mid-1960s, when a pop group from An-

dover self-deprecatingly called themselves the Troggs. Trog continues to be periodically resurrected, usually in middle-class speech.

Trojan *n American* a condom. The word is a trademark name used generically in the USA in the same way as **Durex** in the UK.

troll *vb, n British* (to take a) prowl, wander or **cruise**. This alternative form of 'trawl' has existed since the 15th century. It acquired the sexual sense in the 1930s and was a vogue **gay** term of the 1960s.

↳'Orton insisted the trolling fed his work; but it also fed Halliwell's rage.' (John Lahr, preface to Joe Orton's Diaries, published 1986).

↳'I don't just get married because I enjoy trolling down the aisle.' (Joan Collins, TV talk show, 1988).

trolleys, trollies *n pl British* underpants. A fairly rare public-school expression. It is of uncertain origin but may be related to the archaic 'trolleybobs', a nursery version of trousers. (In her diary entry for 8 January 1934, Barbara Pym mentions buying trollies at Marks and Spencers.)

trombone *n British* a telephone. A rhyming alternative to **dog (and bone)**.

tronk *n British* a foolish, clumsy or contemptible person. A rare schoolchildren's and student's term, possibly related to the Australian synonym **tonk**.

troppo *adj Australian* unhinged, deranged, crazy. The word is an abbreviation of 'tropical' and is usually heard in the phrase **to go troppo**, originally referring to someone overcome by tropical heat but now generalized to mean something like **over the top**. The word originated among armed-service personnel in World War II.

the trots *n British* an attack of diarrhoea. The expression, heard since World War I, evokes swift but controlled movement to the lavatory.

troub, troubs *n British See* **trub**.

trouble (and strife) *n British* wife. A piece of 'cockney' rhyming slang which is still in (mainly jocular, ironic or self-conscious) use; it is now generally shortened simply to trouble by Londoners.

trough *vb British* to eat. A humorous

middle- and upper-class verb evoking (but not necessarily involving) gluttony.

trouser *vb British* to pocket. A humorous alternative term from the 1980s.

↳'*Strobes then insisted on accompanying Chancellor to the prize-giving in Milan, and trousered the cheque himself.*'
(*Private Eye* magazine, 17 March 1989).

trouser *n British* a generic term for males as sex objects. A 1980s women's version of '(a bit of) **skirt**', satirizing the 'predatory' male expression.

trouser bandit *n British* a male homosexual. A humorous though pejorative euphemism, evoking the image of a predatory or promiscuous **gay**. 'Bum bandit' and **arse bandit** are alternative versions.

trouser chuff *n British* a fart. A mock-childish term used by adolescents in the 1980s and popularized in the best-selling *Viz* magazine.

↳'*Johnny Fartpants' "trouser chuffs" always get him into meddlesome scrapes – losing his pocket money or causing the San Francisco earthquake of 1906...*'
(*Time Out* magazine, December 1988).

trouser snake *n* 1 a penis. A young person's joke euphemism adopted by adults; the full version is **one-eyed trouser snake**.

2 a disreputable or reprehensible person. This sense of the expression is typically used in the 1980s by American girls as a term of disapproval applied to males, emphasizing the treachery inspired by 'snake' rather than the sexual aspect of the image.

trout *n See* **old trout**.

trouting *n British See* **out trouting**.

trub, troub(s) *n British* trouble. A shortening used typically in middle-class badinage.

↳'*We've been in a spot of trub recently.*'

trucking *n See* **keep on trucking**.

trumpet *n British* 1 a **fart**. A children's word which enjoyed a vogue in the late 1980s.

↳'*Lucy did a trumpet.*'
(Recorded, 10-year-old boy, Devon, 1986).

2 the telephone. A rare synonym of **trombone**, **blower**, etc.

trustafarian *n British* a young person of wealthy origin frequenting the milieux and/or affecting the manners of London ghetto-dwellers. The humorous coinage blends 'trust-fund' and rastafarian and has remained in use throughout the 1990s.

↳'*But though they seem irredeemably boho, trustafarians are closely related to the dying breed of Sloanes who used to rip it up on the opposite side of Hyde Park.*'
(*Sunday Times*, 20 August 1992).

tsotsi *n South African* 1 the South African patois as spoken in Cape Town and Johannesburg, especially by black speakers. The language is a combination of English, Afrikaans, Xhosa and Sotho.

2 a stylish black male, young gangster.

tub *n* 1 a a boat.

↳'*Can't this tub go any faster?*'
(*Friday 13th part VI*, US film, 1986).

b a car, truck, bus etc.

2 a 'tub of lard', a fat person. A widespread colloquialism.

↳'*She used to call you buttercup?*'
'*What's so funny about that, Norton?*'
'*You were a little cup of butter, now you're a whole tub of lard.*'
(*The Honeymooners*, US TV comedy series, 1950).

tube, the tube *n* 1 the tube television, from the cathode ray tube.

2 the tube the London underground railway system, from the tubular construction of the tunnels. This nickname dates from the turn of the century.

3 *British* a person. A vogue word among teenagers in the late 1980s; it is a synonym for **dude** although it sometimes has the added sense of foolish or gormless.

4 *Australian* a can of beer. (**Tinny** is a slightly later synonym.)

↳'*Alex Buzo, who is minder of the Australian language among his other activities, records that it is 20 years since he last heard beers referred to as tubes.*'
(*Observer* magazine, 13 December 1987).

5 the hollow formed by a breaking wave. A surfer's term from which the term of approbation **tubular** is derived.

tube it *vb American* to fail an examination, test, task, etc. This common campus expression is based on the colloquialism 'down the tubes' in the sense of lost or ruined.

tube steak *n American* penis. A euphemism heard in **hip** circles in the 1980s, from black street-usage of the 1970s. It was originally a jocular term for a frankfurter sausage.

tubular *adj* an all-purpose term of teenage approbation, deriving from riding the **tube** as being the highest form of surfing experience. Like many 1960s surfing terms this expression (often intensified as 'totally tubular') was adopted by **Valley Girls** in the later 1970s and subsequently became a vogue usage in international English in the 1980s.

tuchis *n American See* tush.

tuck, tucker *n* food. The first version of the word is typical of British public-school vocabulary, the second Australian. Both date from the 19th century and probably derive from the verb to tuck in(to), which originally implied the humorous notion of tucking food surreptitiously into oneself or behind one's clothing.

tucked up *adj British* 1 imprisoned, incarcerated. A homely euphemism for a grim reality in the tradition of London working-class usages.

✧*'Adjusting back to normal society is not easy when you've been tucked up for a bit.'*
(Recorded, ex-prisoner, London, 1986).

2 cheated, duped. A London working-class usage paralleling the more widespread **stitch (someone) up**.

tuckered (out) *adj* exhausted. This is originally an American term deriving from an archaic sense of the verb tuck, signifying rebuke or reproach. (In Old English tuck also had the sense of ill-treat.) Now heard in such phrases as 'plumb tuckered out', the word has folksy overtones.

tuck (someone) up *vb British*
a to defeat, capture.

b to confound, dupe. This all-purpose phrase is in use among working-class London speakers, particularly criminals and the police. The image is that of putting a helpless child to bed.

tude *n American* (bad) **attitude**, a surly,

defiant or negative disposition. A short form of the type (**burbs**, **nabe**, **perp**, **tard**) fashionable in adolescent circles in the late 1970s and 1980s and more recently in (often facetious) journalese usage.

tuft hunter *n* a sycophant, toady or 'crawler'. (Titled undergraduates at Oxford and Cambridge were known as 'tufts' after the tassels they were entitled to wear.) This expression is now virtually obsolete.

✧*'He met Kenneth Williams by writing a fan letter to the theatre at Oxford where Kenneth was playing. He's a tuft hunter.'*
(Joe Orton's Diary, 2 May 1967).

tug *n British* 1 an arrest or detention of a suspect (in the jargon of the underworld or police), a **collar**.

✧*''E won't be expecting a tug at that time of night.'*

2 an act of manual sexual stimulation of a male, usually by a female. A less common synonym of **hand-job** in use particularly in Australian speech in the 1990s.

tukus *n American* a version of **tush**, tushie.

tumble *n* 1 an act of sexual intercourse. This fairly inoffensive expression is often elaborated to 'tumble in the hay'.
2 *British* an attempt, try. In working-class usage 'give it a tumble' is the equivalent of 'give it a whirl' (the Australian **give it a burl**).
3 arrest, capture or detention. In criminal and police parlance in both Britain and the USA the word is used in these senses by analogy with a fall suffered by a racehorse or sports contender.

tummy banana *n* the penis. A nursery expression adopted, or perhaps invented for jocular use, by adults. The phrase was first heard in middle-class circles in the early 1970s.

tuna *n American* 1 a a girl or woman. Users of the term, who include teenagers and **preppies**, are often unaware of its origins in the senses which follow.
b sexual activity.
c the female sex organs. The expressions use the seafood (popular in the USA long before it was readily available in Britain) as a euphemism for femininity or femaleness inspired by the piscine quality of the female sexual odour.
2 marihuana. The reason for this usage is

unclear; it may simply be a transference of the idea of tuna as a delicacy or staple food.

tuneage *n American* music. A mock-pompous coinage using the **-age** suffix and recorded among college students in the mid-1990s.

tune in *vb* to attune to one's environment, achieve harmony with one's peer group, the counterculture and/or the cosmos. This **hipster** and **beatnik** term became part of the catchphrase slogan of the **hippy** movement; 'turn on, tune in, drop out': unlike the other two verbs tune in was not itself adopted into mainstream colloquial speech.

tup *vb British* to have sex (with). The country persons' term for the copulation of a ram with a ewe (from the Middle English word for ram, tupe) is by extension used vulgarly of humans.

turbo-crush *n British* an infatuation. 'Turbo-' here is used as an intensifier in the same way as the contemporary and more common **mega-**. '*To have a turbo-crush on someone*' was a vogue term among younger British adolescents in the mid-1990s.

turd *n* 1 a piece of excrement. A descendant of the Anglo-Saxon word 'tord', the term was freely used until about the 17th century, by which time it was being avoided in polite speech and writing. It is still considered vulgar by many speakers, although when referring for example to dog droppings, it is sometimes now used even in broadcasts.

✎'*He said one ancient stool excavated in York, known as the "Lloyd's Bank turd", came from a forbearer who was infested by several hundred whipworms ...*'
(*Independent*, 16 September 1989).

2 an unpleasant and/or despicable person. In this sense the word has the same connotation of obnoxiousness as the literal and figurative synonym, **shit**.

turd burglar *n British* a male homosexual. One of several jocular but hostile phrases of the 1980s (such as **fudgepacker** and **brownie-hound**), used by heterosexuals to suggest the faecal aspects of sodomy.

turf *n* a streetgang or street drug dealer's territory.

✎'*In fact he's a lookout, a lookout for cops and strangers, for other dealers stealing "turf".*'
(*Guardian*, 5 September 1989).

turistas, the turistas, touristas *n American* an attack of diarrhoea. *Turista* is Spanish (or Mexican) for tourist.

turkey-neck *n American* penis. From the supposed resemblance.

✎'*When your mother's crying at the funeral, I'm gonna goose her with my turkey-neck.*'
(*Barfly*, US film, 1987).

turn a trick *vb* to service a (prostitute's) client. The phrase, evoking a neat execution of a deception, stratagem or performance, has been in use since the early years of the 20th century. *See also* **trick**.

turned-on *adj* 1 aware, **hip** or liberated. A term of approbation of the 1960s, deriving from the notion of being 'turned on' by a mood-altering drug. **Switched-on** was a British alternative form.

2 **a** sexually aroused. A slang phrase of the 1950s which has become a common colloquialism.

b stimulated, fascinated. A generalization of the previous sense of the term.

turn-off *n* a depressing, deflating, disappointing or unexciting experience. The phrase was coined by analogy with its opposite, **turn-on**.

✎'*It's really nice that you want to be well groomed, but you get hair in the food. Hair in the food is a turn-off, Joan, sweetie.*'
(*The Serial*, Cyra McFadden, 1976).

✎'*I find all that sort of thing* [male body-building] *a complete turn-off.*'
(Recorded, female social worker, London, 1987).

turn on *vb* **a** to take a drug. The term first referred to hard narcotics, but was later applied to cannabis and LSD. It was originally based on the notion of stimulus at the throw of a switch.

b to allow oneself to experience a heightened or more liberated reality. One of the three 'commandments' of the alternative society of the late 1960s; 'turn on, tune in, drop out'.

✎'*Within a year the league* [for Spiritual Discovery] *will have a million mem-*

bers who will turn on with LSD every seven days.'
(Timothy Leary, *Sunday Times* colour supplement, 1 January 1967).

turn-on *n* **a** a drug, specifically a user's drug of choice.
꿀'*What's your turn-on?*'
b anything arousing or exciting, a sexual stimulus. A back-formation from **turned-on**.
꿀'*I love shoes – patent leather stilettos are a real turn-on.*'

turn (someone) over *vb British*
a to cheat, rob.
꿀'*I never thought my best mate would turn me over.*'
b to attack, beat up.
c to raid and/or search premises. All three sub-senses are in working-class use, particularly in London. The first two have been heard since the 1950s, the third from the mid-19th century.

turtle *n* **a** a passive sexual partner, especially one willing to offer oral or anal sex. The term is in use among prisoners, criminals, etc., and is often applied to male prisoners who offer sexual favours in return for tobacco, etc.
b a woman regarded as a sex object.
꿀'*Lesley Morris, 23, said sailors called the WRENS sluts, slags, splits and turtles.*'
(*Daily Mirror*, 4 February 1997).

turtles *n pl* gloves. An item of rhyming slang (from '*turtle doves*'). This example of the jargon of cat burglars was recorded in *FHM* magazine in April 1996.

tush, tushie *n American* buttocks, backside. These are inoffensive terms used in the family and elsewhere. They derive from Yiddish *tochis*, also written **tokus**, **tukus**, or **tuchis**, which in turn derives from the Hebrew *tokheth*.

tutti-frutti, tootie-fruitie *n* an effeminate, frivolous or ridiculous male. This slang use of the name of the Italian ice cream dish (vanilla with pieces of glacé fruit) originated in the USA where **fruit** denotes a **gay** male. (*Tutti frutti* is Italian for 'all fruits'.)

T.V. *n* transvestism or a transvestite.

twang (the wire) *vb* to masturbate. This word, used only of men, was originally an Australianism with rural overtones.

twanger *n American* the penis.

twannie *n British* a stupid, obnoxious person. The term is a combination of **twat** and **pranny**.

twat, twot *n British* **1** the vagina. A word first recorded in the 17th century. The etymology is obscure but it probably derives from a rural dialect term.
2 a foolish or obnoxious person. The word has had this sense (firstly in London slang) since the late 19th century. Until the early to mid-1960s the word was in widespread use in this context, often by schoolchildren and some adults who were unaware of its provenance (and probably thought it an intensive form of **twit**).
꿀'*What kind of creature bore you/was it some kind of bat?/they can't find a good word for you/but I can/twat.*'
(*A love story in reverse*, poem by John Cooper Clarke, 1978).
꿀'"*We hate tense people," says guitarist John Squire. "The tense people are the twats who are only interested in making money and who ruin things for everybody else."*'
(The Stone Roses, *The Observer*, August 1989).

twat *vb British* to hit, beat up.
꿀'*The drummer went to help and he got twatted as well.*'
(*Fresh Pop*, Channel 4 TV, 17 December 1996).

tweak *vb American* **1** to suffer physical symptoms of drug withdrawal. This 1980s term evokes the irritation and spasmodic nature of drug-induced distress, as well as recalling words such as twitch and weak.
2 to adjust or fine-tune. A piece of jargon applied to motor mechanics and computers, for instance.

tweaked *adj American* eccentric, deranged. An adolescent vogue term of the 1990s.

twerp, twirp *n* an insignificant, silly and/or obnoxious person. An invented word which appeared in the 1930s and gained widespread currency in the 1950s.
꿀'*My stuff is outrageously conceived and devastatingly realised.*'
'*Oh do shut up you boring little twerp!*'
(*Biff* cartoon, 1986).

twig *vb British* to understand, 'catch

on'. A formerly raffish term which since the late 1960s has become a fairly common colloquialism. This usage has been recorded since the 18th century and derives either from 'tweak' in the sense of snatch or grasp, or from a Gaelic verb meaning comprehend.

twig *n See* **drop off the twig.**

twillie, twilly *n British* a foolish, clumsy or stupid person. An adolescent term in use since the early 1970s. It is a blend of **twit** and silly.

✎'*A complete twillie.*'

twimp *n American* a foolish and/or insignificant individual. A high-school term of mild abuse from the late 1980s, blending **twit**, **twerp** and **wimp**.

twimpoid, twimpo *n British* a silly, foolish person. These teenage and pre-teenage vogue terms of disapproval or insult from the 1990s are British versions of the American **twimp**.

twinkie, twinky, twink *n American* **1 a** a male homosexual or effete, fey or eccentric man.

b a cute, attractive person. Both senses of the words derive from the trademark 'Twinkies', a sort of cupcake. The word has echoes of 'twinkle-toes', twinkling and **Tinkerbelle**. Twink is sometimes used as a (usually male) nickname in Britain for someone with sparkle or vim. **2 a** a \$20 bill. An item of black street talk which was included in so-called **Ebonics**, recognized as a legitimate language variety by school officials in Oakland, California, in late 1996.

twirl *n British* a prison officer. An item of prisoners' jargon recorded in the 1990s. 'Twirl' in the sense of a (skeleton) key is an archaic piece of underworld argot dating back to the 19th century.

twirp *n* an alternative spelling of **twerp**.

twist *n American* a girl or young attractive woman. This term, used typically by underworld or working-class speakers, is a rare example of American rhyming slang, from 'twist and twirl': girl.

✎'*M-m-m – goodlooking twist!*'
(*Panic on the 5.22*, US film, 1974).

twister *n American* a person with supposedly perverted sexual taste or preferences.

twit *n British* a foolish or absurd person. A common colloquialism, particularly in the 1950s or 1960s, the word was probably coined in the 1920s under the influence of nitwit, **twat** and **tit**. In the 1970s the word has gained currency in the USA via British TV comedies.

twitch *n British See* **get a twitch on.**

two and eight *n British*
a a fit of agitation.

✎'*What with coming home to find the place burgled, then all these bills arriving, I was in a right two and eight.*' (Recorded, middle-aged woman, London, 1988).

b a dishevelled, disorganized or grotesque person.

✎'*Look at 'er, she's a right two-and-eight.*'

Both senses of the term are London working-class rhyming slang for a 'state'. The rhyming-slang versions were in vogue in the early 1970s.

two-bit *adj American* cheap, penny-pinching, worthless. This Americanism of the mid-19th century is now occasionally used even in countries where 'two bits' does not signify 25 cents (a 'bit' is one-eighth of a dollar).

twoccer, twocker *n British* a joy-rider, car-thief. This term of criminal slang comes from the offence recorded on charge sheets as 'taken without owner's consent', and refers to the culture of **hotting** which grew up in working-class areas in the 1990s.

two-pot screamer *n Australian* a person more than usually unable to cope with the effects of strong drink. A term of disapproval used by hearty males in particular.

✎'*Hi! my husband's pissed again – he's always been a two pot screamer.*' (*The Wonderful World of Barry McKenzie*, Barry Humphries and Nicholas Garland, cartoon strip in *Private Eye* magazine, 1968).

twot *n British* an alternative spelling of **twat**.

uv

Uganda *n See* **discuss Uganda**.

uggers *adj British* ugly. A term popular with adolescents in the late 1990s using the long-established familiarizing suffix **-ers**.

ugly pills *n* an imagined source of repellent physical characteristics, manners or behaviour. The words usually form part of a sardonic speculation that the person in question has been **taking ugly pills**.

u-ie *n* a U-turn. The expression is used by skateboarders as well as drivers, usually in the form '*do a u-ie*' or '*hang a u-ie*'. *See* **hang a louie, hang a ralph**.

uncle *n* **1** *British* a pawnbroker. A use of the word which arose in the 18th century, referring (probably ironically) to the moneylender's avuncular assistance. The term was still heard in London in the 1950s and may survive. From the 1980s it was heard in the British TV series 'Eastenders'.
2 *American* a cry of concession. To **say uncle** or **cry uncle** is to surrender or admit defeat, in playground games for instance. The reason for this choice of word is obscure.
3 *American* the law-enforcement establishment seen as benevolent, protective or rewarding by crooks.
All three main senses of the word derive from the notion of uncle as a potential protector or provider of funds (in the third case perhaps reinforced by **Uncle Sam**). There are many other instances of this, for instance in theatrical jargon where the word equates with **angel**.

uncle, Uncle Dick *adj British* sick. One of many rhyming-slang expressions using 'uncle' and a convenient rhyming Christian name.
↳'*You look a bit uncle to me.*'

(*Minder*, British TV series, 1984).

Uncle Mac *n British* heroin. London drug-users' rhyming slang for **smack**. 'Uncle Mac' was a presenter of children's radio programmes from the 1930s to the 1960s. This sinister borrowing dates from the late 1970s.

Uncle Nab *n See* **nab**.

Uncle Ned *adj, n British* **1** dead.
2 bed.
3 head.
All these senses have been recorded in London rhyming-slang usage; the first is possibly the least dated.

uncool *adj* unacceptably or unfashionably intrusive, assertive, dull, reckless, conventional, etc. An all-purpose negative complement to the all-purpose term of approbation, **cool**. In late 1980s usage uncool perhaps retains unfashionable overtones of the **hippy** era, whereas cool has been enthusiastically adopted by the younger generation.
↳'*Weekend hippies and the like who think "what a groovy joy-ride" and are very, very uncool.*'
(*International Times*, April 1968).

under *n British* sexual activity. A 1960s expression in mainly working-class use, primarily in the phrase **a bit of under**. It is probably a shortening of 'undercover work', used as a euphemism for covert and scandalous behaviour.

underarm *adj British*
a underhand, **dodgy**.
b illegal, illicit.
The use of underarm in these senses stems from the literal sense of passing or carrying something concealed under the arm, reinforced by the supposed offensive nature of the armpit. ('Under the arm' is an archaic expression, once used by vagrants and marginals and meaning bad or inferior.)

underchunders *n pl Australian* underpants (male or female). A humorous vulgarism which employs **chunder** (vomit) as a rhyme, rather than for sense (unless the original image was of a sickening item of clothing).

underdaks *n pl Australian* (men's) underpants. The Australian equivalent of the north of England expression **under-**

kecks, from **daks**, the trade name of a popular brand of casual trousers.

underground *n, adj, adv* (belonging to) the 'alternative society' or counterculture, opposed to bourgeois society. A term from the 1960s adopted from the wartime usage applied to clandestine resistance movements. (The term 'underground railroad' was earlier used for the system of sympathizers/safe houses by which escaped slaves were taken from the Southern States to the North before emancipation.)

under heavy manners *adj, adv* in a state of oppression. A phrase from the counterculture patois of Jamaica which became known in Britain and elsewhere due to its use by reggae musicians in the early 1970s.

underkecks *n pl British* underpants. An extension of the (mainly northern English) use of **kecks** to mean trousers.

underware *n* personal files in a computing system. A piece of jargon in use among computer specialists in the mid-1990s.

underwhelmed *adj* disappointed, unimpressed. A humorous counterpart to the standard English overwhelmed. The coinage began to be heard in the early 1970s and is now in fairly widespread use.

✎ *'I must tell you I was distinctly underwhelmed by what I saw.'*

undie-grundie *n American* the grabbing and twisting of a victim's underwear. A form of jocular attack used by school and college students in the US.

unglued *adj* another version of **untied**.

unhip *adj* unaware, culturally and/or socially out-of-touch, unfashionable. The opposite of **hip**. The word has rarely been heard since the early 1970s, except among the remnants of the 'counterculture'.

unit *n* 1 a the genitals. An unromantic 1970s and 1980s term used by the self-consciously liberated or promiscuous to refer to (usually male) sex organs.

b a potential or actual sexual partner or conquest. A cold-blooded piece of singles-bar jargon from the mid- to late 1970s,

similar in usage and connotation to the more common **item**.

✎ *'Would ya look at that li'l unit in hot-pants, though!'*
(R Crumb cartoon, *Head Comix*, 1970).

See also **t.l.u.**

2 *n Australian* an apartment. The term is an abbreviation of the official designation *'home unit'*, and usually refers to what is known in the UK as a maisonette and in the US as a condominium.

unload *vb*

a to defecate.

b to **fart**.

A vulgarism which is heard all over the English-speaking world but which is particularly popular in Australia.

unmentionables *n pl*

a underwear.

b genitals.

A mock-Victorian euphemism for taboo personal items. The expression was used fairly seriously in the early 1900s; since at least World War II, the usage has invariably been facetious.

unplugged *adj British* behaving naturally and unself-consciously rather than boisterously, particularly towards a partner or friend. This sense of the word, heard among adolescents in the later 1990s and usually referring to male behaviour, is inspired by the use of the term to describe rock and pop musicians performing informal and relaxed acoustic sets as opposed to more contrived electrified stage shows.

unravelled *adj* an alternative version of **untied**.

unreal *adj*

a unbelievably good, excellent.

b outrageous, excessive or unreasonable in behaviour.

Both usages are from the jargon of teenagers, firstly (since the 1960s) in the USA and later elsewhere in the English-speaking world. The expression in fact originated in the **beatnik** era when unreal was an exclamation of hallucinated delight or admiration.

unt-cay *n American* the vagina. An item of pig-Latin based on **cunt**.

unthinkables *n pl British*

a underwear.

b genitals.

A students' facetious mock-Victorian euphemism coined in imitation of **unmentionables**.

↳ *'She left her door open and I got a glimpse of her unthinkables.'*
(Recorded, male university student, London, 1988).

untidy *adj Australian* drunk. A humorous euphemism.

untogether *adj* disorganized, confused, diffuse. This popular **hippy**-era term more often than not refers to the personality or mood of someone who is not in equilibrium emotionally, intellectually or psychically. It postdates its opposite, **together**. Untogether is now rarely heard, but survives in the sociolect of those reaching adolescence in the late 1960s.

up *adj* 1 *American* 'dried', having forgotten one's lines. A theatrical term of uncertain origin.

2 exhilarated or intoxicated, **high**.

up against the wall *exclamation* a shout of rage, defiance or menace. This Americanism, chanted on anti-war or Black Power demonstrations in the late 1960s and early 1970s, and invariably followed by the epithet **motherfucker**, was intended to evoke the righteous rage of a revolutionary mob about to summarily execute their oppressors, and to parody the police instruction when 'spreading' a suspect or captive.

upchuck *vb* to vomit. A humorous reversal of **chuck up** (itself based on 'throw up'), this expression surfaced in the USA in the 1920s and, having spread to British and Australian speech, has enjoyed a limited currency ever since.

up each other/one another *adj, adv Australian* engaged in mutual flattery, 'in cahoots'. The image is that of mutual sodomy, colourfully suggesting an unhealthy or illegally close relationship (often in a political or business context).

upfront *adj* bold, assertive, open, straightforward, trustworthy. The word is usually used approvingly of someone acting honestly or without guile.

uphill gardener *n British* a male homosexual. The term was one of many pejorative synonyms (**stabber**, **fudge-nudger**, **rear-gunner**, etc.) denoting 'active' or 'predatory' homosexuality, heard in the 1990s.

up oneself *adj Australian* self-satisfied, smug, high-handed. A vulgar version of 'full of oneself', evoking autosodomy.

↳ *'They're all up themselves, that lot.'*
(Referring to members of a University Department, teacher, Melbourne, 1988).

uppers *n pl* stimulant drugs such as amphetamines (**pep pills, speed**), cocaine, as opposed to **downers** (barbiturates and sedatives).

↳ *'He acts as if he's on uppers.'*

uppie, uppy *adj British* exhilarating, exciting, powerful. A term from the lexicon of **rave** and dancefloor culture in the northwest of England in the late 1990s.

uppy *adj* aggressive, assertive. The term, often used in the phrase *'getting uppy'*, is heard throughout the English-speaking world but particularly in Lowlands Scots speech.

up shit creek *adj* in serious trouble. Shit creek was a 19th-century nickname (probably coined by British or American sailors) for any stagnant or dangerous backwater or river. The expression is often embellished as *'up shit creek without a paddle'*, sometimes adding *'in a barbed wire canoe'*. *'Up the creek'* is a less offensive version.

upstairs *adj, adv*

a (in) the brain, head, mental or cerebral faculties. Used in such expressions as *'nobody home upstairs'* (i.e. a person is stupid), or *'she's got a lot upstairs'* (i.e. she is intelligent).

b the breast area (referring to women). Used in phrases such as *'there's plenty upstairs'* (of a well-endowed woman).

c (in) heaven. Reference may be made to *'the man upstairs'* (God).

A widely-used colloquial euphemism.

up the duff *adj British* pregnant. A working-class synonym of **up the pole/spout/stick**, here employing the long-established British metaphor of pudding. Duff is an old-fashioned boiled or steamed pudding; the word is a dialect version of 'dough'. It has an all-purpose sexual sense (encompassing gratification, penis, semen, woman and baby).

up the guts *adj Australian/South African* pregnant. A vulgar version of **up the duff/stick**.

up the poke/pole/spout/ stick *adj British* pregnant. These expressions are in mainly working-class use. They are all vulgar, simultaneously evoking the male and female sex organs and the idea of a baby being lodged or jammed. They can describe either the act of conception, as in '*he's put her up the stick*', or the condition, as in '*she's up the stick again*'.

uptight *adj* 1 tense, repressed, humourless, unrelaxed. A black slang term which is probably in origin a short-form of 'wound-up tight' or 'screwed-up tight'. The term was adopted into the **hippy** vocabulary to express the unliberated, repressed characteristics of **straight** society, particularly the authority figures thereof. Since the early 1970s uptight has passed into (mainly middle-class) colloquial usage, although by the late 1980s it had begun to sound rather dated.

↳'*The cops? Oh, just about as uptight and corrupt as in Britain.*'
(Terry Reid interviewed in *Oz* magazine, February 1979).

2 *American* satisfactory, in good order. In black American street-talk the expression retains a second, rare and positive connotation, possibly deriving from 'locked-up tight', meaning fixed, settled, under control, or, alternatively and more probably, from a sexual sense of being 'coupled' or 'snuggled-up tight'.

↳'*It's uptight, everything is all right/Uptight, it's out of sight.*'
(Chorus lyric from 'Uptight' by Stevie Wonder, 1963).

up to one's pots *adj British* drunk. An expression in use among the **gay** theatrical community since the 1960s.

urban surfing *n* riding on the outside of a moving car, bus, train, etc. A dangerous fad of the later 1980s among adolescents, first in the USA and later elsewhere.

u.s. *adj British* useless. Mainly used by middle- and upper-class speakers, the term can apply to objects or people.

↳'*This female razor thing is absolutely u.s.*'

(Recorded, female, Bath, 1986).

user *adj* a habitual drug user, especially referring to a heroin addict.

U.S.G. *n American* a black Afro-Caribbean neighbourhood. The initials stand for '*United States Ghetto*'. An item of black street talk which was included in so-called **Ebonics**, recognized as a legitimate language variety by school officials in Oakland, California, in late 1996.

using *adj* addicted to heroin or habituated to another hard drug. A euphemism employed by law enforcers and drug abusers.

↳'*Looks like she's using again.*'

u.vs *n pl American* ultra-violet rays, sunshine. A **preppie** and **Valley Girl** usage in phrases such as '*catch/cop/grab/soak up some u.vs*'.

V *adj British* very. Often heard in middle-class speech as in 'v. good', 'v. difficult', etc.

vadge *n* the vagina. A vulgarism (it also occurs in the form **fadge**) in use among adolescents in the 1990s and listed in *Viz* comic in 1994. **Vige** is an American synonym.

Vals, Valley Girls *n pl American* a Californian (and later more widespread) youth culture of the early 1980s, based on the habits, mannerisms, and distinctive vocabulary of teenage girls from the San Fernando Valley region of outer Los Angeles. The **Vals**, daughters of affluent parents working typically in the media, music industry or professions, had developed a sybaritic lifestyle in which consumerism ('recreational shopping') and leisure activities were elevated to a social code. The phenomenon was articulated in the US press by Moon Unit Zappa, daughter of the rock musician Frank Zappa, subsequently by *The Valley Girl's Guide to Life* (by Mimi Pond, published 1982) and in Britain by an article in *Harpers and Queen* magazine in 1983. Vals employed a colourful hyperbolic repertoire of slang, typically expressed in a high-pitched, breathless drawl. Their lexicon was partly invented and partly adopted or adapted from the argot of surfers, college and high-school students and other sources. (**Grody**, **gnarly** and **to the max** are examples). Many of these terms became teenage vogue expressions on a wider scale in the mid-1980s.

↳ *'The greatest creative work that any Val does is trying to think of a good slogan for her* [car number] *plate.'*
(*Harpers and Queen* magazine, 1983).

Valspeak *n American* the jargon of **Valley Girls**, as spoken in California in the early 1980s, and subsequently elsewhere.

↳ *'Valspeak is an almost impossible farrago of surfer expressions, Midwesternisms and irrational neologisms, delivered in nasal lockjawed whining tones.'*
(*Harpers and Queen* magazine, 1983).

vamoose *vb American* to leave, go away, get moving. The word, familiar since its use in cowboy-era fiction and subsequent film and TV drama, is a corruption of the Spanish *vamos* ('we're going') or ¡*vamonos*! ('let's go!').

↳ *'OK I think it's time we vamoosed.'*

vamp *vb, n* (to behave as) a seductress. The word is usually employed only semi-seriously to denote an individual (usually but not invariably female), affecting a languid, mysterious and predatory air. The term arose in 1918, inspired by the vampire legend as interpreted by such film stars as Theda Bara.

vamp up *vb British*
a to intensify, make more effective, improve or renovate.
b to improvise, ad-lib.
These colloquial usages are from the standard informal musical sense of 'vamp' (an improvised accompaniment, ultimately from the archaic French *avant-pied*) not, as is often assumed, from the verb **vamp** (to pose as a temptress).

V and T *n British See* **V.A.T.**

vanilla *adj* innocuous, orthodox. The adjective was applied from the early 1980s to otherwise illicit behaviour such as '*vanilla lesbian(ism)*', '*vanilla sex*', etc.

varder, va(h)da(h), vardy, vardo *vb British* to see, look (at). These are forms of the Romany verb to watch (originally rendered as *varter*), used especially in the 1950s and 1960s in the slang of the street market, fairground and theatre. The word was briefly exposed to a wider audience by its use by the **camp** characters 'Julian' and 'Sandy' in the

Kenneth Horne radio comedy shows of the 1960s.

V.A.T. *n British* (a) vodka and tonic. This abbreviation, popular in London in the 1980s, puns on that for Value Added Tax. The American usage 'V and T' is the more usual form.

va-va-voom *exclamation, n American* this imitation of a revving engine or explosive takeoff is used to suggest overwhelming sexual potential or allure. The word was particularly popular (among males) in the 1960s and often featured in *Mad* magazine, usually as the name of a starlet.

veep *n American* a V.I.P., 'very important person'.

veggie, vedgie *n, adj* (a) vegetarian.

veg/vedge-out *vb* to vegetate, idle or loaf. A predominantly adolescent usage, heard in the 1980s, first recorded almost simultaneously in the USA and Australia.

↳ *'I think we'll spend next week just vegging out in front of the TV.'*

velcro *n* **1** a lesbian. The use of the trademark term dates from the late 1980s and is derived from the supposed similarity between the lesbian practice of pressing pubic areas together and Velcro fasteners, consisting of two pieces of rough fabric.
2 *American* also **velcroid**, an intrusive or 'clinging' person, especially a neighbour. A piece of adult or family slang using the trademark name of the fabric-fastening material.

velcro-head *n* a negro. A phrase from the 1980s, deriving from the supposed likeness between Velcro (a trademark name for a fabric fastening material) and a black person's hair. Like **rag-head** and **towelhead** as applied to Arabs, the term is invariably pejorative.

ventilate *vb* to shoot (someone) full of holes. A usage largely confined to crime or western fiction.

ventilate someone's shorts *vb American* to give someone a severe telling-off or dressing-down. A colourful campus phrase of the 1980s invoking the image of a miscreant with backside (and underwear) shredded by a blast of buck-shot.

Vera (Lynn) *n British* (a glass of) gin. Rhyming slang based on the name of the patriotic wartime singer, still heard in the 1990s, often in conjunction with **supersonic**. *Compare* **Veras**.

Veras *n pl British* cigarette papers. This shortening of the London rhyming slang of **Vera Lynns**, meaning **skins**, was popular among younger cannabis-smokers in the 1990s. *Compare* **Vera (Lynn)**.

verbal(s) *n British* 'a verbal is an oral statement of admission or incrimination which is invented by the arresting or interviewing officer and attributed to a suspect' (wrote Deputy Assistant Commissioner David Powis in his *Field Manual for Police* published in 1977). A verbal is in other words a lie. The word can also be used in the phrases 'work the verbal' (synonymous with **work the oracle**) or 'put the verbal in', 'put the verbals on', or as a verb, to **verbal**. These are all items of police jargon in current use.

verboten *adj* forbidden, prohibited. The German term has been used, usually facetiously, in English since World War II as an intensive form of its literal translation.

↪'*Talking to his girlfriend is absolutely verboten.*'

very *adj American*
1a a term of approval, admiration, etc.
↪'*Wow, that bag is, like, very!*'
b a non-commital comment or response.
↪'*What was the hairdo like? Well it was, like, very.*'
These witticisms, formed by excluding the expected qualifying adjective for effect, occur in the affected or mocking speech of adolescents and teenagers in the US, particularly females. (**Totally** is employed in the same way.)

vet *n American* a veteran (soldier). A term best-known in the context of the post-Vietnam war era.

vibe *n* ambience, atmosphere, mood, the latest news. A shortening of **vibrations**, popular in the **hippy** era, vibe was applied catholically to anything that was 'in the air' from an intuitive empathy ('*I like it here. There's a really good vibe about the place*') to an item of hot gossip ('*Hey man, what's the vibe about Mary?*').

The plural **vibes** was a more widespread near-synonym.

vibe on *vb American* to be sympathetic toward, understand, appreciate. A **hippy** term deriving from the notion of having good vibes about someone.

↪'*Some people would say things like, "Oh, that boy's gonna really be great. You don't know how talented that boy is." And the others would say, "Yeah, yeah, yeah, uh-uh, sure." They didn't really vibe on me.*'
(Stevie Wonder, *Musician* magazine, 1984).

vibes *n pl* feeling, atmosphere, mood. A key term and concept in the **hippy** psychic repertoire, vibes denotes the unseen and unheard but nonetheless experienced **vibrations** linking individuals with each other and with the cosmos. The word originated among jazz devotees and **beatniks** and survives in the post-hippy era in limited and usually facetious usage. (James Taylor was ridiculed by British rock journalists when he claimed that he 'grooved to the vibes' at a 1973 Albert Hall concert.)

↪'*Besides, nobody there gave off vibes that heavy. I'd say the heaviest vibes on the premises were on the order of $100,000 a week.*'
(Drug dealer, *IT* magazine, July 1972).

vibrations *n pl* invisible emanations or forces, experienced as psychological sensations; feelings, ambience. A word (and notion) in evidence since its use by 19th-century spiritualists, but in very limited currency until it became part of the vocabulary of jazz musicians, **beatniks** and, most significantly, **hippies**. The word was generally shortened to **vibes**.

vic *n American* a victim, dupe. An underworld term heard in the 1990s.

vicious *adj* impressive, powerful, exciting. A teenage term of approval, admiration or satisfaction on the lines of the more widespread **bad** and **wicked**.

↪'*That's some vicious venue, know what I mean?*'

vige *n American* the vagina. An alternative form of **vadge, fadge**.

village *n, adj British* (someone who is) slow-witted, stupid. This middle-class term, often used by middle-aged speakers, is a shortening of 'village idiot'.

✥ *'I've always considered her rather village.'*

villain *n British* a criminal. The standard police slang designation of a lawbreaker, villain has been used in this way since the inter-war years.

✥ *'Labelled a Black Villain.'*
(Title of autobiography of Trevor Hercules, 1989).

✥ *'He found two villains in possession of stolen goods. They offered him a substantial bribe and he devised a way to get them out of trouble.'*
(Former detective, *Inside the Brotherhood*, Martin Short, 1989).

-ville *suffix* a termination used in **hip** talk, **beatnik** slang and later teenage usage. It denotes place, situation or state of affairs. **Endsville** (the ultimate in either boredom or pleasure) and 'Dullsville' (boredom only) are typical examples. The French form *ville* (town, from Latin *villa*) was used by early American settlers, like '-city' or '-burg', to create placenames.

Vincent Price *n British* ice. An item of rhyming slang used by drinkers and bar staff, (employing the name of the American horror movie star) often in conjunction with **Vera Lynn** and **supersonic**.

vinegar strokes *n pl British* the pelvic thrusting just before the achieving of male orgasm. An item of sexual slang which has been common in armed-forces' usage since World War II, it has more re-

cently been given prominence by alternative comedians such as Frank Skinner, as well as by references in the comic *Viz*.

✥ *'Aye, he'd just got to the vinegar strokes when he were interrupted.'* (*The Viz Big Fat Slags Book*, 1994).

vines *n pl American* clothes. A term, which probably arose in the **beatnik** era, is still heard among adolescents in the 1990s. **Rags**, **threads** and, recently, **garms** are synonyms.

✥ *'Hey, tasty vines.'*

vino *n* wine. This is the Italian and Spanish translation of the English word.

vitamin A *n* LSD, **acid** or **ecstasy**.

vitamin C *n* cocaine.

vitamin E *n* ecstasy.

vitamin X *n* ecstasy.

vogu(e)ing *n American* showing off, behaving ostentatiously. The term, which probably originated in black street slang, denoted a particular style of imitation catwalk posing adopted by hip-hop aficionados and later by the singer Madonna in the 1980s. *Compare* **profiling, styling**.

voice *n See* **throw one's voice**.

vom *vb, n* (to) vomit. A shortening typically used by teenagers and students.

vung *n South African* a car.

wabblefats *n American* an alternative spelling of **wobblefats**.

wack *adj* inferior, worthless, unpleasant. A vogue term in use in the black hip-hop and **rap** subcultures in the early 1980s. The term is probably derived from 'whacky'. By the 1990s it was employed as an all-purpose pejorative, also in use among British and Australian adolescents.

wack, wacker *n British* a term of address between males in working-class speech of the Liverpool area. The word may be connected with **whack** meaning share or portion (as in '*pay one's whack*'). *See also* **whacker**.

wacko *n See* **whacko**.

wacky *adj See* **whacky**.

wacky baccy *n British See* **whacky baccy**.

wad *n*
a a bundle of banknotes, a large quantity of money. Wad had been used in this sense all over the English-speaking world since the end of the 19th century. In Britain the word was heard principally in working-class speech before being adopted as a vogue term in 1988 following its use by the alternative comedian Harry Enfield. One of his **Loadsamoney** character's catchphrases was '*wanna see my wad?*' shouted before brandishing a roll of notes.
b the male genitals. A vulgarism in both homo- and heterosexual use. (Wad had previously signified semen; a metaphor based on the plugs used in loading muskets and cannon. That sense of the word survives in such expressions as **jerkwad**.)
c *British* a bun or (thick) slice of bread.

-wad *combining form American* a termination (denoting a despicable, disgust-ing person) seen in such compounds as **jerk-wad**, **dick-wad**, **butt-wad**. The wad in question originally referred to tissues used as a receptacle for bodily excrescences. **-weed** is a disguised version of the same suffix.

wadge *n British* a variant spelling of **wodge**.

wag *vb Australian* to play truant. A variant of the older British form 'hop the wag', in which the wag in question is a shortening of waggon.

↪ '*And don't you go wagging school this afternoon either – I might be bringing Frank round.*'
(*Richmond Hill*, Australian TV series, 1988).

wag it *vb British* to play truant. A modern version of the phrase 'hop the wag', in which the wag is a shortening of waggon. The Australian **wag** and **wag off** are other modern derivations.

↪ '*"All these kids", says Marjorie disapprovingly. "Wagging it, I suppose".*'
(David Lodge, *Nice Work*, 1988).

wag off *vb* to bunk off, play truant. This 1980s variant on the old phrases 'hop the wag' and 'on the wag', used by schoolchildren, is heard in Britain and Australia. (The word was defined for viewers in a report on *Newsround*, a BBC TV children's programme, in June 1988.) Compare **wag** and **wag it**.

waldo *n American* a fool. An American personification, similar to the British **wally**, in use among teenagers and college students.

walk *vb* 1 to go free. A term popularized by its use in US TV crime dramas and the like.
↪ '*Just give us the names we want and we'll let you walk.*'
2 to escape, leave, disappear.
↪ '*And the guy walked. (He walked with twenty million dollars but he walked.)*'
(*Serious Money*, play by Caryl Churchill, 1987).

walkabout *n, adv See* **go walkabout**.

wall *exclamation* a statement of incomprehension or bafflement. In use among **cyberpunks** and **net-heads**, it originated in the jargon of professional computer specialists.

wallah *n British* a fellow, person. A well-known Anglo-Indian word, surviving into the modern era. The term, often used as a combining form meaning 'person in charge of' as in the obsolescent 'box-wallah' (a peddler or salesman) and modern coinages like 'office-wallah', is from the Hindi *wala* meaning inhabitant (of) or protector (of).

wall-flower *n British* a would-be escapee. An item of prison slang recorded in the 1990s.

wallop *n* strong alcoholic drink. A light-hearted term inspired by the supposed effect of alcohol (although until recently, the word more often denoted beer than spirits).

↳*'A pint of wallop.'*

wallopers *n pl British* police officers. A nickname from the 1950s, now obsolete in Britain but occasionally heard in Australia.

↳*'Please, please Sid. You'll have the wallopers in here in a minute.'*
(*Hancock's Half Hour*, British comedy series, October 1959).

wally, wallie *n British* **1** a pickled gherkin. This old working-class name for a bottled delicacy is still heard in London. It may be a variation of 'olly', a corruption of olives, to which the gherkins were likened by earlier unsophisticated eaters.

↳*'Want a gherkin, Doll?... Charlie calls them Wallys I call them gherkins.'*
(East Ender, *Sunday Times* colour supplement, 2 June 1968).

2 a foolish, ridiculous, clumsy and/or unsophisticated person. This word emerged from obscurity into great popularity between 1976 and 1978 and many theories as to its origin have since been advanced. What seems certain is that the word originated in working-class London usage. The word began to be used in the school playground and in the media from about 1978 (with a meaning very similar to its almost contemporary American counterpart, **nerd**). The term may derive from the earlier sense of a pickled gherkin (**dill** is a synonym in both senses) or from an obscure dialect origin (the archaic Scottish dialect *waly draigle*, meaning weakling has been proposed). **Punks**, who helped to popularize the expression, cited an eponymous Wally, friend and fan of the Sex Pistols and other coevals; it also seems possible that the usage simply arose because of what was felt to be the inherent comicality of the Christian name.

↳*'All the jolly wallies on day-time Radio 1 hate Morrissey's guts. He must be doing something right.'*
(*Independent*, 26 February 1988).

↳*'The George Formby Appreciation Society in plenary session. Until you have seen this herd of wallies, all long past their sell-by dates and playing their ukeleles in time to a film of their diminutive hero, you haven't lived.'*
(John Naughton, *Observer*, 15 January 1989).

3 a cry or chant, heard for example at rock concerts (particularly of the **punk**, post-punk, **hardcore** variety). This phenomenon recalls the street and playground cry '*ollie, ollie, ollie!*' heard in London in the 1950s and 1960s and recorded in cockney use as long ago as the 1870s as a shout of recognition or derision.

wamba, womba *n British* money. A vogue word in 1988 and 1989, emerging from London working-class argot into more general usage (to the extent that it was included in the dialogue in a TV advertisement in summer 1989). Wamba like many other obscure or dated synonyms (**rhino, moolah, spondulicks**, etc.) came into use in the financially oriented atmosphere of the later 1980s. It is presumably an imitation of exotic 'tribal-sounding' words influenced by the Amerindian 'wampum'. **Wonga** was a later variant form.

wand-waver *n American* a sexual exhibitionist, **flasher**. A term in use among police, prostitutes, etc. **Wienie-wagger** is an alternative.

wang, wanger *n* penis. More recent spellings of **whang, whanger**; words which emerged around the turn of the century. They probably derive from an echoic British dialect word meaning beat, hit or slap, with a secondary meaning of strike in the figurative sense of impress or surprise. Although a vulgarism, wang is often considered less offensive than **prick** (but probably more offensive than synonyms such as **dong, willie**, etc.). Unlike many similar terms, wang is not also used to denote a fool.

wanger, wanga *n* **1** *British* a schoolchildren's euphemism for **wanker**. This expression from the late 1980s is apparently sufficiently disguised to allow its use in the presence of adults or even on broadcasts such as the British children's TV series *Grange Hill*.

2 an alternative spelling of **whanger**.

wangler *n British* an ancient taxicab used for practice runs or illicit jobs. An item of taxi drivers' jargon recorded in the London *Evening Standard*, 22 April 1996.

wank *vb British* **1** to masturbate. This very widespread vulgarism (with some recent exceptions still taboo in the printed and broadcast media) is, perhaps surprisingly, of obscure origin. It seems to have entered the spoken language in the late 19th century, significantly at a time when the word **whang** was emerging as a vulgar term for penis. Wank (earlier spelled 'whank') is probably derived from the same source; 'whang' as a dialect word first meaning hit, beat or slap. Wank may be simply a variant pronunciation, or a development of the earlier word influenced by 'whack' and 'yank'. Since the 1960s the word has been used of and by women as well as men.

2 to behave in an ostentatious, self-indulgent and/or futile manner. A usage deriving from the interpretation of masturbation as purposeless and/or offensive.

wanker *n British* **1** a masturbator. For the probable etymology of the word see **wank**.

2 an inconsequential, feeble, self-indulgent or otherwise offensive person. The term of abuse or disapproval (most frequently applied to males) has been in use since the early 20th century, but became extremely common in the 1970s. In the USA the word is known, but its force as a taboo term in Britain is often underestimated by American speakers.

wankered *adj British* extremely drunk. A popular word with students and other adolescents in the 1990s.

wank off *vb British* to masturbate. A longer version of the more widespread term **wank**.

wank stain *n British* a tedious, insignificant and/or obnoxious person. This vulgarism seems to have arisen in the 1970s among adolescents; in the 1980s it became a popular term of abuse, particularly among students. The less offensive shortening, **stains**, was a vogue term of the late 1980s.

wanky *adj British* meagre, inadequate, disappointing. A popular term amongst schoolchildren, also used in the TV comedy *Men Behaving Badly* in 1995, formed from **wank(er)** and possibly influenced by **manky**.

wannabe *n* an aspirant or imitator. A fashionable Americanism of 1986 and 1987 which was quickly adopted in the UK. The wannabe, typically a teenager or young adult, exhibits an envious or ambitious desire, characterized by phrases such as '*I wannabe like Madonna*', 'I wannabe thin', 'I wannabe in the Seychelles', etc.

> '*There are two types of Wannabee. The first kind are the clones – the stagedoor Georges, the Cindy Lauperettes, the Apple scruffs, the Madonna Wannabees (aka Wannabes) – the devoted fans who ape their idols as closely as possible. The other kind are the young urban upstarts with a desperate lust for fame.*'
> (*I-D* magazine, November 1987).

warby *n, adj Australian* (something or someone) filthy, inferior or defective, coarse. This Australianism is a survival of a Scottish dialect term for maggot, archaic in Britain since the 19th century.

warehouse *vb British* to hold or attend an **acid house** party. *See* **warehousing**.

> '*The philologically inclined will note that in Tony's world the word "warehouse" has turned into a verb. "Yea," says Tony, "I warehouse, you warehouse...we was warehoused..." Essentially what it means is this: to overwhelmingly swamp with people.*'
> (*Evening Standard*, 9 October 1989).

warehousing *n British* the practice of arranging or attending **acid house** parties, also known as **orbital raves**; a youth sub-culture phenomenon of 1988 and 1989. The large gatherings in question require meticulous planning, being held in such venues as hangars or warehouses and publicized through semi-underground networks in order to foil police seeking to stop them. (Revellers usually pay to attend.)

warm fuzzies *n American* affection, comfort, friendliness, compliments. A light-hearted phrase from the 1970s, adopted by the business community to denote praise applied deliberately as a motivator. The notion is that of something warm, and perhaps furry, to be nuzzled as a reward or consolation.

warm the bed *vb British* to mobilize personal contacts to ensure a deal. The phrase occurs in the slang of City of London financial traders in the 1990s.

war-paint *n* make-up, female (earlier, theatrical) cosmetics. A humorous usage heard all over the English-speaking world since the mid-19th century.
  ⮞'*She's next door putting on her war-paint.*'

wart *n* an irritating, bumptious or unpleasant person. A term often applied by schoolchildren to younger pupils.

wash *n British*
crack. Washing refers to the chemical purifying of cocaine (with ether for instance) in order to produce freebase (*see* **freebasing**) or the more potent **crack**.

WASP *n* a 'white anglo-saxon protestant', a member of the traditionally dominant ethnic group in the US establishment. This was probably the first of many acronyms, first denoting ethnic subgroups (*see* **Jap**), later social sub-cultures (**yuppie** etc.). WASP originated in the 1960s.
  ⮞'*That's the thing you gotta understand about WASPs – they love animals. They can't stand people.*'
  (*Wall Street*, US film, 1987).
  ⮞'*Brooks Brothers is the natural habitat of the W.A.S.P. The image of the store is synonymous with the white, Anglo-Saxon Protestant male – a virile but wholesome species flourishing in middle America.*'
  (*Independent*, 12 March 1988).

waste (someone) *vb* to kill. A euphemism inspired by 'lay waste'. In the 1950s, US streetgangs used the word to mean defeat, criminals to mean kill. In the Vietnam War era the term first signified devastate and then annihilate and kill.

wasted *adj*
a exhausted, drained of energy.
b intoxicated by drugs (or occasionally alcohol), **stoned**. This is an extension of the sense of devastate, annihilate (arising in the late 1960s) on the pattern of **wrecked**, **smashed**, **blitzed**, etc.
c *American* penniless, broke. A now ob-

solescent sense of the term, heard in the 1950s.

water sports *n pl* urination as part of sex play. A euphemism from the repertoire of pornographers and prostitutes.

wax (out/up) *vb Australian* to share. The verb, heard in the early 1990s, probably derives from the notion of 'wack', meaning portion or share. A synonym is **wack up**.

wax the dolphin *vb American* (of a male) to masturbate. A humorous euphemism employed by adolescent males in the 1990s.

way! *exclamation* a contradiction of '*no way!*', popularized by the cult US film, *Wayne's World*, 1992.

way- *combining form* this intensifier, signifying 'extremely', was fashionable in youth subcultures in the late 1980s and early 1990s, particularly in the phrase **way-cool**.

way-cool *adj* admirable, fashionable. A catchphrase whose usage followed the usual course in moving from street subcultures in the early 1980s to pubescent schoolchildren in the mid-1990s.

wayk, wake, wark *adj British* abbreviated forms of the catchphrase term of approbation **way-cool** in use among teenagers in the later 1990s, often in the form of an exclamation.

Wayne *n British* an alternative personification to **Kevin**. Wayne and his female counterpart, usually **Sharon**, are embodiments of crassness, bad taste, etc. from the late 1970s and 1980s. The names were thought to epitomize working-class adolescents or young adults and were used derisively by those considering themselves socially superior or more sophisticated.

way-out *adj* extreme, excessive, exotic, eccentric. A vogue term first among pre-World War II jazz aficionados, later among **beatniks**. The phrase was picked up by more conventional speakers to refer to unorthodox behaviour and has become a fairly common, if dated expression.

wazoo *n American* anus. This humorous euphemism, usually used figuratively rather than literally, is most often heard in the phrase '*up the wazoo*'.

✎'*I wasn't expecting it but I got it right up the wazoo.*'

wazz *n British* an act of urination. A variant form of the more common **wizz**.

✎'*I've got to go for a wazz.*'
(London cab driver, *Guardian*, February 1994).

weasel *n* **1** a sly, devious, unprincipled and/or vicious person.

2 *British* **a** a dodge, stratagem or half-truth.

b a tip, reward achieved by trickery.

The weasel is a by-word for deviousness in all English-speaking areas. Historically, even its name embodies this; Old English weosule is related to the Latin *virus* and originally meant slimy liquid or poison.

weasel *vb British*

a to behave in a devious, sly or underhand way.

b to carry luggage in order to earn or extract a tip. The second sense is a specific instance of the more prevalent notion of untrustworthiness and unscrupulousness associated with the animal.

weasel words *n* insincere, devious or unscrupulous talk. This well-established usage probably derives from the weasel's claimed ability to suck the contents from an egg without shattering the shell, hence the notion of evasion.

wedding tackle *n British* the male genitals. A humorous phrase which is an elaboration of the earlier 'tackle', (heard in this context since the 18th century). Wedding tackle is a euphemism which is considered inoffensive enough to be broadcast and printed, as well as used in conversational contexts. It was popular during the 1980s but probably dates from much earlier. (Partridge dates the synonym 'wedding kit' to 1918.)

wedge *n* money, wealth. In the 18th century wedge specifically referred to silver, which criminals melted down and re-constituted as 'wedges' (ingots or bars). The term has been used throughout the 20th century by working-class speakers including street traders and criminals. Perhaps unconsciously influenced by **wad** and 'edge' the word has enjoyed renewed popularity like most of its synonyms in the money-conscious environment of the 1980s.

✎'*I've come into a bit of wedge.*'
(*Budgie*, British TV series, 1971).

wedged (-up) *adj British* financially well-endowed, wealthy or 'flush'. A racy working-class back-formation from **wedge** meaning money. Wedged (-up) or 'well-wedged' were adopted in the **yuppie** era by middle-class speakers.

✎'*... the senior partner who spends his lunch hours not at a sandwich bar but at a casino, and every so often comes back "wedged up with more than just a round of tuna mayonnaise".*'
(*Sunday Times*, 15 December 1996).

wee, wee-wee *n* urine, an act of urination. A nursery term in use for the last 90 or so years. The word is an invention probably influenced by **pee**, wet, the word wee meaning small (as opposed to **big jobs**) and the sound of urination.

✎'*One Way Out (BBC1) began unpromisingly for all but doting parents, with talk of wee-wees and poo-poos in the Wendy house, before getting down to the adult business of anatomising Bernard, the Glaswegian psycho-sexual incompetent whose ultimate disposal in a refuse sack we deem reasonable.*'
(Howard Jacobson, *Sunday Correspondent*, 17 September 1989).

wee, wee-wee *vb* to urinate. An inoffensive nursery term, often used facetiously by adults.

weed, the weed *n* **1** marihuana. The plant, *cannabis sativa*, which yields marihuana leaves grows like a weed in warm dry climates, and somewhat resembles nettles.

2 a also **the weed**, tobacco. In this form the word is often used when referring to the harmful nature of the plant and its derivatives.

✎'*Back on the weed again?*'

b a cigarette. A usage popular among American teenagers.

3 *British* a weak, ineffectual person. This usage, beloved of schoolboys in the 1950s and 1960s, is inspired by the visual comparison with a thin etiolated plant.

4 *British* **the weed** a system of extra, unofficial work or a scheme yielding unofficial or illicit income. The sense of the word, used by workers and fairground employees among others is probably now obsolete. It is related to the following verb form.

-weed *combining form American* a disguised or milder version of **-wad**, attached to the same words, as in **dick-weed**, **puss-weed**, etc.

weedhead *n* a marihuana smoker. A term which has been unfashionable since the mid-1960s, but which survives, like its synonym **pothead**, mainly in teenage parlance.

weedy *adj British* weak and ineffectual.

weenie *n American* another spelling of **wienie**.

weenie-wagger *n American See* **wienie-wagger**.

weezer *n American* a weak, eccentric and/or infirm person. The word, perhaps a combination of **wimp** and **geezer**, was adopted as the name of a US rock band in the early 1990s.

weight *n* 1 *British* one pound of hashish or marihuana. The drug dealers' and users' jargon term since the early 1960s; it is a shortening of 'pound weight'.

♦'*He sold them a weight of black.*'

2 *American* narcotics. The word in this context originally had the sense of a necessary or measured amount, but is often generalized to mean heroin or more recently marihuana, cocaine, etc.

♦'*I need some weight.*'

weighted off *adj British* imprisoned. This synonym for 'sent down' has been recorded in this form since at least the 1980s. In the form 'weighed off' it is much older, referring to the assessing of the criminal and subsequent passing of sentence carried out by the judge or prison governor.

weirdie, weirdo *n* a non-conformist, eccentric, a **beatnik** or **hippy**. The terms have been used, typically by disapproving adults, since the end of the 1950s; weirdie was the standard British version ('bearded weirdie' was an elaboration) until about 1966 when the American weirdo became more prevalent. The standard English word 'weird', (from old English wyrd: fate) not only describes the appearance and behaviour of 'deviants' but was a vogue word among beatniks themselves, meaning impressive and acceptable as well as bizarre.

weird out *vb American* to behave eccentrically, undergo a disturbing change of mood. An extension of the use of 'weird' in **hipster**, **beatnik**, **hippy** and later teenage parlance originally frequently used in a drug context, the phrase is currently more often referring to unpredictable or temperamental displays by children, parents etc. To weird someone out is to disorientate or confuse them.

weisenheimer *n American* a know-all, 'wise-guy', **wiseacre** or **wiseass**. The word, dating from the first decade of the 20th century, is an elaboration of the standard term 'wise' into a quasi-German or Yiddish surname (on the lines of Oppenheimer, etc.).

welch, welsh *vb* to fail to repay a loan or wager or to evade another obligation. Now virtually standard English, this term originated as 19th-century racecourse slang inspired by the archaic belief of the dishonesty or meanness of the inhabitants of Wales.

♦'*I knew he'd welch on the deal.*'

welfare-jockey *n American* a recipient of state subsidies, unemployment pay, etc. A pejorative term employed by the right-wing comic writer P. J. O'Rourke, among others.

well *adv British* very. A vogue usage among adolescents and younger schoolchildren since about 1987, from the slang of the streets (used by black **youth** and some white working-class adults) of the earlier 1980s. Typical instances of the word as intensifier are 'well good' and 'well hard'.

well-hung *adj* having large genitals. A vulgarism applied to males, (only very rarely used of large female breasts), for at least two hundred years. *See also* **hung**.

♦'*No male streakers are naff, least of all stupendously well-hung men who invade the pitch at a Test Match and upset Richie Benaud.*'
(*The Complete Naff Guide*, Bryson *et al.*, 1983).

wellie, welly *n British* 1 a force, impetus, power. The word often occurs in the phrase **give it some wellie**.

b brute strength, brawn as opposed to brain.

♦'*It was just welly, welly, welly. The ball must have been screaming for mercy.*'
(Ron Yates characterizing Wimbledon FC's style, *Independent*, May 1989).

2 a dismissal, the sack, as in get the wellie, the order of the wellie.

3 a condom. A term from the late 1980s using the name of one piece of protective rubberwear for another. Also known as a **willie-wellie**.

4 a green welly.

Wellie as a diminutive of wellington (boot) became a household word in the 1970s. It was quickly applied to figurative or metaphorical uses of the word or notion of 'boot', both as a noun and, later, a verb. The first instances of the use of the word have not been definitively identified, although the Scottish comedian Billy Connolly popularized the term, closely followed by several radio disc-jockeys.

5 an unattractive and/or obnoxious female. Coined by analogy with the colloquial '(old) boot'.

wellie *vb British* **1** to kick out, dismiss, sack.

2 to defeat, bully or attack. These are back-formations from the noun form of the word, heard since the end of the 1970s.

wellie-wanging *n British* a sport in which competitors vie to throw a wellington boot the furthest. The pastime enjoyed a vogue at village fêtes, fundraising events, etc. from the end of the 1970s. The 'wanging' component probably echoes the sound of the boot rebounding against turf or concrete, or else is influenced by 'fling' and 'wing'.

well-oiled *adj* drunk. A colloquial synonym for **lubricated**.

well on *adj*

a drunk.

b intoxicated by drugs.

In both senses the euphemism is fashionable in the late 1990s.

welsh *vb British* an alternative spelling of welch.

wenchy *adj American* obnoxious, condescending. Used particularly of and by women, the term is based on a specifically American colloquial sense of 'wench' as a forward, shameless or troublesome female. (In archaic dialect usage in Britain, the word, deriving from an Old English word for a child, had for several centuries signified a promiscuous or immoral woman.)

Wendy *n British* a feeble, ineffectual or contemptible person, a **weed**, **swot** or misfit among schoolchildren. The word is typically applied to schoolboys by their contemporaries in the 1980s. The name is supposed to epitomize 'girlishness' and, like **Tinkerbelle**, probably owes its resonance to a character in *Peter Pan* by J. M. Barrie.

wendy house *n British*

a a theatre, in camp 1960s **parlyaree** slang use.

b the period of the day and place in which prisoners are allowed to socialize, in the slang of inmates and prison officers.

Both usages are based on the children's play-house of the same name.

wet *adj British* **1 a** ineffectual, irresolute, feeble or foolish. A characterization common in service and public-school usage since the early 20th century.

b (of a Tory) having liberal views as opposed to being resolutely 'Thatcherite'. The schoolboy term began to be applied in 1980 as a term of disapproval to MPs with reservations about the style and substance of the current cabinet policies.

2 (of a woman) sexually aroused. Also expressed as **damp**.

wet *n British* **1 a** a weak irresolute or foolish person.

✎ '*Oh Nigel, you're such a wet!*'

b a Tory who is not a wholehearted supporter of the policies of Margaret Thatcher. The word was used by the Prime Minister herself in 1980.

2 the wet *Australian* the rainy season in North Australia.

wetback *n American* an illegal immigrant from Latin America. The term refers specifically to those swimming the Rio Grande, the river which forms the Mexican–US border. It dates from the 1940s.

wet scene *n American* a gory killing. An item of police and secret-service jargon of the 1970s.

✎ '*hellacious wet scene.*'
(Jonathon Kellerman, *Over the Edge*, 1987).

whack *n* **1** *British* a quantity or portion. The word is imitative of a slapping or smacking (down); here in the sense of dumping or depositing spoils onto a table or other surface.

✎ '*He insisted on his full whack.*'

2 *American* a contract killing. A variant of **hit**.

3 heroin. A later variant form of **smack**.

4 *American* a **whacky** person.

See also **wack**.

whack *vb American* to kill. A racier and more recent coinage based on the well-established use of **hit** in this sense.

whacker *n* **1** a **whacky** person, an irresponsible or eccentric individual.

2 an alternative spelling of **wack** or **wacker**.

whacko, wacko *n, adj* (someone who is) crazed, eccentric, insane. This racier version of the colloquial **whacky** has been heard since the mid-1970s. It was popularized by press references to the singer Michael Jackson as 'Wacko Jacko'.

⬥*'We got enough to handle without her going whacko on us.'*

whack off *vb* to masturbate. A vulgarism heard all over the anglophone world. Like many synonymous terms it employs the notion of striking or slapping.

whacko-the-diddle-o! *exclamation Australian* an expression of joy or triumph. This hearty cry, brought to the attention of a British readership via *The Adventures of Barry McKenzie*, the 1960s cartoon strip by Barry Humphries and Nicholas Garland, may be expressed by the shorter 'whacko!' or the equally colourful 'whacko the chooks!' (a **chook** is a chicken).

whack-up *vb* to share, apportion. The phrase is heard particularly in Australian speech.

whacky, wacky *adj* crazed, eccentric, insane. This now widespread colloquialism seems to have originated in northern English dialect meaning a fool (either by analogy with 'slap-happy' or as an imitation of 'quacking' speech). The word was particularly popular in the 1980s.

⬥*'Let's face it, Lady Sylvia is so wacky there are no boundaries of taste.'*
(Amanda Donohoe, *Time Out* magazine, March 1989).

whacky baccy *n* marihuana. A humorous nickname from **whacky** (eccentric or crazy) and **baccy** (tobacco).

whale *n See* **play the whale**.

wham-bam-thank-you-ma'am *n* a catchphrase used to characterize a brusque, cursory sexual act. The expression was heard among American servicemen in World War II (probably adopted from cowboy parlance). Currently the phrase is most often employed disapprovingly by feminists and others to describe a selfish or boorish male attitude to sex.

⬥*'I was hoping for something interesting or exciting, but it was just wham-bam-thank-you-ma'am.'*

whammers, wammers *n pl British* breasts. An adolescent vulgarism heard in the late 1980s.

whammy, the whammie *n American* a supernatural power, spirit or curse, responsible for punishment or retribution. A fanciful evocation, adapting the colloquial term 'wham', imitative of a heavy blow. The word is sometimes part of the phrase 'to put the whammy on someone or something'.

⬥*'Sarge, you got the whammy on me!'* (*Bilko*, US TV series, 1957).

whang, whanger *n* penis. These are earlier (and still current) spellings of **wang, wanger**.

whap *vb American See* **whop**.

what it is! *exclamation* an all-purpose exclamation of greeting, approval, solidarity, which originated in black American speech at the end of the 1980s and by the late 1990s was being heard in British school playgrounds. *'What it like?'* was a similar ritual greeting used by members of rival black street gangs the Crips and the Bloods in Los Angeles.

what to go? *exclamation British* a phrase used by teenage gangs as a provocation or invitation to fight. A synonym is **do me something**. Both phrases are often followed by **then?** The term was recorded in use among north London schoolboys in 1993 and 1994.

wheelie *n* a manoeuvre in which a vehicle is driven at speed on its back wheel(s) only. The term may apply to bicycles, motorcycles or cars: (in the case of cars the term may apply only to the spinning of the rear wheels).

⬥*'Stealing and nicking gives you lots of pleasure and money for everything.*

*And it's easy … you just get an old
lady in your sights and do a 360-de-
gree wheelie on her moustache.'*
(Teenage mugger, *Observer*, 22 May
1988).

wheelman, wheels-man *n* a
getaway driver. A piece of criminal and
police jargon in use in all English-speaking environments.

wheels *n* a car or means of transportation.

wheeze (off) *vb American* destroy,
defeat, frustrate. This adolescent usage
often occurs in the phrase '*wheeze off
someone's gig*' meaning to frustrate their
efforts, spoil their enjoyment, etc.

whiff *vb* 1 to sniff (cocaine).
2 *British* to smell bad. A synonym of **niff**.

whiffy *adj British* having an unpleasant smell. **Niffy** is a synonym.
↳ *'It's a bit whiffy in here, isn't it?'*

whinge *n* a complaint, bout of self-
pity.
↳ *'His "memoirs" are really an extended
whinge at how terribly he's been
treated by the corporation – seldom
offered any work, never appreciated
enough, sneered at by pinkoes, and so
on.'*
(*Private Eye* magazine, 27 October
1989).

whinge, winge *vb* to complain or
make excuses, especially in a wheedling
tone. A blend of 'whine' and 'cringe'
which existed for some time in Australian
usage before becoming established in
Britain in the second half of the 1970s.
The word was originally often found in
the phrase 'whingeing pom', describing
the perpetually complaining British immigrant.
↳ *'English people love a good queue, and
they love a good disaster; they seem
to love a good moan. I think the notion
of the "whingeing Pom" is true. But
I've become a whinger too, since I've
been here.'*
(Australian nurse, *NOW* magazine,
March 1988).

whiplash hustler *n American* a
pedestrian who stages a traffic accident in
order to claim insurance damages. These
pseudo victims are also known as **fender-
benders**. 'The whiplash effect' is medical
jargon for a characteristic – and easily

fakeable – injury in car crashes, colli-
sions, etc.

whipped *adj American* a shortened,
hence disguised and more acceptable version of **pussy-whipped**.

**whip some skull on (some-
one)** *vb American* to perform fellatio. A
phrase (using **skull** as a substitute for
head in a similar context), which was
often used as a ribald exclamation by college boys and **hippies** among others in
the late 1960s and early 1970s.

whirl(e) amount *n British* a large
quantity. This synonym for 'lots' or 'loads'
is usually used in connection with money.
The term was recorded in use among
north London schoolboys in 1993 and
1994.

the whirling pits *n British* a feeling of giddiness and/or nausea, tinged
with hallucination, brought on, for instance, by the combination of alcohol and
a drug such as hashish. The expression
describes a condition characterized by
lying on one's back, unable to move, while
one's stomach heaves and the room
whirls about one's head. **The helicopter**
is a synonym.

whistle *n British* a suit (of clothes).
From the rhyming-slang phrase 'whistle
and flute'. This term dates back to before World War II and has survived into
the late 1980s. It was used by London
mods, for instance, and is now heard
among students as well as working-class
Londoners. Since the 1950s the phrase
has almost invariably been abbreviated to
the one word.

white ant *vb Australian* to denigrate,
undermine. The phrase is based on the
action of the Australian termite and was
given prominence by its use in TV soap
operas such as *Neighbours*.

white bread *n, adj American* (someone) virtuous, well bred, but dull and insipid. A dismissive term, usually applied
to straitlaced or ingenuous people, from
the **preppie** lexicon. The word is also
used in marketing jargon, meaning bland
or inoffensive.

white lady, the white lady *n*
a cocaine.
b heroin. Often used to denote a spectre
in folklore, the phrase is employed here to

romanticize or dramatize the white powders or crystals in question.

↳ *"I've been through pot, white lady and blue lady (forms of synthetic heroin) and I can't go through this much more," says Jean Hobson.'* (*Sunday Times*, 10 September 1989).

white lightning *n* 1 raw spirit, illicitly distilled grain alcohol. The phrase evokes the sudden, devastating effects (and perhaps the accompanying visual disturbance) of the substance in question.
2 a generic nickname given to white tablets or **microdots** of LSD in the late 1960s and early 1970s, in the same fashion as **orange sunshine** or **blue cheer**.

whitener *n British* cocaine. A **yuppie** term.

↳ *'There are guys who blow out, sure, stick too much whitener up their nose.'* (*Serious Money*, play by Caryl Churchill, 1987).

white space *n* free time. **Yuppie** jargon of the late 1980s inspired by blank spaces in an appointment book, but deriving from the jargon of graphic designers, printers, typographers etc. in which white space refers to areas deliberately left blank in a layout.

↳ *'I think I have some white space towards the end of the week.'*

white telephone, big white telephone *n* the toilet bowl or pedestal. The term occurs in phrases such as 'making a call on the big white telephone', evoking the image of someone being noisily, and usually drunkenly, sick. The phrases probably originated in US campus slang of the early 1970s, which also gave synonyms such as **pray to the porcelain god**. One phrase combining both notions is 'call God on the big white phone'.

white trash *n*

a poor whites living in the southern states of the USA. A term coined by black speakers in the mid-19th century to refer to their neighbours, either pejoratively or ruefully. The term was also used by whites and survives into the late 20th century; it is often used with connotations of degeneracy and squalor.
See also **trailer-trash**.

b decadent rich or sophisticated individuals, the 'jet set' or their hangers-on and imitators. The phrase has been extended to refer contemptuously to cosmopolitan socialites (often in the phrase 'International White Trash'). **Eurotrash** is a derivative.

↳ *'She came from South Los Angeles, near Watts, every day and her parents had saved all their lives to buy her in among this rich white trash.'* (Julie Burchill, *The Face* magazine, March 1984).

whitey *n American* a white person. A predictable term used by black speakers to or of individuals and of the white community in general. It is usually, but not invariably, pejorative or condescending. **Pinkie** is a less common Caribbean and British form.

whizz *n See* wizz.

whoopsy, whoopsie, whopsy, woopsie *n British* an act of defecation, excrement. A nursery term sometimes used facetiously among adults, usually in the phrase 'do a whoopsie'.

whop, whap *vb American* to hit, beat, thrash. The terms (used for over 200 years) are echoic and are sometimes extended to mean defeat or trounce.

↳ *'They whopped us good.'*

whore *n* a prostitute. The word has been used in this sense since about the 12th century; before that time it denoted an adulteress and, earlier still, a sweetheart. The ultimate derivation of whore is the Latin *carus*: dear or beloved. In Germanic languages this became *horr* or *hora* (old Norse) and *hore* (old English).

↳ *'Thugs, whores, cabbies, street arabs, gin jockeys – these are by nature conservative folk.'* (*Republican Party Reptile*, P. J. O'Rourke, 1987).

whorehouse *n* a brothel.

↳ *'Pundits summarize [the history of Manila] as "four hundred years in a convent, fifty years in a whorehouse".'* (*Republican Party Reptile*, P. J. O'Rourke, 1987).

wick *n British* 1 penis. This sense of the word combines the candle-wick as phallic image and the London rhyming slang phrase **Hampton Wick** (for **prick**). Hampton Wick is a small community in the southwest London suburbs, familiar to cockneys of the past hundred years as being on their route to the nearby riverside, Hampton Court or Bushy Park. Wick is rarely found alone but rather in the phrases **dip one's wick** or **get on one's wick**.

2 *Irish* nonsense. The standard English word (originally meaning flammable material) is used in colloquial Irish to mean 'rubbish', hence this extended meaning.

wick *adj Irish* uncomfortable, embarrassed, ashamed. This usage may derive from the phrase 'get on one's wick', meaning annoy, irritate or from the second noun sense above.

↳*'Feeling wick.'*

wicked *adj* good, excellent. A US term of approbation adopted by UK teenagers. First in black and streetgang use, the word is now employed by analogy with **bad** but in this sense is probably much older, dating from the turn of the century. By 1989 wicked had become a vogue term even among primary-school children (sometimes in the emphatic form 'well wicked', meaning extremely good, and may sometimes be spelled **wikkid**).

↳*'I know it's a bit sexist, oh alright, misogynistic but the scratching is wicked man, wicked.'*
(*I-D* magazine, November 1987).

↳*'[Oxford University] aristocrats disguise themselves with lingo like: "It's wicked, guy".'*
(*Evening Standard*, 16 June 1988).

wicked pisser *n American* a notable or exceptional person, object or experience. The expression comes from New England and can be used both pejoratively and, more usually, appreciatively.

widdle *n British* an act of urination. This middle- and upper-class nursery vulgarism is a blend of **wee** and **piddle**.

widdle *vb British* to urinate. A combination of **wee** and **piddle**. This nursery term was given prominence when employed by Prince Philip to describe the actions of an ape during a visit to London Zoo.

↳*'Now sneak pictures of Prince William, apparently widdling into a hedge, are published in colour on the front page of the unsavoury Sunday People.'*
(Victoria Mather, *Evening Standard*, 22 November 1989).

wide-o *n* a disreputable, dishonest individual. The term is a variant form of the colloquial term 'wide-boy' where 'wide'

denotes untrustworthy, devious, dishonest.

wide-on *n* a feminine, feminist or jocular female version of **hard-on**.

widget *n* a device, small contraption or product. This synonym for, and adaptation of the word 'gadget' has been in use since before World War II in the USA. In Britain it has been widely used since the 1970s to denote a hypothetical otherwise unnamed product in business simulations, calculations, planning etc.

widgie *n Australian* a female equivalent/counterpart of a **bodgie** (**teddy boy**). The widgie was a less respectable Australian version of the **bobby soxer**, characterized by the wearing of hair tied into a ponytail, a long skirt or blue jeans, often accompanied by 'delinquent' behaviour. The name is said to be a diminutive of 'widgeon', as used as a term of endearment.

widow *n, adj British* (an) American. A piece of now almost obsolete London rhyming slang from around World War II, playing on Widow Twankey (a character in the pantomime *Aladdin*): Yankee.

↳*'Pipe the widow ginger!'*
(Recorded, bookie's runner, London, 1958).

(the) widows' and orphans' fund *n American* money given as bribes. A police euphemism. In Britain the 'policeman's ball' has been employed in a similar euphemistic role.

wienie, weenie, wiener *n American* **1** a frankfurter type sausage. The word is a contracted form of *wienerwurst* (Vienna-sausage).

2 penis. A term which is usually derisive, inspired by the small size and flaccidity of the sausage of the same name.

3 an ineffectual, foolish or tedious person. This sense applies particularly to **swots** in the argot of students.

wienie-wagger, weenie-wagger *n American*
a a male masturbator.
b a male sexual exhibitionist, a **flasher**.

↳*'He's just a wienie-wagger ... that's what the cops call them.'*
(*Lady Beware*, US film, 1987)

wigga, wigger *n* a white person who adopts the mannerisms, appearance and culture of blacks. The word blends white and **nigger** and was first coined by blacks to describe white participants in hip-hop and **rap** subcultures. The word is used appreciatively as well as neutrally or pejoratively.

↳*'Wiggas wannabe black: the word may be only a letter different from a serious case of racial abuse, but London's super-cool young whites carry it with pride.'*
(*Evening Standard*, 21 March 1994).

wigged *adj American* a 1990s variant form of **wiggy**.

wiggle-room, wriggle-room

n American freedom to manoeuvre, especially in a delicate situation. The term was common in the 1990s in armed-forces' and professional usage.

↳*'You've got to let us have some more wiggle-room.'*

wiggy *adj* crazy, eccentric, irresponsible. The word, from the **beatnik** lexicon, was often used approvingly as a synonym for **wild**. It derives from the use of wig to mean head or brain and the notion of 'flipping one's lid'. (**Liddy** is a less common synonym.)

wig out *vb* to go crazy, 'lose one's cool', 'flip one's lid'. A term from the argot of the **beatnik** era, based on wig used as a jocular term for head or brain in pre-World War II **jive** talk.

wikkid *adj* an alternative spelling of **wicked** (in its vogue youth sense of admirable).

wild *adj* exciting, impressive, excellent. This was a vogue term among jazz aficionados, **hipsters** and **beatniks** of the 1950s in the USA. It is inspired by the use of wild to mean enthusiastic in the phrase 'wild about something'. The transferred use of wild as a term of approbation mainly survives in adolescent and pre-teenage speech.

wilding *n* running amok. A black youth vogue term, seemingly first published in the *New York Times* on 22 April 1989.

↳*'A beautiful woman jogger viciously gang-raped and left in a coma by a mob of "wilding" youths in New York's Central Park has woken from the dead.'*
(*People*, 14 May 1989).

wilf *n British* a fool. A mild term of (usually) jocular or affectionate abuse from London working-class speech. The word, typically heard in a school context, is either based on the supposedly inherent comic nature of the name Wilfred, or on the use of that name for a character in the cartoon strip *The Bash Street Kids* appearing in the *Beano* children's comic since the 1950s.

↳*'Come on, don't be such a wilf!'*

William *n British* the police, a police officer. A personification based on **(the) old Bill** and usually used facetiously or ironically.

willie *n British* penis. A schoolchildren's word which is used, usually coyly or facetiously by adults. It is a personification like many similar terms (**Peter, John Thomas**, etc.), in this case first recorded in 1905.

↳*'"genital cold injury"…is described as "Arctic Willy" in the current edition of* The British Medical Journal.'
(*Independent*, 22 December 1989).

willie-wellie *n British* a condom. A humorous expression (**wellie** is a wellington boot), playing on the notion of protective rubberwear.

wiltshire *n British* impotence. A middle- or upper-class embellishment of 'wilt', heard since the early 1970s.

↳*'It was a case of wiltshire, I'm afraid.'*

wimp *n* a feeble, weak or timid person. This now well-established term first appeared as a term of derision employed by US high-school and college students in the mid-1970s. Its exact origins are obscure: suggested derivations are from 'whimper'; from a British undergraduate term for a girl (which was however in very limited use and was obsolete by 1930); from the name Wimpy, given to a character in the Popeye cartoons; or from a blend of weak, simple or **simp**, and limp or **gimp**. By the late 1970s the word had spread to adult speech and beyond the USA.

↳*'Well, goodnight Ralph. It was nice meeting someone so sensitive, aware and vulnerable. Too bad you're such a wimp.'*
(*Real Men Don't Eat Quiche*, Bruce Feirstein, 1982).

↳*'Lunch? You gotta be kiddin'. Lunch is for wimps.'*
(*Wall Street*, US film, 1987).

wimp-bod *n British* a tedious, unfashionable or unsophisticated person. This elaboration of **wimp** was heard in the 1980s particularly in London disco and media society, where it was used to refer disparagingly to those refused entry to exclusive clubs, for instance. *See also* **bod**.

wimp out *vb* to act in a feeble or cowardly manner. A later coinage based on **wimp**, by analogy with the many phrasal verbs employing 'out' (**freak out**, **weird out**, etc.).

↳'*Listen, just pull yourself together; this is no time to wimp out.*'

wimpy, wimpish, wimpo, wimpoid *adj* feeble, weak or cowardly. Formed from the noun **wimp**.

windbag *n* someone who is garrulous, loquacious or full of empty rhetoric. An old and well-established colloquial expression.

↳'*Mr Kinnock appears to be sinking under a barrage of criticism to the effect that he is an ill-educated Welsh windbag carried high by chippy class hatred.*'
(*Evening Standard*, 25 July 1989).

window *n*

a an opportunity.

b a period available for meetings, appointments or other tasks. This fashionable jargon term of the **yuppie** era derives from the use of window in space engineering to denote a set of parameters in time and space. The term was carried over into data processing and other semitechnical usage.

wind someone up *vb British* to provoke, tease, deceive. A London working-class usage which became fashionable at the end of the 1970s in raffish circles. It described the sort of straightfaced manipulation of a victim which discomfits increasingly; the image is probably that of winding up a clockwork toy, or tightening a winch. By the early 1980s the phrase was in widespread colloquial use and was generalized to encompass mockery, deliberate irritation, etc.

↳'*It took me a few minutes to realize that she was winding me up.*'

wind-up *n British* a provocation, teasing or deception. A London working-class back-formation from the verb **wind someone up** which became a fashionable

term in the late 1970s, spreading into general colloquial usage around 1979. (An expert at this kind of deliberate irritation is a 'wind-up artist'.)

wing it *vb* **1** to improvise, ad lib. Rather than being inspired, as is sometimes thought by the phrase 'on a wing and a prayer', this usage almost certainly comes from a 19th-century theatrical term 'to wing', meaning to learn one's lines at the last moment (while standing in the wings, literally or metaphorically).

2 to leave, go away.

wing-nut *n* a person with protruding ears. The jocular pejorative, heard in all English-speaking areas, but particularly the USA, has been applied to Prince Charles, among others.

wing-wong *n British* an object or contraption the name of which is unknown or forgotten. The expression is probably a nursery term, also used among some adults.

winkie, winky *n* **1** *British* penis. A nursery term which is probably a diminutive of **winkle**.

2 *American* the backside, buttocks.

winkle *n British* penis. This nursery term is based on the supposed resemblance between a (peri)winkle (a seafood delicacy traditionally associated with working-class outings) and a child's member.

winkle-pickers *n pl British* shoes with pointed toes. The term was first applied to male footwear in fashion from 1959 to about 1961. (Winkles, a traditional working-class seafood delicacy, were extracted from their shells by pins or toothpicks.)

winnet *n British* an alternative word for **dingleberry**.

wino *n* an alcoholic or habitual drunk. A term particularly applied to vagrants. (In the USA cheap domestic wine is the standard means of intoxication for tramps and poor alcoholics.)

wipe *vb* **1** to kill or destroy. A racier version of the standard phrase wipe out.

2 *Australian* to snub, ignore or **blank** someone. This usage was prevalent in the 1950s.

3 *American* to be repellent, inferior or worthless. A more recent synonym of suck and blow in use principally among adolescent speakers.

ᗷ'*This planet both wipes and sucks – in that order.*'
(*Third Rock From the Sun*, US TV comedy, 1995).

wiped out *adj* 1 a exhausted.
b intoxicated by drink or drugs.
2 devastated, ruined, defeated.
These senses of the phrase are all based on the standard meaning of annihilate or massacre.

wipe out *vb* a to fall off or be capsized by a wave. A surfer's term.
b to fail, particularly in a decisive and/or spectacular way. The second sense is a transference of the first, which came to prominence during the surfing craze of the early 1960s.

wipe-out *n* a failure, particularly a sudden and/or spectacular one.

wired *adj* 1 tense, edgy, manic. The word combines the notion of highly strung with that of electrified. It arose among amphetamine (and later cocaine) users in the 1970s, first in American speech. The word was subsequently adopted in the USA in a non-drug context to denote overstimulated or anxious.

ᗷ'*Frankie man you're all wired, you're all pumped up – you know you're not thinking straight.*'
(*Satisfaction*, US film, 1988).
2 *American* well-connected, integrated in a social or information network.

wiseacre *n American* a know-all, insolent or smug person. The word is an anglicization of the Dutch *wijssegger* (literally 'wise-sayer', originally meaning soothsayer).

wiseass *vb, n American* (to behave as) a know-all, an irritatingly smug or insolent person. This vulgar version of 'wise-guy' has been heard since the early 20th century. (The word wise has flourished in American speech because of reinforcement from the synonymous Dutch *wijs* and German *weise*.)

wiseguy *n American* a member of a mafia family or organized crime syndicate. This item of East Coast US criminal jargon was made famous by Hollywood movies of the 1980s and 1990s.

ᗷ'*It was a glorious time. There were wise-guys everywhere.*'

(*GoodFellas*, US film, 1990).

wisenheimer *n American* an alternative spelling of weisenheimer.

witchy *adj* mysterious, uncanny, fey. This term probably originated in black American speech; it became fairly widespread in the hippy era, describing a bewitching or other-worldly quality or atmosphere.

with-it *adj* fashionable. A vogue term of the early to mid-1960s which in its sense of stylish or up-to-date is still used by the middle-aged in particular, but now sounds dated. It derived from the phrase 'get with it', an essential item of preWorld War II jive talk and postwar beatnik parlance. In its sub-sense of 'on the ball' or in touch with events the phrase may be used by speakers of all ages.

ᗷ'*The "Galerie 55"... has a madly with-it cabaret of saucy "chansons paillardes".*'
(*About Town* magazine, September 1961).

with the edge up! *exclamation* British a cry of defiance used in London working-class speech. The reference is obscure but may refer to a knife or sharp instrument arranged as a dangerous trap. The term was recorded at the end of the 1980s.

witten *n British* an alternative word for dingleberry.

wizz, whizz *n British* amphetamine sulphate, speed. The term, which dates from the later 1970s, is used by the drug abusers themselves.

wizz *vb American* to urinate. An echoic term.

ᗷ'*What can I do?*'
'*Wizz in one of the empty beer bottles in the back.*'
(*Dumb and Dumber*, US film, 1994).

wob *n British* a piece, chunk, lump. A term in mainly middle-class usage in the 1980s. It is a coinage presumably inspired by wodge, 'gob(bet)', 'knob' etc.

wobblefats, wabblefats *n American* an obese person. A term of abuse heard mainly among adolescents.

wobbler, wobbly *n British* a bout of erratic, neurotic or extreme behaviour. The term usually occurs in the phrase throw a wobbly/wobbler. The wobbling in question is probably the unsteadiness

or trembling of a disturbed or uncontrolled subject and the usage may have arisen among medical or psychiatric personnel. The word has been widespread since about 1980.

wobbly eggs *n pl British* temazepam tablets, in the parlance of young drug users in the 1990s. The gelatin-covered capsules of a tranquilizer are roughly ovoid, and both they and their users can be said to wobble.

wodge, wadge *n British* a lump or slice. The word is a blend of wad and wedge and has been in use since at least the mid-19th century.

wog *n British* 1 a foreigner. The word was first used to refer to dark-skinned inhabitants of other countries, and is still usually employed in this sense. First recorded in the late 19th century, the term is derived by some from the initials for 'Westernized Wily Oriental Gentleman', a condescending euphemism supposedly applied to Indians or Arabs working for the British colonial authorities. An equally plausible source is the word 'golliwog' (originally 'golliwogg') denoting a black doll with curly hair; a character invented by the children's writer Bertha Upton in the late Victorian era. The later extension of the term (epitomized in the phrase *'wogs begin at Calais'*) encompasses everyone beyond the chauvinist or racist's own homeland. The word is common in Australia and not unknown in the USA.

꠹*'The only reason I was opposed to them calling me a wog was because I realise that in this country the word is used adversely against dark-skinned people.'*
(Marsha Hunt, *Oz* magazine, July 1969).

2 the wog *Australian* another version of wog gut.

wog box *n British* one of many terms for a **ghettoblaster**. (This is probably the only overtly racist expression, others include **Brixton briefcase**, **boogie box**, **rasta box**.)

wog gut *n* an upset stomach, diarrhoea, **gyppy tummy**. A World War II armed-services term surviving mainly in Australian usage, also in the form the wog.

wok *n British See* **chimney wok**.

wokking *n* smoking **crack**.

wolf *n* a predatory male. This word has been used since the early 1900s in the USA to denote an aggressive womanizer and in the **gay** and criminal subculture, an aggressive, promiscuous and/or violent male homosexual. Since the 1960s the heterosexual sense has been adopted in other English-speaking areas.

꠹*'A self confessed wolf, with the morals of a tom-cat.'*
(The judge in the Argyll divorce case, speaking in March 1963).

womba *n British* an alternative spelling of **wamba**.

wombat *n American* an eccentric and/or grotesque person. The name of the bear-like Australian marsupial has been used in this way since the late 1970s, probably because of the animal's exoticism and comic-sounding name.

womble *n British* a foolish, clumsy or unfortunate person. Since the appearance of the books and television puppets of the same name in the early 1970s, the word has been appropriated, particularly by schoolchildren, to refer to someone considered feeble, contemptible or a misfit. **Gonk** and **muppet**, both names of grotesque creatures, have been used with the same connotations.

꠹*'She hangs around with wombles.'*
(Recorded, schoolgirl, London, 1986).

wonga *n British* a variant form of **wamba**, common in the London area in the 1990s.

wonk *n American* a **swot**, in **preppie** and high-school jargon. The word is probably an arbitrary coinage, although it may possibly derive from the British **wanker**.

wood *n* 1 *American* a shortened form of **peckerwood**.
2 *British see* **get wood**.

woodentop *n British* a uniformed police officer. A term of mild derision used by plain-clothes detectives and disseminated through TV police shows. The Woodentops were a family of puppets featured on British children's television in the 1950s. There is also an obvious parallel with 'woodenhead' meaning fool.

꠹*'You'd better get your uniform cleaned – you'll be down among the woodentops next week.'*
(*Rockcliffe's Babies*, British TV police series, 1989).

woodie, woody *n American* **1 a** an American estate car or station wagon. Wooden exterior trim was a feature of the models manufactured in the 1930s, 40s and 50s.

b any vehicle used by a surfer for transporting people and boards to the beach. Old or customized estate cars were originally favoured for this purpose.

✎ *'I've got a 34 wagon, and we call it a woodie/ You know, it's not very cherry, it's an oldie but a goodie/ Well it ain't got a back seat or a rear window/ But it still gets me where I want to go.'*
('Surf City' written by Jan Berry and Brian Wilson, recorded by Jan and Dean, 1963).

2 an erection. The same notion is conveyed by the British expression **get wood**.

✎ *'Hey go easy, you're giving me a woodie.'*
(*The Mask*, US film, 1994).

woof *n British* an attractive woman. The word, posted on the Internet as an item of new slang in March 1997 by *Bodge World*, may be a variant form of **oof**.

woof, woofter *n British* variant forms of **poof** and **poofter** heard since the mid-1970s.

woof (one's custard) *vb* to vomit. The woof is echoic (in colloquial usage it may also describe 'wolfing down' food).

woofie, woofy *n American* (someone who is) stylish, in the know. The word is probably somehow related to the black slang concept of 'woofing' (itself derived either from the imitation of a dog's bark or from 'wolf') as behaving in a boastful or intimidating manner.

woof ticket *n American See* **buy a woof ticket**.

wool *n American* **1** the female pubic hair.

2 women considered as potential sex partners. Used in this sense the term is a vulgarism, particularly among middle-aged males.

✎ *'She sure is a good-looking wool.'*

Woolloomooloo Yank *n Australian* an Australian who imitates American speech and/or manners, in order to impress or to sell something, etc. This term of contempt applied to hucksters is

noted by Barry Humphries the Melbourne satirist in *A Nice Night's Entertainment* (1981). The term dates from the 1940s and Eric Partridge also records Woolloomooloo Frenchman. (Woolloomooloo is located on the outskirts of Sydney.)

woopsie *n British* an alternative spelling of **whoopsy**.

Woop-woop *n Australian* a very remote region. A synonym for the 'back of beyond' or 'the middle of nowhere', also expressed as **beyond the black stump**. The term was first recorded in the 1920s and was probably an imitation of a native Australian name.

wop *n* an Italian. This derogatory term originating in the USA is now common in all English speaking areas. The word was first applied to young dandified ne'er-do-wells, thugs or pimps in New York's Little Italy in the first decade of the century. It derives from the Sicilian dialect *guappo*, itself from Spanish *guapo*: handsome.

✎ *'"At our last New Year's Eve party, we had 65 wops, and five Brits", says Maro. "They behaved atrociously, all huddled up in a corner".'*
(Maro Gorky, *Harper's and Queen* magazine, November 1989).

word!, word up! *exclamation* an all-purpose term of agreement, solidarity, greeting, etc. (inspired by 'word of honour' or 'the good word'), which appeared first in black street culture of the late 1980s and in **rap** lyrics where it was used as a form of punctuation. In the UK *The Word* was adopted first as the title of a radio programme on the station Kiss FM and then for a controversial TV youth programme of the early 1990s.

✎ *'Enjoying wide usage this winter is my favourite word "Word," which formerly had the sense of "listen" (as in "Word up, man, you be illin'").'*
(Charles Maclean, *Evening Standard*, 22 January 1987).

wordhole *n American* mouth. **Pie-hole** and **hum-hole** are synonyms.

word up *vb American* to speak out, tell the truth, say something meaningful. A street slang expression in the early 1980s, originating in black speech.

working girl *n* a prostitute. A euphemism in use among prostitutes themselves as well as police, **punters**, etc.

✎ *'I'm useful for introducing girls to the*

stars as well. I know most of the working girls in Sheffield, because I work part-time as a bouncer in a massage parlour.'
(Rockstars' minder, *Guardian*, 12 December 1987).

works *n* a hypodermic syringe, in the language of **junkies**. The term may also apply to the other paraphernalia of drug-taking but usually specifies the means of injection.

work the oracle *vb British* to invent an oral statement of guilt on the part of a suspect. A term from police jargon (synonymous with **verbal**).

✎'*I wondered if his return was a consequence of his reluctance to verbal, to "work the oracle" as it is sometimes called....'*
(*Inside the British Police*, Simon Holdaway, 1983).

the worst *n* 1 something considered contemptible, pitiful, miserable, inferior. A straightforward application of the standard word in use among American teenagers and others.

✎'*God, that movie – it's the worst!'*
2 something excellent, admirable, superlative. This sense of the word is by analogy with **bad**, in its black street and youth culture sense of good. The worst was used in this sense by adolescents at least in the 1980s.

wotsit *n* an alternative spelling of **whatsit**.

wowler *n British* an alternative form of **howler**.

wowser, wowzer *n Australian* a spoilsport, puritan or 'wet blanket.' A word which has been recorded in American usage, but not in Britain; wowser originated in the late 19th century and is of uncertain origin. Most suggested etymologies refer to 'wow' as a roar or bark of disapproval or exclamation of shocked surprise.

wrap *n* a portion of a drug such as amphetamine, **ecstasy** or **Crack**. Measured amounts of the drug are wrapped in paper or tinfoil for sale to consumers. This term has been in use in Britain from 1989.

wrecked *adj* intoxicated by drink or drugs. A coinage which parallels such usages as **smashed**, **bombed**, **blitzed**, **destroyed**, etc.

wrinklie, wrinkly *n, adj* (an) old (person). A popular term among adolescents since around 1980, synonyms are **dusty**, **crumbly** and **crinkly**. The word is often used of (middle-aged and elderly) parents.

wrongo *n American* the equivalent of the British **wrong'un**. A fairly rare term.

wrong 'un *n British* 1 a criminal, ne'er-do-well or other undesirable character.

2 something to be avoided, a nuisance. The term has been a common working-class colloquialism since the later 19th century.

✎'*They're petrified that their journey to the western fringes of the Greater London area may result in what they* [cab drivers] *call a "wrong un" – a job, say, to Hillingdon, which takes them only a few miles.'*
(*Observer*, Section 5, 9 April 1989).

wuss *n* 1 *American* a weak, feeble person, and by extension a dupe. A word used by college students and young people from the 1960s and probably inspired by 'puss', 'pussy' or 'pussy-wussy', used as a term of endearment to a kitten.

2 in Swansea and other parts of Wales, the word wuss is commonly heard as a synonym for mate or buddy. This is a shortening and anglicization of the Welsh *gwas* meaning servant.

✎'*Hiya wuss. How's it going?'*

wussy *n American* a variation of (and probably the origin of) the more common **wuss**.

✎'*Come on, toxic waste won't kill you. Don't be such a wussy.'*
(*Armed and Dangerous*, US film, 1986).

wu-wu, woo-woo *n American* the female genitals. An imitation nursery euphemism in adult use.

✎'*You might have to show your wu-wu.'*
(Hollywood agent quoted in ITV documentary *Hollywood Women*, December 1993).

X-Z

X *n* **1** a kiss. A teenagers' term, from the use of the letter x to symbolize a kiss at the end of a letter. The word is used in phrases such as '*give us an x*' or, as an affectionate exclamation, '*x, x, x!*'.
2 the drug **ecstasy**.

X-er *n American* a member of **Generation X**. The term was briefly popular between 1992 and 1994.
⇘'*The narrator of the book is the archetypal X-er. He lives in a rented bungalow (X-ers don't have mortgages) …*'

X-filed *adj British* rejected (by a partner), jilted. The expression puns on the cult US TV series on the paranormal (*The X-Files*) and the notion of an 'ex' partner being filed away. The phrase was used by teenage girls in particular in the late 1990s.

x-out *vb*
a cross out, cancel.
b kill, eliminate, **rub out**.
(The phrase is pronounced 'ecks-out'.)

x-rated *adj*
a salacious, taboo, extremely daring or pornographic. Often used nowadays with at least a degree of irony, the expression is an extension of the categorization applied to films deemed suitable only for those over 18.
⇘'*We had this real x-rated date!*'
b terrifying, horrifying, dreadful. A second sense inspired by the term's application to horror films.
⇘'*She's got this x-rated boyfriend.*'

xtc *n* an alternative spelling of **ecstasy** (the amphetamine-based disinhibiting drug), in vogue in the late 1980s.

yaas *exclamation See* **yass**.

yack *vb, n* an alternative spelling of **yak**.

yacka, yacker *n See* **yakka**.

yackers *n British* money. A variation on **ackers**, in mainly working-class usage.

yaffling irons, yaffling spanners *n pl British* cutlery, knives, forks and spoons as used at the table. The humorous phrase is widespread in the armed forces and derives from the archaic 'yaffle', a dialect term, probably imitative in origin, meaning to consume or eat voraciously.
⇘'*Grab your yaffling irons and let's get scrumming!*'

yah, yaah *n British* an ex-public school young person, a **hooray**. The term, particularly popular in Edinburgh in the early 1990s, derives from the class's characteristic drawling of the word 'yes'.
(**OK, yah** was a catchphrase featured in the Steve Wright radio show and elsewhere in the mid-1980s.)

yahoo *n* a lout, oaf. The word, imitating a wild shout, was used by Jonathan Swift in *Gulliver's Travels* as the name of a race of brutish humans. The modern usage varies slightly in the English-speaking countries. In Britain the word often denotes a boisterous, inconsiderate youth, and is used of **hoorays**, students, etc.; in Australia the word generally equates with **yob**, while in the USA it may mean a stupid and/or coarse person.

yah-yo *n American* cocaine in the street language of the late 1990s. It was included in so-called **Ebonics**, recognized as a legitimate language variety by school officials in Oakland, California, in late 1996.

yak, yack *n* **1** incessant talk, idle chatter. The word imitates the sound of monotonous, grating and/or inane speech. Nowadays variants of the verb form such as **yak away** or **yak on** are often preferred.
⇘'*How much longer are you going to be yakking into that damn phone? We're late.*'
(Recorded, middle-class woman, Bristol, 1989).
2 a laugh, joke or instance of humour. **Yok** is an alternative form, favoured in fashionable journalism.

yakka, yacka, yacker *n Australian* work. The word is a native Aboriginal proper name.

yakkety-yak *vb, n* an elaborated form of **yak** heard especially in the USA and enshrined in the pop song of the same name (written by Jerry Leiber and Mike Stoller and a worldwide hit for the Coasters in the late 1950s). The term often denotes gossip as well as chatter or talk.

yammer *vb*
a to wail, complain or jabber fearfully.
b to talk or shout insistently.
Yammer is probably a modern descendant of an Anglo-Saxon verb meaning to murmur or lament. Its use is reinforced by the influence of words like yell and stammer and, in the USA, by the similarity to the German and Dutch *jammeren*, which means whine or lament and derives from the same Old Germanic root as the English cognate.

yang *n American* penis. This term may be an alteration of the more established **whang**, influenced by the verb to yank; or is perhaps a shortened form of the post-1970s expression **yinyang** (itself possibly containing the Chinese *yang*, meaning masculine principle).
↪'Hanging around toilets waiting for some poor guy to reach for a cop's yang by mistake.'
(*The Switch*, Elmore Leonard, 1978).

yangyang *n American* a variant form of **yinyang**.

yank, yankee *n* an American, a native or inhabitant of the USA. Yankee is the older form of the word and seems to be connected with the early Dutch settlers in Connecticut and the rest of New England. It may be a familiar form (Jan-Kees) of the common forenames Jan and Cornelius, a diminutive Janke ('Johnny'), or an invented epithet Jan Kaas ('John Cheese'), all applied to Dutchmen in general. Other suggestions are that it is from a nickname given to English-speaking pirates and traders by the Dutch, or a deformation of the word 'English' by Amerindian speakers. It may possibly be connected with *yonker*, Dutch for young (noble-)man. In the USA Yankee is used as an epithet by which old-school southerners damn northerners and also as a straightforward designation of an inhabitant of the northeastern states.

yank (off) *v* (of a man) to masturbate. A fairly rare, but geographically widespread term.

yank (someone around/someone's chain) *vb American* to mislead, deceive, harass or irritate. The image on which the expression is based is that of a chained or leashed animal or prisoner being thoughtlessly or maliciously jerked about or led in different directions. (Phrases commencing with **jerk** are used in the same way.)

yank someone's crank/weenie/zucchini *vb American* to mock, mislead or irritate. These expressions are all vulgarizations of 'pull one's leg'.

yap *vb* to talk incessantly and/or inanely. An echoic term also used to depict the persistent high-pitched barking of small dogs.

yap *n* **1 a** talk, idle chatter.
b mouth.
This echoic term is often heard in the form of the British working-class 'shut your yap!'.
2 *American* a country bumpkin. This sense of the word is from an archaic British rural dialect term for simpleton.

yard, the Yard *n* **1** penis. Said to be archaic by most authorities, but still revived from time to time by those in search of a robust or rustic-sounding euphemism.
2 *British* **the Yard** Scotland Yard, the headquarters of the London Metropolitan Police.
3 *American* one thousand. Also one hundred (dollars).
4 Jamaica. A nickname used by the local inhabitants, probably deriving from the notion of 'my own backyard'.
5 home.
↪'This is going to be someone's yard – it used to be a morgue, unfortunately.'
(*Exodus: The Diary*, Channel 4 TV documentary programme, 12 November 1995).

yardbird *n American*
a a military recruit or other person assigned to menial outdoor duties.
b a convict, prisoner.
c a hobo frequenting railyards.

yardie *n Jamaican*

a a member of a secret Jamaican crime-syndicate or gang, said to operate in Britain and the USA since the late 1980s.
b a person from Jamaica or the Caribbean. In Jamaica itself the term has had this more generalized meaning, it comes from the use of **yard** to denote Jamaica or home (probably from 'my own backyard').

yard (on) *vb American* to cheat, be unfaithful to (one's spouse). A black American slang term, deriving from the notion of adulterous trespassing in the back yard. *Compare* **backdoor man**.

yarning *n British* telling stories, especially tall stories. The word, based on the phrase 'to spin a yarn' (itself from nautical rope-making or spinning cloth), is heard particularly among adolescent girls in the later 1990s and probably originated in black usage.

yarra *adj Australian* crazy, mad. There is a psychiatric hospital at Yarra Bend in the state of Victoria.

yarra *n Australian* a stupid and/or obnoxious individual. Like the adjectival form, this derives ultimately from the Yarra river, upon which Melbourne is situated, and refers either to the opacity of its water or to a psychiatric hospital on its banks.

yass, yaas *exclamation* an exclamation of derision, defiance or provocation in black Caribbean English. It is a conflation of '(up) your **ass**'. The expression was briefly adopted by some black Americans and white British speakers in the early 1970s. (The Rolling Stones' use of the term ya-yas in the title of their 1970 live album, *Get yer Ya-Yas out* was a misreading of this expression.)

Yasser *n American* an erection. A shortened form of '*Yasser Crack-a-fat*', an expression punning on the phrase **crack a fat** (have an erection) and on the name of the Palestinian leader, Yasser Arafat. The word was used by male college and high-school students in the later 1990s.

yatter, yatter on *vb* to talk incessantly, frivolously or inanely. This colloquialism is a blend of **yap**, **yak**, chatter and natter.

yawn *n* something extremely boring, dull, uninspiring. A colloquial term, particularly prevalent in middle-class usage.

It is either a noun, as in '*the film was a total yawn*' or an interjection as in '*they took us round the exhibition – yawn!*'. A racier alternative is **yawnsville**.

yawn *vb, n* (to) vomit. Particularly popular in Australia, where it is often embellished as **technicolour yawn**, the usage also exists in Britain and the USA.

yawnsville *n* a boring thing, person or situation. An American teenage expression adopted in Britain and Australia. It uses the common slang suffix **-ville** to denote place, situation or state of affairs.

yecch *exclamation* an American version of **yuk**.

yecchy *adj American* a version of **yukky**.

yegg *n* a safe-cracker or burglar. The word is of unknown origin, but is probably derived either from an archaic dialect verb or from the name of a famous thief. Yegg, but not its obsolete alternative form 'eggman', was introduced to Britain from the USA around the time of World War II, but is rarely heard.

Yehudi *adj British* authentic, trustworthy. A jocular item of middle-class rhyming slang using the name of the Israeli musician 'Yehudi Menuhin', meaning genuine.

yell *n British* **1 a** a good joke or source of hilarity.
↳'*That's a yell!*'
b a riotous party or good time.
↳'*We had a real yell last night.*'
Both usages were heard among young people from the late 1970s. The first is also in use in upper-class and theatrical milieux.
2 an instance of vomiting.
↳'*He's up in the bathroom having a yell.*'

yellow *adj* cowardly, afraid. This now common term is of obscure origin. It is an Americanism of the late 19th century which was quickly adopted into British and Australian English. (In English slang of the 18th and early 19th centuries, yellow meant jealous and/or deceitful.) Some authorities derive the modern sense from the activities of the sensationalist 'yellow press'; other suggestions include a racial slur on the supposedly docile Chinese population of the Western US or reference to a yellow-bellied submissive reptile or animal, but it seems more likely that it is an extension of the earlier pejorative British senses.

yellow-belly *n* a coward. This phrase, learned by modern schoolchildren from the language of Western movies, was probably coined after the turn of the century. The use of **yellow** to denote cowardice is a 19th-century development.

yen shee *n* opium. A term from the vocabulary of drug users in the 1950s and 1960s which is now rare. It derives from the Cantonese *yan* or Mandarin *yen*, meaning smoke and hence opium. *Yen shi* literally means opium user or addict.

yen sleep *n* a waking trance state brought about by the smoking of opium, or, by extension, a drowsy, restless sleep resulting from opium or heroin withdrawal. An expression from the 1950s jargon of drug abusers. The Chinese word *yen*, meaning smoke or opium, is also the source of the English word for a yearning.

yenta, yentl *n* a shrewish woman, gossip or crone. The word is a middle-European Jewish woman's name or title (probably related to forms of the word 'gentile'). The yenta became a comic figure in Jewish folklore, particularly in the American Yiddish theatre before World War II.

yeti *n British* a primitive, repellent or stupid person. A term from the repertoire of schoolboys, army recruits, etc., since the 1970s. The word can be used both with facetious affection (e.g. as a nickname) or to express strong contempt.

yid *n* 1 a Jew. The word is the Yiddish term for a Yiddish-speaking Jew (Yiddish being a Germanic dialect influenced by Hebrew). When used in English the word is invariably racist and derogatory.

2 *British* a supporter of Tottenham Hotspurs ('Spurs') football team. Ever since the fictional racist TV character Alf Garnett, in his capacity as a West Ham supporter, characterized the average Spurs crowd/board, etc. as 'a bunch of Yids', the team/crowd, etc. have been taunted with the name and have adopted it as a badge of pride, replying with cries of 'Yiddo, Yiddo' when challenged.

↳'*West Ham kill yids.*'
  (Graffito, Raynes Park, London, 1989).

yike *n Australian* a brawl or violent quarrel.

yinyang, ying-yang *n American*
1 a the anus.
b (a) sex organ(s).

Yang and **w(h)ang** are both common expressions for penis. Yinyang may be an embellished version of these; it may be a genuine nonsense nursery word for any unnameable thing or part (it was used in a pseudo-Chinese music-hall chorus in the earlier years of the century) or, alternatively, an adult imitation thereof influenced by 'yang' and 'yin' describing the Chinese masculine and feminine principles respectively (given currency in the early 1970s via the *I Ching* and subsequently in therapy and sex manuals).

2 a fool, dupe, inept person, **yoyo**. This use of the phrase probably postdates its other sense of anus or genital(s), by analogy with most other words of similar meaning.

↳'*Well, if it's a yinyang you want, you've got three much better guys for this job.*'
  (*Vice Versa*, US film, 1988).

yippy, yippie *n* a **hippy** activist, a member of the so-called 'Youth International Party' founded by Abbie Hoffman and Jerry Rubin in 1968, the date of the Chicago Democratic Convention where they put forward a pig as a presidential candidate. This short-lived movement was a loose coalition of radicals, anarchists, libertarians and left-wingers concerned with 'situationist' and confrontational political methods. The term was sometimes applied to other politically involved hippies and was one of the sources (a heavily ironical one) of the later word **yuppie**.

↳'*Yippy politics, being made up as it goes along, are incomprehensible.*'
  (*Oz* magazine, 1970).

yob, yobbo *n British* a thug, lout, brutish youth. This is one of the only pieces of **backslang** to enter the popular lexicon; it was heard occasionally in working-class and underworld milieux from the 19th century until the early 1960s, when it became a vogue word and was extensively used in the newly-liberalized entertainment media. Yobbishness, yobbery and even yobbocracy are more recent derivations, often used to refer to brutal behaviour in the social and political context as well as in connection with juvenile delinquency and hooliganism.

✎ '*The London International Financial Futures Exchange, terrible place, full of the most frightful yobs.*'
(*Serious Money*, play by Caryl Churchill, 1987).

✎ '*The Singhs are being threatened by a gang of racist yobs.*'
(*The Sunday Times*, 26 July 1987).

yo-boy *n British* a hooligan, adolescent male. The term was recorded in the south of England particularly in the Slough area from the mid-1980s, and is probably a variation of the older **yob**.

yock *n* an alternative spelling of **yok**.

yodel *vb, n* (to) vomit. An expression used particularly by teenagers and college students.

yodel in the canyon/valley

vb to perform cunnilingus. The first is a jocular expression originating with American college students in the 1960s and now heard elsewhere. The second version is Australian and British. *Compare* **yodel**.

yok, yock *n* a laugh, chortle or instance of humour. A racier version of **yak** or **yuk**, popular for instance with rock-music journalists.

✎ '*There's lots of yoks in this new movie.*'

yomp *vb British* to tramp across rough country wearing or carrying heavy equipment. This item of arcane military slang became known to the general public at the time of the war between Britain and Argentina over the Falkland Islands in 1981. The word is now used by non-military hikers and others, more or less as a synonym for 'trek'. It is either an invented blend, influenced by words like tramp, hump, stomp and jump, or an imitation of the sound of boots slamming into muddy ground.

yoni *n* the vagina. This Sanskrit word (meaning originally 'abode' or 'womb' and later the female equivalent of a religious phallic symbol) is sometimes used jocularly or by writers on sexual matters in place of a taboo or clinical-sounding alternative. It has been familiar to Western readers since the publication of the *Kama Sutra* and other Hindu texts in the early 1960s.

yonks *n British* a very long time, ages. This now popular word began to be heard in the early 1960s, mainly in middle-class usage. Its exact etymology is obscure; it may be a children's deformation of 'years' or alteration of 'donkey's years'.

✎ '*God, I haven't seen her for yonks.*'

yop *vb British* to tell tales, inform on someone. The origin of this 1990s playground usage is obscure.

york *vb* to vomit. The term is echoic and jocular like its synonyms **erp**, **ralph**, **buick**, etc.

you-and-me *n British* tea (the drink or the meal). A surviving example of London rhyming slang. You-and-me is more commonly used to refer to the meal in contrast to **Rosie Lee** for the drink. 'Glory-be' is a less well-known variant. *Compare* **me 'n' you**.

you-dat *exclamation British* an all-purpose phrase indicating mutual respect or approbation. **Respect** itself and **touch-respect** are synonyms. The term was recorded in use among north London schoolboys in 1993 and 1994.

youngblood *n American* a black youth. The term, inspired by its literary use referring to Amerindian braves, is used particularly of a junior member of a street gang. In the late 1980s the word was often shortened to **blood** (which also derives from 'blood brother').

young fogey/fogy *n British* a

youngish person of self-consciously traditional attitudes, manners and aesthetic ideals. Young fogey, by humorous analogy with the colloquial 'old fogey', characterizes another social sub-group of the 1980s. Personified by the fastidious and conservative novelist and critic, A. N. Wilson, these mainly male members of (or aspirers to) the upper-middle-class re-create in their lifestyle and outlook the more refined pre-1960 establishment values ([high] Anglicanism, literary dabbling, a liking for traditional cooking, clothing, etc.).

✎ '*These days a "party" is often a sedate à deux affair at the latest Young Fogy night-spot.*'
(*The Sunday Times*, Men's Fashion Extra, October 1989).

your father's mustache! *ex-*

clamation American a comical cry of contempt or defiance in imitation of the colourful imprecations in use in Latin and Arab cultures.

youth *n Jamaican* a specialized usage of the standard English term, youth means young hero, young gangster or, still in the singular form, young people in general. It is often pronounced 'yoot'.

↳*'There's nothin' round here for the youth. No wonder they out on the street looking for trouble.'*
(Recorded, Jamaican woman, London, 1988).

you wish! *exclamation British* an all-purpose cry of derision or provocation, particularly in response to the expression of an unrealistic hope or desire. The term was recorded in use among north London schoolboys in 1993 and 1994.

yoyo *n* a silly, eccentric or frivolous person. This use of the word, which may be said affectionately of a dizzy noncon-formist or contemptuously with the straightforward meaning of fool, origi-nally referred to someone who vacillated or behaved in an irresolute manner.

yo-yo mode *adj, n* (in) a state of chaos or confusion. The term occurs in the language of computer users. It is often in the form of an exclamation *'full yo-yo mode alert!'*, when a system is going 'hay-wire'.

yuck 1 *n* something or someone dis-gusting.
2 *exclamation* repelled distaste or disap-proval.
3 an alternative spelling of **yuk**.
4 *adj* an alternative spelling of **yucky**.
(In American English this echoic approx-imation of retching is often transcribed as **yecch**.)

yucky, yukky, yecchy *adj* un-pleasant, disgusting, sickly, cloying. A very popular word, particularly since the mid-1970s among children and teenagers, it derives from **yuck** as an ex-clamation of distaste.

yuk *n* an alternative form of **yok** in the sense of laugh.

yumyum(s) *n* anything considered irresistible, such as a potential sexual partner, an illicit drug, or a sum of money. A less-respectable usage of the colloquial and childish, lipsmacking exclamation meaning 'delicious'.

yuppie *n* an acronym for 'young urban professional' (later also interpreted as 'young upwardly-mobile professional') with an added -ie ending in imitation of **hippie**, **yippie**, **surfie**, etc. The word was coined sometime between 1978 and 1980 to denote a new social phenomenon which needed to be distinguished from the existing **preppies**. The yuppie, origi-nally identifiable in New York City by a uniform of a business suit worn with run-ning shoes, is an ambitious work-oriented materialist, usually highly paid and ex-tremely receptive to consumer fashions. The term quickly became established all over the English-speaking world, epitom-izing the 'aspirational' mood of the 1980s. The word is now often used with deroga-tory connotations and has given rise to such forms as **yuppify**, yuppification and yuppiegate (a 1986 financial scandal in New York).

↳*'Yuppie scum fuck off/Kill a yuppie today.'*
(Graffiti protesting the gentrification of the East End, London, 1988).

yuppify *vb*

a to renovate and improve (a neighbour-hood), specifically to create a residential or work environment which will attract wealthy 'young professionals'. The term was coined by analogy with the earlier 'gentrify'.

↳*'Their "bashers" (shacks) will be forcibly removed by police to make way for developers who want to "yup-pify" the Charing Cross area.'*
(*Observer*, 16 August 1987).

b to render less radical or more ambitious and/or materialistic. This sense of the word has been used in the specific context of changes in the image and identity of the Labour Party in the late 1980s.

the Y-word *n* the **yuppie** name for yuppies. A humorous, self-deprecating euphemism on the lines of **the f-word** (**fuck**) or 'the S-word' (sex).

↳*'I have to warn you, they're the essence of the Y-word.'*
(*Cheers*, US TV comedy series, 1988).

za *n American* a pizza, in the jargon of **preppies**.

zaftig *adj American* a version of **zoftig**.

zap *vb*

a to overwhelm, destroy, obliterate (literally or figuratively). The term derives from a comic-book sound effect applied to the action of ray-guns in the 1950s and 1960s.

✎ *'Director Elizabeth Esteve-Coll, zapping the cognoscenti.'*
(Photo caption referring to a leading figure in the staff dispute at London's Victoria and Albert Museum, *Observer*, 12 February 1989).

b to target an individual or organization for protests, picketing, situationist political action, etc. A word from the lexicon of radical **gays** in the 1970s.

✎ *'The Sisters of Perpetual Indulgence... used to go out and zap various things dressed as nuns.'*
(Gay activist, *Out on Tuesday*, British TV documentary series, 1989).

zapper *n* a TV remote control. This term established itself in some households in the 1980s. It was coined perhaps to convey the power and relish experienced by viewers now able to switch channels or turn off at a touch.

zappy *adj* energetic, speedy, dynamic, decisive. A back-formation from **zap**.

zeds *n British* sleep. This use of the term is probably a back-formation from the phrases **stack some zeds/zees** or **cop/bag some zeds/zees**, all meaning to sleep.

zee *n American* a Japanese sports car, in the argot of black street-gangs of the late 1980s.

✎ *'I saw a guy I knew, my age, had a Blazer [a Chevrolet Blazer – 4-wheel drive jeep]. Another guy got a "zee".'*
(Crack dealer, *Independent*, 24 July 1989).

zen out *vb* to enter a blissful, contemplative or inert state. The phrase, based on the notion of mindlessness in Zen meditation, was ascribed to the singer Lisa Stansfield in the *Daily Telegraph* magazine, in October 1993.

zeppelin *n*

a a large cannabis cigarette (**joint**).
b a large penis.

Both senses are inspired by the size and shape of the original Graf Zeppelin airship. The second sub-sense may be influenced by the use of the slang **joint** for both **reefer** and penis.

zero *n* an insignificant individual, dull nonentity.
✎ *'The guy's just a total zero.'*

zero-cool *adj American* extremely, impressive, admirable, nonchalant etc. An intensive form of **cool** probably coined by **hipsters** or **beatniks**, now in use among adolescents.

zero out *vb American*

a to run out of money, to go broke or bankrupt.
✎ *'But, dad, I'm totally zeroed out.'*
(*Maid to Order*, US film, 1987).
b to 'hit rock bottom', reach one's lowest point.
c to fail utterly.

zes *n American See* **z's**.

zhlub *n American* a version of **slob**.

zhooshed, zhush'd *adj British* elaborately dressed and/or made up. The term has been used in **parlyaree** since the 1960s, e.g., to describe the teasing and primping of hair and eyelashes before emerging for a social occasion. The word's origin is unclear: it may simply be an imitation of the sound of appreciative smacking of lips or intake of breath.

zilch *n* **1 a** nothing. The word became common in US speech in the later 1960s, spreading to Britain in the 1980s. It is either an invented alteration of 'zero' or from sense **b**.
b a nonentity. Zilsch or Zilch is a Yiddish/German family name borrowed for a comic character featuring in *Ballyhoo* magazine in the USA in the 1930s.
2 the name of a dice game.

zilch *vb American*

a to defeat (utterly).
b to fail (utterly).

Both usages, found in adolescent speech, are based on the earlier noun form.

zillion *n* a very large number; a humorous coinage by analogy with million, billion and 'trillion'. (**Squillion** is a similar mythical number.)

zine *n* a magazine, particularly a post **punk**-era 'fanzine'. The clipped form of the word is typical of the tendency among American adolescents from the 1980s (as in **za**, **rents**, **burbs**, etc.).

zing *vb American* to deliver a sudden

attack, retort, etc. This use of the word is derived from the colloquial sense of fly, spin, hum or perform zestfully.

↳ *"Did you hear him zing my lawyer?" Mr. Gotti asked reporters. "Bruce should hit him on the chin".'*
(Mafia trial report, *The Times*, 7 February 1990).

zinger *n* something or someone extremely impressive, spectacular, energizing, exciting, etc. The word comes from the use of 'zing' to mean a shrill, high-pitched sound and a lively zestful quality.

zip *n* nothing. Originally often used for a score of zero, the sound of zip evokes brusque dismissal. It has become a fashionable term in racy speech, as have synonyms such as **zilch** and **zippo**. Originating in the USA, zip is now heard in the UK, particularly among **yuppies**.

zip it *vb* shut up, keep quiet. A shortening of **zip one's lip**.

↳ *'Zip it, Fred!'*
(*All of Me*, US film, 1984).

zip one's lip *vb* to shut up, keep quiet. A racier update of **button one's lip**, typically used as a brusque instruction.

zippersniffer *n*
a a male homosexual, particularly one considered to be predatory or importunate. The phrase (originating in the USA, where 'zipper' is used in preference to 'zip') refers to someone giving attention to the trouser fly of another.
b a 'predatory' or sexually importunate female.

zippo *n* nothing. An embellished form of **zip** in the sense of zero. Zippo, originally an Americanism, is now found elsewhere (albeit less often than **zip**).

↳ *'I checked and re-checked and got zippo.'*
(*Hooperman*, US TV series, 1986).

zit *n* a spot or skin blemish. This Americanism has become well established in British usage since the later 1980s, featuring for instance in a TV commercial for anti-acne cream using the slogan *'blitz those zits!'*. The etymology of the word is obscure.

zizz *n, vb* (a period of) sleep or rest, nap. A British coinage dating from the 1920s. The word echoes the sound of light snoring or susurration associated with sleep.

zlub *n American* a version of **slob**.

zod *n American* a dullard, fool, nonentity. A 1980s teenage term of unknown provenance.

zoftig, zophtic, zaftig *adj American* pleasing, luxuriant, voluptuous, succulent. The words are Yiddish forms of **zaftig**: 'juicy', from the German *Saft*: juice. The expression was extended to refer admiringly or lasciviously to women, then to the general sense of pleasurable or satisfactory.

zoid *n* a foolish, clumsy or despised person. This teenage expression is an invention probably influenced by such terms as **zomboid** and 'bozoid'. It originated in the USA, but by the late 1980s was heard in British schools, usually denoting a misfit.

zombie *n* 1 a dull, vacuous or inert person.
2 a UFO or rogue or unidentified object or signal. Both senses derive from the voodoo walking-dead of Haitian folklore.

zomboid *adj* dull, stupid, inert or intoxicated. A coinage from **zombie** with the 'pathological' suffix **-oid**.

↳ *'I mean any man who more-or-less turns the American genocide squad into a bunch of nodding, scratching hepatitic zomboids can't be all bad.'*
(Hashish dealer quoted in *IT* magazine, July 1972).

zoned, zoned out *adj*
stoned, spaced out, semi-conscious. Originally a piece of US drug-users' jargon, the word may now be employed in a non-narcotic context to mean worn out.

zone out *vb* to lose consciousness or concentration, become intoxicated. A drug users' expression related to the notion of **spaced out** and perhaps influenced by the mythical 'twilight zone'. The term has become generalized for use in more innocuous contexts.

↳ *'I didn't really notice – I guess I must have been zoning out.'*
(Recorded, American sub-editor, London, 1989).

zonked, zonko *adj* intoxicated, overwhelmed, stunned. Zonked began as a term evoking the result of a blow to the head (a 'zonk', similar to **'bonk'**), applied to the effects of drink or drugs. The word is now in widespread use and may refer to more innocent sensations such as surprise or exhaustion.

✤ *'I was zonked on enormous quantities of drug cocktails. Once you're on those things it's almost impossible to get off them.'*
(Former patient in a psychiatric hospital referring to his treatment, *Time Out*, February 1988).

zoob, zoobrick, zubrick *n*
penis. The several forms of the word are all derived from the Arabic slang (in which there are variant forms rendered usually as *zob* or *zip*).

zoom *n* amphetamine (**speed**) or cocaine. A drug abuser's nickname. The term refers to the exhilarating **rush** experienced by those using these stimulants.

zooted *adj American* intoxicated by drugs or alcohol. The coinage, probably influenced by **toot** and perhaps **zonked** or **zone(d out)**, appeared in the 1980s, first seemingly referring specifically to the effects of cocaine.

zoot suit *n British* a zipped forensic-evidence bag or 'body bag'. A police term recorded in the 1980s. The phrase was first applied to the fashionable suits with exaggerated lapels and shoulders, drape jacket and wide trousers worn by American youths, pimps and jitterbuggers in the 1930s and 1940s.

zophtic *adj American* an alternative spelling of **zoftig**.

✤ *'A pill and a cup of coffee and Im* [sic] *being already zophtic so who's complaining.'*
(*Requiem for a Dream*, Hubert Selby Jr, 1979).

zos *n South African* food. Recorded as an item of Sowetan slang in the *Cape Sunday Times*, 29 January 1995.

zotz *n American* nothing. A synonym for **zip** and **zilch**, used in the *Prizzi* novels by Richard Condon.

zotz *vb American* to destroy, kill. 'Zot' was an earlier word for a short, sharp blow.

✤ *'Are we just going to wait until one more hooker gets zotzed?'*
(*I Love A Man In Uniform*, Canadian film, 1994).

zow *n South African* a yokel or oaf. Recorded as an item of Sowetan slang in the *Cape Sunday Times*, 29 January 1995.

z's *n American* sleep. From the use of 'z' to indicate the rasping sound of snores, hence sleep, in cartoons. The word pronounced in the American way, is usually part of a phrase such as **grab/cop some z's.**

zucchini *n American* penis. This Italian term for courgettes is also used throughout North America to refer to the vegetable in its singular form. In addition to its culinary usage, it is also a fairly widespread jocularism for the male member.

zulu *n, adj British* a black person. A term of abuse current for instance in the army in the 1980s.

'zup? *question American* this greeting or question – an abbreviated form of 'what's up?' – was fashionable in teenage speech of the 1990s.

zymie, zymotic *adj* unpleasant,
repellent, squalid. The word was used by English teenagers in the 1960s and 1970s. Its users are probably unaware of its etymology: zymotic is in fact a medical or scientific term deriving from the Greek for fermentation, meaning infected or infectious.

IBE B5967